PUBLIC OPINION AND PUBLIC POLICY

Models of Political Linkage

The Dorsey Series in Political Science

Public Opinion and Public Policy

Models of Political Linkage

Edited by

NORMAN R. LUTTBEG
Florida State University

 Revised Edition
1974

THE DORSEY PRESS   Homewood, Illinois 60430
Irwin-Dorsey Limited   Georgetown, Ontario L7G 4B3
Irwin-Dorsey International   London, England WC2H 9NJ

Revised Edition

First Printing, April 1974

ISBN 0-256-01532-5
Library of Congress Catalog Card No. 73-93358
Printed in the United States of America

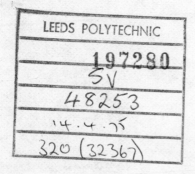

To the memory of my father, an inspiration

Preface

My purpose in this edition as in the last has been to organize the very best information available to aid the student in comprehending how government policy reflects or might be made to reflect public opinion. The editor's role in this is most humble—choosing what he thinks to be the best efforts dealing with the problem at hand. The quality of this reader and its usefulness rests entirely on the intellectual efforts of the authors of the selections. I sincerely thank them for permitting me to reprint their work here.

This reader is directed toward what I believe to be a most important question in a democracy—political linkage, or the interaction between leaders and the led in making democracy public policy. As such, it crosses normal course content divisions dealing with political parties, pressure groups, voting behavior, and public opinion. I very much appreciate the willingness of the many adopters to work with this organization.

In completing the second edition, I owe many thanks to those who helped me. Reviews by John L. Sullivan and Carl C. Hetrick were kind and most helpful as have been the comments by users of the first edition. The comments and suggestions of my colleagues, both faculty and students, about various recent publications and papers brought many selections initially to my attention and confirmed the importance I saw in many new articles. Finally, in the mechanics of getting the manuscript complete, I thank our secretaries, Agnes Raker and Jane Woodruff, and my assistants, Carol Cassel and Marvin Thurston.

March 1974   N.R.L.

Contents

Introduction
Political Linkage in a Large Society

Probably the most widely held conception of democracy is that the government must serve its public. Somehow the policies passed by government must reflect the preferences of the governed and most desirably must reflect the public's best interest. I will ignore the significant and most difficult distinction between what the public wants and what is in its best interest, feeling I can make no additional contribution to existing thought in this matter and knowing of no attempts to evaluate empirically the distinction. Most persons would only be satisfied with a democracy which at least gave some expression to public wants in the policies enacted. This concern with satisfying public wants rests undoubtedly on the belief that a democratic public reacts to an unresponsive government by decreasing public support, perhaps even to the point of resorting to civil strife.[1]

The process of achieving correspondence between public policy and opinion stands out clearly in the idealized New England town meeting and in the Greek city-states wherein the entire society, excepting slaves and outsiders, gathered to vote city policy. Such totally participant democracies are unfeasible in modern nation-states with hundreds of millions of citizens or even in towns with 10,000 to 20,000 persons. The scale of human society has outrun the feasibility of such democracies creating large societies which cannot await the burdensome gathering of all citizens to make decisions on pressing and important matters. In modern large societies, the institution of the elected representative presents the opportunity for democracy.

---

[1] Seymour Martin Lipset, *Political Man* (New York: Doubleday & Co., 1959), chap. 3. Note: Throughout this essay I have referred to the public. In using this concept I do not want to imply that the public is any more than the sum of all of its members. Clearly, as in any assemblage of people such as a town meeting, some will feel the issue is irrelevant, and having no opinions they may not participate. Public opinion in such cases is the opinion of those who have preferences and choose to participate. The saliency of the issue to a given individual and his resulting intense participation might well cause his opinion to weigh more heavily in some linkage processes.

1

The representatives of the public vote the choices of the government in the name of those they represent. Between the masses of the public and the enforced public policy stands the specialist in political participation, the representative. This specialization of effort, with the representative making public policy, frees the less participant masses to invest their time and energy in other concerns, such as earning a living. But the specialization is not without its potential costs as the representative may not perfectly reflect the wishes of those he represents. Along with the institution of the representative comes the need to assure somehow public accountability.

If all men and women held the same opinions as to what public policy should be, such as getting out of Vietnam no matter what the cost or making the automobile pollution free immediately even at the cost of stopping its sale, it would not matter who made public decisions. Any group of people (or for that matter any single person) could be designated the decision makers, and the laws they enacted would reflect opinion and thus would gain public support. At the opposite extreme, if no one shared an opinion on any issue with anyone else, decisions would depend entirely on who made them. Real societies are not so totally individualistic, but it does matter who makes decisions. How can we be assured that the representative acts true to the preferences of his constituents? How can we be assured that the small number of representatives enacts the same policies that the entire society would were they gathered into one stupendous town meeting?

In considering the linkage between public opinion and public policy, the concern here changes to the elite who participate politically and especially to those who hold the formal office of representative be it congressman, member of Parliament, city councilman, or state legislator. Once all technical considerations associated with an issue have been evaluated, such as its expense, impact on the system, and technical feasibility, the representative confronts the decision as to whether he should support or oppose the proposal armed with both his personal opinions and his perception of what various others prefer. Among those various others are the public or segments of it such as the poor, the black, laborers, and college students. Of course the best possible circumstance for the representative is to feel all would agree with him in his vote.[2] While his ultimate decision may be influenced or shaped by a large number of people, situations, and ideas with which he has contact, the question concerning us in this reader rests on whether the policy he and others play a role in enacting is that which the public prefers.

An extensive literature describes the role the public should play in a democracy and the necessary function of representation in large societies. Most of this discussion centers on the public monitoring the actions of their representatives sufficiently to assure that public policy responds to

---

[2] Norman R. Luttbeg and Harmon Zeigler, "Attitude Consensus and Conflict in an Interest Group: An Assessment of Cohesion," *American Political Science Review*, vol. 60 (September 1966), pp. 655–66.

public wishes.[3] The average individual in this literature must be an active political participant. But a parallel literature, originating with Mosca and Pareto, warns of the potential dangers of extensive public participation in the making of public policy. This literature emphasizes the need for a rational, well-conceived, foresightful direction in the affairs of government, all of which might be threatened by an uninformed, immoderate and self-centered public.

Recently explored facts of actual public participation and the quality of the average man's political thoughts allows no resolution to this controversy as to whether greater or lesser public participation is desirable. On the one hand the public is inattentive to politics—relying on their commitment to one of the major political parties or their quick impression of the candidates in deciding how they will vote. And for most, voting is the limit of public involvement in politics. Appeals for attendance at public meetings, for funds, and for campaign efforts fail to spur much public activity. The classic statement of these early voting research finds is *The American Voter*.[4] Such lack of participation may satisfy those apprehensive about broad public participation but are of grave concern to those who see an active public as essential to holding representatives responsible. Similarly, those who would discourage public participation will find any evidence of the public's monitoring of its political leaders and reacting to public policy as dissatisfying. Public support for Wallace, votes against busing, defeats of bond issues and flouridation all may be viewed as regrettable indications of a not totally apathetic public.

While I recognize that some may believe public policy should not be responsive to public opinion, even for them the question of the degree and method of any such response should be important. The organizing concept of this reader is political linkage. Any means by which political leaders act in accordance with the wants, needs, and demands of the public in making government policy is a political linkage. This definition avoids the limiting idea that linkage is either just communication between the representative and the represented or compliance by representatives to public opinion forced on them by public participation. As we will see, some models of political linkage involve communication; others do not. Some models necessitate actions by the average man to assure the correct performance of his elected leaders; others do not. All, however, if fulfilled as prescribed would yield a public policy consistent with public opinion.

I intend to make no statement about the relative desirability of each model or any prescription as to what must be done to improve the quality of American democracy. Rather, my intent in organizing this reader is to gather from disparate sources the conceptual frameworks and pertinent data that will allow the student some grasp of the existing pattern by

---

[3] A valuable summary and critique of this literature is Peter Bachrach, *The Theory of Democratic Elitism* (Boston: Little, Brown and Co., 1967).

[4] Angus Campbell, Philip E. Converse, Warren E. Miller, and Donald E. Stokes, *The American Voter* (New York: Wiley, 1960).

which democratic policy meets its hardest standard, satisfying public opinion.

COERCIVE MODELS OF POLITICAL LINKAGE

The Rational-Activist Model. This model, so popular in civic text-books and in public rhetoric, merely takes the desirable activities on the part of individuals in a small, ideal, democratic society where everyone participates and introduces the element of representation made necessary in a large society. Only the representative and the public act in this ex-planation of political linkage, and both have extensive responsibilities. The average man is expected to be politically informed, involved, ra-tional in reaching decisions, and above all active in elections as well as in the campaigns preceding them. Having formed a personal opinion on each of the various issues based on information personally gathered or presented in speeches and knowing the positions of the various candi-dates for public office, the individual lends his support to those candi-dates most closely supporting his views. The most popular candidates in open and unbiased elections then obtain the offices and after a proper time expect to stand for reelection to give the public an opportunity to express satisfaction with their performance in office. This model posits no distinction as to whether the representative votes his opinions which satisfy the public or votes his perceptions of what the public wants. But assuming the representative desires to remain in office, it seems unlikely that he would not be motivated to try anticipating or evaluating public opinions and to seek thereby broad public approval for his policy votes. Clearly in his day-to-day dealings with constituents, the representative will more than once face constituents' threats to support his opponent should he not vote as they demand.

Extensive information, accurate communication, broad participation, attention to politics, or at least that part that pertains to political linkage, and rational choice based upon clear perception of alternatives charac-terize the expectations of this model on both the representative and the represented.

The Political Parties Model. The political parties model focuses on an intermediate institution, the political party, which because of its de-sire to be victorious by having candidates elected to public office, pro-vides a link between leaders and their public, facilitating the process of political linkage. Because the parties nominate and present candidates for office under their labels, the decision of the public in elections dimin-ishes from one of choosing between several candidates for each office to one of choosing between alternative party slates of candidates. If, for example, there are six offices to be filled each with two candidates, he need only make one decision as to which party he will support rather than six decisions among the candidates for each office. While this nets the individual a substantial saving in decisions, his behavior in evaluating the parties and in voting continues to be that expected of the rational activist voter. He needs to know the parties' platforms, to access their compatibility with his own political preferences in a rational manner, and to be aware of the party's fulfillment of its promise while holding office.

Political parties also have responsibilities under this model as they must be capable of pressing for their platform through their elected officials which should result, if they hold the majority of the particular legislature, in the passage of the platform programs. The minority party's or parties' role is to criticize the performance of the majority and to offer an alternative at each election.

The improbability that the alternatives on each of the complex issues in modern society could be summarized in just two parties' platforms recommends an ideologically more diverse multiple party system. But the impass of many minority parties each trying to enact its platform while thwarting the platforms of all others equally strongly recommends against more than two parties. With more than two parties it is probable that none will have majority control of the legislature and thus none will be capable of implementing their platform without the aid of an opposition party. The debate as to the virtues of two party versus multiple party systems flourishes within the discipline and is further complicated by the fact that multiple party systems have been disturbingly unstable.[5]

The Pressure Groups Model. With the sudden awareness that organized business groups and labor unions actively press their values on government came the awareness of yet another model by which the varied opinion of the public in a large society can be implemented in government policy. The originators of this model see society not as millions of individuals each with idiosyncratic opinions, but rather as thousands or even as few as hundreds of groups with opinion on government policy shared by all members of the group. According to this model groups either originate opinion or summarize it. A man adopting his group's opinion because either he shares experiences with them or feels he must conform illustrates groups originating opinion. Alternatively, existing groups may adopt positions on new social issues to attract and maintain their membership. The individual need only choose among groups exhorting various positions.

Thus, groups are the source of all opinion or they express all opinion of importance.[6] But whichever, this aggregation of opinion within groups greatly reduces the number of actors needing to be considered by government in making policy. The total participation of the town meeting is thus again possible as the number of significant actors is again small enough not to need representatives. All groups, like all people in the town meeting, can participate. But two major problems exist. First, not all the actors weigh equally as would the individuals in the town meeting. Some groups are enormous; others while vocal are quite small. Clearly, the model necessitates some weighting of opinion. Second, these groups cannot directly make public policy but must act through elected officials.

---

[5] Jean Blondel, *An Introduction to Comparative Government* (New York: Praeger, 1969), pp. 164–68.

[6] David B. Truman, *The Governmental Process* (New York: Knopf, 1951), chap. 2.

Ideally, even the representative is immaterial, as decisions can be made on the basis of their popularity among the groups. The representative need only be the tabulator of the votes of groups or the weather vane of group pressures, implementing into policy the predominant direction of their pressures.

Actually, I am aware of no author who expresses the pressure group model in its purest form. Most accept political parties and discuss the pressure groups' activities to make candidates and parties responsive to their needs. Since the pressure groups primarily rely on offers of support and threats to deny support in their relations with political parties, there is debate about the best strategy for dealing with public leaders. If the pressure group strongly identifies with a political party that proves victorious, the pressure group of course is in a far better position to enact its preferences. But if the party loses, the political leaders elected from the other party will feel no need to respond to its demands, and the group loses its access. Thus in reality the groups afford an alternative source of communications and pressure on the representative, supplementing or even contradicting the efforts of the political parties. The compliance of the representative to the will of the group is sought once again, with the intimation that failure to do so will threaten the reelection he seeks.

Some theorists and researchers have argued that the mix of political parties and pressure groups operates to optimize the linkage between the public and its leaders. Thus any alternation of the status quo in the United States to reflect better the nature of the political parties model, as exemplified by the British party system, would potentially threaten the American political system.[7] They argue that a competitive political party system functions best when independent of pressure groups.[8] This amounts to saying that the political parties model will not operate properly in the presence of a functioning pressure group model.

NONCOERCIVE MODELS

Each of the models discussed thus far hinges on the ability of the public or groups of the public monitoring the representatives' behavior and using elections to reward or penalize them. But let us broaden our question from how representatives can be forced to enact public opinion to how public policy can reflect public opinion. The key word dropped in the second phrase is *forced*. Using our earlier distinction between a representative acting on his personal opinion rather than on his perception of others' opinions and adding a distinction as to whether or not he is exposed to coercion which would force him to act responsively, we can conceive of four means by which public policy might correspond with public opinion.

Each of the cells in Figure 1 describes a process by which at least

---

[7] Pendleton Herring, *The Politics of Democracy* (New York: Rinehart, 1940).

[8] Committee on Political Parties of the American Political Science Association, "Toward a More Responsible Two-Party System," *American Political Science Review*, vol. 44 (September 1950), supplement.

FIGURE 1

Means by which Representatives Can Serve the Preferences of the Public

	Coercion of Some Sort Used to Assure Performance	No Means of Coercion Necessary to Assure Performance
Representative acts consistently with his personal preferences	Men whose preferences are preferred by the followers are made representatives. A	Because representatives and the public share many experiences and preferences, representatives in voting their own preferences also vote the preferences of their constituents. C
Representative acts on what he believes to be the preferences of those he leads	Representatives vote the preferences of their followers in fear of being removed from leadership. B	Representatives vote what they believe to be the preferences of their followers and even anticipate public preferences because the representatives believe they should do so. D

some of the representatives might vote a policy consistent with their constituent's opinions. The number of men accurately reflecting public opinion by these processes among any assembly greatly affects the likelihood of a public policy consistent with public opinion, but the major broadening of consideration implicit in the figure is the addition of cells C and D. The previous models which we have discussed necessitate no distinction as to whether the representative acts consistently with his personal preferences or those he believes are preferred by his constituents. His accountability and responsibility depend on his standing for election and being judged by the voters individually, on the basis of his party record, or on the basis of support that groups involved decide to give him.

The distinction as to whose preferences he acts on looms more important in the noncoercive models under the second column of the figure. Discussion earlier was on the polar extremes wherein all opinion is shared among representatives and the represented or no opinion is shared with the decision entirely contingent upon who makes it. The real truth probably lies somewhere between the two extremes, implying that at least on some issues some of the time there is sufficient sharing of opinion within a society that the representative acting on his own preferences does coincidentally vote public opinion.

The Sharing Model. This model merely concedes the possibility that without any coercion by the electorate, such as using election or threatening to take action in elections, certain policies abhorred by the electorate will be equally abhorrent to the representatives, causing them to satisfy public opinion merely by acting on their personal opinions. The positive side of this process can also be expected, as we can hardly expect any legislative body in an American society to make the consumption of apple pie illegal. More seriously, the continuation of certain policies and the exclusion of others seems guaranteed by the sharing model process. American surrender to the will of the Soviet Union, the full socialization of the American economy, the termination of public education, or allowing everyone to the use of services and materials of society to his own taste rather than to his ability to pay fall beyond the scope of public policy-making American legislatures.

The diversity of modern democratic society with the resulting great potential for biases in the preferences of those who govern of course severely limits the scope of issues on which public policy satisfies public opinion by way of the sharing model. But a middle-class representative of a middle-class district, acting only on his own beliefs, can be expected a very large percentage of the time to act consistently with his constituents' opinions. Unlike the previous three models the sharing model is not conceived as a total explanation of political linkage; it merely accentuates a base level of consistency achieved without any conscious efforts on the part of either the representative or the represented.

The Role-Playing Model. In any position we find ourselves in society, such as being a student, a man, or a criminal, we each have ideas about correct behavior. This is also true about the public representative. These ideas about the correct behavior and attitudes for a representative may well be shared by the representative and the public. Edmund Burke captures the most commonly disputed roles associated with being a representative in his famous speech to his constituents in Bristol. He argued that as a representative he was not merely their delegate voicing the most popular opinion among them but rather was their trustee elected by them with the expectation that his wisdom would cause him to act in their interest even if contrary to their immediate opinion. From Burke's perspective, only two distinct roles—the delegate and the trustee—seemed available for that part of the representative's behavior pertaining to his interaction with his constituents. Without roles the representatives might feel that it is perfectly appropriate to steal from the public treasury, to refuse to have any contact with his constituents, to vote for positions which were clearly contrary to both their wants and interests, and even to refuse to stand for reelection threatening bodily harm to those taking exception.

The role-playing model builds on the delegate role in that political linkage can be achieved as shown in cell D of Figure 1. The delegate feels he should be responsive to public sentiments, wants, and desires and strives to enact them even if he feels free of coercion to do so. Again we should note that we do not conceive of this model as describing how all representatives act or how policy is made, but rather how some behavior on the part of representatives can tie public opinion to public policy. The question remains both in this model and in the sharing model how much behavior can be explained by the processes.

While neither the sharing model nor the role-playing model requires coercion to be effective, a finding of shared opinions between representatives and the public need not be only by way of the sharing model. Self-certain men may be elected, do what they wish, and be defeated if their personal attitudes fail to move them to actions preferred by the public.

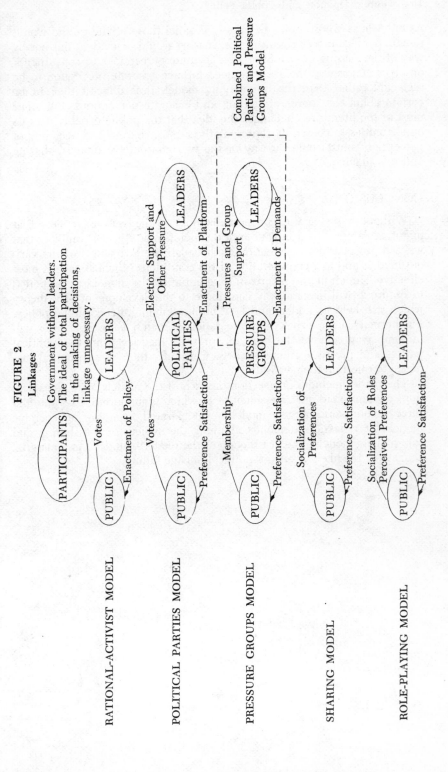

FIGURE 2
Linkages

RATIONAL-ACTIVIST MODEL

Government without leaders.
The ideal of total participation
in the making of decisions,
linkage unnecessary.

PARTICIPANTS

PUBLIC — Votes → LEADERS
PUBLIC ← Enactment of Policy — LEADERS

POLITICAL PARTIES MODEL

POLITICAL PARTIES — Election Support and Other Pressure → LEADERS
POLITICAL PARTIES ← Enactment of Platform — LEADERS

PUBLIC — Votes → POLITICAL PARTIES
PUBLIC ← Preference Satisfaction — POLITICAL PARTIES

Combined Political Parties and Pressure Groups Model

PRESSURE GROUPS — Pressures and Group Support → LEADERS
PRESSURE GROUPS ← Enactment of Demands — LEADERS

PRESSURE GROUPS MODEL

PUBLIC — Membership → PRESSURE GROUPS
PUBLIC ← Preference Satisfaction — PRESSURE GROUPS

SHARING MODEL

PUBLIC — Socialization of Preferences → LEADERS
PUBLIC ← Preference Satisfaction — LEADERS

ROLE-PLAYING MODEL

PUBLIC — Socialization of Roles Perceived Preferences → LEADERS
PUBLIC ← Preference Satisfaction — LEADERS

As only those whose opinions largely parallel those of the public would remain in office in this circumstance, sharing would be evident but not by way of the sharing model. Similarly, accurate perceptions of constituents' opinions may reveal the absolute need to have accurate perception to be reelected rather than the role-playing model. It is difficult then to be certain about the source of sharing and accurate perceptions. But since most of the literature challenges the idea that the public capably uses its opportunities to coerce its representatives, most sharing and accuracy of perceptions must come by way of the two noncoercive models, sharing and role playing.

CONCLUSION

Without a systematic conceptualization of the various models that might explain political linkage in a democratic society, it is unlikely that we will proceed to an evaluation of the relative effectiveness of the various models and to a consideration of the conditions in which each is most effective. Hopefully, my efforts in differentiating the models, as presented in Figure 2, will in some way contribute to the development of a theory which will help us understand how public opinion affects public policy. Furthermore, I hope that the presentation of materials in this reader will in some way remove the aura of "proven" theories from the political parties and pressure groups models. Certainly, there is substantial evidence to question their validity.

The reader includes one section on each of the models, with the selections chosen to aid our assessment as to which is supported. Also the first three sections on coercive models are separated from the noncoercive models by a classic statement containing the nucleus of the sharing and role-playing models. The last section of the reader includes some material suggesting the likely results of political linkage failure.

Section I
The Rational-Activist Model

Bernard Berelson, in our first selection, strives to present systematically the requisites of the rational-activist model. Noting the distinction between theory and fact, he argues that the public's inability to fulfill the requirements of this model should lead to a change in the theory. Furthermore, he questions whether a rational and active public would be healthy to democracy, as people might overtax the political system with their demands and be intolerant of decisions not satisfying them. He conceives of a "political man," who is neither strongly ideological nor totally apolitical. Such men, he claims, are present in American society and help to maintain the balance between conflict and consensus thus stabilizing our democracy. We will repeatedly see this idea of balance throughout the literature on political linkage.

The great outpouring of research in voting behavior, of which Berelson, Paul Lazarsfeld, and William McPhee's *Voting* was an important milestone, threw into the question the ability of the average citizen to use elections to assure that political leaders are responsive to his preferences. The main thrust of the now classic *American Voter*, for example, is the importance of a person's partisan commitment to how he votes. In the reprinted chapter on turnout and the motives people have in voting, the partisan proves to have the virtues attributed to the good citizen, he is politically active and concerned with the outcome of the election. The nonvoter, lacking even the minimal political involvement of the average man, proves quite volatile in choosing a presidential candidate.

The partisan, with his enduring loyalty to one of the major political parties, however, while satisfying the interests and participation standards of the rational-activist model, fails to be responsive to the issues of the campaign. Rather than approaching each election with a rationally formed set of personal preferences, and a receptivity to the positions of the competing candidates, typically one third of the electorate is committed to one of the parties' candidates for president even before the conventions. An additional one third makes up their minds during the conventions, leaving about one third to be convinced by the campaign, quite in violation of the model. Very few people deny a preference for one of the major political parties, and on average only one in seven defects to vote for the opposition. These patterns show little change over time.[1]

Assessing the relative impact of different public evaluations of presidential candidates and the major parties on the average man's decision about which candidate he will support, Stokes challenges the static notion that the 1956 pattern as described in the *American Voter* would apply in later years. Obviously, the sharp decline in support for the Republican presidential candidate between 1956 and 1964 cannot be explained by the party identification of the electorate as it has varied little (the percent calling themselves Democrats has varied between 41 percent and 51 percent since 1956 and the percent Republican, between 24 percent and 29 percent). Indeed, rather than the prime importance of partisan commitment in explaining how people vote, which is the conclusion of the *American Voter,* Stokes finds that the candidates' images—their sincerity, honesty, attractiveness, and other personal virtues which are perceived by the electorate—varies dramatically over the years. This variation is more than enough to change which party wins the presidency.

Edward Dreyer furthers this insight into the irrationality of the voters who decide who will win the presidential election. He finds that those who most closely monitor political information in the mass media prove unlikely to be dissuaded from voting for the political party with which they identify. The less closely a voter follows the available political information, the more likely he is to vote for a different political party than he did in the last election. While impressions of the candidates forced onto a largely inattentive public may largely account for the outcome of presidential elections, such behavior runs contrary to the behavior expected of the rational-activist voter. He would be closely monitoring the available information and would be swayed by his reactions to the issue positions of the candidates, probably often shifting his partisan support between elections.

The late V. O. Key, Jr., took strong exception to the conclusion that the American public was incapable of issue voting. In his last publication, *The Responsible Electorate,* he argues that in any given election, about 12 to 20 percent switch from the political party they voted for in the last election and also that about 15 to 20 percent of the electorate are new voters facing their first presidential election. Thus as much as 40 percent of the electorate will not vote the same as they did in the previous election. Furthermore, in the reprinted selection, Key gives evidence that both standpatters (those voting again for the same party) and the switchers seek consistency between their vote and their attitudes on important issues.

---

[1] Robert S. Erikson and Norman R. Luttbeg, *American Public Opinion: Its Origins, Content and Impact* (New York: Wiley, 1973), chap. 1; and Philip E. Converse, "Change in the American Electorate," in *The Human Meaning of Social Change,* Angus Campell and Philip E. Converse, eds. (New York: Russell Sage Foundation, 1972), pp. 263–338.

Key assumes that his respondents are forming opinions on the issues before they choose their candidate rather than learning to agree with the candidate's positions after selecting him for their vote. Certainly examples of issue positions being taken to be consistent with candidate or party position are common, such as what happened to Democratic and Republican public opinion toward admitting China after the Nixon administration decided to do so. Prior to the policy change, Democrats were more favorable, but after the change, Republicans were more supportive.[2] It seems likely that only the most intense issues would shake the influence of party identification, issues such as civil rights and Vietnam policy.

The 1968 presidential election offered a unique opportunity to assess the impact of issue voting, as Governor George Wallace made one of the strongest third party attempts for the presidency on the basis of several explicit issue positions. A study of this election finds the greatest loss to the Democratic party between the 1964 victory and 1968 loss came from a decline in positive reactions by the public to their 1968 presidential candidate rather than the issues of the campaign or Wallace's third party effort.[3] The Wallace voters, however, were clearly issue motivated. Interestingly the young and the less partisan proved most amenable to the Wallace appeal, indicating that political party identification and its stability over time greatly dampens the influence of issues on the campaign. Political scientists will continue to debate the relative magnitudes of partisan, issue, and image voting. But clearly even the most recent 1972 election study shows public impressions of the candidates themselves (candidate image) most important in accounting for how people vote, and many solely vote their partisan loyalty. Both are contrary to the model.[4]

In a study not reprinted here, Doris Graber assesses the content of a sample of 20 newspapers during the last four weeks of the 1968 presidential campaign.[5] Because newspapers rely heavily on information provided by the candidates and the candidates apparently believe that it is best not to stress issue differences between them and their opponents, newspaper content like public opinion content is composed primarily of the personal qualities of the candidates, not the issues of the campaign. This suggests that public voting is no better than public information, and that the deficiencies of the public in fulfilling its role in the rational-

---

[2] Erikson and Luttbeg, *American Public Opinion*, p. 92.

[3] Philip E. Converse, Warren E. Miller, Jerrold G. Rusk, and Arthur C. Wolfe, "Continuity and Change in American Politics: Parties and Issues in the 1968 Election," *American Political Science Review* (December 1969), pp. 1083–1105.

[4] Arthur H. Miller, Warren E. Miller, Alden S. Raine, and Thad A. Brown, "A Majority Party in Disarray: Policy Polarization in the 1972 Election," a paper presented at the 1973 annual meeting of the American Political Science Association, New Orleans, September 4–8.

[5] Doris Graber, "The Press as Opinion Resource during the 1968 Presidential Campaign," *Public Opinion Quarterly* (Summer 1971), pp. 168–82.

activist model is not attributable to the inherent deficiencies of the public but to the failures of the media and candidates to develop the public.

The Jerrold Rusk and Herbert Weisberg analysis gives additional insights into the public's perceptions of the political arena and into the importance of social issues in the vote. Using what is called a "feeling thermometer," on which a national sample evaluates various groups and presidential candidates, they find the public capable of conceiving of issue dimensions distinct from those they see as represented by the major candidates. This, of course, would suggest that the public is capable of issue voting but perceives the candidates as ordered along a partisan continuum unrelated to the issues. Notably, the few candidates that were seen in 1968 as off the normal partisan dimension, Wallace and McCarthy, by 1970 were seen as less distinctive. Also, between 1968 and 1970 the partisan and issue dimensions better coincided. Either the public was better learning positions which should be taken from their partisan cues, or the political parties are moving to take differing positions on the pressing issues of the day. Unfortunately, their data allow no distinction between these two implications; but this analysis shows the public to be capable of finer distinction than just partisan differences. If they are motivated to escape this condition by seeking partisan cues, they are violating the rational-activist model. If the parties co-opt independent issue positions, making all positions partisan positions, it need not be taken as contrary to the rational-activist model but most supportive of our next model, the political parties model.

Bernard R. Berelson

Democratic Practice and Democratic Theory *

There is always a terrible gulf between the fine and elevating theories about democracy which we read in books on political theory and the actual facts of politics.—Lord Lindsay

I

What does all this mean for the political theory of democracy? For we have been studying not how people come to make choices in general but how they make a political choice, and the political content of the study has broad ramifications beyond the technical interests. In the end, of course, we must leave such theoretical questions to the political theorists and the political philosophers. But the fact that they would not be at home in our empirical material has encouraged us to speak at least briefly to their concerns. Both theory and facts are needed. As Schumpeter says in *Capitalism, Socialism and Democracy:* "The question whether [certain] conditions are fulfilled to the extent required in order to make democracy work should not be answered by reckless assertion or equally reckless denial. It can be answered only by a laborious appraisal of a maze of conflicting evidence."

With respect to politics, empirical-analytic theory and normative theory have only recently become truly separated—and often to their mutual disadvantage and impoverishment. In a recent essay a British scholar comments on "The Decline of Political Theory." That there has been and is now a "decline" seems to be generally accepted. Why? Because, says Alfred Cobban, the theory of the great political thinkers of

* Reprinted from *Voting* by Bernard R. Berelson, Paul F. Lazarsfeld, and William N. McPhee by permission of the University of Chicago Press. Copyright 1954.

The senior author is particularly indebted to his friend and colleague, Edward Shils, for stimulation and instruction on this topic in general and for advice on this chapter in particular.

15

the past was written "with a practical purpose in mind. Their object was to influence actual political behavior. They wrote to condemn or support existing institutions, to justify a political system or persuade their fellow citizens to change it: because, in the last resort, they were concerned with the aims, the purposes of political society." He points out that John Stuart Mill tried to reconcile the demands for state action with established ideals of individual liberty, Bentham to establish a theoretical basis for the legislative and administrative reforms that were then urgently needed, Burke to provide an alternative to the new democratic principle of the sovereignty of the people, Locke to provide a political theory for a generation that had overthrown divine right and established parliamentary government, Hobbes to maintain the primacy of sovereignty in an age of civil wars, etc. From being "formerly the work of men intently concerned with practical issues," the study of political theory

> has become instead an academic discipline written in various esoteric jargons almost as though for the purpose of preventing it from being understood by those who, if they did understand it, might try to put it into practice. . . . Political theory has in this way become disengaged from political facts. Even worse, it has become disengaged on principle, as it has seldom if ever been in the past.

Here, it seems to us, lies one potential use of our data. If the political theorists do not engage directly in politics, they might explore the relevance, the implications, and the meaning of such empirical facts as are contained in this and similar studies. Political theory written with reference to practice has the advantage that its categories are the categories in which political life really occurs. And, in turn, relating research to problems of normative theory would make such research more realistic and more pertinent to the problems of policy. At the same time, empirical research can help to clarify the standards and correct the empirical presuppositions of normative theory. As a modest illustration, this concluding chapter of the volume turns to some of the broad normative and evaluative questions implied in this empirical study.

REQUIREMENTS FOR THE INDIVIDUAL

Perhaps the main impact of realistic research on contemporary politics has been to temper some of the requirements set by our traditional normative theory for the typical citizen. "Out of all this literature of political observation and analysis, which is relatively new," says Max Beloff, "there has come to exist a picture in our minds of the political scene which differs very considerably from that familiar to us from the classical texts of democratic politics."

Experienced observers have long known, of course, that the individual voter was not all that the theory of democracy requires of him. As Bryce put it:

> How little solidity and substance there is in the political or social beliefs of nineteen persons out of every twenty. These beliefs, when examined, mostly resolve themselves into two or three prejudices and aver-

sions, two or three prepossessions for a particular party or section of a party, two or three phrases or catch-words suggesting or embodying arguments which the man who repeats them has not analyzed.

While our data do not support such an extreme statement, they do reveal that certain requirements commonly assumed for the successful operation of democracy are not met by the behavior of the "average" citizen. The requirements, and our conclusions concerning them, are quickly reviewed.[1]

Interest, Discussion, Motivation

The democratic citizen is expected to be interested and to participate in political affairs. His interest and participation can take such various forms as reading and listening to campaign materials, working for the candidate or the party, arguing politics, donating money, and voting. In Elmira the majority of the people vote, but in general they do not give evidence of sustained interest. Many vote without real involvement in the election, and even the party workers are not typically motivated by ideological concerns or plain civic duty.

If there is one characteristic for a democratic system (besides the ballot itself) that is theoretically required, it is the capacity for and the practice of discussion. "It is as true of the large as of the small society," says Lindsay, "that its health depends on the mutual understanding which discussion makes possible; and that discussion is the only possible instrument of its democratic government." How much participation in political discussion there is in the community, what it is, and among whom—these questions have been given answers in an earlier chapter. In this instance there was little true discussion between the candidates, little in the newspaper commentary, little between the voters and the official party representatives, some within the electorate. On the grassroots level there was more talk than debate, and, at least inferentially, the talk had important effects upon voting, in reinforcing or activating the partisans if not in converting the opposition.

An assumption underlying the theory of democracy is that the citizenry has a strong motivation for participation in political life. But it is a curious quality of voting behavior that for large numbers of people motivation is weak if not almost absent. It is assumed that this motivation would gain its strength from the citizen's perception of the difference that alternative decisions made to him. Now when a person buys something or makes other decisions of daily life, there are direct and immediate consequences for him. But for the bulk of the American people the voting decision is not followed by any direct, immediate, visible personal consequences. Most voters, organized or unorganized, are not in a position to foresee the distant and indirect consequences for themselves, let alone

---

[1] A somewhat more general statement is contained in Bernard Berelson, "Democratic Theory and Public Opinion," *Public Opinion Quarterly*, vol. 16 (Fall 1952), pp. 313–30.

the society. The ballot is cast, and for most people that is the end of it. If their side is defeated, "it doesn't really matter."

Knowledge

The democratic citizen is expected to be well informed about political affairs. He is supposed to know what the issues are, what their history is, what the relevant facts are, what alternatives are proposed, what the party stands for, what the likely consequences are. By such standards the voter falls short. Even when he has the motivation, he finds it difficult to make decisions on the basis of full information when the subject is relatively simple and proximate; how can he do so when it is complex and remote? The citizen is not highly informed on details of the campaign, nor does he avoid a certain misperception of the political situation when it is to his psychological advantage to do so. The electorate's perception of what goes on in the campaign is colored by emotional feeling toward one or the other issue, candidate, party, or social group.

Principle

The democratic citizen is supposed to cast his vote on the basis of principle—not fortuitously or frivolously or impulsively or habitually, but with reference to standards not only of his own interest but of the common good as well. Here, again, if this requirement is pushed at all strongly, it becomes an impossible demand on the democratic electorate.

Many voters vote not for principle in the usual sense but "for" a group to which they are attached—their group. The Catholic vote or the hereditary vote is explainable less as principle than as a traditional social allegiance. The ordinary voter, bewildered by the complexity of modern political problems, unable to determine clearly what the consequences are of alternative lines of action, remote from the arena, and incapable of bringing information to bear on principle, votes the way trusted people around him are voting. A British scholar, Max Beloff, takes as the "chief lesson to be derived" from such studies:

> Election campaigns and the programmes of the different parties have little to do with the ultimate result which is predetermined by influences acting upon groups of voters over a longer period. . . . This view has now become a working hypothesis with which all future thinking on this matter will have to concern itself. But if this is admitted, then obviously the picture of the voter as a person exercising conscious choice between alternative persons and alternative programmes tends to disappear.

On the issues of the campaign there is a considerable amount of "don't know"—sometimes reflecting genuine indecision, more often meaning "don't care." Among those with opinions the partisans *agree* on most issues, criteria, expectations, and rules of the game. The supporters of the different sides disagree on only a few issues. Nor, for that matter, do the candidates themselves always join the issue sharply and clearly. The partisans do not agree overwhelmingly with their own party's position, or, rather, only the small minority of highly partisan do; the rest take a rather moderate position on the political considerations involved in an election.

Rationality

The democratic citizen is expected to exercise rational judgment in coming to his voting decision. He is expected to have arrived at his principles by reason and to have considered rationally the implications and alleged consequences of the alternative proposals of the contending parties. Political theorists and commentators have always exclaimed over the seeming contrast here between requirement and fulfillment. Even as sensible and hardminded an observer as Schumpeter was extreme in his view:

> Even if there were no political groups trying to influence him, the typical citizen would in political matters tend to yield to extrarational or irrational prejudice and impulse. The weakness of the rational processes he applies to politics and the absence of effective logical control over the results he arrives at would in themselves suffice to account for that. Moreover, simply because he is not "all there," he will relax his usual moral standards as well and occasionally give in to dark urges which the conditions of private life help him to repress.

Here the problem is first to see just what is meant by rationality. The term, as a recent writer noted, "has enjoyed a long history which has bequeathed to it a legacy of ambiguity and confusion. . . . Any man may be excused when he is puzzled by the question how he ought to use the word and particularly how he ought to use it in relation to human conduct and politics." Several meanings can be differentiated.

It is not for us to certify a meaning. But even without a single meaning —with only the aura of the term—we can make some observations on the basis of our material. In any rigorous or narrow sense the voters are not highly rational; that is, most of them do not ratiocinate on the matter, e.g., to the extent that they do on the purchase of a car or a home. Nor do voters act rationally whose "principles" are held so tenaciously as to blind them to information and persuasion. Nor do they attach efficient means to explicit ends.

The fact that some people change their minds during a political campaign shows the existence of that open-mindedness usually considered a component of rationality. But among whom? Primarily among those who can "afford" a change of mind, in the sense that they have ties or attractions on both sides—the cross-pressured voters in the middle where rationality is supposed to take over from the extremes of partisan feeling. But it would hardly be proper to designate the unstable, uninterested, uncaring middle as the sole or the major possessor of rationality among the electorate. As Beloff points out: "It is likely that the marginal voter is someone who is so inadequately identified with one major set of interests or another and so remote, therefore, from the group-thinking out of which political attitudes arise, that his voting record is an illustration, not of superior wisdom, but of greater frivolity."

The upshot of this is that the usual analogy between the voting "decision" and the more or less carefully calculated decisions of consumers or businessmen or courts, incidentally, may be quite incorrect. For many voters political preferences may better be considered analogous to cultural tastes—in music, literature, recreational activities, dress, ethics, speech, social behavior. Consider the parallels between political preferences and general cultural tastes. Both have their origin in ethnic, sectional, class, and family traditions. Both exhibit stability and resistance to change for individuals but flexibility and adjustment over generations for the society as a whole. Both seem to be matters of sentiment and disposition rather than "reasoned preferences." While both are responsive to changed conditions and unusual stimuli, they are relatively invulnerable to direct argumentation and vulnerable to indirect social influences. Both are characterized more by faith than by conviction and by wishful expectation rather than careful prediction of consequences. The preference for one party rather than another must be highly similar to the preference for one kind of literature or music rather than another, and the choice of the same political party every four years may be parallel to the choice of the same old standards of conduct in new social situations. In short, it appears that a sense of fitness is a more striking feature of political preference than reason and calculation.

II

If the democratic system depended solely on the qualifications of the individual voter, then it seems remarkable that democracies have survived through the centuries. After examining the detailed data on how individuals misperceive political reality or respond to irrelevant social influences, one wonders how a democracy ever solves its political problems. But when one considers the data in a broader perspective—how huge segments of the society adapt to political conditions affecting them or how the political system adjusts itself to changing conditions over long periods of time—he cannot fail to be impressed with the total result. Where the rational citizen seems to abdicate, nevertheless angels seem to tread.

The eminent judge, Learned Hand, in a delightful essay on "Democracy: Its Presumptions and Reality," comes to essentially this conclusion.

> I do not know how it is with you, but for myself I generally give up at the outset. The simplest problems which come up from day to day seem to me quite unanswerable as soon as I try to get below the surface. . . . My vote is one of the most unimportant acts of my life; if I were to acquaint myself with the matters on which it ought really to depend, if I were to try to get a judgment on which I was willing to risk affairs of even the smallest moment, I should be doing nothing else, and that seems a fatuous conclusion to a fatuous undertaking.

Yet he recognizes the paradox—somehow the system not only works on the most difficult and complex questions but often works with distinction. "For, abuse it as you will, it gives a bloodless measure of social forces—

bloodless, have you thought of that?—a means of continuity, a principle of stability, a relief from the paralyzing terror of revolution."

Justice Hand concludes that we have "outgrown" the conditions assumed in traditional democratic theory and that "the theory has ceased to work." And yet, the system that has grown out of classic democratic theory, and, in this country, out of quite different and even elementary social conditions, does continue to work—perhaps even more vigorously and effectively than ever.

That is the paradox. *Individual voters* today seem unable to satisfy the requirements for a democratic system of government outlined by political theorists. But the *system of democracy* does meet certain requirements for a going political organization. The individual members may not meet all the standards, but the whole nevertheless survives and grows. This suggests that where the classic theory is defective is in its concentration on the *individual citizen*. What are undervalued are certain collective properties that reside in the electorate as a whole and in the political and social system in which it functions.

The political philosophy we have inherited, then, has given more consideration to the virtues of the typical citizen of the democracy than to the working of the *system* as a whole. Moreover, when it dealt with the system, it mainly considered the single constitutive institutions of the system, not those general features necessary if the institutions are to work as required. For example, the rule of law, representative government, periodic elections, the party system, and the several freedoms of discussion, press, association, and assembly have all been examined by political philosophers seeking to clarify and to justify the idea of political democracy. But liberal democracy is more than a political system in which individual voters and political institutions operate. For political democracy to survive, other features are required: the intensity of conflict must be limited, the rate of change must be restrained, stability in the social and economic structure must be maintained, a pluralistic social organization must exist, and a basic consensus must bind together the contending parties.

Such features of the system of political democracy belong neither to the constitutive institutions nor to the individual voter. It might be said that they form the atmosphere or the environment in which both operate. In any case, such features have not been carefully considered by political philosophers, and it is on these broader properties of the democratic political system that more reflection and study by political theory is called for. In the most tentative fashion let us explore the values of the political system, as they involve the electorate, in the light of the foregoing considerations.

REQUIREMENTS FOR THE SYSTEM

Underlying the paradox is an assumption that the population is homogeneous socially and should be homogeneous politically: that everybody is about the same in relevant social characteristics; that, if something is a political virtue (like interest in the election), then everyone should have it; that there is such a thing as "the" typical citizen on whom uniform requirements can be imposed. The tendency of classic democratic literature to work with an image of "the" voter was never justified. For, as we will attempt to illustrate here, some of the most important requirements that democratic values impose on a system require a voting population that is not homogeneous but heterogeneous in its political qualities.

The need for heterogeneity arises from the contradictory functions we expect our voting system to serve. We expect the political system to adjust itself and our affairs to changing conditions; yet we demand too that it display a high degree of stability. We expect the contending interests and parties to pursue their ends vigorously and the voters to care; yet, after the election is over, we expect reconciliation. We expect the voting outcome to serve what is best for the community; yet we do not want disinterested voting unattached to the purposes and interests of different segments of that community. We want voters to express their own free and self-determined choices; yet, for the good of the community, we would like voters to avail themselves of the best information and guidance available from the groups and leaders around them. We expect a high degree of rationality to prevail in the decision; but were all irrationality and mythology absent, and all ends pursued by the most coldly rational selection of political means, it is doubtful if the system would hold together.

In short, our electoral system calls for apparently incompatible properties—which, although they cannot all reside in each individual voter, can (and do) reside in a heterogeneous electorate. What seems to be required of the electorate as a whole is a *distribution* of qualities along important dimensions. We need some people who are active in a certain respect, others in the middle, and still others passive. The contradictory things we want from the total require that the parts be different. This can be illustrated by taking up a number of important dimensions by which an electorate might be characterized.

Involvement and Indifference

How could a mass democracy work if all the people were deeply involved in politics? Lack of interest by some people is not without its benefits, too. True, the highly interested voters vote more, and know more about the campaign, and read and listen more, and participate more; however, they are also less open to persuasion and less likely to change. Extreme interest goes with extreme partisanship and might culminate in rigid fanaticism that could destroy democratic processes if generalized throughout the community. Low affect toward the election—not caring much—underlies the resolution of many political problems; votes can be resolved into a two-party split instead of fragmented into many parties (the splinter parties of the left, for example, splinter because their advocates are *too* interested in politics). Low interest provides maneuvering room for political shifts necessary for a complex society in a period of rapid change. Compromise might be based upon sophisticated awareness of costs and returns—perhaps impossible to demand of a mass society—but it is more often induced by indifference. Some people are and should be highly interested in politics, but not everyone is or needs to be. Only the doctrinaire would deprecate the moderate indifference that facilitates compromise.

Hence, an important balance between action motivated by strong sentiments and action with little passion behind it is obtained by heterogeneity within the electorate. Balance of this sort is, in practice, met by a distribution of voters rather than by a homogeneous collection of "ideal" citizens.

Stability and Flexibility

A similar dimension along which an electorate might be characterized is stability-flexibility. The need for change and adaptation is clear, and the need for stability ought equally to be (especially from observation of current democratic practice in, say, certain Latin-American countries).

How is political stability achieved? There are a number of social sources of political stability: the training of the younger generation before it is old enough to care much about the matter, the natural selection that surrounds the individual voter with families and friends who reinforce his own inclinations, the tendency to adjust in favor of the majority of the group, the self-perpetuating tendency of political traditions among ethnic and class and regional strata where like-minded people find themselves socially together. Political stability is based upon social stability. Family traditions, personal associations, status-related organizational memberships, ethnic affiliations, socioeconomic strata—such ties for the individual do not change rapidly or sharply, and since his vote is so importantly a product of them, neither does it. In effect, a large part of the study of voting deals not with why votes change but rather with why they do not.

In addition, the varying conditions facing the country, the varying political appeals made to the electorate, and the varying dispositions of the voters activated by these stimuli—these, combined with the long-lasting nature of the political loyalties they instil, produce an important cohesion within the system. For example, the tendencies operating in 1948 electoral decisions not only were built up in the New Deal and Fair Deal era but also dated back to parental and grandparental loyalties, to religious and ethnic cleavages of a past era, and to moribund sectional and community conflicts. Thus, in a very real sense any particular election is a composite of various elections and various political and social events. People vote for a President on a given November day, but their choice is made not simply on the basis of what has happened in the preceding months or even four years; in 1948 some people were in effect voting on the internationalism issue of 1940, others on the depression issue of 1932, and some, indeed, on the slavery issues of 1860.

The vote is thus a kind of "moving average" of reactions to the political past. Voters carry over to each new election remnants of issues raised in previous elections—and so there is always an overlapping of old and new decisions that give a cohesion in time to the political system. Hence the composite decision "smooths out" political change. The people vote *in* the same election, but not all of them vote *on* it.

What of flexibility? Curiously, the voters least admirable when measured against individual requirements contribute most when measured against the aggregate requirement for flexibility. For those who change political preferences most readily are those who are least interested, who are subject to conflicting social pressures, who have inconsistent beliefs and erratic voting histories. Without them—if the decision were left only to the deeply concerned, well-integrated, consistently-principled ideal citizens—the political system might easily prove too rigid to adapt to changing domestic and international conditions.

In fact, it may be that the very people who are most sensitive to changing social conditions are those most susceptible to political change. For, in either case, the people exposed to membership in overlapping strata, those whose former life-patterns are being broken up, those who are moving about socially or physically, those who are forming new families and new friendships—it is they who are open to adjustments of attitudes and tastes. They may be the least partisan and the least interested voters, but they perform a valuable function for the entire system. Here again is an instance in which an individual "inadequacy" provides a positive service for the society: The campaign can be a reaffirming force for the settled majority and a creative force for the unsettled minority. There is stability on both sides and flexibility in the middle.

Progress and Conservation

Closely related to the question of stability is the question of past versus future orientation of the system. In America a progressive outlook is highly valued, but, at the same time, so is a conservative one. Here a balance between the two is easily found in the party system and in the distribution of voters themselves from extreme conservatives to extreme liberals. But a balance between the two is also achieved by a distribution of political dispositions through time. There are periods of great political agitation (i.e., campaigns) alternating with periods of political dormancy. Paradoxically, the former—the campaign period—is likely to be an instrument of conservatism, often even of historical regression.

Many contemporary campaigns (not, however, 1952) must be stabilizing forces that activated past tendencies in individuals and reasserted past patterns of group voting. In 1948, for example, the middle-class Protestants reaffirmed their traditional Republican position, the working-class Protestants reverted toward their position of the 1930's and the working-class Catholics toward their position not only of the 1930's but of a generation or more earlier. In this sense the campaign was a retreat away from new issues back toward old positions.

Political campaigns tend to make people more consistent both socially and psychologically; they vote more with their social groups and agree more with their own prior ideas on the issues. But new ideas and new alignments are in their infancy manifested by inconsistency psychologically and heterogeneity socially; they are almost by definition deviant and minority points of view. To the extent that they are inhibited by pressure or simply by knowledge of what is the proper (i.e., majority) point of view in a particular group, then the campaign period is not a time to look for the growth of important new trends.

This "regressive tendency" may appear as a reaction to intense propaganda during decisive times. The term "regressive" need not imply a reversion to less-developed, less-adaptive behavior; in fact, one might argue that the revival of a Democratic vote among workers was functional for their interests. What it refers to is simply the reactivation of prior dispositions—dispositions in politics that date back years and decades, often to a prior political era.

Its counterpart, of course, is what we believe to be an important potential for progress during the periods of relaxed tension and low-pressure political and social stimuli that are especially characteristic of America between political campaigns. The very tendency for Americans to neglect their political system most of the time—to be "campaign citizens" in the sense that many are "Sunday churchgoers"—is not without its values. Change may come best from relaxation.

Again, then, a balance (between preservation of the past and receptivity to the future) seems to be required of a democratic electorate. The heterogeneous electorate in itself provides a balance between liberalism and conservatism; and so does the sequence of political events from periods of drifting change to abrupt rallies back to the loyalties of earlier years.

Consensus and Cleavage

We have talked much in the text, and perhaps implied more, about consensus and cleavage. Although there were certain clusters of political opinion in Elmira, at the same time there were a number of opinions that did not break along class or party lines. American opinion on public issues is much too complex to be designated by such simple, single-minded labels as *the* housewife opinion or *the* young people's opinion or even *the* workers' opinion. If one uses as a base the central Republican-Democratic cleavage, then one finds numerous "contradictions" within individuals, within strata and groups, and within party supporters themselves. There are many issues presented, cafeteria-style, for the voter to choose from, and there are overlaps in opinion in every direction.

Similarly there are required *social* consensus and cleavage—in effect, pluralism—in politics. Such pluralism makes for enough consensus to hold the system together and enough cleavage to make it move. Too much consensus would be deadening and restrictive of liberty; too much cleavage would be destructive of the society as a whole.

Consider the pictures of the hypothetical relationships between political preference (e.g., party support) and a social characteristic as presented in this chart:

Percentage for Party Y, by Characteristic X

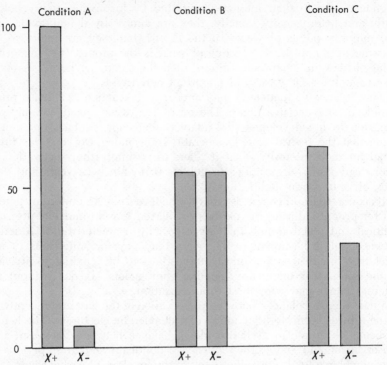

In Condition A there is virtual identity between the characteristics and political preference; all the people of type X+ vote one way, and all the people of X− vote the other way. In Condition B the opposite is the case, and there is no relationship between vote and the characteristic; both parties are supported equally by people of the two types. In Condition C there is neither a complete relationship nor a complete absence; more X+'s than X−'s are partisans of a given side, but there are some members of each type in each political camp.

Now a democratic society in which Condition A was intensified would probably be in danger of its existence. The issues of politics would cut so deeply, be so keenly felt, and, especially, be so fully reinforced by other social identifications of the electorate as to threaten the basic consensus itself. This might be called "total politics"—a conception of politics, incidentally, advanced by such leading theorists of National Socialism and communism as Carl Schmitt and Lenin. This involves the mutual reinforcement of political differences and other social distinctions meaningful to the citizen. The multiplication of Condition B, on the other hand, would suggest a community in which politics was of no "real" importance to the community, in which it was not associated with special interests. Condition C is a combination of Conditions A and B—that is, a situation in which special interests are of some but not of overriding importance. It portrays neither the extremist or fanatical community like A nor the "pure" or utopian community like B.

There is nothing in Elmira that represents Condition A; the closest approximation would be the relationship between vote and religion or minority ethnic status, and even here there are group overlaps in vote amounting to from a quarter to a third of the members. The nearest approximation to Condition B is the relationship between vote and sex, which is another way of saying that there is little relevance of this characteristic to political matters, at least so far as party preference is concerned. The relationships between vote and socioeconomic status or vote and occupation are examples of Condition C.

The social and political correlations we find in places like Elmira (that are not a priori meaningless) are of the C type to a greater or less extent. What this means is that there is a good deal of cross-group and cross-party identification and affiliation within the community. The political lines are drawn in meaningful ways but are not identical with the lines of social groupings. The same social heterogeneity that produces self-interest also produces a cross-cutting and harmonious community interest.

Thus again a requirement we might place on an electoral system—balance between total political war between segments of the society and total political indifference to group interests of that society—translates into varied requirements for different individuals. With respect to group or bloc voting, as with other aspects of political behavior, it is perhaps not unfortunate that "some do and some do not."

Individualism and Collectivism

Lord Bryce pointed out the difficulties in a theory of democracy that assumes that each citizen must himself be capable of voting intelligently:

> Orthodox democratic theory assumes that every citizen has, or ought to have, thought out for himself certain opinions, i.e., ought to have a definite view, defensible by argument, of what the country needs, of what principles ought to be applied in governing it, of the man to whose hands the government ought to be entrusted. There are persons who talk, though certainly very few who act, as if they believed this theory, which may be compared to the theory of some ultra-Protestants that every good Christian has or ought to have . . . worked out for himself from the Bible a system of theology.

In the first place, however, the information available to the individual voter is not limited to that directly possessed by him. True, the individual casts his own personal ballot. But, as we have tried to indicate throughout this volume, that is perhaps the most individualized action he takes in an election. His vote is formed in the midst of his fellows in a sort of group decision—if, indeed, it may be called a decision at all—and the total information and knowledge possessed in the group's present and past generations can be made available for the group's choice. Here is where opinion-leading relationships, for example, play an active role.

Second, and probably more important, the individual voter may not have a great deal of detailed information, but he usually has picked up the crucial *general* information as part of his social learning itself. He may not know the parties' positions on the tariff, or who is for reciprocal trade treaties, or what are the differences on Asiatic policy, or how the parties split on civil rights, or how many security risks were exposed by whom. But he cannot live in an American community without knowing broadly where the parties stand. He has learned that the Republicans are more conservative and the Democrats more liberal—and he can locate his own sentiments and cast his vote accordingly. After all, he must vote for one or the other party, and, if he knows the big thing about the parties, he does not need to know all the little things. The basic role a party plays as an institution in American life is more important to his voting than a particular stand on a particular issue.

It would be unthinkable to try to maintain our present economic style of life without a complex system of delegating to others what we are not competent to do ourselves, without accepting and giving training to each other about what each is expected to do, without accepting our dependence on others in many spheres and taking responsibility for their dependence on us in some spheres. And, like it or not, to maintain our present political style of life, we may have to accept much the same interdependence with others in collective behavior. We have learned slowly in economic life that it is useful not to have everyone a butcher or a baker, any more than it is useful to have no one skilled in such activities. The same kind of division of labor—as repugnant as it may be in some respects to our individualistic tradition—is serving us well today in mass politics. There is an implicit division of political labor within the electorate.

III. CONCLUSION

In short, when we turn from requirements for "average" citizens to requirements for the survival of the total democratic system, we find it unnecessary for the individual voter to be an "average citizen" cast in the classic or any other single mold. With our increasingly complex and differentiated citizenry has grown up an equally complex political system, and it is perhaps not simply a fortunate accident that they have grown and prospered together.

But it is a dangerous act of mental complacency to assume that conditions found surviving together are, therefore, positively "functional" for each other. The apathetic segment of America probably has helped to hold the system together and cushioned the shock of disagreement, adjustment, and change. But that is not to say that we can stand apathy without limit. Similarly, there must be some limit to the degree of stability or nonadaptation that a political society can maintain and still survive in a changing world. And surely the quality and amount of conformity that is necessary and desirable can be exceeded, as it has been in times of war and in the present Communist scare, to the damage of the society itself and of the other societies with which it must survive in the world.

How can our analysis be reconciled with the classical theory of liberal political democracy? Is the theory "wrong"? Must it be discarded in favor of empirical political sociology? Must its ethical or normative content be dismissed as incompatible with the nature of modern man or of mass society? That is not our view. Rather, it seems to us that modern political theory of democracy stands in need of revision and not replacement by empirical sociology. The classical political philosophers were right in the direction of their assessment of the virtues of the citizen. But they demanded those virtues in too extreme or doctrinal a form. The voter does have some principles, he does have information and rationality, he does have interest—but he does not have them in the extreme, elaborate, comprehensive, or detailed form in which they were uniformly recommended by political philosophers. Like Justice Hand, the typical citizen has other interests in life, and it is good, even for the political system, that he pursues them. The classical requirements are more appropriate for the opinion leaders in the society, but even they do not meet them directly. Happily for the system, voters distribute themselves along a continuum:

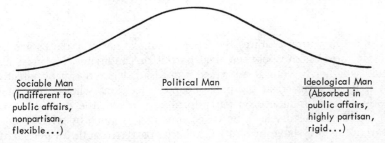

Sociable Man	Political Man	Ideological Man
(Indifferent to		(Absorbed in
public affairs,		public affairs,
nonpartisan,		highly partisan,
flexible...)		rigid...)

And it turns out that this distribution itself, with its internal checks and balances, can perform the functions and incorporate the same values ascribed by some theorists to each individual in the system as well as to the constitutive political institutions!

Twentieth-century political theory—both analytic and normative—will arise only from hard and long observation of the actual world of politics, closely identified with the deeper problems of practical politics. Values and the behavior they are meant to guide are not distinctly separate or separable parts of life as it is lived; and how Elmirans choose their governors is not completely unrelated to the considerations of how they are *supposed* to choose them. We disagree equally with those who believe that normative theory about the proper health of a democracy has nothing to gain from analytic studies like ours; with those who believe that the whole political tradition from Mill to Locke is irrelevant to our realistic understanding and assessment of modern democracy; or with those like Harold Laski who believe that "the decisions of men, when they come to choose their governors, are influenced by considerations which escape all scientific analysis."

We agree with Cobban: "For a century and a half the Western democracies have been living on the stock of basic political ideas that were last restated toward the end of the eighteenth century. That is a long time. . . . The gap thus formed between political facts and political ideas has steadily widened. It has taken a long time for the results to become evident; but now that we have seen what politics devoid of a contemporary moral and political theory means, it is possible that something may be done about it."

Angus Campbell, Philip E. Converse,

Warren E. Miller, and Donald E. Stokes

Voting Turnout*

The act of voting requires the citizen to make not a single choice but two. He must choose between rival parties or candidates. He must also decide whether to vote at all. Since a partisan decision can be effective only if it is expressed at the polls, people's decisions whether or not to vote have great influence on party fortunes. Indeed, the dramatic turns of our electoral history have been accompanied as much by wide changes in turnout as they have by shifts in relative party strength. In percentage terms, the change in turnout between the 1948 and 1952 elections was greater than the change in relative party strength.

Citizen participation at the polls is highly valued in American society, and every national election campaign brings its spate of exhortations to vote. Because of the high value placed on turnout, a good deal of the attention given it in popular discussion has to do with why so many people fail to vote. Despite the great public interest aroused by a presidential contest, our national elections bring less than two thirds of the adult population to the polls.[1] Of course, in any year a great many people are kept from voting by legal barriers—most commonly, in a nation of movers, by the requirements of minimum residence in a state and its lesser divisions.[2] [Ed: This is no longer true.] And many others are kept from voting by political or personal obstacles they could not reasonably overcome. But in each of our national elections millions of people whose way toward registering and voting is relatively clear fail to do so, and this fact has excited wide comment.

---

* Reprinted from Campbell et al., *The American Voter: An Abridgement* (New York: Wiley, 1964), chap. 4.

[1] For example, the 61,522,000 people who voted for president in 1952 constituted 62.7% of the 97,574,000 people the Census Bureau estimated to be civilians of voting age on November 1 of that year. In 1956, 62,027,000 voters comprised 60.4% of an estimated 102,179,000 civilians of voting age.

[2] A comparison of reported length of current residence with state and local residence requirements indicates that these requirements have prevented at least 3 per cent of our respondents from voting. In 1972 the Supreme Court ruled duration of residence to be unconstitutional.

Although accounting for nonvoting is important in understanding the turnout decision, we will conceive the problem of explanation too narrowly if we concentrate solely on failures to vote. The really extraordinary aspect of our presidential elections is that tens of millions of people *do* expend the energy required to reach their polling-places and register their votes. If we are to explain this type of behavior we must find the patterns of motivation that lead these people to vote, as we must find the conditions that keep others from doing so. The explanatory problem is just that of finding what it is that distinguishes the voter from the nonvoter, and we will see as the discussion proceeds that the deviant voter— the person we "expect" *not* to vote yet who does—is somewhat more difficult to explain than is the person we expect to vote who fails to do so.

We assume that the decision to vote, no less than the decision to vote for a given party, rests immediately on psychological forces, although

TABLE 1

Popular Participation in Politics, 1952 and 1956°

	1952	1956
"Do you belong to any political club or organizations?"	2%	3%
"Did you give any money or buy tickets or anything to help the campaign for one of the parties or candidates?"	4	10
"Did you go to any political meetings, rallies, dinners, or things like that?"	7	7
"Did you do any other work for one of the parties or candidates?"	3	3

° Entries are proportions of total samples answering affirmatively.

nonpsychological barriers to action are more prominent among the causes of turnout than they are among the causes of partisan choice. Hence, our quest of understanding begins with an examination of motivational forces, and this chapter will describe a number of psychological influences that affect the likelihood the individual will vote. Yet we assume that the proximate causes of turnout, like the immediate determinants of partisan choice, are intervening variables that express the influence of a wide array of antecedent factors.

MODES OF POLITICAL PARTICIPATION

For most Americans voting is the sole act of participation in politics. Table 1 shows for the two Eisenhower elections the proportion of the electorate that was politically active in each of four elementary ways. The percentages of this table make clear that only small fractions of the public are connected with a party apparatus or help with the work and expense of a campaign. Moreover, since the groups in our samples who did report engaging in these activities are widely overlapping, the percentages cannot be added together to reach an estimate of the total number who were active.

Beyond these modes of participation there are several informal, less well-defined ways in which large numbers of people become "engaged" in a presidential contest. One of the most important of these is informal political discussion. In each of the Eisenhower elections about a fourth of the electorate reported having talked to other people and having tried to persuade them to vote a given way.[3] The casual nature of this behavior should not conceal its importance either as an expression of individual motivation or as a means by which the final distribution of partisan preference in the electorate is achieved. Discussion of this sort is undoubtedly one of the most significant forms of political behavior by a mass public, even if it does not draw the individual directly into organized political activity.

Although it requires still less personal energy, following the campaign through the mass communications media might also be described as a type of informal participation. For some individuals, gleaning the political content of newspapers and magazines and of radio and television is a principal means of relating to politics. For others—presumably for a great majority of Americans—following the campaign in the mass media is a much more passive activity. Yet since the audiences of the media screen out vast amounts of their content, the individual plays at least a minimal role in deciding what he will and will not attend, and in this sense following an election campaign in the media may be called a form of participation.[4] In the Eisenhower elections only about one person in twenty said that the campaign had failed to reach him through any of the principal media of communication.

Since this book is concerned primarily with the act of voting itself, we will fix our attention on turnout rather than on other types of participation in politics. Yet in assessing the determinants of the voting act we are assessing factors which may underlie other modes of behavior by which the individual may participate in the political process. In one other respect the act of voting in a given election can be interpreted as an element of a broader dimension of behavior. It is plausible to think of voting as a type of conduct that is somewhat habitual and to suppose that as the individual develops a general orientation toward politics he comes to incorporate either voting or nonvoting as part of his normal behavior. Certainly we have found a pronounced association between what people tell us their past behavior has been and whether they vote in the elections we have studied. From this viewpoint our inquiry into the determinants of voting turnout is less a search for psychological forces that determine a decision made anew in each campaign than it is a search for the attitude correlates of voting and nonvoting from which these modes of behavior have emerged and by which they are presently supported. As the inquiry proceeds we will find that some of the dimensions of attitude

---

[3] The question "Did you talk to any people and try to show them why they should vote for one of the parties or candidates?" was answered "yes" in 1952 by 27% of our respondents; in 1956 by 28%.

[4] See Angus Campbell, Gerald Gurin, and Warren E. Miller, "Television and the Election," *Scientific American*, Vol. CLXXXVIII (May 1953), p. 47.

that are most helpful in accounting for turnout appear to have the character of orientations to politics much more than they do the character of forces acting on a present decision.[5]

However useful it may be to distinguish turnout and partisan choice analytically, we ought not to suppose that these dimensions of the voting act appear distinct to the individual citizen. It is natural for the individual to perceive that he votes because he wants to make his preference between parties or candidates count, or that he fails to vote because he does not have a clear preference between partisan objects that he feels are equally appealing, unappealing, or without any affective content at all. Almost certainly this perception of the motives for voting overreaches the facts: we will see that the strength of preference only partially accounts for turnout. Yet the perception catches a clear element of motivation, and the relation of turnout to the intensity of preference is the first important fact we should establish in seeking to explain why some people have voted and others have not.

The evidence for this relation is readily seen if we classify people according to the intensity of their preference, and observe what proportion has voted at each level of intensity. Data of this sort from our combined

FIGURE 1

Relation of Intensity of Partisan Preference to Voting Turnout, 1952 and 1956

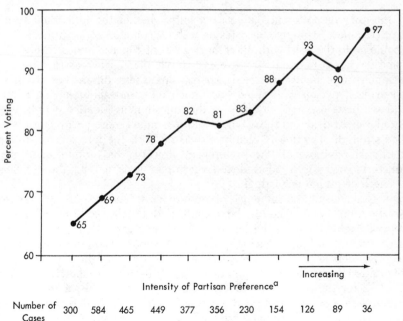

| Number of Cases | 300 | 584 | 465 | 449 | 377 | 356 | 230 | 154 | 126 | 89 | 36 |

---

[5] For a discussion of the causal relation of participation behavior and various psychological dimensions see Heinz Eulau and Peter Schneider, "Dimensions of Political Involvement," *Public Opinion Quarterly*, Vol. XX (Spring 1956), pp. 128–42.

samples of 1952 and 1956 are arrayed in Figure 1. The pattern seen in the figure shows that the probability that a person will vote depends on the strength of his partisan preference. Across virtually the entire range of intensity found in these samples, the greater the strength of the individual's preference, the greater the likelihood he would vote. And the rate of voting at the highest levels of intensity shows that the individual's preference virtually insures his turnout.

TABLE 2

Relation of Perceived Closeness of Election and Intensity of
Partisan Preference to Voting Turnout, 1956

	Election Perceived to Be					
	One Sided Intensity of Preference			Close Intensity of Preference		
	Weak	Medium	Strong	Weak	Medium	Strong
Voted	70%	71%	73%	71%	79%	89%
Did not vote	30	29	27	29	21	11
	100%	100%	100%	100%	100%	100%
Number of cases	130	170	88	301	360	226

Intensity of preference affects not only whether the individual votes; it affects how "strongly" he votes as well. A common observation is that people go to the polls with different degrees of concern about voting. For some the act is imbued with strong positive affect, whereas for others it is much more neutrally toned. To measure these differences we have asked each person who voted how much he cared about having voted, and we have used the answers to this question to identify people who cared a great deal and those who voted in a much more perfunctory way. The strength of voting is plainly associated with the intensity of preference; among those of low preference intensity, the proportion of perfunctory voters is a good deal larger than it is among those whose strength of preference is high.

This sketch of the influence of preference intensity is in one respect overly simple and needs to be complicated by the addition of a perceptual factor. Despite the immediacy of the impact that we would expect strength of preference to have on turnout, its motivational force seems to depend on how close the individual perceives the election to be. The interaction of these factors in the motivation of turnout is shown in Table 2 for the election of 1956. In this table, the levels of intensity in Figure 1 are combined into three broad categories, and the proportion voting in each of these categories is given separately for those who expected the election to be one sided and those who expected it to be close. What the entries of the table have to say about the motivation of turnout is quite clear. The person who thinks the outcome of the election is a foregone conclusion is not more likely to vote if his preference is strong. But the person who thinks the outcome is in doubt is more likely to vote if the intensity of his partisan preference is high. The power of partisan choice to motivate turnout evidently is contingent on the individual feeling, at least in some diffuse way, that his vote may "count."[6] To put the matter another way, the turnout behavior of a person of weak preference is not affected by whether he thinks the election will be close. But the behavior of someone of stronger preference is affected a good deal by his perception of how close the election will be.

The relation between strength of preference and turnout that is seen in our data needs to be interpreted with a greater time perspective. If our measures spanned a broader interval in the life of the individual we would expect to find that the strength of his preference in prior elections has an effect on the likelihood of his voting in later elections. In showing the relation of turnout to the strength of preference in single elections, our data undoubtedly understate the full impact of preference intensity on the decision to vote. A strong commitment to one side or the other in any election tends to involve the individual psychologically more deeply in politics. As a result, the probability of his participating in subsequent elections increases, even though his preference may be substantially less strong in the later campaigns. In this sense, the influence of partisan choice on turnout transcends that shown by the data we have presented here. Yet this secondary effect plainly involves intervening factors. The effect of intensity of preference in time past must be transmitted through forces that act on the individual at the moment of his present behavior.

The need to identify additional psychological forces on the turnout decision is strongly reinforced by a realistic appraisal of how well the intensity of current preference can explain this type of behavior. The findings we have given demonstrate that in a single election someone of strong preference is more likely to vote than is someone of weaker partisan dispositions. Yet Figure 1 should dispel altogether the idea that the strength of partisan choice can by itself fully explain why some people go to the polls and others do not. The inadequacy of strength of preference in accounting for turnout is perhaps most clearly seen in its failure to explain the behavior of those of minimum partisan disposition. Although the proportion voting is lowest in the group having the slightest degree of preference, nearly two-thirds even of these people were found to have cast a vote.

TURNOUT AND POLITICAL INVOLVEMENT

The partial dependence of turnout on preference is of theoretical importance in large part because it implicates everything that may influence

---

[6] The questions we have used to classify respondents according to their expectations about the election have referred to the contest *in the nation as a whole*. Because presidential electors are chosen by states and because all of a state's electors are usually awarded to a single party, we might suppose that how close a person feels the presidential candidates are running in his own state would be of greater importance. But the analysis of answers to a question referring to the presidential race within the respondent's state indicates that it is the election *as a whole* that has cognitive and motivational significance, despite the existence of the Electoral College.

the intensity of preference as a possible influence on the disposition to vote. The fact that one basic dimension of voting is related to the other means that any element in the array of factors leading to partisan choice may lead to turnout as well. The truth of this is recognized at least implicitly in a number of discussions that have explained the disposition to vote in terms of what may strengthen or weaken the disposition to vote a given way.[7] Furthermore, many discussions of the antecedents of partisan choice can throw light on the causes of turnout as well.

Our concern for the moment is not with the antecedents of the intensity of preference but rather with psychological influences on turnout that act apart from the effect of a disposition to vote a given way. In pressing this aspect of our research our major effort has been to relate turnout behavior to what we will call the individual's psychological involvement in politics. We have felt that the individual develops a characteristic degree of interest and involvement in political affairs, which varies widely among individuals but which exhibits a good deal of stability for the same person through successive election campaigns. Postulating a dimension of this sort leads naturally to the hypothesis that the

TABLE 3

Relation of Degree of Interest in Campaign to Voting Turnout, 1956

	Degree of Interest in Campaign		
	Not Much Interested	Somewhat Interested	Very Much Interested
Voted	58%	72%	87%
Did not vote	42	28	13
	100%	100%	100%
Number of cases	540	695	520

stronger the individual's psychological involvement the more likely he is to participate in politics by voting. We have sought to design measures that would catch several aspects of the individual's psychological involvement in politics; in particular, we have measured two sorts of attitudes that describe the individual's orientation to a specific election and two additional attitudes that characterize his orientation to politics and elections more generally.

Interest in the Campaign

The first aspect of involvement we have sought to measure is the degree of a person's interest in the campaign. The presidential contest holds the attention of different people quite unequally, and the degree of

---

[7] It is of central importance, for example, in the discussion of turnout appearing in Seymour M. Lipset et al., "The Psychology of Voting: An Analysis of Political Behavior," *Handbook of Social Psychology*, ed. Gardner Lindzey (Cambridge, Mass.: Addison-Wesley Publishing Co., 1954), Vol. II, pp. 1124–175.

interest has varied widely among the individuals we have interviewed in several election campaigns. The importance of this aspect of involvement for voting turnout is demonstrated by Table 3 with data drawn from the election of 1956. The entries of the table show that the rate of turnout among persons of high interest exceeded that among persons of low interest by nearly 30 per cent. What is more, the incidence of nonvoting among the third of the electorate that is lowest in interest is appreciably greater than it is among the third that is lowest in strength of partisan preference, as shown by Figure 1. Our measure of interest carries us further than the measure of partisan intensity in finding the conditions of nonvoting, although we still need to learn what brought to the polls more than half of those who tell us they are not much interested in the campaign.

Concern over the Election Outcome

A person's orientation to a specific election can be described also in terms of his concern over its outcome. Some people are deeply involved, psychologically speaking, in the electoral result, whereas others are relatively indifferent. Concern over the election result would seem intuitively to be somewhat distinct from political interest, and in our data it is by no means perfectly correlated with interest. Yet the association of the two suggests the influence of a more general involvement factor and leads us to concur in Lane's observation that "questions on 'interest' and 'concern' tend to select out the same populations and to be related to behavior in roughly the same way."[8] The relation we have found between the individual's concern over the outcome and the probability of his voting is shown in Table 4 for 1956. Here again, the effect of involvement on voting turnout seems very clear.

TABLE 4

Relation of Degree of Concern about Election Outcome to Voting Turnout, 1956

	Degree of Concern over Election Outcome			
	Don't Care at All	Don't Care Very Much	Care Somewhat	Care Very Much
Voted	52%	69%	76%	84%
Did not vote	48	31	24	16
	100%	100%	100%	100%
Number of cases	230	367	627	459

Sense of Political Efficacy

Our measures of interest and of concern over the election outcome refer explicitly to the election at hand. As such, they are likely to catch important short-term fluctuations of the individual's political involve-

---

[8] Robert E. Lane, *Political Life* (Glencoe, Ill.: The Free Press, 1959), p. 134.

ment. These measures may tap more enduring orientations to politics as well. The individual does not react *de novo* to each election but tends rather to respond to the stimuli of a new campaign in terms of stable attitudes and dispositions he has toward politics generally. His social environment, immediate and distant, is composed of a number of areas that compete for his emotional energy and in which he comes to have a characteristic level of emotional involvement. Politics is such an area, and most adults have a relatively fixed degree of involvement in it, although their commitment to political affairs, as to work, family, religion, or sports, may vary somewhat over time. This characteristic level of involvement differs widely among people. A really intense commitment to politics probably is limited in American society to a small fraction of political activists, but even in the wider electorate we find substantial differences in the extent of emotional involvement in political affairs.

An important aspect of the individual's response to politics as a general area is the degree to which this response is passive in character. To some people politics is a distant and complex realm that is beyond the power of the common citizen to affect, whereas to others the affairs of government can be understood and influenced by individual citizens. We have assessed the effectiveness the individual feels in his relation to politics by using answers to several questions probing attitudes of this sort to develop a cumulative scale, on which we could array our samples. The influence this dimension of attitude has on the turnout decision is shown by Table 5 for the election of 1956. The rate of voting turnout was found to increase uniformly with the strength of the individual's sense of politi-

TABLE 5

Relation of Sense of Political Efficacy to Voting Turnout, 1956

	Sense of Political Efficacy				
	Low				High
Voted	52%	60%	75%	84%	91%
Did not note	48	40	25	16	9
	100%	100%	100%	100%	100%
Number of cases	263	343	461	501	196

cal efficacy, and more than 40 percentage points separated those whose sense was least developed from those whose sense of effectiveness was strongest.

Sense of Citizen Duty

The final aspect of involvement we have sought to measure also transcends a single election. Wide currency in American society is given the idea that the individual has a civic responsibility to vote. When this norm becomes a part of the value system of the individual, as it has for most of our citizens, it may be regarded as a force acting directly on the

TABLE 6
Relation of Sense of Citizen Duty to Voting Turnout, 1956

| | Sense of Citizen Duty | | | | |
	Low				High
Voted	13%	42%	52%	74%	85%
Did not vote	87	58	48	26	15
	100%	100%	100%	100%	100%
Number of cases	89	78	146	639	812

turnout decision. Of course its strength is not the same for everyone, and the degree to which the individual feels an obligation to vote is an important aspect of his orientation to politics. We have measured the strength of this attitude by constructing a cumulative scale from several questions about the responsibility to vote and classifying those we have interviewed into the categories of the scale. When the proportion voting is shown for each category, as it is in Table 6 for the election of 1956, it is clear that the strength of a person's sense of citizen duty has a very great influence on the likelihood of his voting.

The most striking entries in Table 6 are those indicating that voting is rare among people whose sense of citizen duty is least strong. In those whose sense of citizen duty is weakest we have found a small group whose motivation to participate in politics is so near zero that other forces inducing them to vote only rarely bring them to the polls.

Despite the evidence that the four aspects of political involvement we have measured share an important common component, we have considered separately their relation to turnout because each aspect contributes a distinctive element. However, we can assess how well involvement account for behavior only if we examine the joint relation to turnout of the four measures. In order to make entirely clear what we have *added* to our ability to account for the turnout decision by measuring these aspects of involvement, we will include strength of partisan preference among the explanatory variables so that their *combined* power to account for behavior may be compared directly with that of the intensity of preference alone, as shown in Figure 1.

Such a comparison attests the fundamental role of involvement in motivating turnout behavior. As is seen in Figure 2, the rate of turnout increases steadily with political involvement and partisan preference, and differs by more than 75 per cent from one extreme to the other, whereas the proportions voting at the extremes of low and high intensity of preference alone differed by less than half this much. The fact that persons of the highest involvement are more nearly unanimous in voting than are those of lowest involvement in not voting suggests that we are still beset more by the problem of the deviant *voters* than we are with that of the deviant *nonvoter*. And the existence of any group of similar motivation whose behavior is not homogeneous invites us to push further the quest for explanation.

FIGURE 2

Relation of Intensity of Political Involvement to Voting Turnout, 1956

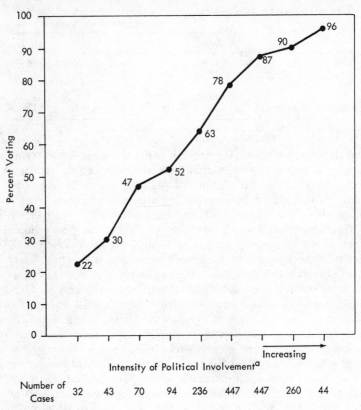

| Number of Cases | 32 | 43 | 70 | 94 | 236 | 447 | 447 | 260 | 44 |

Divergent Cases

Most of the variability in turnout that political involvement fails to explain is found in the middle categories of Figure 2, where the psychological forces we have measured are neither so weak that the individual is highly unlikely to vote nor so strong that he is highly unlikely *not* to vote. In these middle categories other factors, some of them undoubtedly exogenous to our theoretical concerns, have determined whether the individual will vote. But the "error" in Figure 2 that is most interesting is found at the extremes of political involvement, where we would expect to be able to predict with higher confidence whether the individual will in fact vote. The presence of error of this sort leads naturally to an intensive examination of divergent cases to learn why it is that our expectations have proven wrong.

We are better prepared, by the popular lore about voting, for error at the extreme of high involvement. Located here is the person of strong motivation who is kept from voting by personal circumstances he could not reasonably overcome, as the individual who was prevented from voting by a flat tire on his way to the polls. We doubt that this specific factor, which we would unhesitatingly declare exogenous, has had a very high incidence in American politics, but it suggests well the sort of barrier that may keep a highly motivated person from voting. An inspection of our interview protocols provides a number of such cases.

Located here, too, are the individuals of strong motivation who are barred from voting by legal disabilities. Some of our respondents living in states that make no provision for absentee balloting have been away from their homes on election day. Others have changed their residences too recently to satisfy the requirements of minimum residence. Nonregistration ought generally to be regarded as a legal barrier only with caution, since the failure to register may simply reflect the same motivational factors as the failure to vote. Yet in certain cases the impossibility of registering has stood as a clear barrier for those who were motivated to perform the voting act.

Deviant cases of the opposite sort, in which a person of slight motivation has voted, are less familiar in the common lore, except perhaps for what is known of party machines that have voted the dead. An analysis of interviews with people of very low motivation who have gone to the polls indicates that the most important force on their behavior is interpersonal influence, as we have found it to be in inducing deviant partisan behavior. Personal influence seems particularly important within the family group. Of the twelve voters in 1956 who had the least reason for going to the polls in terms of the psychological factors we have measured, nine were women who appeared to respond to the wishes of husbands or of other men in their immediate families.

TABLE 7

Postelection Preference of Nonvoters, 1948 to 1956*

	1948	1952	1956
Would have voted Democratic	82%	52%	28%
Would have voted Republican	18	48	72
Total	100%	100%	100%
Number of cases	192	417	429

* Among nonvoters giving a preference between major-party candidates.

It is the preferences of those who vote that are of primary importance in the wider political system. But the preferences of those who do not are by no means of trivial importance; indeed, in recording substantial shifts over time they prove to be of considerable theoretical interest. Let us examine the partisan preference of nonvoters, as they have been assessed over a twenty-year period.

With the rise of public opinion polls in the 1930's, the first systematic evidence began to appear that nonvoters—or at least people who expected not to vote—were more Democratic than the electorate as a whole. This evidence accumulated through the latter years of the New Deal and the Fair Deal until the generalization that nonvoters tend to be

Democrats had worked itself into the popular understanding of politics. Since it was well known that both partisan preference and voting turnout were related to social class, an explanation of the strongly Democratic color of nonvoters was easily supplied.

The report of partisan preferences we obtained from a national sample interviewed after the election of 1948, the highwater mark of the Fair Deal, was consistent with this description of nonvoters. Whereas the preferences reported by voters were divided very nearly evenly between the parties, the preferences reported by nonvoters favored the Democrats by a margin of more than 4–1. Were it not for the fact that the Truman vote exceeded the advance expectations, the closeness of the Democratic victory in 1948 relative to earlier years would probably have been explained in terms of the lower level of turnout.

If the report taken from those who failed to vote in 1948 supported the contention that nonvoters tend to be Democrats, the postelection reports of 1952 and 1956 dealt this notion severe blows. In our interviews following the election of 1952 only about half of the nonvoters indicating a preference said they would have voted Democratic; in our interviews following the election of 1956 little more than a quarter of the nonvoters giving a preference said they would have voted Democratic. The extreme nature of this shift in the Democratic proportion over an eight-year period is shown by Table 7. Few statistics in all of our studies have shown so violent a change over time as this one.

What can explain so great a shift among nonvoters? Over a period in which the division of preference changed by little more than 10 per cent among voters it changed by more than 50 per cent among nonvoters. How are we to account for the difference? Undoubtedly a number of factors have been at work, but we believe that much of the observed change can be explained by a few central ideas. The major key to understanding is supplied by what we have found to distinguish nonvoters from voters:

TABLE 8

Relation of Degree of Political Involvement to Change in
Partisan Preference of Nonvoters*

	1952 Election		1956 Election	
	Before	After	Before	After
Very much interested	51%	54%	43%	37%
Somewhat interested	56	57	40	37
Not much interested	63	52	42	24

* Entries are percentages favoring Democrats of those giving a preference.

the nonvoter tends to be a person of lower involvement whose emotional investment in politics and its partisan decisions is on the average much less than that of the voter. As a result, we would expect the nonvoter to be less stable in his partisan inclinations than the voter and more responsive to the massive political stimuli that produce shifts of popular attitude over time. And we have little doubt that for the nonvoter a stimulus of great importance in this period, as in any other, was the fact of who was winning elections. For at least part of the way between his position of 1948 and his position of 1956 the nonvoter was riding a psychological bandwagon.

Several kinds of evidence can be marshalled in support of this general view. First of all, if we are right in thinking that the outcomes of these elections were stimuli of relatively greater importance for the nonvoter, we ought to find evidence of the fact in a comparison of the reported preference of nonvoters before and after each election. We do not have the data to make this comparison for the election of 1948, but for each of the Eisenhower elections we may examine the nonvoter's report of preference in the first and second interviews of our brief panel studies spanning the elections. The division of preference among nonvoters shifted in the direction of the winner in each of these years; indeed, the post-election shift toward Eisenhower in 1956 (from 58% to 72%) was 14 percentage points—as great as the shift of preference among voters over the entire period from 1948 to 1956. We would suppose that the Truman victory had much the same effect on the preference of nonvoters—although in the opposite direction—as the Eisenhower victories had in each of the elections that followed.

The most telling evidence for our characterization of change, however, is obtained by further dividing nonvoters according to the degree of their involvement in politics. In any election some individuals whose involvement is high and whose motivation is strong fail to vote. If we can separate these people from individuals who are weakly involved, we should have a clearer sense of the forces inducing change in preference over time. Table 8 makes such a separation for each of the Eisenhower elections by classifying nonvoters according to the extent of their interest in the campaign. Several observations that are important for our formulation of change can be based on this table. First, it is clear for both the 1952 and 1956 elections that change in the Republican direction between the pre- and post-election interviews occurred more among the slightly involved than it did among those of greater involvement. Only the group least interested in the campaign shifted toward Eisenhower in his first victory; hence, the shift seen among nonvoters as a whole rests on the fact that most nonvoters are people of little involvement. Second, the fact that the Democratic percentage prior to the 1952 election was highest among those of slightest interest suggests that these people were most under the influence of past Democratic victories. Yet is it this same group that responded most strongly to the Eisenhower victories and shifted far enough that by the postelection interview of 1956 less than one-fourth of their number favored the Democrats.[9]

---

[9] Of course we have repeated measurements of the preferences of the same persons only within a single election and not over two or more elections. The assumption that the composition of the several involvement groups would be fairly stable over time cannot be validated with these data, and comparisons of their preferences between elections ought to be treated with caution.

This unbroken swing in the Republican direction dissolves the generalization that nonvoters are pro-Democratic and calls attention in the most dramatic way to the importance of psychological involvement in explaining political behavior. We have treated in some detail the shifts of preference among those who fail to vote because these changes suggest the far-reaching effects on behavior of the low involvement that is the nonvoter's primary quality. Yet voters and nonvoters are by no means the only groups within the electorate that differ in the extent of their political involvement, and we shall have occasion in later chapters to examine the behavior of other groups as well for which involvement supplies a key to understanding.

Donald E. Stokes

Some Dynamic Elements of Contests for the Presidency*

Despite the measured pace of American elections, there have now been a number of presidential campaigns since the advent of survey studies of voting. However sparingly, political history slowly has added to the set of distinct configurations of men and events which comprise a contest for the Presidency. The set is still small, whatever the impression created by massed thousands of interviews or by the accompanying files of election returns. Yet it is now large enough to be pressed hard for evidence about the sources of electoral change.

A primary virtue of measurements extended over a series of elections is that they can throw light on the problem of change. So long as the earliest voting studies were confined to cross-sectional relationships, they could deal only very inadequately with changes superimposed on these relationships or with changes in the relationships themselves. In the case of Lazarsfeld's enormously influential Erie County study in 1940, the natural limitations of a single-election study were compounded by the investigators' misfortune in choosing a campaign whose dominant personality and principal issues differed little from those of preceding elections. I have often wondered whether the static social determinism of *The People's Choice* would have emerged from a campaign in which the tides of short-term change were more nearly at flood.[1]

* Reprinted from the *American Political Science Review*, vol. 60 (March 1966), pp. 19–28. Copyright 1966, The American Political Science Association.

[1] Paul F. Lazarsfeld, Bernard Berelson, and Hazel Gaudet, *The People's Choice* (New York: Duell, Sloan and Pearce, 1944). It is paradoxical that Lazarsfeld and his associates should have come to so static a view of party preference, since the desire to observe changes of preference was so central to their original intentions. Had they worked within the context of an election such as that of 1952 it is entirely unlikely that they could have ignored the presence of massive inter-election change, overlaid on the social bases of preference summarized in the Index of Political Predisposition.

I shall examine here some sources of change which are richly evident in the presidential elections of the last two decades. In doing so I shall utilize several time series which can be extracted from the Survey Research Center's interview studies of the American electorate. The presidential contest of 1964 marked the fourth occasion on which the Center's national electoral studies have recorded the public's response to the issues and personalities of a presidential campaign.

This lengthening interval of electoral history contains material enough for the analyst of change. From the Eisenhower victories of the early 1950's, the high-point of presidential Republicanism since the Great Depression overwhelmed Hoover's party, the strength of Eisenhower's successors ebbed away in 1960 and sank in 1964 to a level which can only be regarded as one of the extreme lows of American national party competition. I shall examine some of the attitudinal factors in this extraordinary decline, focusing especially on the importance of changes in the issues and leaders which the electorate is asked to appraise. The relation of these "inputs" to the "output" of the presidential vote is exceedingly complex, but the moral of my piece is that this relationship introduces more dynamism into contests for the Presidency than the stability of party identification or of the social bases of party preference might lead us to expect.

In the course of the discussion I shall utilize a statistical model which has proved useful for measuring various attitudinal forces on the nation's vote. Dealing with a type of behavior which is notoriously subject to multiple influences, this model seeks to discern the relative importance of several dimensions of attitude both for individual choice and for the nation's collective decision.[2] The model treats the behavior of the individual voter as governed in an immediate sense by the direction and strength of his attitudes toward the several political objects he is asked to appraise, attitudes which we have probed in these presidential elections by asking a series of free-answer questions about the parties and presidential candidates. Since a presidential campaign confronts the voter with four main objects—the two parties and the two candidates—it is natural to place each respondent along four dimensions of attitude, and many of the findings reported below will rely on such a four-dimensional model. For other purposes, however, it is more revealing of the content of political attitude to place each respondent along six attitudinal dimensions: (1) attitude toward the Democratic candidate as a person; (2) attitude toward the Republican candidate as a person; (3) attitude toward the parties and candidates which relates to the benefit of various groups; (4) attitude toward the parties and candidates which relates to domestic policy; (5) attitude which relates to foreign policy; and (6) attitude which relates to the general performance of the parties in the nation's affairs. A detailed account of the procedure by which respondents are assimilated to these several dimensions appears in the appended note.

---

[2] For a report of the application of this model to the Eisenhower elections see Donald E. Stokes, Angus Campbell, and Warren E. Miller, "Components of Electoral Decision," *American Political Science Review*, Vol. 52 (June 1958), 367–87.

The appendix also describes the statistical operations by which we obtain definite estimates of each dimension's contribution to the winning majority—the means by which, in effect, the nation's collective decision is resolved into a set of attitudinal components. These methods must of course be regarded as approximate, for reasons of sampling if no other, and I advance no claim to exact measurement; none is really necessary to the central conclusion which I shall draw from the analysis. Nevertheless, the model's success in estimating the direction and size of the winning majority in each of a series of elections does increase our confidence that we have measured dimensions of popular feeling which are deeply involved in changes of party fortune.

The several dimensions of attitude, however, have by no means been equally involved in electoral change. Just as the various components of electoral decision can be very different in their direction and strength at a given point in time, they can exhibit a very different tendency to change over time. In the period of our research some have been relatively stable, others not. By examining the role of each attitude component over twelve years we form several time series which are extraordinarily suggestive of the sources of change during this interval of our national politics.

THE ATTITUDINAL COMPONENTS OVER TIME

The curves described by the components of the six-dimensional model arrange themselves into three interesting pairs. The first of these is a pair whose values have consistently favored the Democrats over the entire period. As shown by Figure 1, partisan evaluations relating to domestic issues and to group benefits have uniformly helped the Democrats more than the Republicans, although the extent of this aid has fluctuated from year to year.[3] To an unusual degree these elements of the party images have roots in the past, extending back at least to the Roosevelt New Deal. Indeed, the benefit to the Democrats from their party's sponsorship of disadvantaged elements of American society is an antique theme of our party politics. Even in the mid-1950's and the early 1960's the volume of comment approving the Democrats and disapproving the Republicans in terms of the interests of the common man was impressive. In the two most recent elections, however, these class-related comments were diminished somewhat and were accompanied by references to religious and racial groups in which the arithmetic of group size was less favorable to the Democrats. For these reasons the group curve in Figure 1 shows the party's advantage to be somewhat less in 1960 and 1964.

---

[3] The vertical coordinate of Figure 1, as well as of Figures 2 and 3, gives the value of the quantity

$$b_t(\overline{X}_t - X_t{}^0)$$

defined in the appendix. As explained there, this quantity may be interpreted either at the individual level as the average amount by which a given dimension has increased (or lessened, in the case of negative values) the probability of the individual's voting Republican or at the level of the whole electorate as the proportion of the total two-party vote by which a given dimension has increased (or lessened) the Republican share.

FIGURE 1

Continuing Democratic Advantage: Groups and Domestic Policy

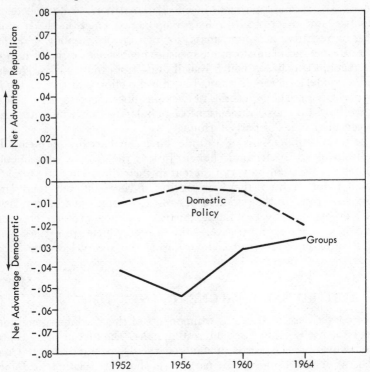

It will be apparent that the concept of "group" is defined here in a very inclusive manner. Likewise, our net has been cast very widely in coding references relating to domestic issues. In particular, many of the comments giving substance to the domestic issue dimension are "valence" or "image" issues, in which the parties or candidates are linked with something which is uniformly approved or disapproved ("the Republicans are the party of depression") rather than "position" issues on which there are genuine differences of party policy. The leading image issue of domestic politics throughout this period was the association of Democrats with good times, the Republicans with bad. This association, which probably had weakened steadily from the height of the Great Depression to the election of 1952, was further attentuated by the prosperity of Eisenhower's first term. But it revived again in the recession of 1958, before the Republican administration had left office, and it has been given fresh substance by the rising prosperity of the Kennedy and Johnson years.

The domestic issue dimension has not, however, been altogether lacking in genuine position issues. One of the peculiar qualities of the Goldwater candidacy is that it converted into position issues a number of image issues on which a broad consensus had hitherto existed between the parties. This fact was not lost upon the general public. Under the Goldwater challenge, the Democrats were rewarded more generously in 1964 than in any of the three prior elections for their sponsorship of social security and of the circle of other social and economic welfare policies which had wide popular approval. Primarily for this reason the domestic issue curve of Figure 1 shows a greater Democratic advantage in 1964 than in the years before.

A second pair of curves is traced by the movement of two components in which a strong initial Republican advantage is seen to have vanished over these four elections. As shown by Figure 2, the Republican party

FIGURE 2

Decaying Republican Advantage: Foreign Policy and Party Performance

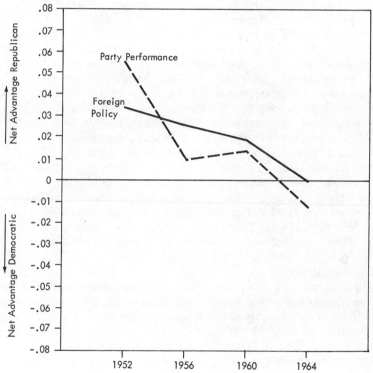

under Eisenhower enjoyed a substantial lead over the Democrats on foreign affairs—preeminently in terms of the great image issue of peace and war. This lead was not greatly lessened when Eisenhower's deputy sought the Presidency in 1960, but Nixon's legacy dissolved altogether in the contest of Goldwater and Johnson. It would be a misreading of the 1964 value, however, to suppose that widely-held foreign policy beliefs consistent with Goldwater's were nicely balanced by widely-held beliefs consistent with Johnson's. According to our evidence, foreign affairs did intrude on the public's consciousness in the 1964 campaign more than in any election since 1952, but popular references to foreign issues in 1964 still had only about a fourth the frequency of references to domestic issues. The loss of Republican advantage on this dimension was due to the final collapse of the belief that the party under Goldwater was more likely to bring peace than were the Democrats under Johnson.[4]

The loss of Republican advantage in foreign affairs is paralleled by the decay of the party's advantage in popular assessments of party performance. The Republicans began this series of elections immensely aided by the mood for a change in 1952. There is no more striking element in all of our attitudinal materials than the public's anger and frustration with the outgoing Democratic administration in that year. Whatever the validity of the public's grievance, it was real enough in motivational terms and contributed handsomely to Eisenhower's first victory. The force of this feeling was easily spent, however, once the Democrats had been driven from office. Yet in 1956 and again in 1960 the Republicans still enjoyed an edge in terms of the electorate's general evaluations of current party performance, a fact which is the more remarkable in view of the stronger hold of the Democrats on the nation's underlying party identifications.[5] By 1964, however, this lingering advantage had been swept away, and the Democrats by a modest margin were now seen as the party better qualified to conduct the country's affairs.

The third pair of curves is traced by the components having to do with popular reactions to the personal attributes of the candidates. As shown in Figure 3, there has been remarkable variety in the appeal of the Republican candidates. The values of this component in 1952 and 1956 attest to General Eisenhower's personal hold on the electorate, an attraction which, if anything, was even more wholly personal after Eisenhower had served four years as President. Mr. Nixon's appeal in 1960 was somewhat less, although his personal appeal to the electorate, especially the sense of his broad experience, was marked. If the eventual account given by the political histories is that Nixon was a weak candidate in 1960, it will be largely myth.

The response to Goldwater, however, was something else again. Whereas Nixon's personal stature helped bring his party to the verge of a third presidential victory against a party enjoying a clear advantage in the country's partisan identifications, popular reaction to Goldwater contributed to his party's electoral ruin. The detailed references to Goldwater are an impressive amalgam of doubts—a wild and erratic campaigner, muddled and unclear, unstable, poorly educated, and so on—with these themes very little offset by references to the advertised qualities of integrity, sincerity, and decisiveness. If our estimates are right,

---

[4] For direct additional evidence on this point see Philip E. Converse, Aage R. Clausen, and Warren E. Miller, "Electoral Myth and Reality: The 1964 Election," *American Political Science Review*, Vol. 59 (June 1965), p. 332.

[5] For evidence on the distribution of party identification in this period see "The Concept of the 'Normal Vote'," in A. Campbell, P. Converse, W. Miller, and D. Stokes, *Elections and the Political Order* (New York: John Wiley and Sons, Inc., 1966), Ch. 1.

FIGURE 3

Greatest Variation: Appeal of Candidates

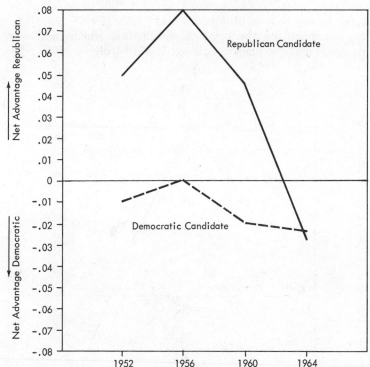

the transition from Nixon to Goldwater cost the Republicans something like 7 percent of the total vote.

Despite immense differences of personal style, the appeal of three successive Democratic candidates was much more nearly equal. And except for Stevenson's second campaign, the response to each of these candidates added to his strength at the polls. Certainly the movement of the Democratic curve in Figure 3 shows Johnson to have been an asset to his own candidacy in 1964: the response to Johnson's attributes apparently did the Democrats about as much good as the response to Goldwater's did. The combined effect of both appears to have moved the two-party vote roughly 5 percentage points toward Johnson.

To emphasize the dymanic implications for party competition of pairing successive candidates for President, Figure 4 combines the effect of the personal appeals of the two men seeking the office in each of these elections.[6] The variation of this summary curve is impressive indeed.

---

[6] The individual and aggregate interpretations of the quantity represented by the vertical coordinate of Figure 4 are the same as before, but the quantity itself is the sum of the components measuring the increment or decrement to Republican strength due to personal attributes of the Republican and Democratic candidates.

From a maximum Republican advantage of nearly 8 percent in the re-match of Eisenhower and Stevenson, the curve falls through more than 13 percentage points to a maximum Democratic advantage of more than 5 percent in the contest of Johnson and Goldwater. A more eloquent statistical comment on the personal contribution which candidates for President can make to electoral change could hardly be given.

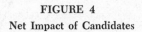

FIGURE 4

Net Impact of Candidates

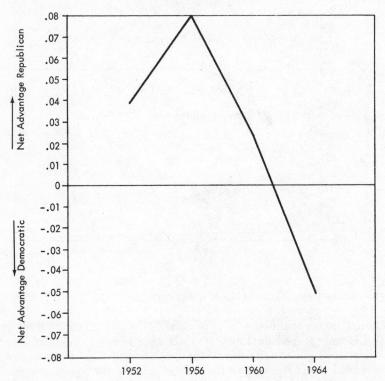

It would be a mistake to read into these figures too simple an expla-nation of the impact of candidate personality on the mass public. Cer-tainly it would be grossly wrong to suppose that the properties of these "stimulus objects" are somehow immediately and directly impressed on the electorate's response. The relation of stimulus and response is re-markably complex, involving an interplay of several quite different fac-tors. Before drawing some general conclusions about the problem of change, it would be well to consider the interaction of the "actual" prop-erties of the stimuli to which the electorate responds, certain response dispositions which the electorate has already learned, and some prop-erties of the communication processes by which the electorate is in-formed of the objects of presidential politics.

STIMULUS PROPERTIES AND RESPONSE DISPOSITIONS IN THE ATTITUDE COMPONENTS

Although the comments below extend to the full range of stimuli to which the public is exposed, some of the subtleties of electoral response can most readily be observed in connection with candidate effects. The men seeking the Presidency bring to a campaign certain "real" properties as stimulus objects. Some of these belong to the past—the candidate's role as war hero, his success as governor or senator, his marital difficulties, and so on—although the communication of these things to much of the public may lie ahead. Other properties have to do with appearance, behavior, and personal style—the candidate's smile, the timbre of his voice, his smoothness in dealing with the teleprompter, his willingness to suffer fools gladly—knowledge of which can reach the electorate in numberless ways.

Impressions of these things, however, do not fall on wholly unprepared ground. Voters display a variety of response dispositions as they form their evaluations of the candidates. One type of response disposition is so evident as to require little comment. A wealth of research evidence, as well as familiar observation, attests the profound influence which partisan loyalties may have on the voter's perceptions of the men seeking office. The stronger the voter's party bias, the more likely he is to see the candidate of his own party as hero, the candidate of the other party as villain. No one who had talked with a sample of voters during a presidential campaign can have failed to note at every hand the processes by which cognitive balance is achieved.[7]

The voter's perceptual predispositions are not, however, limited to party bias. We are confronted at times by striking evidence of other identifications exerting a like influence on candidate images. A vivid example of these is the influence of religion on perceptions of John F. Kennedy during the 1960 election campaign. Because Kennedy was the Democratic candidate, voters identifying with the Democratic party tended to view him more favorably than did voters identifying with the Republican party. But Kennedy was seen by the electorate not only as a Democrat; he was seen as a Catholic as well. As a result, at every point along the party identification continuum, Catholics tended to perceive Kennedy in a more favorable light than did Protestants.

A demonstration of the joint biasing effects of religion and party in 1960 may be found in Figure 5. In that campaign we placed each of our

---

[7] Certainly evidence of it is plentiful enough in the Center's studies. See, for example, Angus Campbell, Philip E. Converse, Warren E. Miller and Donald E. Stokes, *The American Voter* (New York: John Wiley and Sons, 1960), pp. 120–45. An excellent general review of the achievement of cognitive congruence in political attitudes is given by Robert E. Lane and David O. Sears in their *Public Opinion* (Englewood Cliffs, N.J.: Prentice-Hall, 1964). An interesting application of these concepts to attitude change may be found in Denis G. Sullivan, "Psychological Balance and Reactions to the Presidential Nominations in 1960," in M. Kent Jennings and L. Harmon Zeigler (eds.), *The Electoral Process* (Englewood Cliffs, N.J.: Prentice-Hall, 1966), pp. 238–64.

sample respondents along a standard party identification scale, represented here by five ordered groups: Strong Republicans, Weak Republicans, Independents, Weak Democrats, and Strong Democrats. At the
same time we placed each of our Protestant and Catholic respondents on
a scale of religious identification defined here by four ordered groups:
persons strongly identified with a Protestant Church, persons weakly

Influence of Party and Religious Identifications on Perceptions of Kennedy

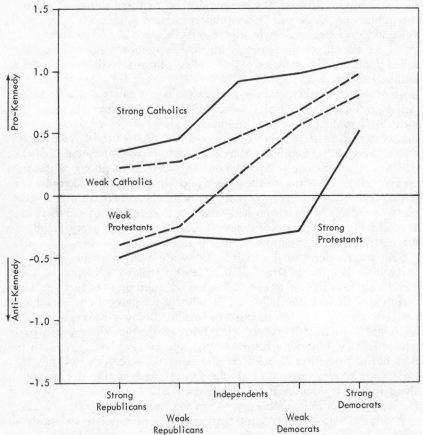

identified with such a church, persons weakly identified with the Catholic Church, and persons strongly identified with the Catholic Church.
These two forms of psychological identification are moderately correlated in American society (that is, Catholics are more likely than Protestants to be Democratic) but not more than moderately so. Crossing the
two here yields twenty groups defined by religion and party at once in
which we may examine the distribution of attitude toward Kennedy.

Figure 5 displays the mean attitude toward Kennedy within each of these twenty groups.[8]

The means exhibit a remarkable pattern. The fact that the curve for each religious group slopes upward to the right shows that, whatever the voter's religious identification, he is more likely to have perceived Kennedy favorably the closer he was to the Democratic end of the party identification dimension. And the march of the four religious curves up the figure shows that, whatever the voter's party identification, he is more likely to have perceived Kennedy positively the closer he was to the Catholic end of the religious dimension. There is even a pattern to the partial discontinuities: the regularity of the curves for weak Protestants and weak Catholics suggests that the biasing tendencies of party identification were generally effective among the mildly religious while the irregularity of the curves for strong Protestants and strong Catholics suggests that party loyalty could have a marked impact on the strongly religious only if a party faith were itself strongly held.

Figure 5 is so rich in evidence of selective perception that we may easily miss what it has to say about the element of Kennedy's image which was not the result of response disposition based on religion and party. The fact that this element was a favorable one ought not to be obscured by the strong pattern of the figure. Any reasonable operation by which we might seek to reconstruct a mean attitude among persons who are religiously and politically neutral would show that Kennedy was likely to be positively seen when his image did not fall prey to strong negative bias. For example, persons who were politically independent perceived Kennedy favorably even if they were weakly identified with a Protestant church.

We ought not to conclude from this that partisan and religious dispositions were the only response biases involved in the electorate's response to Kennedy or that, these dispositions aside, Kennedy was in some absolute sense an attractive candidate. In 1960, as any campaign year, many other kinds of response dispositions underlay the private impressions of the candidates formed by tens of millions of voters. We have identified two of the most important. It would not be difficult to suggest other factors which may have predisposed voters to react positively or negatively to something in the youthful, vigorous, Ivy-educated, Boston-accented stimulus which Kennedy presented.

Perhaps this point can be stated even more forcefully in terms of popular reaction to General Eisenhower, the most attractive presidential candidate since Franklin Roosevelt. The point is simply that "attractive" implies more than something about the candidate himself; it also implies something about the response dispositions of the electorate. Given the

---

[8] In order to standardize the metric used in these comparisons, I have divided each of these means by the sample standard deviation of attitude toward Kennedy. Because the sample contained only seven Weak Catholic Weak Republicans and only seven Weak Catholic Independents the means for these two groups have been adjusted to reduce the probable effect of sampling error.

dominant values of contemporary American society, Eisenhower was enormously appealing. But we can at least imagine his having done very badly before an electorate less resonant to the military conqueror and less susceptible to the charm of a supremely other-directed personality who nevertheless evoked many of the traditional virtues. We might suppose, for example, that Eisenhower would have done very badly indeed before an electorate whose dominant values are those of American university faculties of social science.

Attitudes already formed toward some political objects are of course among the dispositions which can influence response to others. This seems especially true in the case of attitudes toward the candidates. When one rival for the Presidency already is well known, as an incumbent President will always be, the public's attitude toward his opponent will inevitably be colored by its response to the established figure. Thus, in 1940, Roosevelt-haters were quick to discover the virtues of Wendell Willkie when he was thrust onto the presidential stage, as Roosevelt's partisans were quick to discern Willkie's vices. And in the early 1950's, Adlai Stevenson had the misfortune to be paired with a much better established rival who already enjoyed the highest public regard.[9]

Of course the complex relation of candidate stimulus to the public's response also involves important communication factors. In a sense, the only real candidate stimuli are those which reach the voter via the mass media and interpersonal conversation, stimuli which only rarely are complemented by direct voter contact with the candidate. Therefore, the benefit or harm done to a candidate's cause by his actual personal attributes is mediated not only by the response dispositions of the electorate; it is mediated as well by the manner in which these attributes are communicated to the electorate. It is not hard to believe that some of the disarray of Goldwater's popular image was due to his extraordinarily bad press. The candidate properties communicated to the public are not a pure fiction of the media. But neither are they a pure reflection of the candidate himself, as he might have been seen at home in the desert.

What has been said of candidates can be said of any object which has electoral effects. Certainly the political role of domestic and foreign issues involves a similar interplay of stimulus properties, response tendencies, and communication processes. The Korean War's immense profit for the Republicans in 1952, for example, depended on much more than a set of objective events in the Far East and the parties' stand on those events. It depended too on a welter of response dispositions in the electorate—general isolationist or internationalist attitudes, hostility to communism, latent militarist tendencies, the anxieties of farmers over having sons away at harvest time, and the like—as well as the way in which the

---

[9] The voter's attitude toward a given political object may be influenced by the presence of other objects in his perceptual field even when no question of order is involved in the formation of attitude. In such a case, however, it is more reasonable to think of these effects as belonging to the configuration of stimulus objects, rather than to the voter's response dispositions.

public was informed by the communications media of what was happening half a world away. If the political effects of issues and personalities in the wider environment depend partly on what the electorate hears and how it is disposed to react to what it hears, it follows that changes in communication and response tendencies can at times alter the political effects of a stimulus which has not itself changed. A clear example of this is the rapid buildup of a candidate by the mass media when he steps into the charmed circle of leading contenders—or the opposite experience, which many potential candidates have had, of falling through the medias' trap door to oblivion. Instances of marked change of response dispositions while political objects remain unchanged are more difficult to discern, but they undoubtedly occur. Herbert Hoover's high starched collars, a symbol of middle class prosperity in the booming twenties, probably looked quite different from the bread-lines of 1932.

Although changes of communication and of response dispositions can alter the electorate's response to a given political object, it is nevertheless true that a turnover of objects—of the personalities, issues, and events of national politics—is the more important source of short-term electoral change. This is the more true since a stimulus object can affect communication and response dispositions themselves. For example, quite apart from the sort of man he "really" is, a candidate can have wide influence on his treatment by the mass media. If the newspapers gave Mr. Goldwater extraordinarily rough treatment for a Republican candidate, Goldwater's own posture toward the press was part of the reason. Similarly, different candidates engage different response dispositions in the mass public. Unlike any Democratic candidate since Al Smith, Kennedy activated response dispositions based on Catholic and Protestant religious identifications, as we have seen. And candidates can lead the electorate to learn new dispositions, as Kennedy helped make the country receptive to a whole new generation of youthful, vigorous candidates for national and state office.

This type of change is vividly mirrored in the components of electoral decision given here for the past four presidential elections. The evidence of the changing personal impact of the candidates is especially impressive. Yet in a presidential system the turnover of candidates has implications reaching beyond sheer personal appeal. A candidate for the nation's great office is a focus for popular feeling about issues and questions of group benefit as well, and our measurements should be extended to take this fact into account.

RELATIVE CHANGE IN CANDIDATE AND PARTY ATTITUDE

It is hardly surprising that candidates for the Presidency should attract attitudes which are somewhat distinct from those attaching to the parties themselves. The platforms adopted by the nominating conventions are much less binding than the election manifestoes of a British party, for example, and a presidential candidate is notoriously at liberty to take his own stands on major issues and the problems of major social groupings. Equally, on matters requiring congressional action he is free to contradict positions taken by his party in the Senate and House. And on matters of foreign policy, the country is largely dependent on the candidate's record and views to know what his administration would be likely to do in the world. This is the stuff of which a presidential system is made.

Therefore, it is of interest to compare the variability of attitudes toward the parties and their presidential candidates. Neither has been constant over the period of our research, but the two have shown vastly different propensities to change. When we turn from a six- to a four-dimensional model, summarizing popular feeling according to the party or candidate toward which it is directed whether or not it concerns domestic or foreign issues, questions of group benefit, or other matters, the candidate components are found to have moved much more strongly from Republican to Democratic advantage.

This contrast is shown by Figure 6, in which each pair of party and candidate components of the four-dimensional model is added together at each election. The combined party curve has not by any means stood still. The public's full assessment of the parties showed a marked Republican advantage in the mood of 1952. But by 1956 the comparison of parties had moved to the Democrats' benefit, and this trend continued over the later two elections.

The combined candidate curve, however, describes a very much greater change. The public's full assessment of Eisenhower and Stevenson, including issue and group perceptions as well as perceptions of personal qualities, was strongly Republican in 1952 and even more decisively so four years later. In the 1960 election, the comparison of candidates still favored the Republicans, although much more moderately. But between the Kennedy-Nixon campaign and the Johnson-Goldwater campaign the combined candidate component moved a most remarkable distance to the Democrats' advantage. In each contest the candidate curve was the farther removed from the zero-point: indeed, its average displacement from the neutral point has been more than 6 percent, whereas the average displacement of the party curve has been about 2 percent. But the really arresting comparison has to do with relative change: over these elections the variance of the candidate curve has exceeded that of the party curve by more than 10 to 1.

It is therefore evident that the dynamism of popular attitude is peculiarly tied to the emergence of new candidates for the Presidency. The attitudes toward the parties are not inert. The shift in the relative assessment of the parties over the period of this research has been enough to alter the parties' strength by something like six million votes on a turnout equal to that of 1964. But this change, impressive as it is, nevertheless is moderate by comparison with the change induced by succeeding pairs of candidates. The fluctuations of electoral attitudes over these elections have to a remarkable degree focused on the candidates themselves.

All of this is quite out of keeping with the static perspective of the

FIGURE 6

Variation of Party and Candidate Components

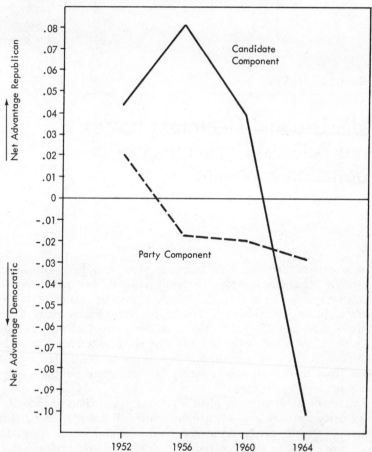

earliest studies of voting. Even if our findings are no more than approximately true, they argue strongly the dynamic implications of changes of the stimulus objects of national politics. This source of change has in fact brought spectacular shifts of presidential voting despite the fact that over the same period there has been almost no perceptible shift in the single most important type of response disposition, the electorate's enduring party loyalties. It may also be noted that the variations of attitude recorded here have been largely independent of secular changes in the structure of American society, although, as we have seen, a turnover of stimulus objects can alter dramatically the facts of social structure which are relevant to political choice. Taken together, changes in the several stimulus objects of presidential politics in this span of years have been quite enough to bring a change of party control, indeed to have induced a drastic transformation of party fortune in the contest for the Presidency.

Edward C. Dreyer

Media Use and Electoral Choices: Some Political Consequences of Information Exposure*

For over two decades, the American voter has been subjected to increasingly meticulous study. Certainly one of the more impressive findings to emerge from this sophisticated probing relates to the electorate's enduring attachment to one or the other major party and the stabilizing influence these loyalties exert on individual voting choices. But quite independent of the serenity that has characterized these basic dispositions is the existence of complex forces of political change that fashion from one election to another the variations in the two-party division of the popular vote.

In an era of stable partisan identifications, explanations of the ebb and flow of party fortunes suggest that the sources of political change are to be found in a wide variety of phenomena. Butler and Stokes, for example, find it convenient to think of political change as arising from at least three sources.[1] The first involves the normal physical turnover in the composition of the electorate. "The importance of this sort of change is obvious," they write. "In any era the young will be unlike the old in many of their attitudes, and some of these differences will extend to politics." A second type of change involves the enduring realignment of the elec-

* From *Public Opinion Quarterly*, vol. 35 (Winter 1971–72), pp. 544–53. Reprinted by permission of the Princeton University Press, copyright owners.

The data for this study were made available through the Inter-University Consortium for Political Research. They were originally collected by the Survey Research Center at the University of Michigan. Neither the Survey Research Center nor the Consortium bears any responsibility for the analysis or interpretations presented here. Financial support for this project was provided through a UMSL Faculty Research Grant. Acknowledgment also is due to the staff of the UMSL Computer Center and to Professors Ruth Jones, Samuel Kirkpatrick, David Leuthold, Dale Neuman, and Stuart Lilie for their helpful comments and suggestions.

[1] David Butler and Donald Stokes, *Political Change in Britain*, New York, St. Martin's Press, 1969, pp. 3–7.

torate's partisan loyalties. Like changes in the basic social and psychological characteristics of the population, shifts in the basic division of voter loyalties may slowly accumulate over the years; or they may occur suddenly as the result of severe social or economic crises of national proportions. The third source of change, and the one that underlies this investigation, concerns the electorate's response to the more or less immediate circumstances that surround a specific election. Admittedly the political changes generated by these short-term partisan forces do not produce the same kinds of long-term political consequences normally associated with population changes or party realignments, but they can have a significant impact on electoral choices and thereby on the tenure of the party currently in power.

Since the pioneering efforts of Berelson and Lazarsfeld, few studies have examined voter responses to the flow of current political information.[2] For the most part only the reinforcing and activating effects of the electorate's surveillance behavior have been emphasized, perhaps because more dramatic impacts are so imperceptible and long-term. In any event, our understanding of the precise impact of the mass media is only fragmentary and based on dated information. Accordingly, this article examines the extent to which the American electorate employs the mass media to monitor the progress of presidential campaigns and the effects this surveillance activity has on the stability of election day turnout and partisan choice. More specifically, the investigation deals with the adequacy of two "floating voter" hypotheses.

THE FLOATING VOTER HYPOTHESES

Any particular election takes place within a context of over-all stability in party identification. Although most voters begin with a "standing decision" to support their party's nominee, the decision is not irrevocable. Many voting studies have shown not only that some people are occasionally "converted" from one candidate or party preference to another but also that certain types of people seem to show a more general tendency toward variation in turnout and changeability in candidate preference. In the six presidential contests between 1948 and 1968, an average of 90 percent or more of the strongly identified Republicans and Democrats cast their ballots for the nominees of their respective parties. The vote of the weak partisans and especially the vote cast by Independents is much more variable. The variability in the partisan choices of these groups suggests that they are more responsive to the transient political forces associated with each presidential election.[3]

The classic formulation of this point of view has been designated as "the floating voter hypothesis" and originated with Lazarsfeld's Erie

[2] Paul Lazarsfeld, Bernard Berelson, and Hazel Gaudet, *The People's Choice*, New York, Columbia University Press, 1944; Bernard Berelson, et al., *Voting*, Chicago, The University of Chicago Press, 1962.

[3] Cf. Edward C. Dreyer and W. A. Rosenbaum, *Political Opinion and Behavior*, 2d ed., Belmont, Calif., Wadsworth Publishing Co., 1970, p. 248.

County study in 1940.[4] In its traditional formulation, the hypothesis asserts that changers—persons who switch their turnout and/or candidate intentions—tend to be people who pay the least attention to politics and absorb the least amount of political information. Converse's more recent analysis proposes two important modifications of this hypothesis.[5] The first, or inter-election version, simply generalizes Lazarsfeld's original finding to cover changes in turnout and partisan choice that occur from one election to the next. The second, or intra-election version, significantly amends the traditional floating voter hypothesis by adding the proviso that short-term partisan change is contingent upon whether or not new political information actually reaches the less politically involved electorate.

INTER-ELECTION PARTISAN CHANGE

A considerable body of data is available for testing the adequacy of the two revised versions of the floating voter hypothesis. The generalized inter-election version is easier and more straightforward to evaluate. Indeed, evidence bearing on this version employs both panel and recall data and can be found in a variety of political settings. A sampling of this data is brought together in Table 1 and provides overwhelming support for the proposition that the least informed or least exposed voters are also the most changeable in the partisan preferences they register from one election to the next. Although these data have no bearing on the simple intra-election version of the floating voter hypothesis, they do lend full support to Converse's expectation that "individuals who vacillate in forming their voting decisions during [any given] campaign period are likely to contribute . . . to such *inter*election voting shifts as do occur. . . ."[6]

The significance Converse assigns to this more generalized version of the traditional floating voter hypothesis has to do with its utility in explaining variations in the turnout and partisanship of the vote in presidential and off-year congressional elections. Since the uninvolved and uninformed segment of the electorate is more susceptible to whatever short-term partisan forces they may encounter, the flow of current political information operates as an important force governing their electoral choices. Thus, in off-year elections the candidates are much less visible to the electorate than they are in presidential contests; party activity is less intense; and the flow of partisan information via the mass media diminishes noticeably. Largely as a result of this reduced yet more diffuse flow of new stimuli, the less involved or floating voter tends to drop out

---

[4] Lazarsfeld et al., *op. cit.*, pp. 69ff. Besides Converse's recent review of the floating voting hypothesis see also H. Daudt, *The Floating Voter and the Floating Vote: A Critical Analysis of American and English Election Studies*, Leiden, Holland, H. E. Stenfert Kroese N. V., 1961.

[5] See Philip E. Converse, "Information Flow and the Stability of Partisan Attitudes," in Angus Campbell et al., *Elections and the Political Order*, New York, Wiley, 1966, pp. 136–58.

[6] Converse, "Information Flow . . . ," p. 137.

TABLE 1

Measures of Inter-Election Change and Stability in Partisan Preferences

	Proportion Supporting Same Party by Exposure to Political Communication				
	Lowest				Highest
Converse's panel, 1956–60*	44%		61%		81%
Butler and Stokes' British panel, 1960–64† ..	57	71	75	80	83
SRC American recalled at‡					
1960–64	47	58	67	67	71
1964–68	50	64	68	66	75

* Recomputed from data presented in "Information Flow and the Stability of Partisan Attitudes," Table 8–1, p. 139.
† *Political Change in Britain,* Table 10.4, p. 221.
‡ Inter-University Consortium for Political Research, 1964 and 1968 Presidential Election Studies.

of the off-year electorate, as evidenced by the rather dependable 10 to 20 percentage point decline in voter turnout when compared with the turnout rate in the preceding presidential contest. Of those who do vote, a large proportion are likely to be strong party identifiers who tend to support their party's nominee more regularly than do the floating in-and-out voters. The fact that turnout and partisan choice in off-year elections is more closely related to strength of party identification tends to produce an aggregate congressional vote that closely resembles the "normal" 54–46 split between Democrats and Republicans. Indeed, in the ten congressional elections between 1950 and 1968, the variation between the actual and the "expected" or "normal" Democratic vote has averaged only three percentage points.

INTRA-ELECTION PARTISAN CHANGE

The more actively one monitors campaign activities through the mass media, presumably the greater the intake of current political information. But this larger intake does not have the same impact as the smaller volume of intake among the less actively exposed; they are far more susceptible to the slightest dose of current information, since their understanding and "mass" of stored political knowledge is so impoverished. Thus, Converse points to the paradox in his revised intra-election hypothesis: the uninvolved voter is most susceptible to short-term change provided new information reaches him, but when the flow of political information is weak, the uninvolved voter is least likely to manifest changes in electoral behavior.

From this point of view it follows that in any single election, the pre-election day intentions of voters who experience no new intake of information should remain perfectly stable, and the votes cast by this group should correlate very strongly with their existing partisan loyalties; or, as Converse puts it, the vote of the less involved should be "a pure party vote."[7] Converse's hypothesis also predicts a dramatic "step

[7] *Ibid.,* p. 143.

change" in the stability of vote intentions from most stable among those who employ no media to most unstable among those who follow the campaign in only one medium; beyond this point, stability should increase with the number of media employed in following the campaign. Thus, instead of a monotonic relationship between change and information intake, Converse argues for the existence of a curvilinear or J-shaped relationship, with both the low and high exposure groups exhibiting the greatest stability in their electoral preferences.

Data from the Survey Research Center's 1952 presidential election study were used by Converse in testing his hypothesis. Since this article attempts to test the same hypothesis with data from all succeeding presidential years, the procedures Converse adopted are followed as literally as possible. Political involvement is measured by the number of media respondents reported using to monitor the progress of the campaign— admittedly a crude but serviceable measure of current surveillance activities.[8] Two different indices are employed to measure stability of electoral choices. The first relies on the turnover rates between pre-election intentions and actual election day behavior.[9] A second index of electoral change or stability involves the defection rates of party identifiers. For both sets of tests, a high tau-beta correlation indicates (1) high stability between pre-vote intention and actual electoral behavior and (2) a high degree of stability between partisan identification and party vote.

When the correlations from the 1952 test are plotted on a coordinate system the predicted J-shaped curves emerge quite clearly. For persons at the lowest end of the exposure continuum information intake is virtually nil and whatever pre-existing dispositions they may possess remain undisturbed. As exposure increases, individuals encounter some new information that may challenge rather weakly held political predispositions; this results in their opinions being the most unstable. As information exposure increases to the maximum level there is a corresponding increase in the strength of internalized partisan predispositions and therefore a greater resistance to change. Among the most active communicators attitude stability is once again quite high. Indeed, in Converse's two-by-two case (party intention by party choice; cf. fn. 9), there is a perfect

---

[8] Converse favors media usage as a measure of political involvement because it taps not only current information intake but also a person's long-term motivation to monitor the political environment. The number of media one employs also correlates quite highly with a person's store of historically rooted political information. See *ibid.*, p. 144 and 145.

[9] Converse explains the rationale behind this measure: "Since the ultimate voting act consisted in a Republican vote, a Democratic vote, or a failure to vote, it was inconvenient to consider any respondents who were unclear as to their vote intention before the election. Thus a three-by-three table could be constructed, and a rank-order (tau-beta) correlation computed for it within subsets of the population, according to whether no media were used or some higher number. Since there might be some question as to the effect of differences in proportions of non-voters upon the correlation, a comparable coefficient was also calculated for the two-by-two table reflecting constancy or change in choice of candidates. These are obviously not independent tests." *Ibid.*

correlation between pre-vote intention and actual vote among those who did not follow the campaign in any of the media. From the evidence Converse presents, those most removed from the flow of political information are among the most stable—as his reformulated version of the floating voter hypothesis predicted they would be. These findings stand in stark contrast to the "traditional" floating voter hypothesis which predicts that the low exposure group should be the most unstable.

In one sense, Converse's reformulated floating voter hypothesis "may appear to be of limited significance, simply because of the meager proportions of voters who fall in the 'no media' cell where presidential campaigns are concerned." In the 1952 tests, for example, calculations for the no media respondents were based on N's of 22 in the two-by-two case and 92 in the three-by-three case. But, as Converse notes, at an earlier point in history the number of no media cases would "have been very much larger, given what we know of changes in conditions of information flow in the past century. In a historical perspective, then, not to mention one which looks toward less developed nations, the refinement is by no means trivial."[10]

Testing the Converse Hypothesis with Pooled Data. By aggregating all observations from 1952 through 1964 we can overcome this problem of small numbers and increase the size of the no media cell by a factor of 3.3 in the three-by-three test and by a factor of 5 in the two-by-two test (the total $N = 5824$).

The correlations that emerge from this aggregated data are presented in Table 2, and they lend rather handsome support to the modified intra-election floating voter hypothesis. If these correlations were plotted on a coordinate chart the predicted J-shaped curves would emerge quite clearly in the three-by-three and two-by-two cases. Moreover, the step changes in the correlations between those who employ no media and those who are only marginally exposed lends credence to the possibility that electoral choices were quite stable in an era when the flow of political information was much weaker than it is now.

The only surprising finding in Table 2 relates to the correlations between partisan identification and the vote, which over the range of media exposure reveals a more linear trend than Converse's hypothesis predicts. In fact in none of the five presidential data sets—including the 1952 data —does a replication of Converse's stated procedure produce a curvilinear trend in the rank-order correlations between these variables. In all cases, the relationships between the vote and party affiliation, as measured by Converse's 2-point and the more standard 3- and 5-point partisan scales, result in a linear trend.[11]

---

10 *Ibid.,* p. 149.

11 Converse alludes to such a pattern at one point early in his article: ". . . our general argument would predict that the magnitude of the correlation between party identification and the actual vote for any election, being an index of the gross amount of defection from party, should vary within the population as a direct function of political comprehension or involvement. In the 1952 and 1956 presidential election data we were able to observe some faint variation of this sort, although the relation-

TABLE 2

Correlations (Tau-Beta) between Stability in Presidential Voting and
Exposure to Political Communication, Combined 1952–1964 Data

| | Exposure to Political Communication | | | | |
	Lowest				Highest
Vote intention by vote choice	.77	.71	.71	.76	.78
	(303)	(819)	(1749)	(1998)	(955)
Party intention by party choice	.87	.82	.87	.91	.90
	(108)	(425)	(1277)	(1685)	(830)
Party identification by party vote ...	.44	.70	.67	.70	.76
	(113)	(405)	(1141)	(1420)	(702)

Testing the Converse Hypothesis in Individual Elections, 1952–1968.
As a result of the interaction between long-term partisan loyalties and the
more transient short-term influences associated with particular campaigns, American electoral contests reveal an interesting mix of both
stability and change. While the stability of party identification and its
influence in structuring the voter's partisan choices characterizes most
electoral studies, there is impressive evidence to suggest that short-term
factors generated in recent presidential campaigns have become increasingly more influential in the electoral calculations of American voters.[12]

Subjecting Converse's hypothesis to each set of post-1952 election data
provides a rather rigorous test of its current relevance and explanatory
capability. If this procedure produces results which conform with Converse's predictions, we will have provided rather strong confirmation of
its current validity. If, on the other hand, the data do not provide this
support, the modified hypothesis is no longer applicable to contemporary
campaigns.

Correlations measuring the stability of partisan attitudes over a series
of four elections and employing the same tests and procedures Converse
used with the 1952 presidential data are contained in Table 3. They in-

ship was more ragged than anticipated." p. 141. The "raggedness" of this relationship
is attributed to the tendency of the weakly involved to change their current party
identifications more readily over rather brief periods of time.

It also should be noted that Converse's data on the relationship between vote and
party identification appears to be based on a simple dichotomization of these variables; independents and non-voters apparently are classified as missing data. But even
under these restrictions Converse's data and my replication of his data do not correspond in every case. With respect to the party identification-party vote relationship,
Converse's reported correlations, from lowest to highest exposure groupings are (approximately) .70, .67, .62, .64 and .72. My replication based on the same data produces tau-beta coefficients that correspond quite closely in all but the "no media"
cell (tau-beta of .63). In the 1952 two-by-two test our correlations also differ significantly despite the fact that they were calculated in the same way and with the same
Ns. In the three-by-three cases, however, our correlations are quite similar.

[12] Walter Dean Burnham, "American Voting Behavior and the 1964 Election,"
Midwest Journal of Political Science, Vol. 12, 1968, pp. 1–40; see also Gerald
Pomper, "Classification of Presidential Elections," *Journal of Politics,* Vol. 29, 1967,
pp. 535–66.

dicate that the tidy set of findings characterizing the 1952 election breaks down with virtually each successive election. Except for one minor deviation in the three-by-three test, the predicted trend holds only for the 1956 contest. In the two-by-two test, the 1968 data set provides the only correlations that conform with the expectations of the modified hypothesis. The predicted step change—from very stable preferences among those with no exposure to very unstable choices among the minimally exposed—also is very uneven and, in most cases, stability tends to increase rather than decrease.

TABLE 3

Tau-Beta Correlations of Attitude Stability, by Exposure to Political Communication and Year of Campaign, 1952–1968

Presidential Year	Exposure to Political Communication				
	Lowest				Highest
A. Vote Intention by Vote Choice[*]					
1952	.69	.65	.64	.69	.65
1956	.75	.61	.77	.74	.88
1960	.86	.75	.74	.81	.75
1964	.75	.75	.72	.77	.81
1968	.68	.70	.66	.70	.80
B. Party Intention by Party Choice[†]					
1952	1.00	.80	.85	.91	.89
1956	.83	.84	.84	.90	.87
1960	.69	.81	.90	.90	.89
1964	.55	.77	.85	.90	.91
1968	.88	.83	.73	.80	.87
C. Party Identification by Party Vote[‡]					
1952	.63	.68	.64	.68	.73
1956	.59	.75	.66	.70	.83
1960	.24	.56	.75	.76	.80
1964	.21	.58	.59	.62	.70
1968[1]	.34	.48	.56	.54	.65

[*] Number of cases for each year from lowest to highest exposure: 1952–92; 208; 464; 525; 228. 1956–108; 276; 472; 435; 212. 1960–61; 183, 434; 572; 278. 1964–43; 152; 377; 466; 237. 1968–40; 169; 358; 397; 168.

[†] Number of cases for each year from lowest to highest exposure: 1952–22; 88; 295; 413; 193. 1956–47; 138; 361; 370; 195. 1960–19; 114; 341; 514; 228. 1964–20; 85; 280; 338; 214. 1968–13; 92; 257; 327; 151.

[‡] Number of cases for each year from lowest to highest exposure: 1952–24; 93; 261; 336; 150. 1956–43; 119; 304; 315; 115. 1960–24; 112; 321; 438; 184. 1964–15; 81; 255; 331; 195. 1968–26; 79; 218; 263; 119.

[1] Because of the three-way race in 1968, tau-chi (a rank-order measure for tables with an unequal number of rows and columns) rather than tau-beta is the appropriate statistic.

But the data most damaging to Converse's modified hypothesis are found in the party identification–party vote test. In none of the elections do the predicted J-shaped curves emerge. More important, the strength of the party identification–party vote relationship not only declines with each passing election but also declines at virtually every level of media exposure. In short, the lack of any consistent support for Converse's modified version of the floating voter hypothesis suggests that perhaps the 1952 findings are the exception rather than the rule. In any event, these observations underscore the necessity of reconsidering the joint impact that stable, long-term partisan identifications and more transient short-term influences have on the voter's electoral choices.

CONCLUSION

According to V. O. Key, the student of political communication would like to be able "to sum up in some comprehensible way what the media do to make people what they are politically. What are the effects of the media on the policy outlooks, preferences, and expectations of the citizenry as a whole?" Unhappily, however, the behavioral sciences have been unable for the most part to shed much light on these questions. "Given the limits of knowledge of the political role and effects of mass communications," Key concluded, "about all that can be done is to make educated guesses around the edges of the problem."[13]

Some "educated guesses" about the impact of political communication on electoral choices suggest the following conclusions. First, with the growing availability of mass media (primarily television since 1952), and the increased utilization of the media by candidates and parties, the flow of short-term political stimuli—both during campaigns and in the lengthy lulls between them—has effectively penetrated all segments of the electorate. These data also suggest that the more or less immediate circumstances that surround any given election have eroded and probably will continue to erode the stabilizing influences normally associated with the electorate's partisan loyalties. This weakening of the party identification—party vote relationship will be manifested across the total electorate. Finally, Converse's modification of the floating voter hypothesis, while probably applicable to an earlier era of rather weak political communication, no longer seems to apply to the current situation. If anything, the data presented in this paper suggest that the traditional floating voter hypothesis applies to both the inter- and intra-election situation.

---

[13] V. O. Key, Jr., *Public Opinion and American Democracy*, New York, Alfred A. Knopf, 1961, p. 345.

V. O. Key, Jr.

The Responsible Electorate*

The apparent stability of the popular support of the political party dominant at the moment excites the curiosity of students of American politics. For relatively long periods one party or the other commands so consistently the votes of a majority that the country is said to be either normally Republican or normally Democratic. From 1932 to 1952 elections appeared to be only reassertions by the standing majority of its continued faith in Democratic leadership. In 1932 Franklin D. Roosevelt drew 59.1 per cent of the two-party vote and in 1936, in an extraordinary expression of popular confidence, 62.5 per cent. The Democratic proportion of the vote declined in succeeding elections bit by bit: 55.0 per cent in 1940; 53.8 per cent in 1944; and 52.3 per cent in 1948. Yet it seemed as if each election was but an occasion for the New Deal to muster again its phalanxes only in slightly diminished strength, march them to the polls, and thereby record its claim to power for another four years.

Elections such as these, in which the party pattern of the preceding election prevails, Angus Campbell calls "maintaining" elections.[1] While this characterization serves happily on a conceptual system for the differentiation of broad types of elections, it tells us nothing about the processes by which a majority party maintains—or does not maintain—its dominance. A satisfactory explanation of those processes would move us toward a better understanding of popular government. Such evidence as can be mustered suggests that the popular majority does not hold together like a ball of sticky popcorn. Rather, no sooner has a popular majority been constructed than it begins to crumble. The maintenance of a supportive majority requires governmental actions, policies, and gestures

---

[1] Angus Campbell, P. E. Converse, W. E. Miller, and D. E. Stokes, *The American Voter* (New York: John Wiley & Sons, 1960), ch. 19.

that reinforce the confidence of those who have placed their faith in the Administration. Yet to govern is to antagonize not only opponents but also at least some supporters; as the loyalty of one group is nourished, another group may be repelled. A series of maintaining elections occurs only in consequence of a complex process of interaction between government and populace in which old friends are sustained, old enemies are converted into new friends, old friends become even bitter opponents, and new voters are attracted to the cause—all in proper proportions to produce repeatedly for the dominant party its apparently stable and continuing majority.

The unbroken series of Democratic victories in the 1930's and 1940's occurred against a background of marked and abrupt innovations in governmental policy. To the extent that interactions between governmental action and public attitudes can be traced, this epoch should be instructive about the processes involved in the maintenance and renewal of a dominant popular coalition. And, thereby, we may also enlarge our information on the behavior of the supposedly errant voter. To speak of these interactions, though, we must recall some of the principal governmental actions of the 1930's. For a substantial part of the population they are by now only vague episodes in a dim and distant history.

The federal government underwent a radical transformation after the Democratic victory in 1932. It had been a remote authority with a limited range of activity. It operated the postal system, improved rivers and harbors, maintained armed forces on a scale fearsome only to banana republics, and performed other functions of which the average citizen was hardly aware. Within a brief time it became an institution that affected intimately the lives and fortunes of most, if not all, citizens. Measures of recovery and of reform—as the categorization of the time went—contributed to this fundamental alteration of federal activities. Legislative endeavors to achieve economic recovery from the Great Depression shaded over into steps toward basic reform; both types of policy touched the interests and hopes of great numbers of people and ignited the fiercest political controversy.

Large-scale measures for the relief of the unemployed made federal policy highly perceptible to millions of destitute persons. Administered at first as direct relief—a dole—by state relief administrations, the program soon came to be conducted by the Works Progress Administration, a federal agency which employed people on projects as diverse as theatricals, road construction, and leaf raking to the accompaniment of a spirited criticism not noticeably shared by those who relied on the WPA for sustenance. Another numerous class of persons received federal assistance through the Home Owners' Loan Corporation, an agency which had $3,000,000,000 to refinance home mortgages to tide necessitous debtors over until a better day. Hard-pressed banks and other business enterprises received infusions of government capital often in the form of loans. Expenditures on a new scale for public works pumped money into the economy. By the Agricultural Adjustment Act, Congress attempted to alleviate the lot of the farmer who had been especially hard hit by the depression. The National Recovery Administration sought, oddly enough, to activate industry by something of a system of legalized cartels, with the inclusion in the cartel agreements (or industry codes) of standards with respect to minimum wages, maximum hours, collective bargaining, and other aspects of the employer–employee relationship.

Only a hazy line divided measures of recovery from those of reform; yet some actions clearly contemplated permanent and often drastic changes in public policy. Some of these new policies had effects of marked visibility. The Social Security Act of 1935 established a system of federal grants to states for programs of assistance to the aged, to the blind, and to dependent children, but it also instituted a system of contributory old-age annuities and a scheme of unemployment compensation, the first national steps into the field of social insurance. The Wagner Labor Relations Act assured to labor the right to organize and imposed on employers an obligation to bargain with employees collectively, an act of fundamental significance in the definition of the structure of the industrial order. In another area the government hoped by the Public Utility Holding Company Act to prevent a recurrence of financial abuses that had been notable, and the Tennessee Valley Authority and various power projects were regarded by the electrical utilities as an entering wedge for a socialism that would ultimately destroy them. Other legislation restrained sharp operators in the securities business who had bilked a goodly number of their fellow men in the halcyon days of the new era of the 1920's.

The merits or demerits of all these actions—and many others—are not our concern. The relevance of their mention is to suggest the considerable range of novel governmental actions with a widespread impact upon the fortunes and aspirations of voters. What kinds of interactions between government and electorate occurred in consequence of this revolution—as American revolutions go—in public policy? The broad effect was, of course, obvious. By 1936 the innovation period of the New Deal had pretty well run its course, and in that year the voters responded with a resounding ratification of the new thrust of governmental policy. Or, if one wishes to be cautious, the electorate resoundingly rejected the Republican alternative, which, as the campaign of 1936 developed, appeared to be a hysterical plea to return to the pre-1932 status quo lest the American system become a dictatorship.[2]

To portray the processes of the maintenance of the New Deal coalition, though, one must go beyond the broad electoral verdict and examine the detailed movements in voter sentiment underlying the grand totals. The maintenance and switching of party positions reflected in part responses to specific and concrete actions of government; they also reflected the responses of voters to the political oratory of the time. As campaigns developed, the commotion over individual policies seemed to be transmuted into the grand abstractions of political debate. The political discussion of the 1930's was heavily tinged with the rhetoric of the conflict of class and interest, and the battle seemed to take the shape of

---

[2] For the tenor of the politics of the time, see A. M. Schlesinger, Jr., *The Politics of Upheaval* (Boston: Houghton Mifflin, 1960).

a competition between rich and poor, or between the American constitutional system and some alien alternative. On the left, evangels, such as Huey Long, preached a doctrine of "share the wealth," while those who had somewhat more than a modicum of wealth organized the Liberty League and other such societies to defend the American system. In 1936 the Republican national committee gloomily forecast that the "American plan of government might be lost forever," if Roosevelt were kept in office.

How might voters be expected to respond to the actions of government and to the campaign oratory of this era? American parties have had historically a multiclass following. Doubtless in 1932, though the data are not available, persons of all classes deserted the Republicans to vote for Franklin D. Roosevelt and a change. The result was that the 1932 Democratic vote probably included large numbers of persons who would not be regarded as "Democratic" in disposition. At any rate, it would be plausible to expect that as the New Deal unfolded, persons of upper-class status and of conservative disposition would be drawn from their Democratic posture to the Republican ranks. Moreover, it might be supposed that a countertendency would also operate as 1932 Republican voters in the lesser economic categories moved over to the Democratic side of the fence. In short, the impact of governmental actions and political rhetoric would be expected to heighten polarization along class and occupational lines.

Some such movement of voters occurred, evidently on a fairly large

TABLE 1

Patterns of Vote Switching in Presidential Elections, 1936–1948,
in Relation to Economic Status*

Status	1936–40†		1940–44‡		1944–48§	
	% of 1936 D's, D–R	% of 1936 R's, R–D	% of 1940 D's, D–R	% of 1940 R's, R–D	% of 1944 D's, D–R	% of 1944 R's, R–D
Wealthy	46	2	35	4	‖	0
Average + ...	30	1	27	5	47	1
Average	28	4	24	7	32	3
Poor + ...	20	5	#	#	#	#
Poor	18	7	19	8	22	6
Old-age assistance	19	4	13	5	18	‖
On relief	14	7	11	‖	‖	‖

* The table entries are the percentages of those with a recall of a vote for a major-party candidate at the first election of the pair of years who expressed a preference for a major-party candidate in surveys in October just prior to the election of the second year of each pair. In each instance several surveys are combined to obtain larger samples in the individual cells. Economic status was that assigned to the respondent by the AIPO interviewer.

† A consolidation of the following AIPO surveys: 215K, 216T, 217, 218K. Roper 22, October 1940, yielded the following percentages of switchers, D-R, in the indicated economic levels: A, 25; ₦, 24; C, 20; D, 12. The corresponding R-D switches were: 2, 3, 5, 9.

‡ A consolidation of AIPO 330, 331, 332, 333, 334.

§ A consolidation of AIPO 430 and 431.

‖ Less than 50 cases.

Data obtained from low-income respondents in 1944 and 1948 were coded only in terms of a "poor" category. There was no "poor +" category.

scale. Many upper-class Democratic voters defected, while relatively fewer working-class Democrats left the ranks. Scarcely any information is available for the election of 1936, but in the elections of 1940, 1944, and 1948 these differentials in party switching existed. Persons at all economic levels at each election moved away from the Democratic party but at rates varying with level of economic status. The differentials in party defection among economic levels, as estimated from Gallup polls of presidential preference, appear in Table 1. The rankings from "wealthy" to "poor" assigned by the interviewers are doubtless not measures of precision; nevertheless, of the "wealthy" 1936 Democratic voters, in the neighborhood of four out of ten deserted to the Republicans in 1940. At the other extreme, less than one in seven persons on relief took that step.

The countermovement, from Republican in 1936 to Democratic in 1940, was relatively small, yet it had a class bias in that relatively more of the poor than of the better-off 1936 Republicans switched to Democratic in 1940. In 1944 involvement in World War II gave the stimuli of the campaign a less class-oriented tone; yet in lesser degree than in 1940 the same class-tinged pattern of party switching prevailed. In 1948, with the war out of the way, the political battle assumed its older form with a more marked difference in switching among economic levels. Though the rates of switching in party preference shown by the pre-election polls analyzed in Table 1 may exceed the switch in the actual vote, they suggest the existence of quite large movements across party lines in these elections which brought voting alignments toward a closer congruity with income classes.[3]

Another test of our expectations about how voters might have responded to the impact of the New Deal appears in Table 2, which shows the switches from Democratic to Republican within broad occupational groups at the same series of elections. Business and professional Democratic voters at one election were far more likely to defect to the Republican candidate at the next election than were unskilled workers. Nevertheless, defections occurred at all occupational levels, a matter not easily explained if one attributes voting behavior largely to the effect of objective economic interest. If one's concern as an unskilled worker governs his voting, by what conceivable reason should an unskilled Democrat of 1936 have become a Republican voter in 1940? The explanation, which will occupy us later, is not immediately apparent; nevertheless, about one in seven of the group in question made that switch. Table 2 incidentally illustrates some of the characteristics of the data with which

---

[3] For the technician it should be noted that the differences in switching rates that appear, for example, in the first column of Table 1 could be attributable in part to a variant of the Maccobyean effect, so called for its identification by Eleanor Maccoby, "Pitfalls in the Analysis of Panel Data: A Research Note on Some Technical Aspects of Voting," *American Journal of Sociology*, LXI (1956), 359–62. The effect may result in an overstatement of differences in rates of change between large and small samples. Random errors in recording responses and in punching data into cards may inflate the rates of change for small N's more than for large N's. The odds are that the potential of the effect is negligible for most of our tables, but comparisons between cells with large and with extremely small N's should be regarded with some wariness.

TABLE 2

Percentages within Occupational Categories Switching from Democratic to
Republican Presidential Preference from Election to Election, 1936–1948, as
Measured by Pre-Election and Post-Election Polls°

Group	1936–40†		1940–44‡		1944–48§	
	Pre	Post	Pre	Post	Pre	Post
Business and professional	33	35	25	18	57	26
White-collar	28	24	22	16	39	21
Skilled and semiskilled	22	19	18	14	23	11
Unskilled	17	15	19	12	23	10
Farmers and farm laborers	23	24	24	16	18	13

° The percentages for the pre-election columns were computed in the same way as the comparable percentages in Table 1. The post-election percentages are derived from surveys conducted during the month after the presidential election; they rest, thus, on reported votes in November as compared with the reported vote of four years before.

† The pre-election column rests on a consolidation of AIPO 216T, 217, 218K, 220, 221. The post-election column represents a consolidation of AIPO 224 and 225. Roper's October 1940 survey produced the following D-R percentages: business and professional, 29; white-collar, 26; wage earners, 15; farmers and farm laborers, 15. The occupational categories were not exactly the same as those of the AIPO.

‡ The pre-election column rests on a consolidation of AIPO 331, 332, 333, 334; the post-election column on AIPO 335 and 336K.

§ The pre-election column rests on a consolidation of AIPO 429, 430, and 431; the post-election column on AIPO 432.

we work; it shows switching as measured both by a pre-election expression of preference and by a post-election report of the vote. Except for the election of 1940, a fairly wide difference exists between the two sets of figures. Probably the "true" figures fell somewhere between the two sets of percentages; the data serve better as indicators of contrasting shifts in attitude of groups of voters than as measures of their absolute rates of switching in the voting.[4]

The pattern of recruitment of new voters into the Democratic ranks resembled the patterns of switching among old voters. Democratic losses among old voters decreased from step to step down the ladder of occupational status; the proportion of new voters preferring the Demo-

----

[4] Several factors contribute to the differences between the pre-election and post-election findings. The two figures are about alike for 1940, probably the result of the practice in that year of screening many prospective nonvoters from the sample at the interview stage. Beyond that, the pre-election figures rest on a consolidation of several surveys during the campaign, a factor that would tend to overestimate switching since during this era the Democratic vote seemed to reach more complete activation as the campaign progressed. The inclusion of potential nonvoters also probably inflates switching rates; the impression develops that this class of persons has a sharp sensitivity to the winds of the moment and would be especially prone under the circumstances of these campaigns to report a switch in preference. The odds also are that, given the tendency for the popular majority to be inflated in surveys reporting past votes, the post-election surveys understate the actual defection rates. The differences between the pre-election and post-election data for 1948 are especially wide, a factor which lends credence to the supposition that in this campaign quite marked shifts in sentiment occurred in the last ten days or so of the campaign. In this campaign the pre-election polls forecast a Republican victory, must to the glee of the critics of the polls whose forecasts were, incidentally, no better.

TABLE 3
Democratic Percentage of Presidential Preference of New Voters, within
Occupational Categories, as Measured by Pre-Election and Post-Election Polls*

Group	1940		1944		1948	
	Pre	Post	Pre	Post	Pre	Post
Business and professional	46	42	49	46	39	48
White-collar	53	54	53	66	44	58
Skilled and semiskilled	68	65	59	64	61	75
Unskilled	68	67	63	59	67	69
Farmers and farm laborers	56	48	42	45	48	61

* Based on same surveys as Table 2. New voters are defined as those who did not vote in the preceding presidential election, either because they were too young or for some other reason.

cratic candidate increased from step to step down the ladder. These variations in the voting inclinations of new voters, that is, those who either were too young or simply failed to vote four years earlier, are shown in detail for each of the elections in Table 3. A significant factor in the maintenance of the position of the "normal" majority probably consists in its success in attracting new voters to its banner. As has been shown (in Table 4), the new voters make up a relatively large proportion of the vote, and a failure to capture the loyalties of a majority of them could within a few elections change the balance of power between the parties. Of greatest importance, of course, is the recruitment of young persons who, once they form partisan attachments, may be expected to remain with the party with fair consistency for many years. Yet the older "new voters" are also a numerous, if heterogeneous, category, not without unimportance in the vote.[5]

So far our analysis follows conventional forms and yields findings that depend upon our reading into the data plausible assumptions about voter motivation. The data suggest that the issues and alternatives of the time tended to sharpen the class cleavage between the parties and in the process produced voter switching on a scale whose magnitude is not commonly suspected. Yet the analysis also generates persistent doubts. It rests on an assumption that voting can best be understood as an expression of motivations induced by the impact of campaign alternatives on short-range, individual economic interest which we assume to be associ-

[5] Over the elections 1940–1960, as shown by Table 4, the Democrats drew a somewhat larger proportion of the "new voters" than of the "old" voters, as measured by expressions of pre-election preference. This Democratic advantage in the recruitment of new support doubtless contributed to the maintenance of its position as the party with the larger number of loyal followers. When the new voters at these elections were grouped into age categories, 21–39, 40–59, and 60 and over, the usual pattern over the period was for the Democratic proportion of the pre-election preference to be highest in the 21–39 age group, which suggested uniformly greater Democratic success in recruiting young voters. The notable exception occurred in 1940 when the Democratic proportion among those 60 and over exceeded the Democratic proportion among those under 40, probably a consequence of the special impact of the old-age security issue on the old folks.

ated with occupation or status. We impute motives to types of individuals, run the cards through the sorter, and, lo and behold, upper-status persons switch in differing degrees and directions than do lower-status persons. Yet the embarrassing fact remains that in the elections examined many lower-status persons also switched preferences from Democratic to Republican; moreover, many lower-status persons maintained a standpat Republican position from election to election. And many well-to-do persons, strange though it may seem, remained steadfast Democrats from election to election.

What would we find if we proceeded directly to motive or attitude and ascertained the relation between vote switching and views on policy? What kinds of relations would be found if we assumed that the voter was a fairly reasonable fellow who voted to promote or to discourage public policies he approved or disapproved, insofar as he could perceive the consequences of his vote? Obviously, all kinds of motives, attitudes, and concerns enter into the voting decision; yet analyses of the available information indicate quite marked correlations between policy attitudes and vote switching. In short, the data make it appear sensible to regard the voter as a person who is concerned with what governments have done or not done and what they propose to do rather than one guided, perhaps unaware, by the imperatives of economic status or the tricks of Madison Avenue.

Our information on the relation of voter switching to policy preferences is not as comprehensive as we might wish. The information on the election of 1936, which was evidently an event of great significance in the reshaping of the American pattern of party loyalties, is especially limited. Nevertheless, in that year the old-age annuity provisions of the Social Security Act turned out to be a major issue. Republicans attacked the act. All citizens would soon be wearing dog tags carrying their social security numbers and less restrained campaign orators treated the system as a fraud. Voters responded with an expression of opinion startling in its clarity. In the neighborhood of four out of ten 1932 Democratic voters who opposed the legislation shifted over to the Republican candidate while about three out of ten of those 1932 Republicans who favored the plan moved to the support of Roosevelt. The details appear in Table 4.*

---

* Editor's note: Key intended to elaborate at some length on the relationship in Table 4 between voters' 1936 presidential preference and their attitude toward the old-age insurance program. Attitudes on the social security issue may have had two broad effects on the 1936 voting. In addition to making voters whose position on the issue was not congruent with their previous presidential vote more likely to switch parties in 1936, it also may have made individuals whose previous presidential vote and policy attitude on the social security question were mutually consistent more inclined to stick with the party they had previously supported. Among 1932 Democratic voters, although four in ten of those who opposed the old-age insurance plan switched to the G.O.P. in 1936, only one in eight of the 1932 Democrats who supported federal old-age pensions left the Democratic party at the next presidential election. On the other hand, 1932 Republican voters who supported the insurance plan were much more likely to switch to the Democratic presidential nominee in 1936 than were 1932 Republican voters who opposed the Social Security pension plan. Three in ten of the 1932 Republican voters who supported the plan switched to Roosevelt in 1936; only 7 per cent of the 1932 Republican voters who opposed the plan deserted the G.O.P. in 1936.

Had the social security issue been the only influence on the vote these switches would have been closer to ten our of ten in each direction. It was not, of course, the only issue.† Nevertheless, an impressive relation between voting behavior and policy preference on this question prevailed, which raises a presumption that the social security issue had a notable power to wrench voters from their 1932 party positions to a vote in accord with their policy preferences.

TABLE 4

Switches in Presidential Voting Preference, 1932–1936, in Relation to Response to Question: "Do you favor the compulsory old-age insurance plan, starting January first, which requires employers and employees to make equal monthly contributions?"°

Response	% of 1932 D's, D-R	% of 1932 R's, R-D	% of New Voters, D†
Yes, favor	12 (1,630)	30 (643)	61 (626)
No	40 (483)	7 (535)	45 (245)
No opinion	13 (315)	16 (175)	71 (170)

° AIPO 53, 9–26–36. This is the only surviving deck of cards for a 1936 survey with a recall of the 1932 vote. Data on the characteristics of the sample are nonexistent, but the addition of the N's to produce a national sample would probably be even more perilous than to the use here made of the data. The N's appear in parentheses. As in Table 1 and other tables, N is the total number of respondents on which the percentage is based. Thus, the figure 1,630 in the first column means that there were 1,630 respondents who recalled having voted for the Democratic candidate in 1932 and who favored the compulsory old-age insurance plan in 1936. Of these 1,630 persons, 12 per cent reported that they intended to support the Republican candidate in 1936.

† New voters are respondents who had not voted in 1932, either because they were too young or for other reasons.

As the election of 1940 approached, newspaper headlines tended to focus on the threat of war; yet voters seemed to be more concerned with the grand issues of domestic politics. Those issues turned broadly around the place and power of business in the American system, and the Democratic Administration occupied the role, in the eyes of business, as the enemy of business and, in the eyes of others, as the protagonist of the generality. The tolerant attitude of government toward the sitdown strikes in the automobile industry in 1937 symbolized the situation. As the 1940 polling neared, however, business protests became sharper as earlier New Deal legislation, made temporarily ineffective by constitutional litigation, began to make its effects felt. The defeat of Roosevelt's plan for the rejuvenation of the Supreme Court heartened business only

† Editor's note: The data in Table 4 do not indicate how important or visible the social security issue was to the members of Dr. Gallup's sample. Some voters, for example, may have duly registered their approval or disapproval of the old-age insurance scheme without really caring very much about its inclusion in the Social Security Act; and Key intended to emphasize that undoubtedly the social security issue was more salient for some voters than for others during the 1936 campaign. Either a lack of concern over the social security question or a greater concern with other issues among some voters could help explain why the relation between policy attitudes on social security and 1936 voting behavior was not even stronger than it was.

temporarily. The Court found ways and means to hold major New Deal legislation constitutional, contrary to the opinions of most of the corporation lawyers in the country. Employers, thus, began to feel the bite of the Wagner Labor Relations Act. Wendell Willkie, an erstwhile Democrat and former president of a utility corporation that had had to sell out to the Tennessee Valley Authority, won the Republican nomination and led the forces of protest against the New Deal.

How did the voters respond to the campaign alternatives? Did their response proceed from their preferences about governmental policy? Or did voters react in a random fashion as the winds of the campaign blew them about? To an astonsihing degree (that is, a degree astonishing to persons with experience in the analysis of polling data) voters in their movements to and fro across party lines and from an inactive to an active voting status behaved as persons who made choices congruent with their policy preferences. In a sense, the question of more or less government control of business bundled up most of the lesser domestic questions of the campaign into a single great issue. Of those 1936 Democratic voters who felt that there should be less government regulation of business, about half expressed an intent to defect to Willkie in 1940. Of the 1936 Republican voters who thought there should be less business regulation, 98 per cent remained steadfastly Republican (and the 2 per cent desertion to the Democrats is not in excess of error that could have been produced in recording interviews and in processing the data). Few 1936 Republican voters favored the existing level of business regulation or more regulation, but those who did succumbed far more frequently to Democratic blandishments; about 15 per cent of them favored Roosevelt. Table 5 contains the details.[6]

An even more marked association prevailed between voter attitudes on farm policy and shifts across party lines. About seven out of ten Democrats of 1936 who became disillusioned about the farm program had a 1940 preference for Willkie. Republican defectors were not numerous but about one out of five 1936 Republicans who approved the Democratic farm program looked favorably on Roosevelt in 1940. Those with the appropriate policy outlooks stood pat in remarkable degree. Only 1 per cent of the 1936 Republicans who disapproved the Administration farm program threatened to vote Democratic. This relationship between

---

[6] For the nontechnical reader, it should be explained that the probability of divergence between the sample percentages in the tables and the true percentages in the sampled population is higher with small samples. Hence, the fact that a poll estimates fairly closely the percentage division of the two-party vote of the nation does not mean that percentages for subdivisions of the sample, for instance, Negroes or unskilled workers, are equally near the true percentages. The chances are high for greater sampling divergencies, on both the high and low sides, for subsamples. Further, the technicians judge that recent polls are superior to earlier ones in their sampling techniques, in their interviewing practices, and in their administration. For the technician, it should be said that the N's of the tables cannot usually be added to produce the total N of a specific survey or combination of surveys; no attempt has been made to account for all the miscellaneous categories of respondents not relevant to our main purpose. The N's may be used, though, to compare the size of the various cells as defined.

TABLE 5

Switches in Presidential Voting Preference, 1936–1940, in Relation to Response to Question: "During the next four years do you think there should be more or less regulation of business by the Federal government than at present?"°

Response	% of 1936 D's, D-R	% of 1936 R's, R-D	% of New Voters, D†
More regulation	10 (856)‡	15 (161)	73 (187)
About same	10 (712)	16 (122)	76 (124)
Less regulation	50 (841)	2 (1,263)	32 (229)
No opinion	14 (637)	8 (158)	68 (148)

° A consolidation of AIPO 215K-T, 10–9–40, and 219K-T, 10–24–40.

† New voters consist of those respondents who had not voted in 1936, either because they were too young or for other reasons.

‡ Here is an illustration of how to read the table entries: these two figures mean that, of the 856 poll respondents in 1940 who said they had voted for Roosevelt in 1936 and who wanted more regulation in the 1940's, 10 per cent expressed an intent to defect to Willkie.

policy outlook and vote (shown in detail in Table 6) doubtless reflected to a degree the tendency of a voter on a specific question to improvise policy views that seem to be consistent with the way he planned to vote for other reasons entirely. A steadfast Democratic partisan might have been expected to opine that the "Roosevent administration has done a good job in handling the farm problem," if the question were put to him in that form. Yet, however such opinions come into being, their supportive function in the political system should be the same.

By 1940 the Supreme Court had held the Wagner Labor Relations Act constitutional; nevertheless, many employers remained hopeful of the ultimate repeal or modification of the act. The only way to fulfill that hope was to defeat Roosevelt. The electorate responded predictably to the impact of the issue. Of the 1936 Democrats who had come to believe that the act should be repealed (which, in the context of the times, was an antilabor move) about one out of two expressed a 1940 Republican

TABLE 6

Switches in Presidential Voting Preferences, 1936–1940, in Relation to Views on Roosevelt Administration's Program for Helping Farmers°

View	% of 1936 D's, D-R	% of 1936 R's, R-D	% of New Voters, D
Approve†	7 (978)	23 (131)	83 (242)
Disapprove	69 (202)	1 (529)	16 (134)
No opinion	22 (269)	6 (170)	60 (130)

° AIPO 215K&T, 10–9–40.

† In this survey the schedule was split and the question was put in a slightly different form in the K and T versions. One question form was: "Do you think the Roosevelt administration has done a good job, or a poor job, in handling the farm problem in this country?" The other was: "In general do you approve or disapprove of the Roosevelt administration's program for helping farmers?" The "approve" version drew 50 per cent approval; the "good" version found only 42 per cent who thought the administration had done a good job. The two surveys are consolidated in this analysis.

preference. Those who thought it should merely be revised defected only about half as frequently. Similarly, Republican loyalties were maintained most steadfastly by those who stood for repeal or revision of the act.

TABLE 7

Switches in Presidential Voting Preference, 1936–1940, in Relation to Response to Question: "Do you think the Wagner Labor Act should be revised, repealed or left unchanged?"*

Response	% of 1936 D's, D-R	% of 1936 R's, R-D	% of New Voters, D
Revised	24 (193)	3 (258)	59 (90)
Repealed	52 (42)	3 (77)	†
Left unchanged	12 (376)	12 (91)	64 (106)
No opinion	22 (497)	5 (283)	59 (192)

* AIPO 215K&T, 10–9–40. The analysis is limited to those who said they had "heard of" the Wagner Act.
† Only 9 respondents fell in this cell; one reported a Democratic preference.

Interestingly, in our sample of 1936 nonvoters only nine respondents turned up favoring the repeal of the act; eight of the nine preferred Willkie. Withal, vote switches occurred in directions consistent with the assumption that voters were moved by a rational calculation of the instrumental impact of their vote. The detailed data are in Table 7.[7]

Roosevelt's candidacy in 1940 ran counter to the two-term tradition, a fact that agitated the citizenry, especially those who opposed him on other groups anyway. And probably those who supported him on other grounds declined in an especial degree to become exercised about the third-term question. In any case, the great shifts of the electorate had a close relationship to attitude on the third-term question, as may be seen from Table 8. Of the 1936 Democrats who felt that under no condition should a President serve three terms, nearly 90 per cent moved over to a Republican preference in 1940. On the other hand, 1936 Republicans who became 1940 Democrats tended to hold moderate views on the third-term matter. They could see the necessity for exceptions. These relations do not, of course, establish that persons opposed to a third term in principle defected from the Democracy [sic] for that reason. An alternative assumption is that they adopted that position because they chose to defect from the Democracy [sic]. Whatever its origin, the congruence of outlook on the constitutional issue and the direction of the vote is of importance, and it is not unreasonable to suppose that a goodly number of persons may very well have been governed in their candidate choice by their policy outlook.

---

[7] The labor issue had begun to take its toll of 1936 Democratic voters by the time of the congressional election of 1938. A survey during the congressional campaign asked: "Do you think the National Labor Relations Board is fair to businessmen and other employers?" Among 1936 Democratc presidential voters who thought the board unfair, 31 per cent favored Republican congressional candidates; among those who thought it fair, only 14 per cent did so. AIPO 135, 10–8–38.

TABLE 8

Switches in Presidential Voting Preference, 1936–1940, in Relation to
Views of Third-Term Question*

Views	% of 1936 D's, D-R		% of 1936 R's, R-D		% of New Voters, D	
Silly and outworn tradition	5	(521)	14	(56)	83	(98)
Not good, but exceptions ..	8	(1,390)	20	(243)	15	(369)
Under no condition	88	(332)	0.3	(989)	5	(189)
Don't know	15	(59)	4	(23)	68	(28)

* Based on Roper survey, October 1940. The question was:
"With which of these statements concerning a third term do you come closest
to agreeing?
"a) The idea that a President should not hold office for three terms is a silly
and outworn tradition.
"b) While it may not generally be a good idea for a President to serve three
terms, there should be no rule at a time of national crisis.
"c) Never under any conditions should a President hold office for three terms."

The opinion surveys during the campaigns of 1944 and of 1948 included few inquiries suitable for the identification of policy-related movements of voters in those elections. From the behavior of persons of different economic and occupational status (presented earlier in Tables 1
and 2) it is a fair assumption that patterns quite similar to those of 1940
prevailed in 1948 and probably to a lesser extent in 1944 when war muted
to some extent the divisive issues of domestic policy.[8] One relevant analysis from the 1948 election appears in Table 9, which presents our familiar pattern of switching in its relation to views on the question whether
the laws governing labor unions were too strict or not strict enough. By
1948 the Wagner Act had been revised by the Taft-Hartley Act to the disadvantage of unions. The AFL and CIO exerted themselves in support
of Harry S Truman who urged repeal of the act, a position which by now
had become a prolabor position. The evidence from this question supports the conventional view that the campaign of 1948 shaped antagonisms along New Deal and anti-New Deal lines. Those few Dewey supporters of 1944 who felt that labor laws were too strict deserted to
Truman at a rate of about one of five in 1948. On the other hand, 1944
Roosevelt supporters who thought the labor laws not strict enough
switched to Dewey with somewhat higher frequency, as the table
indicates.

As the campaign of 1940 approached, the threat of war preoccupied
the pundits and the commentators, who doubtless communicated their
anxieties to the public. Yet the promises made and expectations raised by
the candidates with respect to foreign policy seemed to have far less

---

[8] Unhappiness with wartime economic controls doubtless contributed to Democratic defections in 1944. In a 1944 survey the following question was put: "After the
war in Europe is over, should the following government controls be continued or
discontinued? a) Food rationing? b) Gasoline rationing? c) Price ceilings on things
people buy?" The D-R percentages among "continued" and "discontinued" groups of
1940 Democratic voters were: a) 15 and 20; b) 12 and 21; c) 16 and 21. AIPO 331,
10–6–44.

bearing on the vote than did questions of domestic policy. For a time foreign policy seemed to have been taken out of the campaign, but as the election neared, Willkie, under the prodding of the Republican professionals, stirred up the issue by his forecasts that war would soon come if Roosevelt were re-elected. Democratic campaigners probably became more worried about these charges than did the electorate generally.[9] At any rate, the data indicate a comparatively mild relation between attitudes on foreign policy and vote shifting.

TABLE 9

Switches in Presidential Vote, 1944–1948, in Relation to Response to Question: "As things stand today, do you think the laws governing labor unions are too strict or not strict enough?"*

Response	% of 1944 D's, D-R	% of 1944 R's, R-D	% of New Voters, D
Too strict	8 (304)	22 (76)	74 (80)
About right	15 (357)	9 (218)	68 (118)
Not strict enough	27 (232)	6 (318)	51 (87)
No opinion	15 (181)	10 (101)	64 (58)

* Based on AIPO 432, 11–1–48. Interviews were conducted after the election; the date is the "send-out" date.

The question whether it was more important to keep out of war ourselves or to help England even at the risk of getting into war should have separated persons into the two conflicting camps of the time. Though more of those who thought that we should keep out of war deserted to Willkie, the difference between this figure and the rate of desertion of those who thought we should help England win (Table 10) was not wide enough to indicate that this difference in attitude contributed nearly so heavily to vote switching as did the impact of domestic issues. Similarly, a person's views on the question whether we should have gotten into World War I might be expected to segregate those of isolationist sentiment from their opponents. Those 1936 Democrats who thought our World War I venture was a mistake shifted to Willkie more frequently than did those who held an opposing view; yet again the difference (Table 11) was relatively small.

This is not to say that foreign policy questions invariably command less attention than do domestic questions. Rather in 1940 this seemed to be the case. Probably the more general rule is that the electorate responds most markedly and most clearly to those events it has experienced and observed, vicariously or directly. Voters had enjoyed or not enjoyed eight years of domestic policy of the New Deal and they reacted demonstrably to those experiences. The prospects for the future may generally tend less to engage the voter or to govern his actions. Those prospects tend to be hazy, uncertain, problematic. Voters may respond most as-

[9] On this aspect of the 1940 campaign, see R. E. Sherwood, *Roosevelt and Hopkins* (New York: Bantam, 1950), ch. 8.

TABLE 10

Switches in Presidential Voting Preference, 1936–1940, in Relation to
Opinions on Whether More Important to Keep Out of War or to Help
England Win°

Attitude	% of 1936 D's, D-R	% of 1936 R's, R-D	% of New Voters, D
Keep out of war	31 (1,975)	3 (1,127)	56 (724)
Help England win	19 (2,426)	5 (1,211)	61 (653)
No choice	25 (166)	0 (76)	72 (68)

° A consolidation of AIPO 217, 10–22–40; 220, 10–22–40; 224, 11–19–40.
Note that a post-election survey is combined with two pre-election surveys. The
question was: "Which of these two things do you think is the more important for
the United States to try to do: 1. To keep out of war ourselves, 2. To help England
win, even at the risk of getting into war." The schedules carried the "no choice"
box, though the meaning of this response is unclear.

suredly to what they have seen, heard, experienced. Forecasts, promises,
predicted disaster, or pie in the sky may be less moving.

A kind word needs to be said for that supposedly benighted fellow, the
standpatter, the consistent party voter. So far our attention has centered
on the switcher. The evidence indicates that the shifting voter is far more
numerous than is commonly supposed. Moreover, his reports of his actions and attitudes indicate that as he navigates his way from party to

TABLE 11

Switches in Presidential Vote, 1936–1940, in Relation to Response to
Question: "Do you think it was a mistake for the United States to enter
the last World War?"°

Response	% of 1936 D's, D-R	% of 1936 R's, R-D	% of New Voters, D
Yes, mistake	28 (511)	4 (382)	49 (140)
No	18 (636)	5 (322)	64 (154)
No opinion	20 (258)	6 (118)	67 (108)

° AIPO 224, 11–19–40.

party he moves in a manner that is sensible in the light of his policy preferences. To be sure, partisan loyalties invest the electoral mass with a
degree of inertia and not all voters follow their policy inclinations by
moving from candidate to candidate.[10] What of these voters who remain

---

[10] The data used in this study permit no analyses to ascertain the relation between consistent party support and the sense of party identification which has been
extensively examined by Angus Campbell and his associates of the Survey Research
Center of the University of Michigan. Doubtless the standpatters of our tables who
resist the pull of their policy inclinations toward the opposite party include large
numbers of "strong" party identifiers, that is, persons who regard themselves as
"strong" Republicans or Democrats in their responses to interviewers of the Survey
Research Center.

in the party ranks from election to election? Are they obtuse diehards who swallow their principles to stick by their party?

Almost all the analyses of the preceding pages throw light on the question. On issue after issue those with views consistent with the outlook of their party stood pat in their voting preference. Notably few Republican defections occurred among those who subscribed to sound Republican doctrine. Democratic deserters were uniformly fewest among those who concurred with the pure and orthodox Democratic tenets of the time. No doubt some Republicans and some Democrats adjusted their views to make them conform with their perceptions of the positions of their party. Yet it is the parallelism of vote and policy view that is significant for our analysis, not its origin.

The facts seem to be that, on the average, the standpatters do not have to behave as mugwumps to keep their consciences clear; they are already where they ought to be in the light of their policy attitudes. Tables 12, 13, and 14 demonstrate this point in another way.* Those who vote consistently from one election to the next, the data of those tables indicate, adhere to the party doctrine in high degree. Though partisan groupings of voters are not models of ideological purity, the standpatters of each party manifest fairly high agreement with the party positions as popularly perceived. Thus, well over half of the 1936–1940 D-D's felt that there should be during the next four years about the same degree or more government regulation. Similarly, the Administration's farm program found favor with three fourths of the 1936–1940 D-D's, while only a little more than 10 per cent of the R-R's could bring themselves to approve it. Again far fewer of the 1944–1948 D-D's than of the 1944–1948 R-R's thought that the laws governing labor unions were too strict.[11]

Party switchers move towards the party whose standpatters they resemble in their policy views, a proposition made apparent by the tables.

---

* Editor's note: At this point Key planned to comment further on Tables 12, 13, and 14, and to stress how they differ from Table 11 and some of the other tables presented earlier in this chapter. These earlier tables focused attention on the percentages of persons interviewed who switched parties between two consecutive elections and the presidential preferences of new voters in relation to their position on specified policy questions. The earlier tables emphasized the policy preferences of voters who switched parties from one election to the next. Tables 12, 13, and 14 present data for all voters in each major party camp—new voters, standpatters, and switchers. They indicate the distribution of given policy preferences among each group of voters. Data presented in this form highlight the degree to which the standpatters tend to endorse doctrinal positions usually associated with the party they support.

11 Standpatters, the evidence suggests, acquire their policy attitudes in at least two ways. Some persons more or less deliberately affiliate with the party whose policy emphases appear to parallel their own. Other persons, psychologically identified with a party, adopt those policy outlooks espoused by the more prominent spokesmen of their party. In the course of party life, the acceptance of the cues of party leadership may result in alteration of the attitudes of party followers. This flexible conformity with shifting party doctrine probably occurs most markedly among those strongly identified psychologically with the party. See Angus Campbell and Homer C. Cooper, *Group Differences in Attitudes and Votes* (Ann Arbor, Mich.: Survey Research Center, 1956), pp. 102–4.

TABLE 12

Pattern of Presidential Preference, 1936–1940, in Relation to Distribution of Responses to Question: "During the next four years do you think there should be more or less regulation of business by the Federal government than at present?"°

Response	D-D	R-D	0-D†	0-R†	D-R	R-R
More regulation	32%	28%	34%	18%	13%	8%
About same	27	23	23	10	11	7
Less regulation	18	34	18	55	63	76
No opinion	23	15	25	17	13	9
	100	100	100	100	100	100
N‡	(2,386)	(85)	(403)	(285)	(660)	(1,619)

° A consolidation of AIPO 215K-T, 10–9–40, and 219K-T, 10–24–40 (as in Table 5).
† New voters, i.e., nonvoters in 1936.
‡ As in all tables, the figures in parentheses, technically known as N, are the numbers of survey respondent on which the percentages are based. For example, 2,386 of those interviewed were Democratic standpatters (according to their replies) and 1,619 were Republican standpatters. Of these 1,619, only 8 per cent wanted more regulation of business.

TABLE 13

Patterns of Presidential Preference, 1936–1940, in Relation to Distribution of Views on Roosevelt Administration's Program for Handling Farm Problem°

Response	D-D	R-D	0-D†	0-R†	D-R	R-R
Approve	76%	64%	66%	19%	26%	13%
Disapprove	5	13	7	55	51	66
Don't know	18	21	26	25	22	20
No answer	1	2	1	1	1	1
	100	100	100	100	100	100
N	(1,191)	(47)	(305)	(207)	(274)	(795)

° Based on AIPO 215K&T, 10–9–40, as in Table 6, which see for the form of the question.
† Nonvoters in 1936.

TABLE 14

Patterns of Presidential Preference, 1944–1948, in Relation to Distribution of Responses to Question: "As things stand today, do you think the laws governing labor unions are too strict or not strict enough?"°

Response	D-D	R-D	0-D	0-R	D-R	R-R
Too strict	31%	26%	27%	17%	15%	9%
About right	33	31	36	31	31	31
Not strict enough	19	28	20	35	38	46
No opinion	17	15	17	17	16	14
	100	100	100	100	100	100
N	(909)	(65)	(220)	(123)	(165)	(648)

° Based on AIPO 432, 11–1–48, a post-election survey (interviews were conducted after the election; the date is the "send-out" date).

The D-R's are divided in their policy views in about the same fashion as the R-R's with whom they join in the election, and the R-D's resemble the D-D's to which they attach themselves for the voting. The nonvoters at the preceding election who join the D-D's or the R-R's also have an attitudinal resemblance to the standpatters with whom they ally themselves. Yet, as the tables also indicate, the switchers bear earmarks of their origin. The D-R's are not in quite the same degree as the R-R's attached to the party policy position, and the R-D's also bore traces of their Republican origin. Nevertheless, on balance each of these groups bore far greater resemblance to the standpatters of the party of their destination than to the faithful of the party of their origin.

One major problem remains to be touched on, if not disposed of. That is the problem of the role of personality in the maintenance of the Democratic following during the 1930's and 1940's. How do we cope with the assertion that the series of Democratic victories reflected the massive appeal of the personality of Franklin Delano Roosevelt and nothing more? Even the most cursory reflection destroys this type of explanation in its crude form. It becomes ridiculous immediately if one contemplates what the fate of Franklin Delano Roosevelt would have been had he from 1933 to 1936 stood for those policies which were urged upon the country by the reactionaries of the day. Before 1932 acute political observers had seen him as only a pleasant country gentleman of the Hudson Valley who had a yearning to be president. He became, though, a formidable and wicked opponent to his enemies and a savior to those who regarded him as their champion. His position derived not so much from the kind of a man he was as from the kinds of things for which, and against which, he fought. His personal qualities may have intensified both hatred and love for him. And the popular image of Roosevelt doubtless enabled many persons to support and to oppose him without detailed knowledge of what policies he was for or against; they could accurately regard him as for or against their kind of people.

Neither our data nor the analytical tools of social science permit completely satisfactory appraisals of the place of personality in the determination of the vote. Nevertheless, some wisps of evidence—more or less tautological in nature—have a relevance to the question. In 1940 Dr. Gallup's interviewers asked the respondents in his sample: "If the United States should get into the war, which man would you prefer to have as President—Roosevelt or Willkie?" To ask such a question might be thought to be about the same as to ask, "For whom, as of today, do you plan to vote?" Yet the question raised a perfectly legitimate problem, one to which the citizen should address himself if he is to perform his classical role of recording relevant and responsible decisions as he votes. What did the response to the vote indicate? Some, but not many, 1936 Landon voters opined that Roosevelt would, indeed, be the better man if we got into war, and about half of them, probably reluctantly, had decided to defect from the Republican ranks to support Roosevelt. On the other hand, a goodly number of 1936 Democratic voters liked what they saw in Willkie as a potential wartime leader; 97 per cent of them moved to the Republican side, as Willkie himself had done only a short time before. For the details see Table 15.

In 1944 the National Opinion Research Center put questions to a national sample which showed somewhat similar patterns of voter movement. At the time of this campaign one popular concern was the success-

TABLE 15

Switches in Presidential Voting Preference, 1936–1940, in Relation to Response to Question: "If the U.S. should get into the war, which man would you prefer to have as President—Roosevelt or Willkie?"*

Response	% of 1936 D's, D-R	% of 1936 R's, R-D	% of New Voters, D
Roosevelt	4 (1,158)	47 (59)	93 (341)
Willkie	97 (329)	† (717)	4 (157)
Undecided	51 (71)	0 (54)	45 (44)

* Based on AIPO 220, 10–22–40.
† Less than one half of 1 per cent; one respondent in this cell reported a shift to Roosevelt.

ful conclusion of World War II; moreover, some people were beginning to worry about the shape of public policy when peace came again. The NORC asked in October 1944: "Sometimes one man does a better job of handling certain problems than another man. Do you think Roosevelt or Dewey would do a better job of winning the war?" A very few 1940 Democrats had arrived at the conclusion that Dewey could do a better job of winding up hostilities; most of them switched to Republican in 1944. A much larger number of Willkie voters of 1940 felt obliged to concede that Roosevelt was a better man for this particular job. About a third of them had decided to vote for him, while their fellow Republicans who saw merit in Mr. Dewey stood almost to a man with the G.O.P. The exact figures appear in Table 16. The same survey put a question on whether Dewey or Roosevelt would do better at "providing jobs after the war." The familiar movements and countermovements in consonance with voter judgments on this issue occurred, as Table 17 indicates.

For those who have persevered to this point, a few preliminary reflections on the significance of the information so far assembled are in order. We have established patterns of movement of party switchers from election to election and the patterns of stability of the standpatter that lead us to a conception of the voter that is not often propounded. From our analyses the voter emerges as a person who appraises the actions of government, who has policy preferences and who relates his vote to those

TABLE 16

Switches in Presidential Voting Preference, 1940–1944, in Relation to Response to Question: "Sometimes one man does a better job of handling certain problems than another man. Do you think Roosevelt or Dewey would do a better job of winning the war?"*

Response	% of 1940 D's, D-R	% of 1940 R's, R-D	% of New Voters, D
Roosevelt	6 (828)	35 (114)	87 (144)
Dewey	90 (29)	0 (257)	3 (29)
No difference	44 (100)	3 (335)	12 (48)
Don't know	45 (29)	0 (56)	21 (14)

* NORC 30/229, October 1944.

TABLE 17

Switches in Presidential Voting Preference, 1940–1944, in Relation to
Response to Question: "Sometimes one man does a better job of han-
dling certain problems than another man. Do you think Roosevelt or
Dewey would do a better job of providing jobs after the war?"[*]

Response	% of 1940 D's, D-R	% of 1940 R's, R-D	% of New Voters, D
Roosevelt	3 (747)	52 (63)	93 (124)
Dewey	82 (88)	1 (556)	1 (69)
No difference	25 (73)	12 (92)	42 (19)
Don't know	24 (74)	2 (49)	41 (22)

[*] NORC 30/229, October 1944.

appraisals and preferences. One may have misgivings about the data and
one can certainly concede that the data also indicate that some voters are
governed by blind party loyalty and that some others respond automatically to the winds of the environment of the moment. Yet the obtrusive
feature of the data is the large number of persons whose vote is instrumental to their policy preferences.

These parallelisms of voting patterns and policy preferences may be
dismissed as the meaningless result of the disposition of people to adopt
consistent sets of views on interrelated matters. A survey respondent, be-
deviled by an interviewer, may express a preference for a Democratic
candidate and then, to keep things tidy, adopt a favorable attitude
toward Democratic policy positions. He would, though, in our analysis
fit into the same pigeonhole of the IBM sorter as the person who arrived
at the same consistent constellation of attitudes by a process of anguished
thought and reflection. Doubtless both kinds of respondents are encountered by poll interviewers. Yet, however these patterns of consistent
voting preferences are formed, they can scarcely be regarded as without
political significance. Our correlations, though, should not be taken to
mean that the policy attitudes correlated with changes and continuities
in voting preference necessarily cause those changes or continuities.
Rather they demonstrate the tendency of persons to build up combinations of outlooks and to adopt voting preferences that make sense in the
light of those outlooks.

In another direction our data throw light on the interactions between
government and public and on the functions of the electorate in the democratic process. A notable element of our tables is the extent to which an
Administration seems to lose the votes of its erstwhile supporters who
dissent from actions it has taken. The tables seem to verify the journalistic superstition that the people only vote against; never, for. That appearance results in part from the manner in which the facts have been
presented; an equally strong case could be made for the proposition that
the standpatters stand pat because they are for what has been done. Nevertheless, the fact remains that some erstwhile supporters do vote against
and they tend to disagree with actions that have been taken. Few erstwhile enemies are attracted to a dominant party by its actions, though

some are. A president may, with justification, be anxious lest a projected action draw down his reservoir of popular good will. He cannot proceed on the assumption that inaction will maintain the loyalty of the faithful by antagonizing no one. Yet to govern he must be prepared to expend some of his good will. And to continue to govern he must attempt to offset those losses by policies that attract support from the opposition or from among the new voters.*

The patterns of flow of the major streams of shifting voters graphically reflect the electorate in its great, and perhaps principal, role as an appraiser of past events, past performance, and past actions. It judges retrospectively; it commands prospectively only insofar as it expresses either approval or disapproval of that which has happened before. Voters may reject what they have known; or they may approve what they have known. They are not likely to be attracted in great numbers by promises of the novel or unknown. Once innovation has occurred they may embrace it, even though they would have, earlier, hesitated to venture forth to welcome it.

These tendencies of the electorate, as they obtrude from our many tables, make plain how completely the minority party is a captive of the majority—and of the situation. Critics of the American party system fret because the minority party does not play the role of an imaginative advocate heralding the shape of a new world. In truth, it gains votes most notably from among those groups who are disappointed by, who disapprove of, or who regard themselves as injured by, the actions of the Administration. The opposition can maximize its strength as it centers its fire on those elements of the Administration program disliked by the largest numbers of people. Thus, as a matter of practical politics, it must appear to be a common scold rather than a bold exponent of innovation, though it may propose new (or old) approaches to old questions. The misfortunes of the Republicans over the period 1932–1952 sprang essentially from the simple fact that they could not lay their hands on an issue on which the Democrats had outraged enough people to vote them out of office.

---

* Editor's note: At this point Key intended to elaborate on this "maintenance process"—stressing both the importance to the governing party of maintaining the loyalty of its previous supporters and its need to win converts from the opposition and additional new support among the new voters.

Jerrold G. Rusk and Herbert F. Weisberg

Perceptions of Presidential Candidates: Implications for Electoral Change*

Presidential elections invariably raise questions regarding system change. Frequently, the short-term policy mandate which can be imputed to an election is unclear, but more often the long-term implications of an election for system change are misinterpreted. The classic case is the widespread discussion of the possible demise of the Republican Party after 1964, a topic which seemed irrelevant once a Republican president was elected in 1968. Yet a presidential election often can have important systemic implications which we would not want to overlook. The 1968 election spawned its own discussion of electoral change, with particular interest expressed in the possibility of a party realignment leading to a Republican majority. Our own analysis of 1968 survey data suggested the potential for system change, while emphasizing our lack of suitable longitudinal data for the evaluation of our results.[1]

The mid-term congressional election affords another opportunity for students of voting behavior to assess the relative degree of electoral constancy and change. It lacks the intensity of a presidential election, but it permits replication of previous work to determine which results were more than ephemeral. Therefore, we have employed data from the 1970 national election study of the University of Michigan's Center for Political Studies in order to test the validity of our previous work, as well as to examine whatever change may have occurred between 1968 and 1970.

Our approach is one of analyzing the factional lines of American politics. Presidential contenders in this country represent the various party factions. We examine the extent to which these contenders are perceived along traditional party lines, and the extent to which percep-

* Jerrold G. Rusk and Herbert F. Weisberg, "Perceptions of Political Candidates: Implications for Electoral Change," Midwest Journal of Political Science, vol. 16, no. 3 (August 1972), pp. 388–410. Reprinted by permission of the Wayne State University Press. Copyright 1972, by Wayne State University Press.

[1] A report of the 1968 results is given in Herbert F. Weisberg and Jerrold G. Rusk, "Dimensions of Candidate Evaluation," American Political Science Review, 64 (December 1970), 1167–1185.

tions are molded by a new issue factor. The group context of candidate perceptions will be explored to see whether the candidates fit into the fabric of the new vocal social groups which are emerging, or if they are instead cast in the scenario of older group conflicts. The implications of the present panorama of candidate perceptions for possible changes in party structures will be emphasized—whether increased electoral volatility and eventually realignment will be the pattern of the future, or if such "surface" perceptions merely mask an increasing stability and constancy of the party system. The final section of this report places the results into a theoretical framework of the components of electoral change.

THE THERMOMETER QUESTION

Perceptions of possible contenders for the presidency were measured on a *feeling thermometer* in the 1970 election study. This measuring instrument is a 0-to-100 degree scale on which respondents indicated how they felt toward each candidate. Scores above 50 degrees corresponded to warm feelings, those below 50 degrees represented cold feelings, and 50 degrees signified that the respondent had no feelings about the candidate. The question also sought to obtain "don't know" responses to individual candidates when appropriate.[2] Our ability to compare perceptions across time is enhanced by the availability of similar data collected after the 1968 election.

The selection of names for the study was restricted to those who seemed likely to be contenders in 1972, or who were fairly well-known figures within their parties. Such candidates included President Nixon, Vice-President Agnew, Ronald Reagan, John Lindsay, George Wallace, and a series of Democratic hopefuls—Edmund Muskie, Hubert Humphrey, Ted Kennedy, Eugene McCarthy, and George McGovern.[3] The scores received by the candidates inevitably reflect the post-election timing of the study, those most active in the congressional campaign being most affected in this regard. Another aspect of the timing of this research is the fact that we describe public reactions two years before the 1972 election, well before the media campaigns increase the salience of the actual candidates. This means that our 1970 measurements were obtained at a less intense point in time than our 1968 data, so that some of the differences between the two sets of observations represent only the necessary differences, particularly in salience, between presidential and midterm election settings.

---

[2] The full wording of the question is given in the Appendix of Weisberg and Rusk, "Dimensions of Candidate Evaluation," p. 1185. The thermometer card handed to the respondent is also shown in this article, although it was inadvertently placed on page 1175.

[3] The comparable candidate list for the 1968 election study included seven candidates listed in the 1970 study (President Nixon, Vice-President Agnew, Ronald Reagan, George Wallace, Edmund Muskie, Hubert Humphrey, and Eugene McCarthy), plus Robert Kennedy, Lyndon Johnson, Nelson Rockefeller, George Romney, and Curtis LeMay.

A SPATIAL MAPPING OF CANDIDATE PERCEPTIONS

Perceptual data on the candidates can tell us much about how the public views the factional structure of politics—the basic conflicts and cleavages which exist in the political world today. Candidates both initiate and represent such conflicts, their nature and intensity most often become apparent in the presidential race, and the differences people perceive between the candidates center on the underlying structure of political conflict.

Inter-Candidate Correlations

An analysis of this underlying structure of political conflict must first start with an examination of which candidates are perceived as similar to one another and which are not. Clusters of candidates viewed as similar to one another and the relationships between these clusters provide a rough guideline to ascertain the underlying factional bases of perceptions of candidates. Correlation values will be used to summarize the perceptual similarity or dissimilarity of pairs of candidates. Candidates being perceived in a similar fashion should have substantial positive correlations and fall into the same cluster; those seen as quite dissimilar from one another should have sizable negative values and fall into different clusters. Correlations near zero indicate an absence of shared perceptions between given pairings of candidates.

Using this logic in 1968, we found that the set of candidate correlations revealed four basic clusters—the members within each cluster being viewed by the public as similar in certain ways, while candidates residing in different clusters were perceived as dissimilar to each other. The four clusters consisted of (a) mainstream Democrats (Humphrey, Muskie, Johnson, and Kennedy), (b) mainstream Republicans (Nixon, Agnew, and Reagan), (c) American Independent Party candidates (Wallace and LeMay), and (d) bipartisan liberals (McCarthy, Rockefeller, and Romney). Shades of both partisan and issue cleavages were evident in such candidate perceptions—representing the major elements of political competition.

The candidate clusters visible in the 1970 data were similar but not identical to those found in 1968. A mainstream Republican cluster was again evident, since the correlations between Nixon, Agnew, and Reagan ranged from .51 to .58. Humphrey, Muskie, Kennedy, McCarthy, McGovern, and Lindsay formed a second cluster (correlations ranged from .21 to .60) which could be decomposed into two more familiar sub-clusters—the Democratic mainstream group of Humphrey, Muskie, and Kennedy (correlations between .43 and .50) and the Democratic and Republican liberal group of McCarthy, McGovern, and Lindsay (correlations between .34 and .60). Wallace, as in 1968, tended to be isolated from the other clusters.

Greater change was evident in the relationships between the clusters. Wallace's correlations with the mainstream Republican cluster in 1970 were all positive and larger than before. This could have resulted from less concentration on the unique aspects of Wallace's candidacy in the off-year, from policy convergence between the administration and Wallace, or both. Whatever the exact cause, one side effect of this was that the strongest negative correlations in 1970 were between the partisan clusters, whereas in 1968 the strongest negative correlations had been between the Democrats and Wallace. Hence, Wallace was both seen as closer to the Republican position (or vice-versa), and not as the polar object to the Democrats, the Republicans being polar to the Democrats in 1970.

These elements of continuity and divergence suggest the possibility once again of mapping the American competitive space into partisan and issue terms, while at the same time, implying that the partisan factor had a greater weight in 1970 than in 1968 (as might be expected in an off-year election). But at this stage such projections of candidate perceptions along these factional lines are mainly conjectural. Based on our experience in 1968, the correlations do not present a ready or systematic comprehension of the underlying competitive structure from simple inspection alone. What is needed is to transform such correlational information into a geometric representation of the perceived differences between the candidates. By use of the Shepard-Kruskal scaling technique, we can arrive at a *candidate space* based on the correlational data; such a technique places the candidates in a space so that those with the highest correlations are closest together, while those with the most negative values are furthest apart. This monotonic rule may not provide a perfect solution within a space of small dimensionality, but the technique seeks a solution for any given number of dimensions, attempting to come as close as possible to satisfying the rule of monotonicity between correlation values and candidate distances.[4]

---

[4] Shepard-Kruskal scaling is a nonmetric, multidimensional scaling algorithm. A nonmetric technique has been employed because the order of the correlations is more invariant under the vagaries affecting the measurement than are the exact correlation values. Multidimensional scaling is preferable to factor analysis in that the latter overestimates the dimensionality of the data. See Weisberg and Rusk, "Dimensions of Candidate Evaluation," footnote 12, pp. 1173–1174.

Of more fundamental importance is our decision to analyze correlation coefficients rather than directly analyzing the individual preference orders. Since the correlations measure the covariation in the ratings of candidate pairs while controlling for idiosyncratic variation unique to each given candidate, the resultant spatial representation is particularly suitable for determining the common dimensions of conflict. Yet a space based directly on the individual preference orders would be better suited for describing the distribution of voters in the candidate space and discussing candidate strategies in competing in that space. Each approach has its own utility and limitations; we consider the correlational space appropriate for present purposes, but we expect future work to give more emphasis to the preference space. See George B. Rabinowitz, *Spatial Models of Electoral Choice: An Empirical Analysis* (Ph.D. dissertation in progress, University of Michigan). Also see Hans Daalder and Jerrold G. Rusk, "Perceptions of Party in the Dutch Parliament," in Samuel C. Patterson and John C. Wahlke, eds., *Comparative Legislative Behavior: Frontiers of Research* (New York: John Wiley and Sons, 1972), pp. 143–98, for a comparison of the two methods on Dutch elite data. In this latter report, the correlation approach revealed traditional dimensions of conflict, while the focus on individual preference order data highlighted a party coalition strategy space (analogous to the voter-candidate strategy space on the mass level).

The Candidate Space

By using this technique, we get a "physical picture" of the candidates —how close together or far apart they are from one another. Such a space gives us a better grasp of what competitive dimensions the public views as pulling some candidates together and others apart. Figure 1 shows the two-dimensional representation of the correlation coefficients.[5] The Re-

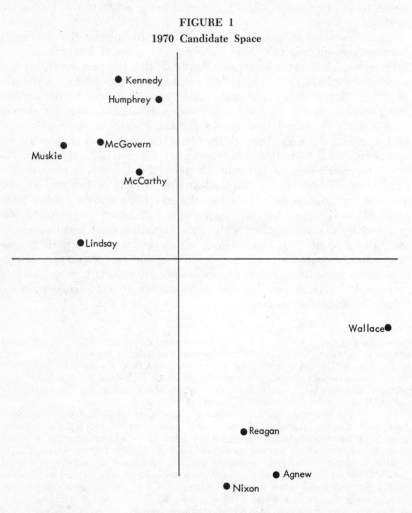

FIGURE 1
1970 Candidate Space

[5] This solution was obtained from Kruskal's MDSCAL program (version 5). See Joseph B. Kruskal, "Multidimensional Scaling by Optimizing Goodness of Fit to a Nonmetric Hypothesis," *Psychometrika*, 29 (March 1964), 1–27. The extent of monotonicity between the correlations and spatial distances is summarized by a measure known as stress, ranging in value from 0 for a perfect solution to a maximum value of 1. The solution shown in Figure 1 has a stress of .060 which Kruskal would term "excellent." A "good" one-dimensional representation (stress = .177) could be ob-

publican and Democratic clusters suggested in the discussion of the correlations are evident here, with Lindsay being closest to the Democratic cluster. Wallace is seen to be separated from the two main clusters, but closer to the Republican one. The vertical axis, running from Nixon and Agnew to Humphrey and Kennedy, corresponds to a partisan factor. The Republicans are separated from the Democrats in the public's mind—certainly the essential basis of all political competition—with Wallace and Lindsay occupying the middle positions as a reflection of their ambiguous party positions. The horizontal axis places Wallace at one end and Lindsay and Muskie at the other. This second dimension has left-right overtones, but its exact meaning cannot be specified from Figure 1 alone.

This spatial representation is basically similar to the candidate space we obtained from the 1968 data. To illustrate this point, we have rotated the 1970 solution to obtain the best fit with the 1968 space.[6] This result is shown in Figure 2, the two solutions being superimposed on one another. The general structures of the two spaces resemble each other in the overall clustering and in the relations between the clusters. It is evident that the two partisan clusters remain largely intact over the two year period, the 1968 and 1970 clusters for each party adhering closely to one another while the main clusters of the two parties reside in opposite parts of the space. Also, Wallace is separate from the partisan clusters in both measurements.

While the overall reading is one of stability in candidate perceptions, Figure 2 also calls attention to some elements of movement and change. The fourth cluster evident in our 1968 space—McCarthy, Rockefeller, and Romney—does not exist in 1970. In part this reflects the omission of the latter two candidates from our 1970 measurement, but it also denotes a movement of McCarthy toward the mainstream Democratic cluster, something that is more noticeable here than in our earlier discussion of the correlations taken alone. Essentially, McCarthy is not viewed as distinct from his party as he was in 1968. Lindsay seems to occupy a position similar to McCarthy's in 1968, but he does not form a separate cluster entirely by himself, his ties to the Democrats putting him in a middle position.

---

tained with the mainstream Republicans and Wallace on one end of the dimension and the other candidates at the opposite end (Nixon and Kennedy being at the respective extremes). However, such a solution places Wallace too close to the Republican mainstream candidates and Lindsay too far from them, problems remedied by the two-dimensional solution given in Figure 1. The stress values cited here are larger than those in our previous article because we have switched to Kruskal's second stress formula which leads to values about twice as large as those given by his first formula. The axes are arbitrary in multidimensional scaling; we have chosen a varimax rotation around the centroid of the space for the figures presented in this paper.

[6] Schönemann and Carroll's least squares matrix comparison procedure has been used on configurations of the candidates common to both thermometer measurements. This procedure is described in Peter H. Schönemann and Robert M. Carroll, "Fitting One Matrix to Another Under Choice of a Central Dilation and A Rigid Motion," *Psychometrika*, 35 (June 1970), 245–55.

FIGURE 2

1970 Candidate Space Rotated to 1968 Candidate Space

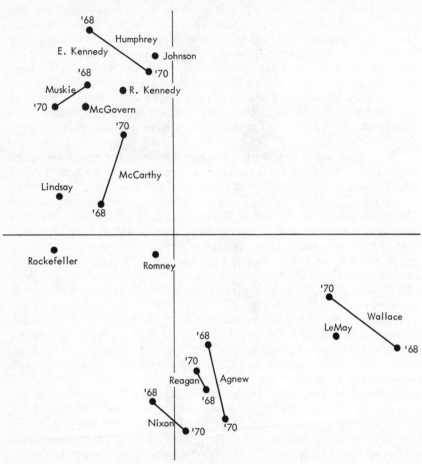

The largest movements between the two years involve Wallace, Mc-Carthy, and Agnew. Wallace is viewed as less extreme than in 1968, due presumably to the lower intensity of the 1970 election and its lessened focus on Wallace *per se*. McCarthy's move toward the Democratic cluster has resulted as circumstances causing him to deviate from his party have receded in the public memory. Agnew's move toward the end of the Republican scale reflects his greater embodiment of the Republican partisan position in 1970. His increasing salience and intense partisan rhetoric over the two year period undoubtedly explain this movement. Such movements add the flavor of change to perceptions of the candidates these past two years, but they are perhaps even more noteworthy because they stand against a backdrop of remarkable stability between the two candidate configurations. The basic notions of the vertical axis being a partisan factor and the horizontal one representing some type of left-right stance on the issues (or at least a Wallace versus non-Wallace position on the issues) remain unchallenged, the movement of Wallace, McCarthy, and Agnew only bolstering these interpretations by providing further reference points in such a discussion.

Societal Mappings

The essence of our interpretation thus far centers on the idea that conflict space of the kind we have described mirrors people's perceptions of the candidates. A further test of this contention would be to relate the public's perceptions of various social groups associated with these conflicts to how people view the candidates. If there is a firm relationship between the two sets of perceptions, then we have additional evidence that political conflict, whether partisan or issue-oriented, is the underlying basis for perceptions and evaluations of the candidates.

Our measurement of people's group perceptions is again based on the feeling thermometer, enhancing the comparability between these perceptions and those of the candidates. In the 1970 election study, we had respondents score some seventeen groups on the thermometer, ranging from standard partisan and racial groups to such new social groups as urban rioters and marijuana users. While the average popularities of candidates varied between 32 and 59 on the thermometer scale, the means for the seventeen groups used ranged from 8 (for urban rioters) to 80 (for police). The mean scores for most of the groups were more extreme than those of the candidates. In short, the groups clearly evoked strong feelings, making the evaluations of the candidates look pallid by comparison.

Figure 3 portrays the scaling of the candidates with the groups. While it essentially retains the structure of the earlier candidate space (see Figure 1), some of the candidate positions have moved somewhat in order to satisfy the additional constraints imposed by the inclusion of the new data set on groups. To satisfy these additional constraints, a three-dimensional solution was required. The vertical dimension in this solution is partisan, as before—the Republican and Democratic candidates loading high on opposite ends of the dimension, with Wallace being the only candidate not having his highest loading here. The vertical dimension poses President Nixon at one end of the axis to the Democratic candidates at the other.

Other items which loaded highly on this dimension include the Republican and Democratic partisan groups and the "conservative" and "liberal" groups. We would expect the Republicans and Democrats to be located on this dimension, lending further validation to its being a partisan factor, but why the conservative and liberal groupings? The answer lies in the fact that such terms have a very restricted meaning to the public—referring mainly to "government spending," a referent first attached to these terms in the social welfare, New Deal days, and one which became closely associated with people's party identification over

FIGURE 3

1970 Candidate-Group Space

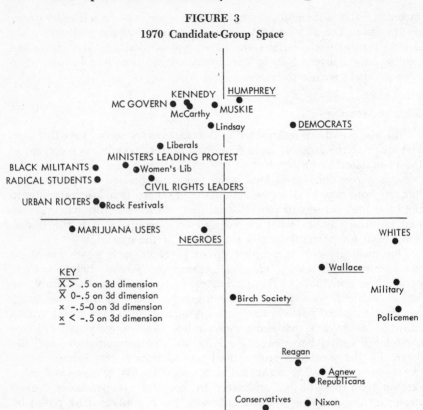

the years (a point evident in the 1968 data and one which will again be demonstrated below for the 1970 materials).[7] Suffice it to say that such terms or groupings basically are not identified by the public with general ideological belief systems or left-right positions on the new political issues of the 1960s, but instead are associated with the partisan conflicts centering on "government spending" that originally arose in the New Deal days of the 1930s.

The horizontal dimension involves the left-right distinctions associated with some of the new issues and groups which have dominated political headlines in the past few years. The police and military seem posed at one end of the dimension, contrasted with the marijuana users, urban rioters, black militants, radical students, rock festival followers, protest march ministers, and women liberators at the other. Implications of a social or moral issue factor come to mind. Wallace, Agnew, Nixon, and Reagan are viewed on the *traditional* side of the dimension, while McGovern, Kennedy, McCarthy, and Lindsay tend toward the *change*

---

[7] See Philip E. Converse, "The Nature of Belief Systems in a Mass Public," in David E. Apter, ed., *Ideology and Discontent* (New York: Free Press, 1964), pp. 206–56.

side. This political-social dichotomy remains when we place specific issues into the space with the candidates. The third dimension has a special character of its own. It is concerned primarily with the racial question, pitting the blacks and civil rights leaders against Wallace. However, the John Birch Society also loads highly on the conservative side of this dimension, indicating that its meaning may be somewhat broader than a strictly civil rights interpretation. Both the second and third dimensions highlight a conflict structure underlying candidate perceptions which involves left-right cleavages over the new political issues of the day, and the groups associated with them.

The spaces displayed thus far point to the fact that no one dimension alone shapes perceptions of the candidates. However, the vertical dimension—the partisan factor—has the strongest explanatory power, although it cannot account for perceptions of some of the candidates and most of the social groups. Ideological and life style considerations can begin to account for some of the differences we have shown, but these are matters best confronted when we add issues to our universe, a point to which we now turn.

ISSUES OF CONTEMPORARY SOCIETY

In the 1968 election study, the public gave notice that a new issue area was an object of their concern, one that centered on such problems as the plight of the cities, civil rights, Viet Nam, protest, and law and order. In 1970, the public was still very much concerned with these issues. About 63 percent of the respondents in the 1970 election study continued to mention these issues as the major problems facing the country, compared to 75 percent two years earlier. Viet Nam was still the specific issue most mentioned though its salience as a problem fell from 42 percent to 30 percent in the two year span as Nixon began winding down the war. There were other changes in emphasis within the new issue context, such as less concern with urban riots and more concern with campus disorder. But, the overall concern with the new issues remained central as before. While there was much discussion in the media about the effect of economic issues on the 1970 election, we found that public concern over economic questions was still minimal, only increasing from 3 percent mentioning such problems in 1968 to 12 percent doing so in 1970.

We have mentioned this new set of problems as if it were a coherent issue area. The relationships among these issues are, however, far from perfect, a situation which is typical of attitudinal survey data. This limitation aside, we do find a tendency for attitudes on these issues to cohere. The 1970 study included attitude questions concerning possible solutions to eight problems: urban unrest, campus unrest, rights of accused criminals, government aid to minorities, Viet Nam, inflation, pollution, and government health insurance. The first five of these issues formed a distinct cluster, as one would expect if a new issue area really existed. The correlation values ranged from .20 to .50. The remaining items showed very little relationship to one another or to the new issue cluster.

The relationship between these issues and party tells us much about the direction of partisan competition. The new issues had very small correlations with party in 1968, correlations ranging from .02 to .15 but with an average of only .07. The new issues were correlated somewhat more with party in 1970, although the correlations remained low. The average 1970 correlation with party was .12, ranging from .09 to .17. Two of the items were asked in both years: attitudes on urban unrest became less partisan as a Republican president had to face responsibility for such problems (.15 to .11), while attitudes on Viet Nam became more partisan as leading Democratic candidates moved to a more dovish position on the war (.02 to .08). Of the remaining items, government health insurance had the highest correlation with party (.23), coming closest to tapping the social welfare concerns out of which present partisan divisions developed during the New Deal.

The Candidate-Issue Space

We have shown a spatial representation of the candidate perceptions. Now we can add issue items to that space, to show the relationship between the candidates and these issues. We employed four attitudinal items for this purpose: party identification and government health insurance as representative of traditional concerns, and urban unrest and Viet Nam as representative of the new issue concerns. If our contention is correct that a conflict structure underlies candidate perceptions, we should be able to use these attitudinal items as validation, much as we did with the earlier social group items.

Adding these items to the space results in the solution shown in Figure 4.[8] The familiar partisan element seems to be the dimensional basis for candidate perceptions along the vertical axis. The array of candidates here resembles the cast of contenders in 1968, with Nixon and Humphrey occupying the polar positions on the continuum and Wallace, the third party candidate, found relatively near the middle. Buttressing the partisan interpretation is the fact that the Republican and Democratic codings of party identification load very highly on this dimension. These party items are also located close in space to their respective clusters of candidates. The government health insurance item is found near these clusters and the party items, and this finding fits well with the partisan interpretation since social welfare was the major issue of government spend-

---

[8] We should emphasize that issues are being added to the space to facilitate interpretation of the two-dimensional candidate space, and not as a separate test of the dimensionality of the space. We include in Figure 4 both the liberal and conservative poles of the issue items to draw attention to the placement of the issues with respect to the full set of candidates within the confines of the two dimensions of Figure 1. Additional issues could have resulted in added dimensions, as in Figure 3 where the dimensionality of the 17 groups predominates over that of the 10 candidates. However, our choice of issue areas is based on the analysis of the major problems cited by the respondents in the 1970 election study, with the cluster analysis testifying to the integrity of the issue areas. In particular, the racial problem is part of the new issue cluster and is implicit in the urban unrest item.

FIGURE 4
1970 Candidate-Issue Space

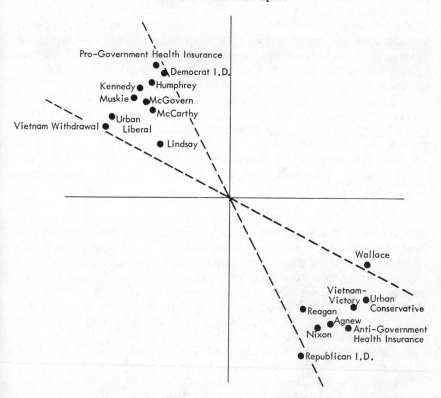

ing arising out of the Roosevelt period, during which present party loyalties were molded.

The second dimension pits Wallace against Muskie, and among issue items, the conservative ends of the urban unrest and Viet Nam issues with their liberal counterparts. The position of these issue items indicates the effect which new issue and political forces have had on how the public perceives the candidates. Also, it indicates some breaking away from the traditional partisan conflicts of the past, from a total reliance on party to screen and color one's perceptions of the other forces in the political environment. The separation of the new issues and some of the candidates from party is hardly complete, but it begins to give indications of what might develop as a major force in the future.

We found a similar two-dimensional solution in 1968, but one important difference exists between the two years. In 1968, the two dimensions of candidate perception, party, and the new issue factor, were largely independent of one another; in 1970, they were not. One can see readily that many of the candidates in the 1970 space have moderate loadings on both dimensions. The dotted lines in Figure 4 indicate this fact of correlated dimensions in 1970, while the solid lines show how the solution would look within the confines of an orthogonal structure. The correlation of these oblique axes in 1970 was a high .81, whereas a similar set of axes for the 1968 solution yielded a correlation of only .24 between the dimensions.

A fundamental question is, "Why were the two dimensions uncorrelated in 1968 but correlated in 1970?" Several possible answers can be given, answers which are not necessarily mutually exclusive and which cannot be completely verified with the data at hand. One obvious explanation would be the fact that an off-year election, without the presidential race, is relatively issue-less, with a stronger emphasis on party loyalties. Basically, congressional races are partisan campaigns, the contestants hewing to party appeals and the party line. What is all the more remarkable is that, despite this partisan climate in an off-year election, the issue dimension still was clearly visible in the electorate's mind. Even in an off-year election, there are enough tensions in the system to preclude total reliance on party.

A second explanation is that the parties and their leading presidential candidates have moved closer to the new issue dimension. With Johnson removed from the scene, Democratic candidates have more flexibility to deal with the new issues, particularly more ability to assume a dovish stand on the war. A Republican administration inevitably has the effect of forcing its party to take positions on these issues; and thereby associate Republican candidates with those positions, as when Nixon had to act on the Viet Nam war and hence identify his party with his position on that issue. This process is not only partly inevitable, given a change of administration following on the heels of wide dissension in the previous administration's party concerning its policies, but also it may be the result of a more conscious effort on the part of one or both parties to merge the new issues with traditional party appeals. Viewed in this light, the consolidation process has gone far, but still remains incomplete.

All told, the issue space, just as the social group space above, has presented the picture of both partisan and issue cleavages underlying perceptions of the candidates. While a tendency existed in 1970, unlike 1968, for the partisan and issue factors to merge, the circle has by no means been closed. Some candidates are still seen more in partisan than in issue terms, and others reflect the opposite pattern. Our next question will be to assess the relatively explanatory weights these two factors have for each of the candidates.

Determinants of Candidate Ratings

A discussion of the results portrayed in Figure 4 has given some initial idea of the relative influences of party and issue factors on candidate perceptions. How close a candidate is to the extremity of a dimension obviously indicates the extent to which the public identifies him with the content of that dimension. A further and more direct aid to understanding the relative influence of these two factors is to partial out the effects of one factor in order to ascertain the independent explanatory power the other factor possesses when related to the public's perceptions of the candidates.

Table 1 presents partial regression statistics which summarize the relative importance of party identification and two of the new issue items in determining candidate ratings.[9] For example, the values in the party

TABLE 1

Effects of Party Identification, Urban Unrest and Viet Nam Attitudes on
Candidate Ratings, 1968 and 1970

| | Beta Coefficients | | | | | | Multiple Correlation Coefficients | |
| Candidates | Party Identification | | Urban Unrest | | Viet Nam | | | |
	1968	1970	1968	1970	1968	1970	1968	1970
Muskie	.29	.28	.16	.17	.08	.14	.35	.39
Humphrey	.44	.41	.22	.15	.19	.07	.54	.46
Johnson	.42	–	.17	–	.10	–	.48	–
Kennedy, R.	.31	–	.20	–	.15	–	.43	–
Kennedy, E.	–	.41	–	.19	–	.10	–	.49
McCarthy	.09	.18	.14	.13	.17	.07	.24	.24
McGovern	–	.25	–	.12	–	.15	–	.34
Lindsay	–	.03	–	.12	–	.18	–	.22
Rockefeller	.10	–	.11	–	.10	–	.15	–
Romney	.09	–	.15	–	.10	–	.18	–
Agnew	.25	.33	.03	.16	.09	.13	.24	.42
Nixon	.42	.49	.03	.09	.09	.13	.42	.54
Reagan	.25	.36	.14	.09	.12	.09	.32	.40
LeMay	.10	–	.22	–	.20	–	.35	–
Wallace	.13	.09	.32	.27	.32	.18	.45	.38

identification columns indicate the effect of partisan loyalty on candidate perceptions after the impact of attitudes on urban unrest and Viet Nam have been controlled. Data for both 1968 and 1970 given in the table to facilitate comparisons between the two years.

Party is the major determinant of candidate ratings for a large majority of the candidates. The only instances in which one of the new issues is more important than party are with Wallace and Lindsay in 1970 and Wallace, LeMay, McCarthy, Rockefeller, and Romney in 1968. The principal change between the two years is in perceptions of McCarthy; McCarthy is seen in more partisan terms than earlier, a result which fits with his changing position in the multidimensional scaling space (see Figure 2). Since issue conflicts recede in an off-year election while partisan cleavages become intensified, it is little wonder that party is the dominant perceptual cue for candidates in 1970, maintaining a much stronger position in this regard than it did in 1968. Other factors are more important than party in 1970 only in those rare cases in which the candi-

---

[9] The figures reported here are partial beta coefficients produced by Multiple Classification Analysis, a multivariate technique which assumes additive but not linear effects. See Frank Andrews, James Morgan, and John Sonquist, *Multiple Classification Analysis* (Ann Arbor, Michigan: Institute for Social Research, University of Michigan, 1967).

date's partisan location has become blurred by having conducted campaigns for office as an Independent and having, at the same time, become labelled as a party renegade.

Increases are visible in the partisan images of several of the candidates. McCarthy's turn in this direction has already been noted, reflecting the fact that the public has, to some extent, forgotten his bold and independent moves to upset his party's incumbent president in 1968. The mainstream Republicans—Nixon, Agnew, and Reagan—are also viewed as more partisan in 1970 than in 1968, due, in part, to the administration's active campaign in the partisan off-year elections. Senator Edward Kennedy is another who is seen in heavily partisan terms in 1970, the public obviously projecting its strong partisan image of his late brother to its perceptions of the senior senator from Massachusetts.

Table 1 also calls attention to shifts in the issue images of many of the candidates. Nixon, Agnew, and Muskie are perceived more in new issue terms in 1970 than in 1968. This increase, even if mild, is important since it was registered in a relatively issueless partisan election year. The issue positions of the Republican administration and the Democratic front-runner have become better known over the two year period, and issue partisans correspondingly differ more in their assessments of the candidates. On Viet Nam policy and urban problems, the soft-liners have become increasingly disenchanted with the administration positions, while Muskie has lost favor among Viet Nam hawks.

One important qualification must be added to this discussion of the impact of public attitudes on candidate perceptions. The combined impact of party and issues is only moderate at best. Much of the variation in candidate ratings is due to individual response differences among those interviewed which have not been controlled, to unclear public images of some of these figures, and to candidate personality factors which go beyond parties and issues (such as "charisma"). Little of the variation in the responses given to Lindsay and McCarthy are explained by party or the issues in the 1970 ratings (and the same was true for Rockefeller, Romney, McCarthy, and Agnew in 1968). A similar pattern is evident for McGovern, although the public's highly superficial knowledge of the South Dakota senator may well explain why he was identified more in party than in issue terms. All three—Lindsay, McCarthy, and McGovern—have more of a potential for an issue candidacy than is evidenced here, but it is contingent on their becoming salient to the public and communicating their positions to that public.

In summary, the mixture of partisan and issue cleavages is apparent, with party being the dominant element shaping perceptions of candidates. However, the fact that the issue dimension continues to persist into 1970 logically raises the question of what its impact may be on future elections and on the party structures competing in those elections. The extent to which issue dimension is correlated with party also raises the question of how party and issues will interact in the future in forming candidate perceptions. Will the new issue dimension merge with party, or will it break away in 1972 to achieve the same independent status it had in 1968? What will the implications of such cleavages be on an electorate that is increasingly characterized as highly volatile in nature? Implications to the broader panorama of electoral change and party realignment are evident in the way people perceive candidates for the highest office in the land.

ELECTORAL CHANGE: TOWARD REALIGNMENT OR VOLATILITY?

The study of electoral behavior is fundamentally concerned with the study of long-term and short-term electoral change. On the short-term level, the prime question is whether there will be a change in the party and administration in power. Nixon's narrow victory in 1968 makes his position unusually vulnerable. Data from the 1970 election study indicate that he has captured the advantage in the two-year interim, but the data cannot tell us how safe that lead is.

While popular interest in short-term change is well-justified, our concern must also concentrate on the implications for long-term change. One basic bundle of long-term system components is *party alignment*—the number of parties, their group bases, their issue appeals, and most fundamentally, their levels of strength. A second bundle of long-term system components centers on the level of electoral *volatility*—the adhesion of the electorate to the party system and the fidelity of individual voters to their own party. Identification of the entire public with the parties, coupled with strict party voting, results in low system volatility; large numbers of Independent identifiers and sizable deviations from party voting indicate high levels of volatility. Increased volatility is inevitable as party alignments shift, with a corresponding decrease in volatility as voting patterns restabilize after a realignment period. Volatility can increase without realignment occurring, but increased volatility should heighten the potential for realignment.[10]

Evidence from the late 1960s is unequivocal in its indication of increasing volatility of the electorate. The proportion of Independent identifiers has risen, as has the extent of partisan defection.[11] The sizable vote gathered by Wallace in 1968 is further evidence of increased volatility in the system. There are those who see the end of political parties in these developments. However, the parties still have a long life remaining to them if their speed of demise remains constant. Volatility may be on the increase, but does this imply changing party alignments?

Party identification, a basic survey measure of party strength, has been astoundingly stable since the early 1950s. But party identification by itself is an imperfect measure of changes in party alignments. The

---

[10] For a recent clarification of the conceptual questions involved in what constitutes a realignment as well as analysis of recent survey data in this regard, see Bruce D. Merrill, *Party Realignment and Social Class: 1958–1970* (unpublished Ph.D. dissertation, University of Michigan, 1971).

[11] See Philip E. Converse, "Change in the American Electorate," in Angus Campbell and Philip E. Converse, eds., *The Human Meaning of Social Change* (New York: Russell Sage, in press).

party identification measure may mask a balance between the partisan-ships of those entering the electorate and those leaving the electorate during this period, or it may conceal changes among those who were in the electorate throughout this period which were balanced by the dif-ferences in the partisanship of those entering and leaving the electorate. The overall stability of party identification provides no clue to whether the group bases of the parties and their issue appeals have changed. Our discussion of a new issue dimension points to the possibility of changing issue appeals.

The popular press has made much of Scammon and Wattenberg's presentation of a new "Social Issue" composed of such elements as crime (safe streets and the law and order theme), race, youth (campus unrest and the drug culture), values (changing standards in the areas of sexual mores and dress), and Viet Nam dissent (and the reaction to it).[12] Yet theirs is basically a *style issue*—one on which there is general agreement (no one really favors unsafe streets and few members of the electorate favor disruptive demonstrations) which can damage candidates who find themselves associated with the unpopular side. Elections can turn on style issues, but the party disadvantaged by style issues usually manages to defuse them before they cause irreparable harm.

By contrast, we would emphasize the *position issue* aspect of our new issue cluster. There are style overtones to the problems of the cities, civil rights, and Viet Nam, but they are fundamentally issues on which actors (parties, candidates, and voters) take differing stands. The emergence of an important new position issue introduces the possibility of major system realignment if that issue polarizes the electorate in a manner un-related to existing partisan divisions. In 1968 the importance of the new issues and their virtual independence from traditional party appeals signified that the necessary conditions were met for a changing party alignment based on issue appeals.

How do parties cope with the development of a new issue dimension? One possibility would be to ignore the new issues with the hope that they would recede in importance. We have seen that the importance of these issues to the public decreased only slightly by 1970, and we would not expect the urban and racial problems to vanish. Party leaders could still feel that the issues are not yet intense enough to require the parties to take positions on them. Increased volatility is the likely consequence. Third and fourth party movements become more probable. Greater fluc-tuations between elections may occur, with the possibility of a series of one-term presidents. The question of which party is the dominant party may not change, but that dominant party would find itself losing a greater proportion of the elections. There is every evidence of these de-velopments occurring up through 1968. If the issues were extremely in-tense and the parties did not respond to them, we would expect new parties to replace the major parties, but even Wallace's efforts did not seriously challenge the dominant positions of the major parties in 1968.

---

[12] Richard Scammon and Ben J. Wattenberg, *The Real Majority* (New York: Coward-McCann, 1970).

Alternately, the parties could directly address the new issues, taking opposite positions on them and thereby absorbing the new issue dimension. Convergences between the new issues and party would mean that the parties would remain intact but with corresponding changes in party alignment. There is evidence of such developments between 1968 and 1970. The increased correlation between party and the new issues indicates a degree of convergence, though that convergence is still far from perfect. That this convergence could be caused by the inevitable off-year concentration on partisanship rather than issues means that it may only be temporary. However, we have also argued that the polarization-convergence process (polarization of parties and convergence of dimensions) is partly inevitable. The administration must take stands which associate its party with the new issues while the out-party, freed from the associations of the previous administration, is able to move to a position of opposition to the new issue policies of the administration. The issue bases of the parties are changing, slowly but unmistakably. Leadership bolts have occurred more frequently than is often the case in major realignments, with a number of southern Democrats becoming Republican and with Mayor Lindsay becoming a Democrat. The extent to which the group basis of politics changes in the process is not yet apparent. No doubt the process is not yet finalized. The intense attitudes toward the new groups mentioned earlier suggests that the party system is not yet able to accommodate these new groups so that continuing modification is likely.

A gradual realignment process can change the balance of the parties. Phillips has seen this resulting in the emergence of a Republican majority, in large part a consequence of the administration's southern strategy.[13] We find no evidence of a new Republican majority. A high level of volatility makes such a result possible, but it also makes possible the further solidification of the Democratic majority.

The enfranchisement of the 18–20 year olds further increases the potential for volatility. Even before that development, we argued that the coming of age of the post-war baby-boom was going to increase electoral volatility in 1972.[14] The infusion of this doubly large group is particularly significant because their attraction in sizable numbers to one party or another in their first presidential vote could give that party an advantage for a series of elections. Our data suggest that young voters would not be necessarily enthusiastic in their reactions to most of the candidates, with the exception of a strong positive reaction to Senator Kennedy. There is also some tendency for them to be enthusiastic about McCarthy, McGovern, and Lindsay, but relatively unenthusiastic about Humphrey and Republicans Agnew, Reagan, and Nixon. The minority party has accepted the enfranchisement of a set of voters which could cause that party's demise if it were attracted in large and permanent numbers to the majority party by an appealing candidate. What happens

---

[13] Kevin P. Phillips, *The Emerging Republican Majority* (New Rochelle, New York: Arlington House, 1969).

[14] Weisberg and Rusk, "Dimensions of Candidate Evaluation," p. 1185.

depends on the identity of the Democratic candidate, but the potential for large scale realignment resulting from the stream of new voters is unusually high.

A mid-term election does not afford a suitable setting for the resolution of questions concerning electoral change. However, it does provide an effective opportunity for sharpening our questions about future directions. We see electoral change as occurring presently, but as being incomplete. We see signs of increased volatility in the system, but we do not consider them as foreshadowing the end of parties or the emergence of long-term minor parties. We recognize the potential for a Republican majority, but we would also emphasize the possibility of the Democrats so increasing their majority as to make the Republican position untenable. We find the issue appeals of the parties to be changing, but with only limited effect to date on the group bases of these parties. The stability of indicators in the issueless 1950s desensitized analysts to the possibility that continued stability during the issue-packed 1960s could hide real change. The 1970s should witness the culmination of this process. Our mid-term assessment is one of increased volatility with some realignment of the issue bases of the parties; the scope of the realignment and its ultimate implications for the partisan balance are questions which must be put off for a later report.

Section II
The Political Parties Model

The last section's reading revealed the active part played by political party identification in the average man's reactions to and evaluations of his elected officials. But political party identification is not an essential part of the political parties model, and may even be contrary to its proper functioning. Like the rational-activist model, the political parties model demands that citizens be open-minded to the vote appeals of both parties and ever ready to support the opposition if elected officials fail to fulfill promises made when they were elected. Loyalty to a political party from one election to the next violates both models as it does not encourage political linkage.

While one might argue that there is a circumstance in which a candidate or party might deserve loyalty for having consistently satisfied the voters, in no case should the voter fail to give full evaluation of the alternative candidates and their positions in reaching his decision late in the campaign. And the switcher or less party loyal voter should show no less involvement in the system. The first two selections in this section focus on public behavior in congressional, off-year elections, considering factors which affect how a person votes and especially whether his vote is affected by his position on issues. Actual behavior in both 1958 and 1970, the authors find, fails to satisfy the requisites of the political parties model. Donald Stokes and Warren Miller conclude that the congressman generally need not concern himself with his constituents' reactions to his votes because they are not "looking." Stanley Freedman finds little change in this pattern.

Although one cannot deny some changes in the American electorate since 1956, such as sharply improved education, a slight increase in those calling themselves independents, some increase in the number claiming to see differences in the political parties (from 50 percent in 1956 to 60 percent in 1968), and improved consistency in the viewing of Democrats as liberals, the changes noted in this study of 1970 versus 1958 congressional voting show very little difference. Perhaps the changes noted merely reveal the impact of education and better or more consistent communication of political cues with no change in the public's commitment to voting more consistently with the expectations of either the rational-activist or the political parties models.

Gerald Pomper notes that the *American Voter* by Angus Campbell and associates found little belief among Americans in the early 1950s that the political parties took different positions on the major issues of the day or that one party was consistently the more liberal, but more recent data finds an improvement. Across six national issues he finds a 9 percent increase from the 51 percent who saw a party difference in 1956; and among those seeing a party difference, he finds a 24 percent increase from the 59 percent who saw the Democrats as the liberal party in 1956. This still leaves better than half of the public not seeing the Democrats as liberal as distinct from the conservative Republican party. More troubling, however, is the fact that while 96 percent of the strong Democrats saw the Democratic party as the liberal party, 42 percent of the strong Republicans would not concede that the other party was more liberal. Research by Paul Messick notes, moreover, that people seek consistency between their personal opinions and those they attribute to their preferred political party.[1] Table 1 exemplifies the consistencies he finds. The

TABLE 1

Perception of Party Differences on Government Guarantee of Job by
Strength of Party ID and Issue Opinion

	Favorable				Unfavorable			
	Demo-crat	Repub-lican	No Differ-ence	(N)	Demo-crat	Repub-lican	No Differ-ence	(N)
Strong Democrat	89%	1%	10%	(147)	54%	5%	42%	(97)
Democrat	72	3	25	(116)	48	9	43	(141)
Independent	40	17	43	(103)	38	16	46	(220)
Republican	34	29	37	(38)	50	16	34	(104)
Strong Republican ...	18	61	21	(28)	49	29	22	(69)
N				(432)				(631)

Gamma = .55
Significant at .05 level

Gamma = −.05
Significant at .05 level

overall pattern finds people's perceptions of which party favors a program depend on both their party identification and their personal opinion about the issue. Thus while 89 percent of strong Democrats who favor federally guaranteed jobs believe their party also favors this program, among their counterparts who oppose the program only 54 percent see the Democrats as the party favoring the program and 42 percent claim to see no difference. People adjust their perceptions of which political party favors a program to suit their personal opinions on the program rather than agreeing regardless of party preference and issue position as to which party favors the program. Both the preference to see one's party

---

[1] Paul J. Messick, "Party Issue Positions and Personal Attitudes: Misperceiving for Attitude Consistency," an unpublished paper.

as the liberal party and the misperception of a party's position to get consistency in one's beliefs contradict the policy-party tie seen as a desirable trend by Pomper and seemingly necessary for the functioning of the political parties model.

The third selection by Kenneth Prewitt poses a serious problem for all coercive models. He finds that many of the city councilmen he studies are initially appointed and then stand for election in very low turnout local elections, resulting in most incumbents being reelected. Thus many representatives never face electoral challenge and tend to think of office holding as satisfying a civic duty. One can well imagine how affronted a representative who feels he is holding office to fulfill his civic duty would feel if he were defeated at the polls. Prewitt gives scattered evidence of the prevalence of this "volunteerism" at different levels of government.

The selection by John Sullivan and Robert O'Connor assesses what they call the "two neglected conditions of the linkage process," whether candidates of the two political parties differ in issue positions and whether they vote consistently with their preelection attitudes. Both conditions are satisfied, but no consistent choice is voiced by the American electorate in terms of the representatives they send to Congress. The winners in the 435 congressional seats in 1966 differ little from the losers. Recalling the Freedman article, we might explain this as evidencing the absence of issue voting by the electorate. But alternatively, one region's selection of liberal Democrats may be offset by another's choice of conservatives which when viewed on a national basis reveals no pattern of preferences. Most importantly, they show that the political parties show consistency in the ideological positions of their candidates and that the electorate in nearly all districts has a meaningful choice. The deficiency of the political parties model evident in their data is a deficiency of the electorate, not the parties.

Donald E. Stokes and Warren E. Miller

Party Government and the Saliency of Congress*

Any mid-term congressional election raises pointed questions about party government in America. With the personality of the President removed from the ballot by at least a coattail, the public is free to pass judgment on the legislative record of the parties. So the civics texts would have us believe. In fact, however, an off-year election can be regarded as an assessment of the parties' record in Congress only if the electorate possesses certain minimal information about what that record is. The fact of possession needs to be demonstrated, not assumed, and the low visibility of congressional affairs to many citizens suggests that the electorate's actual information should be examined with care.

How much the people know is an important, if somewhat hidden, problem of the normative theory of representation. Implicitly at least, the information the public is thought to have is one of the points on which various classical conceptions of representation divide. Edmund Burke and the liberal philosophers, for example—to say nothing of Hamilton and Jefferson—had very different views about the information the public could get or use in assessing its government. And the periods of flood tide in American democracy, especially the Jacksonian and Progressive eras, have been marked by the most optimistic assumptions as to what the people could or did know about their government. To put the matter another way: any set of representative institutions will work very differently according to the amount and quality of information the electorate has. This is certainly true of the institutional forms we associate with government by responsible parties. A necessary condition of party responsibility to the people is that the public have basic information about

* From *Public Opinion Quarterly*, vol. 26 (Winter 1962), pp. 531–46. Reprinted by permission of the Princeton University Press, copyright owners.

The research from which this report is drawn was supported by grants of the Rockefeller Foundation and the Social Science Research Council. The authors also gratefully acknowledge the skilled assistance of Ralph Bisco, Jon Faily, Julie Crowder, and Arthur Wolfe.

the parties and their legislative record. Without it, no institutional devices can make responsibility a fact.

To explore the information possessed by those who play the legislative and constituent roles in American government, the Survey Research Center of the University of Michigan undertook an interview study of Congressmen and their districts during the mid-term election of Eisenhower's second term. Immediately after the 1958 campaign the Center interviewed a nationwide sample of the electorate, clustered in 116 congressional districts, as well as the incumbent Congressmen and other major-party candidates for the House from the same collection of districts.[1] Through these direct interviews with the persons playing the reciprocal roles of representative government, this research has sought careful evidence about the perceptual ties that bind, or fail to bind, the Congressman to his party and district. We will receive some of this evidence here for the light that it throws on the problem of party cohesion and responsibility in Congress.

THE RESPONSIBLE-PARTY MODEL AND THE AMERICAN CASE

What the conception of government by responsible parties requires of the general public has received much less attention than what it requires of the legislative and electoral parties.[2] The notion of responsibility generally is understood to mean that the parties play a mediating role between the public and its government, making popular control effective by developing rival programs of government action that are presented to

---

[1] The 116 districts are a probability sample of all constituencies, although the fact that the study was piggy-backed onto a four-year panel study of the electorate extending over the elections of 1956, 1958, and 1960 made the design of the 1958 representation sample unusually complex. In particular, since metropolitan areas and nonmetropolitan counties or groups of counties, rather than congressional districts, were used as primary sampling units when the panel sample was originated in 1956, the districts represented in our 1958 sample did not have equal probability of selection and the efficiency of the sample of districts was somewhat less than that of a simple random sample of equal size. Descriptions of the sample design may be obtained from the Survey Research Center.

[2] For example, the 1950 report of the American Political Science Association's Committee on Political Parties, the closest approach to an official statement of the responsible-party view as applied to American politics, concentrates on the organization of Congress and the national parties and deals only very obliquely with the role of the public. See *Toward a More Responsible Two-Party System* (New York: Rinehart, 1950). In general, theoretical and empirical treatments of party government have focused more on the nature of party *appeals*—especially the question of whether the parties present a real "choice"—than on the cognitive and motivational elements that should be found in the *response* of an electorate that is playing its correct role in a system of responsible-party government. For example, see the excellent discussion in Austin Ranney and Wilmoore Kendall, *Democracy and the American Party System* (New York: Harcourt, Brace, 1956), pp. 151–52, 384–85, 525–27.

It should be clear that the data of this report are taken from a particular election of a particular electoral era. We would expect our principal findings to apply to most recent off-year elections, but they are of course subject to modification for earlier or later periods.

the electorate for its choice. The party whose program gains the greater support takes possession of the government and is held accountable to the public in later elections for its success in giving its program effect. Two assumptions about the role of the public can be extracted from these ideas. *First,* in a system of party government the electorate's attitude toward the parties is based on what the party programs are and how well the parties have delivered on them. The public, in a word, gives the parties *programmatic* support. And, in view of the importance that legislative action is likely to have in any party program, such support is formed largely out of public reaction to the legislative performance of the parties, especially the party in power.

Second, under a system of party government the voters' response to the local legislative candidates is based on the candidates' identification with party programs. These programs are the substance of their appeals to the constituency, which will act on the basis of its information about the proposals and legislative record of the parties. Since the party programs are of dominant importance, the candidates are deprived of any independent basis of support. They will not be able to build in their home districts an electoral redoubt from which to challenge the leadership of their parties.[3]

How well do these assumptions fit the behavior of the American public as it reaches a choice in the off-year congressional elections? A first glance at the relation of partisan identifications to the vote might give the impression that the mid-term election is a triumph of party government. Popular allegiance to the parties is of immense importance in all our national elections, including those in which a President is chosen, but its potency in the mid-term congressional election is especially pronounced. This fact is plain—even stark—in the entries of Table 1, which

TABLE 1

1958 Vote for House Candidates, by Party Identification
(in per cent)

	Party Identification*			
	Democratic	Independent	Republican	Total
Voted Democratic	53†	2	6	61
Voted Republican	5	3	31	39
Total	58	5	37	100

* The Democratic and Republican party identification groups include all persons who classify themselves as having some degree of party loyalty.

† Each entry of the table gives the per cent of the total sample of voters having the specified combination of party identification and vote for the House in 1958.

---

[3] This assumption does not imply that pressures toward party cohesion come *only* from the mass public. Other sanctions against party irregularity are of equal or greater importance, especially those available in the nominating process and within the legislative parties themselves. To cite the most celebrated empirical case, the cohesiveness of the British parliamentary parties is not enforced primarily, if at all, by the British electorate. Nevertheless, the public ought not to give aid and comfort to the legislative party irregular; the idea of the candidate building a local bastion of strength from which he can challenge the party leadership is clearly contradictory to the party-government model.

break down the vote for Congress in 1958 into its component party elements. The table makes clear, first of all, how astonishingly small a proportion of the mid-term vote is cast by political independents. Repeated electoral studies in the United States have indicated that somewhat fewer than 1 American in 10 thinks of himself as altogether independent of the two parties.[4] But in the off-year race for Congress only about a twentieth part of the vote is cast by independents, owing to their greater drop-out rate when the drama and stakes of the presidential contest are missing.

Table 1 also makes clear how little deviation from party there is among Republicans and Democrats voting in a mid-term year. The role of party identification in the congressional election might still be slight, whatever the size of the party followings, if partisan allegiance sat more lightly on the voting act. But almost 9 out of every 10 partisans voting in the off-year race support their parties. Indeed, something like 84 per cent of *all* the votes for the House in 1958 were cast by party identifiers supporting their parties. The remaining 16 per cent is not a trivial fraction of the whole—standing, as it did in this case, for 8 million people, quite enough to make and unmake a good many legislative careers. Nevertheless, the low frequency of deviation from party, together with the low frequency of independent voting, indicates that the meaning of the mid-term vote depends in large part on the nature of party voting.

THE SALIENCY OF THE PARTIES' LEGISLATIVE RECORDS

If American party voting were to fit the responsible-party model it would be *programmatic* voting, that is, the giving of electoral support according to the parties' past or prospective action on programs that consist (mainly) of legislative measures. There is little question that partisan voting is one of the very few things at the bottom of our two-party system; every serious third-party movement in a hundred years has foundered on the reef of traditional Republican and Democratic loyalties. But there is also little question that this voting is largely nonprogrammatic in nature. A growing body of evidence indicates that party loyalties are typically learned early in life, free of ideological or issue content, with the family as the main socializing agency. Certainly the findings of adult interview studies show that such loyalties are extremely longlived and, summed across the population, give rise to extraordinarily stable distributions.[5] The very persistence of party identification raises suspicion as to whether the country is responding to the parties current legislative actions when it votes its party loyalties.

That this suspicion is fully warranted in the mid-term election is indicated by several kinds of evidence from this research. To begin with, the electorate's perceptions of the parties betray very little information about current policy issues. For the past ten years the Survey Research Center has opened its electoral interviews with a series of free-answer questions designed to gather in the positive and negative ideas that the

---

[4] See Angus Campbell, Philip E. Converse, Warren E. Miller, and Donald E. Stokes, *The American Voter* (New York: John Wiley & Sons, 1960), p. 124.

[5] For evidence on this point, see *ibid.*, pp. 120–67.

public has about the parties. The answers, requiring on the average nearly ten minutes of conversation, are only very secondarily couched in terms of policy issues. In 1958, for example, more than six thousand distinct positive or negative comments about the parties were made by a sample of 1,700 persons. Of these, less than 12 per cent by the most generous count had to do with contemporary legislative issues. As this sample of Americans pictured the reasons it liked and disliked the parties, the modern battlefields of the legislative wars—aid-to-education, farm policy, foreign aid, housing, aid to the unemployed, tariff and trade policy, social security, medical care, labor laws, civil rights, and other issues—rarely came to mind. The main themes in the public's image of the parties are not totally cut off from current legislative events; the political activist could take the group-benefit and prosperity-depression ideas that saturate the party images and connect them fairly easily with issues before Congress. The point is that the public itself rarely does so.

How little awareness of current issues embodied in the congressional vote also is attested by the reasons people give for voting Republican or Democratic for the House. In view of the capacity of survey respondents to rationalize their acts, direct explanations of behavior should be treated with some reserve. However, rationalization is likely to increase, rather than decrease, the policy content of reasons for voting. It is therefore especially noteworthy how few of the reasons our respondents gave for their House votes in 1958 had any discernible issue content. The proportion that had—about 7 per cent—was less even than the proportion of party-image references touching current issues.

Perhaps the most compelling demonstration of how hazardous it is to interpret party voting as a judgment of the parties' legislative records is furnished by the evidence about the public's knowledge of party control of Congress. When our 1958 sample was asked whether the Democrats or the Republicans had had more Congressmen in Washington during the two preceding years, a third confessed they had no idea, and an additional fifth gave control of the eighty-fifth Congress to the Republicans. Only 47 per cent correctly attributed control to the Democrats. These figures improve somewhat when nonvoters are excluded. Of those who voted in 1958, a fifth did not know which party had controlled Congress, another fifth thought the Republicans had, and the remainder (61 per cent) correctly gave control to the Democrats. However, when a discount is made for guessing, the proportion of voters who really *knew* which party had controlled the eighty-fifth Congress probably is still not more than half.[6]

---

[6] Plainly, some deduction has to be made for guessing. One model of the situation would be to think of the sample as composed of three types of people: those who knew, those who didn't know and said so, and those who didn't know but guessed. Assuming that for those who guessed $p = q = \frac{1}{2}$, where p is the probability of guessing Republican, we would deduct from the Democratic answers a percentage equal to the 18 per cent who guessed Republican incorrectly, hence reducing the proportion of voters who really knew which party controlled Congress to 43 per cent. This model may be too severe, however, in view of the presence of the Republican President. It may be more reasonable to admit a fourth type of person, those who

It would be difficult to overstate the significance of these figures for the problem of party government. The information at issue here is not a sophisticated judgment as to what short of coalition had *effective* control of Congress. It is simply the question of whether the country had a Democratic or a Republican Congress from 1956 to 1958. This elementary fact of political life, which any pundit would take completely for granted as he interpreted the popular vote in terms of party accountability, was unknown to something like half the people who went to the polls in 1958.

It is of equal significance to note that the parties' legislative record was no more salient to those who *deviated* from party than it was to those who voted their traditional party loyalty. It might be plausible to suppose that a floating portion of the electorate gives the parties programmatic support, even though most voters follow their traditional allegiances. If true, this difference would give the responsible-party model some factual basis, whether or not the greater part of the electorate lived in darkness. But such a theory finds very little support in these data. In 1958 neither the issue reasons given for the congressional vote nor the awareness of party control of the eighty-fifth Congress was any higher among those who voted *against* their party identification than it was among those who voted *for* their party, as the entries of Table 2 demon-

TABLE 2

Issue Responses and Awareness of Which Party Controlled
85th Congress among Party Supporters and Voters
Who Deviated from Party

	Of Party Identifiers Who	
	Voted for Own Party	Voted for Other Party
Per cent aware of party control:		
Uncorrected	61	60
Corrected for guessing*	44	35
Per cent giving issue reasons		
for House vote	6	7

* This correction deducts from the proportion attributing control to the Democrats a percentage equal to the proportion attributing control to the Republicans. See footnote 6.

strate. If anything, correcting perceived party control for guessing suggests that voters who deviated from their party in 1958 had poorer information about the course of political events over the preceding two years.

Nor do the perceptions of party control of Congress that *are* found supply a key to understanding the congressional vote. Whatever aware-

did not guess but were misled by Republican control of the White House. Or we might think of the guessers as following a probability law in which $p > \frac{1}{2} > q$. In either of these cases something less than 18 per cent would be deducted from the Democratic answers; hence, the proportion of voters who *knew* which party controlled Congress would lie somewhere between 43 and 61 per cent.

ness of control the electorate had in 1958 was remarkably unrelated to its support of candidates for the House. To make this point, Table 3 analyzes deviations from party according to three perceptions held by party identifiers voting in 1958: *first,* whether they thought the country's recent domestic affairs had gone well or badly; *second* (to allow for the complication of divided government), whether they thought Congress or Presi-

TABLE 3
**Percentage of Party Identifiers Voting against Party in 1958,
by Perception of Party Control of Government
and Course of Domestic Affairs**

Thought That Domestic Affairs	Thought That More Effective Branch of Government Was Controlled by	
	Own Party	*Other Party*
	I	II
Had gone well	16	22
	(N = 43)	(N = 46)
	III	IV
Had gone badly	14	13
	(N = 152)	(N = 122)

dent had the greater influence over what the government did; and, *third,* whether they thought the Democrats or Republicans had controlled Congress. To recreate the basis on which the voter might assign credit or blame to the parties, the second and third of these perceptions may be combined; that is, partisans may be classified according to whether they thought their own party or the opposite party had controlled the more effective branch of government. Crossing this classification with perceptions of whether domestic affairs had gone well yields four groups for analysis, two of which (I and IV) might be expected to show little deviation from party, the other two (II and III) substantially more. In fact, however, the differences between these groups are almost trifling. According to the familiar lore, the groups that thought affairs had gone badly (III and IV)are the ones that should provide the clearest test of whether perceptions of party control are relevant to voting for the House. Moreover, with a recession in the immediate background, most people who could be classified into this table in 1958 fell into one of these two groups, as the frequencies indicate. But when the two groups that felt there had been domestic difficulties are compared, it seems not to make a particle of difference whether the Democrats or Republicans were thought to have controlled the actions of government. And when the two groups (I and II) that felt things had gone well are compared, only a slight (and statistically insignificant) difference appears. Interestingly, even this small rise in the rate of deviation from party (in cell II) is contributed mainly by Democratic identifiers who wrongly supposed that the Congress had been in Republican hands.

The conclusion to be drawn from all this certainly is not that national political forces are without *any* influence on deviations from party in the mid-term year. Clearly these forces do have an influence. Although the fluctuations of the mid-term party vote, charted over half a century or more, are very much smaller than fluctuations in the presidential vote or of the congressional vote in presidential years, there is *some* variation, and these moderate swings must be attributed to forces that have their focus at the national level.[7] Even in 1958 one party received a larger share of deviating votes than the other. Our main point is rather that the deviations that *do* result from national forces are not in the main produced by the parties' legislative records and that, in any case, the proportion of deviating votes that can be attributed to national politics is likely to be a small part of the total votes cast by persons deviating from party in a mid-term year. This was specifically true in 1958.

If the motives for deviations from party are not to be found primarily at the national level, the search moves naturally to the local congressional campaign. A third possibility—that deviations are by-products of state-wide races—can be discounted with some confidence. Despite the popular lore on the subject, evidence both from interview studies and from aggregate election statistics can be used to show that the influence of contests for Governor and Senator on the outcome of House races is slight in mid-term elections, although these contests can have an immense influence on turnout for the House.[8] In our 1958 sample, a majority of those who deviated from party in voting for the House *failed* to deviate also at the state level; more often than not, what had moved them into the other party's column at the House level was dissociated from the contests for Governor or Senator in which they voted. Moreover, the fact that an elector deviates from his party in voting both for the House and some office contested on a state-wide basis is not conclusive evidence that the state race has influenced his choice for the House, rather than the other way round. When the possibility of *reverse* coat-tail effects is allowed for, the reasons for believing that the state-wide race is a potent

---

[7] A simple but persuasive comparison is this: from 1892 to 1960 the standard deviation of the two-party division of the mid-term congressional vote was 3.9 per cent; of the presidential-year congressional vote, 5.5 per cent; of the presidential vote, 8.2 per cent. Moreover, if the realignment of party loyalties that occurred in the early 1930's is taken into account by computing deviations from pre- and post-1932 means, rather than from a grand mean for the whole period, the standard deviation of the mid-term congressional vote is found to have been 2.4 per cent, compared with a standard deviation of 7.5 per cent for the presidential vote. Some of the remaining variability of the mid-term vote may be due to fluctuations of turnout that do not involve deviations from party. Yet, even ignoring this possibility, the bounds within which national political forces can have influenced the off-year vote by inducing deviations from party appear narrow indeed.

[8] A remarkable fact is that while the total vote for the House increased by 3 million between 1954 and 1958, more than 2 million of this increase was contributed by New York, where Rockefeller sought the governorship; by Ohio, where a fierce referendum battle was fought over the issue of "right-to-work"; and by California, where the fantastic Knight-Knowland-Brown free-for-all was held.

force on the House vote seem faint indeed.[9] As we search for the motives for deviation from party, analysis of the local congressional race pays greater dividends.

THE SALIENCY OF CONGRESSIONAL CANDIDATES

By the standards of the civics text, what the public knows about the candidates for Congress is as meager as what it knows about the parties' legislative records. Of the people who lived in districts where the House seat was contested in 1958, 59 per cent—well over half—said that they had neither read nor heard anything about either candidate for Congress, and less than 1 in 5 felt that they knew something about both candidates. What is more, these remarkable proportions are only marginally improved by excluding nonvoters from the calculations. Of people who went to the polls and cast a vote between rival House candidates in 1958, fully 46 per cent conceded that they did so without having read or heard anything about either man. What the other half *had* read or heard is illuminating; we will deal with its policy content presently. Many of our respondents said they knew something about the people contesting the House seat on the basis of very slender information indeed.

The incumbent candidate is by far the better known. In districts where an incumbent was opposed for re-election in 1958, 39 per cent of our respondents knew something about the Congressman, whereas only 20 per cent said they knew anything at all about his nonincumbent opponent. The incumbent's advantage of repeated exposure to the electorate is plain enough. In fact, owing to the greater seniority and longer exposure of Congressmen from safe districts, the public's awareness of incumbents who were unopposed for reelection in 1958 was as great as its awareness of incumbents who had had to conduct an election campaign that year.

The saliency of a candidate is of critical importance if he is to attract support from the opposite party. However little the public may know of those seeking office, any information at all about the rival party's candidate creates the possibility of a choice deviating from party. That such a choice occurs with some frequency is shown by the entries of Table 4, whose columns separate party identifiers in contested districts in 1958 according to whether they were aware of both candidates, the candidate of their own party or the other party only, or neither candidate. The con-

---

[9] This conclusion is fully supported by an analysis of the variance of turnout and party vote in the mid-term congressional elections of the 1950's. If state-wide races have a major influence on local House races, the election results for the several congressional districts of a state should vary together; similar changes of turnout and party division should be seen in the districts that are influenced by the same statewide contests. An analysis of the variance of the differences between the 1954 and 1958 turnout level and partisan division for all congressional districts in states having at least two districts indicates that state races have a large effect on turnout; the intraclass correlation expressing the ratio of the between-state variance to the total variance of turnout was more than .45. But this analysis shows, too, that statewide races have almost no effect whatever on the party division of the House vote; the intraclass correlation expressing the ratio of the between-state variance to the total variance of the party division was not more than .02.

TABLE 4

Percentage Voting for Own Party Candidate and Other Party Candidate
for House in 1958, by Saliency of Candidates in
Contested Districts

	Voter Was Aware of			
Voted for Candidate	Both Candidates (N = 196)	Own Party Candidate Only (N = 166)	Other Party Candidate Only (N = 68)	Neither Candidate (N = 368)
Of own party	83	98	60	92
Of other party	17	2	40	8
Total	100	100	100	100

dition of no information leads to fairly unrelieved party-line voting, and
so to an even greater degree does the condition of information only about
the candidate of the voter's own party. But if partisan voters know something about the opposition's man, substantial deviations from party appear. In fact, if such voters know *only* the opposition candidate, almost
half can be induced to cast a vote contrary to their party identification.
In the main, recognition carries a positive valence; to be perceived at all
is to be perceived favorably. However, some *negative* perceptions are
found in our interviews, and when these are taken into account the explanation of deviation from party becomes surer still. For example, if we
return to Table 4 and select from the third column only the voters who
perceived the candidate of the other party *favorably*, a clear majority is
found to have deviated from party allegiance in casting their votes. And
if we select from the first column only the handful of voters who perceived the candidate of their own party *negatively* and of the opposite
party *positively*, almost three-quarters are found to have deviated from
their party loyalty in voting for the House.

What our constituent interviews show about the increment of support
that accrues to the salient candidate is closely aligned to what the candidates themselves see as the roots of their electoral strength. Our interviews with incumbent and nonincumbent candidates seeking election to
the House explored at length their understanding of factors aiding—or
damaging—their electoral appeal. In particular, these interviews probed
the candidates' assessment of four possible influences on the result: traditional party loyalties, national issues, state and local contests, and the
candidates' own record and personal standing in the district. Caution is
in order in dealing with answers to questions that touch the respondent's
self-image as closely as these. Specifically, we may expect some overstatement of the candidate's own importance, particularly from the victors, and we may expect, too, that too large a discount will be applied to
party allegiance, since this "inert" factor, having little to do with increments of strength, is so easily taken for granted.

After these allowances are made, it is still impressive how heavy a
weight the incumbent assigns his personal record and standing. The Con-

gressman's ranking of this and the other factors in the election is shown in Table 5. As the entries of the table indicate, more than four-fifths of the incumbents re-elected in 1958 felt that the niche they had carved out in the awareness of their constituents had substantial impact on the race, a proportion that exceeds by half the percentage who gave as much weight to any of the three other factors. This difference is more than sheer puffing in the interview situation, and the perceptual facts it reveals deserve close attention. Among the forces the Representative feels may enhance his strength at the polls, he gives his personal standing with the district front rank.

TABLE 5
Relative Importance of Factors in Re-election
as Seen by Incumbent Candidates in 1958
(in per cent)

Perceived as	Personal Record and Standing	National Issues	Traditional Party Loyalties	State and Local Races
Very important	57	26	25	14
Quite important	28	20	21	19
Somewhat important	9	20	24	27
Not very important	3	27	18	19
Not important at all	3	7	12	21
	100	100	100	100

In view of the way the saliency of candidates can move the electorate across party lines, great stress should be laid on the fact that the public sees individual candidates for Congress in terms of party programs scarcely at all. Our constituent interviews indicate that the popular image of the Congressman is almost barren of policy content. A long series of open-ended questions asked of those who said they had any information about the Representative produced mainly a collection of diffuse evaluative judgments: he is a good man, he is experienced, he knows the problems, he has done a good job, and the like. Beyond this, the Congressman's image consisted of a mixed bag of impressions, some of them wildly improbable, about ethnicity, the attractiveness of family, specific services to the district, and other facts in the candidate's background. By the most reasonable count, references to current legislative issues comprised not more than a thirtieth part of what the constituents had to say about their Congressmen.

The irrelevance of legislative issues to the public's knowledge of Representatives is underscored by the nature of some primary *determinants* of saliency. A full analysis of the causes of constitutional awareness of candidates goes beyond the scope of this paper. Although our investigation has given a good deal of attention to communication factors and to characteristics of Congressmen and constituents themselves that determine the probability a given Congressman will be known to a given constituent, this interplay of causes cannot be explored very deeply here.

However, it *is* noteworthy in the present discussion that many factors increasing the saliency of candidates are unlikely to enhance what the public knows about their stands on issues. An excellent example is sex. Both for incumbents and nonincumbents, a candidate property that is related to saliency is gender; one of the best ways for a Representative to be known is to be a Congress*woman*. How irrelevant to policy issues this property is depends on what we make of the causal relation between sex and salience. The fact of being a woman may make a candidate more visible, but a woman may have to be unusually visible (like a Congressman's widow, say) before she can be elected to the House, or even become a serious candidate. If the first of these inferences is even partially right, the salience of the candidate is not likely to be in terms of positions taken on legislative issues.

Given the number of women who run for Congress, the role of sex may seem a trivial example to demonstrate the irrelevance of issue stands to saliency. However, the same point can be made for a much wider set of districts by the greater saliency of candidates who live in the constituent's home community. Just as there is enormous variety in the communities that make up the American nation, so there is the widest possible variation in how well a congressional district coincides with a natural community, and the goodness of this fit is a fundamental way of typing districts. At one extreme is the constituency whose area is lost within one of the country's great metropolitan centers, comprising at best a small fraction of the whole community. At the middle of the range is the district that is itself a natural community, consisting of a single medium-sized city and its environs. At the other extreme is the district whose territory includes a great number of small communities, as well as surrounding open country that goes on, in some cases, for hundreds of miles. In all but the metropolitan districts the salience of the candidate for the voter differs markedly according to whether candidate and voter live in the same community. The fact of common residence—of being "friends and neighbors"—stands for important facts of communication and community identification. Candidates will be joined by formal and informal communication networks to many of the voters living in the same community, and they may also be objects of considerable community pride.

The reality of this local effect is demonstrated by Table 6. As the entries of the table show, dividing a nationwide sample of constituents according to whether they live in the same community as their Congressman or his opponent produces marked differences of saliency. The "friends and neighbors" effect made familiar by studies of primary voting in one-party areas has a counterpart in voting for Representatives throughout the country, apart from the large metropolitan areas.[10] And despite the fact that localism is found here in the context of as tightly

---

[10] See V. O. Key, Jr., *Southern Politics*, New York, Knopf, 1949, pp. 37ff. We have demonstrated the "friends and neighbors" effect in terms of candidate salience because of our interest in the policy content of candidate perceptions. However, owing to the impact of salience on the vote, living in the same community with the candidate has a clear effect on voting as well.

TABLE 6

Influence of "Friends and Neighbors" Factor
on Saliency of Candidates for Voters°
(in per cent)

Voter Is	Incumbent Candidate Lives in		Non-incumbent Candidate Lives in	
	Same Community as Voter (N = 269)	Other Community than Voter (N = 414)	Same Community as Voter (N = 304)	Other Community than Voter (N = 447)
Aware of candidate	67	45	47	22
Not aware of candidate	33	55	53	78
Total	100	100	100	100

° Metropolitan and large urban districts, for which the notion of the candidate living outside the voter's community has no clear meaning, are excluded from the analysis.

party-determined an election as any in American politics, the irrelevance of local appeal to legislative issues is probably as great as it is in the wide-open, one-party primary.

CONCLUSION

What the public knows about the legislative records of the parties and of individual congressional candidates is a principal reason for the departure of American practice from an idealized conception of party government. On the surface the legislative elections occurring in the middle of the President's term appear to be dominated by two national parties asking public support for their alternative programs. Certainly the electorate whose votes they seek responds to individual legislative candidates overwhelmingly on the basis of their party labels. Despite our kaleidoscopic electoral laws, the candidate's party is the one piece of information every voter is guaranteed. For many, it is the only information they ever get.

However, the legislative events that follow these elections diverge widely from the responsible-party model. The candidates who have presented themselves to the country under two party symbols immediately break ranks. The legislative parties speak not as two voices but as a cacophony of blocs and individuals fulfilling their own definitions of the public good. Party cohesion by no means vanishes, but it is deeply eroded by the pressures external to party to which the Congressman is subject.

The public's information about the legislative record of the parties and of Members of Congress goes far toward reconciling these seemingly contradictory facts. In the congressional election, to be sure, the country votes overwhelmingly for party symbols, but the symbols have limited meaning in terms of legislative policy. The eddies and cross-currents in Congress do not interrupt a flow of legislation that the public expects but fails to see. The electorate sees very little altogether of what goes on in the national legislature. Few judgments of legislative performance are associated with the parties, and much of the public is unaware even of which party has control of Congress. As a result, the absence of party discipline or legislative results is unlikely to bring down electoral sanctions on the ineffective party or the errant Congressman. What the public's response to the parties lacks in programmatic support is not made up by its response to local congressional candidates. Although perceptions of individual candidates account for most of the votes cast by partisans against their parties, these perceptions are almost untouched by information about the policy stands of the men contesting the House seat. The increment of strength that some candidates, especially incumbents, acquire by being known to their constituents is almost entirely free of policy content. Were such content present, the Congressman's solidarity with his legislative party would be no means be assured. If the local constituency possessed far greater resources of information than it has, it might use the ballot to pry the Congressman away from his party quite as well as to unite him with it. Yet the fact is that, by plying his campaigning and servicing arts over the years, the Congressman is able to develop electoral strength that is almost totally dissociated from what his party wants in Congress and what he himself has done about it. The relevance of all this to the problem of cohesion and responsibility in the legislative party can scarcely be doubted.

The description of party irresponsibility in America should not be overdrawn. The American system *has* elements of party accountability to the public, although the issues on which an accounting is given are relatively few and the accounting is more often rendered by those who hold or seek the Presidency than by the parties' congressional delegations. Especially on the broad problem of government action to secure social and economic welfare it can be argued that the parties have real differences and that these have penetrated the party images to which the electorate responds at the polls.

Nevertheless, American practice does not diverge widely from the model of party government, and the factors underlying the departure deserve close analysis. An implication of the analysis reported here is that the public's contribution to party irregularity in Congress is not so much a matter of encouraging or requiring its Representatives to deviate from their parties as it is of the public having so little information that the irregularity of Congressmen and the ineffectiveness of the congressional parties have scant impact at the polls. Many of those who have commented on the lack of party discipline in Congress have assumed that the Congressman votes against his party because he is forced to by the demands of one of several hundred constituencies of a superlatively heterogeneous nation. In some cases, the Representative may subvert the proposals of his party because his constituency demands it. But a more reasonable interpretation over a broader range of issues is that the Congressman fails to see these proposals as part of a program on which the party—and he himself—will be judged at the polls, because he knows the constituency isn't looking.

Stanley R. Freedman

The Salience of Party and Candidate in Congressional Elections: A Comparison of 1958 and 1970*

The function of political parties in a modern democracy has, for many years, been the subject of continuing controversy. Of particular importance is the role of the party in the electoral process. Some view the party as a keying mechanism, devoid of issue content, from which the voter gives continuing electoral support to candidates in much the same way as he roots for athletes of his favorite sports team. On the other hand, the party may be vital to the achievement of a link between public opinion and public policy. This idea of parties acting responsible "is understood to mean that the parties play a mediating role between the public and its government, making popular control effective by developing rival programs of government action that are presented to the electorate for its choice. The party whose program gains the greater support takes possession of the government and is held accountable to the public in later elections for its success in giving its program effect."[1] There are two assumptions which can be derived from this framework. The first, labeled party salience, is that the voter makes his choice between parties on the basis of which party's platform most closely reflects his own personal preferences. Second, an aware and knowledgeable public evaluates legislative candidates on the basis of their link to party platform. This concept is termed candidate salience.

Stokes and Miller examine these two assumptions in some detail. They conclude that the public fails on both assumptions primarily because they

---

* The data utilized in this publication were made available by the Inter-University Consortium for Political Research. The data were originally collected in the 1970 Congressional Election Study. Neither the Center for Political Studies nor the Consortium bears any responsibility for the analyses or interpretations presented here.

[1] Donald E. Stokes and Warren E. Miller, "Party Government and the Saliency of Congress," *Public Opinion Quarterly*, XXVI (Winter, 1962), p. 533.

fail to monitor and be guided by candidate and party issue positions. Their data, drawn from 1958, however, may not reflect voter behavior today. The intent of this study is to directly replicate the earlier work of Stokes and Miller, using current data.

DESIGN

As did Stokes and Miller, we used a mid-term congressional election in the hope that the coattail effects of the President would be removed, and a true assessment of the impact of the parties on the electorate could be made. The 1970 election data used in this replication is provided by the Inter-University Consortium for Political Research, The University of Michigan, and are a representative cross-section of persons living in the United States, at least 18 years of age. The unweighted cross-section sample of 1,580 is used in the analysis. Wherever possible, the variables and tables used by Stokes and Miller are exactly replicated. Exceptions to this will be noted where applicable. Party salience will be determined by examining, in the aggregate, the individual's partisan position on various issues, his perception of which of the major parties will do what he wants on these issues, his congressional vote by party, and his party identification. Candidate salience will be determined by the extent to which the public knows the congressional candidates, and partisan voting. Democratic and Republican identifiers include all those persons classifying themselves as having some degree of partisan leanings. Thus along the traditional seven point scale, strong, weak, and independent Democrats are classified as Democrats.

FINDINGS

The relationship between party ties and partisan voting is shown in Table 1. In 1958, 84 percent of all votes were cast by partisans voting for

TABLE 1
Vote for House Candidates by Party Identification in 1970
(array percents)

	Party Identification			
	Democratic	Independent	Republican	Total
Voted Democratic	44	4	6	54
Voted Republican	10	4	32	46
Total	54	8	38	100

their party, while in 1970 this figure drops to slightly more than 75 percent. The most striking difference can be found in the Democratic column, with nearly twice as many shifting in 1970 as did 12 years before. Looking at only partisan identifiers, we find that 85 percent voted for party in 1958 compared with 83 percent in 1970. Although there does appear to be more partisan vote switching in 1970 than in 1958, Stokes and Miller's overall conclusion of the high degree of association between congressional voting and partisanship remains largely unchanged.[2]

Our first assumption calls for programmatic support for the parties from their citizen supporters. In 1958 and again in 1970 there seems to be little evidence of this type of electoral support. The public's knowledge of party control of Congress remains minimal. In 1958 only 47 percent of the public knew that the Democrats controlled Congress.[3] In 1970 the figure reached 49 percent.

Of even greater importance is the relationship between deviation from partisan voting and the saliency of a party's legislative record. It could be argued that while most individuals do vote their partisan loyalties, there is a smaller group of voters who are aware of party positions, and cast their vote on the basis of their personal preferences. For them, at least, this responsible party framework would hold true. Thus one would expect to find substantial differences in awareness of party control of Congress between those who vote their party loyalty and those who deviate from it, with party control being more salient to those who deviate. This does not appear to be the case. In 1970 as in 1958, awareness among those who voted for their own party (61 percent in 1958 and 64 percent in 1970) differed little from those who deviated from it. (60 percent in 1958 and 66 percent in 1970).[4]

The 1958 assessment of the number of party identifiers who voted against their party, controlling for the perception of party control of the most effective branch of government and satisfaction with the course of domestic affairs, can not be replicated exactly for 1970. The questions on domestic affairs and the most effective branch of government were not asked. The respondent's satisfaction with his financial situation, and the perception of which party controls the House of Representatives were substituted for the two control variables. Having noted these differences, we can go on to infer from the responsible party framework that those voters satisfied with affairs and believing the opposition party in control, and those dissatisfied with affairs and believing their own party to be in control would rank as the highest defectors from their parties. Thus cells II and III should have the highest frequencies. This is not the case. In 1958 there was little difference between groups, and 1970 conforms to the same distributions and differences with one major exception.[5] The highest cell frequency and the one which deviates the most from the others is IV—those voters dissatisfied with financial affairs and perceiving the other party as controlling the House. This means that the largest proportion of dissatisfied partisan vote shifters actually voted for the party they believed to be in control, rather than the party out of power as would be expected. Needless to say this is highly inconsistent with the concept of programmatic support.

2 Stokes and Miller, p. 534.
3 Stokes and Miller, p. 536.
4 Stokes and Miller, p. 537.
5 Stokes and Miller, p. 538.

TABLE 2

Percentage of Party Identifiers in 1970 Voting Against Party
by Perception of Party Control and Satisfaction

Thought That His Own Financial Situation in the Past Year	Thought That the House Was Controlled by	
	Own Party	Other Party
Had gotten better I	II	
	17	18
	(N = 86)	(N = 91)
Had gotten worse III	IV	
	15	27
	(N = 48)	(N = 37)

Carrying the investigation of programmatic support beyond the Stokes and Miller analysis, we examined the interrelationship between partisan loyalty, partisan voting, and voter perception of party proximity to personal position on three issues. The issue areas are Vietnam, the power of the Federal government, and school integration. For each issue, over half of the voters in 1970 perceived no difference between the parties. Vietnam led the way with 59 percent seeing no party difference, followed by integration (54 percent) and government power (51 percent). Either the parties are not providing alternative policy outcomes for most of the public, or the public is incapable of recognizing alternatives when presented. In either case, this lends little credence to the idea that parties receive programmatic support from the voters.

What of those individuals who do perceive a difference between the parties? Do they base their support on party programs or party loyalty? We can indirectly answer this question by looking at those situations where perception of party proximity to personal position and partisan loyalty conflict. If when making his decision the voter tends to lean more heavily toward his perception of a party's issue position than to partisan loyalty, then we would have reason for believing in the existence of programmatic support.

Table 3 depicts the above mentioned relationship. We are looking at party identifiers who perceive differences between parties, by partisan vote in 1970. It is clear that in most instances there is agreement between party's position, voters issue position, and partisan choice. Clearly, the greatest proportion of voters are those whose party's and personal issue positions and vote all agree. Unfortunately this does not tell us how many of these individuals are casting issue oriented rather than party oriented votes. A more instructive portion of the table depicts those individuals whose own position and party's position is in disagreement. In every instance, at least twice as many voters still vote for their own party than switch. The responsible party framework implies that just the opposite will take place.

The conclusion to be drawn from this analysis is clear. In 1970, just as in 1958, there appears to be little correspondence between a party's legislative record and vote choice for those individuals who disagreed

TABLE 3

Percent Agreeing/Disagreeing with Their Own Party's Stand
on Three Issues, by Vote for Own/Other Party in 1970
(array percentages)

Vietnam	Correspondence of Own Position to Party's Position	
	Agreement	Disagreement
Voted for own party 80		6
Voted for other party 12		3
Government Power		
Voted for own party 80		4
Voted for other party 14		2
Integration		
Voted for own party 72		10
Voted for other party 14		4

with their party. This lack of programmatic support would indicate a low
saliency of the parties' legislative records.

The saliency of congressional candidates is of greater importance in
accounting for partisan deviation than is the party's legislative record,
although the actual saliency of candidates is rather low. In 1970 when
the respondents were asked if they could remember the names of their
congressional candidates, only 43 percent claimed that they could. Of
these, 29 percent incorrectly named the candidates. Table 4 depicts the
percentage voting for their own party's or other party's candidate for the
House, by saliency of candidates. An individual was said to be aware of
a candidate if he correctly named him, not if he named his party. The
candidate's party was then determined, and the "own/other" correspondence was made with the respondent's partisan identification. In both
1958 and 1970, as the knowledge of the other party's candidate increased,
so did the tendency to vote for him. But, while the general trend is the
same in 1970 as it was in 1958, there are two interesting differences. First,
as noted in the relationship of party identification with partisan voting,
there is more overall partisan vote shift in 1970 than in 1958. Secondly,
in 1970 a majority of partisans abandoned their party when their knowl-

TABLE 4

Percentage Voting for Own Party and Other Party Candidate
for House, by Saliency of Candidates in Contested
Races, in 1970

Voted for Candidate	Both Candidates (N = 150)	Own Party Candidate Only (N = 128)	Other Party Candidate Only (N = 60)	Neither Candidate (N = 228)
Of own party	75	99	43	84
Of other party	25	1	57	17
Total	100	100	100	101

edge was limited to only the other party's candidate. In 1958 the majority of voters in this category still held fast to their traditional party loyalty.

CONCLUSION

Partisan defection does not appear to be associated with awareness of party control or a combination of party control and satisfaction with domestic affairs. Thus, no changes between 1958 and 1970 are evident. In addition there appeared to be little programmatic support for the parties even among the less than half of the voters who did perceive differences. Whether this is a result of faulty perceptions or lack of real differences, it still leads to the same conclusion, a lack of programmatic ' support for parties.

These findings run contrary to some of the current work being done on issue voting. Gerald Pomper, who examines the impact of issues over time, contends that there has been a marked increase in voter consciousness of issues in the period from 1956 to 1968.[6] He further argues that the 1964 campaign may have marked a "(c)larification and realignment of the parties' policy positions . . . (which leads to) the possible development of a 'responsible two-party system' in the United States."[7] The data presented here do not support Pomper's conclusion. One possible explanation for the discrepancy may be found in the fact that Pomper deals with presidential elections where candidate saliency is generally higher than in congressional races, and the impact of a candidate's image may confound any measure of issue voting. Coupled with this, we have seen that as knowledge of the opposition candidate increases, the rate of partisan defection increases. This phenomenon is stronger in 1970 than in 1958, to the point where exclusive awareness of the opposition candidate finds a majority shift away from party. Thus what we may be witnessing is an increase in the impact of candidate image on partisan choice, rather than the rise of a responsible party framework with its accompanying rise in issue voting. Indeed, the study of the 1972 presidential election finds that candidate image has a greater impact on vote choice than does issue or party identification.[8]

---

[6] Gerald M. Pomper, "From Confusion to Clarity: Issues and American Voters, 1956–1958," *American Political Science Review*, LXVI (June, 1972), pp. 416–20.

[7] Pomper, p. 426.

[8] Arthur H. Miller et al.: "A Majority Party in Disarray: Policy Polarization in the 1972 Election" (A Paper presented at the Annual Meeting of the American Political Science Association, New Orleans, Louisiana, September 1973), p. 67.

Gerald M. Pomper

From Confusion to Clarity: Issues and American Voters, 1956–1968*

Students of politics, from Plato to Marcuse, have frequently sneered at the inability of the "masses" to discern political reality. Whether citizens are misled by the shadows on the wall of the cave or by the shadows of the television tube, they are deemed to be fundamentally unequipped consciously to control political elites and rationally to direct public policy.

In contemporary times, such conclusions have been unintentionally strengthened by selected and often distorted findings of empirical voting research. In broad terms, political scientists have found voters to have limited interest in politics, to be strongly attached to their traditional parties and social groups, and to lack ideological coherence in their views of political issues.[1] Of particular concern here is the electorate's perception of issues, of coherent ideologies, and of the links between issue pref-

* Reprinted from the *American Political Science Review*, vol. 66 (1972), pp. 415–28. Copyright 1970, The American Political Science Association.

Mr. Thomas O'Donnell deserves many thanks for his work in arranging and computing the data on which this paper is based. I also appreciate the many suggestions of my colleagues at Rutgers University particularly Benjamin Barber, W. Carey McWilliams, Stephen Salmore, and Gordon Schochet, and the comments of John Kessel and Rick Piltz.

[1] The most important past works are, chronologically: Paul Lazarsfeld, Bernard Berelson, and Helen Gaudet, *The People's Choice*, 2nd ed. (New York: Columbia University Press, 1948); Bernard Berelson, Paul Lazarsfeld and William McPhee, *Voting* (Chicago: University of Chicago Press, 1954); Angus Campbell, Gerald Gurin and Warren Miller, *The Voter Decides* (Evanston: Row, Peterson, 1954); Eugene Burdick and Arthur Brodbeck, eds., *American Voting Behavior* (New York: The Free Press, 1959); Campbell, Philip Converse, Warren Miller, and Donald Stokes, *The American Voter* (New York: Wiley, 1960), Ithiel de Sola Pool, Robert Abelson and Samuel Popkin, *Candidates, Issues and Strategies* (Cambridge: M.I.T. Press, 1964); Philip Converse, "The Nature of Belief Systems in Mass Publics," in David Apter, ed. *Ideology and Discontent* (New York: The Free Press, 1964); and Campbell, Converse, Miller and Stokes, *Elections and the Political Order* (New York: Wiley, 1966). Important recent works will be cited below.

132

erences and partisan preferences. Much voting research has indicated that these perceptions are cloudy. Large proportions of voters have "no opinion" or "don't know" their opinion on specific policy issues.[2] Only 12 per cent of the citizenry has been found to hold an ideological view of the parties.[3] The links between issue preferences and party choice are weak. Party identification was found in *The American Voter* to have little relation to general ideology,[4] and McClosky, dealing with the same period, found "that substantial differences of opinion exist among the electorate on only five of the 24 issues" he examined.[5] The Michigan volume indicated that there was little belief among the electorate that the parties differed on particular issues, and little agreement on the direction of whatever differences were perceived.[6] Although the findings were carefully qualified, their general thrust justified the conclusion: "The electoral decision gives great freedom to those who must frame the policies of government. If the election returns offer little guidance on specific policies, neither do they generate pressures that restrict the scope of President and Congress in developing public policy."[7]

Reaction to these conclusions has varied. Some publicists or would-be "hidden persuaders" have selectively drawn from the voting studies to compose a picture of an irrational voter, easily manipulated by possessors of this arcane knowledge. Thus, a widely quoted book on "the New Politics" is taken seriously when it warns, "These new managers . . . can play upon the voters like virtuosos. They can push a pedal here, strike a chord there, and presumably, they can get precisely the response they seek."[8] To Bernard Berelson, the voting findings offered the occasion to develop a new theory of democracy, in which stability depended on the limited involvement of the population.[9]

V. O. Key saw the danger that the findings of voting research could be misused to convert popular democracy into a system of elitist manipulation, in which, "fed a steady diet of buncombe, the people may come to expect and to respond with highest predictability to buncombe."[10] In his last work, he sought to revive the notion that issue and voting preferences are closely related. While he did demonstrate a certain consistency in the electorate's choices, he could not prove a causal connection. Key's work,

---

[2] V. O. Key, Jr., *Public Opinion and American Democracy* (New York: Knopf, 1961), Chap. 4; Campbell et al., *The American Voter*, p. 174.

[3] Campbell et al., *The American Voter*, p. 249.

[4] Campbell et al., *The American Voter*, chap. 9.

[5] Herbert McClosky, Paul J. Hoffman, and Rosemary O'Hara, "Issue Conflict and Consensus among Party Leaders and Followers," *American Political Science Review*, 54 (June, 1960), p. 419. Among party leaders, by contrast, differences existed on 23 of 24 issues.

[6] Campbell et al., *The American Voter*, pp. 182–84.

[7] Campbell et al., *The American Voter*, p. 544.

[8] James M. Perry, *The New Politics* (New York: Clarkson Potter, 1968), p. 213.

[9] Berelson, Chap. 14.

[10] V. O. Key, Jr., *The Responsible Electorate* (Cambridge: Harvard University Press, 1966), p. 7.

along with Arthur Goldberg's,[11] however, did bring a renewed emphasis on the analysis of policy preferences to electoral studies.

In the past few years, this renewed emphasis has been evident in a number of independent reappraisals of *The American Voter's* finding of ideological unawareness among the electorate. One set of authors argues that mass ideological awareness has always been present to a greater degree than found by Campbell, Converse, Miller and Stokes, but that appropriate methods have not been employed to observe this awareness. Thus, focusing on local concerns, Luttbeg found considerable "constraint" or coherence, in mass attitudes.[12] Similarly, using a series of prepared statements, Brown found no difference in ideological awareness between political articulates and inarticulates.[13] Most notable is the work of Lane, who was able to discern a developed ideology among New Haven workers through lengthy interviews.[14] These strands suggest that previous studies demonstrated not the absence of ideology, but the absence of the ability to articulate hidden ideology.[15]

Another criticism is that the findings of *The American Voter* are time-bound. They may show a low degree of ideology among voters in 1956, but only because the 1956 election did not stimulate ideological feelings. Replicating the Michigan study for the contrasting 1964 election, in which ideology was emphasized, Field and Anderson found a substantial increase in ideological awareness. In the Goldwater-Johnson context, a third of the respondents are classified as ideological, more than double the proportion of 1956 voters, and nearly three times the proportion of the total sample in the earlier study.[16]

The recent work of Pierce combines these two revisions. Using three measures of ideological awareness derived from Survey Research Center materials, instead of only one, Pierce also tested the change in awareness over time. A greater proportion of the sample was classified as ideological under the three-pronged analysis, and the proportion was found to have

---

[11] Arthur Goldberg, "Discerning a Causal Pattern among Data on Voting Behavior," *American Political Science Review*, 60 (December, 1966), 913–922; "Social Determinism and Rationality as Bases of Party Identification," *American Political Science Review*, 63 (March, 1969), 5–25.

[12] Norman Luttbeg, "The Structure of Beliefs among Leaders and the Public," *Public Opinion Quarterly*, 32 (Fall, 1968), 398–409.

[13] Steven R. Brown, "Consistency and the Persistence of Ideology," *Public Opinion Quarterly*, 34 (Spring, 1970), 60–68.

[14] Robert Lane, *Political Ideology* (New York: The Free Press, 1960).

[15] See John Plamenatz, "Electoral Studies and Democratic Theory: I. A British View," *Political Studies*, 6 (February, 1958), 9.
A choice is reasonable, not because the chooser, when challenged, can give a satisfactory explanation of why he made it but because, if he could give an explanation, it would be satisfactory. The reasoning that lies behind the choice is often made in private language which the chooser never learns to translate into words intelligible to others because there is ordinarily no need for him to do so.

[16] J. O. Field and R. E. Anderson, "Ideology in the Public's Conceptualization of the 1964 Election," *Public Opinion Quarterly*, 33 (Fall, 1969), 380–98. While the coding in this research differs somewhat from that of *The American Voter*, the changes were essentially those made necessary by new procedures of the Survey Research Center.

increased considerably from 1956 through 1960 to 1964.[17] These recent findings suggest an increased awareness of politics among American voters. The analysis below provides further evidence to support this conclusion.

CHANGING PERCEPTIONS OF PARTIES AND POLICIES

The research presented here does not deal with general ideology, but with voter opinions and perceptions on the six precise policy questions which have been asked consistently of the national Survey Research Center sample in each quadrennial study since 1956. I will analyze the relationship between issue preferences and three partisan variables: party identification, the awareness of differences between the parties on these six issues, and the consensus among the electorate on the positions of the parties on these issues. In each of the three instances, we will find an increase in voter consciousness during the 1956–1968 period.

The six policy issues are: federal aid to education, government provision of medical care, government guarantee of full employment, federal enforcement of fair employment and fair housing, federal enforcement of school integration, and foreign aid. Although the questions are not worded identically in the four surveys, they are sufficiently close to be highly comparable. Moreover, we are not concerned with the trend of opinion itself, but rather with comparisons of the structure of opinion in each of the election years, so that identical wording is not critical.[18]

---

[17] John G. Pierce, "Party Identification and the Changing Role of Ideology in American Politics," *Midwest Journal of Political Science*, 14 (February, 1970), 25–42. Confirming evidence is found in the recent work of David E. RePass, "Issue Salience and Party Choice," *American Political Science Review*, 65 (June, 1971), 389–400. Using responses to open-ended questions, RePass finds considerable mass concern for issues, an increase in issue awareness from 1960 to 1964, a close relationship between issue position and partisanship, and a significant partial correlation of .23 in 1964 between issue partisanship and vote, controlling for candidate image and party identification.

[18] The differences in wording consisted largely of changes in form. In 1956 and 1960, the questions were asked as statements with which the respondent could agree or disagree (and also indicate the intensity of his opinion), e.g., "If cities and towns around the country need help to build more schools, the government in Washington ought to give them the money they need." In 1964 and 1968, the respondent was offered a choice between two policies, each of which was advocated by "some people," such as—"the government in Washington should help towns and cities provide education," or "this should be handled by the states and local communities." There are two differences in wording of possible substance. In 1956 and 1960, the question dealing with full employment asks whether or not "the government in Washington ought to see to it that everybody who wants to work has a job and a good standard of living," while the later alternative does not include "who wants to work." In the earlier surveys, the question on racial equality asks whether, "If Negroes are not getting fair treatment in jobs and housing, the government should see to it that they do," while in later years the question is more narrowly presented as dealing with jobs alone. I believe the basic thrust of these questions is not affected by these changes. The questions used are, by deck and column numbers, in 1956: 3/12, 3/18, 3/21, 3/24, 3/33, 3/54; in 1960: 4/59, 4/67, 4/55, 4/63, 4/72, 4/61; in 1964: 4/45, 4/56, 4/61, 5/11, 5/14, 4/67; in 1968: 4/54, 4/58, 4/60, 4/74, 4/76, 5/29. The surveys of 1948 and 1952 could not be used because questions were insufficiently comparable.

In Table 1, positions on these issues are presented along a five-point scale of party identification. The statistic reported is the percentage taking the "liberal" position (i.e., in favor of federal government action). For 1956, the data clearly support the contention of *The American Voter* that issue preferences were essentially unrelated to party identification. A linear relationship between the two variables existed only on the issue of medical care. The situation changed substantially, however, over the next twelve years. By 1968, a linear relationship existed essentially on all issues but foreign aid. The change was not gradual, but became suddenly apparent in the election of 1964. When John Kennedy was elected President, the relationship of opinion and party identification was hardly different from that of the Eisenhower period. By 1964, however, linear relationships were evident on four of the six issues, and they began to appear on the other two as well.

The same pattern is evident in the increasing spread between the extremes. Strong Democrats and Strong Republicans were already distinct on the issue of medical care in 1956, but the difference almost doubled in 1964 and remained considerably widened in 1968. The same pattern is evident on the other issues as well. Party differences became quite high by 1964 and then decreased slightly (on job guarantees, fair employment, and foreign aid) or increased slightly (on aid to education and school integration) four years later.

The increased policy distinctiveness of partisans is summarized by the increases in the ordinal correlation (*gamma*) included in the last row of Table 1. Policy and party preferences became far more congruent in 1964, and the correlation was very similar in 1968. The only major exception is the issue of school integration. For the first three elections in this period, no meaningful correlation existed between party identifica-

TABLE 1

Party Identification and Policy Position, 1956, 1960, 1964 and 1968
(in percentages supporting "liberal" position)

Party Identification	Aid to Education				Medical Care				Job Guarantee			
	'56	'60	'64	'68	'56	'60	'64	'68	'56	'60	'64	'68
Strong Democrat ..	80.0	66.8	51.0	53.6	74.2	74.5	78.2	81.3	75.6	71.2	52.6	53.1
Weak Democrat ...	78.1	59.0	44.1	38.3	67.3	60.2	65.2	72.1	64.0	62.4	38.4	39.7
Independent	71.0	53.2	39.3	32.9	55.8	56.7	57.2	55.3	55.0	56.6	31.0	27.0
Weak Republican ..	68.7	39.1	21.5	22.5	51.4	47.5	43.5	39.3	59.5	43.9	25.9	24.9
Strong Republican .	67.7	44.5	15.5	12.0	45.9	54.2	23.6	42.7	51.5	52.7	16.1	25.4
Gamma	.15	.20	.34	.36	.24	.18	.45	.41	.19	.16	.31	.25

Party Identification	Fair Employment				School Integration				Foreign Aid			
	'56	'60	'64	'68	'56	'60	'64	'68	'56	'60	'64	'68
Strong Democrat ..	73.3	63.0	56.3	61.9	38.7	39.8	53.7	58.9	49.5	51.4	64.7	51.3
Weak Democrat ...	71.3	63.1	42.9	43.5	44.4	37.5	43.2	44.6	55.4	48.8	59.2	45.8
Independent	66.6	65.4	50.3	37.7	48.8	47.1	49.0	37.3	49.9	53.2	57.5	42.7
Weak Republican ..	70.8	62.7	36.3	37.8	49.3	43.0	50.5	37.4	48.2	54.0	56.6	47.0
Strong Republican .	66.8	65.9	20.6	31.3	38.8	41.5	34.8	31.5	51.4	61.5	49.7	41.8
Gamma	.04	−.02	.22	.24	.04	−.01	.08	.43	.01	−.03	.08	.04

tion and support of federal action on the issue (*gammas* = .04, −.01, .08). But by 1968, there was a considerable relationship, and the *gamma* statistic (.43) is higher than in any other instance. On five of the six issues—all but foreign aid—party identification meant something by 1968 other than a traditional reaffirmation: it was now related to the policy preferences of the voter.

TABLE 2

Perceptions of Parties on Policy Issues, by Party Identification
(percentages of those with opinions perceiving party differences)

| | Existence of Party Differences | | | | | | | | | | | |
| | Aid to Education | | | | Medical Care | | | | Job Guarantee | | | |
Group	'56	'60	'64	'68	'56	'60	'64	'68	'56	'60	'64	'68
Strong Democrat ..	58.1	62.8	73.8	75.7	63.2	68.6	86.4	85.8	73.0	74.5	80.3	78.1
Weak Democrat ...	44.2	53.2	60.9	53.0	48.9	59.0	77.2	71.2	54.2	66.3	69.3	65.4
Independent	43.4	52.3	53.5	48.0	41.2	45.3	77.4	62.3	36.4	57.6	55.2	54.2
Weak Republican ..	48.0	41.8	58.9	53.3	50.0	68.6	75.3	65.8	50.3	50.5	61.3	64.1
Strong Republican .	59.0	63.0	78.4	73.3	64.9	66.7	87.7	75.9	63.7	42.5	76.7	79.1
Total Sample	52	55	66	59	54	58	82	71	55	64	70	63

| | Fair Employment | | | | School Integration | | | | Foreign Aid | | | |
Group	'56	'60	'64	'68	'56	'60	'64	'68	'56	'60	'64	'68
Strong Democrat ..	50.0	52.5	77.5	78.5	55.6	50.6	70.0	75.9	46.5	44.7	61.5	64.7
Weak Democrat ...	46.9	38.7	70.1	64.9	55.6	34.9	63.7	62.5	40.4	37.5	52.7	43.8
Independent	38.5	38.7	58.8	55.0	42.3	30.8	59.0	51.1	33.6	32.7	50.8	39.3
Weak Republican ..	46.0	44.3	53.2	47.7	50.0	36.4	52.1	53.1	50.0	32.0	50.3	42.8
Strong Republican .	52.3	50.0	75.0	60.5	57.5	39.2	66.2	60.5	63.9	47.4	61.8	48.0
Total Sample	47	44	69	62	51	36	64	60	49	39	56	46

A second change is evident in the awareness of party differences on these six policy questions. In 1956, the Survey Research Center found little awareness of differences. It subjected its respondents to a series of questions on each policy question. It eliminated those who had no interest in, or opinion on, an issue, as well as those who, holding an opinion on the issue, could not decide if "the government is going too far, doing less than it should, or what?" This latter question typically eliminated more respondents than the query on the issue itself. Those who were left after the multiple screening were then asked whether there was a difference between the parties. This remaining sample was presumably a relatively knowledgeable group, but in 1956 even *they* found rather little distinction between the parties on most issues.[19] In later surveys, the

---

[19] The answers of 1956 respondents can be found in Table 8–3 of Campbell et al., *The American Voter*, p. 182. It might be argued that 1956 voters were far more issue-conscious than the data reveal, but that they were thinking about different issues than those raised by the parties or the survey. This argument seems hardly plausible, since it would require a degree of ideological originality for which there is no evidence among any mass public.

question on the government's program was eliminated. Therefore, the remaining sample asked to differentiate the parties was larger, and presumably less informed. Nevertheless, they perceived more of a difference between the parties. This changing awareness is seen in Table 2. Over time, the parties have come to be seen as more different on questions of federal government power. Again, the issue of foreign aid is exceptional. The critical effect of the 1964 election is evident once more, as the proportions seeing party differences changed most dramatically in the Goldwater-Johnson contest. In 1968, there was a regression downward toward lessened perceptions of party splits, although it was not a full regression. Only on the distinct issue of foreign aid was the perception of party difference in 1968 at or below the level of the Eisenhower period. For the other issues, during the decade of the 1960s, a significant and apparently enduring political lesson was learned about the existence of party differences. The lesson was particularly well learned by the stronger partisans. On virtually all issues and in all elections, the strong partisans were more likely to see party differences than were weak partisans, who in turn were more likely to see differences than independents. These results clearly accord with the concept and significance of party identification.

A more important finding is involved in the third change, relating to the ideological identity of the parties. In 1956, even among the sample remaining after various filterings, there was relatively little consensus on the position of the parties. The greatest consensus existed on another question dealing with ownership of electric power and housing. On this item, three-fourths of those who saw a party difference also agreed that the Republicans were more favorable to private ownership of these industries.[20] The identification of the parties' ideological positions was lower on the six issues we are considering. (The item on power and housing was not used in later surveys, so it cannot be analyzed here.)

By 1968, as seen in Table 3, each of the two parties seemed to have a much clearer identity. The proportion seeing the Democrats as the more liberal or activist party had risen on every question, even on foreign aid. It is particularly significant that in almost all cases the perceptions of the parties showed a consensus greater than that which existed on the exceptional issue of ownership of industry in the Eisenhower period. By 1968, in other words, to judge by six important items, the majority of the electorate had become more aware of party differences and had come to agree that the Democratic party was the liberal party.[21]

---

[20] Campbell et al., *The American Voter*, p. 182.

[21] The perceptions of party are asked in different ways in the four surveys, so the data must be handled differently. In 1956, respondents were asked which party "is closer to what you want." To locate those who believe the Democrats are liberal on federal aid to education, for example, one must combine those who favor the policy, and think the Democrats are closer to their own position, with those who oppose the policy, and think the Republicans are closer. In 1960, 1964 and 1968, the question was asked in a straightforward manner, which party is likely to favor federal aid to education. These data are located, in 1956: two columns to the right of the policy question; in 1960: in decks and columns 4/60, 4/70, 4/56, 4/64, 4/75, 4/62; in 1964: 4/45, 4/60, 4/63, 5/13, 5/18, 4/69; in 1968: immediately after the policy question, except for party stands on school integration, 4/79.

TABLE 3

Consensus on Positions of Parties on Policy Issues, by Party Identification
(percentage of those perceiving difference selecting democrats as liberal)

Group	Consensus on Party Positions											
	Aid to Education				Medical Care				Job Guarantee			
	'56	'60	'64	'68	'56	'60	'64	'68	'56	'60	'64	'68
Strong Democrat ..	90.5	95.2	96.5	94.1	93.9	95.8	98.2	98.8	85.5	98.8	98.8	97.0
Weak Democrat ...	86.5	90.5	93.6	82.6	84.6	90.4	95.8	88.7	71.8	93.3	93.9	88.5
Independent	66.3	74.6	83.8	64.3	76.4	87.7	93.5	82.7	61.9	82.3	89.3	71.4
Weak Republican ..	37.2	60.9	55.8	58.7	64.3	52.2	77.6	85.0	60.0	67.3	72.5	69.4
Strong Republican .	31.6	47.9	55.0	41.2	57.8	51.3	79.8	63.6	47.0	32.3	63.8	53.9
Total Sample	67	76	81	73	77	81	92	87	69	80	88	80

Group	Fair Employment				School Integration				Foreign Aid			
	'56	'60	'64	'68	'56	'60	'64	'68	'56	'60	'64	'68
Strong Democrat ..	64.6	83.5	96.9	97.3	39.1	34.7	96.2	95.3	57.1	80.9	98.1	93.0
Weak Democrat ...	63.6	65.5	93.9	88.3	51.5	42.5	90.3	87.1	53.0	60.2	94.2	89.2
Independent	49.4	53.4	89.5	75.6	45.8	46.4	91.8	83.4	54.5	46.8	88.1	83.1
Weak Republican ..	23.6	18.3	81.0	70.2	45.1	49.3	83.9	75.4	46.2	13.0	67.8	81.5
Strong Republican .	6.0	17.2	67.6	56.4	59.4	48.5	71.3	69.5	29.3	21.4	70.8	61.6
Total Sample	48	52	89	83	48	44	89	86	43	49	88	85

The change in perceptions of the parties' positions is not affected by controls for party identification. In all partisan groups, the Democrats were increasingly recognized as the liberal party on each of the six issues. Democrats were most likely to make this judgment, but by 1964 a majority even of Strong Republicans recognized the liberal credentials of the opposition. In 1956, by contrast, the Strong Republicans conceded this "honor" to the Democrats on only two issues.

The acceptance of the liberalism of the Democrats is most evident in the 1964 survey, conducted during the contest of Goldwater and Johnson. It was not solely related to that election, however, for important changes in perceptions of party position on the economic issues of aid to education, medical care, and job guarantees can be located as early as the 1960 campaign. The identification of the Democratic party as the liberal faction largely persisted through the 1968 election as well, although there was some lessening of perceived party positions, most notably on the issue of federal aid to education.

The most striking change occurred on racial issues. In 1956, there was no consensus on the parties' stands on the issues of school integration and fair employment. Differences between the parties were less likely to be seen, and Republicans were as likely as Democrats to be perceived as favoring federal action on civil rights. A startling reversal occurred in 1964: all partisan groups recognized the existence of a difference on this issue, and all were convinced that the Democrats stood more for government programs on behalf of blacks. Even Strong Republicans conceded the point they argued in the Eisenhower years. The identification of the

Democrats with civil rights was slightly attenuated in 1968, but it still was a clearer perception than existed on any other issue.

SOURCES OF CHANGE

What accounts for these shifts? The increasing correspondence of party identification with policy preferences is probably related to the new perceptions of the parties as holding relatively distinctive and identifiable positions on these issues. Generational change is one possible explanation of these new perceptions. Younger, more ideologically attuned voters may have replaced older and less sensitive electors. To test this possibility, age is controlled in Table 4. Respondents in the age groupings used in the 1956 survey are compared to cohorts four, eight, and twelve years older in 1960, 1964, and 1968, respectively. If generational replacement is the main reason for the changed perceptions, the greatest differences would be seen between the upper-right and lower-left seg-

TABLE 4

Perceptions of Parties on Policy Issues, by Age
(percentages of those with opinions perceiving party differences)

Existence of Party Differences

Group		Aid to Education				Medical Care			
Age in '56	Age in '68	'56	'60	'64	'68	'56	'60	'64	'68
————	Under 27	—	—	60.0	52.2	—	—	84.7	64.6
Under 25	27–36	49.1	67.2	58.4	56.7	57.8	74.0	83.9	68.7
25–34	37–46	49.1	45.7	65.3	59.8	49.0	51.4	82.5	77.8
35–44	47–56	45.2	53.1	72.7	62.9	50.2	66.1	81.0	68.6
45–54	57–66	53.3	58.0	65.9	59.6	54.0	52.0	76.6	71.4
55–64	Over 66	52.2	58.8	55.2	56.5	59.0	58.0	78.1	74.9
65 and over	————	54.0	59.3	—	—	53.5	52.6	—	—

Group		Job Guarantee				Fair Employment			
Age in '56	Age in '68	'56	'60	'64	'68	'56	'60	'64	'68
————	Under 27	—	—	65.8	65.8	—	—	78.1	60.5
Under 25	27–36	46.6	68.7	66.0	61.5	50.7	57.3	69.9	64.3
25–34	37–46	55.3	66.3	73.0	70.8	51.5	37.8	68.1	63.3
35–44	47–56	49.5	66.0	68.2	74.6	44.1	39.0	66.3	65.0
45–54	57–66	58.0	62.3	71.8	62.2	50.2	48.5	66.8	54.0
55–64	Over 66	63.9	59.0	66.2	70.3	39.1	42.6	65.6	58.2
65 and over	————	58.8	54.5	—	—	52.7	46.7	—	—

Group		School Integration				Foreign Aid			
Age in '56	Age in '68	'56	'60	'64	'68	'56	'60	'64	'68
————	Under 27	—	—	75.6	56.2	—	—	54.5	42.2
Under 25	27–36	58.2	41.1	67.1	59.6	42.5	42.3	55.1	39.2
25–34	37–46	52.7	38.4	61.6	65.4	48.8	38.9	60.6	49.3
35–44	47–56	50.2	46.6	64.9	57.7	40.4	37.4	55.0	47.5
45–54	57–66	49.3	40.6	61.9	61.3	44.5	37.8	55.6	47.2
55–64	Over 66	53.1	28.5	54.7	56.9	44.9	33.0	54.8	50.6
65 and over	————	50.0	34.4	—	—	47.2	46.6	—	—

ments of each set of percentages. If political aging is not an explanation, changes would be most evident among cohort groups.[22] The data show that both conclusions are valid to some extent but that generational turnover is not an adequate explanation in itself. In virtually all comparisons, the new generation (below age 23 in 1964 or below age 27 in 1968) was more aware of party differences and more perceptive of Democratic liberalism than those it replaced (those 65 or older in 1956, or 69 or older in 1960, who were too depleted by 1964 and 1968 to be included). These differences are not as large, however, as are the changes of matched cohorts. Some political learning occurred in all age groups. Thus, in 1956 and 1960, most age groups did not see a party difference on racial issues, and all of them tended to identify the Republicans as more liberal. Particularly in 1964 and even in 1968, all age groups

TABLE 4—(continued)
(percentages of those perceiving differences selecting Democrats as liberal)

Consensus on Party Positions

Group		Aid to Education				Medical Care			
Age in '56	Age in '68	'56	'60	'64	'68	'56	'60	'64	'68
————	Under 27	—	—	89.9	65.6	—	—	96.7	86.0
Under 25	27–36	51.8	77.9	86.2	72.3	73.8	82.4	92.2	88.6
25–34	37–46	66.0	73.5	84.8	79.4	78.9	89.4	94.1	91.5
35–44	47–56	75.8	74.6	77.4	67.0	81.6	80.0	87.5	87.6
45–54	57–66	69.7	90.2	86.5	73.1	80.2	82.7	95.5	83.3
55–64	Over 66	67.1	72.6	74.0	73.1	72.0	71.3	90.6	80.8
65 and over	————	51.8	60.8	—	—	64.5	75.9	—	—

Group		Job Guarantee				Fair Employment			
Age in '56	Age in '68	'56	'60	'64	'68	'56	'60	'64	'68
————	Under 27	—	—	92.0	79.0	—	—	93.6	83.7
Under 25	27–36	76.0	82.6	92.7	78.3	54.7	55.4	93.0	83.0
25–34	37–46	65.0	82.4	88.5	85.9	43.6	52.5	88.3	83.5
35–44	47–56	72.2	81.6	85.4	66.7	42.7	45.3	85.8	84.7
45–54	57–66	65.8	85.2	89.0	83.9	53.0	63.1	91.5	82.0
55–64	Over 66	62.5	72.1	90.8	74.5	48.0	42.0	89.3	75.6
65 and over	————	71.4	64.9	—	—	47.7	56.2	—	—

Group		School Integration				Foreign Aid			
Age in '56	Age in '68	'56	'60	'64	'68	'56	'60	'64	'68
————	Under 27	—	—	91.2	85.5	—	—	87.5	85.2
Under 25	27–36	50.0	34.9	92.6	84.5	34.8	50.0	90.6	85.8
25–34	37–46	42.6	44.6	92.0	90.0	60.1	44.0	88.1	87.7
35–44	47–56	46.8	40.0	85.8	85.3	40.6	46.0	86.5	85.9
45–54	57–66	51.0	50.0	90.0	84.6	48.1	60.1	88.0	83.2
55–64	Over 66	57.2	35.2	86.9	79.6	47.3	50.0	83.7	80.5
65 and over	————	49.0	52.3	—	—	38.6	46.0	—	—

[22] On the method of cohort analysis, see Neal E. Cutler, "Generation, Maturation and Party Affiliation: A Cohort Analysis," Public Opinion Quarterly, 33 (Winter, 1969–70), 583–92.

came to perceive a party difference, and there was intergenerational agreement on the Democratic party's greater support of fair employment and school integration.

The data give some indication of greater growth in awareness among older, rather than younger voters. The cohort aged 25–34 in 1956 (37 to 46 in 1968) appears to have become particularly aware of Democratic liberalism in 1964 and to have held to its new perceptions in 1968. Speculating on the source of this change, we could note that this group came of age politically just after the realignment of the New Deal. Hence this group may not have been immediately affected by the political events of

TABLE 5-A

Perceptions of Parties on Policy Issues, by Education
(percentages of those with opinions perceiving party differences)

| | Existence of Party Differences | | | | | | | | | | | |
| | Aid to Education | | | | Medical Care | | | | Job Guarantee | | | |
Group	'56	'60	'64	'68	'56	'60	'64	'68	'56	'60	'64	'68
Elementary school .	45.7	51.8	61.6	56.1	49.2	53.4	76.0	70.7	59.9	65.3	68.8	63.7
High school	52.2	55.4	61.6	53.0	50.0	60.0	80.6	68.0	52.3	71.2	65.5	61.4
Some college	49.0	58.2	66.9	61.7	57.0	63.8	84.3	68.9	48.1	56.4	71.2	68.1
College graduate ..	65.2	60.2	73.2	67.4	61.7	63.9	87.8	84.1	55.2	56.5	71.9	74.9

| | Fair Employment | | | | School Integration | | | | Foreign Aid | | | |
Group	'56	'60	'64	'68	'56	'60	'64	'68	'56	'60	'64	'68
Elementary school .	47.2	45.9	68.2	62.5	50.0	35.2	63.3	61.9	40.2	39.0	51.0	46.3
High school	49.1	36.3	67.7	61.2	54.1	37.3	61.3	57.1	43.1	35.5	54.8	47.5
Some college	46.5	48.3	67.5	63.1	51.7	34.4	66.7	60.2	47.1	42.3	55.7	42.2
College graduate ..	44.3	44.4	65.8	57.6	51.8	41.2	58.9	61.7	62.0	36.5	68.3	51.6

TABLE 5-B

Perceptions of Parties on Political Issues, by Education
(percentage of those perceiving differences selecting Democrats as liberal)

| | Consensus on Party Positions | | | | | | | | | | | |
| | Aid to Education | | | | Medical Care | | | | Job Guarantee | | | |
Group	'56	'60	'64	'68	'56	'60	'64	'68	'56	'60	'64	'68
Elementary school .	65.7	71.8	86.4	75.0	70.9	75.3	92.7	84.0	68.8	78.0	90.1	82.0
High school	62.3	73.9	77.6	70.3	75.5	85.0	90.3	87.0	69.9	83.6	87.2	76.2
Some college	67.5	78.9	77.4	71.6	82.9	81.1	89.4	86.4	65.0	80.0	85.6	79.2
College graduate ...	75.8	88.7	86.9	75.8	89.0	93.9	95.4	92.0	72.2	82.9	90.0	84.4

| | Fair Employment | | | | School Integration | | | | Foreign Aid | | | |
Group	'56	'60	'64	'68	'56	'60	'64	'68	'56	'60	'64	'68
Elementary school .	49.7	53.7	91.6	79.7	45.5	51.5	87.2	84.8	46.5	47.8	88.4	84.8
High school	53.0	63.8	88.5	81.3	44.5	41.7	91.2	83.3	40.6	58.2	86.0	83.5
Some college	39.2	44.0	85.3	83.6	51.0	36.7	87.0	87.7	51.0	40.5	83.6	84.3
College graduate ...	46.5	39.5	91.3	88.9	56.0	35.8	96.6	87.0	56.0	54.8	97.2	86.4

that period but may have been particularly susceptible to the effect of similar issues in 1964.

Degree of educational achievement might be an alternative explanation. The average level of schooling has increased considerably in the United States in this twelve-year period. Greater perception might result from the intellectual upgrading of the population, with less informed grade school or high school graduates being replaced by informed college alumni. Controlling for education would reveal this effect by indicating relatively little change by educational level. This control is presented in Table 5, which clearly shows that educational upgrading does not explain the shift in perceptions. Awareness has increased at all educational levels.

In fact, the disparities in perceptions among persons of varying schooling have tended to lessen, particularly in regard to identifying the Democrats as the liberal party. This effect was most marked in the 1964 campaign; in that year, on every issue, respondents with only a grade school education were clearer in their perceptions of the parties than college graduates were in 1956. The educational gap widened slightly in 1968, but the level of awareness remained substantially higher in all educational strata. In one sense, therefore, the political events of this period provided a tax-free learning substitute for the political education that might otherwise have occurred in high school and college classrooms. (The vocational implications for political science faculty members might best be left aside.)

A final control may be made for region and race, as in Table 6, since the changed perceptions noted above may have been concentrated in particular segments of the population. Such differences are evident in Table 6, although the changes are also apparent in both the North and South, and among whites as well as blacks. Southern whites particularly stand out. Their perceptions varied widely over the course of the four elections, but the net result has been relatively little change in their awareness of party differences or in their ideological identifications of the parties. They changed almost exclusively in their identification of the Democrats as the more liberal party on issues of civil rights. These changing perceptions may well be related to the growth of Republican voting in the white South.[23]

Blacks' opinions also varied widely, but the net result has been a substantially increased awareness of party differences and a clear identification of the Democrats as the liberal party. While this change is most dramatically evident on the civil rights issues, and among southern

---

[23] See: Bernard Cosman, "Republicanism in the South," *Southwestern Social Science Quarterly*, 48 (June, 1967), 13–23; Philip Converse, Warren Miller, Jerrold Rusk and Arthur Wolfe, "Continuity and Change in American Politics: Parties and Issues in the 1968 Election," *American Political Science Review*, 63 (December, 1969), esp. 1095–1101. The Wallace Campaign in 1968 did not substantially affect the perceptions of the major parties' positions on civil rights. In noting the parties' stands, a respondent could answer that there was no difference between the major parties, but Wallace did represent a distinctive position. Few respondents chose this option; those who did were included in this analysis with the "no-difference" group.

TABLE 6-A

Perceptions of Parties on Policy Issues, by Region and Race
(percentages of those with opinions perceiving party differences)

Existence of Party Differences

Group	Aid to Education				Medical Care				Job Guarantee			
	'56	'60	'64	'68	'56	'60	'64	'68	'56	'60	'64	'68
North White	48.0	57.3	61.1	58.0	51.2	53.6	81.1	71.5	52.4	63.2	66.4	65.2
North Black	66.7	80.0	71.8	72.6	61.5	57.9	83.3	79.2	75.0	79.0	78.8	77.0
South White	51.0	49.3	68.8	50.2	54.6	57.6	78.3	65.3	61.5	62.2	69.8	61.0
South Black	62.4	50.8	80.8	87.7	54.7	45.7	83.3	88.1	64.5	68.3	81.8	90.9

Group	Fair Employment				School Integration				Foreign Aid			
	'56	'60	'64	'68	'56	'60	'64	'68	'56	'60	'64	'68
North White	43.2	44.2	63.5	59.2	49.5	37.3	59.2	57.6	43.3	36.2	53.2	45.0
North Black	79.5	73.2	88.2	87.5	57.5	57.2	85.7	81.2	43.5	50.9	57.8	45.1
South White	52.7	36.4	67.4	56.1	57.0	30.6	64.3	56.0	49.7	39.1	57.9	44.9
South Black	70.0	60.0	89.3	89.9	58.5	46.0	82.2	88.1	61.8	38.1	63.3	75.0

TABLE 6-B

Perceptions of Parties on Political Issues, by Region and Race
(percentages of those perceiving differences selecting Democrats as liberal)

Consensus on Party Positions

Group	Aid to Education				Medical Care				Job Guarantee			
	'56	'60	'64	'68	'56	'60	'64	'68	'56	'60	'64	'68
North White ..	66.4	75.9	81.2	68.0	74.8	81.7	93.1	87.0	66.0	78.8	88.8	79.0
North Black ..	77.2	84.4	100.0	95.0	81.2	91.0	97.5	100.0	76.0	91.1	97.3	96.0
South White ..	63.8	80.8	74.3	70.0	81.9	79.3	83.6	79.0	67.4	82.5	81.3	72.4
South Black ..	75.0	53.3	98.4	100.0	82.3	71.4	98.7	98.2	80.0	86.1	98.6	100.0

Group	Fair Employment				School Integration				Foreign Aid			
	'56	'60	'64	'68	'56	'60	'64	'68	'56	'60	'64	'68
North White ..	47.1	78.8	88.8	81.1	54.2	48.3	91.2	84.0	45.2	52.2	89.5	84.1
North Black ..	65.7	83.7	98.0	100.0	60.8	32.1	100.0	100.0	70.0	57.1	84.6	86.9
South White ..	34.8	48.0	79.0	75.0	34.4	37.4	77.5	79.6	45.7	41.4	83.2	82.4
South Black ..	60.6	53.8	100.0	100.0	35.3	17.6	100.0	100.0	61.5	43.8	100.0	100.0

blacks, it is not confined to these issues or to the former Confederacy. Negroes of both regions also became more cognizant of differences between the parties and of Democratic liberalism on economic issues. It is interesting to note, moreover, that within each region in all years, blacks tended to be more conscious of political differences than whites. Given their perceptions of increasing differences between the parties, it is not surprising that blacks now overwhelmingly identify with and vote for the Democrats.[24]

[24] Of the 1968 SRC sample, only 3 of the 149 blacks identified themselves as Republicans, and only 3 voted for Nixon.

There is no obvious demographic cause for the changed awareness of party differences by the electorate. Neither the passing of generations, nor improved education, nor regional and racial variations provides a simple explanation. The fact remains that, during these twelve years, all segments of the population displayed considerable political learning (or misperception, depending on one's view of the "real" character of the parties). The alternative to a demographic explanation is a directly political one: the events and campaigns of the 1960s, I suggest, made politics more relevant and more dramatic to the mass electorate. In the process, party differences were developed and perceived. Democrats divided from Republicans, Democrats became more liberal, and voters became more aware.

There are many correspondences between the events of the political world and the voters' perceptions of the parties. In the 1960 campaign, John Kennedy and Richard Nixon, and the Democratic and Republican platforms, differed on federal aid to education[25]—and the voters became more likely to regard the Democrats' position on the issue as the more liberal. Medicare became a major partisan issue during the Kennedy administration, resulting in a series of partisan Congressional roll calls on the issue, and a platform conflict during the 1964 campaign. Perceiving this disagreement, the voters were much more likely in 1964 to see a difference between the parties on the issue of medical care and to identify the Democrats as more favorable to governmental action on the issue. When a Republican administration acted vigorously to promote school integration, as in Little Rock, the voters tended to believe that the G.O.P. was more favorable to this policy. This opinion was particularly common in 1956 and 1960 among Southerners and blacks. When a Democratic administration came to support new civil rights legislation, when it sent marshals and National Guardsmen to desegregate the University of Alabama and the University of Mississippi, when it reacted sympathetically to the protests of Martin Luther King in Birmingham and Selma, the voters drew the conclusion that there was a difference between the parties and identified the Democrats as more favorable to the cause of the Negroes. When the Republican party adopted a "Southern strategy" in 1968 and its candidate largely ignored the issue of civil rights, the voters continued to hold this position and clearly to distinguish the parties.[26]

The most important electoral event of this period appears to be the 1964 Presidential campaign. Senator Barry Goldwater consciously sought to clarify and widen the ideological differences between the parties. The evidence presented here indicates that he accomplished his goal, although it did not benefit the Republican party. Voters, previously unable to see differences between the parties, learned the lesson of "a choice, not an echo." They accepted the Senator's characterization of the Republicans as conservative and the Democrats as liberal, and, on the specific

---

[25] Kirk Porter and Donald Johnson, *National Party Platforms*, 3rd ed. (Urbana: University of Illinois Press, 1966), pp. 590–614.

[26] On the development of medicare, civil rights and other programs in this period, see James L. Sundquist, *Politics and Policy* (Washington: Brookings Institution, 1968).

issues involved, they preferred the liberal alternative.[27] This process of education was not confined to the insightful young, or to the formally-trained college population, or to committed White segregationists and Black integrationists. This political education was general and apparently persistent. The party characteristics which had been so clearly marked in 1964 remained relatively evident to the voters four years later. The lessons remained learned even though differences between the candidates had narrowed considerably, and although some of the previous issues, such as aid to education and medical care, had been partially resolved. Differences were not perceived as clearly in 1968 as in 1964, but they were far more apparent to the voters than in the Eisenhower years.

IMPLICATIONS OF THE DATA

The data developed in this article lead to three implications. First, the central importance of the 1964 campaign lends support to the supposition that this election was a critical election, initiating a new political era in the United States, rather than the aberrant event it appeared at the time. A critical election, such as that of the New Deal, is one in which a deep and enduring cleavage in the electorate becomes evident.[28] Characteristic of such elections is increased voter consciousness of policy questions, and the later electoral persistence of group divisions based on the policy questions raised in the critical election.[29] These hallmarks of a critical period are evident in the upsurge of mass perceptions of party differences in 1964 and the persistence of these perceptions in 1968. While the voters did not respond ideologically in the full sense of the term, they did respond to the specific issues presented to them, and they did align their partisan loyalties far closer to their policy preferences. Such readjustments occur rarely, but they are the decisive moments in American political history.

Research at the time of the 1964 election led to the conclusion the electorate did not respond primarily in ideological terms,[30] although there already were signs available that deeper forces were moving the voters.[31] Subsequent work by younger scholars, perhaps less committed

---

[27] Also see Lloyd Free and Hadley Cantril, The Political Beliefs of Americans (New Brunswick: Rutgers University Press, 1967), Chap. 2.

[28] V. O. Key, Jr., "A Theory of Critical Elections," Journal of Politics, 17 (February, 1955), pp. 3–18. The concept and its significance have been deeply researched in Walter Dean Burnham, Critical Elections and the Mainsprings of American Politics (New York: Norton, 1970).

[29] The point is elaborated well in Everett C. Ladd, American Political Parties (New York: Norton, 1970), pp. 1–10, and illustrated historically in the body of this book.

[30] See Philip Converse, Aage R. Clausen, and Warren E. Miller, "Electoral Myth and Reality: The 1964 Election," American Political Science Review, 59 (June, 1965), 330–335.

[31] See: Walter Dean Burnham, "American Voting Behavior and the 1964 Election," Midwest Journal of Political Science, 12 (February, 1968), 1–40; John Kessel,

to prevailing commonplaces, has shown the growth of ideological constraints and divergent "party images" during the turbulent decade of the 1960s.[32] Moreover, the most current controversies are tending to emphasize the ideological division between the parties. Partisan conflicts on such issues as national health insurance, federal revenue sharing, or enforcement of equal employment opportunities are likely to reinforce the popular belief that Democrats favor increased federal government action and Republicans prefer private or state governmental action.[33] Perceptions of party differences are therefore likely to be confirmed and extended.

Confirming evidence is needed to demonstrate a critical election in 1964. Such evidence would include shifts in party identification among substantial groups of voters and the emergence of new issues. The data presented here do not speak to these questions. Indeed, they deal only with issues already evident in 1956. We do find, however, increased coherence of policy positions within each party following, and new sharp cleavages associated with racial issues. These findings are congruent with those expected in a period of realignment.

Clarification and realignment of the parties' policy positions leads to a second implication, the possible development of a "responsible two-party system" in the United States. Such a system was advocated by a committee of the American Political Science Association in 1950.[34] That committee, however, expected more of voters than was possible at the time. To effectuate the system of party government advocated in the APSA *Report*, the voter must perceive a relationship between his policy preferences and his partisan choices. Furthermore, for the parties to serve as links between voter preferences and public policies, their programs must be perceived as somewhat distinct and reasonably clear. These are necessary but not sufficient conditions for developing a responsible party system in which parties put forth programs, receive popular approval of these programs, and then carry out the popular mandate.

That these conditions did not exist at the time of the APSA *Report* is indicated by our data for the 1956 election. On most issues, the voters did not relate their policy preferences to their partisan affiliations nor did they see a difference between the parties, nor did they agree on the

---

The *Goldwater Coalition* (Indianapolis: Bobbs Merrill, 1968), pp. 301–8; Gerald Pomper, *Elections in America* (New York: Dodd, Mead, 1968), Chap. 5; David Segal, "Partisan Realignment in the United States: The Lesson of the 1964 Election," *Public Opinion Quarterly*, 32 (Fall, 1968), 441–44; RePass, "Issue Salience and Party Choice," 398–400.

[32] See: David Nexon, "Hacks, Fanatics, and Responsible but Dense Voters," (Unpublished M.A. Thesis, University of Chicago, 1970); and Rick S. Piltz, "Mass support for the Political Parties: Bases for Realignment," (Ph.D. Dissertation, University of Michigan, in progress).

[33] See the roll calls listed in *Congressional Quarterly Weekly Report*, 29 (January 29, 1971), 220–22, dealing with the 91st Congress.

[34] American Political Science Association, Committee on Political Parties, "Toward a More Responsible Two-Party System," *American Political Science Review*, 44 (September, 1950), Supplement.

relative positions of the two parties. In recent years, however, the situation has changed. There is a sizeable statistical correlation now between party identification and policy preference on the particular issues studied. Voters now do see a difference between Democrats and Republicans and agree on their ideological character.

Parties can now meaningfully stand as "groups of like-minded men" offering particular stances toward public issues. Their victories in elections can now reasonably be interpreted as related to the mass choice of one set of issue positions over another. To this extent, the conditions for a responsible party system have been fulfilled.

Other necessary conditions, however, have not been met. Greater voter awareness of party differences does not in itself create a mandating election system. It would also be necessary to show that votes are actually cast *because of* issue preferences. Moreover, a responsible party system requires not only a responsible electorate to provide direction, approval, or castigation for the parties. It also requires coherent, effective, and relatively disciplined parties. In fact, both in the APSA *Report* and in the British party system which its authors cited with admiration, party government is crucially dependent on the internal discipline of the parties, even more than on the electorate.[35] There is comparatively little evidence of the development of cohesive parties in the United States.[36] Many developments in fact have tended in the opposite direction, such as the diffusion of party power to wealthy individuals, media specialists, and campaign managers; the challenge to entrenched party leaders through party primaries and the decentralizing reforms of national conventions; and the separation of national, state, and local elections. The electorate is more ready today than in the 1950s for a responsible party system, but the parties may be too weakened for the task.

The final implication of the data relates to the study of American voting behavior. Because of the excellence with which the Michigan studies have been conducted and presented, we have tended to overgeneralize the findings of such studies as *The American Voter*. We have assumed that this superb analysis of the 1950s is a study of the electorate of all time. Because voters of the Eisenhower period did not respond to the parties in ideological terms, we have often concluded that they could not respond in such terms. Yet, Key reminded us that "the voice of the people is but an echo . . . The people's verdict can be no more than a selective reflection from among the alternatives and outlooks presented to them."[37] If the parties do not emphasize issues, or do not present distinct

---

35 On the British electorate, see David Butler and Donald Stokes, *Political Change in Britain* (New York: St. Martin's Press, 1969), esp. Part IV.

36 Sundquist, however, in *Politics and Policy*, Chaps. 9 and 12, argues that Democratic party actions in the 1950s and 1960s already constituted the creation of a responsible party system. In contrast, see Donald E. Stokes and Warren E. Miller, "Party Government and the Saliency of Congress," in *Elections and the Political Order*, Chap. 11. Originally published in 1962, the latter work shows the absence of conditions for responsible parties, at least before the possibly critical election of 1964.

37 Key, *The Responsible Electorate*, 2.

and clear positions, the voters are unlikely to invent party programs. When there *are* party positions and differences, the voters can perceive them. Students of electoral behavior must be sensitive to these changing stimuli and reactions.

In observing electoral behavior and mass ideology, we particularly must beware of our own ideological biases. It is instructive to remember that *The American Voter* was written at the time of "the great American celebration," when the dominant academic ideology was that the United States had reached the "end of ideology" through a consensual agreement on twentieth-century liberalism.[38] It was therefore comforting and appropriate to find that ideology was absent among the mass public. In the absence of ideology, basic social change was difficult to imagine. The existing political system was therefore seen as stable and relatively insulated from change. Throughout the Michigan studies, the emphasis is on the inertial elements of American politics, an emphasis that, in keeping with the tone of the era, plays down the possibility and desirability of basic social change.[39]

In the last decade, after a series of political shocks, ideological conflict has been resurrected, and consensus has been severely disrupted, if not destroyed. Basic issues have been raised again, and the electorate has shown itself able to comprehend and respond to such conflicts. Furthermore, an emphasis on ideological passivity is itself seen to be ideological. Earlier findings on the electorate remind us of the dangers of overgeneralization from data derived from a limited temporal or spatial context.

More generally, we must remember to be aware of the political context of voting behavior. Perhaps the major fault of the Michigan studies has been the comparative neglect of the political environment as an independent variable. The methodology of survey research has brought an overemphasis on the individual behavior of isolated respondents. The influences upon these respondents have been studied only indirectly, through the voters' personal perceptions and actions.[40] But voters in fact are not isolated, for they are affected by their environment,[41] the mass media, the economic system, and the prevailing ideology. More attention must be devoted to these shaping influences.

---

[38] Daniel Bell, *The End of Ideology* (New York: The Free Press, 1960); Louis Hartz, *The Liberal Tradition in America* (New York: Harcourt, Brace and World, 1955).

[39] For example, note the concluding chapter of *The American Voter* or Chaps. 2, 8, 10, 12 of *Elections and the Political Order*, which are largely reprints of earlier articles.

[40] Note the criticisms of Kenneth Prewitt and Norman Nie, in "Revisiting the Election Studies of the Survey Research Center," a paper prepared for delivery at the 1970 meeting of the American Political Science Association, p. 18:
The SRC group has written persuasively regarding the implications for American politics of the findings about citizen information and awareness. They have less critically discussed the implications for voter rationality of their findings about election processes and alternatives.

[41] Warren Miller recognized this point in "One Party Politics and the Voter," *American Political Science Review*, 50 (Sept., 1956), 707–25.

Most critically, we must emphasize in this context the effect upon voters of the stimuli they receive from the parties and other electoral actors. If these stimuli are issueless and static, as they largely were in the 1950s, the citizenry is likely to respond in the manner described in *The American Voter*. If these stimuli are more ideological and dynamic, we are likely to see different perceptions and behavior, such as that evidenced in the 1964 and 1968 elections.[42] "In the large the electorate behaves about as rationally and responsibly as we should expect, given the clarity of the alternatives presented to it and the character of the information available to it."[43] Confused voters reflect confused parties; clarity among the voters follows from clear-headed parties.

---

[42] The recent work of the Survey Research Center has given more emphasis to dynamic elements. See Donald Stokes, "Some Dynamic Elements of Contests for the Presidency," *American Political Science Review*, 60 (March, 1966), 19–28; and Converse et al., "Continuity and Change in American Politics."

[43] Key, *The Responsible Electorate*, 7.

Kenneth Prewitt

Political Ambitions, Volunteerism, and Electoral Accountability*

A generally accepted interpretation of American politics today is associated with the "theory of electoral accountability." The salient features of this theory are well known. The thesis was initially shaped in Schumpeter's classic work on democracy, and since has been elaborated by a generation of scholars.[1] The elaboration, especially where grounded in empirical studies, has established (1) that the public, being largely apathetic about political matters and in any case ill-informed regarding public issues, cannot provide the necessary and sufficient conditions for the maintenance of democratic procedures; (2) that a liberal political and social elite are committed to the preservation of democratic forms, at least more committed than the average citizen; therefore, (3) what maintains the democratic tradition is not extensive public participation in political policy-making, but, instead, competition among elites whose behavior is regulated by periodic review procedures. Competition among elites and review by citizens of political leaders are provided by elections. Thus elections hold political leaders accountable to nonleaders.[2]

* Reprinted from the *American Political Science Review*, vol. 64 (March 1970), pp. 5–17. Copyright 1970, The American Political Science Association.

The larger project of which this analysis is a part, the City Council Research Project, is sponsored by the Institute of Political Studies, Stanford University, and is supported by the National Science Foundation under grants GS 496 and GS 1898. I am indebted to several colleagues who read and sharply criticized an earlier version of this paper. I leave them unnamed for it is very possible they would prefer not to be associated with even this version.

[1] Joseph Schumperter, *Capitalism, Socialism and Democracy* (New York: Harper & Row, 1947).

[2] Relevant studies are Bernard Berelson, et al., *Voting* (Chicago: University Press, 1954), especially chapter 14; Robert A. Dahl, *Preface to Democratic Theory* (Chicago: University of Chicago Press, 1956) and Dahl, *Who Governs?* (New Haven: Yale University Press, 1961); V. O. Key, *Public Opinion and American Democracy* (New York: Knopf, 1961), especially chapter 21; S. M. Lipset, *Political Man* (New York: Doubleday & Co., Inc., 1960, Anchor Books edition, 1963); David Truman, "The American System in Crisis," *Political Science Quarterly*, 73 (December, 1959, pp. 481–97).

Writers associated with this general position have recently come under scholarly attack. The critique, directed at the first two assertions, can be reviewed briefly: although true that the public is not well-informed politically and is not actively engaged in political life, this is not to be attributed to the inherent traits of citizens so much as to the structure of political opportunities in the United States.[3] Moreover, although true that research has detected among political leaders a greater commitment to democratic procedures than is the case for the ordinary citizen, this commitment is to procedures in which only the leaders participate. It is a commitment neither to substantive justice nor to widespread political participation.[4] The critics propose that the facts of American politics have been misinterpreted in such a manner as to disguise the extent to which democracy falls short of its promise. Further, in misinterpreting the facts, contemporary political science actually impedes the realization of a more democratic politics.[5]

The critical exchange about the propositions and findings associated with the theory of accountability has given little attention to the third assertion, that elections hold the few who govern accountable to the many who are governed.[6] This is surprising, for with respect to democratic theory a proposition linking elections and accountability is necessarily a central one. Ours is an inquiry into the conditions under which elections do insure accountability.

I. ELECTIONS, AMBITIONS, ACCOUNTABILITY

A very few leaders govern the very many citizens. Although the many are often politically ignorant and apathetic, the few who govern are nevertheless responsive to the preferences of the many *because*, as elected officials, the few can be and are held accountable for their actions. Ac-

[3] Important statements are to be found in Peter Bachrach, *The Theory of Democratic Elitism* (Boston: Little, Brown and Co., 1967); and Jack L. Walker, "A Critique of the Elitist Theory of Democracy," this REVIEW, Vol. LX (June, 1966), 285–95. A data article consistent with the thesis is Walter Dean Burnham's "The Changing Shape of the American Political Universe," this REVIEW, 59 (March, 1965), 7–28. A book which anticipates much of this critical literature is T. B. Bottomore's *Elites and Society* (London: Penguin Books, 1964), especially ch. VI.

[4] It has been the substantial accomplishment of Geraint Parry to explicate this point. He writes that although elites may be disagreed on policy, "they may share similar views as to the appropriate decision-making process, namely negotiation between elites." *Political Elites* (London: George Allen and Unwin Ltd., 1969), p. 90. The complete implications of Parry's point cannot be developed at this time. It is evident, though, that elites can simultaneously be committed to democratic norms *and* to a process of decision-making in which only they participate. It should be remembered that the data base for arguing that political leaders are committed to democracy is primarily survey items on civil liberties and not items on the wisdom of the participation of the "average" citizens in the decision processes.

[5] I do not mean to imply that the scholars listed in footnotes three and four necessarily associate themselves with this critique of the political science discipline.

[6] An exception to this is Murray Edelman who has very creatively called into question some of our assumptions about what elections do and do not do. See in particular the first chapter of *The Symbolic Uses of Politics* (Urbana: The University of Illinois Press, 1967).

countability is assured because men want to gain and to continue in office and because these men recognize that the voting public determines who will hold office. Therefore, since the electorate through periodic elections grants or withholds the privilege of governing, men who wish to govern select policies they believe to be in accord with voter preferences. This thesis has an honorable tradition. Schumpeter's famous definition of democracy is a useful beginning point: "The democratic method is that institutional arrangement for arriving at political decisions in which individuals acquire the power to decide by means of a competitive struggle for the people's vote."[7] In his most frequently cited essay on democracy Lipset writes of a "social mechanism which permits the largest possible part of the population to influence major decisions by choosing among contenders for political office."[8] Or, as more succinctly stated by Downs, contestants for office "formulate policies in order to win elections, rather than win elections in order to formulate policies."[9] Dahl has been the most influential writer in the Schumpeter tradition. In a theoretical statement about democracy he notes that the effective political elites operate within limits "set by their expectations as to the reactions of the group of politically active citizens who go to the polls."[10] This hypothesis is generally confirmed in his empirical study of New Haven; "elected leaders keep the real or imagined preferences of constituents constantly in mind in deciding what policies to adopt or reject."[11]

The works of Schumpeter, Lipset, Downs, and Dahl, have been very influential among scholars theorizing about democracy. It has been the accomplishment of these scholars to examine a political process which provides a measure of citizen control over the few who are selected as political leaders. Thus the somewhat banal observation that fewer men issue commands than must obey them is converted into the more powerful theory that elections hold those few accountable for the commands they issue.

The theory of electoral accountability can be reviewed from another, complementary perspective to the one already suggested. Carl Freidrich's "rule of anticipated reactions"[12] provides the hint for this other perspective and Schlesinger's "ambition theory of politics"[13] makes it explicit. Men in office anticipate the likely response of voters because the incum-

---

[7] Schumpeter, op. cit., p. 269.

[8] S. M. Lipset, op. cit., p. 27.

[9] Anthony Downs, An Economic Theory of Democracy (New York: Harper & Row, 1957), p. 28.

[10] Dahl, Preface, op. cit., p. 72.

[11] Dahl, Who Governs?, op. cit., p. 164.

[12] Carl J. Freidrich, Man and His Government (New York: McGraw-Hill, 1963), pp. 199–215. Of course Freidrich's "rule" is much broader than what is implied by my use; he develops a theory of political influence based on the rule which refers to nearly all political interactions, not just to relationships between electorates and representatives. A study which applies the "rule of anticipated reaction" and comes to conclusions similar to those advanced here is Roy Gregory, "Local Elections and the 'Rule of Anticipated Reactions,' " Political Studies, XVII (March, 1969), pp. 31–47.

[13] Joseph A. Schlesinger, Ambition and Politics (Chicago: Rand McNally & Co. 1966).

bents want either to retain that office or to move to a more elevated one. This perspective on accountability assumes that there is a supply of men intent on gaining and then holding political office. This assumption links directly to thinking about accountability. For if men are uninterested in gaining and holding office, why should they guide their actions in a manner sensitive to voter preferences?

Schlesinger has stated this point vigorously. "Ambition lies at the heart of politics," writes Schlesinger. He reasons, with particular relevance to democratic theory,

> To slight the role of ambition in politics, then, or to treat it as a human failing to be suppressed, is to miss the central function of ambition in political systems. A political system unable to kindle ambitions for office is as much in danger of breaking down as one unable to restrain ambitions. Representative government, above all, depends on a supply of men so driven; *the desire for election and, more important, for reelection becomes the electorate's restraint upon its public officials.* No more irresponsible government is imaginable than one of high-minded men unconcerned for their political futures.[14]

We can now reformulate the theory of electoral accountability as we understand it.

> Since periodic elections hold officeholders accountable, these officeholders select policies in anticipation of voter response and thus choose policies which broadly reflect the preferences of the governed.

This thesis, in turn, rests upon a prior assumption:

> Men in political office work to gain their positions and wish to retain them.

II. SOME PUZZLING RESPONSES

In a study of the men who govern eighty-two cities of the San Francisco Bay Area, more than 400 city councilmen were interviewed with a lengthy and largely open-ended questionnaire. A wide variety of topics were covered, and councilmen were given ample opportunity to state the decision criteria they invoked as they set about the task of governing their communities. In reading these protocols it becomes evident that often the sentiments voiced by these councilmen do not match well with what the "rule of anticipated reactions" leads us to predict. Indeed, if the reader of the protocols is bearing in mind the observation that elected leaders "formulate policies in order to win elections," then the responses can only be described as puzzling. For it is very clear that councilmen infrequently refer to elections and, when they do, it often is in a manner which directly contradicts the premises of a theory of electoral accountability.

---

14 *Ibid.*, p. 2, italics added.

For example, councilmen were asked if they felt it were easy or difficult to go against majority preferences when choosing community policies.

> Easy, I am an independent type of individual. I don't feel the weight of voter responsibility. I am not all fired up for a political career.
> You don't always follow the majority; you shouldn't give a damn whether you get elected or not. Don't be afraid to be defeated.
> Yes, it is easy because I don't really care if I get elected or not.
> I am free to do as I feel. In general it is easy to vote against the majority because I don't have any political ambitions.

Responding to a related question, another councilman explains why he and his colleagues ignore the pressures which mount from community influentials:

> I doubt if the City Council would consider preferentially the opinion of such a person. This City Council doesn't give a damn if it is reelected.

More of the same is voiced in response to questions about the councilmen's political futures. One respondent, not sure whether he will stand for reelection, makes his position clear.

> I won't know until my time is up. I don't think a councilman can do a good job if he is concerned about counting votes. If something is best for the city, you have to go against some groups. And you don't want to have to worry that these groups may not vote for you in the next election if you vote wrong.

Another doubtful candidate,

> I promised myself I wouldn't decide ahead of time whether to run or not. I don't want to do things to collect votes.

These quotations, although clearly contradicting the theory of electoral accountability, do not constitute a data base on which to confirm or falsify anything. For one thing, the quotations were selected to make a point. Moreover, they are responses from one small population of elected officials—nonsalaried, nonpartisan city councilmen from one region of one state. Yet these responses should not be dismissed too readily. The manner in which councilmen reflect on their relationships with the public indicates that the rule of anticipated reactions does not always operate. It is in order to ask whether there are political conditions which, if present, would make these councillor responses less puzzling. This inquiry is best initiated by specifying more exactly a proposition in the theory of electoral accountability.

III. THE SELECTION AND DISPLACEMENT OF POLITICAL LEADERS

A very crude classification permits categorizing theories of democracy as having one of two emphases. One emphasis stresses widespread citizen participation in the making of public policy. Of relevance to scholars in this tradition are issues such as expansion of suffrage, citizenship training, methods of citizen petitioning, rights of association and free speech, mobilization of the public, and so forth. The second emphasis stresses procedures of leadership selection and displacement. Relevant issues are extent of organized competition for office, availability of regularized review procedures, tenure limitations, access of all social groups to political recruitment channels, circulation of elites, and so forth. Though no scholar is faced with an either-or choice, individual scholars as well as schools of thought tend to concentrate on one or the other set of issues.

The theory of electoral accountability largely directs attention to analysis of leadership selection and displacement. Schumpeter takes "the view that the role of the people is to produce a government." He continues, "it should be observed that in making it the primary function of the electorate to produce a government (directly or through an intermediate body) I intended to include in this phrase also the function of evicting it. The one means simply the acceptance of a leader or a group of leaders, the other means simply the withdrawal of this acceptance. . . . electorates

TABLE 1

Proportion of Councils with Various Appointment Rates
(N = 81)

Percentage of Councilmen Initially Appointed to Office	Percentage of Cities with Different Appointment Rates
Fewer than ten	19%
10 to 19	16
20 to 29	23
30 to 39	11
40 to 49	10
50 to 74	14
75 to 100	7
	100%

normally do not control their political leaders in any way except by refusing to reelect them or the parliamentary majorities that support them."[15] Lipset advances a similar argument: "Democracy, however, implies permanent insecurity for those in governing positions; and the more truly democratic the governing system, the greater the insecurity of the incumbent. Thus every incumbent of a position of high status within a truly democratic system must of necessity anticipate the loss of his position by the operation of normal political processes."[16] The processes which provide for democracy are sustained competition for political office and regularized procedures for review by electorates of leaders; parties establish the former, and elections establish the latter of these conditions.

[15] Schumpeter, op. cit., p. 269, 272.

[16] S. M. Lipset, Martin Trow, and James Coleman, Union Democracy (Garden City: Anchor Books, Doubleday & Co., Inc., 1962), p. 241.

Since the present task is to explain some "puzzling" responses of elected officials, attention should turn to the procedures for selecting and displacing these officials. The study of the city councils reveals four relevant facts, two related to the selection of the legislators and two related to the manner in which they are displaced.

1) *The Frequency of Appointment to Elected Office.* The theory of electoral accountability makes the tacit assumption that persons holding elected office earned them by competing for voter support. This need not be the case; nearly one-fourth (24 per cent) of the city councilmen interviewed had initially reached office by being appointed to fill an unexpired term. Such frequent use of a method of leadership selection which circumvents the election process will undoubtedly affect how the leaders, appointed as well as those who do the appointing, think about the sanctioning power of elections. Table 1 shows the frequency with which the appointment strategy is used among the cities in the study. These data are taken from aggregate election statistics over a ten-year period, five elections for each city. (Data are available for 81 of the 82 cities in the study.) In seventeen cities half or more councilmen are initially appointed to office. More than four-fifths of the cities have at least one member appointed (councils are never fewer than five members). In cities where appointment is a regularly employed method of selecting some or most leaders, there may occur a nonchalance about elections.

2) *The Electorate as a (Small) Constituency.* It is well known that relatively few citizens express their preferences in local elections. This generalization holds true for the cities we are studying. Averaged over five elections, fewer than one in three of the adult citizens cast a ballot in the councilmanic elections. Although low voter turnout is normal, what is interesting is to consider the interaction between low turnout and the plurality method of counting ballots. The cities being studied are all nonpartisan and use some variant of at-large election procedures. Depending on the number of vacancies, the two or three candidates with the most votes win. Except in a very few cases, there are no run-off elections. Low turnout and plurality elections mean that a very small number of citizens can elect a candidate to office. Table 2 presents illustrative data showing, for five different size cities, the *minimum* number of votes it took to gain a council seat averaged for five elections. For instance, in a city of more than 13,000 residents, on the average as few as 810 voters elected a man to office. Such figures sharply question the validity of thinking that "mass electorates" hold elected officials accountable. For these councilmen, even if serving in relatively sizable cities, there is no "mass electorate"; rather there are the councilman's business associates, his friends at church, his acquaintances in the Rotary Club, and so forth which provide him the electoral support he needs to gain office.

These two observations, one pointing out the frequency of appointments and the other suggesting that the effective electorate for any given officeholder can be very small in local, plurality elections, give pause to interpretations of politics which emphasize that selection to office is controlled by large electorates indirectly voicing policy preferences. In the present research site, selection of leaders is less controlled by a voting

TABLE 2

Minimum Number of Votes Needed to Win
Office in Different Size Cities

City Population (1964 estimate)	Average Total Vote of Lowest Winner— Five Elections* (1955-65)
71,000	5,298
28,750	1,931
13,450	810
6,675	518
500	64

* To compute the average total vote of the lowest winner, we simply added the votes of lowest winner for five elections and divided by five. Except in special elections, there are never fewer than two winners for any council election.

public than might be necessary for the conditions of electoral account-ability to hold. What about the electorates' power to evict the governors?

3) *The Infrequency of Election Defeat.* Implicit in the theory of electoral accountability is the assumption that voters frequently enough remove men from office that election defeat is seen by officeholders as a threat to tenure. It is difficult to know how frequent is "frequent," but the success of incumbents at gaining reelection is commonly taken for granted by students of American politics. Over the ten-year period, four out of five incumbent councilmen who stood for reelection were successful. This figure, though high, is even somewhat lower than one reported for members of the House of Representatives. During the years 1924–1956, 90 per cent of the congressmen who sought reelection were returned by the voters.[17] Once in elected office men can feel relatively secure about staying there. Indeed, in 20 of the 82 cities studied, over a ten-year time period not one single incumbent seeking another term failed to be reelected. Table 3 presents pertinent data.

Two speculations can be derived from this table, both of which run counter to the assumption that elections insure accountability. The frequency with which officeholders are returned to office suggests that they are unlikely to be constantly preoccupied with voter preferences. Moreover, the voting public, which already constitutes a minority of the eligible population, evidently does not see in elections the means by which to force leadership turnover.

4) *The Frequency of Voluntary Retirement from Elected Office.* In the cities we are studying, more men by far depart from elected office voluntarily than because of election defeat. Officeholders simply conclude that the obligations of office exceed the rewards. Among the nearly 500 men who govern the cities of the San Francisco Bay Area, about one-

---

[17] David A. Leuthold, *Electioneering in a Democracy* (New York: John Wiley & Sons, 1968), p. 127.

TABLE 3

Proportion of Cities with Various Incumbent Win Ratios
(N = 81)

Percentage of Incumbents Who Successfully Sought Reelection	Percentage of Cities with Different Incumbent Win Ratios
90 to 100	30%
80 to 89	20
70 to 79	19
60 to 69	15
50 to 59	7
25 to 49	6
0 to 24	3
	100%

fifth will be planning to retire voluntarily at the end of the present term and another 30 to 50 per cent will be planning to retire after only one more term. It is not the electorate jealously guarding its power to sanction officeholders which establishes tenure limitations. Rather, there are widely shared norms among these councilmen which lead to self-imposed limitations. The single most important reason for voluntary departures is simply "I've been on long enough" or "I have done my duty." As one typical councillor states it:

No, I won't run again. I think this is the end. If I had my way, I'd limit it to two terms anyway. You get a lot of new blood that way. New ideas are needed and new councilmen can provide them. Give the next guy a chance.

Thus it is that norms held by the councilmen themselves often lead to turnover among officeholders, not the behavior of an aroused or impatient electorate. Table 4 presents data.

TABLE 4

Proportion of Cities with Various Voluntary
Departure Rates
(N = 81)

Percentage of Councilmen Who Left Office Voluntarily	Percentage of Cities with Different Voluntary Departure Rates
90 to 100	1%
80 to 89	5
70 to 79	9
60 to 69	28
50 to 59	22
40 to 49	11
30 to 39	14
20 to 29	7
Fewer than 20	3
	100%

IV. THE NORM OF VOLUNTEERISM

This brief attention to the manner in which men enter and depart elected office in 82 California cities points uniformly in one direction. The quotations earlier reported, though puzzling when read in terms of electoral accountability perspectives, are not puzzling when read in the context of the cumulative impact of (1) the frequent reliance on appointment as a route to office, (2) the smallness of the electorate which can send and retain a man in office, (3) the overwhelming electoral advantage held by the incumbent, and (4) the high rate of voluntary retirement from office. Men enter and leave office not at the whim of the electorate, but according to self-defined schedules.

To the extent this is so, it is likely that a strong norm of volunteerism is at work in these city councils. This appears to result directly from the process by which councilmen are recruited into office, the images they hold of council service, and the manner in which they vacate office. They treat council service as a "citizen duty" in much the same manner as they treat service in the Chamber of Commerce, the PTA, the Library Board, and other such community service organizations. As we pointed out elsewhere, the norm of volunteerism "can serve to undermine an already weakened election system. Although the volunteer in office, especially if relatively indifferent to staying there, may be a devoted public servant as he defines the role, he is unlikely to be constantly sensitive to voter preferences. His political thinking has been formed by a series of experiences which minimize for him the importance of mass electorates."[18]

Volunteerism and the Theory of Electoral Accountability

It is clear why electoral accountability is weakened to the extent that volunteerism dominates in a political community. Both the choosers and the chosen come to think of movement into and out of political office as being regulated by self-selection and self-elimination patterns rather than electoral challenges. We have shown elsewhere that in communities where elections seldom evict governors, the officeholders tend to act in response only to their own image of what the community needs. The council which does not face the threat of election defeat is less likely than a council which does to respond either to attentive publics or to ad hoc issue groups.[19] We can now carry this analysis a step further, by classifying cities with respect to the "norm of volunteerism."[20]

For present purposes, two indicators of volunteerism are used: the frequency of appointment as a route to elective office and the frequency

[18] Kenneth Prewitt, *The Recruitment of Political Leaders: A Study of Citizen-Politicians* (Bobbs-Merrill, in press). This book includes a more detailed analysis of the survey data.

[19] Kenneth Prewitt and Heinz Eulau, "Political Matrix and Political Representation," this REVIEW, LXIII (June, 1969), pp. 427–41.

[20] In this analysis the council in contrast to the individual councilman is taken as the unit of analysis. The theoretical rationale for this as well as some methodological considerations are spelled out in Prewitt and Eulau, *ibid.*

of voluntary departure from office. Cities were ranked high to low on each of these measures; they were then divided at the median and cities above the median on both measures are said to be the most characterized by the norm of volunteerism. Cities below the median on both measures are least characterized by this norm. Cities high on one measure but low on the other are for present purposes simply left as intermediate. Two indicators, then, are combined to construct an ordinal measure of volunteerism.

The hypothesis is very simple: councils characterized by volunteerism will exhibit traits which contradict what the theory of electoral accountability predicts about elected legislatures. Table 5 confirms this hypoth-

TABLE 5

Relationship between Extent of Volunteerism in Leadership Selection and Seven Dependent Variables Related to the Theory of Accountability

| Attribute of Council | Extent of Volunteerism* | | |
	Most Present (15)	Mixed (49)	Least Present (17)
a. Council votes with perceived majority public opinion	35%	49%	53%
b. Council senses demands from the public	29	51	73
c. Council reflects concern with next election	29	45	60
d. Council activates constituencies in connection with policy-making	35	43	73
e. Council views many groups as politically influential	29	51	67
f. Council facilitates group access	35	61	60
g. Council performs services for constituents	29	41	67

* The councils scored as "most volunteerism" are those above the median of all councils with respect to frequency of appointment to the council and rate of voluntary retirement; those scored as "least volunteerism" are those below the median on these two measures; the "mixed" councils are high on one of the measures but low on the other.

esis. Where the norm of volunteerism is more prevalent, councils are (a) more likely to vote against what they see as majority opinion, (b) less likely to feel under pressure from the public, (c) less likely to consider the upcoming election when choosing among policy alternatives, (d) less likely to involve constituencies as part of the strategy of policy-making, (e) less likely to view political groups as having an influential part to play in city politics, and (f) less likely to facilitate group access to the council, and (g) less likely to perform services for constituents.[21]

Each item in Table 5 merits discussion, for each one relates in its own manner to a theory of electoral accountability. For instance, if the an-

---

[21] In every case the dependent items in Table 5 derive from some method of aggregating the responses of individual councilmen into a group measure. Two procedures are represented. With respect to all items but 'c' and 'd' the responses of individual councilmen were summed, a mean was computed, and the distribution of means was then used to assign councils as either above or below the median of all councils. With respect to the remaining items, a procedure relying on coder judgment to assign a score to each council was used. Footnote 9 in Prewitt and Eulau, *ibid.*, describes the procedure.

ticipated reactions of the voting public are thought to be relevant to policies chosen by governors, then elected councils will likely involve constituencies as the council carries out its deliberations. Yet it is clear that councils characterized by volunteerism seldom mobilize constituencies as part of the activities which surround the making of policy. Or, another example, elected councils will feel under some pressure from publics if indeed the councils are keeping the preferences of constituents in mind as they govern their cities. But we note that fewer than one-third of the more volunteeristic councils report being under such pressure. And so forth.

It would detract from the central argument to pursue every theoretical lead suggested by Table 5. Instead, a general summary observation can be advanced. The theory of accountability is both confirmed and confounded by the evidence of Table 5. On the one hand, councils in cities where elections play a greater role in the selection and eviction of governors appear to be more sensitive to public constituencies. On the other hand, there are processes at work, summarized by the term volunteerism, which weaken the capacity of elections to insure the accountability of the elected legislature to the voters.

This summary inference from Table 5 suggests, in turn, several ways in which to speculate about volunteerism, elections, and democratic accountability. First, however, it is important to raise the nagging question: How unusual are the Bay Area councils with respect to the norm of volunteerism?

Scattered Evidence about the Distribution of Volunteerism in American Politics

Although the measures used in this study forced some variation among the cities, it is plausible that if all political units in the U.S. could be arrayed along a continuum from the most to the least volunteeristic, the 82 units here studied would cluster well toward the "most volunteeristic" end. Systematic data for determining the accuracy of this guess are not readily available; however, there is sufficient evidence to confirm that volunteerism is far from being limited to a few Bay Area nonpartisan councils.

It has been noted already that the frequency with which incumbents are returned to office when they seek reelection is uniformly high for all types of legislatures in the United States. The rate of voter turnout is a more problematic variable because of the ambiguity of determining what is "high" and what is "low" turnout; however, both survey and aggregate data readily confirm that voter turnout fluctuates widely from one type of election to the next and, in the thousands upon thousands of elections below the state level, elections very often involve only small minorities of the eligible electorate. Data on appointment as a route to elective office are not available, but a reasonable guess is that the figure reported here (approximately one-fourth) does not greatly exaggerate the proportion of appointees to school boards, city and township councils, and so forth. The proportion of appointees to state legislatures and to the national congress should be much lower.

There are more systematic data on the frequency with which elected officials voluntarily depart from office, the remaining indicator of volunteerism. James Young's *The Washington Community—1800–1828,* is a good beginning point. Evidence reported by Young indicate that the federal congresses of the early decades should be placed well toward the "most volunteerism" end of a hypothetical continuum; indeed, the legislative body empowered to guide the nation in its early years had higher rates of voluntary departure than the councils presently governing the Bay Area cities. "From 1797 to 1829 (5th through 20th Congresses) more Senators resigned than failed to be reelected by their state legislatures." And, "Each new Congress, moreover, brought a host of new faces to the community, drastically reconstituting its membership every two years. For the first four decades of national government between one-third and two-thirds of the congressional community left every two years not to return."[22] On the average, the biennial turnover during the first decades of the founding was 41.5 per cent of the total legislative membership. Young's study is a prototype for investigating how voluntary turnover affects the governing process and especially the means by which accountability is insured. The burden of his analysis is that the legislators were "remote" from the citizens they were to govern and, in effect, that they were not held accountable for the policies they pursued.[23]

To move to more recent times, and from the national to the state level, it is instructive to review the data on voluntary retirement collected by Charles Hyneman three decades ago. He reports that much turnover among state legislators is due not to election defeat, but to voluntary retirement. In his extensive study of twenty-five state chambers between 1925 and 1935, he found that fewer than one-third of the retirements from state legislative office were due to election defeats; only 16 per cent came from general election defeats, the presumed sanction of the voting public. After his exhaustive study of turnover he commented, "The real task is to find why so many legislators, senators and representatives alike, choose not to run again."[24] Eulau, writing about state legislators some twenty years after the Hyneman study, reports similar figures. The proportion of legislators in each of four states who either intend not to stand for reelection or are doubtful about it is as follows: Tennessee—66 per cent; Ohio—40 per cent; California—34 per cent; and New Jersey—24

---

[22] James S. Young, *The Washington Community—1800–1828* (New York: Columbia University Press, 1966), p. 57, 89.

[23] Young writes of the "remoteness of the rulers from the citizenry and remoteness of the citizenry from the rulers" and that the "isolated circumstances of the early governing group must have afforded a freedom of choice as nearly uninhibited as any representative government could have." *Ibid.,* p. 34, 36. Young, of course, is making much of the sheer fact of geographical isolation whereas volunteerism implies a distance between rulers and citizenry established not by geography but by the processes of leadership selection.

[24] Charles S. Hyneman, "Tenure and Turnover of Legislative Personnel," *Annals of the American Academy of Political and Social Science,* Vol. 195 (1938), p. 20.

per cent.[25] Barber's study of Connecticut state legislators provides similar data. In Connecticut, "election defeat accounted for less than 26 per cent of retirement from the House in seven elections between 1946 and 1958. Thus, by far the largest proportion of retirements may be classified as pre-election turnover."[26] Among the first-term representatives interviewed by Barber, 35 per cent report that they definitely or probably would not be willing to serve more than two or three terms.

Additional confirmation that leadership turnover is often voluntary is to be found in data collected by Schlesinger. For twenty-nine states between 1914 and 1958, in only 17 per cent of 542 gubernatorial elections was the incumbent defeated. For thirty-six states during the same time period, in only one-fifth of the 616 senatorial elections was the incumbent defeated.[27] Although it is not possible to derive rates of voluntary retirement directly from these figures, Schlesinger presents other data which support the conclusion that rates of voluntary retirement are high even for governors and senators.[28]

This sketchy review suggests an hypothesis: there is an inverse relationship between volunteerism and perceived political stakes. "Important" legislatures have less volunteerism than "unimportant" ones. There are several variants on this theme. For instance, the higher the level of government, the fewer the number of voluntary departures from office. Another variant, the more professionalized (or better paid) the legislature, the lower the rate of volunteerism.[29] Further, the greater the competition to enter the legislature, the less volunteerism there is. And so on. Thus, whereas in the extent of volunteerism the national congresses of the 1800's may parallel nonpartisan city councils in the 1960's, the 80th Congress in no way resembles the 8th Congress.

Such qualifications, though important, do not negate the thesis developed in this paper. The thesis is theoretical—showing the relationship

25 John Wahlke, Heinz Eulau, William Buchanan, Leroy C. Ferguson, *The Legislative System* (New York: John Wiley & Sons, 1962), computed from Table 6.1, p. 122.

26 David Barber, *The Lawmakers* (New Haven: Yale University Press, 1965), p. 8.

27 Schlesinger, *op. cit.*, p. 63 (Table IV–2).

28 This inference seems warranted on the basis of evidence Schlesinger presents on p. 144, regarding the frequency with which the candidates for gubernatorial and senatorial elections differ from their predecessors, and his statement on p. 146 that the opportunity for men to be nominated for these offices is "impressively high, indicative of a great deal of fluctuation at the very top of the pyramid within state parties." His data, of course, include controls for tenure limitations. There are two interpretations possible. Either the political parties habitually fail to renominate the incumbent, or the rates of voluntary retirement are high for governors and senators. The latter seems the more reasonable inference.

29 Schlesinger writes that the "impact of ambitions upon the behavior of public officials will be greater on those in high than in low office, greater upon congressmen than upon state legislators, greater upon United States Senators than upon United States Representatives." *Ibid.*, p. 193. Although this observation is intuitively persuasive, it is relevant to record that it is an inference and in no way is it directly confirmed by the massive amounts of evidence Schlesinger imaginatively analyzes. Evidence suggesting that salary differentials may promote or retard political ambitions at the state level is suggested by John W. Soule, "Future Political Ambitions and the

among variables pertinent to accountability theories, but also descriptive —discovering something about the likely distribution of these variables. To review the thesis: the theory of electoral accountability predicts that elected officials keep in mind the preferences of ordinary citizens because these officials are determined to remain in office. This proposition has been confirmed in several empirical studies, and, in fact, is confirmed in Table 5. What is generally ignored by scholars associated with the accountability theory is (1) clearly establishing the conditions under which elections hold the representatives accountable, and (2) providing evidence regarding the distribution of these conditions. Our analysis speaks to both of these points: where the methods of selecting and displacing political leaders encourage the norm of volunteerism, electoral accountability is weakened; moreover, though undoubtedly more prevalent at the local than the state and at the state than the national level, the norm of volunteerism in some degree is present in most legislatures.

A postscript to this latter point is in order. The overwhelming majority of the half-million elected legislators in the United States serve in legislatures where some recognizable degree of volunteerism is present. The skeptic can say that these legislative bodies—city councils, school boards, village governments, etc.—are "unimportant" because they deal with "low-stake issues." While true that the House Committee on Education and Labor is far more important to the education of American citizens than any single school board, the cumulative impact of nearly 35,000 school boards is in turn far greater than the action of a Congressional Committee. Thus, whereas there is one national legislature and 50 state legislatures (where already evidence of volunteerism is apparent), there are in excess of 3,000 county governments, in excess of 35,000 municipalities, towns, and townships, nearly 35,000 school boards, as well as 18,000 special districts.

I do not deny the symbolic as well as material importance of the central government, yet if the ordinary citizen is subject at the local level to legislatures seemingly remote and indifferent, that citizen's "experience with democracy" falls short not only of the classical model but also of the neo-classical model which emphasizes electoral accountability. It is in this context that we should interpret survey results such as, for instance, McClosky's finding that approximately half of the general electorate "perceive government and politicians as remote, inaccessible, and largely unresponsive to the electorate's needs or opinions."[30] Volunteer-

---

Behavior of Incumbent State Legislators," *Midwest Political Science Review*, XIII (August, 1969), pp. 443–44. For a study indicating that as a legislature becomes more professionalized over time, the incidence of volunteerism should drop, see Nelson Polsby, "The Institutionalization of the U. S. House of Representatives," this REVIEW, LXII (March, 1968), 144–68. To read Polsby's study side-by-side with Young's analysis of the early congresses is very instructive, and indicates why volunteerism as an attribute of a legislature is variable over time.

[30] Herbert McClosky, "Consensus and Ideology in American Politics," this REVIEW, LVIII, (June, 1964), 361–82. For instance, as reported on pp. 370–71, more than half the general electorate agree that "It seems to me that whoever you vote for, things go on pretty much the same" and "There is practically no connection between what a politician says and what he will do once he gets elected," and "Nothing I ever do seems to have any effect upon what happens in politics."

ism among elected officials may well be connected with political disillusionment among the electors.

V. SPECULATIONS AND CONCLUSIONS

Perhaps the most efficient manner in which to summarize the thesis and findings presented here is to organize the conclusions around a few general speculations. Speculations permit us to review prominent themes in writings about electoral accountability, from the viewpoint of findings about volunteerism, and yet avoid the dangers of premature precision.

Leadership Turnover, Accountability, and Volunteerism. To consider democratic politics from the perspective of electoral accountability theories has, for many writers, implied sharing with Lipset the belief that permanent insecurity for those in governing positions makes for democratic politics. When leaders are entrenched they form an oligarchy; and oligarchies are inimical to political processes which would insure some fit between the preferences of non-leaders and the policies of leaders. Insecure tenure, in contrast, assures that leaders will attempt to retain their high status positions by satisfying the policy demands of at least some sizable part of the citizenry.

This formulation seems reasonable until we encounter volunteerism in the methods of leadership selection. When movement into and out of office is self-determined, rapid turnover of elected leaders, far from being an indicator of insecurity and, hence accountability, is more likely related to an indifference among the elected to the sanctions of the ballot box. Indeed, when we discovered in the city council study that leadership turnover was not necessarily linked to election defeats, we were led to distinguish between the "circulation of elites" and the "replaceability of elites." The former term implies that leadership turnover is associated with changes in the mood of the citizens and thus with changes in policies; the latter term makes no such assumptions. Where there is recruitment by replaceability, a procession of like-minded men move through public office with relatively little resultant shift in policies.

Civic Duty, Social Status, and Malrepresentation of Social Groups. The inquiry into volunteerism also encourages some revised thinking about a topic closely related to the issue of tenure insecurity. There is in the study of democratic politics considerable attention to the topic of social class and political recruitment. One perspective on this question treats the political processes which accentuate and those which depress the tendency for the members of the relatively better-off social groups in society to be significantly overrepresented in political leadership circles.

Where electoral accountability is fully operating, this tendency should be depressed. Candidates for office must appeal to a relatively wide range of social groups in order to reach and to hold political office. Where volunteerism affects leadership selection, class bias in the composition of the legislature is likely to be accentuated. The reasoning here is simple.

First, the smallness of the voting constituency increases the probability that the constituency is socially homogeneous, and, based on what we know about the correlates of voting behavior, consequently increases the probability that the constituency is middle and upper-middle class.[31] Second, a more complicated but possibly more critical factor relates to the motives for seeking office. When the selection of leaders is characterized by volunteerism, the recruitment processes necessarily further careers of the self-selected. For the cities we study this implies that the pool of eligible recruits for city office are those citizens with a strong sense of civic duty. That the positions are nonsalaried adds to this tendency. Although the term "civic duty" can imply many things, among the citizens who govern cities and towns, school boards and special districts, and so forth, it very often implies a belief that one has the duty to direct the political community.[32] This belief is never randomly distributed across all socio-economic groupings in society. Political socialization studies show that white middle and upper-middle class children, more so than children from less well-to-do social groups, are taught to believe in their "duties" as citizens and their "responsibilities" as community leaders. Civic duty tends to be little more than a middle-class version of *noblesse oblige;* it is not nobility status which obligates but bourgeois status. Political volunteerism derives from citizen duty, and malrepresentation of social groups in legislatures is one consequence.

Status Inequality, Ambitions, and Volunteerism. The investigation of volunteerism might make a contribution to a related inquiry which attempts to link accountability to issues of social status. Lipset, elaborating on Michels, notes that democratic accountability is threatened when the status difference between political leaders and political followers grows too great.[33] If there is great status inequality, those in office will have cause to resist leadership turnover and, moreover, will have the superior resources it requires to forestall challenges from an opposition. The difficulties of establishing constitutional democracy in several African nations lends support to this hypothesis.

A contrary position has been advanced by May[34] and, indirectly, by Schlesinger. When political office confers no status, then the motive for seeking office is not political ambition but, for instance, civic duty. Schlesinger reminds us that the absence of ambition in politics can be inimical to representative democracy: "No more irresponsible government is im-

---

[31] An interesting study which shows that the socio-economic composition of legislatures is related to voter turnout is that of Rosalio Wences, "Electoral Participation and the Occupational Composition of Cabinets and Parliaments," *American Journal of Sociology,* vol. 75 (September, 1969), pp. 181–92. A related discussion is in Kenneth Prewitt, "From the Many Are Selected the Few," *American Behavioral Scientists,* November, 1969.

[32] A finding of McClosky's is instructive in this context. One of the very few items on which political influentials measured higher than the general electorate was as follows: "Most politicians can be trusted to do what they think is best for the country." Seventy-seven percent of the influentials agreed and fifty-nine percent of the electorate did. *op. cit.,* p. 370.

[33] Lipset, et al., *op. cit.,* especially pp. 239–47.

[34] A paper by John D. May, unfortunately not yet published, is particularly insightful on this issue. See his "Democracy and Inequality," unpublished paper, Chicago, 1969.

aginable than one of high-minded men unconcerned for their political futures."[35] The earlier cited responses of elected councilmen lends support to this point; as one councilman stated it, "I am free do do as I feel. In general it is easy to vote against the majority because I don't have any political ambitions."

The data on volunteerism helps clear up the contradiction between the "status inequality" hypothesis and the "ambition" hypothesis. The question is not whether political leaders have higher status for, as Eulau reminds us, this is almost certainly the case.[36] At issue is not the status distance, but whether office confers status or whether office is simply a by-product of previously achieved status, which is to say previously acquired prestige, wealth, leisure, security, and so forth. Where political office is but a by-product, the conditions leading to volunteerism will be accentuated. Electoral accountability can be expected to suffer.

Volunteerism and the Political Formula. Inquiry into political representation, following Burke's lead, has established that representatives define their relationship with constituencies according to a trustee role-orientation, a delegate role-orientation, or, possibly, some mixture.[37] Available evidence testifies to the widespread presence of the trustee orientation among legislators in the United States; and though theories of electoral accountability have never been joined with studies of representational role-orientations, it is a reasonable speculation that trusteeship and volunteerism can comfortably coexist in the same legislative system.[38] Moreover, volunteerism and trusteeship are congenial to an interpretation of elections which stresses the ceremonial and ritualistic function they perform.

To suggest that volunteerism in political recruitment, trusteeship in political representation, and ritualism in political elections form a compatible package does not mean that these political phenomena necessarily coexist. But that they might coexist suggests an entirely new perspective on the theory of electoral accountability. Mosca will help us to sharpen this perspective.

For Mosca, the power of any political class rests upon a political formula or the set of moral principles which justifies the political hierarchy to those toward its bottom as well as those toward its top. Mosca describes the political formula in the United States: "The powers of all lawmakers, magistrates and governmental officials in the United States

---

[35] Schlesinger, *op. cit.,* p. 2.

[36] Heinz Eulau, "Changing Views of Representation," in Ithiel de Sola Pool (ed) *Contemporary Political Science* (New York: McGraw-Hill, Inc., 1967), p. 80.

[37] Wahlke, Eulau, et al., *op. cit.,* is the most elaborate application of the Burkean categories to the empirical study of legislators.

[38] A measure of a council attribute related to trusteeship is something we term the "city father ethos;" a term which describes an orientation of paternalistic responsibility among the councilmen. Where volunteerism was most present, 65% of the councils are characterized by this orientation; where volunteerism is least present, 40% of the councils are characterized by the orientation. A great deal of additional analysis remains to be completed, however, before we can confirm that volunteerism and trusteeship are empirically linked.

emanate directly or indirectly from the vote of the voters, which is held to be the expression of the sovereign will of the whole American people."[39] That Mosca himself considered this belief to be myth does not make it so. That he was correct in asserting that the vast majority of Americans believe in the formula, however, cannot be denied. One need only consult a portion of the data stored in political socialization studies, survey data, civics textbooks, political histories, journalistic imagery, and campaign speeches to conclude, with Mosca, that political leaders in this society are granted legitimacy because they are elected.

It has been the accomplishment of theorists working with electoral accountability notions to effect a subtle translation of Mosca's observation. Mosca's insight into the process which *legitimates* political leaders has been converted into a statement about the process which holds them *accountable*. But this is to confuse what should be separate issues. The electors and the elected can share a belief in the legitimacy of the political hierarchy because votes are cast and counted, without the same counting of ballots necessarily leading to accountability.

The operative political formula as described by Mosca is considered to be congenial to electoral accountability; less often noted is that the political formula is equally congenial to a politics where accountability does not proceed from electoral sanctions. Volunteerism in political recruitment, trusteeship in political representation, and ritualism in elections provide appropriate conditions. Political leaders are legitimated without feeling accountable. This would be so if, first, the norms shared by political leaders stress mutual responsibility for the public interest (trusteeship) without at the same time stressing accountability; such norms bring leaders closer together while simultaneously widening the distance between any given set of leaders and the constituency it represents.[40] And if, second, the political norms widely shared by citizens are such as to temper direct and regular involvement in political activities; that such is the case in the United States is the burden of much survey data.[41]

Two points remain to be made. First, the speculation advanced in these last few paragraphs refers to electoral accountability and not to whether leaders consult the preferences of non-leaders. The question of consultation is separate from the issue of accountability. The point we stress is that if the consultative process occurs to any significant extent where volunteerism is present, it is for reasons other than an accountability forced by electoral sanctions.

---

[39] Gaetano Mosca, *The Ruling Class* (New York: McGraw-Hill, Inc., 1939), p. 70.

[40] I have paraphrased the argument advanced in Parry, *op. cit.*, in this sentence. It has been the substantial and brilliant contribution of Theodore Lowi, in his *The End of Liberalism* (New York: W. W. Norton & Co., Inc., 1969), to document exactly this tendency in contemporary politics. See, for instance, chapter 3, where he relates his thesis to the problem of holding leaders accountable for their actions.

[41] Gabriel Almond and Sidney Verba, *The Civic Culture* (Princeton: Princeton University Press, 1963), especially pp. 476–87. The authors actually refer to their finding as constituting a myth. The citizen's perception that he can be influential "may be in part a myth, for it involves a set of norms of participation and perceptions of ability to influence that are not quite matched by actual political behavior," p. 481.

Second, the last few decades of empirical research have seen an emphasis on electoral accountability as the process which links the few who govern and the many who are governed. The study of politics has been advanced by this insight. But if the theory of electoral accountability has added to an understanding of democratic politics, it has also distracted attention from political processes which weaken electoral sanctions. Volunteerism is one of these processes. Volunteerism as well as other political processes which weaken electoral sanctions are undoubtedly present in the strikingly large number of legislative systems in the United States. There are very many small groups of citizens elected to make laws for the greater number of citizens. It is a research task of practical as well as theoretical significance to discover what, if anything, establishes democratic controls over legislatures somewhat immune from electoral sanctions.

John L. Sullivan and Robert E. O'Connor

Electoral Choice and Popular Control of Public Policy: The Case of the 1966 House Elections*

DEMOCRATIC THEORY AND ELECTORAL CHOICE

Recent democratic theorists define democracy procedurally, providing lists of necessary and sufficient conditions for a democratic system. They require a free press, free and open elections, universal suffrage, one-person one-vote; they require that candidates or parties with the most votes must win, that minorities must be allowed equal opportunity to become majorities, and so on. Certainly this description fits such theorists as Dahl,[1] Downs,[2] and Mayo,[3] all of whom feel that the basic meaning of democracy is deciding who shall govern. Typical is the following definition of democracy: "One test of an electoral system is the extent to which it is democratic, that is, the extent to which everyone is permitted to participate in the choice (of rulers)."[4]

* Reprinted from the *American Political Science Review*, vol. 66 (December 1972), pp. 1256–65. Copyright 1973, The American Political Science Association.

This paper could not have been written without the assistance of several individuals. Milton C. Cummings and Donald R. Matthews helped us obtain the data. A special debt is owed to I. A. Lewis, Manager of NBC News, Election Unit. He allowed us access to the data and provided us with technical assistance. The data were originally collected by *Congressional Quarterly* for NBC News. Financial assistance was provided by the National Science Foundation and the National Institute of Mental Health. The first-named author would like to express his gratitude to the Psychology and Politics Program of Yale University and to NIMH for time and financial assistance in the form of a Postdoctoral Fellowship.

[1] Robert Dahl, *A Preface to Democratic Theory* (Chicago: Univ. of Chicago Press, 1956), chapters 3 and 5.

[2] Anthony Downs, *An Economic Theory of Democracy* (New York: Harper, 1957), pp. 23–24.

[3] Henry B. Mayo, *An Introduction to Democratic Theory* (New York: Oxford University Press, 1960), chapter 4.

[4] Walter Berns, "A Critique of Berelson, Lazarsfeld, and McPhee's *Voting*," in *Public Opinion and Public Policy: Models of Political Linkage*, ed. Norman R. Luttbeg (Homewood, Illinois: Dorsey, 1968), p. 32.

It is argued that since the size and complexity of modern nations have made direct popular control of policies impossible, the best test of democracy is popular selection of decision makers. According to this criterion, we have in the United States in the 1970s an approximation to democracy, since there is considerable popular choice of leaders in a large majority of congressional districts, senate races, and in all presidential elections.

Is this the highest level of democracy? Logically, we can imagine a higher level in which the people would control both the leaders *and* the policies. Popular control of leaders is not necessarily popular control of policies. If popular control of, for example, legislative policies exists, then the legislator's voting behavior is consistent with the attitudes of his constituents. If this relationship between congressmen's voting behavior and constituency opinion were to hold for every district, laws (legislative outputs) would closely reflect public opinion. This is what we mean by popular control of legislative outputs.

We have asserted that popular control of leaders exists. Does popular control of policy also exist? Miller and Stokes found correlations between constituency attitudes and the roll-call behavior of representatives of approximately −0.09 in the policy area of foreign affairs, 0.30 in social and economic welfare, and 0.60 in civil rights.[5] It appears that in at least one, and perhaps two, major policy areas, the relationship is weak enough to argue that constituency control does not exist.

Political scientists have made considerable effort to explain the absence of a strong linkage between constituency attitudes and public policy.[6] Generally this effort has focused upon two necessary conditions for a strong linkage: first, that voters perceive the issue positions of the candidates, and second, that voters cast their ballots on issue grounds. Popular control of policies is dependent upon these two conditions.

Popular control of policies is also dependent upon two other conditions which have been neglected by political scientists.[7] These conditions are: third, that opposing candidates (for the same office) differ attitudinally on the issues, and fourth, that the winners vote in accordance with their pre-election attitudes.[8]

Although it has been demonstrated that there are real differences in the voting behavior of congressmen from the two major parties,[9]

---

[5] Warren E. Miller and Donald E. Stokes, "Constituency Influence in Congress," *American Political Science Review*, 57 (March, 1963), 49.

[6] See, for example, Philip E. Converse, "The Nature of Belief Systems in Mass Publics," *Ideology and Discontent*, ed. David Apter (New York: Free Press, 1964), pp. 206–61, and Luttbeg, *Public Opinion and Public Policy*.

[7] An exception to this statement is found in Jeff Fishel, "Party, Ideology, and the Congressional Challenger," *American Political Science Review*, 63 (December, 1969), 1213–1232.

[8] John L. Sullivan, "Linkage Models of the Political System," *Public Opinion and Political Attitudes: A Reader*, ed. Alan R. Wilcox, forthcoming.

[9] See, among others, David B. Truman, *The Congressional Party* (New York: Wiley, 1959); Julius Turner, *Party and Constituency: Pressures on Congress* (Baltimore: The Johns Hopkins University Press, 1951); and Duncan MacRae, *Dimensions of Congressional Voting* (Berkeley: University of California Press, 1958).

. . . any ideological differences (or similarities) between Democratic and Republican challengers could be quite deceptive from the viewpoint of alternatives presented the electorate in specific districts. It is possible that nonincumbents are more like their incumbent opponents in most districts while pairs of congressional candidates differ from district to district.[10]

This third condition—that opposing candidates for the same elective office must differ in their attitudes toward the issues—is an essential component of any realistic linkage model of the political system of the United States.[11]

The fourth condition, that winners vote in accordance with their pre-election attitudes, also is essential for popular control of policies. If voters prefer the more conservative candidate but if, once elected, he behaves as his more liberal opponent would have, the electorate has been deceived in its efforts to exercise control of policies.

What we have referred to as the third and fourth conditions should be the first conditions examined by political scientists. If the third and fourth conditions are false, nonrealization of the two well-researched conditions of the linkage process is not surprising. If many candidates do not differ appreciably from one another, or if the winners fail to vote in Congress on the basis of their pre-election attitudes, there is little reason for voters to become familiarized with the issue positions of the candidates or to vote on the basis of these issue positions.[12] If the conditions of choice and of winners voting their expressed positions are not met, elections may still perform valuable functions,[13] but they cannot permit a strong linkage between public opinion and public policy.

This paper examines the two neglected conditions of the linkage process in an effort to evaluate an alternative explanation (other than voter apathy and ignorance) of why the linkage between public policy and constituency attitudes appears to be so weak.

DATA

The data consist of attitudinal measures for all candidates for the House of Representatives in 1966. For all nonincumbents the data consist of answers to a questionnaire, while for all incumbents the data consist of both past roll-call behavior and responses to the questionnaire. The questions asked and the roll calls employed fall in three general areas: foreign affairs, civil rights, and domestic programs. The questions focus

---

[10] Fishel, p. 1221.

[11] Sullivan, Part V.

[12] The individual voter cannot arrive at this conclusion unless he has first familiarized himself with the issue positions of the candidates and the later roll-call behavior of the winners. We know that the possession of this information is the exception rather than the rule. If, however, a district (or an entire political system) has in the recent past offered little choice, it may become part of the collective attitude of the citizenry that all attempts to gather this type of information are wasted.

[13] Richard Rose and Harve Mossawir, "Voting and Elections: A Functional Analysis," *Political Studies*, 15 (June, 1967), 173–201.

upon issues that were considered both substantively important and likely to be voted upon by the 90th Congress.[14]

Each of the eight items of the questionnaire received a score of one (liberal response), two (moderate response) or three (conservative response). The items scale across issues and can be combined into an overall liberalism-conservatism scale vis-à-vis public policy. The candidates' scores vary from eight (liberal on all eight items) to twenty-four (conservative on all eight items).

One condition for linkage involves candidates' attitudinal differences toward public policy for each congressional district. Candidate differences are obtained by subtracting the score of a given candidate from that of his opponent in each district. On this measure the minimum score possible is zero, meaning that the candidates do not differ on this liberalism-conservatism continuum; the maximum is sixteen, meaning that a conservative on every issue faces a liberal on every issue.

The other condition of linkage examined in this study is that winners vote in a manner consistent with pre-election attitudes. For this we compare the roll-call behavior of the winners of the 1966 election with our pre-election measures.[15]

CHOICE

Table 1 evinces the magnitude of differences between candidates' attitude scores within districts. The modal category is represented by a score of zero. This finding reflects the fact that 57 Congressmen faced no opposition in the general election. If we focus momentarily only on contested seats, the median score rises to eight, the mean score to seven, and the modal category to nine.[16]

The distribution of Table 1 is based on differences on the overall liberalism-conservatism scale. The analysis presented in Appendix A makes it clear that it is possible for two candidates to have the same score on this scale, yet arrive at them by giving somewhat different responses.

---

[14] See Appendix A for the questionnaire, roll calls, and scaling. *Congressional Quarterly* was able to obtain a 100 per cent response rate by making ample use of telephone followups. In several cases, aides answered the questions, but presumably they gave the same answers the candidate would have given. If the incumbent was absent for a roll call, he was asked how he would have voted had he been present.

[15] The roll calls for the 90th Congress are presented in Appendix B. If the representative was absent but announced for or against, we accepted this announcement as indicating how he would have voted had he been present. If there was no information available, we coded his response as a moderate one, except where otherwise noted (Table 7).

[16] One complicating factor is the amount of choice offered in the primary elections. The available evidence, however, suggests that issues only weakly define primary elections. See V. O. Key, Jr., *Southern Politics* (New York: Knopf, 1949), pp. 105, 117, 142. The evidence further suggests that the amount of choice offered in primary elections in safe districts is not great. For example, Julius Turner, "Primary Elections as the Alternative to Party Competition in 'Safe' Districts," *Journal of Politics*, 15 (May, 1953), 197–210, found that, between the years 1944–1950, only half the primaries in safe districts were even contested. No doubt the candidates differed only marginally on the issues in at least some of the contested primaries.

TABLE 1

Intradistrict Differences in House Candidates' Attitudes
(liberalism-conservatism scale)

Score	Frequency	Percent	Score	Frequency	Percent
0	69	16	8	40	9
1	19	4	9	46	11
2	28	6	10	35	8
3	31	7	11	21	5
4	21	5	12	14	3
5	24	6	13	9	2
6	28	6	14	5	1
7	41	9	15	3	1
			16	1	0
				435	99

Mean = 5.9
Median = 6

We think it important then to show (Table 2) the sum of the absolute differences, question by question. The average amount of choice, when choice is conceptualized as differences in response to eight individual questions, rather than as differences in overall liberalism-conservatism, rises from a mean of 5.9 to a mean of 6.5. Because the individual questions are highly scalable, the difference between these distributions is slight. That is to say, those who are more liberal on one set of issues also tend to be more liberal on other sets of issues.

One is faced with the problem of determining how much choice is sufficient to satisfy the third linkage condition. Does the election offer the electorate a chance to affect policy outputs in a significant manner? Our approach to the problem is to examine aggregate differences among the candidates. This determines whether or not the election of one aggregate set of candidates over another set would have made any differences in the balance of power in Congress. Would the most *liberal* Con-

TABLE 2

Intradistrict Differences in House Candidates' Attitudes
(absolute differences)

Score	Frequency	Percent	Score	Frequency	Percent
0	61	14	8	42	10
1	5	1	9	56	13
2	20	5	10	43	10
3	18	4	11	24	6
4	19	4	12	14	3
5	31	7	13	9	2
6	36	8	14	5	1
7	48	11	15	3	1
			16	1	0
				435	100

Mean = 6.5
Median = 7

gress which could have been elected, in the aggregate, be quite different from the most *conservative* Congress which might have been chosen? Table 3 presents the attitude distributions of five hypothetical Congresses and of the real 90th Congress on the foreign policy questions. The most liberal and most conservative hypothetical Congresses are composed of the candidates having the lower or higher score, respectively, for each district on the foreign policy attitude scale.[17]

TABLE 3
Hypothetical Congresses—Frequency of Scale Scores on Foreign Policy

Score†	Winners N	Unchallenged Winners and Losers N	Most Democratic* N	Most Republican* N	Most Liberal N	Most Conservative N
2 liberal	31	45	58	18	73	3
3 moderate-liberal	51	60	76	35	91	20
4 moderate	177	173	224	126	203	147
5 moderate-conservative	104	71	49	126	48	127
6 conservative	72	86	28	130	20	138
	435	435	435	435	435	435
Mean	4.3	4.2	3.8	4.7	3.7	4.9
Median	4	4	4	5	4	5

* "Most Democratic" Congress includes Democrats plus unchallenged Republicans; "Most Republican" Congress includes Republican plus unchallenged Democrats.
† See Appendix A for a clarification of scale scores by issue area.

The actual 90th Congress is very much like the hypothetical Congress of losers; the winners have only fourteen fewer liberals and nine fewer moderate liberals among their number than have the losers. The balance of power resides with the moderates in both the actual Congress and the Congress of losers, since no liberal or conservative majority can be obtained without the support of a considerable number of moderates. This finding suggests that the election entailed much interdistrict canceling. In many districts the more liberal candidate won, but in many other districts the more conservative candidate won. The attitudinal composition of the Congress would not have been much different if all the losers had won. Perhaps even if we "threw all the rascals out," the new Congress-

[17] In each case, the most liberal and most conservative Congresses are based on the scores within the issue domain considered, rather than on the overall scale scores. Again, because of the scalability of the items, the most liberal and most conservative Congresses do not differ appreciably even when the overall scale scores are used to determine which candidate is more liberal. In no case is the mean or median different from those presented in Tables 3–5 because there are very few cases where one candidate is more liberal on the overall liberalism-conservatism scale but more conservative on one of the within-issue area scales, or vice versa. It was done this way to ensure that Tables 3–5 present the most conservative and most liberal Congresses possible in each issue cluster. The same procedure is followed in the data presented in Table 12.

men would give us the same policies. We must throw them out selectively if we wish significant policy changes.

If only the more liberal losers had won, however, the 90th Congress would have been very different. In the most liberal Congress, only 68 members would have favored a "tougher" policy toward Red China and in Vietnam. In the most conservative Congress, 265 members, a clear majority, would have favored a harder foreign-policy line. In the most liberal Congress, however, only 164 members would have preferred a softer foreign policy; the most liberal Congress would have provided a moderate balance of power, only slightly more liberal than the actual 90th Congress. The difference, or choice, presented in the election of 1966 on foreign policy was between a moderate, or status quo, policy (the moderate response on both questions was support for the present policy) or a more conservative policy. Even the most liberal Congress would not have resulted in a more liberal national policy without additional support from the moderates.

The civil rights data of Table 4 are comparable to those of Table 3. Again, the Congresses of winners and losers are similar (although the

TABLE 4
Hypothetical Congresses—Frequency of Scale Scores on Civil Rights

Score†	Winners N	Unchallenged Winners and Losers N	Most Democratic* N	Most Republican* N	Most Liberal N	Most Conservative N
2 liberal	201	162	257	106	272	92
3 moderate-liberal	15	65	36	44	32	48
4 moderate	110	103	64	149	59	154
5 moderate-conservative	17	16	6	27	6	27
6 conservative	92	89	72	109	66	114
	435	435	435	435	435	435
Mean	3.5	3.5	3.1	4.0	3.0	4.0
Median	4	3	2	4	2	4

° "Most Democratic" Congress includes Democrats plus unchallenged Republicans; "Most Republican" Congress include Republican plus unchallenged Democrats.
† See Appendix A for a clarification of scale scores by issue area.

Congress of losers would allow a liberal majority without the support of any moderates), the Democrats are consistently more liberal than the Republicans, the most liberal and the most conservative hypothetical Congresses are very different, and the most Democratic and most liberal Congresses are quite similar, as are the most Republican and the most conservative Congresses. If the electorate had chosen the most conservative Congress, the balance of power on civil rights would have lain with the moderates. No conservative or liberal majority could emerge without the support of the moderate faction. On the other hand, if the most liberal Congress had been elected, there would have been enough civil rights liberals to enact civil rights legislation without any moderate support. In fact, there would have been a surplus of 54 confirmed liberals, without any support from moderate liberals. These data suggest that if Riker is right,[18] legislation even more liberal than the open-housing bill would have been seriously proposed, debated, and quite possibly passed.

The actual 90th Congress began with only 216 liberal or moderately liberal civil rights supporters, but more than 40 Congressmen shifted in the liberal direction to pass the Open Housing Act of 1968. These shifts, probably in response to civil disturbances and to the assassination of Dr. Martin Luther King, Jr., still would not have been sufficient to pass the legislation had the most conservative Congress been in office. In the area of civil rights, the electorate had a choice only between two positions— a liberal or a moderate balance of power in Congress, rather than among three positions—a liberal, a moderate, or a conservative balance.

Table 5 indicates that the electorate also had an opportunity to affect policy outcomes on domestic issues. Again the losers and winners look relatively similar, although the winners are more conservative. Also, the fits between the most Democratic and most liberal Congresses on the one hand, and the most Republican and most conservative Congresses on the other, are even closer than in the cases of foreign policy and civil rights. These correspondences on domestic issues support the notion that the major issues dividing the two parties are bread-and-butter issues, i.e., domestic economic and welfare policies.

If the most liberal Congress had been elected, there would have been only 78 conservatives or moderate conservatives, while 290 members would have favored most of the liberal items of social legislation. If the liberals had been able to obtain the support of slightly more than half of

TABLE 5
Hypothetical Congresses—Frequency of Scale Scores on Domestic Issues

Score†	Winners N	Unchallenged Winners and Losers N	Most Democratic* N	Most Republican* N	Most Liberal N	Most Conservative N
4 liberal	79	57	129	7	130	6
5–6 moderate-liberal	81	105	161	25	160	26
7–9 moderate	43	85	64	64	67	61
10–11 mod.-conservative	70	90	28	132	33	128
12 conservative	162	98	53	207	45	214
	435	435	435	435	435	435
Mean	8.7	8.3	6.6	10.5	6.5	10.5
Median	10	8	6	11	6	11

* "Most Democratic" Congress includes Democrats plus unchallenged Republicans; "Most Republican" Congress includes Republican plus unchallenged Democrats.
† See Appendix A for a clarification of scale scores by issue area.

[18] William Riker, The Theory of Political Coalitions (New Haven: Yale University Press, 1962).

the moderate liberals, a clear liberal majority would have resulted. On the other hand, if the most conservative Congress had been elected, there would have been only 32 liberals or moderate liberals, leading to a clear conservative majority with the support of only a small number of the 128 moderate conservatives. The median domestic scale score for the most liberal Congress is 6 (toward the moderate end of the moderate-liberal category); for the most conservative Congress it is 11 (toward the conservative end of the moderate-conservative category). This is a meaningful difference because different electoral outcomes imply majority support for different policies.

ATTITUDES AND BEHAVIOR

We have been talking about attitudes toward public policy. It must be emphasized, however, that our measures for nonincumbents consist entirely of responses to a questionnaire and represent what are conventionally referred to as verbal attitudes, while our measures for incumbents consist partially of actual roll-call behavior. The questionnaire asked the nonincumbents if they supported certain programs which had been voted on in the previous Congress. As a result, the attitude-behavior distinction should be at a minimum, but it would be risky to assume, without a thorough empirical examination, that the questionnaire data and the roll-call data are comparable.[19]

The general question of the relationship between verbal attitudes and overt behavior has never been adequately resolved. In a review of more than 32 studies, Wicker concluded:

> Taken as a whole, these studies suggest that it is considerably more likely that attitudes will be unrelated or only slightly related to overt behaviors than that attitudes will be closely related to actions. Product-moment correlation coefficients relating the two kinds of responses are rarely above .30, and often are near zero.[20]

Taken at face value, this conclusion does seem to resolve the problem: there is no predictable relationship. Yet under the appropriate conditions, he implies, there ought to be a strong positive relationship. Wicker goes on to inventory the kinds of factors—personal and situational—that determine the strength of the relationship between verbal attitudes and overt behavior. Personal factors include other attitudes relevant to the observed behavior: competing motives; verbal, intellectual, and social abilities; and activity levels. Situational factors include the degree of privacy, normative prescriptions of behavior, alternative behaviors avail-

---

[19] Miller and Stokes, "Constituency Influence in Congress," p. 48, report correlations between the true opinion of Congressmen (as measured by a questionnaire) and their roll-call behavior of 0.75 among those who felt their attitudes were expressed in their roll calls, but only 0.04 among those who felt that they were not.

[20] Allan W. Wicker, "Attitudes versus Actions: The Relationship of Verbal and Overt Behavioral Responses to Attitude Objects," *Journal of Social Issues*, 25 (Autumn, 1969), 65.

able, specificity of attitude objects, unforeseen events, and consequences of the act, expected or actual.[21] Without attempting a complete enumeration, we will suggest the effects of some of these variables in the present research.

The fact that we are comparing actual behavior with behavioral intentions of high specificity, rather than with general attitudes toward the attitude object in question, enhances the relationship between the two different types of measurements. For example, competing motives in this case could easily include the conflict between attitude toward civil rights and the desire to get re-elected. If questioned about his attitude toward civil rights, a representative may have indicated a positive response yet voted against a civil rights bill because he felt that his constituency opposed it and would not re-elect him if he voted for it. This conflict should be lessened because the questionnaire did not ask the challengers whether or not they favored civil rights, but rather whether they would have supported (voted for) a particular civil rights bill. Presumably, they considered these conflicting motives in the same manner they would have if actually faced with the behavioral decision. Undoubtedly there is slippage, since some candidates may not have been aware of all the conflicting motives they would encounter if they actually had to make a behavioral decision. The point is that the slippage should be minimal as compared to less behaviorally specific attitudes.

Or consider activity level. The attitude-behavior relationship is hypothesized to be considerably stronger for the active as opposed to the more apathetic individual. Certainly the candidates in the 1966 congressional elections were sufficiently active to produce a strong relationship between attitude and behavior vis-à-vis the major issues of the day.

It seems, therefore, that although the questionnaire and roll-call data are not isomorphic, they ought to be directly comparable. We can examine this congruence empirically, at least indirectly, in the form of

TABLE 6

Relationship between Scale Positions on Pre-Election Attitudes and Postelection Roll-Call Behavior: Nonincumbents, Domestic Issues

Postelection Roll-Call Scale Position	Pre-election Attitude Scale Position							
	3	4	5	6	7	8	9	Totals
3	1	2	1	0	1	2	0	7
4	0	0	0	0	0	0	1	1
5	0	0	0	1	0	1	1	3
6	0	0	0	0	1	0	1	2
7	0	0	0	1	3	3	3	10
8	0	0	0	0	2	1	1	4
9	2	0	0	4	3	12	31	52
Totals	3	2	1	6	10	19	38	79

gamma = .48
Somer's d_{xy} = .37

---

[21] Wicker, pp. 67–74.

predictive validity. If both sets of pre-election data predict subsequent roll-call behavior with equal accuracy, we can feel secure about comparability. Thus the examination of the relationship between pre-election data and postelection roll-call behavior serves two functions. It allows us to examine and judge the comparability of the two types of pre-election data, and it allows us to determine the validity of the fourth linkage condition, i.e., that the pre-election differences between candidates are the basis of post-election roll-call differences.

In order to examine this relationship empirically, additional data were collected from the *Congressional Quarterly Almanac, 1968*. These data are the roll-call votes of all winners of the 1966 Congressional elections on the same issues which constitute our pre-election data.[22]

Table 6 illustrates the relationship between the nonincumbents' pre-election attitudes and subsequent roll-call behavior on selected domestic issues. Table 7 illustrates the relationship between the incumbents' roll-call behavior before the election and their postelection behavior on the same issues.[23] The relationship is very strong for the incumbents, while it is moderately strong for the nonincumbents. This difference requires a note of caution regarding the assumption of strict comparability of the questionnaire and pre-election roll-call data, at least on domestic welfare issues. But clearly the relationship, when compared with Wicker's dismal conclusion, is considerably stronger than his upper limit of .30.

Generally the winners voted as our pre-election scores indicated they would. Among the nonincumbents, there are 11 winners whose postelec-

---

[22] There were no roll calls comparable to the foreign affairs, labor, or voting rights items of the pre-election scale. Therefore, in the tables that follow, these items have been dropped from the initial measures. The included roll calls are listed in Appendix B. It should also be noted that the foreign affairs data are questionnaire responses for both incumbents and nonincumbents (See Appendix A). Therefore, although we cannot examine the linkage condition in foreign affairs, the methodological question of comparability does not arise.

[23] Gamma is stronger than Sommer's d_{xy} because it ignores all ties. It considers only the concordant and discordant pairs, while Somer's d_{xy} is penalized for every case in which the dependent variable varies but the independent variable does not vary. The actual theoretical relationships of Tables 7–10 are probably overestimated by the strength of gamma because if two cases are tied on one variable but not on the other, they ought not to be ignored unless the theory predicts that this should happen. This is not the case here. Conversely, Somer's d_{xy} probably underestimates the relationship because some of the cases which lower Somer's d_{xy}, cases which differ on the dependent variable but not on the independent variable, do so because of measurement error. Two nonincumbents whose pre-election scores are 8 on domestic issues might be expected to differ in postelection behavior because the intermediate option is not so easily taken on roll calls as it is on questionnaires, and their reasons for hedging on one issue in the pre-election questionnaire may be quite different, leading to a different postelection roll-call decision. Somer's d_{xy} is included, however, to illustrate the range of values obtained, depending on the method of handling ties. Somer's d_{xy} was selected over d_{yx}, which is reduced by cases which vary on the independent but not the dependent variable, because of the nature of the two different kinds of measurement. The questionnaire allowed more options than a roll call, in that abstention on a roll call is more difficult than selecting the intermediate option on a questionnaire. Therefore, the situation of variation on the independent variable coupled with ties on the dependent variable is slightly more likely to occur than is variation on the dependent variable coupled with ties on the independent variable.

TABLE 7

Relationship between Scale Positions on Pre-Election
and Postelection Roll-Call Behavior: Incumbents, Domestic Issues

Postelection Roll-Call Scale Position	Pre-election Roll-Call Scale Position							Totals
	3	4	5	6	7	8	9	
3	63	16	46	1	5	0	0	131
4	11	3	6	1	1	1	1	24
5	3	0	8	0	5	0	5	21
6	1	0	2	1	2	1	1	8
7	1	0	3	0	2	3	20	29
8	0	0	0	0	1	4	15	20
9	0	0	1	1	6	9	102	119
Totals	79	19	66	4	22	18	144	352*

gamma = .86
Somer's d_{xy} = .72

* Among the 356 incumbent winners, there were no postelection data for four: both Younger (R-Calif.) and Fogarty (D-R.I.) had died, Powell (D-N.Y.) was excluded from the House, and McCormack (D-Mass.), as Speaker, did not vote.

tion score is two or more points more liberal than their pre-election scores. There are 9 whose postelection scores are two or more points more conservative than their pre-election scores. The figures for incumbents are 88 more liberal and 16 more conservative, illustrating a shift in the liberal direction. This shift was strong enough to cause slippage between the representation some voters might be expected to believe they would get and what they actually received on domestic legislation, but it was not sufficient to alter the moderate-conservative balance of power predicted on the basis of pre-election scores, as evidenced by Table 8. (Compare Table 8 to the winners column of Table 5.) Therefore, although individual voters may have been misled, the aggregate effect of such crossovers was not extensive enough to affect domestic policy. We may thus conclude that on domestic welfare issues the data support both the methodological contention that the pre-election data are comparable, and the substantive and theoretical contention that the pre-election candidate differences lead to postelection policy differences.

Tables 9 and 10 present the relationships between pre-election and

TABLE 8

Actual Congress, Frequency of Postelection
Roll-Call Scores, Domestic Issues

Score	N
3 liberal	138
4–5 moderate-liberal	49
6 moderate	10
7–8 moderate-conservative	63
9 conservative	171
	431
Mean	6.3
Median	7

TABLE 9

Relationship between Scale Scores on Pre-
Election Attitudes and Postelection Roll-Call
Behavior: Nonincumbents, Open Housing

Postelection Roll-Call Scale scores	Pre-election Attitude Scale Scores			
	1	2	3	Totals
1	15	7	7	29
2	0	0	1	1
3	4	6	39	49
Totals ..	19	13	47	78

gamma = .80
Somer's d_{xy} = .58

postelection measures on open housing for nonincumbents and incumbents, respectively. Again, the measures of association for the incumbents are higher, although they are also very high for the nonincumbents. This finding indicates a very strong link between attitudes and behavior, and comparability of the pre-election measures in the area of civil rights. The inferences about civil rights policy in the section on hypothetical Congresses seem to be supported. Generalizing the strength of the attitude-behavior relationship to those nonincumbents who lost, one can readily see that they would have voted as their attitudes indicated they would.

Unlike the shifts on domestic welfare, the shifts on civil rights *were* sufficient to affect policy. Fifteen nonincumbents shifted in the liberal direction, ten in the conservative direction; the figures for the incumbents are 33 vs. 12. As Table 11 illustrates, this shift resulted in a balance of power favoring the liberals (i.e., the bill passed). When compared to the balance of power predicted before the election (winners column and marginals, Table 4; pre-election attitudes, Tables 9 and 10) this change represents a shift from the moderate position. A shift on civil rights was to be expected, as this was a roll-call vote with only abstention representing a middle alternative. Therefore we have the paradoxical situation in which pre-election attitude is a better predictor of roll-call behavior on

TABLE 10

Relationship between Scale Scores on Pre-
Election and Postelection Roll-Call Behavior:
Incumbents, Open Housing

Postelection Roll-Call Scale scores	Pre-election Roll-Call Scale Scores			
	1	2	3	Totals
1	169	3	25	197
2	3	1	5	9
3	9	0	137	146
Totals	181	4	167	352

gamma = .97
Somer's d_{xy} = .78

TABLE 11

Actual Congress, Frequency of Postelection
Roll-Call Scores, Civil Rights

Score	N
1 liberal	226
2 moderate	10
3 conservative	195
	431
Mean	1.9
Median	1

civil rights than on domestic welfare issues, yet the fewer civil rights crossovers result in a new balance of power. This result is entirely due to the precarious balance of power on civil rights issues, plus the events, such as the assassination of Dr. Martin Luther King, which influenced the passage of the Open Housing Act of 1968.

SUMMARY AND DISCUSSION

This paper essentially presents three simple findings: (1) that the electorate in the aggregate was offered a substantively significant choice in the Congressional election of 1966, (2) that winning candidates in that election generally voted as their pre-election issue positions predicted, and (3) that the Democratic candidates were almost invariably more liberal than their intradistrict Republican competitors.

These simple empirical findings have broad implications for democratic theory. Concerning the linkage question, the data suggest that the relatively weak linkage between public opinion and policy outputs is neither a result of the party system's failure to provide choices on issue positions nor of the system's providing oral choices later ignored in roll-call behavior. The voters could have established a strong overall linkage.

The findings also fuel the discussion about voter rationality. In all three cases, the most liberal Congress is very similar to the Congress composed of Democrats and unchallenged Republicans. Similarly, the most conservative Congress resembles the most Republican Congress. Only 19 of the Republican candidates were more liberal than their Democratic opponents on the overall scale, even though they may have been more liberal than many Democratic candidates in other districts. This finding has interesting implications in light of studies which have bemoaned the electorate's supposedly limited awareness of public affairs and the limited extent of policy-oriented voting. If a voter in 1966 wanted to vote conservatively, he only had to know that the Republican party is generally more conservative than the Democratic party in order to cast his ballot correctly in light of his values. If our findings may be generalized to other elections, party may be said to provide a valid cue for the policy-oriented voter who does not have a thorough awareness of the issues or the policy positions of the candidates.

If informational costs for policy-oriented voters are so low, why did Miller and Stokes fail to find strong linkages between public opinion and public policy? Perhaps one answer lies in the way rationality has been defined, namely in terms of a liberal-conservative scale on national issues. Although we have found that Congressional candidates' attitudes do scale unidimensionally along a liberal-conservative dimension, there is little evidence that mass attitudes fall along the same continuum. This suggests not that mass attitudes are in some way irrational but that candidates' attitudes are to some extent inconsistent with the attitudes of many voters. For example, a voter may be hawkish, anti-civil rights, and a proponent of liberal domestic programs. He may have to choose between a Democrat who is more liberal than his opponent in all three cases, and a Republican who is more conservative in all three policy areas. By our scale, this citizen has a wide choice. But the choice is not easy, for he must choose on the one hand to support civil rights policies and foreign policies that he really opposes, or on the other to help defeat domestic programs he supports. Either way this voter's ability to help forge a linkage between public opinion and public policy is limited.

To reiterate: We have examined choice only in terms of a liberal-conservative dimension, not in terms of whatever dimensions seem most relevant to individual voters. There is evidence which suggests that from the voters' own points of reference, their behavior is quite rational.[24] The crux of the matter is that even though the electorate is presented with a choice in elite attitudes, elite attitudes seem to be ordered along a different dimension than are mass attitudes.[25] Therefore the linkage must of necessity be weak on some issues whether voters are issue-oriented or not.[26]

Another factor weakening the linkage between public opinion and public policy is the large number of safe districts where the challenger has no realistic chance of winning.[27] Using the criterion that if more than

---

[24] Michael J. Shapiro, "Rational Political Man: A Synthesis of Economic and Social-Psychological Perspectives," *American Political Science Review*, 63 (December, 1969), 1106–1119.

[25] Steven R. Brown and Richard W. Taylor, "Objectivity and Subjectivity in Concept Formation: Problems of Perspective, Partition, and Frames of Reference," paper delivered at the sixty-sixth annual meeting of the American Political Science Association, Los Angeles, California, September, 1970.

[26] Miller and Stokes, p. 50, report correlations between constituency majority and congressional roll-call votes of 0.4, and between district majority and nonincumbent candidate attitudes of −0.4, in the social welfare policy domain. This suggests that within the confines of the amount and kind of choice presented, the masses are indeed selecting those elites whose attitudes are most congruent with their own. The fact that the congruency is not higher may be due primarily to the differing attitudinal structures of elites and nonelites.

[27] If the electorate votes primarily on the basis of party identification and if these identifications are unevenly distributed within a large percentage of districts, the result is a lack of intradistrict competition. If this uneven distribution of identifications reflects an equally uneven distribution of opinions and preferences on issues, then linkage could occur without a choice of candidates who differ in their issue positions. Therefore the optimal amount of choice in each district would depend on its internal distribution of opinion. Since data of this nature are not available, this analysis has focused on the systemic, rather than district, consequences of choice. From this framework, the more choice, the greater the opportunity for the electorate as a whole to exercise control over policy.

55 per cent of the vote goes to the winner, the district is noncompetitive, we found that only 73 of the 435 districts both were competitive and offered a policy choice. To quote Turner, "The alternative candidates must have nearly equal chances of success in the election, or else the voter is not presented with realistic alternatives."[28] As our data clearly show, the *opportunity* to affect policy outcomes via the electoral process certainly existed in 1966. To verify this linkage condition in no way vitiates the somewhat different but related point that the *probability* that the electoral process would affect policy in 1966 was somewhat lower.

To illustrate this point, the most liberal and most conservative Congresses were recomputed in all three issue clusters, assuming that a noncompetitive district offered a choice of zero regardless of how much the competing candidates may have differed. The results are presented in Table 12.

Table 12

Hypothetical Congresses, Frequency of Scale Scores in Three Areas Controlling for Party Competition

Score	Foreign Policy		Civil Rights		Domestic Issues	
	N Most Liberal	N Most Conservative	N Most Liberal	N Most Conservative	N Most Liberal	N Most Conservative
liberal	36	26	220	181	88	73
moderate-liberal	62	42	11	20	104	66
moderate	187	169	106	116	42	41
mod.-conservative	90	114	12	24	52	84
conservative	60	84	86	94	149	171
	435	435	435	435	435	435
Mean	4.2	4.4	3.4	3.6	8.3	9.0
Median	4	4	2	4	8	10

This makes it clear that although the "outer limits" of choice in the election were sufficient to verify the linkage condition in question, the realities of party competition narrowed these limits considerably. Realistically, the most the election meant was the difference between a liberal vs. moderate balance of power on civil rights and a moderate-conservative vs. moderate balance of power on domestic issues. Regardless of the outcome of the election, given the large number of relatively safe districts, the balance of power had to reside with the moderates on foreign policy.[29] This finding merely serves to clarify the nature of our analysis. We have not found that the 1966 election significantly affected public policy. Rather we have found that the opportunity for it to affect policy was present, and that this opportunity is all that is necessary to provide a means of policy control for the electorate.

---

[28] Turner, "Primary Elections," p. 198.

[29] In all three issue clusters, the actual Congress resembles the most conservative Congress probable, given the existence of a large number of safe districts. To the extent that it makes sense to label an election a liberal or a conservative victory, the 1966 House election was a conservative victory.

Section III
The Pressure Groups Model

The pressure groups model conceives of society as composed of very few individuals unassociated with at least one group and government policy as the product of competition among groups each fighting for its preferences. Few would argue that groups are not active in seeking to shape the public policy at national, state, and local levels, but whether they are the sole forces shaping policy remains undemonstrated. It is quite questionable whether the opinions of various groups concerned with an issue, such as abortion laws, equal the opinion of the general public. Many Americans belong to no groups. Typically, 50 to 60 percent of the public report memberships in various groups, clubs, unions, or other voluntary organizations, which is high relative to other countries but certainly far enough short of full involvement to question whether those who are members accurately mirror the opinions of those who do not belong.[1] Furthermore, one study found that only 40 percent of the group members thought that their group was involved in political affairs, meaning that only about one citizen in four belongs to a politically active group.[2] Finally, a study of group memberships in Florida found no more than 10 percent of the public belonged to groups to which they would turn for advice or information.[3]

As discussed in the Introduction, in its purist form the pressure groups model gives no independence to the elected representative; he merely tabulates the thrust of interested groups. But only about one legislator in three in a study of state legislators felt he should be so facilitating of

[1] Charles R. Wright and Herbert H. Hyman, "Voluntary Association Membership of American Adults: Evidence from National Sample Surveys," *American Sociological Review*, vol. 23 (1958), reprinted in *American Political Interest Groups: Readings in Theory and Research*, Betty H. Zisk, ed. (Belmont, Calif.: Wadsworth, 1969); Gabriel A. Almond and Sidney Verba, *The Civic Culture* (Princeton: Princeton University Press, 1963), p. 302; and Sidney Verba and Norman Nie, *Participation in Democracy* (New York: Harper Row, 1972), p. 41.

[2] Almond and Verba, *Participation in Democracy*, p. 306.

[3] Robert S. Erikson and Norman R. Luttbeg, *American Public Opinion: Its Origins, Content, and Impact* (New York: Wiley, 1973), p. 306.

groups.[4] The groups then, if they are to be heard and serve to achieve political linkage, must be able to mobilize their memberships to force compliance from representatives. They must obviously be able to control the direction of the members' political activities. But the first selection reproduced here assesses various groups' ability to shape their members' votes. Angus Campbell and his associates find groups can align their members' votes with a seemingly sympathetic political party over a period of years under the proper circumstances. But the process is slow and certainly not manipulatable to the political purpose of the groups' leaders from one election to the next. Labor, for example, can get most involved members to vote Democratic with some effort, but certainly cannot swing the labor vote to the Republican party one year because of less Democratic response to the demands of labor.

If groups are to serve as communicators of their members' opinions before government, group leaders should be able to express accurately the favored positions of their membership. Norman Luttbeg and Harmon Zeigler consider whether leaders accurately perceive members' opinions or personally share those opinions. Leaders in representing their membership can act either on their own opinions or on those they think to be held by their membership. In this professional teachers' organization acting on either would cause leaders to misrepresent actual teachers' opinions.

Turning to the relations between elected representatives and lobbyists for groups, Zeigler finds substantial variation between states. Massachusetts lobbyists face frustratingly unresponsive legislators, while Oregon legislators seem to work quite well with groups in their state. Is the pressure group model then more effective in some circumstances; if so, what are they? Zeigler gives some speculation on this.

A study of the type of person to whom Iowa legislators turn for advice concludes the selections on this model. G. R. Boynton, Samuel Patterson, and Ronald Hedlund find these advisors or "political middlemen" hardly satisfy any expectation under the pressure group model that group leaders would be the prime advisors. Instead locally elected officials predominate. Judging from their personal characteristics, these men also cannot be viewed as conduits of public opinion to representatives as they do not mirror the Iowa public in age, education, occupation, or party identification.

If the findings in this section are correct, group leaders misrepresent the opinions of even the small minority which hold membership in politically active groups. And many group leaders face hostile representatives who seek advice from men not representing groups.

---

[4] John C. Wahlke, Heinz Eulau, William Buchanan, and Leroy C. Ferguson, *The Legislative System* (New York: Wiley, 1962), p. 327.

Angus Campbell, Philip E. Converse,
Warren E. Miller, and Donald E. Stokes

Membership in Social Groupings*

During each political campaign we hear comment about the "Catholic vote," the "Negro vote," the "labor vote," and so on. Unlike the political parties, these groups stand at one remove from the political order. Their reason for existence is not expressly political. The labor union exists to force management to provide more liberally for the worker; the Catholic church exists for religious worship. But members of these groups appear to think and behave politically in distinctive ways. We assume that these distinctive patterns are produced, in one fashion or another, by influence from the group.

THE PROBLEM OF GROUP INFLUENCE

Groups have influence because we tend to think of them as wholes, and come to respond positively or negatively to them in that form. In this sense, even people who are not members of a group may be influenced by the position that a group takes in politics. Groups can become reference points for the formation of attitudes and decisions about behavior; we speak then of *positive* and *negative reference groups*. People who are actually members of the group are likely to have a more differentiated image of it. But there remains a sense of norms and values attributed to a generalized "group": these are the expectations concerning appropriate behavior for the "loyal" Catholic or union member. It is the group standards that are psychologically real and are responsible for influence when it occurs.

In this chapter we are concerned with the apparent political influence exerted among major, nationwide groupings such as the labor unions, Negroes, Catholics, and Jews. This is not the only level at which political influence dependent on social contact may be examined. Much influence is exerted in smaller, face-to-face "primary" groups such as families, circles of friends, and the like. In fact, there is some evidence that when primary-group influences run counter to secondary-group political stan-

* Reprinted from Campbell, et al., *The American Voter: An Abridgement* (New York: Wiley, 1964), chap. 11.

189

dards, the more intimate contacts may more often than not carry the day.[1] Nonetheless, although many of the mechanisms of influence may be the same in both cases, the study of secondary-group effects has its own unique fruits. It is probably accurate to assume that influence ramifies through primary groups at the grass roots of the nation in a manner fairly constant for both parties. The success or failure of influence at a face-to-face level is not likely to account for the gross trends of the sort constituted by secondary-group voting. If every man managed to influence his wife to vote as he does, we would have no more than a "multiplier" effect on both sides of the political fence. In contrast, successful influence by secondary groups can cause a large-scale, unidirectional shift in the partisan division of the national vote. We are interested in understanding the conditions under which these group pressures are more or less successful.

When we discussed the political parties, it seemed reasonable to speak in terms of a "psychological group," in part because the boundaries of the parties are so poorly delimited by the fact of official membership. In secondary membership groups like labor unions, these formal group boundaries are quite clear. We do not have to ask our informants whether they "consider" they belong to one or another groups; membership is a factual matter. But as we examine these groups more closely, it turns out that the concept of group identification and psychological membership remains extremely valuable. Individuals, all of whom are nominal group members, vary in *degree* of membership, in a psychological sense; and this variation provides us with an excellent tool for breaking apart a voting "bloc," like the American Negro community, in order to understand the workings of influence within the secondary group.

The significance of group identification in all social groupings provides us with a foundation for a more general model of group influence in politics. The scheme would tell us what dimensions of the situation were important for measurement, and how these measures should be combined once they were taken. Appropriate measurements based on such a scheme would allow us to anticipate the direction and degree of the influence that the grouping would wield in the specific situation.

In this chapter we treat membership in social groupings by sketching the outlines for a general model of this sort. The specific currents observed in the Negro vote in the 1956 election become, in this light, substance of a case study to lay against the more abstract elements called for by the scheme. Likewise, the distinctive behavior of union members toward the objects of politics becomes a special case of the broad phenomenon of group influence.

THE ELEMENTS OF THE MODEL

A model for group influence should perform two distinct services:
1. Increase our understanding of deviation from group political stan-

---

[1] Norman Kaplan, "Reference Group Theory and Voting Behavior" (unpublished doctoral dissertation, Columbia University, 1955).

dards by individual members. If the group exerts influence on its membership, and these individuals are members, how and why do they resist?

2. Increase our understanding of the waxing and waning of distinctive political behavior on the part of certain social groupings in the population. What specific conditions govern this variation in group political "strength"?

The same system of variables can handle both problems, for the problems are closely related. If we can specify the conditions under which an individual fails to be influenced by his group, then it is likely that the decline of group potency in politics will result from the extension of these conditions to an increasing proportion of the membership.

At the simplest level, there is a triangle of elements involved in the situation: (1) the individual, (2) the group, and (3) the world of political objects. This triangle suggests three different relationships among these elements: (a) the relationship of the individual to the group; (b) the relationship of the group to the political world; and (c) the relationship of the individual to the political world. These three relationships determine the types of variables that we take into account. A full model will call for measurements that adequately capture the important dimensions of each relationship, if we are to understand the way in which the individual will respond to politics *given the presence of a group that is real in the sense that it can exert a greater or lesser influence on his behavior.*

The relationship of the individual to the world of politics represents a combination of group and nongroup forces. The group forces in the field are predictable as a function of two "background" terms; the relationship of the individual to the group and the relationship of the group to the world of politics. The nongroup forces are, of course, independent of either of these terms. An analysis of the social origins of political motives therefore involves (1) the manner in which the two background terms interact to produce group forces; and (2) the manner in which group forces interact with other forces in the immediate field of political attitudes.

Two important implications are suggested by a logical exercise of this sort. On one hand, we must arrive at some means of sorting the group forces in which we are interested from nongroup forces, within the total field that characterizes the relationship of the individual to the world of politics. But if we pay little systematic attention to the total relationship of the individual to the political world in elaborating this portion of the model, we must not forget that these nongroup forces exist. In fact, this is a first-level answer to the problem of member deviation from group political standards. Group members do not make political decisions in a psychological field limited to group forces, any more than nonmembers make decisions in a vacuum. The current objects of orientation in the political world are available to everybody and, if perceived, have characteristics that can be distorted only within limits.

Our immediate concern lies with the strength of group-generated forces. We wish to understand the conditions under which that strength varies, over time, from individual to individual and from group to group.

For this task we can conceptually ignore other forces in the field, which derive from the relation of the individual to politics, *group considerations aside*. But we must remember that these forces exist and contribute to the final attitudes and behavior.

ESTABLISHING THE FACT OF GROUP INFLUENCE

The immediate problem is to find ways to estimate the strength of group forces on the individual. With other forces present in the field, it is easy to mistake their effects for the effects of group influence.

First, it is important to think in terms of the *distinctiveness* of group behavior, rather than its absolute nature. For example, a majority of Catholics in our 1956 sample voted Republican. Traditionally, there has been a Democratic norm among Catholics. Does this finding mean that the norm has died away, or that the group now has new, pro-Republican standards? It means neither. The Catholic Republican vote moved only slightly above the 50 per cent mark, when the nation as a whole was voting 57 per cent Republican. The group force was weak and nongroup forces pushing toward a Republican vote were strong; the nongroup forces were dominant enough to pull a majority of Catholics into the Republican camp, but the presence of group forces in a Democratic direction remains detectable, *relative to the behavior of nongroup members*.

With vote distinctiveness as a criterion, Table 1 summarizes the behavior of several key secondary membership groups with traditional Democratic voting norms over a period of three presidential elections. Several aspects of the table are striking. First we find that there is considerable variation in *degree* of distinctiveness, from election to election and from group to group. We also find that each group seems to vary within a characteristic range. Catholics tend to be least distinctive throughout; the labor unions fall in a middle range. Negroes, despite a sharp drop in distinctiveness between 1952 and 1956, remain on the high side along with Jewish voters.

Nevertheless, there is room for dissatisfaction with distinctiveness, cast in this form, as a working measure of influence. The fact of membership in secondary groupings of the type we are considering locates the person in a peculiar position in social structure, which *in itself* ensures a distinctive pattern of life experience. For example, Negroes have been kept in the lower levels of the nation's status structure; they tend to predominate in the least desirable occupations, receive the lowest pay, are least well educated, and so on. Their high birth rate means that young people are more numerous among Negroes than among other elements in the population. In the North, they tend to reside in metropolitan areas; in the South, in small towns and rural areas. All of these distinctive characteristics have a potential effect on their reactions to politics; and this would be true *even if the group did not exist as an entity cognized by its members*. Northern Negroes as a group made a massive shift of allegiance from the Republican to the Democratic Party during the 1930's. Was this group cohesiveness in response to an Administration interested in the

TABLE 1
The Distinctiveness of Voting Behavior among Several Social Groupings with Democratic Norms, 1948–1956*

	1948	1952	1956
Members of union households†	+35.8	+19.8	+18.1
Union members	– ‡	+24.9	+21.4
Catholics	+16.2	+12.8	+7.1
Negroes	– §	+41.2	+24.7
Non-South	– §	+50.8	+33.1
South	– §	+17.6	−1.1
Jews	– §	+31.9	+40.8

* The entry in each cell represents the deviation in per cent Democratic of the two-party vote division from the comparable per cent among the residual, non-member portion of the total sample. A positive deviation indicates that the group vote was more Democratic; a negative deviation indicates that the group was more Republican than the residual nongroup.

† "Members of union households" includes both union members, where interviews were conducted with the member himself, and other nonunion individuals living in a household that contained a union member. In most cases, the non-member is the wife of a member.

‡ Members and nonmembers were not separated within our sample of union households in 1948.

§ Due to the reduced size of the 1948 sample and the small proportion of Negroes and Jews in the parent population, insufficient cases are available for presentation.

welfare of the Negro community, or was it simply the independent reaction of a set of individuals to economic pressures, part and parcel of the nationwide establishment of Democratic dominance at the lower status levels? In the one case, we would speak of group influence; in the other, we would turn to considerations of social class and economic deprivation.

Of course, we cannot ignore the fact that group influence is in part contingent upon the life situations of the membership. But the important point remains that group influence *is* an additional element in the picture; shared membership provides a focus and direction for behavior that is lacking among nongroup members who happen to be placed in the same life situation. Therefore, it is important to distinguish between the

TABLE 2
Distinctiveness of Presidential Vote among Certain Groups, with Life Situation Controlled, 1956*

	1956 Presidential Vote
Members of union households	+17.1
Union members	+20.4
Catholics	+2.9
Negroes	
Non-South	+11.6
South	+15.4
Jews	+45.4

* The entry in each cell represents a deviation in per cent Democratic of the two-party vote within the test group from a comparable per cent computed for control groups matched with the test groups for a variety of conditions of life situation.

patterns of behavior that develop from the life situations of group members, without reference to the group *qua* group, and the residual distinctiveness that may be traced directly to the fact of group membership.

Hence we must contrast behaviors of group members not simply with those of the remainder of the population, but with the restricted part of that population that shares the peculiar life situations of group members. We want to isolate a "control" group of nonmembers that matches the "test" group of members on all important aspects of life situation save the fact of membership.

With life situation controlled, our estimate of group distinctiveness should be materially improved. Table 2 summarizes this new estimate for our groups in the context of the 1956 election. If we compare the figures for vote distinctiveness with those in Table 1, we find that much of the picture has remained the same. Catholic distinctiveness has almost disappeared, and the estimate of Jewish distinctiveness has risen slightly. But the major change has been a substantial reduction in the estimate of distinctiveness of the non-Southern Negro vote. This group remains significantly Democratic; but taking into account its extremely low status, its relative youth, and its Southern origins leaves it less Democratic than might appear at first glance.[2]

With such controls, we have more nearly reduced the relationship between the individual and the world of politics to its group-relevant aspects. In effect, we have arrived at an improved estimate of the strength of group forces in the total field at the time of the voting act. The estimate is not perfect and depends on an aggregation of cases; we cannot say that any specific group member is more swayed by the group than any other, although we get the clear impression that some groups exert more effective influence than others. We must now turn to other elements in the model for this variation in influence.

THE RELATIONSHIP OF THE INDIVIDUAL TO THE GROUP

The first variables to be considered must define the way in which the individual relates himself to the group. We would like to measure aspects of the individual-group relationship that are meaningful for the relationship of *any* individual to *any* group, whether or not that group ever expends effort in political affairs.

Let us think of the group as a psychological reality that exerts greater or lesser attractive force upon its members. Whatever the nominal membership status of the individual, there is room for a great deal of variation in the degree of psychological membership that characterizes the relationship. Just as party identification measures the sense of personal attachment to a political party, so a measure of group identification will indicate the closeness or "*we* feeling" that an individual senses with regard to his membership group.

---

[2] The application of the Southern-origin factor to Negroes represents one point at which we lack information to exercise controls prudently. As the matter stands, the distinctiveness of the Negro group may be underestimated in Table 2.

We have measured group identification by asking members of various politically significant groups the following questions:

Would you say that you feel pretty close to (e.g.) Negroes in general or that you don't feel much closer to them than you do to other kinds of people?

How much interest would you say you have in how (e.g.) Negroes as a whole are getting along in this country? Do you have a good deal of interest in it, some interest, or not much interest at all?

From responses to these items an index of group identification was prepared. The first hypothesis that the model suggests is as follows: *the higher the identification of the individual with the group, the higher the probability that he will think and behave in ways which distinguish members of his group from nonmembers.*

Actually hypotheses much like this have found supporting evidence in other empirical work on voting behavior. Therefore, we are not surprised to find that if we take all members of groups that vote distinctively Democratic, the people who are highly identified with these groups vote even more distinctively Democratic than members who are less highly identified. The least identified third voted 43 per cent Democratic, a figure not very different from the vote proportion in the population as a whole. Medium identifiers, however, voted 56 per cent Democratic; and those most highly identified with these groups voted 69 per cent Democratic. In general, then, the hypothesis receives clear support, and strength of group identification deserves a place as a variable in our model.

Secondary groups that are not primarily political take little interest in some issues, and in these cases group members do not hold attitudes that differ significantly from those of nonmember control groups nor do high identifiers differ from more peripheral members. But as a general rule, whenever a group holds distinctive beliefs about some issue, then within the group a differentiation appears between members according to the strength of their group identification.

This combination of facts argues most conclusively that we are dealing here with a true group-influence phenomenon. To ascertain that influence exists is but a first step, however. We are also interested in assessing the relative strength of influence exerted by various groups and the conditions under which this strength increases or decreases. We find considerable variation in the degree of disparity in presidential vote between strong and weak identifiers within various groups. Table 3 summarizes this variation. If we compare these figures with those in Table 2, we find some interesting similarities in the rank ordering of the groups. Vote distinctiveness *within the group* bears some relation to distinctiveness between the group and a control group matched for life situation, as we would expect if both were taken to reflect strength of group political influence. But there are differences, also: high identifiers are more distinct in the union case and less distinct in the Negro case than Table 2 would lead us to expect. Most Negroes are highly identified with their group; therefore the total group is more clearly Democratic than it might appear

TABLE 3

Vote Division within Four Test Groups, According to
Strength of Group Identification, 1956°

	Highly Identi- fied	Weakly Identi- fied	Discrepancy
Members of union households	64	36	+28
Catholics	51	39	+11
Negroes			
Non-South	72	63	+9
South	− †	− †	− †
Jews	83	55	+28

° The entries in the first two columns represent the per cent Democratic of the two-party vote division. The final column summarizes the differences between percentages in the first two, a plus indicating the high identifiers in the group voted more strongly Democratic.

† Southern Negro voters in the sample are too few for further subdivision.

if the proportion of high and low identifiers within the Negro group was closer to that found within the union group. But part of the discrepancy results from other factors to be added to the model shortly.

Group identifications help to answer the two primary questions with which a theory of group influence must deal. At the individual level, we may sort out a set of nominal members who are most likely to deviate from the group position under nongroup forces. They are the people who do not strongly identify with the group, who are psychologically peripheral to it.

A similar proposition can be formulated at the group level. Some groups boast memberships intensely loyal to group purposes and interests. Others have trouble maintaining member identifications. We shall call a group enjoying high member identification a *cohesive group*.[3]

TABLE 4

Relation of Group Cohesiveness to Group Identification, 1956

Cohesiveness	Mean Identification Score°	Group
High	2.5	Southern Negro
	2.2	Non-Southern Negro
	2.2	Jewish
Low	1.8	Union member
	1.6	Catholic
	1.6	Member, union household

° The responses to the two identification questions (see p. 159) are scored such that a maximum value on the index is 3.0, when the most positive response is made to both items. The corresponding minimum value is 0.0, when the most negative response is made to both items. About 61 per cent of Southern Negroes responded positively toward the group on both items; the corresponding proportion among Catholics was 28 per cent.

3 Dorwin P. Cartwright and Alvin Zander, *Group Dynamics: Research and Theory* (Row, Peterson and Co., Evanston, Ill., 1953), Part II, pp. 71–134.

Group cohesiveness is one determinant of the influence which a group can wield over its membership.

If a group has generated distinctive political attitudes and behavior among its members, this distinctiveness will fade if group cohesiveness is destroyed. Cohesiveness itself must depend on a number of factors according to the type of group and the setting involved. Within the large and far-flung social groupings under discussion in this chapter, a prime determinant may simply be the degree to which group members feel set apart from other people by virtue of social barriers. If we set up a mean identification score as a simple index of cohesiveness for each group, the resulting array (see Table 4) seems to support this hypothesis.

THE RELATIONSHIP OF THE GROUP TO THE WORLD OF POLITICS

If the relationship between individual and group is summarized by the concept of identification, attempts to deal with the relationship of the group to the world of politics focus upon a vaguer concept of *proximity*. All of our secondary membership groups except the political party have their basic existence outside of the political order. At this point it becomes important to specify this distance from the world of politics more precisely.

If we analyze our intuitions concerning proximity, we find that they depend upon the frequency with which we have seen the group *qua* group associated intimately with objects that are clearly political—issues, candidates, and parties. We would think, for example, of lobbying activity, political pronouncements, and candidates who publicize the fact of membership in that group. We would consider what we know of the primary goals of the group, and their apparent relevance to politics. The perceived relationship between the group and the world of politics has substantial grounding in objective events, constituted largely by the actions of group leaders. But we could not expect that all individuals, or even all group members, would perceive the relationship of the group to politics in precisely the same manner. Thus we shall think of proximity as a subjective dimension, a tendency to associate group and politics at a psychological level.

Where proximity has partisan significance we would hypothesize that: *as proximity between the group and the world of politics increases, the political distinctiveness of the group will increase.*

Or, at the individual level: *as perception of proximity between the group and the world of politics becomes clearer, the susceptibility of the individual member to group influence in political affairs increases.*

The concept of proximity will have to undergo further refinement before these hypotheses have full meaning. We must specify a good deal more precisely the dimensions that are involved in our general sense of proximity, and attempt to measure them more objectively.

We have suggested that perceptions of proximity between one's group and the world of politics rest upon associations that have been built up between the group and the political objects. How do these links become established? In some cases, the associations are directly given, as when the political candidate is a highly visible member of the group. The link is, so to speak, "built into" the object of orientation itself. We shall discuss phenomena of this sort under the general heading of *group salience* in politics. More often, however, the establishment of associations between the group and politics depends on conscious effort by elements within the group to propagate certain standards of member behavior. This *transmission of standards* is a communication process, and its effectiveness depends on the clarity with which the standard is transmitted and the insistence that accompanies it.

But the perceived proximity of the group to the world of politics depends on more than the perception of a group standard at a point in time. While the successful transmission of a group standard in a particular situation may increase the member's sense of proximity, we would propose that the effect of any particular standard, once received, will vary according to the individual's generalized, preexisting sense of proximity between group and politics. In part, then, proximity is dependent upon reception of past standards; in part, too, it is dependent on the individual's sense of the *fitness* of group activity in politics. Underlying values that deny the group a legitimate role in the world act as barriers to reduce the sense of proximity, however clearly standards may be received.

What we have roughly labeled proximity, then, has a number of dimensions that demand independent treatment, and we shall discuss several of these. Throughout, we encounter evidence that the perceived relationship of the group to politics, like the relationship of the individual to the group, bears directly upon the strength of group forces in the field at the time of political decision.

The Transmission of Group Political Standards

Whatever the process of communication that alerts the member to a partisan group standard, we can think of group norms as forces, having a given direction and varying degrees of strength. The standard prescribes support of one party, candidate, or issue position, and forbids support of the other. And these prescriptions are propagated with varying amounts of urgency or intensity.

There are two conditions in which group standards may lack sufficient clarity to permit influence. The end result of each is the same—a lack of distinctiveness in the aggregate group vote—but the differences are of considerable theoretical interest. In one case, the usual channel for communication of such norms is silent as to a particular standard, or emits it very weakly. For example, within international unions where standards were most clear according to the content analysis of pre-election editions of official journals, the vote division among members in our sample was 67 per cent Democratic. This fell to 55 per cent, then to 51 per cent, and finally to 44 per cent where standards were least clear. These differences occurred even though the proportion of high identifiers from category to category varied over a range of only 3 per cent, so that we cannot explain the variation in vote by differences in group cohesiveness.

In the other case, conflicting standards are conveyed to the membership. When standards conflict, there are several possible outcomes. At one extreme, we might find that no single member became aware of the conflict in standards, but that various sets of members felt pressures in opposing directions. Here is the point at which analysis of influence at the individual level becomes more accurate than that at a group level. For in such a situation, even if every member responded to influence, the aggregate outcome might lead the observer to believe that no influence had occurred at all.

At the other extreme, all members may be aware of a conflict in standards. To some degree, the group force is cancelled out: even if the member is concerned with respectability in the eyes of the group, he can pick the standard that would best suit his desires independent of group considerations and act accordingly without feeling guilt. If, however, the situation is ripe for influence—if the individual is motivated to conform to the group—it is unlikely that events will work out in just this way. A conflict in group standards usually occurs as a result of decentralization of leadership. Few large and far-flung groups can long maintain a leadership with monolithic control over group standards. Among the secondary membership groups this is especially true. But if an unwieldy group tends to develop its subgroups with their conflicting standards, the general model still applies. Although awareness of different standards among other elements of the total group may relax group pressures to some degree, the individual is likely to feel most strongly the forces from the subgroup with which he is most strongly identified.

Conflicting Standards: A Case Study

We have found the Negro community to be the most cohesive of the groups we have surveyed. Furthermore, Negroes, as we shall see, are almost unanimous in their belief that the group has a right to further its ends by political activity. Several of the necessary conditions for influence are fulfilled. In 1952, there was a good deal of solidarity among Negro leaders in their endorsement of the Democratic presidential ticket. And the Negro vote itself in 1952 was very distinctively Democratic.

In 1956, however, Negro leaders were much less enthusiastic about the Democratic Party, owing in part to the role of Southern Democratic legislators in blocking civil rights legislation and in part to Republican sympathy with Negro aspirations. The National Association for Advancement of Colored People adopted a posture of watchful waiting, with occasional executive threats of a Republican endorsement. The two senior United States Congressmen from the Negro community gave clear public support to opposing candidates for the presidency: Adam Clayton Powell in New York City endorsed Eisenhower, whereas William L. Dawson of Chicago supported Stevenson.

This conflict in standards was reflected in the perceptions of Negroes in our sample. When asked how they thought Negroes around the country would vote in the 1956 election, responses had shifted sharply away from the near Democratic unanimity that the same question elicited in

1952. Furthermore, the conflict was most clearly perceived at the level of the leadership. Almost as many Negroes saw the leadership voting Republican as Democratic in 1956. The distinctiveness of the Negro vote fell off sharply.

We hypothesized that when a secondary group fragments into subgroups propagating standards that conflict, much the same influence process goes on, with identification focused on the appropriate subgroup rather than the total group. In Chicago, where Dawson had stood firm for the Democrats, there was an overall decline of 5 per cent in the Democratic presidential vote, by comparison with 1952. Within the city, three of the most clearly Negro wards declined 4 per cent, 4 per cent, and 9 per cent—close to the city average. In New York City, the picture was different. In the heavily colored New New York Assembly Districts 11 and 12, which included much of Powell's constituency, the Democratic presidential vote fell about 15 per cent. And this occurred despite a fraction of a per cent increase in the Stevenson vote in New York County as a whole. The effect of conflicting standards is to reduce the distinctiveness of the total group vote; but where we can isolate subgroups, we find evidence of influence.

The Political Salience of the Group

In some situations, the need for active propagation of group standards is at a minimum, because the standard is self-evident. This is the case when important political objects of orientation embody group cues, so that the course of behavior characteristic of a "good" group member cannot be held in doubt. Fundamentally, this situation is no more than a special case of the transmission of clear and strong standards. But it deserves separate treatment because it implies a simpler and less fallible communication process and because it involves a stratagem dear to the hearts of political tacticians. This dimension is one component of the model that is especially subject to short-term variation, since salience usually depends on the most transient objects of political orientation: the candidates and the issues.

Political salience of the group is high, for example, when a candidate for the election is recognized as a member of the group. Attracting the votes of members of a particular group by nominating a candidate who is a group member is, of course, a time-worn strategy in the art of political maneuver. Frequent executive appointment of group members to high posts is of the same order, although perhaps less potent in creating salience. It is our thesis that the success of the maneuver among group members depends upon the values of other variables in the total model. High salience alone does not create a unanimous group response.

The political salience of the group can also be increased by a coincidence between group goals and current political issues. The degree of salience that accrues with regard to issues in any particular situation is some joint function of the importance of the issue in the campaign and the importance of the goal to the group. One of the central issues of the 1948 campaign was the Taft-Hartley Act, which union leadership felt threatened vital aspects of the movement. To the degree that these elements communicated to the rank and file, the labor union ought to have been particularly salient for members voting in the election. Since that time, civil rights controversies have tended to increase the political salience of Negro membership.

Salience: A Case Study

The behavior of Catholic voters toward Catholic candidates for the United States Congress allows us to examine the salience phenomenon. We recall that in Table 2 the presidential vote among Catholics in 1956

TABLE 5
Political Salience: The Vote of Catholics for Catholic
Congressional Candidates in Races Involving Non-Catholics, 1956°

	Catholic Identification		
	High	Low	Total Group
Catholic voters	63%	59%	61%
	(43)	(51)	(94)
Catholic	—	—	49%
			(76)

° The per cent entry refers to the proportion of the indicated group voting for the Catholic candidate in the split-religion congressional race. The figure in parentheses indicates the number of cases involved in each proportion.

was barely more Democratic than that among a Catholic control group (a margin of 3 per cent). We find a much more distinctive vote if we shift the scene to those congressional races in which a Catholic candidate was pitted against a non-Catholic (Table 5). Furthermore, Catholic voters are quite willing to cross party lines to support a candidate of the same creed. Thus if we decompose Table 5 we find that where the Catholic candidate is a Democrat, Catholics vote over 10 per cent more Democratic than their control group; but where the Catholic candidate is Republican, Catholics vote over 10 per cent more *Republican* than their controls.

By sacrificing a large proportion of our cases, we can refine the data in a manner that sharpens these relationships further. Obviously, the theory underlying the salience hypotheses demands that the voter recognize the candidate as a group member if salience effects are to emerge. If we restrict attention to those voters (one-third of the total) who can refer to their congressional choices by name after the election, we should clear away some individuals for whom we could little expect salience to be operative.

Although the cases for analysis are few, Table 6 shows a group vote much more distinctive yet than that in Table 5. And the inadequate number of cases is offset somewhat by the fact that similar results are to be found when we look for the same patterns within the 1956 U.S. senatorial races in which Catholics were involved. These similarities emerge even though the Catholic voters appearing in both segments of the table are few indeed.

There is, therefore, substantial evidence that the salience of a group membership, created by group cues in the political object, intensifies group forces in the member's psychological field at the time of the vote decision. On the other hand, we should note that the sharpening of findings from Table 5 to Table 6 indicates that lack of attention to candidates for House and Senate may make severe inroads upon the vote increment which the aspirant can reap from salience effects.

TABLE 6

Group Salience: The Vote of Catholics for Catholic Candidates
Whose Names Can Be Recalled, in Races Involving
Non-Catholics, 1956*

	Catholic Identification		
	High	Low	Total Group
U.S. House of Representatives:			
Catholic voters	85%	69%	77%
	(13)	(13)	(26)
Catholic control	−	−	51%
			(25)
U.S. Senate:			
Catholic voters	86%	57%	70%
	(22)	(28)	(50)
Catholic control	−	−	49%
			(47)

* The per cent entry refers to the proportion of the indicated group who voted for the Catholic candidate in the split-religion congressional or senatorial race. The figure in each parenthesis indicates the number of cases involved in each proportion.

The Legitimacy of Group Political Activity

However strong the group identification, and however firm the association between group and political objects, the member may resist the intrusion of "nonpolitical" groups upon the political scene. There are cultural values bound up with beliefs about democracy and the individual that inveigh against such activity. The sophisticated view of democracy as a competition between interest groups does not have great popular currency. Voting, whether at the mass or the legislative level, is morally a matter of individual judgment and conscience; recognition of group obligation and interests is thoroughly taboo to some Americans.

We asked members of various groups whether they felt it was "all right" for organizations representing the group to support legislative proposals and candidates for office. The responses to these questions showed a fairly strong relationship with the group identification variable. The more highly identified a group member, the more likely he was to grant the group a right to engage in political activity. Within each level of group identification, however, members of the two religious groups—

Catholics and Jews—show much greater reluctance to accept the legitimacy statements than either of the two more secular groupings—Negroes and union members. Also, with identification controlled, there is somewhat less readiness to grant legitimacy among older people. This fact would conform with the impressions that popular values opposing frank interest-group politics represent an older America.

The Backgrounds of Group Identifications

We have indicated some of the sources of feelings about legitimacy. It is natural to inquire as well concerning the roots of group identification. Why do some group members identify with the group, whereas others fail to?

This is a difficult problem, and our evidence to date is fragmentary. But we can draw a few general conclusions about major determinants of identification. There are numerous groups, of course, that are created for the purpose of political and ideological persuasion, such as the National Economic Council or the American Civil Liberties Union. Members are recruited and come to identify with the group on the basis of pre-existing beliefs and sympathies. Here the case for influence is much less clear, except as group activity serves to reinforce and guide member efforts. But in most groups formed along occupational, ethnic, or religious lines membership is more likely to determine attitudes than are attitudes to determine membership.

There is little doubt of this fact in the groups we have watched most closely. Except in some semiorganized areas of the South, even membership in the labor union is effectively involuntary. If labor union members vote distinctively, we cannot say that only workers with certain attitudes join the union; rather, we must concede that influence exists. But if membership is involuntary, identification is not. How can we be sure that high union identification plays a formative role in the development of political attitudes?

There is a clear and substantial relationship between strength of union identification and length of membership in the union. The longer an individual has belonged to the union, the more likely he is to identify strongly with it, and we can find no other causative factors that begin to approach this relationship in strength. A relationship between age and union identification has been observed before, but it was never clear whether the relationship existed because of simple contact with the union over time, or because the unusual "barricades" generation of the 1930's would currently constitute the bulk of older union members. Our data show clearly that older men who have recently joined the union have weak identification with it, whereas younger men aged 25 and 30 who have belonged to the union for longer periods show stronger identifications with it. In fact, if we control length of union membership, we find that the relationship between age and union identification is somewhat negative. The later in life a person joins a union, the less completely he will be identified with it given any particular length of membership. His identification will still increase with length of membership, but the level will not be quite as strong at it would be for a person who had joined when younger.

This cluster of findings is of considerable theoretical significance. In the first place, it makes it difficult to maintain that identification with the union results as a rule from existing political attitudes similar to those represented by the union. Instead, we get a sense of an acculturation process—slow and cumulative influence over a period of time, with identification as the key intervening factor. It appears that a potent force in the growth of group identifications is simple contact and familiarity, just as an immigrant comes to identify with the new country and accept its customs as time passes. Furthermore, like the immigrant, identifications never become as strongly rooted if the initiate is no longer young.

These findings are important from another point of view as well. For the pattern of relationships between age, length of membership, and strength of identification is precisely the same as we found where the group involved is the political party. That is, party identification appears to grow stronger with age; but the critical variable, instead of being age, is length of psychological membership in the party. With length of membership controlled, age is negatively related to party identification, just as it is in the union case.

Those few persons who have been union members for long periods of time yet who have remained unidentified are less likely to vote Democratic than any of the other union subgroups isolated. Not only are they much more Republican in their vote than union members generally; they are even more Republican than the control group matched with union members on aspects of life situation (33 per cent Democratic vote among those who have been members 15 years or more, as opposed to 36 per cent for the control group). Thus lack of identification among long-standing members of the union may have actively negative implications not present among new members who are not yet strongly identified.

We find no such clear relation between age and group identification among Catholics, Negroes, or Jews. Age, in these groups, logically coincides with "length of membership." There is some faint increase in identification among older Catholics, and an equally faint decrease in identification among older Negroes. We would expect these differences to appear if Catholic cohesiveness is waning and if the current civil rights ferment is beginning to sharpen cohesiveness among Negroes. But these tendencies are very weak, and there is no trend visible at all in the Jewish situation. We must conclude that no reliable relationship is present.

The contrast in the development of identification between these groups and the union or party is sharp. We are led to consider differences in the characteristics of the several groups that might account for such variation. It is obvious that the individual takes on serious membership in a union or in the psychological group represented by a political party later in life than is the case with the other groups. The individual grows up within the atmosphere of a religious or ethnic group in a much more inclusive sense than with either the party or the union.

Thus, different patterns of identification may be traced to basic differences in types of groups. But it is possible to suggest a more general proposition to cover all cases: instead of considering age or even the absolute length of time of group membership as the proper independent variable, let us employ the *proportion of the individual's life* spent as a member. Recast in this fashion, the presence of the strong positive relationship between length of membership and identification, the negative relationship between age and identification with length of membership constant, and the fact that certain ascribed groups show no variation with age would all be predicted by a single independent variable. If there is no relationship between "length of membership" and identification among Catholics, Jews, and Negroes, it is because members of these groups have held membership for 100 per cent of their lives, and variation in their identification must be explained with other factors. We arrive at the general proposition that one fundamental determinant of group identifications is the proportion of one's life spent in close (psychological) contact with the group.

SECONDARY GROUPS, THE POLITICAL PARTY, AND THE INFLUENCE PROCESS

If the political party, and psychological membership in it, fit a more general model for social memberships and political influence, it is equally clear that the party has a peculiar location in the space that the model encompasses. We have laid out with some care what seem to be the components of the relationship between any group and the world of politics. This effort was necessary because the secondary groups with which we dealt were not at base political, and this fact turns out to be a crucial limitation in the political influence they can wield. Now if we were to fill in the values that the scheme requires for prediction, we would find that in the case of the party, proximity is at an upper limit, for the party has a central position in the world of politics. In all major elections, its salience is absolutely high: one candidate is always a group member, the prime group goal is political victory, and all controversial issues represent subordinate goals that the group has assumed. The legitimacy of its activity in politics goes without question, for the major parties at least, and the communication of their standards is perfect. Therefore, we would expect that the political influence of psychological membership in a party would be extremely potent, relative to other secondary memberships. If we take distinctiveness of political attitudes and behavior as a criterion, this proposition cannot be questioned.

We are most directly interested, at this point, in suggesting the processes by which nonpolitical membership groups come to have a certain amount of political influence. Thus far we have paid little attention to the fact that these processes have duration over time. The political influence of secondary memberships, as witnessed in the distinctiveness of a group vote, is not necessarily a product of the immediate situation. The labor union need not indoctrinate its membership anew at each election. If the labor vote was distinctive in 1956, there is no need to presume that this distinctiveness represents only the political action of the union during the 1956 campaign. Influence, when successful, has enduring effects, and in this sense the distinctiveness of a group vote at any point in time represents cumulative influence. We hypothesize that the political party plays a crucial role in the durability of this influence.

When a political candidate is a member of one's group, or when the issues of politics bear directly upon goals important to the group, membership in that group becomes salient in the individual's orientation to politics. In these instances, the need for political translation, for communication of specific standards regarding proper group behavior, is slight. But under normal circumstances, when salience is not high, the group, if it is to have influence, must lend the observed world political meaning in terms relevant to the group.

Now issues and candidates are transient political objects; the entity that endures is the party. If group influence leads the identified member to take on identification with the party, then little renewal of influence is needed. The individual has, as it were, acceded to a self-steering mechanism, that will keep him politically "safe" from the point of view of group standards. He will respond to new stimuli as a party member and code them properly. As time passes, his identification with the party will increase of its own accord, because the individual will find that event after event demonstrates—in nongroup matters as well as group matters now—the rectitude of his own party and the obnoxiousness of its opponent.

If there were no parties, but only a flux of candidates and issues, it does not follow that there would be no political influence exerted by other membership groups. The psychological economy of the individual demands parties as an organizing principle, and if bereft of this, there might be much more straightforward dependence on other groups for guidance. In situations of this sort, secondary groups with quite apolitical origins have in fact come to function as political parties.[4] But where parties exist, influence from nonpolitical secondary groups is likely to have a good deal of continuity.

Given the flux of objects like candidates and issues, group influence is likely to be most effective when meaningful contact is established between the group and the party, for parties subsume candidates and issues and, more important, endure over time. However, this proposition is true only if we define influence in a very particular way, that is, as cumulative over time. An individual led to a Democratic orientation by a group membership in 1930 may still be registering a manifestation of that influence in 1956.

But for the practical politician who wants to know how many votes a group leader can "deliver" to one party or the other in a specific election, influence may have a rather different meaning. Here we encounter a paradox. If party identification is a trustworthy bridge from group identification to "proper" political behavior, it is also a structure which, once

---

[4] As an example, see Key's treatment of factionalism in the South. Secondary groups constitute one type of nucleus for the factions that compete for political power in a one-party system. V. O. Key, *Southern Politics in State and Nation* (Alfred Knopf, New York, 1950), pp. 52–57.

laid down, is not readily moved. Thus the mechanisms that are best calculated to build a reliably distinctive group vote are at the same time mechanisms that tend to undermine the maneuverability of the group in politics.

When political events cause a group leadership to switch official support to the opposing party, the strong party loyalties that it has helped to create and reinforce may be reserved only with great difficulty.[5] We can imagine that these loyalties, even when direct creations of group influence, gain some functional autonomy as they grow stronger. They come to have a force of their own, rather than remaining dependent on forces from the nonpolitical secondary group. And, since the political party can exert unusually intense influence on political motives, this force may turn out to be stronger than any counter-force that the nonpolitical group can bring to bear *in politics* at a later date. It would follow from the general outlines of our theory that when such reversals of group standards occur, the new influence will have most effect among the youngest group members.

The political party may be treated, then, as a special case of a more general group-influence phenomenon. The party may be located within our model, and values on appropriate dimensions may be calculated for the party member at any point in time. The nature of the group, so located, ensures the power of its influence within the world of politics. But of great significance also is the role of the party as a bridge between other social groupings and that political world. The influence of other secondary groups in politics comes to have more enduring effects as loyalties directed toward them may be transferred to abiding political loyalties.

---

[5] It is interesting to note that for large-scale, secondary groups at the national level, these switches are rare and tend to be limited to rebellious factions. Many aspects of political process seem to converge toward maintenance of these continuities. Factors such as the dependence of the party on group support and the loyalties and interpersonal commitments built up between group leaders and the party enhance the temptation to work for reform within the chosen party when things go awry. These facts make treatment of influence in its cumulative sense the more meaningful.

Norman R. Luttbeg and Harmon Zeigler

Attitude Consensus and Conflict in an Interest Group: An Assessment of Cohesion*

In America, interest groups operate within the democratic frame of reference. Like all political organizations, they are accorded more legitimacy when they can show that they are representative of the attitudes and values of a particular segment of the population. Consequently, the leaders of interest groups frequently spend a great deal of time explaining just how democratic their organizations are. If one examines the testimony of interest group leaders at state and national legislative hearings, he is likely to find that much of it is begun with an introductory statement explaining that the leadership of the testifying group is merely the voice of the membership. The personal values of the interest group leader are played down, and his function as representative (as distinguished from delegate) is exaggerated.

On the other hand, relatively few political interest groups have systematic and formalized means of ascertaining the desires of members. We know that most of the devices used to solicit member opinion are not very effective. Truman has shown that the affairs of most interest groups are run on a day-to-day basis by a fraction of the total membership. The mass of the membership takes a relatively passive role with regard to the formation of public policies by the organization.[1]

Communication between leaders and followers is spasmodic and cannot provide efficient guidelines for the actions of leaders. Whether or not leadership of an organization seeks to become a manifestation of Michel's iron law of obligarchy, the realities of communication within an organi-

* From *The American Political Science Review*, vol. 60 (September 1966), pp. 655–65. Copyright 1966, The American Political Science Association.

The research reported here was made possible by a grant from the Center for the Advanced Study of Educational Administration, University of Oregon.

[1] David B. Truman, *The Governmental Process* (New York: Alfred A. Knopf, Inc., 1951), pp. 129–39.

zation suggest that most of the communication undertaken by leaders will be with other members of the leadership clique rather than with the larger body of followers in the group.

This situation is not necessarily dysfunctional for the organization. By many criteria the leader's decision is superior to that of the average member. Leaders have more time to give to matters of special concern to the organization. The information on which they make their decisions is likely to be more extensive than that of the average member, and they are likely to be more cognizant of the long-term impact of a particular decision. Unlike the average member, however, the leader's decision is complicated by his need to consider the extra-group and intra-group impact of his various alternative decisions and actions.

In the area of extra-group considerations, he must estimate the probable responses of other actors in the political process and the effect of these responses upon the chances of achieving a desired goal, assuming that he does not possess all capabilities of realizing this goal himself. Concerning intra-group considerations he must consider how the followers will respond to a decision. Will they be aware of it? Do they care about the alternatives, and if so, how will they respond to a decision which is contrary to their desires?

Even in the absence of efficient consultative mechanisms, leaders and followers exist in a functional relationship.[2] That is to say, leaders are limited by the followers' expressed or latent values and expectations. Regardless of the efficiency of corrective mechanisms and apart from how extensive the violation of the followers' values must be before the corrective mechanism comes into play, the leader's position is less secure if he fails to satisfy the followers. If another leader is vying with him for the followers' support, the implications of failing to satisfy the followers are even more threatening. In a political interest group, the functional relationship of leaders to followers is keyed to the necessity for cohesion as a weapon in extra-group competition. The actuality or at least the appearance of unity is essential.[3]

Assuming that the leader desires to maintain an extra-group competitive position, he will therefore undertake efforts toward the fostering of intra-group cohesion. In a voluntary organization, one of the prime requisites for this cohesion is the extent to which the membership is satisfied with the performance of leaders.[4] There are three ways in which a leader may satisfy the desires of an organization's membership. First, he may unconsciously act consistently with their desires. For example, he may decide to act on the basis of his evaluation of extra-group factors in such a way that the membership will be entirely satisfied. Second, he may respond entirely in terms of his personal attitudes and beliefs and, be-

[2] William Haythorn, et al., "The Effects of Varying Combinations of Authoritarian and Equalitarian Leaders and Followers," *Journal of Abnormal and Social Psychology*, Vol. LIII (September, 1956), 210–19.

[3] Truman, *op. cit.*, pp. 167–87.

[4] Herbert Simon, *Administrative Behavior* (New York: The Macmillan Co., 1957), pp. 110–22.

cause he so accurately reflects the attitudes of his membership, again satisfy their desires. Third, a leader may consciously seek to do what he believes the membership of the organization desires. His success in satisfying the membership by this effort is dependent upon the accuracy of his perceptions of their attitudes and expectations.

RESEARCH DESIGN

In this paper we examine the latter two dynamics by which leaders can satisfy members. Our data were gathered from the membership of the Oregon Education Association. Three sets of information were collected: the beliefs and attitudes of the members of the Association, the beliefs and attitudes of the leaders of the Association, and the perception of the attitudes of the members as held by the leaders. The analysis consists of comparing these three sets of information and noting changes in their interrelationships on different attitudes. The nature of the analysis is illustrated by Figure 1.

FIGURE 1

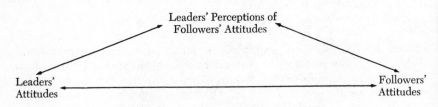

Leaders' Perceptions of
Followers' Attitudes

Leaders'
Attitudes

Followers'
Attitudes

The sample of group members used in this study is a clustered stratified random sample of 803 high school teachers. This represents 14% of the high school teachers in Oregon.[5]

The sample of leaders includes all nine of the OEA's top administrative officials. These are the members of the executive staff, which is employed by the organization's Board of Trustees. Its official responsibility is to implement the policies of the Representative Council, which consists of 200 representatives elected by local teachers' organizations. The Representative Council is the official policy-making body of the Association. However, both the Representative Council, which meets only once a year, and the Board of Trustees, which is supposed to deal with the specifics of the council's directives, are part-time functions. Thus, the permanent administrative staff is often forced to act in areas in which directives are vague or nonexistent. As is frequently the case in formal organizations, therefore, the permanent administrative staff has great flexibility and is a major delineator of policy.

In interviewing the leaders, we used a majority of the questions included in the teachers' interview schedule. Certain modifications in word-

---

[5] Attitudes were assessed by personal interviews. There were 91 teachers in the original sample with whom interviews were not completed.

ing were made to allow for differences in organizational position. Leaders were first asked to answer the questions in terms of their own attitudes. They were then asked to take the point of view of the "average teacher" answering the same questions as they thought the "average teacher" would answer them. Only one of the leaders displayed any difficulty in assuming this attitude perspective; he had difficulty in keeping from answering questions in terms of what the teachers *should* believe rather than what he thought they actually *did* believe. The little difficulty the leaders experienced in answering these questions is evidenced that the distinction between personal attitudes and the attitudes of the membership is a meaningful one for them.

These three sets of attitudes (teachers' attitudes, leaders' attitudes, and leaders' perceptions of teachers' attitudes) are studied in four attitudinal contexts. They are:

1. Mandates for organizational action,
2. Expectations and satisfaction with the direction of leadership behavior,
3. Abstract political values, and
4. Norms of teachers' political participation.

The mandates for organizational action consist of two parts: expectations of behavior on the part of leaders themselves and expectations of action undertaken by teachers' organizations. In both cases, the satisfaction of the members with a particular action is dependent upon a congruence of the attitudes of the leaders with the actual attitudes of the followers.

Attitudes related to satifaction with the direction of leadership are concerned with three of the Oregon Education Association's most strenuous activities; efforts toward salary improvement, efforts to raise teacher standards and accreditation, and efforts toward the establishment of a state sales tax with the revenues going to the public schools.

Abstract political values describe a set of attitudes, many of which are clichés often used by persons to persuade others to accept their position. They represent the basic "truths" of both the conservative and liberal points of view. A leader perceiving the membership as adhering to conservative values is ascribing conservatism to the membership and at the same time indicating that he believes an argument for action based upon these values would draw support from the membership.

The attitudes dealing with teachers' political participation concerned a broad set of politically related activities which might be undertaken by teachers in the classroom or during leisure time. The leadership's ability to satisfy members in this regard will be reflected in their efforts or lack of efforts to support teachers in trouble in their local communities for various political activities and in the formal or informal articulation of a professional ethic with respect to these activities.

Although it would be possible to analyze these data using contingency tables, the existence of 50 attitude items and three comparisons for each item would tax the reader's ability to follow the analysis. A single measure which characterizes the relationship on each comparison of attitudes is therefore required. Although numerous measures of association and correlation were considered for this purpose, we settled upon Kendall's tau chi (τ_c).[6] This measure has its faults, the principal one being that its maximum value is dependent upon the marginals of the table. Our tables frequently have marginals of 803 and 9 (the N's of our two samples). Such great differences will yield a correlation of only .044 for a perfect relationship on a 2×2 table.. Since we are more interested in finding a measure to characterize the comparison of attitude distributions of leaders and followers than in using the measure as a test of statistical significance, it was decided to rely upon a new measure, τ_c over τ_c maximum.

As we are using this measure in comparing the distributions of attitudes of leaders and followers, a high correlation would indicate a strong relationship between attitudes and the person holding them. That is to say, a high correlation would indicate that leaders hold attitudes different from those of the followers. The sign of the measure will indicate the direction of this difference. Notice that a correlation of .000 indicates that leaders share the attitudes of the followers or that the two sets of attitudes compared have the same distribution.

Some may inquire of the statistical significance of the findings. There are two problems with the application of statistical significance tests to these data. First, one of the samples is not a sample at all but the universe of the administrative leaders of the Oregon Education Association. Thus, with no sampling error contributed by the leadership sample the comparing of leaders' and followers' attitudes does not necessitate as strong a relationship to achieve statistical significance as would be normally required. In the data comparing leaders' attitudes and their perceptions of followers' attitudes, clearly no statistical significance tests are applicable because the differences are real differences for the universe of leaders. Even if the leaders did constitute a sample, their small number places an unnecessarily strict requirement on the strength of the relationship necessary to achieve statistical significance.[7] In general, therefore, greater reliance is placed upon the consistency of a relationship within

---

[6] Our data justify the use of ordinal measures of association, but there are several characteristics of our data and properties of various measures of association which complicate the choice of such a measure. First, on some of the items only two responses are possible while others are seven-point Likert scales. Thus any measure which is sensitive to the shape of the contingency table from which it is computed will decrease the comparability of the data across items. A measure which reached unity when only one cell is zero is also undesirable, as instances in which the leaders are in perfect agreement while the followers differ are common in our data. Such measures would be insensitive to the degree of followers' disagreement with the leaders. The final difficulty is that some measures are sensitive to the marginals of the contingency table. No measure was discovered which did not have at least one of the characteristics. See Hubert Blalock, *Social Statistics* (New York: McGraw-Hill Book Co., 1960), p. 323; and Leo A. Goodman and William H. Kruskal, "Measures of Association for Cross Classifications," *Journal of the American Statistical Association*, Vol. XLIX (December, 1954), p. 750.

[7] David Gold, "Some Problems in Generalizing Aggregate Associations," *American Behavioral Scientist*, Vol. VIII (December, 1964), p. 18.

an attitude area rather than on the statistical significance of any one item. However, those single-item relationships which are significant are indicated by a small "s" in the tables (the Kruskal-Wallis h test is used to test statistical significance).

FINDINGS

Leaders' Perceptions of Their Roles

Before comparing the three sets of attitudes contained in this study, some discussion should be made of the leaders' perceptions of their roles within the organization. We refer here to the extent to which leaders believe they should act primarily in accordance with their own personal values rather than trying to reflect the desires of those whom they lead. We are asking whether leaders believe they should be delegates or representatives.[8]

Two questions were included in the leaders' interview schedule dealing with the problem of whose attitudes should be acted upon, those of the leaders or those of the followers. In one question the leaders were offered a brief dialogue between two persons, one arguing that a leader must do as the members wish and the other arguing that the leader must do what he personally believes to be correct. The leader was given the opportunity of selecting the argument which he found most satisfactory. Only one leader answered that the membership's desires should rule. Five answered that the leader should do what he personally believes to be right, although they added the comment that they thought the problem would occur very infrequently. Three of the leaders said that if this problem could not be resolved the leader should resign.

The second question approached the problem from a slightly different angle and achieved very dissimilar results. The leaders were asked if they felt the organization should do pretty much what the average teacher wants, what the more influential teachers want, what the school administrators want, or what they themselves want. The "pretty much" phrase in the first alternative apparently was easier to accept than the wording in the other question, as five leaders chose this alternative. Two altered the second response to indicate that they believed they should do what the "more informed" teachers wanted while two indicated that they would prefer to do what they themselves thought best.

It would seem, therefore, that the leaders accept the maxim that they should do what the followers want, but they are also jealous of their autonomy to do what they think best. There appears to be a clear in-

---

[8] The terms "delegate" and "representative" are borrowed from the literature on the legislative process, whereby they are applied to the role perceptions of legislators. Heinz Eulau presents three legislative role orientations in John C. Wahlke, Heinz Eulau, William Buchanan, and LeRoy C. Ferguson, *The Legislative System* (New York: John Wiley and Sons, Inc., 1962), pp. 267–86. The "trustee" of Eulau's scheme has traditionally been described as a "delegate" while the "delegate" corresponds to "representative." These roles are the extremes, with "politico" falling somewhere between them.

ternalized conflict between the representative and delegate roles. Obviously the best of all possible worlds for the leaders would be perfect consensus between them and the members. In the absence of this consensus, they appear unable to reach a clear resolution of the conflict and to find a stable definition of their roles.

The leaders' acute awareness of the problem of communication with followers is indicated by a final question. Leaders were asked what policies of the Oregon Education Association they were most dissatisfied with. Seven volunteered the answer that the greatest problem was the OEA's failure to be true to the desires of its membership. Two of the leaders who gave this response explicitly criticized the administrative structure for not administering impartially the policy decisions of the Representative Council. It appears, therefore, that the representative nature of the organization is not only meaningful to leaders but is also potentially divisive of the leadership.

TABLE 1

Comparison of the Three Attitude Sets in the Area of Mandate for Actions by
Leaders, Teachers' Organizations, and the OEA

Questions	Sets of Attitudes Compared		
	Followers' Attitudes vs. Leaders' Attitudes	Followers' Attitudes vs. Leaders' Perception of Followers' Attitudes	Leaders' Attitudes vs. Leaders' Perception of Followers' Attitudes
Leaders should:			
1. Fight attacks on educational principles and methods.	−.1	−.1	.0
2. Fight against dismissal of teachers.	−.1	−.1	.0
3. Defend teachers from public attacks from getting involved in controversial issues.	−.1	−.1	.0
4. Eliminate political liberals from staff.	+.3	+.1	−.2
5. Give helping hand to school board members coming up for election.	−.3(s)	+.2	+.5
Teachers' organizations should:			
6. Endorse political candidates.	−.4(s)	+.2	+.6
7. Take sides on public issues.	−.4(s)	+.2	+.6
OEA should:			
8. Endorse candidates in school elections.	−.4(s)	+.1	+.4
9. Try to influence legislation.	.0	.0	.0

Expectations Concerning Organizational Activity

The exact nature of this potential conflict within the organization will become clearer as we proceed to the analysis of the four attitude areas. We will first consider the mandates for organizational activity.

Table 1 presents the correlations for each of the attitude comparisons for each of the questions. In this, as in the tables which follow, the first column presents the objective attitudes, the "real world," and thus measures the extent of actual conflict. The second column shows the degree to which leaders are accurate in their perceptions of followers' attitudes, while the third column measures the extent of conflict as seen by the leaders. The negative sign of the correlation means that the bottom set of attitudes is more heavily weighted in the direction of believing that leaders of the organization *should* undertake a particular action. For example, in the first column a negative sign means that leaders believe more than the followers that they or the organization should undertake a given activity. In the second column the negative sign means that the leaders perceive the followers as being more in favor of undertaking a particular action than they actually are. The positive sign in the second column means that the followers are more in favor of undertaking a particular activity than the leaders believe them to be. A negative sign in the third column means that the leaders perceive the followers as more supportive of a particular activity than the leaders are. A positive sign in the third column indicates the reverse.

The table indicates that, with the single exception of eliminating from the OEA staff people believed to be politically extreme, the leaders are more inclined to favor the involvement of the organization in each of the actions presented. This is shown by the fact that in seven of the nine cases the signs of the first column are negative. The first three of these items are the more clearly "professional" of the set. They involve the traditional academic values of freedom of expression and the protection of teachers against hostile forces in the community. These are at best *quasi* political activities. Yet even here the followers are more restrained than the leaders. Note that on the question of eliminating political liberals from the OEA staff, the followers are more in favor of such action than are the leaders. However, it is true that the greatest discrepancy between followers' and leaders' attitudes occur on those questions involving the more purely political aspects of the organization, such as endorsing political candidates, taking sides on public issues, and taking part in the electoral activities of school board members.

With regard to these political activities, the followers are much more restrained than they are concerning more purely educational activities. Granted that the distinction between quasi-political and political is arbitrary at best, the followers do appear to make it. Thus, they are much more inclined to support the activities of the OEA if it defends teachers against public attacks than they would be if the teachers' organization endorsed political candidates.

The glaring exception to the general reluctance of the teachers to support the OEA's political activities is on the question of lobbying. Here there is nearly perfect agreement between leaders and followers. Lobbying is perceived by teachers to be an absolutely legitimate function of the organization. Teachers, therefore, are making a distinction between legislative politics and electoral politics.[9] The Association is currently

---

[9] Cf. Gabriel Almond and Sidney Verba, *The Civic Culture* (Boston: Little, Brown, and Co., 1965), pp. 250–51.

engaged in a vigorous lobbying program at the state legislative level. With regard to lobbying, it is interesting to notice that not only do the attitudes of the leaders and followers converge, but also the leaders perceive that the followers support the lobbying activities. This is indicated by the zero correlation in the second and third columns.

Notice also that with regard to the first three activities (fighting attacks on educational principles and methods, fighting against the dismissal of teachers, and defending teachers from public attacks) the leaders see *more* support among the teachers than actually exists. Since the leaders overestimate the enthusiasm of followers, they see a consensus which does not hold true in the "real world." Hence the perfect correla-

TABLE 2

Comparison of the Three Attitude Sets in the Areas of Expectations and Satisfaction with Leaderships' Actions

Questions	Followers' Attitudes vs. Leaders' Attitudes	Followers' Attitudes vs. Leaders' Perception of Followers' Attitudes	Leaders' Attitudes vs. Leaders' Perception of Followers' Attitudes
		Sets of Attitudes Compared	
1. How important do you think has been the role played by the OEA in getting improved salaries and benefits?	+.6(s)	+.0	−.7
2. How about the Teachers' Union; how important do you think its role was in getting improved salaries and benefits?	−.3	−.1	+.2
3. Do you think the OEA is doing enough to improve teachers' salaries and benefits?	−.3	−.4	−.1
4. How about the Teachers' Union; is it doing enough in improving teachers' salaries and benefits?	−.4	−.4	.0
5. Do you think the OEA is doing enough in its support for higher teacher standards and accreditation to improve professional status?	−.0	−.0	.0
6. Do you think there should be a state sales tax with the revenue going to the schools?	+.3	+.4	+.1

tion in the third column between the leaders' attitudes and their perceptions of teachers' attitudes is based upon faulty perceptions. This is not true with regard to the consensus about lobbying.

It is in the more purely electoral activities of the organization that discrepancies occur. Notice that on questions five, six, seven, and eight, the negative signs of the first column become positive signs in the second column. This means that, whereas leaders are more likely to want to engage in the electoral activities than are followers, the leaders perceive the followers as far more hesitant than the followers actually are. Consequently, these electoral activities can be contrasted with the professional and lobbying activities. In these professional and lobbying activities, the third column indicates that the leaders see little or no discrepancy between their point of view and the point of view of the followers, whereas the correlations on items five, six, seven, and eight in the third column indicate that the leaders see a considerable conflict between their values and those of the followers. With regard to these political activities, the leaders are correct in perceiving conflict although conflict also exists in educational activities but is missed by the leaders.

At this point in its organizational history, the OEA is in fact more likely to engage in professional and lobbying activities than it is in electoral activities. It is these activities in which the leaders see the followers as being entirely supportive of the organization, although they are correct only with regard to lobbying. If the OEA were to increase its electoral activities, therefore, it would be engaging in practices which are less favored by the followers. However, the fact that the teachers are perceived as being more reluctant to support these activities than they actually are might result in the leaders engaging in these activities to a lesser extent than would be tolerated by the followers.

Evaluations of Organizational Performance

Turning from the extent to which leaders and followers are in agreement as to what the organization should do, we consider now the relationships between sets of attitudes concerning the extent of satisfaction with the actual behavior of the leaders of the organization. In Table 2 a negative sign indicates that the bottom set of attitudes is less satisfied with the performance of the teachers' organization. A positive sign indicates that the bottom set is more satisfied.

In the first analysis, we found that the leaders consistently underestimate the followers' activism. In Table 2 we find a similar tendency with several notable exceptions. On the question of the importance of the OEA's role in getting improved salaries and benefits in the past, we find a great discrepancy between leaders' and followers' attitudes: the followers are inclined to give the OEA less credit than are the leaders. However, the second column shows that the leaders' perception is accurate. Hence, they perceive followers as exhibiting more dissatisfaction with past performance than the leaders do. Leaders, intimately involved in the successes and failures of the organization, see their role as more significant than do the more passive followers. Only about one-third of the followers think that the OEA was "very important" in securing past benefits, whereas all the leaders are of this opinion.

With regard to current performance a different situation exists. The leaders are more dissatisfied with the performance of the organization and its constant fight for better salaries. Once again, however, they perceive more dissatisfaction among the followers than actually exists. Although accurate in their perceptions of teacher satisfaction with past performance, leaders fail in their evaluation of current satisfaction. In fact, 56% of the followers indicated that they think the OEA is doing enough about salaries. This is not exactly an overwhelming vote of confidence, but it is apparent that more satisfaction exists in reality than is perceived by the OEA leadership.

In view of the current conflict between teachers' unions and professional organizations for the loyalties of teachers, it is interesting to note that the OEA leaders are more likely to denigrate the efforts of the teachers' union than are the teachers themselves. This is indicated by the negative sign of the correlations in column one considering the role of the union in past and present efforts toward salary increases. Again column two tells us that in both of these cases leaders perceive that followers are more dissatisfied with the union than they actually are. This distinction between past and present produces some curious results in the third column, showing the extent of conflict perceived by leaders. While they exaggerate the extent of dissatisfaction on the part of followers, perhaps projecting their own desires more than an objective evaluation would indicate, they recognize that the followers are more impressed with past union performance than they (the leaders) are. Yet they persist in seeing perfect agreement between themselves and teachers concerning current union performance, an agreement which does not exist. These distortions lead the leadership to assume a "what-have-you-done-for-me-lately" attitude somewhat along the lines of old fashioned bread and butter unionism. It seems likely that these perceptions will cause them to channel more of their resources into salary increase efforts at the risk of providing less satisfactory efforts in other areas. On the other hand this risk does not appear to be very great. For example, the leaders are extremely accurate in their perceptions of teacher satisfaction with regard to support for higher professional standards and accreditation. A consensus only slightly weaker than that regarding lobbying exists here.

The final item in the table dealing with the question of state sales tax enables us to return once again to lobbying. We may well ask "Lobbying for what?" The OEA has been strongly lobbying for a state sales tax with revenues going to the public schools, but only a slight majority (53%) of the teachers agree that a state sales tax should be enacted, while more than two-thirds of the leadership favor the tax. This is apparently an elite-derived effort enjoying only weak support from the followers. In this case, however, the leaders perceive far more support than actually exists. They actually believe that followers support this effort more than the leaders do, whereas the opposite is the case. Thus, although high consensus is achieved on the legitimacy of lobbying, leaders do not show a great capability of deciding how much effort should be devoted to the pursuit of certain policies by means of lobbying. The leaders want a sales tax, perceive the followers as wanting a sales tax, and pursue this effort vigorously. It is possible that if the efforts to achieve a sales tax are continued with increased intensity, membership support might be reduced beyond the bare majority it enjoys now, and intra-group conflict may result. If this happens the perceptual errors of the leaders could prove costly.

Abstract Political Values

Up to this point we have been considering the explicit programs of the Oregon Education Association, and the extent to which there is a congruence between leaders' and followers' values with regard to these programs. Members of organizations, however, may have values which are not directly translatable into explicit programs but which nevertheless color the relationship between leaders and followers. The overall ideo-

TABLE 3

Comparison of the Attitude Sets in the Area of Orthodox Values

Questions	Sets of Attitudes Compared		
	Followers' Attitudes vs. Leaders' Attitudes	Followers' Attitudes vs. Leaders' Perceptions of Followers' Attitudes	Leaders' Attitudes vs. Leaders' Perceptions of Followers' Attitudes
Conservative			
1. The American form of government may not be perfect, but it's the best type of government yet devised by man.	−.1	+.1	+.2
2. Democracy is considered the ideal form of government by most of the world. ...	−.2	−.7	−.4
3. Private enterprise could do better most of the things the government is now doing.	+.4	−.2	−.6
4. The participation of the federal government in local affairs leads to undesirable federal controls.	+.6(s)	−.4	−.9
5. Communis‚n is a total evil.	+.1	−.5	−.6
6. People of most underdeveloped countries are by nature incapable of self-government.	+.3	−.2	−.5
7. Private enterprise is the only really workable system in the modern world capable of satisfying our economic needs.	+.3	−.2	−.5
Liberal			
8. Economic and social planning by government does not necessarily lead to dictatorship.	−.3	+.1	+.4
9. Man is the maker of his own society, such events as wars and depressions could be controlled by man.	−.1	+.2	+.3
10. The growth of large corporations makes government regulations of business necessary.	−.2	+.1	+.3
11. We could increase spending for many government services without harming the nation's economy	−.4	+.0	+.4
12. The federal government represents the needs of most people better than local government.	−.0	+.3	+.3
13. The government should increase its activities in matters of health, retirement, wages, and old-age benefits.	−.2	−.0	+.2

logical pattern of leaders and followers is, therefore, a component in determining the extent to which leaders represent the followers' values. It is this assumption which leads us to inquire about abstract political values. The items in Table 3 are offered as important in the leaders' evaluations as to what programs might appeal to the followers and also what the nature of appeals to the membership for support on a given issue might be. On the basis of their content, the items are separated into those indicating conservatism and those indicating liberalism. The first seven questions are the conservative questions, and the last six are the liberal questions. For each group, a negative sign indicates that the bottom set of attitudes shows greater acceptance to the item.

Looking at the first column, it can readily be seen that the leaders are more likely to disagree with the conservative items and more likely to agree with the liberal items than are the followers. Furthermore, the high correlations in the third column show that the leaders believe that the followers differ greatly from them with regard to these items. Once again, however, the leaders' perceptions of teachers' attitudes tends to exaggerate the differences. In eleven of the thirteen cases, leaders perceive followers to be more conservative and less liberal than they actually are. Thus, although the OEA leaders are a biased section of the teachers with respect to their political and economic values, they tend to perceive their atypical posture as more extreme than it actually is. This discrepancy in perception is likely to influence the leaders to use more conservative appeals to the followers in the urging support of particular programs than would be called for by an accurate inventory of their values.

Combined with the bread and butter perception described previously, this perceived conservatism of teachers leads the leaders into the path of heavy emphasis on salaries and other basic issues while at the same time forcing them to restrict their activities in the realm of expansion of organizational activities. If the leadership seeks to venture into untried areas which are not specifically related to educational problems, it may be hesitant to begin for fear that the programs are too liberal for the membership.

Of course, as Krech and Crutchfield point out, the degree of association between cognitive attitudes and action-orientated attitudes is not necessarily great.[10] Thus, a person holding conservative beliefs does not automatically favor conservative actions by government. To ascertain the extent to which abstract values are translatable into immediate preferences for governmental action, we administered the items from the Survey Research Center's domestic attitude scale.[11] As in the abstract value index, the leaders proved to be much more liberal than the fol-

[10] David Krech and Richard Crutchfield, *Theory and Problems of Social Psychology* (New York: McGraw-Hill Book Co., 1948), p. 251.

[11] See Angus Campbell, et al., *The American Voter* (New York: John Wiley and Sons, 1960), pp. 194–98. V. O. Key gives the items used in this scale. See V. O. Key, Jr., *Public Opinion and American Democracy* (New York: Alfred A. Knopf, 1961), p. 561.

lowers. Also, the leaders saw the followers as not being as liberal as they actually are. In this case, however, the leaders are not so greatly more liberal and they do not see the followers as so greatly more conservative than they actually are. The main thrust of the conservative scale is identical to that of the abstract political value index, but the discrepancies are not as great. It may be, therefore, that the leaders are less in danger of undercutting the cohesion of the organization should they lend its support to an explicit governmental program outside the realm of education related issues. The danger to cohesion may be not so much in the undertaking of new programs but in the appeal to followers on the basis of their perceived conservatism.

The Political Role of the Teacher

Teachers, like the holders of any social position, have perceptions of what is permissible behavior by holders of their social position. Others who do not hold this position also have expectations. The interaction of these two expectations constitutes a role. Table 4 presents the comparisons between the three sets of attitudes with regard to norms of teachers' political participation. A negative sign indicates that the bottom set of attitudes in the comparison favors teacher participation more than does the top set of attitudes.

Here we see a remarkably consistent pattern. Leaders are, in every case save one, more supportive of actions by teachers in these areas than are the teachers. This is even true of joining a teachers' union, but it is not true of striking to secure higher salaries and other benefits. In this latter case, the teachers are slightly more likely than leaders to be willing to undertake this activity and are much more likely to be willing to strike than leaders perceive them to be. This is the single example of followers being more "activist" than leaders to achieve liberal goals. In every other case, no matter what type of action is involved, leaders are more willing to take a risk, more willing to engage in controversial activity than are followers. When we examine the leaders' perception of followers' attitudes, we find once again the consistent pattern of underevaluation of the experimental nature of teachers. Leaders perceive teachers as being unlikely to engage in these activities whereas teachers themselves, although less anxious than leaders to take part in these activities, are more willing to do so than leaders believe them to be. Thus, the teachers are more willing to join teachers' unions, political party organizations, or racial organizations than leaders believe them to be.

CONCLUSIONS

To summarize the findings of this analysis, the following points may be offered. As is true of most organizations, the leaders of the Oregon Education Association are more active than the followers. They are more liberal than the followers and they are more willing than the followers to expand the activities of the organization, but they consistently exaggerate the atypical nature of their position. They see the followers as

TABLE 4

Comparison of the Attitude Sets in the Area of the Norms of Teachers'
Political Participation

Questions	Sets of Attitudes Compared		
	Followers' Attitudes vs. Leaders' Attitudes	Followers' Attitudes vs. Leaders' Perceptions of Followers' Attitudes	Leaders' Attitudes vs. Leaders' Perceptions of Followers' Attitudes
Teachers should if they want to:			
1. Join a teachers' union.	−.1	+.5(s)	+.7
2. Go on strike to secure higher salaries and other benefits.	+.1	+.3(s)	+.3
3. Join a political party organization. ...	−.0	+.2	+.2
4. Serve as party precinct worker in pre-election activities.	−.1	+.3	+.3
5. Publicly criticize local government officials.	−.3	+.5(s)	+.8
6. In a presidential election, outside school time, make speeches or give other services on the behalf of a candidate.	−.1	+.3(s)	+.4
7. Run for political office.	−.1	+.5(s)	+.6
8. In a presidential election, explain to class reasons for preferring one candidate.	−.1	+.3	+.3
9. Belong to the NAACP or CORE. ...	−.1	+.3(s)	+.4
10. Take part in a CORE or NAACP demonstration, such as public picketing.	−.1	+.5(s)	+.6
11. Allow an atheist to address the class.	−.1	+.4(s)	+.6
12. Argue in class against the censoring of literature by people who feel it is pornographic.	−.2	+.0	+.3
13. Speak out in class against the John Birch Society and groups like it.	−.2	+.2	+.3
14. Speak in favor of nationalizing the steel industry and the railroads.	−.2	+.3	+.6
15. Speak in class in favor of the Medicare program.	−.2	+.3	+.4
16. Speak in class in favor of the United Nations.	−.0	+.3	+.3
17. Allow the distribution of anticommunist literature put out by the National Association of Manufacturers.	−.3	+.2	+.4
18. Speak in class favorably about socialism.	−.1	+.2	+.3
19. Argue in class that labor unions should be more regulated or controlled by the government.	−.2	+.2	+.3
20. Allow the distribution of anticommunist literature put out by the John Birch Society.	−.4(s)	+.1	+.6

being more conservative and restrained than they actually are. These discrepancies, both in perception and in actual attitudes, lead us to speculate as to how they came about. Is the relative activism of leaders a function of their social role, their organizational position, or their personality? It is certainly not feasible to argue that leadership positions somehow recruit more daring people. It is more feasible to seek explanations within the nature of the organization and the teaching profession. Consider, for example, the items dealing with political participation by teachers. Leaders would be subject to none of the pressures that teachers would feel from their community. Also, while teachers can recall relatively few cases in which the community made demands upon the school system for the dismissal of a teacher for engaging in controversial activity, those who can recall such incidents are of the opinion that the teachers' organization was ineffective in the defense of teachers. It is also true that the teachers look upon the local affiliates of the Oregon Education Association much more favorably than they look upon the statewide organization which employs the leaders considered in this study. In arguing for organizational position as a fundamental contributor to differential perception, we draw added support from the reaction of the leaders to the competition of the union. Leaders behave in much the same fashion as political party leaders.[12] They are more emotionally committed to the organization than are the rank and file. Hence, they find it difficult to comprehend the problems of teaching and the restrictions traditionally imposed upon teachers by the community.

It might be useful to know something about the leaders' backgrounds. All have at one time been teachers and all have passed through some lower administrative position before achieving their present status. Most have taken graduate work, usually in educational administration. All earn in excess of ten thousand dollars per year. Thus, although they do have a teaching background, they are much more upwardly mobile than the average teacher and make more money. They are also substantially better educated. The upward mobility of the leaders of the OEA can be gleaned from the backgrounds of their fathers. Most of their fathers had less than a high school education and held low status occupations. Thus holding a position in the OEA marks more of a step up than does teaching. Perhaps, therefore, the leaders consider themselves as more sophisticated and advanced than teachers.

When we consider the fact that serving as an OEA administrator is in a sense moving beyond a teaching position, the explanation offered above becomes more plausible. Combine this with the fact that leaders have interaction with a more heterogeneous environment and their perception of teachers becomes even more understandable. Unlike the teachers, who interact mostly with teachers, students, principals, and parents, the OEA administrative staff interacts with lobbyists, legislators, state officials, and national educational officials.

---

[12] Herbert McClosky, "Consensus and Ideology in American Politics," *American Political Science Review*, Vol. LVIII (June, 1964), 361–82.

As a final alternative to the explanation offered above, we considered the possibility that, whereas the leaders incorrectly perceive the political values and political role perceptions of teachers, they may base their reactions upon communication with a biased sample. There are, of course, many different shades of opinion among teachers just as there are among the general public. Is it true that the OEA leaders interact with a segment of the teaching population which is more conservative and more restrained? If this is true, then their perceptions of followers' attitudes might not be a function of their social position but might be the result of an unrepresentative sample of opinion being communicated to them. However, our evidence indicates quite clearly that there is no relationship between political conservatism and participation in organizational affairs. There is no evidence that the conservative teachers have any more interaction with OEA leaders than do the liberal teachers. Also, those teachers who take a restrained view of the political role of the teacher are no more likely to communicate with OEA leaders than are those teachers who take a more expansionist view.[13] Thus, we can say that there is no weighting of communication which comes to the attention of OEA leaders in favor of conservatism and restraint.

Assuming, therefore, that being a leader in an organization contributes to a discrepancy between leaders' and followers' attitudes, we may inquire finally into the possibility of having a democratic interest group without frequent and carefully supervised consultative mechanisms. Can leaders be representative simply because they intuitively comprehend what is required of them? In considering this question, let us note that, with the exception of the last table, the discrepancy between leaders' attitudes and followers' attitudes is generally *greater* than the errors made by leaders in perceiving these attitudes. Thus, OEA leaders operating entirely upon their personal values would not be representative of the values of their followers. On the other hand, if they adopted a purely representative role, they would become more conservative and restrained than the teachers would prefer. Yet, with exception of the last set of attitudes, the error would be less than would be true if followers' wishes were ignored. That is to say, if they followed their understanding of followers' values, the resulting conservatism and restraint would be closer to the actual desires of teachers than would be true if leaders used their personal values as the sole criteria of judgment. "Virtual" representation in an interest group cannot serve as a substitute for actual representation, because the position of group leader contributes to the development of attitudes which differ from those of the followers.

---

[13] It is true, however, that there is more interaction between leaders and small-town teachers; these teachers are considerably more conservative and restrained than their big-city counterparts.

Harmon Zeigler

The Effects of Lobbying: A Comparative Assessment*

Heinz Eulau once asked a question which might appear to "realistic" students of American politics as absurd. He asked: "What would politics in America be like without lobbies and lobbyists?"[1] To a generation of political scientists raised on the writings of Bentley and Truman, the question seems, at first glance, not only absurd, but *reactionary*. When the "behavioral revolution" reached a fever pitch in the 1950's, political scientists turned first to those writers who rejected the legalism of the past in an effort to describe the interaction of individuals rather than the structure of institutions. Arthur Bentley clearly stood out as a potential source of inspiration. Anybody who, in 1908, could write that "formal study of the most external characteristics of governing institutions" is worthless and must be replaced by the enterprise of getting hold of "political institutions, legislatures, courts, executive officers, and get them stated as groups, in terms of groups. . . ."[2] appeared as a logical Marx for the behavioral revolution.

Although most political scientists did not pay much attention to Bentley, various case studies of "pressure groups in action" began to appear, culminating in the summary statement of Truman.[3] While there are

* The author wishes to acknowledge the support of the Center for the Advanced Study of Educational Administration during a portion of the time he devoted to the preparation of this paper. CASEA is a national research and development center which was established at the University of Oregon under the provisions of the Cooperative Research Program of the U.S. Office of Education. I wish to acknowledge the assistance of Heinz Eulau, who carefully evaluated an earlier draft and made numerous suggestions for improvement.

[1] Heinz Eulau, "Lobbyists: The Wasted Profession," *Public Opinion Quarterly*, Vol. XXVIII (Spring 1964), p. 27.

[2] Arthur Bentley, *The Process of Government* (San Antonio, Texas: Principia Press of Trinity University, 1949), p. 210.

[3] David Truman, *The Governmental Process* (New York: Alfred A. Knopf, Inc., 1951).

enough ambiguities in Bentley to make a direct application of his theories virtually impossible, interest groups approached the status of a "first cause" of public policy. Of course, Truman (who replaced Bentley) never really said that in order to study legislation one need only to account for the activities of formal groups, but such an inference was made by readers of *The Governmental Process*, if only because the data to support his theories were not easily obtained from formal organizations.

TWO CONTRASTING MODELS OF THE GROUP BASIS OF POLITICS

The belief that interest groups are, by definition, powerful has been described as a "mechanistic" theory. In some extreme cases perhaps it was. Yet the better writers on the subject did not argue that all groups were powerful, nor did they believe that legislators made decisions solely as a result of their interactions with lobbyists. However, the "group theorists" did, if all their writings are summed up, outline a model of the political process roughly along the following lines. Individuals within a society have a variety of needs, some of which can be achieved only, or at least more efficiently, through governmental activity. Most of the values and beliefs of individuals are derived from the groups that they belong to or that they have contact with. Some of these groups are determined *for* an individual; others are joined voluntarily. Yet even the voluntary joining of an association has its roots in the deeper group affiliations of the individual. Since most of the needs of the individual derive from his group affiliations, the logical method of translating needs into demands is through formal groups. Of course, groups do not automatically become formal organizations. The formalization of group relationships occurs when, through intense and sustained interaction, individuals systematize their relationships. Hence farmers, druggists, doctors, or automobile workers find that their shared attitudes make it efficient to be represented by an interest group. The interest group, by means of its lobbyists, relates to the decision makers the needs of its members.

Viewed from this angle, group theorists were suggesting that interest groups are *transmission belts* between individual needs and governmental institutions. Other possible channels of communication, especially political parties, were not considered to be as effective primarily because they were too heterogeneous to be capable of presenting a cohesive point of view.

Crucial to the theory is the notion that, as societies become more complex, secondary associations replace primary associations as the essential group-referents of individuals. Consequently, in a complex industrial society such as America, formal associations are the essential means of communication. Froman has provided a useful summary of the function of interest groups, as defined by the group theorists. Interest groups channel communications to decision makers, help structure alternative policy choices, act as buffers between the government and the people, help check demands made by others, provide functional representation, compartmentalize access to decision makers, lead to a system of minorities rule, and provide people with an emotional outlet.[4]

Of course, such a brief outline of traditional group theory hardly does justice to many of its complexities and modifications. The essence of their theories is that interest groups are powerful because they monopolize access to governmental decision makers. The difficulty with this body of knowledge is that most of the empirical justifications assumed the validity of the theory, and many of them were case studies of a single legislative episode or a single interest group. Although in some cases this research involved interviewing legislators and lobbyists, the assumption that lobbyists were (naturally) influential lead to some distortions of the findings to fit the mechanistic model.

The writer can provide personal evidence of the confusion which results from an unquestioning acceptance of the mechanistic model. In writing *The Politics of Small Business*, it was discovered that the lobbyists for small business organizations described themselves as intimately involved in the affairs of the House and Senate Small Business Committees and of the Small Business Administration. However, members of these committees, their staffs, and the administrators of the Small Business Administration not only did not share this evaluation, but in many cases did not know the names of the lobbyists! It seemed as if the decision makers regarded the interest groups as without either power or legitimacy.[5] This was, of course, only a single case study of one area of public policy. However, it seemed to fit with what Donald R. Matthews was finding out at about the same time. His interviews with legislators led him to conclude that the effects of lobbying were greatly exaggerated.[6] Actually, the research of those not committed to group-theoretical notions gave support to Matthews' assessment. Studies of Congressional decision making did not emphasize groups unless such an emphasis was the a priori purpose of the investigation. Zeigler concluded in 1964 that "Since interest groups do not monopolize the communication of demands to the legislature, it is not likely that the effects of lobbying are as great as lobbyists themselves or journalistic writers seem to believe."[7] Empirical evidence was inadequate, however.

Evidence was soon forthcoming; in fact, some already existed. Wahlke, Eulau, Buchanan, and Ferguson, in a comparative study of four state legislatures, assessed the attitudes of state legislators toward interest groups. Categorizing legislators into "facilitators," "neutrals," and

---

[4] Lewis A. Froman Jr., "Some Effects of Interest Group Strength in State Politics," *American Political Science Review*, Vol. LX (December 1966), p. 954.

[5] Harmon Zeigler, *The Politics of Small Business* (Washington: The Public Affairs Press, 1961).

[6] Donald R. Matthews, *U.S. Senators and Their World* (Chapel Hill: University of North Carolina Press, 1960), pp. 195–96.

[7] Harmon Zeigler, *Interest Groups in American Society* (Englewood Cliffs: Prentice-Hall, Inc., 1964), p. 276.

"resistors," they found that while a minority of legislators were overtly hostile to lobbyists, there was substantial state-by-state variation.[8] In other words, in some political systems interest groups were dominant while in others they were not. There are some problems in interpreting these data which relate primarily to the fact that the sole measure of legislators' relationships with lobbyists is their attitude rather than their actual interaction. These problems will be taken up again. For the moment, it is important to observe that, in the Wahlke, Eulau, Buchanan, Ferguson study, the role of the legislator vis à vis lobbyists was an open question.

Shortly after the publication of *The Legislative System,* two studies of lobbying in Washington took direct issue with traditional group theory. Bauer, Pool, and Dexter, echoing an earlier protest by Cohen that the legend of "pressure group potency . . . appears to be accepted and passed on without evidence. . . . ,"[9] discovered that, with regard to reciprocal trade legislation, lobbyists and the organizations they represented were a relatively minor factor in the ultimate decision: ". . . the groups did not appear to have the raw material of great power. We noted shortages of money, men, information, and time."[10] Although the authors are careful to disclaim any intention to suggest that their particular case is typical, their conclusions certainly strike at the heart of the stereotype of the powerful, active interest group. Bauer, Pool, and Dexter speculated about the extent to which lobbyists aided in the perpetuation of the myth. However, Milbrath, interviewing a random sample of Washington lobbyists, generally supported the conclusions of Bauer, Pool, and Dexter.[11] He discovered that legislators did not feel very dependent upon the information supplied by lobbyists; consequently, only a small portion of lobbyists (9 percent) are consulted frequently. Milbrath uses the responses of lobbyists, suggesting that legislators and their staffs do not need them, to argue that the net result of lobbying is minimal.

THE NATURE OF THIS EXPLORATION

Thus we have come full circle. The mechanistic model has been buried, and we are now in the position of arguing that interest groups (or at least the lobbyists who represent them) could very easily be eliminated from the decision-making process without any appreciable change in public policy. This strikes me as a curious situation. Do we have to decide that the "truth" lies in either one direction or the other? Clearly, we do not. The research problem is to try to measure the effects of in-

8 John C. Wahlke et al., *The Legislative System* (New York: John Wiley & Sons, Inc., 1962), pp. 311–42.

9 Bernard C. Cohen, *The Influence of Non-Governmental Groups on Foreign Policy-Making* (Boston: World Peace Federation, 1959), p. 2.

10 Raymond A. Bauer et al., *American Business and Public Policy* (New York: Atherton Press, 1963), p. 398.

11 Lester Milbrath, *The Washington Lobbyists* (Chicago: Rand McNally and Co., 1963).

terest groups in different decision-making arenas and to offer some explanations as to the variations that can be expected to exist. This seems
to be the thrust of the recent arguments by Eulau. In evaluating Milbrath's book, he agrees that the concept of "pressure" is too "strong" to be
useful as an explanatory device. There is probably substantial consensus
that "pressure group" is a misnomer. However, Eulau maintains that
Milbrath's alternative explanatory model, "communications," is too
"weak." By this he means that attempting to define the lobbying act as a
communications process cannot provide a guide to reliable explanations
because the concept is too inclusive. Obviously, lobbying is communications because *every* social interaction is an example of the communications process. Correct in his assessment of the nature of communications,
Eulau seems to deny Milbrath's communications model its real virtue; it
indicates that the interactions between legislators and lobbyists (albeit
slight) takes a variety of forms, with "pressure" being a very minor one.
That is to say, the concept of communications includes the notion of pressure, along with the transmission of information.

The real virtue of Eulau's criticism is his plea that we should address
ourselves to "the critical problems of the impact of lobbying on governmental decisions."[12] I gather that Eulau believes this problem is best
approached by means of a model which depends heavily upon a description of the *total* role definition system of legislators. In order to understand the attitude of legislators toward interest groups (and, by inference, the behavior of legislators with regard to lobbyists), we have to
understand their self-perceptions in relation to their colleagues, constituents, parties, and any other source from which legislators derive cues.

One can hardly quarrel with Eulau's plea, as far as it goes. However,
there are alternative ways of approaching the problem. A conspicuous
gap in The Legislative System is the failure of the authors to pay more
than cursory attention to the total environment in which the legislators
perform their functions. This gap is made even more troublesome because of recent research on outputs. Recent efforts by Dye, Hofferbert,
Grumm, and others to explain the outputs of state legislatures has led to
the conclusion that knowing the characteristics of the political system
(such as extent of malapportionment, strength of parties, and party cohesion) does not enable one to predict what kinds of decisions a given
state will make.[13] Knowing something about the economic and social
environment, on the contrary, enables us to make relatively strong predictions about state outputs. Thus, one can ask the same question of party
organizations that Eulau asked about interest groups: what would happen if they were to disappear? Clearly, the time has not yet come to make
the statement that nothing would happen, but this kind of research has
made compelling the need to look at total environment. This is not to
assert, however, that environmental conditions *necessarily* influence the

12 Eulau, *op. cit.*, p. 35.

13 This literature is evaluated in John G. Grumm, "Structure and Policy in the
Legislature" (manuscript presented at the Conference on the Comparative Study of
State Politics, University of Michigan, August 1–12, 1966).

behavior of interest groups; rather it is to suggest the desirability of *asking* whether or not they do. It may be true that behavioral patterns, unlike outputs, are not related.

The interaction of legislators and lobbyists, and the relative effect of interest groups which flows from this interaction, must be placed within the context of total environment in order to ascertain the existence of a relationship between environment and behavior. Some of the more obvious aspects of environment can be derived from aggregate statistics. For instance, I used percentage of the population residing in urban areas, per capita income, and industrialization to hypothesize that interest groups are strongest in less urban, less wealthy, less industrial states.[14] Consequently, more group-oriented activity can be expected in these areas. Although urban, industrial societies generate more membership in voluntary associations, a more open and competitive group system reduces the chances of any one interest becoming dominant. Therefore, interest groups would be more likely to achieve a monopoly of communications in low-participant states with a low potential for group politics. Since the nonurban, nonindustrial, less wealthy states are those with the *least* participation and the *strongest* interest groups, the theory "fits." However, this argument is based upon a very unreliable measure of interest group strength. Indeed, due to the questionable nature of the measure, it remains an open question as to whether there is a relationship between the socioeconomic environment and the strength of the interest group system. To anticipate a later argument, this article will suggest that there is *not*.

Whereas cross-national research is an obvious testing ground for theories concerned with environmental variables, so are the American states. The states, because of their relative accessibility to researchers, are more useful than cross-national studies. Further, there appears to be as much variety among the states as there is between various national political cultures. Finally, while there are large varieties in the socioeconomic nature of the states, there are enough institutional similarities to make the task of comparative research less trying. The data for this research is interviews conducted with legislators and lobbyists in Oregon, North Carolina, Utah, and Massachusetts.[15] The states were selected to provide a maximum dispersion of socioeconomic conditions. Table 1 outlines some of the dimensions of these differences. There is, of course, no way

---

[14] Harmon Zeigler, "Interest Groups in the States," in Herbert Jacob and Kenneth Vines, eds., *Politics in the American States* (Boston: Little, Brown and Co., 1965), pp. 101–46.

[15] Interviews were conducted during February and March 1966. Efforts were made to interview each legislator and lobbyist. For the legislators, the percentage of completed interviews is: Massachusetts, 87%, North Carolina, 97%, Oregon, 94%, and Utah, 94%. For lobbyists, the percentage interviewed is more difficult to assess. In Utah, there is no list of registered lobbyists and in the other states it was found that some lobbyists do not register. In Massachusetts and North Carolina, the number of completed interviews exceeds the number of registered lobbyists. In Oregon, 94% of the registered lobbyists were interviewed. In Utah, since we first had to construct a list based upon preliminary interviews with experienced legislators, newspaper reporters, and more visible lobbyists, no percentage calculation can be given.

of causally linking these variables to the behavior of lobbyists and legislators. However, one could infer that empirically observed differences in behavior are related to differences in environment. Conversely, if it appears that environmental differences are randomly distributed in regard to the behavior of legislators and lobbyists, one can assume that no relationship exists.

Attention to environment is not intended to submerge the importance of individual role perceptions, but rather to provide them with a setting. Indeed, most of the empirical portions of this paper are based directly upon perceptions of self and perceptions of others. The basic assumption, derived directly from Eulau rather than in opposition to him, is that ". . . one should conduct empirical work . . . at both ends of the legislator-lobbyist relationship."[16] This points to another criticism of *The Legis-*

TABLE 1
Cultural Variations in Four States

	Massachusetts	North Carolina	Oregon	Utah
Total population	5,296,000	4,787,000	1,999,000	971,000
Percent increase: 1960-63 .	2.9	5.1	4.7	9.0
Percent urban	83.6	39.5	62.2	74.9
Percent Negro	2.2	24.5	1.0	0.5
Percent foreign parentage .	28.8	1.0	13.0	12.0
Population mobility: percent of 1960 population residing in different county than 1955 residence	13.5	15.6	25.7	21.2
Percent living in largest SMSA	49.7	6.7	39.9	45.6
Per capita income	2,853	1,807	2,502	2,119
Percent failure, Draft Board Mental Tests, 1963	14.1	43.8	6.9	5.5
Median school years completed	11.6	8.9	11.8	12.2
Industrialization index° ...	98.7	86.7	92.1	94.0
Voter turnout in gubernatorial and senatorial elections in non-Presidential years	58.8	25.1	55.9	64.3
Ranney index of party competititon (adjusted)†	.0227	.3793	−.1455	−.0395
Percent Democratic, 1964 Presidential election	76.5	56.2	63.9	54.7
Number of days in legislative session, 1963-64 ..	505	145	163	63
Bills considered per day ..	18.9	14.2	9.8	17.0
Percent bills passed	18.3	66.0	45.5	20.3

° Percentage of population not employed in agriculture, forestry, or fishing.
† .5000 equals perfect competition.

---

[16] Heinz Eulau and Katherine Hincley, "Legislative Institutions and Processes," in James A. Robinson, ed., *Political Science Annual* (Indianapolis and New York: The Bobbs-Merrill Co., Inc., 1966), p. 147.

lative System (derived, as noted, from one of the authors of the book). It is difficult to draw inferences about the actual nature of the lobbying process without talking to both lobbyists and legislators. When this is not done, the assumption that legislators are the best judge of what is actually happening is tacitly made. Garceau and Silverman, and Lockard indicate that in some cases legislators are actually *not* aware of the "real" world.[17] On the other hand, lobbyists are not necessarily any more reliable. The inability of either set of participants to provide an "accurate" assessment of the situation is not a function of dishonesty but is simply an obvious illustration of the fact that two actors participating in the same act might have entirely different perceptions of the situation. This is true because ". . . the essential features of the interpersonal behavior event . . . may be thought of as a process . . . in which the action of one person is a response to the second person . . . the actions of each are in reference to the other."[18] Hence, the role definitions of lobbyists and legislators are derived as a consequence of their interaction, although neither lobbyist nor legislator need have shared assumptions about the purpose of the encounter. Indeed, certain behavior might be a consequence of misperceptions. Note that this model does not necessarily imply that the only way to understand the legislator-lobbyist relationship is to account for the *total* network of interactions and expectations that each actor has. Rather the idea is that the best approach is to understand expectations with *regard to each other.*[19]

Thus the research is simply the analysis of encounter between legislators and lobbyists within the context of political culture. The purpose of the research is an assessment rather than a theory. Eulau is right in saying that neither the mechanistic nor the communications theory is adequate. He is also correct in wondering, if lobbyists do not perform the functions normally ascribed to them, who does? However, the generalizations about the lack of impact of lobbyists is not comparative, but rather is drawn from various studies of Washington. The only comparative study of lobbying is *The Legislative System,* which does not describe the perceptions of lobbyists. Consequently, the time is right for a comparative assessment. We need to know: (1) how much interaction between legislators and lobbyists actually takes place, (2) what is the nature of this interaction, and (3) what is the effect of this interaction.

How Much Communication Takes Place?

To be effective, lobbyists have to interact with legislators on a regularized and frequent basis. State legislators are busy, and the sources com-

---

[17] Oliver Garceau and Corinne Silverman, "A Pressure Group and the Pressured: A Case Report," *American Political Science Review,* 43 (September 1954), pp. 672–91; Duane Lockard, *New England State Politics* (Princeton: Princeton University Press, 1959), p. 42.

[18] David Krech et al., *Individual in Society* (New York: McGraw-Hill, 1962), p. 4.

[19] On this point, see Edward E. Jones and John W. Thibaut, "Interaction Goals as Bases of Inference in Interpersonal Perception," in Renato Tagiuri and Luigi Petrullo, *Person Perception and Interpersonal Behavior* (Stanford: Stanford University Press, 1958).

peting for their time are many. Therefore, the beginning of an assessment of interest group strength must be frequency of interaction. Legislators and lobbyists were asked how many contacts (of any kind) occurred per week during the legislative session.[20] The following table indicates, first, that there are substantial interstate differences and, second, with regard to interstate differences, that the perceptions of legislators and lobbyists differ (Table 2). It seems quite clear that both legislators and lobbyists

TABLE 2
Mean Interactions per Week as Reported by Legislators and Lobbyists

	Mean	N
Massachusetts		
Legislators	7.8	244
Lobbyists	10.7	185
North Carolina		
Legislators	8.5	164
Lobbyists	25.9	132
Oregon		
Legislators	34.0	84
Lobbyists	31.0	193
Utah		
Legislators	16.0	90
Lobbyists	18.5	134

report more contact in Oregon. More interaction takes place in Oregon than in any other state, regardless of who is making the judgment. It also is clear that legislators and lobbyists have the fewest number of interactions in Massachusetts. Utah falls between the two extremes, and again there is substantial consensus. The real problem is North Carolina. In each of the other states legislators and lobbyists are relatively close in their assessment of the extent of interactions, but in North Carolina legislators think little interaction takes place, while lobbyists would "rank" their state second only to Oregon. Here we encounter a basic problem in Eulau's suggestion that both actors in the interaction should be examined. Who is right? One possibility is, of course, that lobbyists are exaggerating their importance, as McAdams has suggested in another context, while legislators, conforming to their perception of the good legislator, believe they are acting "independently."[21] This explanation has the obvious flaw of failing to account for the tendency of legislators in other states to approximate the estimates of lobbyists. In Oregon, legislators see *more* interaction than do lobbyists.

Still, there might be some truth in the explanation. North Carolina is less urban, less industrialized, and less wealthy than the other states. It

---

[20] It is obviously better to *observe* the number of interactions than to ask the participants to recall them, but to do so would have been impossible both in terms of comparative research and in terms of time involved. The table should be interpreted as an estimate.

[21] Alan K. McAdams, *Power and Politics in Labor Legislation* (New York: Columbia University Press, 1964), p. 193.

also has the lowest rate of political participation. These conditions generally contribute to the strength of the interest group system, but at the same time might contribute to the reluctance of legislators to discuss interest groups, or to the failure of legislators to be able to offer accurate assessments. North Carolina has, according to Elazar, a *traditionalistic political culture*. The essential attributes of such a culture are "a paternalistic and elitist concept of the commonwealth." Consequently, such a culture confines "real political power to a relatively small and self-perpetuating group drawn from an established elite" who have a "right" to govern.[22] If legislators reflect these kinds of attitudes, they would admit very little "outside" influence, whether from party, interest group, or constituents. Eulau's evaluation of Tennessee—a state with essentially the same political culture as North Carolina—is suggestive of this conclusion. There are more "trustees" in Tennessee than in any of the other states examined.[23] Trustees define their legislative role as that of free agent, relying on their own conscience and principles rather than the advice of any external forces. Therefore, they would be reluctant either to place much reliance on lobbyists or, perhaps, to *admit* that they do so.

The fact that interest groups seem to be such a minor part of the Massachusetts legislative system might be a function of the strong party cohesion in that legislature. Further, Massachusetts is a populous, ethnically diverse state which might, on the one hand, produce more demands for legislative action, but at the same time increase the number of competitors for rewards (still, there are fewer registered lobbyists in Massachusetts than in Oregon).

In addition to the strength of party, Massachusetts has nearly three times as many legislators as does either Oregon or Utah, making the task of interaction difficult purely on the basis of the ratio of legislators to lobbyists.[24] Boston is a large city in which one can easily submerge oneself in anonymity; Salem, Oregon, is a small town with the legislature as the main focal point of activity. Salt Lake City, between Boston and Salem in population, yields an interaction rate also between these two extremes. Of course, one can hardly maintain that the size of the capital city per se is a basic contributor to the rate of interaction, but coupled with the limited visibility of interest groups in comparison to the strong political parties of Massachusetts, it might be a reinforcement. The weakness of groups in North Carolina and Massachusetts appears easier to explain than the strength of groups in Oregon and Utah. As the explanation develops, attempts will be made to correct this deficiency.

The fact that legislators and lobbyists have different perceptions of the extent of communication might be indicative of actual *patterns* of

---

22 David Elazar, *American Federalism: A View from the States* (New York: Thomas Y. Crowell Co., 1966), p. 93.

23 Wahlke et al., *op. cit.*, p. 281.

24 The idea of the difficulty of the lobbyists' job being related to the size of the audience can be explored by examining the interaction rates of the state senates, which have fewer members. In Massachusetts and Utah there is substantially more interaction in the Senate than in the House. However, in North Carolina, there is substantially less contact in the Senate, while in Oregon the interaction rates are virtually the same.

interaction. Both sets of judges might be correct. Assuming this is true, we might conclude that in the states in which legislators perceive more communication than do lobbyists, the bulk of the contact comes from a *few* lobbyists trying to communicate with a large body of legislators. The target of communications might be large. The best examples of this possibility are Oregon and Utah. The larger targets of lobbyists might reflect the relatively open decision-making structure of these legislatures. Neither strong parties nor traditionalistic cultures would restrict the number of legislators who might be viewed as useful targets for communication. The strategy would thus be to contact as many legislators as possible, whether or not they hold important party or legislative positions. Yet, since a relatively small proportion of lobbyists are full-time "professionals" who make lobbying a business, this relatively large body of legislators would interact with a smaller proportion of lobbyists. In Oregon, in contrast to Utah, more lobbyists are "professionals" and put in longer hours on the job. In this state, therefore, there is both the necessity of contacting a larger body of legislators and a larger number of lobbyists trying to interact.

Two contrasting patterns are presented by North Carolina and Massachusetts, neither of which have broad target areas. In Massachusetts, few legislators interact with few lobbyists. In North Carolina, many lobbyists interact with few legislators. Thus, the rigidity of party control in Massachusetts might eliminate the rank-and-file from the communication process, while the traditionalism and value placed upon experience might do so in North Carolina. In North Carolina, however, the case for a restricted target zone appears strengthened because of the greater activity of lobbyists. North Carolina brings to mind the research of Garceau and Silverman, which suggested that many Vermont legislators are unaware of intense lobbying activity, and of Wahlke, Eulau, Buchanan, and Ferguson, who find Tennessee legislators uninformed, but draw a different sort of conclusion: that there not much lobbying takes place. It is clear, in North Carolina, that most legislators are not involved in the lobbying process, but this does not necessarily mean that little lobbying takes place.

The problem would not have existed had only legislators been interviewed, but the description emerging from a single set of interviews would have been less valid. One approach to the problem is to find out what *kinds* of lobbyists and legislators are most likely to interact. For instance, it may be that interaction increases with the experience of both or either sides. In the case of lobbyists, it may take time to locate key decision makers, become familiar with the rules of the game, learn the technicalities of legislation, establish a reputation, and get on friendly terms with legislators. Legislators might have increased contact with lobbyists if they have had considerable legislative experience and if their position in the legislature is sufficiently important to attract the attention of lobbyists. Since turnover in the ranks of both groups is fairly high, perhaps a minority really get involved. To some extent these speculations are supported by the data, but not in a clear fashion. In all states except Utah, the experienced lobbyists do interact more with legislators than do the novices. However, the Oregon novice lobbyists interact with legislators as much as do the experienced lobbyists in North Carolina. Thus, intense interaction is limited in North Carolina but is more "open" in Oregon. In Utah, the novice lobbyists actually have more contacts with legislators than do the experienced ones. Assuming that the experienced lobbyists know more about their jobs, this suggests that a better strategy is to limit contact. Both North Carolina (52 percent) and Utah (44 percent) have a higher proportion of experienced lobbyists than Oregon (30 percent) and Massachusetts (29 percent).[25] However, in spite of the relative experience of their lobbyists, the two states differ markedly with respect to intensity of interaction.

A similar pattern emerges for legislators; those with the most experience have the greatest contact with lobbyists, except for North Carolina, which is a puzzling development. We have described North Carolina as a relatively "closed" state in which only the more experienced lobbyists actually get into the act of contacting a few legislators. But the experienced legislators do not absorb the bulk of the efforts of lobbyists, as they do in other states. Nor do committee chairmen or party leaders receive more communications from lobbyists than nonleaders, as is generally true.[26] The structure of power in North Carolina's legislature—insofar as it can be ascertained from the efforts of lobbyists—is totally unrelated to the formal structure of the institution.

On the basis of interaction—without concern for the *effects* of interaction—Oregon and Massachusetts stand at opposite ends of a continuum with North Carolina (depending upon the judges) and Utah falling in between. Of course, interaction need not be an indicator of effect. Perhaps one contact by a good lobbyist is worth 100 contacts by an amateur. Also, perhaps the greater the contact—indicating a more intense set of demands—the less effective any one contact is likely to be. Further, intensity of interaction might simply be a function of how busy legislators are. The more bills there are to consider, the more frequent will be the interaction (assuming that interest groups are the basic communicator of demands). Such an assumption clearly does not work because Massachusetts, with its low rate of interaction, considers almost twice as many bills per day (19) as does Oregon (10).

Although the explanation of the reasons for varied rates of interaction is parted at this point, let us proceed to the next step in the argument. The question is: to what extent does frequency of interaction provide clues both about the nature and effects of the interaction?

What Is the Nature of the Interaction?

Although a communications model may be too weak, communicating with legislators is what lobbyists are supposed to do. It is certainly true that the purpose of *any* communication is to change behavior, yet the communications and mechanistic models offer markedly different interpretations of the nature of communications. The supporters of the com-

---

[25] The cut-point for experience is eleven years (the mean).
[26] From data to be reported in the future.

munications model believe that lobbyists transmit *information* to legislators. The consequences of this assumption are: (1) most interaction occurs between two partisans: "Its [the interest group's] role became that of an auxiliary service bureau for a senator with whom it was in complete agreement,"[27] and (2) successful lobbyists are those upon whom legislators know they can rely for accurate information, preferably information which is available most conveniently (or exclusively) from lobbyists. One lobbyist phrased the job of the informant in these words: "I will try to establish a reputation for having certain . . . technical information which is otherwise unavailable to them [legislators]."

The assumptions of the mechanistic model are fundamentally different. Lobbyists have as their fundamental goal the *persuasion* of legislators. Subscribers to the mechanistic theory believe: (1) lobbyists com-

TABLE 3

Percentage of Legislators and Lobbyists Classifying Their Roles as:

	Persuader	*Informant*	*Both*	*N*
Massachusetts				
Legislators	30	42	28	244
Lobbyists	54	18	28	185
North Carolina				
Legislators	20	53	27	164
Lobbyists	45	29	27	132
Oregon				
Legislators	26	55	19	84
Lobbyists	48	34	19	193
Utah				
Legislators	29	57	14	90
Lobbyists	38	36	25	134

municate with opponents or undecided legislators, and (2) successful lobbyists are those able to convert opponents into supporters and firm up waverers. According to one such lobbyist: "Well, I may as well be honest about it. We are trying to influence votes on certain measures. We spend most of our time trying to influence votes on legislative measures."

Just as Eulau argues that neither the mechanistic nor the communications models are entirely correct, it is reasonable to assume that there is a bit of truth in the behavioral consequences which flow from either model. Certainly the data suggest that this is the case (Table 3).

Legislators and lobbyists are categorized according to whether they spend more of their time sending or receiving messages with a content either primarily informational or persuasive.[28] Obviously, such a categorization of the nature of communication is ideal. Information is cer-

---

[27] Bauer et al., *op cit.*, p. 357.

[28] The categorization is derived from the "purposive" and "non-purposive" distinction found in the literature of communications. See Bruce H. Westley and Malcolm S. MacLean, Jr., "A Conceptual Model for Communications Research," in James H. Campbell and Hal W. Helper, eds., *Dimensions in Communication* (Belmont, Calif.: Wadsworth Publishing Co., Inc., 1965), pp. 61–62.

tainly an instrument of persuasion, and most messages are probably a "mix." Nevertheless, respondents were able to decide what the perceived essential purpose of a message was. The table is illustrative of some fundamental concepts in the examination of the interaction process. The evaluation of an encounter will be based upon self-perceptions and perceptions of the other person, as is illustrated by Figure 1. To apply the

FIGURE 1
A Model Interaction

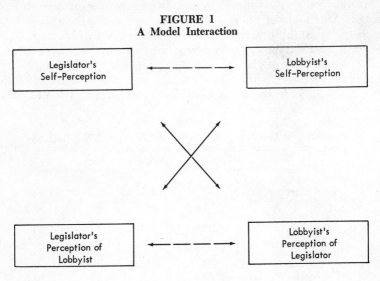

figure to the table, it will be noticed that the nature of the interaction is seen quite differently by the two participants. The pattern is quite consistent from state to state. In every case, a higher proportion of lobbyists are classified as persuaders and a higher proportion of legislators define their role as receivers of information. These contrasting perceptions of the encounter can be expected to have an impact upon the behavior of the actors. As we have argued, the nature of the encounter is defined by the perceptions of the participants. It stands to reason that the more congruent the perceptions of the participants, the less ambiguous will be the encounter. In this case, the effectiveness of the lobbyist should be related to the extent of harmony between his perceptions and that of the legislator. In other words, the clearer the mutual expectations, the more effective will be the lobbyist.

Table 3 provides categories based solely upon whether or not one type of communication outweighs another. To get an idea of the extent of congruence, let us examine the rate of congruence, let us examine the rate of interaction spent in either informational or persuasive communication (Table 4). We can now see that the greatest congruence concerning perception of persuasion occurs in Oregon, followed by Utah, North Carolina, and Massachusetts. Thus, the two states with the highest interaction have the greatest congruence. It will be argued shortly that Oregon and Utah are the states with the strongest groups, thus supporting

TABLE 4
Interaction Rates of Legislators and Lobbyists
Devoted to Persuasion or Information

	Persuasion	Information
Massachusetts		
Legislators	.25	.33
Lobbyists	.46	.22
North Carolina		
Legislators	.09	.17
Lobbyists	.33	.22
Oregon		
Legislators	.21	.30
Lobbyists	.37	.25
Utah		
Legislators	.23	.38
Lobbyists	.33	.32

the idea of the relationship between congruence and effectiveness. Further, the fact that there is greater congruence in states with high interaction indicates that stereotypic perceptions probably dictate the terms of an *initial* encounter, but that more accurate images develop as the interactions become more frequent. Hence, Massachusetts and North Carolina, with the lowest rates of interaction, also have the least congruence and the least effective lobbyists. Notice also that there is uniformly greater congruence concerning informational communication. This may indicate a greater acceptance of the legitimacy of this type of communication and, incidentally, suggest an introductory chapter to a textbook for beginning lobbyists.

The Effects of Lobbying

Measuring the effects of lobbying is especially difficult in view of contrasting perceptions, and because of the existence of at least two functions of lobbying. If lobbying is persuasion, we need to know how often this goal is achieved. If lobbying is information, we need to know how much confidence is placed in this information. The point to be made is that a single measure of influence is not able to account for the *ends* attached to various lobbying *means*. Mention was made earlier of the report by Zeller.[29] Political scientists were asked to describe the influence of interest groups in their states as "strong," "moderate," or "weak." The defects of this method are apparent. The panel of judges is, at best, questionable. Asking people to evaluate the effects of interest groups in terms of such an ambiguous concept as "power" compounds the felony. A better method was devised by Wahlke, Eulau, Buchanan, and Ferguson. Their measure was based on questions dealing with both the legislators' awareness of interest groups and their acceptance of the legiti-

[29] Belle Zeller, ed., *American State Legislatures* (New York: Thomas Y. Crowell Co., 1954), pp. 190–91.

macy of lobbying. By combining legislators' attitudes (as measured by a series of scales) and awareness (as measured by ability to identify certain organizations), legislators were classified into three role-orientations: facilitators, neutrals, and resistors. Thus, in no case is anybody simply asked about the power of interest groups. However, as I noted earlier, there are some problems with this scheme. The classifications are only minimally behavioral. They do not deal with the effects of actual interaction but only with attitudes. Wahlke reasons that legislators can be expected to behave according to their role definitions and that the behavioral consequences follow naturally from role definitions.

Whereas this assumption may be correct, no actual behavior is described.[30] Our data does indicate, in support of Wahlke, that the extent of contact, effect of contact, and attitudes toward lobbyists are clearly interrelated. However, one of the conclusions of *The Legitimate System*, that percentage of resistors declines as legislative experience increases, is challenged. It was found that, whereas the *attitudes* of legislators toward lobbyists become more favorable as experience increases, legislators *do not* become more persuadable. The lack of connection between behavior and attitude is illustrated by Wahlke's discussion of the potential for interest group politics in the various states, avoiding a discussion of what happens in favor of an estimate of what might happen. Finally, the potential and the actuality are gradually merged until the distinction is lost.

There is no clear way out of these dilemmas. The approach offered here is to consider lobbying as both a persuasive and informational process and to assess the effects of both attempts, relying upon reports of behavior more than upon assessment of attitudes.

Initially, we might observe some apparent differences between lobbying in the states and lobbying in Washington. In Washington, where informational lobbying seems typical, lobbyists talk to sympathetic legislators. In the states, where there is more persuasion, opponents seem to have considerable contact with each other. It is true that more contact takes place among like-minded lobbyists and legislators than among those who do not see things in the same way, but in all states at least a third of the legislators and lobbyists indicate substantial contact with opponents. In Oregon, to use a slightly atypical case, about the same number of contacts take place among those with conflicting points of view as between those in agreement. In fact, lobbyists tend to lean toward contacts with legislators whose position is unclear. In short, lobbyists appear to "lobby" in the traditional stereotype more in the states than in Washington. Concerning stereotypes, the younger lobbyists are more likely to talk to opponents and to define their role as persuader than are the older lobbyists; hence, they fit the stereotype more easily. There is a sort of professionalization process which reduces the stereotypic behavior of lobbyists as they begin to learn the rules of the game.

---

[30] Since this analysis is based upon reports of behavior rather than independent observations of behavior, the point of the objection is questionable. Nevertheless, in using reports as a surrogate for behavior, the effort to describe behavior is made clear.

Such a process of professionalization is certainly related to the number of interactions. The greater the number of interactions, the more realistic become the actors' images of each other. Hence, younger lobbyists who do not get "into the game" very much have not had the opportunity to correct their stereotypes.

Another aspect of stereotypic behavior which is probably related to extent of interaction concerns the notion of "pressure." According to popular and some scholarly characterizations, pressure groups do just what the name implies. No one is really sure what pressure tactics are available to lobbyists, and the research in the Washington setting of Milbrath and Bauer, Pool, and Dexter suggests that "information groups" is a more appropriate appellation. Nevertheless, the image persists. To legislators and lobbyists, pressure is an undesirable connotation. When a legislator says that he is being pressured, he means that he perceives the lobbyist to be trying vigorously to overcome his resistance by any available means.

The perceived incidence of pressure varies from state to state and between legislators and lobbyists. Massachusetts lobbyists, who report very little contact with legislators, believe that they engage in pressure tactics far more so than do the lobbyists of the other states. In Massachusetts, as is true for the other states, legislators tend to see less pressure than lobbyists, but the discrepancy between the perceptions of the two judges is substantially greater.[31]

By contrast, Oregon, which appears to have the greatest interaction, also appears to have the lowest perception of pressure tactics on the part of both legislators and lobbyists. The general rule seems to be that interaction and perceptions of pressure exist in a functional relationship. The greater the interaction between legislators and lobbyists, the more favorable become the evaluations of the encounter. The exception if Utah, which is a high interaction state with high perceptions of pressure. Indeed, Utah legislators believe themselves to be more pressured than the legislators of any other state. As will become evident shortly, although Utah and Oregon seem to be the two states in which interest groups are most active, the attitudes of legislative participants in these states is quite able become the evaluations of the encounter. The exception is Utah, to accept interest groups as legitimate, even though they come into frequent contact with them. It can be demonstrated that, whereas the interaction frequency in Utah is either the same or slightly less than that in Oregon, the effects of interaction are somewhat less in Utah.

Effectiveness of lobbying is measured by three questions based upon the assumptions of Guttman scaling. Legislators were asked, first, whether they could recall being influenced by a lobbyist to the point of questioning their position about any given issue. Next, they were asked if they could recall being influenced by a lobbyist to the extent of changing their opinion on an issue so that the positions of legislator and lobbyist were not as far apart as they were initially. Finally, legislators were asked if they could recall being influenced to the extent of reaching total

---

[31] From data to be reported in the future.

agreement with the position of the lobbyist. Thus, the first question represents minimum effect and the last question represents maximum effect. Lobbyists were also asked these questions with appropriate modification in wording so that the legislators became the object rather than the subject of persuasion. The assumptions require that the frequency of success would decrease with the difficulty of the task. The assumptions held true for lobbyists. In terms of what they think they are doing, the more difficult the task, the fewer the favorable responses. According to lobbyists, they are able to produce "questioning" and "leaning" responses more often than they are able to produce a "conversion" (Table 5).

TABLE 5

Percentage* of Legislators and Lobbyists Believing that They Have (Have Been) Influenced to the Extent of:

	Questioning a Previously Held Opinion	Leaning More toward the Views of the Lobbyist	Changing from One Position to Another	N
Massachusetts				
Legislators	34	31	20	244
Lobbyists	51	39	26	185
North Carolina				
Legislators	22	20	18	164
Lobbyists	76	70	39	132
Oregon				
Legislators	45	42	51	84
Lobbyists	79	52	41	193
Utah				
Legislators	32	38	42	90
Lobbyists	77	66	48	134

* Percentages are of those who indicate that a particular event has occurred "frequently" or "occasionally."

With legislators, the assumptions are not so neatly fulfilled. In both Oregon and Utah, more legislators indicate that they have changed positions more often than they have undergone more moderate forms of persuasion. The table confirms pretty well what we have learned so far about the four states under examination. Massachusetts lobbyists are far more skeptical about their ability to achieve successful results than are the lobbyists in any other states. This pessimism is shared to some extent by legislators, although the gap between perceptions is far less severe than it is in North Carolina. North Carolina lobbyists see their influence as far greater than do legislators. Indeed, the difference between the North Carolina lobbyists (whose legislators consider them impotent) and the Oregon lobbyists (whose legislators consider them powerful), is minimal and in one case the North Carolina lobbyists appear to be more optimistic. The table also firms up the argument that Oregon and Utah appear to be strong lobbying states, whereas Massachusetts and North

Carolina appear to be weak lobbyist states, especially if we consider the attitudes of legislators.

Naturally, lobbyists exaggerate the impact of their efforts. However, there is one exception to the rule of lobbyists' overestimation which deserves mention. In Oregon, more legislators than lobbyists believe that conversion has occurred. The difference in Oregon is especially striking. In this particular case, lobbyists are underestimating substantially the impact of their communications. The differences in the perceptions between legislators and lobbyists is least in Oregon and in Massachusetts, with both judges in Oregon agreeing that lobbyists are powerful and both in Massachusetts agreeing that lobbyists are ineffective (Table 6).

TABLE 6
Differences in the Effects of Communication as Reported
by Legislators and Lobbyists

	Questioning a Previously Held Position	Leaning More toward the Views of the Lobbyist	Changing from One Position to Another	Average
Massachusetts	−17*	− 8	− 6	−10
North Carolina	−54	−50	−21	−42
Oregon	−34	−10	+10	−15
Utah	−44	−28	− 6	−26

* Entries are differences between the percentages reported in Table 5. Negative signs indicate a higher percentage of lobbyists reporting on effects; positive signs indicate the reverse.

These sorts of realistic appraisals are, of course, not found in North Carolina or in Utah. The optimism of the Oregon lobbyists is earned, as is the pessimism of the Massachusetts lobbyists. To a lesser extent, the optimism of the Utah lobbyists is realistic, but the optimism of the North Carolina lobbyists is apparently without foundation.

Finally, conversion does occur more frequently than the research on national legislation has suggested. We would expect legislators to underestimate the extent of conversion; but even taking this into account, a slight majority of Oregon lawmakers and a large minority of Utah legislators indicated that they have been switched from one position to another by lobbyists. Even in Massachusetts, 34 percent of the legislators have been influenced by lobbyists, albeit to the limited extent of questioning a previously held opinion. These data assume, of course, that the job of the lobbyist is that of changing minds. In fact, we have seen that there are two role definitions of the job of the lobbyist: that of persuader and that of informant. Needless to say, these role definitions are not mutually exclusive, making it possible for lobbyists to perform different roles at separate points in time or even simultaneously. Further, the data should not be interpreted to mean that more subtle, less explicit modes of communication cannot have a persuasive consequence.

This paper is not concerned with lobbying strategies, but rather with an assessment of lobbying strengths. Nevertheless, one source of strength, and indeed perhaps a crucial source, is the extent to which legislators accept the lobbyist as a legitimate source of information. Our data indicate that, whereas there is no relationship between the amount of contact between legislators and lobbyists and the persuasability of legislators, there is a clear and strong relationship between the extent of communication *initiated* by legislators and this degree of persuasability (Table 7). Legislators who seek out lobbyists are more likely to be persuaded by

TABLE 7
Percentage° of Legislators Reporting Influence Related to the
Extent of Interaction Initiated by the Legislator

	Questioning a Previously Held Opinion	Leaning More toward the Views of the Lobbyist	Changing from One Position to Another	N‖
Massachusetts				
Low†	28	26	24	156
Medium‡	51	42	44	41
High§	47	53	60	15
North Carolina				
Low	19	18	15	130
Medium	32	32	23	22
High	38	13	38	8
Oregon				
Low	29	33	42	24
Medium	63	53	57	30
High	46	50	63	24
Utah				
Low	24	32	44	50
Medium	39	46	39	26
High	60	50	50	10

° Percentage indicating that an event had occurred "frequently" or "occasionally."
† Less than five contacts per week.
‡ Six to twenty-five contacts per week.
§ Twenty-six or more contacts per week.
‖ "Don't know's" are excluded.

them in comparison to legislators who do not initiate as much interaction. Consequently, one source of the strength of interest groups in Oregon and Utah might be found in the fact that two thirds of the legislators in these states indicate that they solicit the opinions of lobbyists when an issue arises about which they have legitimate concern. In contrast, only slightly more than one third of the legislators in Massachusetts and North Carolina do so.

We would assume that the seeking out of lobbyists indicates an acceptance on the part of the legislators of the legitimacy of interest groups in the legislative process. However, by a variety of measures it appears that the attitude of Utah legislators toward lobbyists is far more hostile than their behavior would indicate. Consider, for example, a question approaching legitimacy from a slightly different angle. Legislators were asked if they believed it was proper to be seen socially with a lobbyist. Whereas 83 percent of the Oregon legislators indicated that it was proper to be seen with a lobbyist, 68 percent of those in Utah indicated that it was proper. Although more Utah legislators are uneasy in the presence of lobbyists than Massachusetts legislators (75 percent), they are exceeded only by North Carolina legislators (58 percent). Thus, legislators in one of the "strong lobby states" indicate more circumspection in the presence of lobbyists than legislators in a "weak lobby state."

This pattern can be amplified further by the return to the problem of the relationship between attitudes and behavior. We noted that there was a relationship between the two, but the caveat should be added that this relationship does not emerge very clearly in Utah. For instance, there is no relationship in Utah between the attitudes of legislators toward interest groups and the extent of interaction.[32] Those who have an unfavorable attitude are just about as likely to interact as those who do not. Also, more legislators in Massachusetts than in Utah believe that lobbyists are "absolutely necessary" in the legislative process. A good illustration of the suspicion of the lobbying process in Utah can be seen in Table 8, which presents the attitudes legislators have toward the information they receive from lobbyists.

It can be seen that Utah legislators depend upon lobbyists for information almost as much as they do in Oregon, but that the confidence they have in this information is substantially less. Also, only a minority of Utah legislators in contrast to Oregon find this information especially helpful. Indeed, they appear almost as unimpressed with such information as the Massachusetts legislators. Thus, it is clear that the dependence of Utah legislators upon the services of lobbyists is not based solely upon a facilitating attitude. It appears that the interaction of Utah lobbyists and legislators is not entered into in a purely voluntary way. The interaction seemed forced upon each actor, somewhat in the nature of the exception Homans cites to his principle that interaction and attraction are related.[33]

TABLE 8

Attitudes of Legislators Toward Information Received
from Lobbyists: Percent Indicating They:

	Depend upon Information from Lobbyists*	Have Confidence in Information from Lobbyists†	Find Information from Lobbyists Helpful‡	N
Massachusetts	50	55	41	244
North Carolina	41	56	28	164
Oregon	83	88	61	84
Utah	80	70	43	90

* Percentage reporting they depend upon information from lobbyists "a good deal" or "some" of the time.
† Percentage indicating they have "a lot" and "quite a bit" of confidence in information.
‡ Percentage indicating "all" or "most" of the information is helpful.

---

[32] From data not reported in this article.

[33] See George C. Homans, *The Human Group* (New York: Harcourt, Brace and World, 1950), pp. 116–17.

In political systems there are compelling reasons for the continual functioning of a system in spite of private attitude systems; the interaction system is more compelling than the attitude system. Certain things have to be done; laws have to be passed, information must be gathered. There are very few staff services in Utah, and the legislators are very inexperienced in comparison to the other states. Thus, attitudes alone do not explain the nature of the Utah legislative system. The Utah legislators' attitudes are perhaps traceable to the fact that two thirds of them are Mormons (in contrast to less than half the population of the state). Utah is the only state in which a religio-economic group controls a majority of the seats. Since the Mormon church has such total access it is naturally not seen as an interest group. The dominance of the Mormon church probably diminishes the favorable attitude of legislators toward other "outside" groups. In addition, there is a stern moralism associated with the Utah legislature. Perhaps one source of these hostile attitudes is an orientation booklet which tells the beginning legislator:

> Perhaps the most overwhelming experience for any new legislator is his first contact with the lobbyist—the person representing a special interest. Since each lobbyist is committed to advancing the cause of his own group, the legislator can expect to encounter considerable pressure to vote a narrowly seen "right way." There is nothing wrong with listening to the case presented by a lobbyist. He may provide valuable information. But the legislator should always remember that the lobbyist will volunteer only information which is helpful to his cause; that which is contrary must be learned elsewhere.[34]

In spite of these pressures against lobbyists, Utah still has a strong interest group system.

Services Provided by Lobbyists

Since we know that a favorable persuasive situation is created when the legislator asks the lobbyist to perform a service for him, we now need to know the nature of the services performed by lobbyists. We have previously discussed the nature of the interaction between lobbyists and legislators in terms of either persuasion or information. A slight modification needs to be made with respect to the kinds of services performed. Here we are dichotomizing services into those involving a display of power or influence and those involving the provision of information. Three kinds of services are selected as being typical of the use of lobbyists as sources of influence by legislators. They are, first, calling upon lobbyists to have them influence other legislators; second, calling upon lobbyists to have them help amass public opinion in favor of a legislator's position; third, including lobbyists in planning strategy in an effort to negotiate a bill through the legislature. The extent to which lobbyists are called upon to perform these services are given in Table 9.

[34] *The Utah Legislator's Orientation Manual* (1966), p. 6.

TABLE 9
Percentage° of Legislators and Lobbyists Interacting for "Influence" Services

	Influencing Other Legislators	Mobilizing Public Support	Participating in Planning Strategy	N
Massachusetts				
Legislators	11	17	17	244
Lobbyists	22	38	36	185
North Carolina				
Legislators	25	27	39	164
Lobbyists	51	65	73	132
Oregon				
Legislators	53	32	65	84
Lobbyists	55	46	64	193
Utah				
Legislators	46	45	42	70
Lobbyists	68	65	73	134

° Percentages indicate those who "frequently" and "occasionally" request (or are requested to) perform a service.

Considering only the relative importance of lobbying in the various states, nothing new is learned by this table. Oregon still appears as the most lobbying-oriented state; Utah runs a close second, with North Carolina and Massachusetts bringing up the rear. However, there are some variations both in the kinds of services likely to be performed within a given state and in the extent to which the perceptions of legislators and lobbyists differ. For instance, participation in the planning strategy preceding the introduction of a bill seems relatively more important in Oregon and North Carolina than it does in Utah and Massachusetts. At the same time, helping to amass public opinion does not seem as prominent in Oregon as it should be in comparison to the relative utilization of other services. It appears that a greater amount of the services performed by Oregon lobbyists are kept within the internal politics of the legislature. This type of service is not found to the same extent in any other state. Indeed, the amassing of public opinion is the single item on which both sets of judges in Utah "rank" their state higher than Oregon.

The other type of service which lobbyists can perform consists of the provision of information. We consider here two types of such services: the communication to the legislator of the opinions of other legislators or lobbyists, and the actual conducting of research for the legislators for use in the presentation of arguments for or against legislation. The first kind of service is, essentially, the utilization of lobbyists for the "nose-counting" which usually precedes any decision by the legislator concerning strategy. The second kind of service, the actual production of information based upon technical research, is usually performed in Washington by staffs. Since state legislators typically do not have staff assistants, legislators come to rely upon lobbyists more than any other service, as Table 10 indicates.

The tables, considered together, suggest that even though informational services are more frequently provided than are influence-type serv-

TABLE 10

Percentage° of Legislators and Lobbyists Interacting
for "Informational" Services

	Communicating with Other Lobbyists	Researching a Bill	N
Massachusetts			
Legislators	25	46	244
Lobbyists	22	43	185
North Carolina			
Legislators	19	47	164
Lobbyists	51	71	132
Oregon			
Legislators	40	89	84
Lobbyists	53	73	193
Utah			
Legislators	49	78	90
Lobbyists	63	63	134

° Percentages indicate those who "frequently" or "occasionally" request
(or are requested to) perform a service.

ices, lobbyists apparently do not consider them as glamorous. With the
exception of North Carolina, the general tendency is for legislators to
agree with lobbyists that informational services are typical of the legislator–lobbyist relationship. Thus, an examination of the differences between the percentages indicates that there is a mean difference of about
21 percent between the perceptions of legislators and lobbyists with regard to influence services as compared to a difference of 7 percent with
respect to informational services (Table 11).

TABLE 11

Differences in Legislators' and Lobbyists' Perception of
the Services Performed by Lobbyists°

	Influence	Information
Massachusetts	−17%	+ 3%
North Carolina	−37	−28
Oregon	− 5	+ 2
Utah	−25	+ 1

° Entries are the average differences in the answer of legislators
and lobbyists reported in Tables 9 and 10. Negative signs indicate
that more lobbyists than legislators believe the service is performed.

Indeed, only in North Carolina do the differences between the perceptions of legislators and lobbyists with respect to informational services approach the magnitude of the difference on influence services.
When evaluating influence services, lobbyists exaggerate (or legislators
minimize). When evaluating informational services, both legislators and
lobbyists see lobbyists' performance in a similar manner. In Oregon and
Utah, for example, legislators indicate they call upon lobbyists for re-

search quite a bit more than do lobbyists. It should also be noted, however, that the differences in perception in Oregon are relatively small no matter whether influence or informational services are being evaluated, indicating a high congruence in perception in comparison to the other states. Nevertheless, it does appear that these answers are somewhat indicative of idealized roles. It appears that legislators look upon lobbyists as providers of information, but lobbyists like to think of themselves as agents of influence.

These findings support the earlier conclusions with respect to how lobbyists spend their time. At any rate, pedestrian though it may be, it is clear that even in weak lobbying states, such as Massachusetts, lobbyists are frequently called upon to provide legislators with facts. In strong lobbying states there is a considerable amount of influence-trading, but even here research is the basic task.

To lobbyists, the prominence of research means that persuasion has to be accomplished by indirect means. We noted earlier that experienced lobbyists are inclined to define their role as that of informant. Concurrently, legislators indicate a substantial preference for the services of experienced lobbyists, especially if they have had previous governmental experience. In all states, these kinds of lobbyists are sought out for services far more than are the inexperienced lobbyists. The experienced lobbyists frequently engage in an explicit attempt to define their role to the legislators. Consider, for example, the following statement: "Last session there were eleven people on the House Financial Affairs Committee. Five of them were freshmen. My first job was to introduce myself to them and let them know that I would be around, be at the Committee meetings, and that I am the fount of all information with respect to the insurance industry and if they have questions they should call on me. Certainly I try to persuade them, but I try to persuade them with information." In this case the lobbyist is seeking to establish a relationship based solely upon his role as informant. The purpose is to produce perceptions on the part of the legislators congruent with the lobbyists' self-perceptions. If successful, this lobbyist would have built a substantial influence base, resting upon the willingness of legislators to seek him out.

SUMMARY AND CONCLUSIONS

This comparative analysis has probably raised more questions than it has provided answers to existing questions. In the first place, it is obvious that neither the mechanistic nor the communications model are universally applicable, suggesting that less inclusive theories are more useful. There seems to be little question that interest groups are very powerful in Oregon and very weak in Massachusetts. To phrase the conclusions in terms of Eulau's rhetorical question, very little would happen in Massachusetts if there were no lobbies, but the legislature would function in an entirely different fashion in Oregon were this situation to come to pass. On the other hand, in the case of North Carolina and Utah it would be very difficult to say what the consequences would be because the perceptions, especially in North Carolina, are so incongruent. Also, in Utah the high activity and moderate impact of lobbyists is not matched by a favorable set of attitudes on the part of Utah legislators. Attitudinally, Utah is as similar to Massachusetts as it is to Oregon.

To return to the initial question about the effect of environmental variables, it appears that they are randomly distributed. The "weak lobby states"—Massachusetts and North Carolina—have little in common. Massachusetts is urban, heterogeneous, industrialized, with a relatively wealthy, well-educated population. North Carolina is the reverse. Massachusetts is competitive, North Carolina is not. Indeed, Massachusetts is more similar to the "strong lobby states"—Utah and Oregon—in its degree of party competition, than it is to North Carolina.

On the other hand, Utah and Oregon seem somewhat more similar. Yet, on a variety of measures they are approximations of Massachusetts. The population of Utah and Oregon is quite a bit more mobile than that of the weak lobby states. Indeed, this is the only characteristic which is consistent.

The socioeconomic environment does not appear to effect interaction of legislators or lobbyists and consequences of the lobbying effect, with the exception of mobility. Mobility, however, is in reality an artifact of a more fundamental distinction between weak and strong lobby states which is more *developmental* than environmental. To illustrate this point, let us add to our sample of four states two states examined by Wahlke, Eulau, Ferguson, and Buchanan: California, which is clearly a strong lobby state, and Tennessee, which is clearly a weak lobby state.[35] We can now see that a basic distinction is between the newer, late developing states, and the older, now established political systems. California, Oregon, and Utah did not develop viable *stakes* for the political game until the twentieth century. By the time that Massachusetts, Tennessee, and North Carolina had developed enough complexity to support an interest group system, the rules of the game of politics had been established and, in a sense, closed to interest groups. In the South, legislators are likely to view *all* "outsiders" (interest groups, parties, constituents) as having doubtful legitimacy. In Massachusetts, interest groups have a difficult time competing with established parties. In both areas, therefore, there is an oligarchical type of politics which do not include interest groups.

In contrast to the old New England or southern states stands the new west. Political systems and interest groups developed simultaneously in a much more open fashion. Interest groups did not have to fight existing political institutions; they shared in the developing of the political system; also, political development coincided with economic development. Lobbyists and politicians "grew up" together. Finally, the western political tradition—nonpartisanship, open primaries, a high rate of participation—invites interest groups, along with everybody else, to compete for the stakes of politics.

A further possibility is raised by this notion of the stakes of politics. We have explained high interaction and the effects so far without refer-

---

[35] Ohio and New Jersey are excluded because their classification is less certain.

ence to the obvious possibility that interest groups will be attracted to the arenas where important decisions are being made—where the stakes are the biggest. Do the stakes vary from state to state? Do some states do a "bigger business" than others? If so, how does this relate to patterns of group politics? To answer this question, consider Table 12, which com-

TABLE 12
Expenditure and Revenue of Strong and Weak Lobby States

	Strong			Weak		
	Oregon	California	Utah	Massachu-chusetts	Tennessee	North Carolina
Revenue: per capita	$257	$251	$251	$185	$171	$183
Expenditure: per capita ..	$260	$254	$255	$190	$164	$171

pares the per capita revenues and expenditures of the strong and weak lobby states. Clearly the strong lobby states have a greater output than the weak lobby states. In the research of Dye, Hofferbert, and others mentioned earlier, the environment influences the output. In this case, a sort of reverse of this suggestion is developed. The magnitude of the outputs influences the pattern of activity accompanying the output.

G. R. Boynton, Samuel C. Patterson, and
Ronald D. Hedlund

The Missing Links in Legislative
Politics: Attentive Constituents*

In democratic theory one of the central postulates is that linkages
between representatives and the represented provide for access, representation, and accountability. Some research has been focused on these linkages, but it has been confined largely to relations between legislators and
the general publics of their districts.[1] It is very unlikely, however, that
representatives actually think of their constituents *en masse*.[2] There is
also some evidence that political interest groups organized on a system-
wide basis do not supply the major linkage between constituents and
representatives.[3] Rather, the major linkage appears to be through the

* Reprinted from the *Journal of Politics*, vol. 31, no. 3 (August 1969), pp. 700–21.
Copyright 1969.

This report is part of the research of the Iowa Legislative Research Project, supported by grants and other assistance from the National Science Foundation, the
Social Science Research Council, and the Laboratory for Political Research and Computer Center of the University of Iowa. For their major part in the gathering and
processing of the data, we are especially indebted to Ted Hebert, Norman Elliott
and Nancy Cohen of the Laboratory for Political Research, and to Glenn Roberts,
Director of the Research Department and Iowa Poll of the *Des Moines Register and
Tribune*.

1 Warren E. Miller and Donald Stokes, "Constituency Influence in Congress,"
American Political Science Review, 57 (March 1963), 45–56.

2 See the comments of Ralph K. Huitt in "Congress, the Durable Partner," in
Lawmakers in a Changing World, ed. by Elke Frank (Englewood Cliffs, N.J.; Pren-
tice-Hall, Inc., 1966), 26–27, and Malcolm E. Jewell and Samuel C. Patterson, "The
Legislator and His Constituents," in *The Legislative Process in the United States*
(New York: Random House, 1966), 339–357.

3 Henry Teune, "Legislative Attitudes Toward Interest Groups," *Midwest Journal
of Political Science*, 11 (November 1967), 489–504; and John Jackson, "Some Indirect Evidences of Constituency Pressure on the Senate," in *Public Policy*, ed. by
John D. Montgomery and Albert O. Hirschman, XVI (Cambridge: Harvard University Press, 1967), 253–270.

politically active subculture in legislative constituencies, those middle-men in politics who, in a variety of ways, mediate between mass publics and representative elites.

V. O. Key thought these middlemen constituted a "missing piece of the puzzle" in research efforts "to assemble the elements that go into the construction of a democratic regime."[4] Variously characterized as middlemen, political activists, or influentials, Key thought the "thin stratum" lying across the structural path between mass opinion and the upper layer of the political elite was critical to the maintenance and persistence of democratic regimes. He argued that these middlemen could constitute a distinctive political subculture sufficiently independent and diverse to provide the pluralism necessary for the democratic formula, sufficiently active and involved to be able to acquire and exploit access to both the narrower circles of political leadership and the wider circles of political participation, and sufficiently imbued with common motives and values as to help maintain and promote a general public trust, a restraint in the exploitation of public opinion, and etiquette in the conduct of opposition politics. Although Key assigned to the middlemen of politics a vital place in democratic regimes, he lamented the fact that little data about them had been assembled by research on the attributes and attitudes of the mass population. Thus, he argued that "systematic knowledge of the composition, distribution in the social structure, and patterns of behavior of this sector of the political system remains far from satisfactory."[5] Dwaine Marvick's recent analysis of research on political middlemen, although it indicates that some progress has been made, gives current confirmation to Key's rueful assessment.[6]

We have sought, in a particular intra-elite context, to identify at least some important part of the thin stratum of middlemen standing athwart the path between legislators and the mass public, and we will refer to them as *attentive constituents*. Without presuming that one modest investigation would answer all of Key's implicit and explicit queries about the structure, values, and role of these middlemen, we sought to give form to Key's puzzle by assembling some evidence as to the composition, perspectives, and activities of attentive constituents in one legislative system. Further, we sought to acquire the kind of data that would permit comparisons of these attentive constituents with both legislators and the general adult population. We wanted to be able to characterize these attentive constituents in terms of their socioeconomic status, political awareness, and political activity. We wished to assess their linkage capacity by probing the extent to which they engage in communications above and below them in the political structure. We hoped to examine their role in recruiting members of the top elite. Finally, we wanted to

---

[4] V. O. Key, Jr., *Public Opinion and American Democracy* (New York: Alfred A. Knopf, 1961), 536–543. The quotations are on 536.

[5] *Ibid.*, 537.

[6] Dwaine Marvick, "The Middlemen of Politics," in *Approaches to the Study of Party Organization*, ed. by William J. Crotty (Boston: Allyn and Bacon, Inc., 1968), 341–374. This paper can be consulted for further bibliographical material.

254 Public Opinion and Public Policy

investigate their perspectives on the legislature as an institution, and their support for it.

It is obvious that dealing with these matters requires a minimum of three discrete sets of survey data—for the mass public, for attentive constituents, and for legislators. Identifying legislators is easy; accordingly, we were able to complete interviews with 181 of the 185 members of the 1967 session of the Iowa legislature.[7] Sampling the adult population of Iowa presented no great difficulty, and in the latter part of 1966 we interviewed 1,001 adult Iowans by way of a random household probability sample.[8] In identifying attentive constituents, we proceeded on the assumption that they should, by and large, be salient to legislators themselves, and thus it should be possible for legislators to identify at least the major attentive constituents in their own districts.[9] Accordingly, when we interviewed Iowa legislators in 1967, we asked them to nominate persons in their own counties whom they regarded as politically knowledgeable and aware, and whose advice they might seek out about legislative issues or problems. From the more than 600 names given us by legislators, we selected and interviewed 484 nominated constituents who matched the communities in which our general population respondents resided.[10] The survey schedule for each set of respondents consisted of a common core of comparable interview items, so that a host of direct comparisons can be made across the three samples.

COMPOSITION OF ATTENTIVE CONSTITUENTS

Knowledge about political influentials in general naturally leads to the expectation that attentive legislative constituents are composed of persons occupying high status. As Table 1 makes very clear, Iowa's attentive constituents and legislators differed markedly from the general adult population in terms of occupational status and educational attainment. While the proportions of lawyers among attentive constituents and legislators were very similar, a considerably higher percentage of attentive constituents were in professional and managerial occupations and less than half as many were farmers. Attentive constituents also achieved a somewhat higher level of education than legislators.

Legislators, attentive constituents, and the public did not differ greatly in religious affiliation, although Protestants were somewhat over-repre-

[7] These interviews, taken in April and May during the legislative session in Des Moines, were conducted by the staff of the Laboratory for Political Research under the direction of Ronald D. Hedlund.

[8] These interviews occurred in November 1966, and were taken by the field staff of the Iowa Poll under the direction of Director Glenn Roberts.

[9] Although we were seeking reference individuals for legislators, our research problem bears some resemblances to those encountered in other research on influentials. See Wendell Bell, Richard J. Hill and Charles Wright, *Public Leadership* (San Francisco: Chandler Publishing Company, 1961).

[10] The Laboratory for Political Research prepared a list of names and addresses from the legislator interview protocols and other sources. Respondents in this sample were interviewed in July and August 1967 by the field staff of the Statistical Laboratory, Iowa State University, Ames.

TABLE 1

Attributes of Legislators, Attentive Constituents, and Public in Iowa
(in percentages)

Attributes	Legislators 1967	Attentive Constituents 1967	Public 1966
Occupation			
Lawyer	14	15	0
Other professionals	8	16	7
Managerial	36	41	7
Farmers	33	15	9
Sales-clerical	1	1	7
Blue-collar workers	5	3	15
Housewives	2	4	35
Retired	2	4	13
Other	0	1	6
Total	101	100	99
Education			
Grade School	2	3	26
Attended high school	7	4	14
High school graduate	14	21	39
Attended college	33	18	13
College graduate	17	19	4
Postgraduate education	27	35	4
Total	100	100	100
Religion			
Protestant	77	81	76
Catholic	15	17	20
Jewish, other none	1	3	2
No response	8	0	2
Total	101	101	100
Age			
18–35	13	5	24
36–65	75	82	53
66–89	11	13	23
Total	99	100	100
Residence			
City over 50,000	23	29	25
City 5,000–50,000	28	31	24
City 2,500–5,000	11	13	6
Town under 2,500	36	13	23
Farm	2	14	22
Total	100	100	100
No. of cases	181	484	1,001

sented among attentive constituents. Both legislators and attentive constituents differed from the general population in their over-representation of those from thirty-six to sixty-five years of age, and in their under-representation of the younger and very old population. On the average, attentive constituents were their legislators' elders. The comparisons in Table 1 for place of residence present some interesting results which illustrate that among legislators small cities and towns are greatly overrepresented *vis-a-vis* the general public, and Iowans actually living on farms were greatly under-represented. Nearly half of the 1967 legislators resided in cities and towns under 5,000 people, and only two percent actually lived on farms. At the same time, only about a third of the adult citizens of Iowa lived in small cities, and nearly a quarter of them lived on farms. Interestingly for a state ordinarily thought of by outsiders as almost wholly agricultural, though a third of the legislators described themselves as farmers, very few of them in fact resided on farms. They owned, managed, or worked on farms, but most of them lived in small towns and cities. The small-town bias reflected among legislators was not shown among attentive constituents, more of whom actually lived on farms or in the larger cities of the state.

The 484 attentive constituents constituted a comparatively highly politicized middle-elite group. Among attentive constituents were a substantial proportion who were occupying, or had occupied, public or political party offices. Beyond that, attentive constituents were highly involved in politics generally, highly aware of legislative affairs, and heavily committed in their political identifications. Their location in the political structure is indicated by the fact that more than two-thirds (64.7 percent) had held, or were holding, some public office. Thirty-one percent had been elected to public office, 16 percent held appointive offices, and another 18 percent had served in both elective and appointive public office. Among those who had held public office a wide variety of offices were represented, although these were almost wholly at the city or county levels. For instance, about a fourth of the attentive constituents (23.1 percent) had served in elected municipal offices, and most of these were city councilmen, mayors, and city attorneys. Another fourth (25.4 percent) had county office experience, as supervisors, county attorneys, or judges. The remainder of those who had served in a public office had been elected to school boards, and a few had served in elected (7.9 percent) or appointed (10.5 percent) state offices. Of the 484 attentive constituents, only 34 were ex-legislators.

While two-thirds of the attentive constituents had public officeholding experience, only about a fourth (25.6 percent) were party leaders in the sense of holding grassroots political party offices. Thus, it seems clear enough that our 484 respondents were attentive constituents from the legislators' perspective very largely because of their places in the governmental structure of the local communities in legislative districts. Although attentive constituents were highly politicized in partisan terms, as we shall show in a moment, it would appear that linkages between citizens and legislators tend to occur through local governmental structures more than through political party organizations at the local levels.

Attentive constituents were overwhelmingly more aware of the existence of the day-to-day legislature than the general adult population (See Table 2). In the public, very few citizens could respond correctly to the most elementary questions about the legislature, such as how many legislators there were from their county, to which party their legislators belonged, and how often the legislature meets. Although few Iowans knew to which political party their own legislator belonged, two-thirds

TABLE 2

Legislative Awareness of Attentive Constituents and Public
(in percentages)

	Correct Responses	
Items	Public 1966	Attentive Constituents 1967
How many legislators represent county in House and Senate?	22	88
Which party do they belong to?	16	83
How often does the legislature meet in regular session?	24	98
For how long a term are Representatives elected?	67	98
For how long a term are Senators elected?	34	84
Which party controlled the House during the last session?	64	96
Which party controlled the Senate during the last session?	63	96
No. of cases	1,001	484

knew which party controlled the legislature as a whole. In contrast, attentive constituents were very substantially capable of correctly answering basic questions about the legislature. Almost all of them knew how often the legislature meets, how long their representatives' terms are, and which party controls each house of the legislature. More than 80 percent knew how many representatives were elected in their county, to which party they belonged, and the terms of state senators.

Similarly, attentive constituents are, compared with the general public, overwhelmingly involved in political life and engaged in political activity (See Table 3). About one-fifth of all Iowans reported a great deal of interest in politics, and a third said they were very interested in election campaigns. In contrast, 85 percent of the attentive constituents reported high political interest and over 90 percent reported great interest in election campaigns. Similar contrasts can be drawn between the public and attentive constituents in their respective tendencies to follow political developments in the communications media. A third of the general population sample said they talked to people about voting for a party or candidate, while nine-tenths of the attentive constituents reported doing so. Three-quarters of the attentive constituents reported campaign activity which they substantiated by wearing a campaign button or putting a campaign sticker on their automobile, while only a fifth of the public reported similar participation. Finally, in contrast to the 70 percent of the general public who reported voting in the mid-term 1966 election, less than one percent of the attentive constituents indicated that they had not voted.

Attentive constituents also exhibit marked differences from the general public in their commitment to political parties. Table 4 shows the partisan identifications of legislators, attentive constituents, and public. The

TABLE 3

Political Involvement of Attentive Constituents and Public
(in percentages)

Items	Public 1966	Attentive Constituents 1967
Interested in politics a great deal	18	85
Very interested in election campaigns	33	92
Follow reports of political and governmental affairs nearly every day	44	94
Read magazines for information about public affairs weekly or more often	28	83
Talk to people about voting for parties or candidates	34	90
Worn campaign button or put sticker on car	21	75
Voted in November 1966 election	70	99
No. of cases	1,001	484

distribution for the general public indicates the close parity between Democratic and Republican parties in Iowa in terms of partisan attachments—38 percent identified themselves as Democrats, 39 percent identified themselves as Republicans, and 20 percent were independents. The Republican party is stronger in Iowa from the point of view of relative party identification than in the country as a whole, but Iowa is now clearly a competitive two-party state in terms of the basic partisan commitments of its potential electorate.

The 1967 legislature was much more Republican than was the state as a whole. In 1967, 72 percent of the House seats and 48 percent of the Senate seats were held by Republican legislators. Since they were nominated by the legislators themselves, Republicans were over-represented among attentive constituents. In addition, the linkage between legisla-

TABLE 4

Party Identification of Legislators, Attentive Constituents and Public in Iowa
(in percentages)

Party Identification	Legislators 1967	Attentive Constituents 1967	Public 1966
Strong Democrat	24	18	19
Weak Democrat	12	3	19
Independent	0	8	20
Weak Republican	15	10	18
Strong Republican	50	59	21
Other, don't know	0	1	4
Total	101	99	101
No. of cases	181	484	1,001

tors and the attentive constituents whom they nominated is very sharp in terms of party identification. Of the attentive constituent nominations made by Democratic legislators, 68 percent were Democrats and 23 percent were Republicans. Of nominations made by Republican legislators, 83 percent were Republicans and only 7 percent were Democrats. So, not only were there more Republican legislators to make nominations of attentive constituents, but Republican legislators were also more likely than Democratic legislators to nominate attentive constituents of their own political party. To consider it from the attentive constituents' viewpoint, 88 percent of the Weak Republican and 92 percent of the Strong Republican constituents were nominated by Republican legislators. Forty-four percent of the Weak Democratic constituents and 77 percent of the Strong Democrats were nominated by Democratic legislators. The extent of inter-party connections is suggested by the fact that a fifth of the Strong Democratic attentives and 56 percent of the Weak Democrats were actually nominated by Republican legislators, and that three-fourths of the politically independent attentive constituents were Republican-nominated.

From the standpoint of strength of partisan attachment, legislators and attentive constituents differ sharply from the public as a whole. Seventy-four percent of the legislators and 77 percent of the attentive constituents were strong identifiers, compared with only 40 percent of the general public. In addition, attentive constituents reported much greater consistency of party voting in state legislative elections. Nearly half of the general citizenry (47.9 percent) reported that they had voted for candidates of different parties for state legislative office, while fewer than a fifth of the attentive constituents (19.4 percent) reported similar irregularity.

In their personal and social attributes, attentives in legislative constituencies are much more like the legislators than they are like rank-and-file constituents. They are, to a considerable extent, occupants of important positions in the governmental structures of local communities. They are very knowledgeable about legislative affairs and highly involved in political life. Not only are they powerfully committed to political life generally, but they also exhibit very strong partisan attachments. Politics is much more salient for them than for ordinary citizens, and they are more consistent in their political choices. Many of them have themselves had experience in public office. These are the "folks back home" with whom legislators most regularly maintain contact. These are the leading figures among the middlemen of legislative politics who provide the linkages between the legislator and the mass of his constituents. In terms of communications, what capabilities do these middlemen seem to have for linking mass constituents to their representatives?

LINKAGE CAPACITY OF ATTENTIVE CONSTITUENTS

Our evidence about the capability of attentive constituents to link legislators and mass constituents together is not as full as we would like, but the parameters of attentives' linkage capacity are fairly sharply drawn in our data. While we do not have detailed evidence dealing with attentives' contacts with rank-and-file citizens, we do know that 90 percent of the attentive constituents reported talking to citizens about voting for parties or candidates in connection with election campaigns. We think it is fair to assume that most of these contacts were not intramural, and that our attentive constituents were "opinion leaders" in their communities.

But if our data concerning the communications links of attentives with the mass constituencies are not entirely conclusive, our evidence for their linkages with legislative and other political elites is unmistakable. Nearly all of the attentive constituents talked about public or governmental problems with national, state, or local public officials, and 85 percent reported doing so often (see Table 5). Similar proportions of the atten-

TABLE 5

Extent to Which Attentive Constituents Report Talking to Public Officials

Item		Percent
Talk about public problems with governmental officials, either local, state or national		99
Quite often	59	
Often	26	
Not very often	14	
Talk to state legislators from their districts about public problems		98
Quite often	58	
Often	26	
Not very often	14	
No. of cases	484	

tive constituents reported talking to state legislators from their districts. These middlemen were in almost constant touch with their state legislators, and more were in contact with state legislators than with any other public leaders. But their communications net was cast well beyond members of the legislature; 56 percent of the attentive constituents reported talking about public problems regularly with national political leaders, and 42 percent reported regular discussions with county and city officials. Forty-three percent of the attentive constituents talked frequently to members of Congress. It seems likely from this fact that many of our 484 attentives served in overlapping middlemen roles and constituted part of the attentive, active, and responsive public for several constituencies.[11] The contacts these middlemen maintained at the state and national levels of government were almost wholly *legislative* in character. Very few reported talking regularly to national or state administrative officials

---

[11] See Joseph Schlesinger's interesting comments about "enclaved constituencies" in *Ambition and Politics: Political Careers in the United States* (Chicago: Rand McNally & Company, 1966), 127–133.

(only 4.5 percent in the case of the national level, and 14.5 percent at the state level).

The attentive constituent not only talks with his legislators a great deal, he also reports substantial attempts to influence them as well. In contrast to the rank-and-file citizen who rarely reported attempts to influence legislative decisions, attentives by very wide margins reported having done so. As Table 6 indicates, 71 percent of the public-sample

TABLE 6

Influence Attempts of Attentive Constituents and Public
(in percentages)

Item	Public 1966	Attentive Constituents 1967
Have met state legislators or seen them at a meeting	53	98
Have done something to try to influence a decision by the state legislature		
Often	1	36
Several times	8	50
Once or twice	17	10
Never	71	4
No response	3	1
Likelihood of success of efforts to change a state law considered harmful or unjust		
Very likely	4	10
Moderately likely	8	28
Somewhat likely	21	43
Not at all likely	61	16
No response	6	3
Likelihood of actually doing something to change a legislative enactment considered harmful or unjust		
Very likely	13	72
Moderately likely	13	18
Somewhat likely	29	7
Not at all likely	40	2
No response	5	1
No. of cases	1,001	484

respondents said they never had done anything to try to influence a decision by the legislature, while only 4 percent of the attentive constituents reported such restraint. When reference is made specifically to changing legislative enactments that they might consider harmful or unjust, almost all attentive constituents indicated the likelihood that they would actually try to do something, while 40 percent of the general public sample considered it unlikely that they would do anything. Finally, attentive constituents perceived a fairly strong likelihood that they would be successful in changing a state law they considered unjust or harmful. Eighty-one percent thought they would have some chance of success, whereas nearly two-thirds of the rank-and-file citizens took a dim view of their influence in such an effort.

We asked attentive constituents what they talked to state legislators about. Some reported talking about local governmental affairs, but the overwhelming numbers discussed state-wide policy issues. More talked about state financial problems and education than about other issues. Fifty-nine percent said they discussed budgetary and tax problems with their legislators, and among them the most prominent issue was that of property-tax relief. Eighty-seven percent reported talking about other legislative policy issues, the most consequent being that of education (26.0 percent). Notably missing from the reported content of discussion between attentive constituents and legislators is strictly political content —patronage, personnel, reelection problems, party-organizational issues, or political strategy. If issue considerations are of minimal consequence in the mass public, they clearly dominate discussions between attentive constituents and legislators.[12] Our data make it plain that the communications channels are open very wide and that they are substantially filled with discussions of policy questions.

Attentive constituents have a remarkable capacity for linking mass citizen and legislator. Most of them talk politics regularly with others. Many report persistent discussion with county, city, and other local public officials. These attentives are in very heavy contact with legislators, they attempt to influence, and they have a high sense of efficacy about their attempts. In this interaction between legislators and attentive constituents the public policy content of the political process becomes prominent. But in addition to finding attentive constituents suffused in the heavy atmosphere of policy-issue politics, we expected them to play an active part in the recruitment of legislators.

RECRUITMENT CAPABILITY OF ATTENTIVE CONSTITUENTS

The commitment of attentive constituents to legislative politics is clearly revealed in their considerable role in the recruitment process. Undoubtedly many of them are part of the recruitment pool for higher public office, in light of the fact that more than two-thirds of them have had experience in public office. But beyond that, the attentive constituents served as middlemen in the recruitment of other candidates for political office.

We asked attentives whether any candidates talked to them about running for office before they announced their candidacies, and whether the attentives had ever suggested to someone that he ought to run for public office. Attentive constituents were able to estimate the number of times they had entered the recruitment process in these ways, and these estimates of their recruitment contacts are shown in Table 7. Only 15 percent said that no candidate for office had ever discussed running for

---

12 Philip E. Converse, "The Nature of Belief Systems in Mass Publics," in *Ideology and Discontent*, ed. by David Apter (New York: Free Press, 1964), 206–261.

TABLE 7

Attentive Constituents and Public Recruitment
(in percentages)

Extent of Reported Recruitment Contacts	Candidates Talked to Attentives before Announcing Candidacy	Attentives Suggested Candidacy for Office
Many (11 or more)	21	14
Several (4–10)	34	27
Few (1–3)	30	37
None (0)	15	21
Don't know	– °	1
Total	100	100
No. of cases	484	484

° Less than 1%.

office prior to his announcement, and only a fifth said they never had suggested to someone that he be a candidate. For 55 percent of the attentives, prior discussion of candidacy for public office was a fairly frequent occurrence, and 41 percent said that they had frequently suggested to people that they run for office. In a political system where self-started political careers are not unusual, the extent to which these attentive constituents are involved in recruiting candidates for office appears to be reasonably heavy.[13]

While attentive constituents were involved in the recruitment of national, state, and local officials, their recruitment role was focused on legislative office and, in particular, on the state legislature. Table 8 shows that about a third of the attentives received candidacy contacts from prospective members of Congress, and slightly more than a fifth suggested candidacies for Congress. A higher proportion (49.0 percent and 47.3 percent respectively) of these attentive constituents were involved in the recruitment of candidates for county and city offices, spread rather widely across the variety of such offices available. But it is at the level of state offices that the recruitment role of attentive constituents is most pronounced. Three-fourths of the attentives reported that candidates for state offices discussed their candidacies with them, and two-thirds suggested candidates for state offices. Of these, the overwhelming proportion were candidacies for the state legislature. Forty-two percent of the attentives said that candidates for the state House of Representatives dis-

---

[13] On self-starters in four state legislatures, see John C. Wahlke, Heinz Eulau, William Buchanan, and LeRoy C. Ferguson, *The Legislative System: Explorations in Legislative Behavior* (New York: John Wiley & Sons, 1962), 98–101. We have dealt with self-starters and the role of grass-roots party leaders in recruitment in Lewis Bowman and G. R. Boynton, "Recruitment Patterns Among Local Party Officials: A Model and Some Preliminary Findings in Selected Locales," *American Political Science Review*, 60 (September 1966), 667–676; Samuel C. Patterson, "Characteristics of Party Leaders," *Western Political Quarterly*, 16 (June 1963), 332–352; and Phillip Althoff and Samuel C. Patterson, "Political Activism in a Rural County," *Midwest Journal of Political Science*, 10 (February 1966), 39–51.

TABLE 8

Political Recruitment Role of Attentive Constituents
(in percentages)

Offices	Attentive Constituents to Whom Candidates Talked before Announcing Candidacy	Attentive Constituents Who Suggested to Someone That He Ought to Run for Office
National Office		
Congressman	21	17
Senator	9	4
Other	1	1
Total°	31	22
State Office		
Representative	42	35
Senator	18	14
Governor	9	7
Other	9	7
Total	74	63
Local Office		
County supervisor	11	9
Other county offices	27	22
City councilmen	6	4
Mayor	5	4
Other local offices	7	8
Total	49	47
No. of Cases	484	484

° Because of some overlapping of responses, totals do not always equal
the sum of internal categories.

cussed their candidacies with them prior to announcing, and 18 percent
stated that senatorial candidates had prior discussions with them. Again,
35 percent of the attentives reported that they had suggested candidacies
to prospective senators.

These data underscore the proximity of the linkage between attentive
constituents and legislators in political terms. They indicate not only that
attentive constituents are very much in communication with legislators
and are communicating to a substantial degree in policy terms, but also
that they are, to a considerable extent, *recruitment influentials* as well.
We cannot know to what degree the recruitment efforts of the attentive
constituents were successful in terms of actual legislative candidacies,
but it is plain enough that many attentives conceived of themselves as
important actors in the legislative recruitment process.

ATTENTIVE CONSTITUENTS' CONCEPTIONS
OF THE LEGISLATIVE FUNCTION

Given the scope and character of the linkage that attentive constituents provide between the mass public and the legislative elite, we would
anticipate that attentives' perspectives on the institutional role of the

legislature would differ from those of the general population. We certainly expected that a higher proportion of attentive constituents would be able to describe the functions of the legislature, and that their perspectives on the legislative institution would be more sophisticated than would be true of the public-at-large. We were not at all sure what particular differences between attentives and public would emerge.

We asked both groups, "How would you describe the job of the state legislature, that is, what are the things that it ought to do when it meets in Des Moines?" From a wide variety of concrete responses, it was possible to characterize respondents' perspectives under four major substantive rubrics. The first of these was the *procedural* perspective. Those whose perspective was procedural viewed the legislature primarily as a law-making machine; their focus was upon the legislative organization and procedures that produce laws. The second category was the *representative* perspective. Many respondents could view the legislature in terms of the representative role of the legislators, or the representativeness of the legislature as a whole. A third perspective was the *purposive* orientation to the legislature. Those who took a purposive perspective expressed general norms about how the legislature should operate—that the legislature should take care of pressing problems, that they should "give bills a good going over," that they should work hard and accomplish something. Finally, many respondents viewed the legislature from a *policy-oriented* perspective. They saw the legislature as an arena in which issues were resolved, programs developed, and policies adopted. They talked about the legislature in terms of making policy changes, raising taxes, providing welfare programs, providing for schools, providing more roads, and regulating traffic. Of course, these are not mutually exclusive categories; the real-world legislature may be thought of as being characterized by all of these attributes. Many respondents were able to conceive of the legislature as a multi-faceted institution.

Table 9 shows the comparison of attentive constituents and public in their conceptions of the role of the legislature under these rubrics. A third of the general population sample could not find a way to describe the job of the legislature, whereas almost all of the attentive constituents

TABLE 9
Conceptions of the Role of the Legislature Held by
Attentive Constituents and Public
(in percentages)

Job of the Legislature	Public 1966	Attentive Constituents 1967
Procedural	31	39
Representative	13	37
Purposive	15	41
Policy-oriented	35	48
Other, vague response	5	3
Could not describe the job of the legislature	31	1
No. of cases	1,001	484

could do so. The greater legislative sophistication of attentive constituents is underscored by the fact that their mean number of responses was 2.14, while the average number of responses for the general public was only 1.14. We are impressed by the considerable proportion of respondents in the general population sample who could characterize the legislature in policy-oriented terms (34.6 percent), but as we suspected a substantially higher percentage of attentive constituents viewed the legislature in these terms (48.1 percent). Comparatively speaking, the representative and purposive aspects of the legislative institution were only dimly seen by the general public, while attentive constituents were able to conceive of the legislature in more sophisticated, more abstract, and more varied ways. We suggest that this means, in line with conventional expectations, that attentive constituents have a more complete and realistic conception of what the legislature is than do people in the general population.

ATTENTIVE CONSTITUENTS AND SUPPORT FOR THE LEGISLATURE

Attentive constituents are more like legislators than they are like the mass public, they are knowledgeable and highly involved politically, they have a high capacity for providing communication linkages between public and legislators, they are substantially involved in recruiting legislators, and they exhibit, when compared with the mass public, highly sophisticated conceptions of the role of the legislative institution in the political system. Because of their strategic position in the legislative system, we would expect them to play a crucial part in the support structure of the legislature. If, as it seems probable, demands in the legislative system are very likely to be crystallized and communicated through attentive constituents, then we would expect the attentives to interject high levels of support into the system as well.

One way to think about support for the legislature is to evaluate the performance of a particular legislative session. In our interviews with attentive constituents and the general population sample, we asked, "In general, would you say that the Iowa state legislature does an excellent job, a good job, a fair job, or a poor job?" Attentive constituents were interviewed some six months after the interviews with respondents in the population sample. The legislative session that was immediately past for the public sample would have been the session in 1965, while attentive constituents were interviewed just after the 1967 session of the legislature. Both sessions were atypical in certain respects. In both, there was a very high turnover of legislators, especially in the House of Representatives. The Democrats controlled both Senates, but the Democrats had a majority in the 1965 House and the Republicans a majority in the 1967 House. The same governor, Harold E. Hughes, was in office for both sessions. Both legislatures were reasonably well-apportioned, and, by Iowa standards, both enacted unusually progressive legislation. Still, we cannot know to what extent these two sessions of the legislature constituted different referents for attentive constituents and the general public. We have no way of overcoming the time and referential differences that may be involved here. This caveat notwithstanding, the evaluations of attentive constituents and public are interesting (they are shown in Table 10). In their evaluations of the legislature, the two groups did not

TABLE 10
Evaluations of the Legislature by Constituency Influentials and Public
(in percentages)

Iowa Legislature Does an:	Public 1966	Attentive Constituents 1967
Excellent job	5	5
Good job	47	53
Fair job	38	33
Poor job	4	8
Don't know	7	1
Total	101	100
No. of cases	1,001	484

differ greatly. A higher proportion of attentive constituents (57.6 percent) rated the legislature as having done a good or excellent job than did respondents in the public (51.0 percent), but more public respondents gave the legislature only fair (38.4 percent), and more attentive constituents rated the legislature as poor (8.3 percent). If we score the ratings on a 4 to 1 scale, giving excellent a 4 and poor a 1, the mean rating of attentive constituents was somewhat higher than for the public (2.52 as against 2.38). We incline to the view that attentive constituents were about as critical of the legislature as the public generally, although perhaps for different reasons.

But evaluation of the performance of a particular legislative session is, in a sense, ephemeral and evanescent. We certainly can imagine a citizen thinking that the last legislature did a very poor job and still strongly supporting the legislature as a symbol, as an institution, as a process. We wanted to probe beneath mere performance rating to measure support for the legislative institution.[14] Accordingly, we asked our three sets of respondents a set of seven questions designed to measure diffuse legislative support. The questions, calling for Likert-type agree-disagree responses, were these:

(1) There are times when it almost seems better for the citizens of the state to take the law into their own hands rather than wait for the state legislature to act.

---

[14] A complete discussion of our conceptualization of legislative support is in G. R. Boynton, Samuel C. Patterson, and Ronald D. Hedlund, "The Structure of Public Support for Legislative Institutions," *Midwest Journal of Political Science*, 12 (May 1968), 163–180.

(2) If you don't particularly agree with a state law, it is all right to break it if you are careful not to get caught.

(3) There are times when it would almost seem better for the Governor to take the law into his own hands rather than wait for the legislature to act.

(4) Even though one might strongly disagree with a state law, after it has been passed by the state legislature one ought to obey it.

(5) One should be willing to do everything that one could to make sure that any proposal to abolish the state legislature was defeated.

(6) If the Iowa legislature continually passed laws that the people disagreed with, it might be better to do away with the legislature altogether.

(7) It would not make much difference if the constitution of Iowa was rewritten to reduce the powers of the state legislature.

Responses to these seven items for all three groups of respondents together were factor analyzed, and respondents were factor scored across all seven items. In the process, we lost 51 general population respondents because of the incidence of "don't know" responses, so our base number for this group is 950 in this analysis. We divided the legislative support scores into three groups, labeling them "High," "Medium," and "Low," roughly by terciles.[15] The appropriate comparisons are shown in Table 11. The data provided dramatic evidence of the ladder structure of sup-

TABLE 11

Support for the Legislative Institution among Legislators,
Attentive Constituents and Public
(in percentages)

Legislative Support	Legislators 1967	Attentive Constituents 1967	Public 1966
High	64	50	16
Medium	29	31	32
Low	7	18	52
Total	100	99	100
No. of cases	181	484	950

port for the legislative institution. In the general population, support was relatively low; 52 percent of the public sample fell roughly into the lower third of the support scores. The word *relatively* should be underlined

---

[15] Respondents were factor-scored from the first factor of a principal component analysis. Then mean factor scores were computed, and respondents were categorized in terms of deviations from the mean. The "High" category consisted of those whose support scores were one-half a standard deviation above the mean; the "Low" category included those whose scores were one-half a standard deviation below the mean; and, the "Medium" group included those whose scores were between one-half a standard deviation above and one-half a standard deviation below the mean. The "High," "Medium," and "Low" groups were very nearly equal in size.

here because actually the level of public support for the legislature was quite high. Instead of low, medium, and high, it might be better to read the support levels in Table 11 as high, higher, and highest. But the level of support in an absolute sense is not at issue here; we are interested in comparing public, attentive constituents, and legislators. In that comparison, attentive constituents were vastly more supportive of the legislature as an institution than was the general public. Half the attentives were in the highest third of the support scores. Finally, legislators themselves were the most supportive of the legislature; two-thirds of them were in the high category. Diffuse support for the legislative institution was skewed in the supportive direction by the very high support inputs from the middlemen who provide a vital linkage between legislative elites and the mass public.

CONCLUSION

We have sketched the profile of the middlemen in legislative politics as sharply and fully as we can. We have suggested the critical role in the legislative system we think attentive constituents exert. Our data contribute to V. O. Key's hope for new knowledge about the form and structure of the middlemen in politics. We have shown, as Key asked to be shown, that attentive constituents are a socially diverse group, although strongly biased toward the upper socioeconomic end of the scale. We have shown that the political middlemen are highly aware and active politically, that they have access to wide circles of political leadership, and that they are heavily committed to involvement in the recruitment of the top echelon of leaders. Finally, we have shown that attentive constituents provide a powerful input of loyalty to, or support for, the legislative institution.

Key hoped, further, for evidence that the middlemen of politics constituted a special subculture, highly imbued with democratic values yet sufficiently incohesive so that alternatives would be available among competing elites. Attentive constituents do share subculture values about the virtue of the legislative way of life, but they are sharply divided in their political loyalties. In future reports we hope to show the content and structure of other kinds of value sharing among attentive constituents, and to probe more deeply into the cross-cutting effects of party differences in the linkage role of political middlemen.

Section IV
Representation in a Pluralist Democracy

The preceding selections hardly depict a politically active and ideologically rational public closely monitoring their elected officials to assure governmental responsibility. But as Berelson notes, one can see benefits to the political system in the low levels of political involvement found to exist in the United States, namely the stability of our country in an otherwise unstable world. Some might conclude that democracy is a sham because of the public's limited ability to achieve political linkage by way of the preceding coercive models, but the pluralist position as extolled by Berelson and in the selection by Robert Dahl reprinted here not only sees hope in the existing system but also great success. The pluralist position hardly encourages easy testing as to its accuracy. The final two models of political linkage, the sharing and role-playing models, however, spring from their optimism that the public interest is served.

Robert A. Dahl

The Polyarchy Model*

THE AMBIGUITY OF LEADERSHIP

One of the difficulties that confronts anyone who attempts to answer the question, "Who rules in a pluralist democracy?" is the ambiguous relationship of leaders to citizens.

Viewed from one position, leaders are enormously influential—so influential that if they are seen only in this perspective they might well be considered a kind of ruling elite. Viewed from another position, however, many influential leaders seem to be captives of their constituents. Like the blind men with the elephant, different analysts have meticulously examined different aspects of the body politic and arrived at radically different conclusions. To some, a pluralistic democracy with dispersed inequalities is all head and no body; to others it is all body and no head.

Ambiguity in the relations of leaders and constituents is generated by several closely connected obstacles both to observation and to clear conceptualization. To begin with, the American creed of democracy and equality prescribes many forms and procedures from which the actual practices of leaders diverge. Consequently, to gain legitimacy for their actions leaders frequently surround their covert behavior with democratic rituals. These rituals not only serve to disguise reality and thus to complicate the task of observation and analysis, but—more important—in complex ways the very existence of democratic rituals, norms, and requirements of legitimacy based on a widely shared creed actually influences the behavior of both leaders and constituents even when democratic norms are violated. Thus the distinction between the rituals of power and the realities of power is frequently obscure.

Two additional factors help to account for this obscurity: First, among all the persons who influence a decision, some do so more directly than others in the sense that they are closer to the stage where concrete alternatives are initiated or vetoed in an explicit and immediate way. Indirect influence might be very great but comparatively difficult to observe and weigh. Yet to ignore indirect influence in analysis of the distribution of influence would be to exclude what might well prove to be a highly significant process of control in a pluralistic democracy.

Second, the relationship between leaders and citizens in a pluralistic democracy is frequently reciprocal: leaders influence the decisions of constituents, but the decisions of leaders are also determined in part by what they think are, will be, or have been the preferences of their constituents. Ordinarily it is much easier to observe and describe the distribution of influence in a political system where the flow of influence is strongly in one direction (an asymmetrical or unilateral system, as it is sometimes called) than in a system marked by strong reciprocal relations. In a political system with competitive elections, such as New Haven's, it is not unreasonable to expect that relationships between leaders and constituents would normally be reciprocal.

One who sets out to observe, analyze, and describe the distribution of influence in a pluralistic democracy will therefore encounter formidable problems. It will, I believe, simplify the task of understanding New Haven if I now spell out some of the theory and assumptions that guided our story of the distribution of influence.

The Political Stratum

In New Haven, as in other political systems, a small stratum of individuals is much more highly involved in political thought, discussion, and action than the rest of the population. These citizens constitute the political stratum.

Members of this stratum live in a political subculture that is partly but not wholly shared by the great majority of citizens. Just as artists and intellectuals are the principal bearers of the artistic, literary, and scientific skills of a society, so the members of the political stratum are the main bearers of political skills. If intellectuals were to vanish overnight, a society would be reduced to artistic, literary, and scientific poverty. If the political stratum were destroyed, the previous political institutions of the society would temporarily stop functioning. In both cases, the speed with which the loss could be overcome would depend on the extent to which the elementary knowledge and basic attitudes of the elite had been diffused. In an open society with widespread education and training in civic attitudes, many citizens hitherto in the apolitical strata could doubtless step into roles that had been filled by members of the political stratum. However, sharp discontinuities and important changes in the operation of the political system almost certainly would occur.

In New Haven, as in the United States, and indeed perhaps in all pluralistic democracies, differences in the subcultures of the political and the apolitical strata are marked, particularly at the extremes. In the political stratum, politics is highly salient; among the apolitical strata, it is remote. In the political stratum, individuals tend to be rather calculating in their choice of strategies; members of the political stratum are, in a sense, relatively rational political beings. In the apolitical strata, people are notably less calculating; their political choices are more strongly influenced by inertia, habit, unexamined loyalties, personal attachments, emotions, transient impulses. In the political stratum, an individual's political beliefs tend to fall into patterns that have a relatively high degree of coherence and internal consistency; in the apolitical strata, political orientations are disorganized, disconnected, and unideological. In the political stratum, information about politics and the issues of the day is extensive; the apolitical strata are poorly informed. Individuals in the political stratum tend to participate rather actively in politics; in the apolitical strata citizens rarely go beyond voting and many do not even vote. Individuals in the political stratum exert a good deal of steady, direct, and active influence on government policy; in fact some individuals have a quite extraordinary amount of influence. Individuals in the apolitical strata, on the other hand, have much less direct or active influence on policies.

Communication within the political stratum tends to be rapid and extensive. Members of the stratum read many of the same newspapers and magazines; in New Haven, for example, they are likely to read the *New York Times* or the *Herald Tribune*, and *Time* or *Newsweek*. Much information also passes by word of mouth. The political strata of different communities and regions are linked in a national network of communications. Even in small towns, one or two members of the local political stratum usually are in touch with members of a state organization, and certain members of the political stratum of a state or any large city maintain relations with members of organizations in other states and cities, or with national figures. Moreover, many channels of communication not designed specifically for political purposes—trade associations, professional associations, and labor organizations, for example, serve as a part of the network of the political stratum.

In many pluralistic systems, however, the political stratum is far from being a closed or static group. In the United States the political stratum does not constitute a homogeneous class with well-defined class interests. In New Haven, in fact, the political stratum is easily penetrated by anyone whose interests and concerns attract him to the distinctive political culture of the stratum. It is easily penetrated because (among other reasons) elections and competitive parties give politicians a powerful motive for expanding their coalitions and increasing their electoral followings.

In an open pluralistic system, where movement into the political stratum is easy, the stratum embodies many of the most widely shared values and goals in the society. If popular values are strongly pragmatic, then the political stratum is likely to be pragmatic; if popular values prescribe reverence toward the past, then the political stratum probably shares that reverence; if popular values are oriented toward material gain and personal advancement, then the political stratum probably reflects these values; if popular values are particularly favorable to political, social, or economic equality, then the political stratum is likely to emphasize equality. The apolitical strata can be said to "govern" as much through the sharing of common values and goals with members of the political stratum as by other means. However, if it were not for elections and competitive parties, this sharing would—other things remaining the same—rapidly decline.

Not only is the political stratum in New Haven not a closed group, but its "members" are far from united in their orientations and strategies. There are many lines of cleavage. The most apparent and probably the most durable are symbolized by affiliations with different political parties. Political parties are rival coalitions of leaders and subleaders drawn from the members of the political stratum. Leaders in a party coalition seek to win elections, capture the chief elective offices of government, and insure that government officials will legalize and enforce policies on which the coalition leaders can agree.

In any given period of time, various issues are salient within the political stratum. Indeed, a political issue can hardly be said to exist unless and until it commands the attention of a significant segment of the political stratum. Out of all the manifold possibilities, members of the political stratum seize upon some issues as important or profitable; these then become the subject of attention within the political stratum. To be sure, all the members of the political stratum may not initially agree that a particular issue is worthy of attention. But whenever a sizable minority of the legitimate elements in the political stratum is determined to bring some question to the fore, the chances are high that the rest of the political stratum will soon begin to pay attention.

Although political issues are sometimes generated by individuals in the apolitical strata who begin to articulate demands for government action, this occurs only rarely. Citizens in the apolitical strata are usually aware of problems or difficulties in their own circle; through word of mouth or the mass media they may become aware of problems faced by people in other circles. But to be aware of a problem is by no means equivalent to perceiving a political solution or even formulating a political demand. These acts are ordinarily performed only by members of the political stratum. Within the political stratum, issues and alternatives are often formulated by intellectuals, experts, and reformers, whose views then attract the support of professionals. This is how questions as abstract and difficult as the proper rate of growth in the Gross National Product are injected into national politics; and, as we shall see, this is roughly the route by which urban redevelopment came into the politics of New Haven.

However, in gaining attention for issues, members of the political stratum operate under constraints set by party politicians with an eye on the next election. Despite the stereotype, party politicians are not necessarily concerned *only* with winning elections, for the man who is a party politician in one role may, in another, be a member of a particular interest group, social stratum, neighborhood, race, ethnic group, occupation, or profession. In this role he may himself help to generate issues. However, simply qua party politician, he not only has a powerful incentive to search for politically profitable issues, but he has an equally strong motive for staying clear of issues he thinks will not produce a net gain in his votes in the next election.

Because of the ease with which the political stratum can be penetrated, whenever dissatisfaction builds up in some segment of the electorate party politicians will probably learn of the discontent and calculate whether it might be converted into a political issue with an electoral payoff. If a party politician sees no payoff, his interest is likely to be small; if he foresees an adverse effect, he will avoid the issue if he can. As a result, there is usually some conflict in the political stratum between intellectuals, experts, and others who formulate issues, and the party politicians themselves, for the first group often demands attention to issues in which the politicians see no profit and possibly even electoral damage.

The independence, penetrability, and heterogeneity of the various segments of the political stratum all but guarantee that any dissatisfied group will find spokesmen in the political stratum, but to have a spokesman does not insure that the group's problems will be solved by political action. Politicians may not see how they can gain by taking a position on an issue; action by government may seem to be wholly inappropriate; policies intended to cope with dissatisfaction may be blocked; solutions may be improperly designed; indeed, politicians may even find it politically profitable to maintain a shaky coalition by keeping tension and discontent alive and deflecting attention to irrelevant "solutions" or alternative issues.

In his search for profitable issues, the party politician needs to estimate the probable effects various actions he might take will have on the future votes of his constituents. Although he is generally unaware of it, he necessarily operates with a theory, a set of hypotheses as to the factors that influence the decisions of various categories of voters and the rough weights to assign to these factors.

The subculture of the political stratum provides him with the relevant categories—businessmen, Italians, wage earners, and the like. It also furnishes him with information as to the voting tendencies of these groups, e.g., their predisposition to vote Democratic or Republican. Given a category and its voting tendency, the party politician typically operates on the simple but sound assumption that human responses can be influenced by rewards and deprivations, both past and prospective. His task then is to choose a course of action that will either reinforce the voting tendency of categories predisposed in favor of him or his party, or weaken the voting tendency of categories predisposed to vote against him or his party. This he does by actions that provide individuals in these categories with rewards or the expectation of rewards.

Some Political Axioms

Most of the people in the political stratum at any given moment take for granted a number of assumptions so commonplace in the political culture of the time and so little subject to dispute that they function as "self-evident" axioms. The axioms include both factual and normative postulates. In New Haven, the most relevant current axioms among the political stratum would appear to be the following:

1. To build an effective political coalition, rewards must be conferred on (or at least promised to) individuals, groups, and various categories of citizens.

2. In devising strategies for building coalitions and allocating rewards, one must take into account a large number of different categories of citizens. It would be dangerous to formulate strategies on the assumption that most or all citizens can be divided into two or three categories, for a successful political coalition necessarily rests upon a multiplicity of groups and categories. (In the early decades of the century a minority in the political stratum, leaders of the Social Democratic and Socialist Labor parties, pursued a strategy that reflected a confident belief in the existence of a bipolar socioeconomic structure in which political beliefs and actions were almost wholly determined by working-class or white-collar ways of making a living. But because this strategy failed to win elections, it has never been widely approved, least of all among the party politicians in the two major parties.)

3. Although a variety of attributes are relevant to political strategy, many different attributes can either be subsumed under or are sometimes overridden by ethnic, racial, and religious affiliations.

4. In allocating rewards to individuals and groups, the existing socioeconomic structure must be taken as given, except for minor details. (The local political stratum has not been strongly reformist, certainly not on social and economic matters. Except perhaps for socialists, local reform movements have concentrated on defects in the political system, not the socioeconomic structure of the society. And except for a few men who dreamed and spoke of changing the face of the city, until recently the political stratum has assumed that the physical and economic features of the city are determined by forces beyond their control.)

5. Although a certain amount of legal chicanery is tolerable, legality and constitutionality are highly prized. The pursuit of illegal practices on a sizable scale is difficult to conceal; illegal actions by public officials ordinarily lead, when known, to loss of public office; unconstitutional action is almost certain to become entangled in a complex network of judicial processes. The use of violence as a political weapon must be avoided; if it were used it would probably arouse widespread alarm and hostility.

6. The American creed of democracy and equality must always be given vigorous and vociferous support. No one who denies the validity of this creed has much chance of winning political office or otherwise gaining influence on the local scene. Among other things, the creed assumes that democracy is the best form of government, public officials must be chosen by majority vote, and people in the minority must have the right to seek majority support for their beliefs.[1]

---

[1] On the extent of belief in this creed in two cities (Ann Arbor, Michigan, and Tallahassee, Florida) see James W. Prothro and Charles M. Grigg, "Fundamental Principles of Democracy: Bases of Agreement and Disagreement," *Journal of Politics*, Vol. XXII (1960), pp. 276–94. See "Stability, Change, and the Democratic Creed" below, p. 216.

7. In practice, of course, universalistic propositions in the American creed need to be qualified. Adherence to the creed as a general goal and a set of criteria for a good government and a good society does not mean that the creed is, or as a practical matter can be, fully applied in practice. (Some elements in the political stratum are deeply disturbed by the gap between ideal and reality. Most people in the political stratum, however, are probably either unaware of any sharp conflict between ideal and reality, or are indifferent to it, or take the gap for granted in much the same spirit that they accept the fact that religious behavior falls short of religious belief.)

STABILITY, CHANGE, AND THE PROFESSIONALS

New Haven, like most pluralistic democracies, has three characteristics of great importance to the operation of its political system: there are normally "slack" resources; a small core of professional politicians exert great influence over decisions; and the system has a built-in, self-operating limitation on the influence of all participants, including the professionals.

Slack in the System

Most of the time, as we have already seen, most citizens use their resources for purposes other than gaining influence over government decisions. There is a great gap between their actual influence and their potential influence. Their political resources are, so to speak, slack in the system. In some circumstances these resources might be converted from nonpolitical to political purposes; if so, the gap between the actual influence of the average citizen and his potential influence would narrow.

The existence of a great deal of political slack seems to be a characteristic of pluralistic political systems and the liberal societies in which these systems operate. In liberal societies, politics is a sideshow in the great circus of life. Even when citizens use their resources to gain influence, ordinarily they do not seek to influence officials or politicians but family members, friends, associates, employees, customers, business firms, and other persons engaged in nongovernmental activities. A complete study of the ways in which people use their resources to influence others would require a total examination of social life. Government, in the sense used here, is only a fragment of social life.

The Professionals

The political system of New Haven is characterized by the presence of two sharply contrasting groups of citizens. The great body of citizens use their political resources at a low level; a tiny body of professionals within the political stratum use their political resources at a high level. Most citizens acquire little skill in politics; professionals acquire a great deal. Most citizens exert little direct and immediate influence on the decisions of public officials; professionals exert much more. Most citizens have political resources they do not employ in order to gain influence over the decisions of public officials; consequently there is a great gap between their actual and potential influence. The professionals alone narrow the gap; they do so by using their political resources to the full, and by using them with a high degree of efficiency.

The existence of a small band of professionals within the political stratum is a characteristic of virtually all pluralistic systems and liberal societies. The professionals may enjoy much prestige or little; they may be rigidly honest or corrupt; they may come from aristocracies, the middle strata, or working classes. But in every liberal society they are easily distinguished by the rate and skill with which they use their resources and the resulting degree of direct influence they exert on government decisions.

Probably the most important resource of the professional is his available *labor time*. Other citizens usually have occupations that demand a large part of their labor time; they also feel a need for recreation. Measured by the alternatives he has to forego, the average citizen finds it too costly to sacrifice at most more than a few hours a week to political activities.

The professional, by contrast, organizes his life around his political activities. He usually has an occupation that leaves him freer than most citizens to engage in politics; if he does not, he is likely to change jobs until he finds one that fits easily into political routines. Celentano was an undertaker, Lee a public relations man for Yale, DiCenzo a lawyer, Golden an insurance broker—all occupations that permit innumerable opportunities for political work. As a public official, of course, the politician can work virtually full-time at the tasks of politics.

Most citizens treat politics as an avocation. To the professional, politics is a vocation, a calling. Just as the artist remains an artist even as he walks down a city street, and the scientist often consciously or unconsciously remains in his laboratory when he rides home in the evening, or the businessman on the golf course may be working out solutions to his business problems, so the successful politician is a fulltime politician. The dedicated artist does not regard it as a sacrifice of precious time and leisure to paint, the dedicated scientist to work in his laboratory, nor the dedicated businessman to work at his business. On the contrary, each is likely to look for ways of avoiding all other heavy claims on his time. So, too, the dedicated politician does not consider it a sacrifice to work at politics. He is at it, awake and asleep, talking, negotiating, planning, considering strategies, building alliances, making friends, creating contacts—and increasing his influence.

It is hardly to be wondered at that the professional has much more influence on decisions than the average citizen. The professional not only has more resources at the outset than the average citizen, but he also tends to use his resources more efficiently. That is to say, he is more *skillful*.

Skill

Skill in politics is the ability to gain more influence than others, using the same resources. Why some people are more skillful than others in politics is a matter of great speculation and little knowledge. Because skill in politics is hard to measure, I shall simply assume here that professionals are in fact more skillful. However, two hypotheses help to account for the superior skill of the politician.

First, the stronger one's motivation to learn, the more one is likely to learn. Just why the professional is motivated to succeed in politics is as obscure as the motives of the artist, the scientist, or the businessman. But the whole pattern of his calling hardly leaves it open to doubt that the professional *is* more strongly motivated to acquire political skills than is the average citizen.

Second, the more time one spends in learning, the more one is likely to learn. Here the professional has an obvious advantage, as we have just seen: he organizes his life, in effect, to give him time to learn the art of politics.

I have just said the *art* of politics. Although politicians make use of information about the world around them, and hence depend on "scientific" or empirical elements, the actual practice of politics by a skilled professional is scarcely equivalent to the activities of an experimental physicist or biologist in a laboratory.

Even the professional cannot escape a high degree of uncertainty in his calculations. If the professional had perfect knowledge of his own goals, the objective situation, and the consequences of alternative strategies, then his choice of strategy would be a relatively simple and indeed a "scientific" matter. But in fact his knowledge is highly imperfect. He cannot be sure at which point rival professionals will begin to mobilize new resources against his policies. When new opposition flares up, he cannot be sure how much further the battle may spread or what forces lie in reserve. He cannot even be certain what will happen to his own resources if he pursues his policies. He may lose some of his popularity; campaign contributions may fall off in the future; the opposition may come up with a legal block, an ethnic angle, a scandal.

Because of the uncertainty surrounding his decisions, the politician, like the military leader, rarely confronts a situation in which his choice of strategies follows clearly and logically from all the information at his disposal, even when he happens to be well-informed as to his own goals. Surrounded by uncertainty, the politician himself necessarily *imputes* a structure and meaning to the situation that goes beyond empirical evidence and scientific modes of analysis. What the politician imputes to the situation depends, in sum, not only on the information at his disposal but also on his own inner predispositions. His strategy therefore reflects his predispositions for caution or boldness, impulsiveness or calculation, negotiation or toughness, stubbornness or resilience, optimism or pessimism, cynicism or faith in others. The strategies of professionals may vary depending on the forces that generate needs for approval, popularity, domination, manipulation, deception, candor, and so on. The effect of inner dispositions on a professional's strategies is by no means clear or direct. But as one works back from a given situation with all its uncertainties to the professional's interpretation of the situation and his choice of strategies, usually some element in the interpretation or the choice is difficult to account for except as a product of his own special dispositions imposing themselves on his selection of strategies.

Differences in predispositions that result in differences in strategies often reveal themselves in dramatic differences in the style of a chief executive: the differences between a Roosevelt and Eisenhower, for example, or a Wilson and a Coolidge, or the early Truman doubtful of his inherent fitness for the presidency and the later, cocky, self-confident President. Differences also show up at the local level—for example, the contrast between the cautious demeanor of Mayor Celentano and the aggressive, programmatic behavior of Mayor Lee.

Just as individuals vary, so professionals vary in the extent to which they use all the resources at their disposal. Some professionals seem driven not only to use all the resources they have but to create new resources and thus to pyramid their influence. They are a kind of political entrepreneur. In an authoritarian milieu perhaps the political entrepreneur might even be driven to dictatorship. But in a pluralistic political system, powerful self-limiting tendencies help to maintain the stability of the system.

The Art of Pyramiding

We have seen that in the pluralistic political system of New Haven, the political order that existed before 1953—the pattern of petty sovereignties—was gradually transformed into an executive-centered order. How could this change take place? There were few formal changes in the structure of government and politics. The city charter not only remained unaltered, but as we have seen a proposed charter that in effect would have conferred full legality and legitimacy on the executive-centered order was turned down decisively in the same election in which the chief of the new order was reelected by one of the greatest popular majorities on record.

The transformation of petty sovereignties into an executive-centered order was possible only because there were slack resources available to the mayor which, used skillfully and to the full, were sufficient to shift the initiative on most questions to the chief executive. Initially the new mayor had access to no greater resources than his predecessor, but with superb skill he exploited them to the limit. In this way, he managed to accumulate new resources; he rose to new heights of popularity, for example, and found it increasingly easy to tap the business community for campaign contributions. His new resources in turn made it easier for him to secure the compliance of officials in city agencies, enlarge his staff, appoint to office the kinds of people he wanted, obtain the cooperation of the Boards of Finance and Aldermen, and gain widespread support for his policies. Thus the resources available to the mayor grew by comparison with those available to other officials. He could now increase his influence over the various officials of local government by using these new resources fully and skillfully. An executive-centered order gradually emerged.

This transformation had two necessary conditions. First, when the new mayor came into office he had to have access either to resources not available to his predecessor or to slack resources his predecessor had not used. In this instance, the new mayor initially relied on a fuller and more efficient use of substantially the same resources available to his predecessor. By using slack resources with higher efficiency the new mayor moved his actual influence closer to his potential influence. Then because of his greater influence he was able to improve his access to resources. In this fashion he pyramided both his resources and his influence. He was, in short, a highly successful political entrepreneur.

There is, however, a second necessary condition for success. The policies of the political entrepreneur must not provoke so strong a countermobilization that he exhausts his resources with no substantial increase in his influence.

What then stops the political entrepreneur short of dictatorship? Why doesn't the political entrepreneur in a pluralistic system go on pyramiding his resources until he overturns the system itself? The answer lies in the very same conditions that are necessary to his success. If slack resources provide the political entrepreneur with his dazzling opportunity, they are also the source of his greatest danger. For nearly every citizen in the community has access to unused political resources; it is precisely because of this that even a minor blunder can be fatal to the political entrepreneur if it provokes a sizable minority in the community into using its political resources at a markedly higher rate in opposition to his policies, for then, as with the White Queen, it takes all the running he can do just to stay in the same place. Yet almost every policy involves losses for some citizens and gains for others. Whenever the prospect of loss becomes high enough, threatened citizens begin to take up some of the slack in order to remove the threat. The more a favorable decision increases in importance to the opposition, the more resources they can withdraw from other uses and pour into the political struggle; the more resources the opposition employs, the greater the cost to the political entrepreneur if he insists on his policy. At some point, the cost becomes so high that the policy is no longer worth it. This point is almost certain to be reached whenever the opposition includes a majority of the electorate, even if no election takes place. Normally, however, far before this extreme situation is approached the expected costs will already have become so excessive that an experienced politician will capitulate or, more likely, search for a compromise that gives him some of what he wants at lower cost.

Three aspects of Mayor Lee's situation made it possible for him to avoid costly opposition. These were: the wide degree of latent support for redevelopment that already existed in New Haven and needed only to be awakened; the evident need for a high degree of coordination among city agencies if redevelopment were to be carried out; and the Mayor's unusual skill at negotiating agreement and damping down potential disagreements before they flared into opposition. These aspects of Lee's situation are not prevalent in New Haven all the time, nor, certainly, do they necessarily exist in other cities. In the absence of any one of them, opposition might have developed, and the attempt to transform the independent sovereignties into an executive-centered order might have become altogether too costly.

Thus the distribution of resources and the ways in which they are or are not used in a pluralistic political system like New Haven's constitute an important source of both political change and political stability. If the distribution and use of resources gives aspiring leaders great opportunities for gaining influence, these very features also provide a built-in throttle that makes it difficult for any leader, no matter how skillful, to run away with the system.

These features are not, however, the only source of stability. Widespread consensus on the American creed of democracy and equality, referred to many times in the previous pages, is also a stabilizing factor. The analysis in the preceding pages surely points, however, to the conclusion that the effectiveness of the creed as a constraint on political leaders depends not only on the nature of the political consensus as it exists among ordinary citizens but also as it exists among members of the political stratum, particularly the professionals themselves. This is the subject of the following pages.

STABILITY, CHANGE, AND THE DEMOCRATIC CREED

Leaving to one side as a doubtful case the elected oligarchy that governed New Haven during its first century and a half, public officials in New Haven have been selected for the last century and a half through democratic institutions of a rather advanced sort. For more than a century, indeed, New Haven's political system has been characterized by well-nigh universal suffrage, a moderately high participation in elections, a highly competitive two-party system, opportunity to criticize the conduct and policies of officials, freedom to seek support for one's views, among officials and citizens, and surprisingly frequent alternations in office from one party to the other as electoral majorities have shifted. (Hereafter, when I speak of the political system of New Haven, I will assume what I have just enumerated to be the defining characteristics of that system: "stability" will mean the persistence of these characteristics.)

During this period New Haven has not, so far as I can discover, fallen at any time into the kind of semi-dictatorship occasionally found in other American communities. Violence is not and seems never to have been a weapon of importance to New Haven's rulers. Party bosses have existed and exist today; the parties tend to be highly disciplined, and nominations are centrally controlled. But despite occasional loose talk to the contrary, today the parties are too competitive and the community too fragmented for a party boss to be a community boss as well.

Like every other political system, of course, the political system of New Haven falls far short of the usual conceptions of an ideal democracy; by almost any standard, it is obviously full of defects. But to the extent that the term is ever fairly applied to existing realities, the political system of New Haven is an example of a democratic system, warts and all. For the past century it seems to have been a highly stable system.

Theorists have usually assumed that so much stability would be unlikely and even impossible without widespread agreement among citizens on the key ideas of democracy, including the basic rights, duties, and procedures that serve to distinguish democratic from nondemocratic systems. Tocqueville, you will recall, concluded that among the three causes that maintained democracy among the people of the United States —their physical, social, and economic conditions, their laws, and their customs—it was the customs that constituted "the peculiar cause which renders that people the only one of the American nations that is able to support a democratic government." By "customs," he explained, he meant "the whole moral and intellectual condition of a people." Considering his remarkable eye for relevant detail, Tocqueville was uncharacteristically vague as to the specific nature of these customs. But the general import of his argument is perfectly clear. "Republican notions insinuate themselves," as he says at one place, "into all the ideas, opinions, and habits of the Americans and are formally recognized by the laws; and before the laws could be altered, the whole community must be revolutionized."[2]

Before the days of the sample survey it was difficult to say with confidence how widely shared various ideas of democracy actually were in the United States, or even in New Haven. The data are still inadequate. However, some recent findings[3] cast doubt on the validity of the hypothesis that the stability of the American democratic system depends, as Tocqueville and others seem to argue, on an almost universal belief in the basic rules of the democratic game. These studies offer support for some alternative hypotheses. First, although Americans almost unanimously agree on a number of general propositions about democracy, they disagree about specific applications to crucial cases. Second, a majority of voters frequently hold views contrary to rules of the game actually followed in the political system. Third, a much higher degree of agreement on democratic norms exists among the political stratum than among voters in general. Fourth, even among the political stratum the amount of agreement is hardly high enough to account by itself for the stability of the system.

I propose, therefore, to examine some alternative explanations. Because my data on New Haven are not wholly adequate for the task at hand, the theory I shall sketch out might properly be regarded more as reflections on the process of creating consensus than as a testing of theory by a hard examination of the facts in New Haven. But New Haven will provide a convenient reference point.

Some Alternative Explanations

There are at least five alternative ways (aside from denying the validity or generality of recent findings) to account for the stability of the political system in New Haven.

---

[2] Tocqueville, *Democracy in America*, pp. 310, 334, 436.

[3] Especially Samuel Stouffer, *Communism, Conformity and Civil Liberties* (New York: Doubleday, 1955) and James W. Prothro and Charles M. Grigg, *op. cit.*

First, one may deny that New Haven is "democratic" and argue that it is in fact run by a covert oligarchy of some sort. Thus the problem, it might be said, is illusory. Yet even in the absence of comparable studies our findings argue strongly that New Haven is not markedly *less* democratic than other supposedly democratic political systems. Some of these, we know, have proved to be unstable; hence the problem does not vanish after all.

Second, one might argue that things were different in the good old days. Yet it is hardly plausible to suppose that in 1910, when slightly less than half the population of New Haven consisted of first- and second-generation immigrants (many of them from countries with few democratic traditions), democratic beliefs were more widespread than they are now. In any case, the main characteristics of the political system—majority rule, the legitimacy of opposition, and so on—do not show any signs of disappearing.

Third, it might be said that the political system of New Haven is scarcely autonomous enough to furnish us with adequate explanations of its own stability, for stability may depend much less on the beliefs of citizens locally than on state and national institutions. There is much truth in this objection, but it does not altogether explain why some American towns, cities, and counties have at various times moved a good deal farther from democratic norms than New Haven has.

Fourth, one might argue that the system has not been entirely stable, that in fact most seemingly stable democratic systems are constantly in transition. Surely this is a valid point, but it is one that cuts both ways. In New Haven, as elsewhere, the rules of the game have altered in quite important, one is tempted to say fundamental, ways over the past century and a half. For example, organized, overt political competition, which was anathema to the patrician oligarchy, seems to have been fully legitimate since about 1840. Consider the electorate—the active voters. Partly as a result of the abolition of property qualifications in 1845, but probably more as a result of party organization and competition, the proportion of voting adults shot up and then stabilized at a moderate level. In most elections from 1800–33 the voters comprised less than a quarter of the adult males and sometimes less than 10 per cent; since 1834, however, they have made up from a half to three-quarters of the adult male (and since 1920, female) population. A final example: throughout the nineteenth century, an implicit norm excluded persons of foreign birth or non-Yankee origins from nomination or election to the mayoralty; since the mayoralty election of 1899, the norm has very nearly come to operate in reverse.

Because of, or in spite of, these changes, however, the essential characteristics of the political system as I described them have remained substantially intact for the past century. With appropriate techniques, probably one could detect and describe significant fluctuations in the "intensity," "degree," or "magnitude" of the various characteristics, but this line of inquiry would not help much in the present problem.

Fifth, one might argue that the stability of New Haven's political system does not depend on a widespread belief that certain democratic norms, rules, or procedures are highly desirable or intrinsically preferable to other rules; in some circumstances a democratic system could be highly stable if a substantial part of the electorate merely *accepted* them. A majority of voters who do not really believe in extending freedom of speech to individuals and groups beyond the pale of popular morality—and who would readily say so during an interview—might nonetheless acquiesce in such extensions on a variety of pragmatic grounds.

There is, I think, a good deal more truth in this view than many enthusiastic democrats care to admit. Let me suggest some circumstances in which this explanation might be valid.

Whenever the costs of disagreement are believed to be very high, there are innumerable conditions under which a collection of people might knowingly agree on a choice that no one preferred, simply because this was the only choice on which they could agree. Stable systems of international politics, such as the balance of power system in the nineteenth century, surely have been of this kind. Or suppose that 80 per cent of the voters are in favor of a more restricted suffrage than actually exists. Suppose that 40 per cent would like to restrict the suffrage to taxpayers, another 40 per cent would like to restrict it to college graduates, and only 20 per cent would like to retain the present suffrage. Suppose further that their other choices were as shown in the table below. One

	40% prefer:	40% prefer:	20% prefer:
First choice:	Taxpayers	College graduates	Present requirements
Second choice: ..	Present requirements	Present requirements	College graduates
Third choice: ...	College graduates	Taxpayers	Taxpayers

does not need to assume a great amount of rationality to conclude that they would retain the existing broad suffrage requirements, even though this would be the preferred choice of only a minority.

Moreover, this example hints at the fact that the stability of a political system, even a democratic one, is not merely a matter of the *numbers* of persons who adhere to it but also of the *amount of political resources* they use—or are expected to use—in acting on their beliefs. The amount of political resources an individual is likely to use is a function, among other things, of the amount of resources he has access to, the strength or intensity of his belief, and the relevance he sees in political action as a way of acting on his beliefs. Other things being equal, rules supported only by a wealthy, educated minority (money and knowledge being important political resources) and opposed by the rest of the voters are surely likely to endure longer than rules supported only by a poor, uneducated minority and opposed by the rest of the voters. Likewise, rules that are *strongly* believed in by a minority and weakly opposed by the rest are more likely to endure than rules *weakly* believed in by a majority and strongly opposed by a minority.

In addition to numbers and resources, however, skill is obviously a critical factor. Rules supported by a politically skillful minority may withstand the opposition of a less skilled majority, and in any case are likely to endure longer than if they are supported only by an unskilled minority.

Let us now imagine a society with a political system approximately like that in New Haven. Suppose the rules, procedures, and essential characteristics of this system are strongly supported by a minority which, in comparison with the rest of the population, possesses a high degree of political skill. Suppose further that a majority of voters would prefer rules different from those prevailing, though they might not all prefer the same alternatives. Suppose finally that the majority of voters have access to fewer resources of influence; that their preferences for other rules are not salient or strong; that because of their relative indifference they do not employ what potential influence they have; and that they are not very skillful in using their political resources anyway. Such a political system, its seems to me, might be highly stable.

On the other hand, if any of the characteristics of this hypothetical minority were to shift to the majority, then the system would surely become less stable. Instability would increase, then, if the minority favoring the system no longer had superior resources, or if it became less skillful, or if the question of rules became salient and urgent to a majority of voters.

I should like to advance the hypothesis that the political system we have just been supposing corresponds closely to the facts of New Haven, and in all probability to the United States. If it errs, it is in supposing that *even among the political stratum* the level of agreement on the rules of the game is, at any given moment, high enough to explain the persistence of the rules.

Consensus as a Process

Most of us, I suppose, are ready to recognize long-run changes in the beliefs expressed by the more articulate segments of the political stratum and the intelligentsia, and we can infer from various kinds of evidence—all of it, alas, highly debatable—that changes of some sort take place over long periods of time in the attitudes about democracy held in the general population. We tend to assume, however, that except for these long-run shifts beliefs about democracy are more or less static. I want to propose an alternative explanation, namely that democratic beliefs, like other political beliefs, are influenced by a recurring *process* of interchange among political professionals, the political stratum, and the great bulk of the population. The process generates enough agreement on rules and norms so as to permit the system to operate, but agreement tends to be incomplete, and typically it decays. So the process is frequently repeated. "Consensus," then, is not at all a static and unchanging attribute of citizens. It is a variable element in a complex and more or less continuous process.

This process seems to me to have the following characteristics:

1. Over long periods of time the great bulk of the citizens possess a fairly stable set of democratic beliefs at a high level of abstraction. Let me call these beliefs the democratic creed. In Ann Arbor and Tallahas-

see, Prothro and Grigg found that very nearly everyone they interviewed agreed with five abstract democratic propositions.[4] We can, I think, confidently conclude that most Americans believe in democracy as the best form of government, in the desirability of rights and procedures insuring a goodly measure of majority rule and minority freedom, and in a wide but not necessarily comprehensive electorate. At a somewhat lower level of agreement, probably the great majority of citizens also believe in the essential legitimacy of certain specific American political institutions: the presidency, Congress, the Supreme Court, the states, the local governments, etc.

2. Most citizens assume that the American political system is consistent with the democratic creed. Indeed, the common view seems to be that our system is not only democratic but is perhaps the most perfect expression of democracy that exists anywhere; if deficiencies exist, either they can, and ultimately will, be remedied, or else they reflect the usual gap between ideal and reality that men of common sense take for granted. Moreover, because leading officials with key roles in the legitimate political institutions automatically acquire authority for their views on the proper functioning of the political institutions, as long as these various officials seem to agree, the ordinary citizen is inclined to assume that existing ways of carrying on the public business do not violate, at least in an important way, the democratic creed to which he is committed.

3. Widespread adherence to the democratic creed is produced and maintained by a variety of powerful social processes. Of these, probably formal schooling is the most important. The more formal education an American has, the more democratic formulas he knows, expresses, and presumably believes. But almost the entire adult population has been subjected to *some* degree of indoctrination through the schools. Beliefs acquired in school are reinforced in adult life through normal exposure to the democratic creed, particularly as the creed is articulated by leading political figures and transmitted through the mass media.

These social processes have an enormous impact on the citizen, partly because they begin early in life and partly because the very unanimity with which the creed is espoused makes rejection of it almost impossible. To reject the creed is infinitely more than a simple matter of disagreement. To reject the creed is to reject one's society and one's chances of full acceptance in it—in short, to be an outcast. (As a mental experiment, try to imagine the psychic and social burdens an American child in an American school would incur if he steadfastly denied to himself and others that democracy is the best form of government.)

To reject the democratic creed is in effect to refuse to be an American. As a nation we have taken great pains to insure that few citizens will ever want to do anything so rash, so preposterous—in fact, so wholly un-

---

[4] "Democracy is the best form of government." "Public officials should be chosen by majority vote." "Every citizen should have an equal chance to influence government policy." "The minority should be free to criticize majority decisions." "People in the minority should be free to try to win majority support for their opinions." Prothro and Grigg, *op. cit.*, pp. 282, 284.

American. In New Haven, as in many other parts of the United States, vast social energies have been poured into the process of "Americanization," teaching citizens what is expected in the way of words, beliefs, and behavior if they are to earn acceptance as Americans, for it was obvious to the political stratum that unless the immigrants and their children quickly accepted American political norms, the flood of aliens, particularly from countries with few traditions of self-government, would disrupt the political system. In a characteristic response, the Board of Education of the city of New Haven created a supervisor for Americanization (a post, incidentally, that still exists). Something of the feeling of urgency and accomplishment that must have prevailed in many segments of the political stratum shines through these enthusiastic words in the annual report of the New Haven superintendent of schools in 1919:

> The public school is the greatest and most effective of all Americanization agencies. This is the one place where all children in a community or district, regardless of nationality, religion, politics, or social status, meet and work together in a cooperative and harmonious spirit. . . . The children work and play together, they catch the school spirit, they live the democratic life, American heroes become their own, American history wins their loyalty, the Stars and Stripes, always before their eyes in the school room, receives their daily salute. Not only are these immigrant children Americanized through the public school, but they, in turn, Americanize their parents carrying into the home many lessons of democracy learned at school.[5]

For their part, the immigrants and their children were highly motivated to learn how to be Americans, for they were desperately, sometimes pathetically, eager to win acceptance as true Americans.

In one form or another the process of Americanization has absorbed enormous social energies all over the United States. As a factor in shaping American behavior and attitudes, the process of Americanization must surely have been as important as the frontier, or industrialization, or urbanization. That regional, ethnic, racial, religious, or economic differences might disrupt the American political system has been a recurring fear among the political stratum of the United States from the very beginning of the republic. Doubtless this anxiety was painfully stimulated by the Civil War. It was aroused again by the influx of immigrants. Throughout the country then the political stratum has seen to it that new citizens, young and old, have been properly trained in "American" principles and beliefs. Everywhere, too, the pupils have been highly motivated to talk, look and believe as American should. The result was as astounding an act of voluntary political and cultural assimilation and speedy elimination of regional, ethnic, and cultural dissimilarities as history can provide. The extent to which Americans agree today on the key propositions about democracy is a measure of the almost unbelievable success of this deliberate attempt to create a seemingly uncoerced nation-wide consensus.

---

[5] "Report of the Superintendent of Schools," *Annual Report of the Board of Education of the New Haven City School District*, 1919.

4. Despite wide agreement on a general democratic creed, however, citizens frequently disagree on specific applications. Many citizens oppose what some political philosophers would regard as necessary implications of the creed. Many citizens also disagree with the way the creed is actually applied—or perhaps it would be more accurate to say, with the existing rules of the game, the prevailing political norms. Again and again, for example, surveys indicate that a large number of Americans, sometimes even a majority, do not approve of the extension of important rights, liberties, and privileges to individuals and groups that do in fact enjoy them.

A citizen is able to adhere to these seemingly inconsistent beliefs for a great variety of reasons. For one thing, he himself need not see any inconsistency in his beliefs. The creed is so vague (and incomplete) that strict deductions are difficult or impossible even for sophisticated logicians. Moreover, propositions stated in universal terms are rarely assumed by men of common sense to imply universality in practice; to the frequent dismay of logicians, a common tendency of mankind—and not least of Americans—is to qualify universals in application while leaving them intact in rhetoric. Then, too, the capacity for (or interest in) working out a set of consistent political attitudes is rather limited. As the authors of *The American Voter* have recently shown, most voters seem to operate at a low level of ideological sophistication; even among intelligent (though not necessarily highly educated) citizens, conceptions of politics are often of a simplicity that the political philosopher might find it hard to comprehend.[6] In addition, most citizens operate with a very small fund of political information; often they lack the elementary information required even to be aware of inconsistencies between their views and what is actually happening in the political system, particularly if the subject is (as most questions of rights and procedures are) arcane and complex. Again, questions that bother theorists are often not interesting or salient to most voters; their attention and energies are diverted elsewhere, usually to activities that lie entirely outside the political arena. As long as a citizen believes that democracy is the best political system, that the United States is a democracy, and that the people in office can be trusted, by and large, to apply the abstract creed to specific cases, issues of democratic theory and practice hotly discussed by political philosophers, or even by publicists and columnists, are likely never to penetrate through the manifold barriers to abstract political thinking that are erected by the essentially apolitical culture in which he lives. Finally, even if the issues do manage to get through, many citizens feel themselves incompetent to decide them; this, after all, is what Supreme Court judges, presidents, and members of Congress are supposed to do. Worse yet, many citizens feel that no one in public office will care much about their opinions anyway.

5. Members of the political stratum (who live in a much more politicized culture) are more familiar with the "democratic" norms, more consistent, more ideological, more detailed and explicit in their political

---

[6] A. Campbell, P. E. Converse, W. E. Miller, D. E. Stokes, *The American Voter* (New York, Wiley, 1960), chs. 9 and 10.

attitudes, and more completely in agreement on the norms. They are more in agreement not only on what norms are implied by the abstract democratic creed but also in supporting the norms currently operating. This relatively higher degree of support for the prevailing norms in the existing political system is generated and maintained by a variety of processes. Because members of the political stratum have on the average considerably more formal education than the population as a whole, they have been more thoroughly exposed to the creed and its implications. Because they are more involved in, concerned with, and articulate about politics, they invest more time and effort in elaborating a consistent ideology. Because they participate more extensively in politics, they more frequently express and defend their views, encounter criticism, and face the charge of inconsistency. They know more about politics, read more, experience more, see more.

Within the political stratum, the professionals tend to agree even more on what the norms should be, what they are, and the desirability of maintaining them substantially as they are. Agreement among the professionals is generated by all the factors that account for it among the rest of the political stratum and even among the apolitical strata. Mastery over the existing norms of the political system represents the particular stockpile of skills peculiar to the professional's vocation. Norms also tend to legitimate his power and position in the political system, furnish an agreed-on method of getting on with the immediate tasks at hand, carry the authority of tradition, and help to reduce the baffling uncertainty that surrounds the professional's every choice. Finally, the professional is likely to support the existing norms because his own endorsement of existing norms was initially a criterion in his own recruitment and advancement; complex processes of political selection and rejection tend to exclude the deviant who challenges the prevailing norms of the existing political system. Most of the professionals might properly be called democratic "legitimists."

6. The professionals, of course, have access to extensive political resources which they employ at a high rate with superior efficiency. Consequently, a challenge to the existing norms is bound to be costly to the challenger, for legitimist professionals can quickly shift their skills and resources into the urgent task of doing in the dissenter. As long as the professionals remain substantially legitimist in outlook, therefore, the critic is likely to make little headway. Indeed, the chances are that anyone who advocates extensive changes in the prevailing democratic norms is likely to be treated by the professionals, and even by a fair share of the political stratum, as an outsider, possibly even as a crackpot whose views need not be seriously debated. No worse fate can befall the dissenter, for unless he can gain the attention of the political stratum, it is difficult for him to gain space in the mass media; if he cannot win space in the mass media, it is difficult for him to win a large following; if he cannot win a large following, it is difficult for him to gain the attention of the political stratum.

7. Sometimes, of course, disagreements over the prevailing norms occur within the political stratum and among the professionals themselves. But these disagreements need not, and perhaps ordinarily do not,

produce much effort to involve the general public in the dispute. The disagreements are not, to be sure, secret; the electorate is not *legally* barred from finding out about the conflict and becoming involved. It does not need to be. Given the low salience of politics in the life of the average citizen, most conflicts over the prevailing norms might attract more attention if they were held behind locked doors. Unless a professional is willing to invest great resources in whipping up public interest, he is not likely to get much effective support. In any case, public involvement may seem undesirable to the legitimist, for alterations in the prevailing norms are often subtle matters, better obtained by negotiation than by the crudities and oversimplifications of public debate.

8. Among the rules and procedures supported strongly by the legitimists in the political stratum, and particularly by the professionals, are some that prescribe ways of settling disagreements as to rules and procedures. These involve appeals to authorities who give decisions widely accepted as binding, authoritative, and legitimate—though not necessarily as "good" or "correct." Typically these include appeals to courts or quasi-judicial institutions that ostensibly arrive at their decisions by appeals to norms, codes, formulas, and beliefs that appear to transcend partisan and policy differences in the political stratum.

9. Ordinarily, then, it is not difficult for a stable system of rights and privileges to exist that, at least in important details, does not have widespread public support and occasionally even lacks majority approval. As long as the matter is not a salient public issue—and whether it is or not depends partly on how the political stratum handles it—the question is substantially determined within the political stratum itself. When disagreements arise, these are adjudicated by officials who share the beliefs of the political stratum rather than those of the populace; and even when these officials adopt positions that do not command the undivided support of the political stratum, members of the political stratum, and particularly the professionals, tend to accept a decision as binding until and unless it can be changed through the accepted procedures. This is the essence of their code of democratic legitimism.

10. Occasionally, however, a sizable segment of the political stratum develops doubts that it can even achieve the changes it seeks through accepted procedures that are, in a sense, internal to the political stratum and the professionals. One or more of these dissenters may push his way into the professional group, or the dissenters may be numerous and vocal enough to acquire a spokesman or two among the professionals. The strategy of the dissenters may now begin to shift. Instead of adjudicating the matter according to the accepted procedures, the dissenters attempt to arouse public support for their proposals, hoping that when a sufficient number of voters are won over to their cause, other professionals—legitimists or not—will have to come around.

The professionals, as I have said, live in a world of uncertainty. They search for omens and portents. If the auguries indicate that the appeal to the populace has failed, then the legitimists may confidently close ranks against the dissenter. But if the auguries are uncertain or unfavorable, then the legitimists, too, are forced to make a counter-appeal to the populace. Since public opinion is often as difficult to interpret as the flights of birds or the entrails of a sheep, political professionals may and frequently do misread the auspices. In October 1954, the Survey Research Center discovered that only 12 per cent of their sample said they would be more likely to vote for a candidate who had the support of Senator McCarthy; 37 per cent said they would be less likely, and 43 per cent said it would make no difference.[7] In retrospect, these proportions do not look wildly off, but in 1954 belief in McCarthy's mass following was widespread throughout the whole political stratum and not least among the professionals. The legitimists could probably have ignored the late Senator with impunity—as they later did—but he followed a classic strategy—(required, I am suggesting, by the tendency of the legitimists to monopolize the internal devices for adjudicating disputes over norms)—by taking the issue out of the hands of the professionals, where the rules of the game were bound to run against him, and appealing instead to the populace.

If the dissenters succeed in forcing the issue out beyond the political stratum, and dissenters and legitimists begin making appeals to the populace, then the nature of the debate begins to change. Technical questions, subtle distinctions, fine matters of degree are shed. The appeal is now shaped to the simple democratic creed which nearly every citizen believes in. Because the creed does not constitute a tightly logical system, it is possible for the legitimists to demonstrate that existing norms are necessary consequences of the creed, and for the dissenters to show that existing norms run counter to the creed. Because the creed is deeply laden with tradition and sentiment, emotion rises and reasoned discussion declines.

11. Ordinary citizens who normally remain outside these debates now find their attention—and their votes—solicited by both sides. They become aware that the very officials who ordinarily decide these matters, to whom the citizen himself turns for his cues as to what is legitimate and consistent with the creed, are locked in deadly, heated battle. These citizens must now find ways of applying the creed to the issue. One way is to withdraw even more deeply into the political shadows; a citizen can simply refuse to choose. Many do. In March 1937, at the height of the debate over President Roosevelt's proposal to enlarge the Supreme Court, 50 per cent of the people interviewed in a Gallup poll had listened to neither of the President's two recent radio speeches defending his plan. A month later, one out of seven persons who were asked whether Congress should pass the President's bill expressed no opinion.[8] In New Haven, after several years of public discussion and debate over charter reform, when a sample of registered voters was asked in 1959 whether they personally would do anything if a revision of the charter was pro-

[7] Angus Campbell and Homer C. Cooper, *Group Differences in Attitudes and Votes, A Study of the 1954 Congressional Election* (Ann Arbor, Mich.: University of Michigan Survey Research Center, 1954), p. 145.

[8] Hadley Cantril, ed., *Public Opinion, 1935–1946* (Princeton: Princeton University Press, 1951), p. 150.

posed that would make the mayor stronger, over 40 per cent of those who disapproved of such an idea said they would do nothing to oppose it, and nearly three-quarters of those who approved said they would do nothing to support it. (These seemed to be tolerably honest responses; in the preceding election, after wide discussion among the political stratum and hot debate among the professionals over a new charter, less than half the voters who went to the polls even bothered to vote on the charter.) Thus when dissenters and legitimists appeal to the populace to settle questions they ordinarily decide among themselves, they cannot be at all sure that they will actually produce much of a response no matter how much they try to stir up the public.

However, citizens who *do* make up their minds must find some ways for arriving at a choice. For many citizens the decision is eased by their existing loyalties to parties or political leaders. In April 1937, 68 per cent of the Democrats in a Gallup poll said that Congress should pass Roosevelt's court plan; 93 per cent of the Republicans said Congress should not. Those who had no strong party identifications were, as one might expect, split—42 per cent in favor and 58 per cent against.[9] In 1954, attitudes toward McCarthy were closely related to party identifications. Among strong Democrats, those who said that McCarthy's support would make them *less* likely to vote for a candidate were six times as great as those who said his support would make them *more* likely; strong Republicans, by contrast, split about evenly. Among Catholics who were strong Democrats, the ratio was two to one against McCarthy; among Catholics who were strong Republicans it was nearly two to one in his favor.[10]

If the parties give no clear guidance, citizens may look to particular leaders or institutions. They may turn to spokesmen in their churches, for example, or trade unions, or regions. They often turn, of course, to attitudes prevalent in their own circle of intimates, friends, associates, acquaintances. If their search yields no consistent cues, they may give up. In the struggle over charter reform in New Haven in 1958, when Democratic leaders were split from the top down, judging from a sample of registered voters interviewed shortly after the election the proportion of people who went to the polls and voted on the general election but did not vote either for or against the charter was higher among Democrats than among either Republicans or independents.

12. An appeal to the populace may terminate in several ways. The appeal may simply fail to create a stir. Interest in political matters wanes rather quickly; since complex issues of democratic norms nearly always lack a direct relation to the ongoing life of an individual, they have even less capacity for holding attention than many other issues. However passionately the dissenters feel about their case, life does move on, old questions become tiresome, and the newspapers begin to shove the conflict to the inside pages. Perhaps the legitimists, buoyed by their reading of the

---

[9] *Ibid.*

[10] Campbell and Cooper, *Group Differences in Attitudes,* Tables VI–VIII (p. 92) and B–81 (p. 149). See also Nelson W. Polsby, "Towards an Explanation of McCarthyism," *Political Studies, 8,* No. 3 (1960), 250–71.

electorate, defeat the dissenters in a clear-cut trial of strength and, having done so, close ranks and go on to the next business. Perhaps the dissenters win, or a compromise is worked out; if so the dissenters, like as not, turn into the next generation of legitimists.

The Role of Democratic Beliefs

The specific beliefs of the average citizen thus have a rather limited though important function. Ordinarily, conflicts over democratic norms are resolved among the professionals, with perhaps some involvement by parts of the political stratum but little or no involvement by most citizens. Thus the fact that a large number of citizens do not believe in the political norms actually applied, particularly extending political liberties to unpopular individuals and groups, has slight effect on the outcome.

The beliefs of the ordinary citizen become relevant only when professionals engage in an intensive appeal to the populace. Even then, the actual outcome of the appeal does not necessarily reflect majority attitudes at all accurately. These are not always known; they are guessed at in a variety of inaccurate ways, and they have to be filtered through the tighter mesh of the political stratum and the professionals before they can become public policy.

Nonetheless, wide consensus on the democratic creed does have two important kinds of consequences. On the one hand, this very consensus makes occasional appeal all but inevitable, for the creed itself gives legitimacy to an appeal to the populace. On the other hand, widespread adherence to the creed limits the character and the course of an appeal. It insures that no appeal is likely to succeed unless it is framed in terms consistent with the creed—which is perhaps not so small a constraint. Some solutions pretty evidently are *not* consistent. Because an appeal must take place in the face of criticism from legitimists and extensive appraisal by members of the political stratum, blatant inconsistencies are likely to be exposed. Moreover, because the appeal is legitimized by the creed, it provides an orderly way to conduct a dispute that exceeds the capacities of the professionals to resolve among themselves.

No one, I imagine, has ever supposed that the existence of the creed entails no risks. People can be deceived by appeals intended to destroy democracy in the name of democracy. Dissenters who believe in the democratic creed may unwittingly advocate or legitimists may insist on preserving rules of the game destined to have unforeseen and unintended consequences disastrous to the stability and perhaps the survival of the democracy.

Nonetheless, we can be reasonably sure of this: even if universal belief in a democratic creed does not guarantee the stability of a democratic system, a substantial decline in the popular consensus would greatly increase the chance of serious instability. How the professionals act, what they advocate, what they are likely to believe, are all constrained by the wide adherence to the creed that exists throughout the community. If a substantial segment of the electorate begins to doubt the creed, professionals will quickly come forth to fan that doubt. The nature and course of an appeal to the populace will change. What today is a question of applying the fundamental norms of democracy will become tomorrow an inquiry into the validity of these norms. If a substantial number of citizens begin to deny not merely to *some* minorities but to minorities *as such* the rights and powers prescribed in the creed, an appeal to the populace is likely to end sooner or later in a call to arms.

Thus consensus on political beliefs and practices has much in common with other aspects of a democratic system. Here, too, leaders lead—and often are led. Citizens are very far indeed from exerting equal influence over the content, application, and development of the political consensus. Yet widely held beliefs by Americans in a creed of democracy and political equality serve as a critical limit on the ways in which leaders can shape the consensus.

Neither the prevailing consensus, the creed, nor even the political system itself are immutable products of democratic ideas, beliefs, and institutions inherited from the past. For better or worse, they are always open, in some measure, to alteration through those complex processes of symbiosis and change that constitute the relations of leaders and citizens in a pluralistic democracy.

Section V
The Belief-Sharing or Consensus Model

So long as leaders are not treated from their early childhood as a class apart, they will share life experiences with other citizens and be exposed to the same culture. To the degree that experiences are common and lead to the same likes and dislikes, leaders like all others will be disposed to certain actions as new problems and events arise. Were personal experiences common to all, and were everyone totally in agreement on all values, it would matter little who governed as all would agree with the actions taken by leaders. Sharing in this case would be complete. There seems little question, however, that an American consensus falls far short of including all people or all political actions and that political leaders are more likely to come from the middle rather than working classes, thus casting suspicion on their representativeness. A 1970 CBS poll of Congress and the public, by contrast, did find substantial agreement between senators and representatives and the public. Across five national issues, including Vietnam and civil rights, representatives' opinions differed only 8 percent from the public and senators', only 22 percent. To be sure, such agreement could come by way of the more deviant congressional candidates being unsuccessful in seeking reelection. But in the face of serious questions about the public's ability to coerce unresponsive leaders noted in previous sections, sharing rather than coercion may best explain the consistency between leaders and public opinion.

While opinion polls provide an opportunity to get the opinions of the inattentive who would fail to express themselves by voting and who would certainly be unheard at public meetings, their answers to polls are also troublesome. Experience with polls has shown many answers are less than thoughtful. Some people seemingly answer randomly, much like the unprepared student guessing on an examination. Others always agree with statements regardless of what is asked. Philip Converse in the seminal article reprinted here finds public opinion not only fails to be ordered in the liberal-conservative way common to political leaders and other political activists but seems largely shaped by "nonopinions". Nonopinions are those given by a person in an unfamiliar area solely to satisfy the questioner. Obviously, it is meaningless to look for sharing of opinion between representatives and their constituents if public opinion is random guesses expressing no personal concern.

The publics in two northwestern communities show more thought in their responses to various community issues perhaps because of more personal relevance seen in local issues. Leaders in these communities also fail to mirror the liberal or conservative stances found by Converse among his congressmen, but the pattern of responses to local issues by these local leaders is not the same as that of the public. Sharing in these communities is possible on specific issues, but it is inappropriate to speak of the public not sharing the conservatism of local leaders.

Testing the question of whether there are differences between the policies which the two major political parties would seek to enact if elected, Herbert McClosky, Paul Hoffman, and Rosemary O'Hara find leaders of the parties (delegates to the party conventions of 1956) differ far more sharply than do public supporters of the parties. Across a broad range of issues the public is given a clear choice, but neither party shares the opinions of the public. In fact Democratic party leaders actually better reflect Republican party supporters' opinions than do Republican leaders. These findings have been replicated in more recent studies. John Soule and James Clarke found 1968 delegates to the major party conventions continued to differ sharply between parties.[1] Moreover, delegates' candidate preferences mirrored their opinions. This would suggest that each party's candidate would tend to reflect the moderate middle of party opinion. Indeed, Edmond Costantini in a 1960 study of the California Democratic delegation found that at each stage of the party's moving people to higher echelons in the party, those with more extreme positions were passed over, meaning that top officials more closely shared public opinion.[2] Finally, the most recent study (1972) by William Shaffer, Ronald Weber, and Robert Montjoy of county party chairmen of both parties compared with public opinion closely paralleled McClosky et al. findings of substantial party differences in opinion with the Republican leaders deviating most from public opinion.[3]

The propensity of national politicians to order their political world consistently with liberal or conservative alternatives to government policy while the public does not clearly runs counter to the sharing model. Such distinctiveness between Republicans and Democrats may be supportive of the political parties model as others have already noted in Section II, but even there the public failed to use the choice. Either a decline in leader orderings along the liberal-conservative dimensions or

---

[1] John W. Soule and James W. Clarke, "Issue Conflict and Consensus: A Comparative Study of Democratic and Republican Delegates to the 1968 National Conventions," *Journal of Politics* (February 1971), pp. 72–91.

[2] Edmond Costantini, "Intraparty Attitude Conflict: Democratic Party Leadership in California," *Western Political Quarterly* (1963), pp. 956–72.

[3] William R. Shaffer, Ronald E. Weber, and Robert S. Montjoy, "Mass and Political Elite Beliefs about the Policies of the Regime," a paper presented at the 1973 Annual Meeting of The American Political Science Association, New Orleans, September 4–8.

an acceleration of a very weak tendency for the public to order their opinions and party support along this dimension would better fulfill the sharing model.[4] Also, the moderation of opinion among higher echelon party officials, while contrary to the political parties model, may yield greater opinion sharing between decision makers and the public.

The final selection by Robert Jackman looks to a commonly noted greater tolerance among political leaders for respecting the right of minorities, especially unpopular ones, to participate in public discussion. The sharing of such intolerant opinions might satisfy political linkage at the price of democracy. Jackman finds complete sharing between leaders and those members of the public who have the same personal characteristics with education being the most important characteristic. While leaders' attitudes on specific issues seem undetermined by their social characteristics, tolerance to the rights of minorities springs from the education of leaders rather than from their participation in politics.

---

[4] See Robert S. Erikson and Norman R. Luttbeg, *American Public Opinion: Its Origins, Content, and Impact* (New York: Wiley, 1973), chap. 3.

Philip E. Converse

The Nature of Belief Systems in Mass Publics*

Belief systems have never surrendered easily to empirical study or quantification. Indeed, they have often served as primary exhibits for the doctrine that what is important to study cannot be measured and that what can be measured is not important to study. In an earlier period, the behaviorist decree that subjective states lie beyond the realm of proper measurement gave Mannheim a justification for turning his back on measurement, for he had an unqualified interest in discussing belief systems.[1] Even as Mannheim was writing, however, behaviorism was undergoing stiff challenges, and early studies of attitudes were attaining a degree of measurement reliability that had been deemed impossible. This fragment of history, along with many others, serves to remind us that no intellectual position is likely to become obsolete quite so rapidly as one that takes current empirical capability as the limit of the possible in a more absolute sense. Nevertheless, while rapid strides in the measurement of "subjective states" have been achieved in recent decades, few would claim that the millennium has arrived or that Mannheim could now find all of the tools that were lacking to him forty years ago.

This article makes no pretense of surpassing such limitations. At the same time, our substantive concern forces upon us an unusual concern with measurement strategies, not simply because we propose to deal with belief systems or ideologies, but also because of the specific questions that we shall raise about them. Our focus in this article is upon differences in the nature of belief systems held on the one hand by elite political actors and, on the other, by the masses that appear to be "numbered" within the spheres of influence of these belief systems. It is our thesis that there are important and predictable differences in ideational

* This abridged selection is reprinted with permission of The Macmillan Company from *Ideology and Discontent* by David Apter. Copyright © The Free Press of Glencoe, a division of The Macmillan Company, 1964.

[1] Karl Mannheim, *Ideology and Utopia* (New York, 1946), especially pp. 39ff.

worlds as we progress downward through such "belief strata" and that these differences, while obvious at one level, are easily overlooked and not infrequently miscalculated. The fact that these ideational worlds differ in character poses problems of adequate representation and measurement.

The vertical ordering of actors and beliefs that we wish to plumb bears some loose resemblance to the vertical line that might be pursued downward through an organization or political movement from the narrow cone of top leadership, through increasing numbers of subordinate officials, and on through untitled activists to the large base formally represented in membership rolls. It is this large base that Michels noted, from observations of political gatherings, was rarely "there," and analogues to its physical absence do not arise accidentally in dealing with belief systems. On the other hand, there is no perfect or necessary "fit" between the two orderings, and this fact in itself has some interest.

That we intend to consider the total mass of people "numbered" within the spheres of influence of belief systems suggests both a democratic bias and a possible confusion between numbers and power or between numbers and the outcomes of events that power determines. We are aware that attention to numbers, more or less customary in democratic thought, is very nearly irrelevant in many political settings. Generally, the logic of numbers collides head on with the logic of power, as the traditional power pyramid, expressing an inverse relation between power and numbers, communicates so well. "Power" and "numbers" intersect at only one notable point, and that point is represented by the familiar axiom that numbers are one resource of power. The weight of this resource varies in a systematic and obvious way according to the political context. In a frankly designed and stable obligarchy, it is assumed to have no weight at all. In such a setting, the numbers of people associated with particular belief systems, if known at all, becomes important only in periods of crisis or challenge to the existing power structure. Democratic theory greatly increases the weight accorded to numbers in the daily power calculus. This increase still does not mean that numbers are of overriding importance; in the normal course of events it is the *perception* of numbers by democratic elites, so far as they differ from "actual" numbers, that is the more important factor. However this may be, claims to numbers are of some modest continuing importance in democratic systems for the legitimacy they confer upon demands; and, much more sporadically, claims to numbers become important in nondemocratic systems as threats of potential coercion.

I. SOME CLARIFICATION OF TERMS

A term like "ideology" has been thoroughly muddied by diverse uses.[2] We shall depend instead upon the term "belief system," although there

---

[2] Minar has compiled a useful if discouraging survey of this diversity. See David W. Minar, "Ideology and Political Behavior," *Midwest Journal of Political Science,* 5 (November 1961), No. 4, 317–31.

is an obvious overlap between the two. We define a *belief system* as a configuration of ideas and attitudes in which the elements are bound together by some form of constraint or functional interdependence.[3] In the static case, "constraint" may be taken to mean the success we would have in predicting, given initial knowledge that an individual holds a specified attitude, that he holds certain further ideas and attitudes. We depend implicitly upon such notions of constraint in judging, for example, that, if a person is opposed to the expansion of social security, he is probably a conservative and is probably opposed as well to any nationalization of private industries, federal aid to education, sharply progressive income taxation, and so forth. Most discussions of ideologies make relatively elaborate assumptions about such constraints. Constraint must be treated, of course, as a matter of degree, and this degree can be measured quite readily, at least as an average among individuals.[4]

In the dynamic case, "constraint" or "interdependence" refers to the probability that a change in the perceived status (truth, desirability, and so forth) of one idea-element would *psychologically* require, from the point of view of the actor, some compensating change(s) in the status of idea-elements elsewhere in the configuration. The most obvious form of such constraint (although in some ways the most trivial) is exemplified by a structure of propositions in logic, in which a change in the truth-value of one proposition necessitates changes in truth-value elsewhere within the set of related propositions. Psychologically, of course, there may be equally strong constraint among idea-elements that would not be apparent to logical analysis at all, as we shall see.

We might characterize either the idea-elements themselves or entire belief systems in terms of many other dimensions. Only two will interest us here. First, the idea-elements within a belief system vary in a property we shall call *centrality*, according to the role that they play in the belief system as a whole. That is, when new information changes the status of one idea-element in a belief system, by postulate some other change must occur as well. There are usually, however, several possible changes in status elsewhere in the system, any one of which would compensate for the initial change. Let us imagine, for example, that a person strongly favors a particular policy; is very favorably inclined toward a given political party; and recognizes with gratification that the party's stand and his own are congruent. (If he were unaware of the party's stand on the issue, these elements could not in any direct sense be constrained within the same belief system.) Let us further imagine that the party then changes its position to the opposing side of the issue. Once the information about the change reaching the actor has become so unequivocal that he can no longer deny that the change has occurred, he has several

---

[3] Garner uses the term "constraint" to mean "the amount of interrelatedness of structure of a system of variables" when measured by degree of uncertainty reduction. Wendell R. Garner, *Uncertainty and Structure as Psychological Concepts* (New York, 1962), pp. 142ff. We use the term a bit more broadly as relief from such polysyllables as "interrelatedness" and "interdependence."

[4] Measures of correlation and indices of the goodness of fit of a cumulative scale model to a body of data are measures of two types of constraint.

further choices. Two of the more important ones involve either a change in attitude toward the party or a change in position on the issue. In such an instance, the element more likely to change is defined as less central to the belief system than the element that, so to speak, has its stability ensured by the change in the first element.[5]

In informal discussions of belief systems, frequent assumptions are made about the relative centrality of various idea-elements. For example, idea-elements that are logically "ends" are supposed to be more central to the system than are "means." It is important to remain aware, however, that idea-elements can change their relative centrality in an individual's belief-system over time. Perhaps the most hackneyed illustration of this point is that of the miser, to whom money has become an end rather than a means.

Whole belief systems may also be compared in a rough way with respect to the *range* of objects that are referents for the ideas and attitudes in the system. Some belief systems, while they may be internally quite complex and may involve large numbers of cognitive elements, are rather narrow in range: Belief systems concerning "proper" baptism rituals or the effects of changes in weather on health may serve as cases in point. Such other belief systems as, for example, one that links control of the means of production with the social functions of religion and a doctrine of aesthetics all in one more or less neat package have extreme ranges.

By and large, our attention will be focused upon belief systems that have relatively wide ranges, and that allow some centrality to political objects, for they can be presumed to have some relevance to political behavior. This focus brings us close to what are broadly called *ideologies*, and we shall use the term for aesthetic relief where it seems most appropriate. The term originated in a narrower context, however, and is still often reserved for subsets of belief systems or parts of such systems that the user suspects are insincere; that he wishes to claim have certain functions for social groupings; or that have some special social source or some notable breadth of social diffusion.[6] Since we are concerned here about only one of these limitations—the question of social diffusion—and since we wish to deal with it by hypothesis rather than by definition, a narrow construction of the term is never intended.

II. SOURCES OF CONSTRAINT ON IDEA-ELEMENTS

It seems clear that, however logically coherent a belief system may seem to the holder, the sources of constraint are much less logical in the

---

[5] Definitions of belief systems frequently require that configurations of ideas be stable for individuals over long periods of time. The notion of centrality fulfills this requirement in a more flexible way. That is, once it is granted that changes in the perceived status of idea-elements are not frequent in any event and that, when change does occur, the central elements (particularly in large belief systems) are amply cushioned by more peripheral elements that can be adjusted, it follows that central elements are indeed likely to be highly stable.

[6] Minar, *loc. cit.*

classical sense than they are psychological—and less psychological than social. This point is of sufficient importance to dwell upon.

Logical Sources of Constraint

Within very narrow portions of belief systems, certain constraints may be purely logical. For example, government revenues, government expenditures, and budget balance are three idea-elements that suggest some purely logical constraints. One cannot believe that government expenditures should be increased, that government revenues should be decreased, and that a more favorable balance of the budget should be achieved all at the same time. Of course, the presence of such objectively logical constraints does not ensure that subjective constraints will be felt by the actor. They will be felt only if these idea-elements are brought together in the same belief system, and there is no guarantee that they need be. Indeed, it is true that, among adult American citizens, those who favor the expansion of government welfare services tend to be those who are more insistent upon reducing taxes "even if it means putting off some important things that need to be done."[7]

Where such purely logical constraint is concerned, McGuire has reported a fascinating experiment in which propositions from a few syllogisms of the Barbara type were scattered thinly across a long questionnaire applied to a student population. The fact that logical contingencies bound certain questions together was never brought to the attention of the students by the investigator. Yet one week later the questionnaire was applied again, and changes of response to the syllogistic propositions reduced significantly the measurable level of logical inconsistency. The conclusion was that merely "activating" these objectively related ideas in some rough temporal contiguity was sufficient to sensitize the holders to inconsistency and therefore to occasion readjustment of their beliefs.[8]

On a broader canvas, such findings suggest that simple "thinking about" a domain of idea-elements serves both to weld a broader range of such elements into a functioning belief system and to eliminate strictly logical inconsistencies defined from an objective point of view. Since there can be no doubt that educated elites in general, and political elites in particular, "think about" elements involved in political belief systems with a frequency far greater than that characteristic of mass publics, we could conservatively expect that strict logical inconsistencies (objectively definable) would be far more prevalent in a broad public.

Furthermore, if a legislator is noted for his insistence upon budget-balancing and tax-cutting, we can predict with a fair degree of success that he will also tend to oppose expansion of government welfare activi-

---

[7] See A. Campbell, P. E. Converse, W. Miller, and D. Stokes, *The American Voter* (New York, 1960), pp. 204–9.

[8] William J. McGuire, "A Syllogistic Analysis of Cognitive Relationships," in Milton J. Rosenberg, Carl I. Hovland, William J. McGuire, Robert P. Abelson, and Jack W. Brehm, *Attitude Organization and Change*, Yale Studies in Attitude and Communication, Vol. 3 (New Haven, 1960), pp. 65–111.

ties. If, however, a voter becomes numbered within his sphere of influence by virtue of having cast a vote for him directly out of enthusiasm for his tax-cutting policies, we cannot predict that the voter is opposed as well to expansion of government welfare services. Indeed, if an empirical prediction is possible, it may run in an opposing direction, although the level of constraint is so feeble that any comment is trivial. Yet we know that many historical observations rest directly upon the assumption that constraint among idea-elements visible at an elite level is mirrored by the same lines of constraint in the belief systems of their less visible "supporters." It is our argument that this assumption not only can be, but is very likely to be, fallacious.

Psychological Sources of Constraint

Whatever may be learned through the use of strict logic as a type of constraint, it seems obvious that few belief systems of any range at all depend for their constraint upon logic in this classical sense. Perhaps, with a great deal of labor, parts of a relatively tight belief system like that fashioned by Karl Marx could be made to resemble a structure of logical propositions. It goes without saying, however, that many sophisticated people have been swept away by the "iron logic" of Marxism without any such recasting. There is a broad gulf between such logic and the quasi-logic of cogent argument. And where the elements in the belief system of a population represent looser cultural accumulations, the question of logical consistency is even less appropriate. If one visits a Shaker community, for example, one finds a group of people with a clear-cut and distinctive belief system that requires among other things plain dress, centrality of religious concerns, celibacy for all members, communal assumptions about work and property, antagonism to political participation in the broader state, and a general aura of retirement from the secular world. The visitor whose sense of constraint has been drawn from belief configurations of such other retiring sects as the Amish is entirely surprised to discover that the Shakers have no abhorrence of technological progress but indeed greatly prize it. In their heyday, a remarkable amount of group energy appears to have been reserved for "research and development" of labor-saving devices, and among the inventions they produced was a prototype of the washing machine. Similar surprise has been registered at idea-elements brought together by such movements as Perónism and Italian Fascism by observers schooled to expect other combinations. Indeed, were one to survey a limited set of ideas on which many belief systems have registered opposite postures, it would be interesting to see how many permutations of positions have been held at one time or another by someone somewhere.

Such diversity is testimony to an absence of any strict logical constraints among such idea-elements, if any be needed. What is important is that the elites familiar with the total shapes of these belief systems have *experienced* them as logically constrained clusters of ideas, within which one part necessarily follows from another. Often such constraint is quasi-logically argued on the basis of an appeal to some superordinate value or posture toward man and society, involving premises about the nature of social justice, social change, "natural law," and the like. Thus a few crowning postures—like premises about survival of the fittest in the spirit of social Darwinism—serve as a sort of glue to bind together many more specific attitudes and beliefs, and these postures are of prime centrality in the belief system as a whole.

Social Sources of Constraint

The social sources of constraint are twofold and are familiar from an extensive literature in the past century. In the first place, were we to survey the combinations of idea-elements that have occurred historically (in the fashion suggested above), we should undoubtedly find that certain postures tend to co-occur and that this co-occurrence has obvious roots in the configuration of interests and information that characterize particular niches in the social structure. For example, if we were informed that dissension was rising within the Roman Catholic Church over innovations designed to bring the priest more intimately into the *milieu* of the modern worker, we could predict with a high degree of success that such a movement would have the bulk of its support among the *bas-clergé* and would encounter indifference or hostility at the higher status levels of the hierarchy.

Of course, such predictions are in no sense free from error, and surprises are numerous. The middle-class temperance movement in America, for example, which now seems "logically" allied with the small-town Republican right, had important alliances some eighty years ago with the urban social left, on grounds equally well argued from temperance doctrines.[9] Nonetheless, there are some highly reliable correlations of this sort, and these correlations can be linked with social structure in the most direct way. Developmentally, they have status similar to the classic example of the spurious correlation—two terms that are correlated because of a common link to some third and prior variable. In the case of the belief system, arguments are developed to lend some more positive rationale to the fact of constraint: The idea-elements go together not simply because both are in the interest of the person holding a particular status but for more abstract and quasi-logical reasons developed from a coherent world view as well. It is this type of constraint that is closest to the classic meaning of the term "ideology."

The second source of social constraint lies in two simple facts about the creation and diffusion of belief systems. First, the shaping of belief systems of any range into apparently logical wholes that are credible to large numbers of people is an act of creative synthesis characteristic of only a miniscule proportion of any population. Second, to the extent that multiple idea-elements of a belief system are socially diffused from such creative sources, they tend to be diffused in "packages," which consumers

---

9 Joseph R. Gusfield, "Status Conflicts and the Changing Ideologies of the American Temperance Movement," in Pittman and Snyder, eds., *Society, Culture and Drinking Patterns* (New York, 1962).

come to see as "natural" wholes, for they are presented in such terms ("If you believe this, then you will also believe that, for it follows in such-and-such ways"). Not that the more avid consumer never supplies personal innovations on the fringes—he is very likely to suppress an idea-element here, to elaborate one there, or even to demur at an occasional point. But any set of relatively intelligent consumers who are initially sympathetic to the crowning posture turns out to show more consensus on specific implications of the posture as a result of social diffusion of "what goes with what" than it would if each member were required to work out the implications individually without socially provided cues.

Such constraint through diffusion is important, for it implies a dependence upon the transmission of information. If information is not successfully transmitted, there will be little constraint save that arising from the first social source. Where transmission of information is at stake, it becomes important to distinguish between two classes of information. Simply put, these two levels are what goes with what and why. Such levels of information logically stand in a scalar relationship to one another, in the sense that one can hardly arrive at an understanding of why two ideas go together without being aware that they are supposed to go together. On the other hand, it is easy to know that two ideas go together without knowing why. For example, we can expect that a very large majority of the American public would somehow have absorbed the notion that "Communists are atheists." What is important is that this perceived correlation would for most people represent nothing more than a fact of existence, with the same status as the fact that oranges are orange and most apples are red. If we were to go and explore with these people their grasp of the "why" of the relationship, we would be surprised if more than a quarter of the population even attempted responses (setting aside such inevitable replies as "those Communists are for everything wicked"), and, among the responses received, we could be sure that the majority would be incoherent or irrelevant.

The first level of information, then, is simple and straightforward. The second involves much more complex and abstract information, very close to what Downs has called the "contextual knowledge" relevant to a body of information.[10] A well informed person who has received sufficient information about a system of beliefs to understand the "whys" involved in several of the constraints between idea-elements is in a better position to make good guesses about the nature of other constraints; he can deduce with fair success, for example, how a true believer will respond to certain situations. Our first interest in distinguishing between these types of information, however, flows from our interest in the relative success of information transmission. The general premise is that the first type of information will be diffused much more readily than the second because it is less complex.

It is well established that differences in information held in a cross-section population are simply staggering, running from vast treasuries of well organized information among elites interested in the particular sub-

---

[10] Anthony Downs, *An Economic Theory of Democracy* (New York, 1957), p. 79.

ject to fragments that could virtually be measured as a few "bits" in the technical sense. These differences are a static tribute to the extreme imperfections in the transmission of information "downward" through the system: Very little information "trickles down" very far. Of course, the ordering of individuals on this vertical information scale is largely due to differences in education, but it is strongly modified as well by different specialized interests and tastes that individuals have acquired over time (one for politics, another for religious activity, another for fishing, and so forth).

Consequences of Declining Information for Belief Systems

It is our primary thesis that, as one moves from elite sources of belief systems downward on such an information scale, several important things occur. First, the contextual grasp of "standard" political belief systems fades out very rapidly, almost before one has passed beyond the 10% of the American population that in the 1950s had completed standard college training.[11] Increasingly, simpler forms of information about "what goes with what" (or even information about the simple identity of objects) turn up missing. The net result, as one moves downward, is that constraint declines across the universe of idea-elements, and that the range of relevant belief systems becomes narrower and narrower. Instead of a few wide-ranging belief systems that organize large amounts of specific information, one would expect to find a proliferation of clusters of ideas among which little constraint is felt, even, quite often, in instances of sheer logical constraint.[12]

At the same time, moving from top to bottom of this information dimension, the character of the objects that are central in a belief system undergoes systematic change. These objects shift from the remote, generic, and abstract to the increasingly simple, concrete, or "close to home." Where potential political objects are concerned, this progression tends to be from abstract, "ideological" principles to the more obviously recognizable social groupings or charismatic leaders and finally to such objects of immediate experience as family, job, and immediate associates.

Most of these changes have been hinted at in one form or another in a variety of sources. For example, "limited horizons," "foreshortened time perspectives," and "concrete thinking" have been singled out as notable characteristics of the ideational world of the poorly educated. Such observations have impressed even those investigators who are dealing with

---

[11] It should be understood that our information dimension is not so perfectly correlated with formal education as this statement implies. Since educational strata have a more ready intuitive meaning, however, we shall use them occasionally as convenient ways of measuring off levels in the population. In such cases, the reader may keep in mind that there are always some people of lesser education but higher political involvement who are numbered in the stratum and some people with education befitting the stratum who are not numbered there because their interests lie elsewhere and their information about politics is less than could be expected.

[12] There is a difference, of course, between this statement and a suggestion that poorly educated people have no systems of belief about politics.

subject matter rather close to the individual's immediate world: his family budgeting, what he thinks of people more wealthy than he, his attitudes toward leisure time, work regulations, and the like. But most of the stuff of politics—particularly that played on a national or international stage—is, in the nature of things, remote and abstract. Where politics is concerned, therefore, such ideational changes begin to occur rapidly below the extremely thin stratum of the electorate that ever has occasion to make public pronouncements on political affairs. In other words, the changes in belief systems of which we speak are not a pathology limited to a thin and disoriented bottom layer of the *lumpenproletariat;* they are immediately relevant in understanding the bulk of mass political behavior.

It is this latter fact which seems to be consistently misunderstood by the sophisticated analysts who comment in one vein or another on the meaning of mass politics. There are some rather obvious "optical illusions" that are bound to operate here. A member of that tiny elite that comments publicly about political currents (probably some fraction of 1% of a population) spends most of his time in informal communication about politics with others in the same select group. He rarely encounters a conversation in which his assumptions of shared contextual grasp of political ideas are challenged. Intellectually, he has learned that the level of information in the mass public is low, but he may dismiss this knowledge as true of only 10 to 20% of the voters, who affect the course of mass political events in insignificant ways if at all.[13] It is largely from his informal communications that he learns how "public opinion" is changing and what the change signifies, and he generalizes facilely from these observations to the bulk of the broader public.[14]

III. ACTIVE USE OF IDEOLOGICAL DIMENSIONS OF JUDGMENT

Economy and constraint are companion concepts, for the more highly constrained a system of multiple elements, the more economically it may be described and understood. From the point of view of the actor, the idea organization that leads to constraint permits him to locate and make sense of a wider range of information from a particular domain than he would find possible without such organization. One judgmental dimen-

---

[13] This observation is valid despite the fact that surveys showing ignorance of crucial political facts are much more likely to run in a range from 40–80% "unaware." At the height of the 1958 Berlin crisis, 63% of the American public did not know that the city was encircled by hostile troops. A figure closer to 70% is a good estimate of the proportion of the public that does not know which party controls Congress.

[14] In this regard, it was enlightening to read the stunned reactions of the political columnist Joseph Alsop when, during the 1960 presidential primaries, he left the elite circuits of the East Coast and ventured from door to door talking politics with "normal" people in West Virginia. He was frank to admit that the change in perceived political worlds was far greater than anything he had ever anticipated, despite his prior recognition that there would be some difference.

sion or "yardstick" that has been highly serviceable for simplifying and organizing events in most Western politics for the past century has been the liberal-conservative continuum, on which parties, political leaders, legislation, court decisions, and a number of other primary objects of politics could be more—or less—adequately located.[15]

The efficiency of such a yardstick in the evaluation of events is quite obvious. Under certain appropriate circumstances, the single word "conservative" used to describe a piece of proposed legislation can convey a tremendous amount of more specific information about the bill—who probably proposed it and toward what ends, who is likely to resist it, its chances of passage, its long-term social consequences, and, most important, how the actor himself should expect to evaluate it if he were to expend further energy to look into its details. The circumstances under which such tremendous amounts of information are conveyed by the single word are, however, twofold. First, the actor must bring a good deal of meaning to the term, which is to say that he must understand the constraints surrounding it. The more impoverished his understanding of the term, the less information it conveys. In the limiting case—if he does not know at all what the term means—it conveys no information at all. Second, the system of beliefs and actors referred to must in fact be relatively constrained: To the degree that constraint is lacking, uncertainty is less reduced by the label, and less information is conveyed.

The psychological economies provided by such yardsticks for actors are paralleled by economies for analysts and theoreticians who wish to describe events in the system parsimoniously. Indeed, the search for adequate overarching dimensions on which large arrays of events may be simply understood is a critical part of synthetic description. Such syntheses are more or less satisfactory, once again, according to the degree of constraint operative among terms in the system being described.

The economies inherent in the liberal-conservative continuum were exploited in traditional fashion in the early 1950s to describe political changes in the United States as a swing toward conservatism or a "revolt

---

15 The phrase "less adequately" is used to show recognition of the frequent complaint that the liberal-conservative dimension has different meanings in different politics at different times. More importantly, it takes into account the fact that in most politics new issues are constantly arising that are difficult before the fact to relate to such a yardstick. Some of these intrinsically "orthogonal" issues may remain unrelated to the dimension, and, if they become of intense importance, they can split existing parties and redefine alignments. More typically, however, elites that are known on some other grounds to be "liberal" or "conservative" ferret out some limited aspect of an issue for which they can argue some liberal-conservative relevance and begin to drift to one of the alternative positions in disproportionate numbers. Then, either because of the aspect highlighted or because of simple pressures toward party competition, their adversaries drift toward the opposing position. Thus positions come to be perceived as "liberal" or "conservative," even though such alignments would have been scarcely predictable on logical grounds. After the fact, of course, the alignments come to seem "logical," by mechanisms discussed earlier in this paper. Controversy over British entry into the European Common Market is an excellent example of such a process. Currently the conservatives are officially pro-entry, and Labour leadership has finally declared against it, but the reverse of this alignment had frequently been predicted when the issue was embryonic.

of the moderates." At one level, this description was unquestionably apt. That is, a man whose belief system was relatively conservative (Dwight D. Eisenhower) had supplanted in the White House a man whose belief system was relatively liberal (Harry Truman). Furthermore, for a brief period at least, the composition of Congress was more heavily Republican as well, and this shift meant on balance a greater proportion of relatively conservative legislators. Since the administration and Congress were the elites responsible for the development and execution of policies, the flavor of governmental action did indeed take a turn in a conservative direction. These observations are proper description.

The causes underlying these changes in leadership, however, obviously lay with the mass public, which had changed its voting patterns sufficiently to bring the Republican elites into power. And this change in mass voting was frequently interpreted as a shift in public mood from liberal to conservative, a mass desire for a period of respite and consolidation after the rapid liberal innovations of the 1930s and 1940s. Such an account presumes, once again, that constraints visible at an elite level are mirrored in the mass public and that a person choosing to vote Republican after a decade or two of Democratic voting saw himself *in some sense or other* as giving up a more liberal choice in favor of a more conservative one.

On the basis of some familiarity with attitudinal materials drawn from cross-section samples of the electorate,[16] this assumption seems thoroughly implausible. It suggests in the first instance a neatness of organization in perceived political worlds, which, while accurate enough for elites, is a poor fit for the perceptions of the common public. Second, the yardstick that such an account takes for granted—the liberal-conservative continuum—is a rather elegant high-order abstraction, and such abstractions are not typical conceptual tools for the "man in the street." Fortunately, our interview protocols collected from this period permitted us to examine this hypothesis more closely, for they include not only "structured" attitude materials (which merely require the respondent to choose between prefabricated alternatives) but also lengthy "open-ended" materials which provided us with the respondent's current evaluations of the political scene in his own words. They therefore provide some indication of the evaluative dimensions that tend to be spontaneously applied to politics by such a national sample. We knew that respondents who were highly educated or strongly involved in politics would fall naturally into the verbal shorthand of "too conservative," "more radical," and the like in these evaluations. Our initial analytic question had to do with the prevalence of such usage.

It soon became apparent, however, that such respondents were in a very small minority, as their unusual education or involvement would suggest. At this point, we broadened the inquiry to an assessment of the

[16] All American data reported in this paper, unless otherwise noted, have been collected by the Survey Research Center of The University of Michigan under grants from the Carnegie Corporation, the Rockfeller Foundation, and the Social Science Research Council.

evaluative dimensions of policy significance (relating to political issues, rather than to the way a candidate dresses, smiles, or behaves in his private life) that seemed to be employed *in lieu of* such efficient yard-sticks as the liberal-conservative continuum. The interviews themselves suggested several strata of classification, which were hierarchically ordered as "levels of conceptualization" on the basis of *a priori* judgments about the breadth of contextual grasp of the political system that each seemed to represent.

In the first or top level were placed those respondents who did indeed rely in some active way on a relatively abstract and far-reaching conceptual dimension as a yardstick against which political objects and their shifting policy significance over time were evaluated. We did not require that this dimension be the liberal-conservative continuum itself, but it was almost the only dimension of the sort that occurred empirically. In a second stratum were placed those respondents who mentioned such a dimension in a peripheral way but did not appear to place much evaluative dependence upon it or who used such concepts in a fashion that raised doubt about the breadth of their understanding of the meaning of the term. The first stratum was loosely labeled "ideologue" and the second "near-ideologue."

In the third level were placed respondents who failed to rely upon any such over-arching dimensions yet evaluated parties and candidates in terms of their expected favorable or unfavorable treatment of different social groupings in the population. The Democratic Party might be disliked because "it's trying to help the Negroes too much," or the Republican Party might be endorsed because farm prices would be better with the Republicans in office. The more sophisticated of these group-interest responses reflected an awareness of conflict in interest between "big business" or "rich people," on the one hand, and "labor" or the "working man," on the other, and parties and candidates were located accordingly.

It is often asked why these latter respondents are not considered full "ideologues," for their perceptions run to the more tangible core of what has traditionally been viewed as ideological conflict. It is quite true that such a syndrome is closer to the upper levels of conceptualization than are any of the other types to be described. As we originally foresaw, however, there turn out to be rather marked differences, not only in social origin and flavor of judgmental processes but in overt political reactions as well, between people of this type and those in the upper levels. These people have a clear image of politics as an arena of group interests and, provided that they have been properly advised on where their own group interests lie, they are relatively likely to follow such advice. Unless an issue directly concerns their grouping in an obviously rewarding or punishing way, however, they lack the contextual grasp of the system to recognize how they should respond to it without being told by elites who hold their confidence. Furthermore, their interest in politics is not sufficiently strong that they pay much attention to such communications. If a communication gets through and they absorb it, they are most willing to behave "ideologically" in ways that will further the interests of their group. If they fail to receive such communication, which is most unusual, knowledge of their group memberships may be of little help in predicting their responses. This syndrome we came to call "ideology by proxy."

The difference between such narrow group interest and the broader perceptions of the ideologue may be clarified by an extreme case. One respondent whom we encountered classified himself as a strong Socialist. He was a Socialist because he knew that Socialists stood four-square for the working man against the rich, and he was a working man. When asked, however, whether or not the federal government in Washington "should leave things like electric power and housing for private business-men to handle," he felt strongly that private enterprise should have its way, and responses to other structured issue questions were simply un-correlated with standard socialist doctrine. It seems quite clear that, if our question had pointed out explicitly to this man that "good Socialists" would demand government intervention over private enterprise or that such a posture had traditionally been viewed as benefiting the working man, his answer would have been different. But since he had something less than a college education and was not generally interested enough in politics to struggle through such niceties, he simply lacked the contextual grasp of the political system or of his chosen "ideology" to know what the appropriate response might be. This case illustrates well what we mean by constraint between idea-elements and how such constraint depends upon a store of relevant information. For this man, "Socialists," "the work-ing man," "non-Socialists" and "the rich" with their appropriate valences formed a tightly constrained belief system. But, for lack of information, the belief system more or less began and ended there. It strikes us as valid to distinguish such a belief system from that of the doctrinaire socialist. We, as sophisticated observers, could only class this man as a full "ideologue" by assuming that he shares with us the complex under-girding of information that his concrete group perceptions call up in our own minds. In this instance, a very little probing makes clear that this assumption of shared information is once again false.

The fourth level was, to some degree, a residual category, intended to include those respondents who invoked some policy considerations in their evaluations yet employed none of the references meriting location in any of the first three levels. Two main modes of policy evaluation were characteristic of this level. The first we came to think of as a "nature of the times" response, since parties or candidates were praised or blamed primarily because of their temporal association in the past with broad societal states of war or peace, prosperity or depression. There was no hint in these responses that any groupings in the society suffered differen-tially from disaster or profited excessively in more pleasant times: These fortunes or misfortunes were those that one party or the other had de-cided (in some cases, apparently, on whim) to visit upon the nation as a whole. The second type included those respondents whose only approach to an issue reference involved some single narrow policy for which they felt personal gratitude or indignation toward a party or candidate (like social security or a conservation program). In these responses, there was no indication that the speakers saw programs as representative of the broader policy postures of the parties.

The fifth level included those respondents whose evaluations of the political scene had no shred of policy significance whatever. Some of these responses were from people who felt loyal to one party or the other but confessed that they had no idea what the party stood for. Others devoted their attention to personal qualities of the candidates, indicating disinterest in parties more generally. Still others confessed that they paid too little attention to either the parties or the current candidates to be able to say anything about them.[17]

The ranking of the levels performed on *a priori* grounds was corroborated by further analyses, which demonstrated that independent measures of political information, education, and political involvement all showed sharp and monotonic declines as one passed downward through the levels in the order suggested. Furthermore, these correlations were strong enough so that each maintained some residual life when the other two items were controlled, despite the strong underlying relationship between education, information, and involvement.

The distribution of the American electorate within these levels of conceptualization is summarized in Table 1. The array is instructive as

TABLE 1

Distribution of a Total Cross-Section Sample of the American Electorate and of 1956 Voters, by Levels of Conceptualization

	Proportion of Total Sample	Proportion of Voters
I. Ideologues	2½%	3½%
II. Near ideologues	9	12
III. Group interest	42	45
IV. Nature of the times	24	22
V. No issue content	22½	17½
	100%	100%

a portrait of a mass electorate, to be laid against the common elite assumption that all or a significant majority of the public conceptualizes the main lines of politics after the manner of the most highly educated. Where the specific hypothesis of the "revolt of the moderates" in the early 1950s is concerned, the distribution does not seem on the face of it to lend much support to the key assumption. This disconfirmation may be examined further, however.

Since the resurgence of the Republicans in the Eisenhower period depended primarily upon crossing of party lines by people who normally considered themselves Democrats, we were able to isolate these people to see from what levels of conceptualization they had been recruited. We found that such key defections had occurred among Democrats in the

---

[17] This account of the "levels of conceptualization" is highly abbreviated. For a much more detailed discussion and rationale, along with numerous illustrations drawn at random from interviews in each stratum, see Campbell et al., *op. cit.*, Chapter 10.

two bottom levels at a rate very significantly greater than the comparable rate in the group-interest or more ideological levels. In other words, the stirrings in the mass electorate that had led to a change in administration and in "ruling ideology" were primarily the handiwork of the very people for whom assumptions of any liberal-conservative dimensions of judgment were most farfetched.

Furthermore, within those strata where the characteristics of conceptualization even permitted the hypothesis to be evaluated in its own terms, it was directly disproved. For example, the more sophisticated of the group-interest Democrats were quite aware that Eisenhower would be a more pro-business president than Stevenson. Those of this group who did defect to Eisenhower did not, however, do so because they were tired of a labor-oriented administration and wanted a business-oriented one for a change. Quite to the contrary, in the degree that they defected they did so *in spite of* rather than *because of* such quasi-ideological perceptions. That is, their attitudes toward the respective interests of these groups remained essentially constant, and they expected misgivings about an Eisenhower vote on precisely these grounds. But any such worries were, under the circumstances, outweighed by admiration for Eisenhower's war record, his honesty, his good family life, and (in 1952) his potential for resolving the nagging problem of the Korean War. Among respondents at higher levels (ideologues and near-ideologues), there was comparable attraction to Eisenhower at a personal level, but these people seemed more careful to hew to ideological considerations, and rates of Democratic defection in these levels were lower still. In short, then, the supposition of changing ideological moods in the mass public as a means of understanding the exchange of partisan elites in 1952 seems to have had little relevance to what was actually going on at the mass level. And once again, the sources of the optical illusion are self-evident. While it may be taken for granted among well educated and politically involved people that a shift from a Democratic preference to a Republican one probably represents a change in option from liberal to conservative, the assumption cannot be extended very far into the electorate as a whole.

IV. RECOGNITION OF IDEOLOGICAL DIMENSIONS OF JUDGMENT

Dimensions like the liberal-conservative continuum, as we have observed, are extremely efficient frames for the organization of many political observations. Furthermore, they are used a great deal in the more ambitious treatments of politics in the mass media, so that a person with a limited understanding of their meaning must find such discussions more obscure than enlightening. Aside from active cognitive use, therefore, the simple status of public comprehension of these terms is a matter of some interest.

It is a commonplace in psychology that recognition, recall, and habitual use of cognized objects or concepts are rather different. We are capable of *recognizing* many more objects (or concepts) if they are directly presented to us than we could readily *recall* on the basis of more indirect cues; and we are capable of recalling on the basis of such hints many more objects (or concepts) than might be *active* or *salient* for us in a given context without special prompting. In coding the levels of conceptualization from free-answer material, our interest had been entirely focused upon concepts with the last status (activation or salience). It had been our assumption that such activation would be apparent in the responses of any person with a belief system in which these organizing dimensions had high centrality. Nevertheless, we could be sure at the same time that if we presented the terms "liberal" and "conservative" directly to our respondents, a much larger number would recognize them and be able to attribute to them some kind of meaning. We are interested both in the proportions of a normal sample who would show some recognition and also in the meaning that might be supplied for the terms.

In a 1960 reinterview of the original sample whose 1956 responses had been assigned to our levels of conceptualization, we therefore asked in the context of the differences in "what the parties stand for," "Would you say that either one of the parties is more *conservative* or more *liberal* than the other?" (It was the first time we had ever introduced these terms in our interviewing of this sample.) If the answer was affirmative, we asked which party seemed the more conservative and then, "What do you have in mind when you say that the Republicans (Democrats) are more conservative than the Democrats (Republicans)?" When the respondent said that he did not see differences of this kind between the two parties, we were anxious to distinguish between those who were actually cynical about meaningful party differences and those who took this route to avoid admitting that they did not know what the terms signified. We therefore went on to ask this group, "Do you think that people generally consider the Democrats or the Republicans more conservative, or wouldn't you want to guess about that?" At this point, we were willing to assume that if a person had no idea of the rather standard assumptions, he probably had no idea of what the terms meant; and indeed, those who did try to guess which party other people thought more conservative made a very poor showing when we went on to ask them (paralleling our "meaning" question for the first group), "What do people have in mind when they say that the Republicans (Democrats) are more conservative than the Democrats (Republicans)?" In responding to the "meaning" questions, both groups were urged to answer as fully and clearly as possible, and their comments were transcribed.

The responses were classified in a code inspired by the original work on levels of conceptualization, although it was considerably more detailed. Within this code, top priority was given to explanations that called upon broad philosophical differences. These explanations included mentions of such things as *posture toward change* (acceptance of or resistance to new ideas, speed or caution in responding to new problems, protection of or challenge to the *status quo*, aggressive posture toward problems *vs.* a *laissez-faire* approach, orientation toward the future or lack of it, and so forth); *posture toward the welfare state, socialism, free enterprise, or capitalism* (including mention of differential sensitivity to social problems, approaches to social-welfare programs, governmental interference with private enterprise, and so forth); *posture toward the expanding power of federal government* (issues of centralization, states' rights, local autonomy, and paternalism); and *relationship of the government to the individual* (questions of individual dignity, initiative, needs, rights, and so forth). While any mention of comparably broad philosophical differences associated with the liberal-conservative distinction was categorized in this top level, these four were the most frequent types of reference, as they had been for the full "ideologues" in the earlier open-ended materials.

Then, in turn, references to differences in attitude toward various interest groupings in the population; toward spending or saving and fiscal policy more generally, as well as to economic prosperity; toward various highly specific issues like unemployment compensation, highway-building, and tariffs; and toward postures in the sphere of foreign policy were arrayed in a descending order of priority, much as they had been for the classifications into levels of conceptualization. Since respondents had been given the opportunity to mention as many conservative-liberal distinctions as they wished, coding priority was given to the more "elevated" responses, and all the data that we shall subsequently cite rests on the "best answer" given by each respondent.[18]

The simple distributional results were as follows. Roughly three respondents in eight (37%) could supply no meaning for the liberal-conservative distinction, including 8% who attempted to say which party was the more conservative but who gave up on the part of the sequence dealing with meaning. (The weakest 29% will, in later tables, form our bottom stratum "V," while the 8% compose stratum "IV.") Between those who could supply no meaning for the terms and those who clearly did, there was naturally an intermediate group that answered all the questions but showed varying degrees of uncertainty or confusion. The situation required that one of two polar labels (conservative or liberal) be properly associated with one of two polar clusters of connotations and with one of two parties. Once the respondent had decided to explain what "more conservative" or "more liberal" signified, there were four possible patterns by which the other two dichotomies might be associated with the first. Of course, all four were represented in at least some interviews. For example, a respondent might indicate that the Democrats were the more conservative because they stood up for the working man against big business. In such a case, there seemed to be a simple error consisting in reversal of the ideological labels. Or a respondent might

---

[18] Some modest internal support for the validity of the distinction between those who spoke in terms of broad philosophy and those who offered narrower explanations may be seen in the fact that only 5% of the former category had previously judged the Democrats to be more conservative than the Republicans. Among those giving less elevated "best answers," 14% deemed the Democrats the more conservative party. And, to give some sense of the "continental shelf" being explored here, among those who had responded that a certain party was more conservative than the other but who subsequently confessed that they did not know what the distinction implied, 35% had chosen the Democrats as the more conservative, a figure that is beginning to approach the 50–50 assignment of sheer guesswork.

say that the Republicans were more liberal because they were pushing new and progressive social legislation. Here the match between label and meaning seems proper, but the party perception is, by normal standards, erroneous.

The distribution of these error types within the portion of the sample that attempted to give "meaning" answers (slightly more than 60%) is shown in Table 2. The 83% entered for the "proper" patterns is artifi-

TABLE 2

Association of Ideological Label with Party and Meaning

Ideological Label	Meaning	Party	Proportion of Those Giving Some Answer
Conservative	Conservative	Republican	
Liberal	Liberal	Democrat	
Conservative	Liberal	Republican	83%
Liberal	Conservative	Democrat	5
Conservative	Conservative	Democrat*	
Liberal	Liberal	Republican	6
Conservative	Liberal	Democrat	
Liberal	Conservative	Republican	6
			100%

* While this pattern may appear entirely legitimate for the southern respondent reacting to the southern wing of the Democratic Party rather than to the national party, it showed almost no tendency to occur with greater frequency in the South than elsewhere (and errors as well as lacunae occurred more frequently in general in the less well educated South). Data from a very different context indicate that southerners who discriminate between the southern wing and the national Democratic Party take the national party as the assumed object in our interviews, if the precise object is not specified.

cially increased to an unknown degree by the inclusion of all respondents whose connotations for liberalism-conservatism were sufficiently impoverished so that little judgment could be made about whether or not they were making proper associations (for example, those respondents whose best explanations of the distinction involved orientations toward defense spending). The error types thus represent only those that could be unequivocally considered "errors." While Table 2 does not in itself constitute proof that the error types resulted from pure guesswork, the configuration does resemble the probable results if 20–25% of the respondents had been making random guesses about how the two labels, the two polar meanings, and the two parties should be sorted out. People making these confused responses might or might not *feel* confused in making their assessments. Even if they knew that they were confused, it is unlikely that they would be less confused in encountering such terms in reading or listening to political communications, which is the important point where transmission of information is concerned. If, on the other hand, they were wrong without realizing it, then they would be capable of hearing that Senator Goldwater, for example, was an extreme conservative and believing that it meant that he was for increased federal spending (or whatever other more specific meaning they might bring to the term). In either case, it seems reasonable to distinguish between the people who belong in this confused group at the border of understanding and those who demonstrate greater clarity about the terms. And after the confused group is set aside (stratum III in Tables 3–4), we are left with a proportion of the sample that is slightly more than 50%. This figure can be taken as a maximum estimate of reasonable recognition.

We say "maximum" because, once within this "sophisticated" half of the electorate, it is reasonable to consider the quality of the meanings put forth to explain the liberal-conservative distinction. These meanings varied greatly in adequacy, from those "best answers" that did indeed qualify for coding under the "broad philosophy" heading (the most accurate responses, as defined above) to those that explained the distinction in narrow or nearly irrelevant terms (like Prohibition or foreign-policy measures). In all, 17% of the total sample gave "best answers" that we considered to qualify as "broad philosophy."[19] This group was defined as stratum I, and the remainder, who gave narrower definitions, became stratum II.

Perhaps the most striking aspect of the liberal-conservative definitions supplied was the extreme frequency of those hinging on a simple "spend-save" dimension *vis-à-vis* government finances. Very close to a majority of all "best" responses (and two-thirds to three-quarters of all such responses in stratum II) indicated in essence that the Democratic Party was liberal because it spent public money freely and that the Republican Party was more conservative because it stood for economy in government or pinched pennies. In our earlier coding of the levels of conceptualization, we had already noted that this simple dimension seemed often to be what was at stake when "ideological" terms were used. Frequently there was reason to believe that the term "conservative" drew its primary meaning from the cognate "conservation." In one rather clear example, a respondent indicated that he considered the Republicans to be more conservative in the sense that they were ". . . more saving with money and our *natural resources*. Less apt to slap on a tax for some non-essential. More conservative in promises that can't be kept." (Italics ours.)

Of course, the question of the proportion of national wealth that is to be spent privately or channeled through government for public spending has been one of the key disputes between conservatives and liberal "ideologies" for several decades. From this point of view, the great multitude of "spend-save" references can be considered essentially as accurate matching of terms. On the other hand, it goes without saying that the conservative-liberal dialogue does not exhaust itself on this narrow question alone, and our view of these responses as an understanding of the differences depends in no small measure on whether the individual sees this point as a self-contained distinction or understands the link between it and a number of other broad questions. On rare occasions, one encounters a respondent for whom the "spend-save" dimension is intimately bound up with other problem areas. For example, one respondent feels

---

[19] In all candor, it should probably be mentioned that a teacher grading papers would be unlikely to give passing marks to more than 20% of the attempted definitions (or to 10% of the total sample). We made an effort, however, to be as generous as possible in our assignments.

that the Republicans are more conservative because " . . . they are too interested in getting the budget balanced—they should spend more to get more jobs for our people." More frequently when further links are suggested, they are connected with policy but go no further:

> [Republicans more conservative because] "Well, they don't spend as much money." [What do you have in mind?] "Well, a lot of them holler when they try to establish a higher interest rate but that's to get back a little when they do loan out and make it so people are not so free with it."

Generally, however, the belief system involved when "liberal-conservative" is equated with "spend-save" seems to be an entirely narrow one. There follow a number of examples of comments, which taken with the preceding citations, form a random drawing from the large group of "spend-save" comments:

> [Democrats more conservative because] "they will do more for the people at home before they go out to help foreign countries. They are truthful and not liars."
>
> [Republicans more liberal judging] "by the money they have spent in this last administration. They spent more than ever before in a peace time. And got less for it as far as I can see."
>
> [Republicans more conservative because] "Well, they vote against the wild spending spree the Democrats get on."
>
> [Republicans more conservative because] "they pay as you go."
>
> [Democrats more conservative because] "I don't believe the Democrats will spend as much money as the Republicans."
>
> [Republicans more conservative because] "it seems as if the Republicans try to hold down the spending of government money." [Do you remember how?] "Yes," [by having] "no wars."

From this representation of the "spend-save" references, the reader may see quite clearly why we consider them to be rather "narrow" readings of the liberal-conservative distinction as applied to the current partisan scene. In short, our portrait of the population, where recognition of a key ideological dimension is concerned, suggests that about 17% of the public (stratum I) have an understanding of the distinction that captures much of its breadth. About 37% (strata IV and V) are entirely vague as to its meaning. For the 46% between, there are two strata, one of which demonstrates considerable uncertainty and guesswork in assigning meaning to the terms (stratum III) and the other of which has the terms rather well under control but appears to have a fairly limited set of connotations for them (stratum II). The great majority of the latter groups equate liberalism-conservatism rather directly with a "spend-save" dimension. In such cases, when the sensed connotations are limited, it is not surprising that there is little active use of the continuum as an organizing dimension. Why should one bother to say that a party is conservative if one can convey the same information by saying that it is against spending?

Since the 1960 materials on liberal-conservative meanings were drawn from the same sample as the coding of the active use of such frames of reference in 1956, it is possible to consider how well the two codings match. For a variety of reasons, we would not expect a perfect fit, even aside from coding error. The earlier coding had not been limited to the liberal-conservative dimension, and, although empirical instances were rare, a person could qualify as an "ideologue" if he assessed politics with the aid of some other highly abstract organizing dimension. Similarly, among those who did employ the liberal-conservative distinction, there were no requirements that the terms be defined. It was necessary therefore to depend upon appearances, and the classification was intentionally lenient. Furthermore, since a larger portion of the population would show recognition than showed active use, we could expect substantial numbers of people in the lower levels of conceptualization to show reasonable recognition of the terms. At any rate, we assumed that the two measures would show a high correlation, as they in fact did (Table 3).

TABLE 3

Levels of Conceptualization (1956) by Recognition and Understanding of Terms
"Conservatism" and "Liberalism" (1960)

	Stratum	Ideologue	Near Ideologue	Group Interest	Nature of the Times	No Issue Content
			Levels of Conceptualization			
Recognition and understanding*	I ...	51%	29%	13%	16%	10%
	II	43	46	42	40	22
	III	2	10	14	7	7
	IV	2	5	6	7	12
	V	2	10	25	30	49
Number of cases		100% (45)	100% (122)	100% (580)	100% (288)	100% (290)

* The definitions of the strata are: I. recognition and proper matching of label, meaning, and party and a broad understanding of the terms "conservative" and "liberal"; II. recognition and proper matching but a narrow definition of terms (like "spend-save"); III. recognition but some error in matching; IV. recognition and an attempt at matching but inability to give any meaning for terms; V. no apparent recognition of terms (does not know if parties differ in liberal-conservative terms and does not know if anybody else sees them as differing).

Of course, very strong differences in education underlie the data shown in Table 3. The 2% of the sample that occupy the upper left-hand cell have a mean education close to seven years greater than that of the 11% that occupy the lower right-hand cell. Sixty-two per cent of this lower cell have had less formal education than the least educated person in the upper corner. The differences in education show a fairly regular progression across the intervening surface of the table (see Table 4). Although women have a higher mean education than men, there is some sex bias to the table, for women are disproportionately represented in the lower right-hand quadrant of the table. Furthermore, although age is negatively correlated with education, there is also rather clear evidence that the sort of political sophistication represented by the measures can accumulate with age. Undoubtedly even sporadic observation of politics over long enough periods of time serves to nurture some broader view of

TABLE 4

Levels of Conceptualization (1956) and Term Recognition (1960)
by Mean Years of Formal Education

| | Stratum | Levels of Conceptualization | | | | |
		Ideologue	Near Ideologue	Group Interest	Nature of the Times	No Issue Content
Recognition and understanding‡	I	14.9†	14.2	12.3	11.1	11.9
	II	13.9	11.9	10.7	10.7	11.5
	III	°	11.1	10.6	9.8	9.6
	IV	°	°	10.4	9.9	10.3
	V	°	10.0	9.5	8.5	8.2

° Inadequate number of cases.

† The cell entry is mean number of years of formal education. Partial college was arbitrarily assumed to represent an average of 14 years, and work toward an advanced degree an average of 18 years.

‡ See Table 3 for definitions of the five strata.

basic liberal-conservative differences, although of course the same sophistication is achieved much more rapidly and in a more striking way by those who progress greater distances through the educational system.

It is not surprising that political sophistication goes hand in hand with political activism at the "grass roots" (Table 5). The relationship is certainly not perfect: About 20% of those in the most sophisticated cell engaged in none of the forms of participation beyond voting that were surveyed (see †footnote, Table 5) in either the 1956 or 1960 election campaigns, and there is more "stray" participation than has sometimes been suspected among those who express little interest in politics or

TABLE 5

Amount of 1956–1960 Political Activity by Level of Conceptualization (1956)
and Term Recognition (1960)

| | Stratum | Levels of Conceptualization | | | | |
		Ideologue	Near Ideologue	Group Interest	Nature of the Times	No Issue Content
Recognition and understanding‡	I	3.8†	2.6	2.5	2.6	2.2
	II	3.4	3.0	1.7	1.8	1.3
	III	°	2.5	2.2	1.5	1.1
	IV	°	°	1.9	1.5	.8
	V	°	1.7	1.0	.8	.4

° Inadequate number of cases.

† The cell entry represents a mean of the number of acts of political participation exclusive of voting reported for the two presidential campaigns of 1956 and 1960. For 1956, a point was awarded to each respondent for party membership, campaign contributions, attendance at political rallies, other party work, attempts to convince others through informal communication, and displaying campaign buttons or stickers. In 1960, essentially the same scoring applied, except that on two items more differentiated information was available. A point was awarded for attending one or two political rallies, two points for three to six rallies, and three points for seven or more. Similarly, a second point was awarded for people who reported having attempted in 1960 to convince others in more than one class (friends, family, or coworkers). A total score of 15 was possible, although empirically the highest score was 14. Only about 1% of the sample had scores greater than 9.

‡ See Table 3 for definitions of the five strata.

comprehension of party differences yet who may, for example, happen on a political rally. Furthermore, even the active hard core is not necessarily sophisticated in this sense: Two of the thirteen most active people fall in the lower right half of the table, and their activism is probably to be understood more in terms of mundane social gratifications than through any concern over the policy competition of politics.

Nonetheless, persistent and varied participation is most heavily concentrated among the most sophisticated people. This fact is important, for much of what is perceived as "public reaction" to political events depends upon public visibility, and visibility depends largely upon forms of political participation beyond the vote itself. Anyone familiar with practical politics has encountered the concern of the local politician that ideas communicated in political campaigns be kept simple and concrete. He knows his audience and is constantly fighting the battle against the overestimation of sophistication to which the purveyor of political ideas inevitably falls prey. Yet, even the grass-roots audience that forms a reference point for the local politician is, we suspect, a highly self-selected one and quite sophisticated relative to the electorate as a whole.

Since we have 1960 information on the number of political rallies attended by each of our respondents, we may simulate the "sophistication composition" of the typical political gathering. "Typical" is loosely used here, for real gatherings are various in character: A dinner for the party faithful at $15 a plate obviously attracts a different audience from the one that comes to the parade and street rally. Nonetheless, the contrast between the electorate and an hypothetical average rally is instructive (Table 6). People located in the three upper left-hand corner cells of the

TABLE 6
The Sophistication Composition of a "Typical" Political Rally, Compared to the Composition of the Total Electorate*

	A Rally					The Electorate				
	High				Low	High				Low
High	5%	5%	11%	11%	2%	2%	3%	6%	3%	2%
	6	8	11	11	4	1	4	18	9	5
	0	5	9	0	†	†	1	6	1	2
	†	0	1	†	†	†	*	3	2	3
Low	†	2	7	1	0	†	1	11	7	11

* Both five-by-five matrices are those employed in Tables 3, 4, and 5. Aside from rounding error, the proportions entered in each matrix total 100%. The table should be read by observing differences between proportions in the same regions of the two tables. For example, the three least sophisticated cells in the lower right-hand corner constitute 21% of the electorate and 1% of a typical rally audience.
† Less than half of 1%.

matrix (6% of the electorate) form more than 15% of the composition of such rallies, and probably, in terms of further rally participation (vocal and otherwise), seem to form a still higher proportion. Yet on election day their vote (even with a 100% turnout) is numerically outweighed by those votes mustered by people in the single cell at the opposite corner of the table who do not attend at all.

One of the most intriguing findings on the surface of the matrix is that strength of party loyalty falls to one of its weakest points in the upper left-hand corner cell of the matrix. In other words, among the most highly sophisticated, those who consider themselves "independents" outnumber those who consider themselves "strong" partisans, despite the fact that the most vigorous political activity, much of it partisan, is carried on by people falling in this cell. If one moves diagonally toward the center of the matrix, this balance is immediately redressed and redressed very sharply, with strong partisans far outnumbering independents. In general, there is a slight tendency (the most sophisticated cell excepted) for strength of party loyalty to decline as one moves diagonally across the table, and the most "independent" cell is that in the lower right-hand corner.[20]

This irregularity has two implications. First, we take it to be one small and special case of our earlier hypothesis that group-objects (here, the party as group) are likely to have less centrality in the belief system of the most sophisticated and that the centrality of groups as referents increases "lower down" in the sophistication ordering. We shall see more handsome evidence of the same phenomenon later. Second, we see in this reversal at least a partial explanation for the persistence of the old assumption that the "independent voter" is relatively informed and involved. The early cross-section studies by Lazarsfeld and his colleagues turned up evidence to reverse this equation, suggesting that the "independent voter" tends instead to be relatively uninformed and uninvolved. Other studies have added massively to this evidence. Indeed, in many situations, the evidence seems so strong that it is hard to imagine how any opposing perceptions could have developed. The perception is somewhat easier to understand, however, if one can assume that the discernment of the informed observer takes in only 5, 10, or 15% of the most sophisticated people in the public as constituting "the public." This "visible" or "operative" public is largely made up of people from the upper left-hand corner of our preceding tables. The illusion that such people are the full public is one that the democratic sample survey, for better or for worse, has destroyed.

V. CONSTRAINTS AMONG IDEA-ELEMENTS

In our estimation, the use of such basic dimensions of judgment as the liberal-conservative continuum betokens a contexual grasp of politics that permits a wide range of more specific idea-elements to be organized

---

20 This cell is laden, of course, with people who are apathetic and apolitical, although more than half of them vote in major elections. Flanigan, working with the total sample, set aside those who never vote as politically inconsequential and then set about comparing the remainder of self-styled independents with strong partisans. Some of the customary findings relating political independence with low involvement and low information then became blurred or in some cases reversed themselves altogether. Our highly sophisticated independents contribute to this phenomenon. See William H. Flanigan, "Partisanship and Campaign Participation" (Unpublished doctoral dissertation, Yale University, 1961).

into more tightly constrained wholes. We feel, furthermore, that there are many crucial consequences of such organization: With it, for example, new political events have more meaning, retention of political information from the past is far more adequate, and political behavior increasingly approximates that of sophisticated "rational" models, which assume relatively full information.

It is often argued, however, that abstract dimensions like the liberal-conservative continuum are superficial if not meaningless indicators: All that they show is that poorly educated people are inarticulate and have difficulty expressing verbally the more abstract lines along which their specific political beliefs are organized. To expect these people to be able to express what they know and feel, the critic goes on, is comparable to the fallacy of assuming that people can say in an accurate way why they behave as they do. When it comes down to specific attitudes and behaviors, the organization is there nonetheless, and it is this organization that matters, not the capacity for discourse in sophisticated language.

If it were true that such organization does exist for most people, apart from their capacities to be articulate about it, we would agree out of

TABLE 7

Constraint between Specific Issue Beliefs for an Elite Sample and a
Cross-Section Sample, 1958*

	Domestic					Foreign		
	Em-ploy-ment	Edu-cation	Hous-ing	F.E.P.C.	Eco-nomic	Mili-tary†	Isola-tionism	Party Pref-erence
Congressional candidates								
Employment	–	.62	.59	.35	.26	.06	.17	.68
Aid to education ..		–	.61	.53	.50	.06	.35	.55
Federal housing ..			–	.47	.41	–.03	.30	.68
F.E.P.C.				–	.47	.11	.23	.34
Economic aid					–	.19	.59	.25
Military aid						–	.32	–.18
Isolationism							–	.05
Party preference ..								–
Cross-section sample								
Employment	–	.45	.08	.34	–.04	.10	–.22	.20
Aid to education ..		–	.12	.29	.06	.14	–.17	.16
Federal housing ..			–	.08	–.06	.02	.07	.18
F.E.P.C.				–	.24	.13	.01	–.04
Economic aid					–	.16	.33	–.07
Soldiers abroad† ..						–	.21	.12
Isolationism							–	–.03
Party preference ..								–

* Entries are tau-gamma coefficients, a statistic proposed by Leo A. Goodman and William H. Kruskal in "Measures of Association for Cross Classification," *Journal of the American Statistical Association*, 49 (Dec. 1954), No. 268, 749. The coefficient was chosen because of its sensitivity to constraint of the scalar as well as the correlational type.

† For this category, the cross-section sample was asked a question about keeping American soldier abroad, rather than about military aid in general.

hand that the question of articulation is quite trivial. As a cold empirical matter, however, this claim does not seem to be valid. Indeed, it is for this reason that we have cast the argument in terms of constraint, for constraint and organization are very nearly the same thing. Therefore when we hypothesize that constraint among political idea-elements begins to lose its range very rapidly once we move from the most sophisticated few toward the "grass roots," we are contending that the organization of more specific attitudes into wide-ranging belief systems is absent as well.

Table 7 gives us an opportunity to see the differences in levels of constraint among beliefs on a range of specific issues in an elite population and in a mass population. The elite population happens to be candidates for the United States Congress in the off-year elections of 1958, and the cross-section sample represents the national electorate in the same year. The assortment of issues represented is simply a purposive sampling of some of the more salient political controversies at the time of the study, covering both domestic and foreign policy. The questions posed to the two samples were quite comparable, apart from adjustments necessary in view of the backgrounds of the two populations involved.[21]

For our purposes, however, the specific elite sampled and the specific beliefs tested are rather beside the point. We would expect the same

---

[21] As a general rule, questions broad enough for the mass public to understand tend to be too simple for highly sophisticated people to feel comfortable answering without elaborate qualification. The pairings of questions, with those for the mass public given first, are as follows:

Employment. "The government in Washington ought to see to it that everybody who wants to work can find a job." "Do you think the federal government ought to sponsor programs such as large public works in order to maintain full employment, or do you think that problems of economic readjustment ought to be left more to private industry or state and local government?"

Aid to Education. "If cities and towns around the country need help to build more schools, the government in Washington ought to give them the money they need." "Do you think the government should provide grants to the states for the construction and operation of public schools, or do you think the support of public education should be left entirely to the state and local government?"

Federal Housing. "The government should leave things like electric power and housing for private businessmen to handle." "Do you approve the use of federal funds for public housing, or do you generally feel that housing can be taken care of better by private effort?"

F.E.P.C. "If Negroes are not getting fair treatment in jobs and housing, the government should see to it that they do." "Do you think the federal government should establish a fair employment practices commission to prevent discrimination in employment?"

Economic Aid. "The United States should give economic help to the poorer countries of the world even if those countries can't pay for it." "First, on the foreign economic aid program, would you generally favor expanding the program, reducing it, or maintaining it about the way it is?"

Military Aid. "The United States should keep soldiers overseas where they can help countries that are against Communism." "How about the foreign military aid program? Should this be expanded, reduced, or maintained about as it is?"

Isolationism. "This country would be better off if we just stayed home and did not concern ourselves with problems in other parts of the world." "Speaking very generally, do you think that in the years ahead the United States should maintain or reduce its commitments around the world?"

general contrast to appear if the elite had been a set of newspaper editors, political writers, or any other group that takes an interest in politics. Similarly, we would expect the same results from any other broad sampling of political issues or, for that matter, any sampling of beliefs from other domains: A set of questions on matters of religious controversy should show the same pattern between an elite population like the clergy and the church members who form their mass "public." What is generically important in comparing the two types of population is the difference in levels of constraint among belief-elements.

Where constraint is concerned, the absolute value of the coefficients in Table 7 (rather than their algebraic value) is the significant datum. The first thing the table conveys is the fact that, for both populations, there is some falling off of constraint *between* the domains of domestic and foreign policy, relative to the high level of constraint *within* each domain. This result is to be expected: Such lowered values signify boundaries between belief systems that are relatively independent. If we take averages of appropriate sets of coefficients entered in Table 7 however, we see that the strongest constraint *within* a domain for the mass public is less than that *between* domestic and foreign domains for the elite sample. Furthermore, for the public, in sharp contrast to the elite, party preference seems by and large to be set off in a belief system of its own, relatively unconnected to issue positions (Table 8).[22]

TABLE 8
Summary of Differences in Level of Constraint within and between
Domains, Public and Elite (based on Table 7)

| | *Average Coefficients* | | | |
	Within Domestic Issues	*Between Domestic and Foreign*	*Within Foreign Issues*	*Between Issues and Party*
Elite	.53	.25	.37	.38
Mass	.23	.11	.23	.11

It should be remembered throughout, of course, that the *mass* sample of Tables 7 and 8 does not exclude college-educated people, ideologues, or the politically sophisticated. These people, with their higher levels of constraint, are represented in appropriate numbers, and certainly contribute to such vestige of organization as the mass matrix evinces. But they are grossly outnumbered, as they are in the active electorate. The

---

[22] We are aware that drawing an average of these coefficients has little interpretation from a statistical point of view. The averages are presented merely as a crude way of capturing the flavor of the larger table in summary form. More generally, it could be argued that the coefficients might be squared in any event, an operation that would do no more than heighten the intuitive sense of contrast between the two publics. In this format, for example, the elite-mass difference in the domestic-issue column of Table 8 would shift from .53 *vs.* .23 to .28 *vs.* .05. Similarly, that in the party column would become .15 *vs.* .01.

general point is that the matrix of correlations for the elite sample is of the sort that would be appropriate for factor analysis, the statistical technique designed to reduce a number of correlated variables to a more limited set of organizing dimensions. The matrix representing the mass public, however, despite its realistic complement of ideologues, is exactly the type that textbooks advise against using for factor analysis on the simple grounds that through inspection it is clear that there is virtually nothing in the way of organization to be discovered. Of course, it is the type of broad organizing dimension to be suggested by factor analysis of specific items that is usually presumed when observers discuss "ideological postures" of one sort or another.

Although the beliefs registered in Table 7 are related to topics of controversy or political cleavage, McClosky has described comparable differences in levels of constraint among beliefs for an elite sample (delegates to national party conventions) and a cross-section sample when the items deal with propositions about democracy and freedom—topics on which fundamental consensus among Americans is presumed.[23] Similarly, Prothro and Grigg, among others, have shown that, while there is widespread support for statements of culturally familiar principles of freedom, democracy, and tolerance in a cross-section sample, this support becomes rapidly obscured when questions turn to specific cases that elites would see as the most direct applications of these principles.[24] In our estimation, such findings are less a demonstration of cynical lip service than of the fact that, while both of two inconsistent opinions are honestly held, the individual lacks the contextual grasp to understand that the specific case and the general principle belong in the same belief system: In the absence of such understanding, he maintains psychologically independent beliefs about both. This is another important instance of the decline in constraint among beliefs with declining information.

While an assessment of relative constraint between the matrices rests only on comparisons of absolute values, the comparative algebraic values have some interest as well. This interest arises from the sophisticated observer's almost automatic assumption that whatever beliefs, "go together" in the visible political world (as judged from the attitudes of elites and the more articulate spectators) must naturally go together in the same way among mass public. Table 7 makes clear that this assumption is a very dangerous one, aside from the question of degree of constraint. For example, the politician who favors federal aid to education could be predicted to be more, rather than less, favorable to an internationalist posture in foreign affairs, for these two positions in the 1950s were generally associated with "liberalism" in American politics. As we see from Table 7, we would be accurate in this judgment considerably more often than chance alone would permit. On the other hand, were we

[23] Herbert McClosky, "Consensus and Ideology in American Politics," *American Political Science Review,* 58 (June 1964), No. 2, pp. 361–82.

[24] James W. Prothro and C. W. Grigg, "Fundamental Principles of Democracy: Bases of Agreement and Disagreement," *Journal of Politics,* 22 (May 1960), No. 2, 276–94.

to apply the same assumption of constraint to the American public in the same era, not only would we have been wrong, but we would actually have come closer to reality by assuming no connection at all.

All the correlations in the elite sample except those that do not depart significantly from zero exhibit signs that anybody following politics in the newspapers during this period could have predicted without hesitation. That is, one need only have known that Democrats tended to favor expansion of government welfare activities and tended to be internationalists in foreign affairs, to have anticipated all the signs except one. This exception, the −.18 that links advocacy of military aid abroad with the Republican Party, would hold no surprises either, for the one kind of international involvement that Republicans came to accept in this period limited foreign aid to the military variety, a view that stood in opposition to "soft" liberal interests in international economic welfare. If these algebraic signs in the elite matrix are taken as the culturally defined "proper" signs—the sophisticated observer's assumption of what beliefs go with what other beliefs—then the algebraic differences between comparable entries in the two matrices provide an estimate of how inaccurate we would be in generalizing our elite-based assumptions about "natural" belief combinations to the mass public as a whole. A scanning of the two matrices with these differences in mind enhances our sense of high discrepancy between the two populations.

To recapitulate, then, we have argued that the unfamiliarity of broader and more abstract ideological frames of reference among the less sophisticated is more than a problem in mere articulation. Parallel to ignorance and confusion over these ideological dimensions among the less informed is a general decline in constraint among specific belief elements that such dimensions help to organize. It cannot therefore be claimed that the mass public shares ideological patterns of belief with relevant elites at a specific level any more than it shares the abstract conceptual frames of reference.

Constraints and Overt Behavior

There is still another counter-hypothesis that deserves examination. This view would grant that the political belief systems of the less well educated may be more fragmented and chaotic. It would maintain at the same time, however, that this fact is inconsequential in the determination of behavior. The presence, absence, or incoherence of these "intervening" psychological states is thus epiphenomenal: Social structure commits behavior to certain channels quite independent of specific cognitions and perceptions of the actors themselves.[25] In other versions, researchable

---

[25] There is unquestionably a class of social behaviors for which this description is more rather than less apt, although one need not have recourse to mystical or unexplained terms to understand the processes involved. In any social system, some beliefs and behavior patterns are learned by the young in such a way that there is no awareness of the possibility of alternatives. Where beliefs are concerned, a phrase like "unspoken cultural assumptions" provides an appropriate description, and there are analogues in socially learned behaviors. Most of politics, however, involves competi-

intervening mechanisms are suggested. The "opinion leader" model is one of them. If it is true that the mass of less knowledgeable people rely upon informal communication from a few more informed people for cues about desirable or appropriate behavior, then the lines of behavior choices followed in politics might indeed show strong sociostructural patterns, even though many uninformed actors have little of the opinion leaders' coherent and organized understanding of why one behavior is more appropriate than another. What these points of view have in common is the insistence that strong constraints can be expected to operate between sociostructural terms and conscious behavior choices quite apart from the presence or absence of appropriate intervening psychological "definitions of the situation."

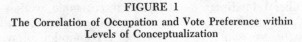

FIGURE 1

The Correlation of Occupation and Vote Preference within
Levels of Conceptualization

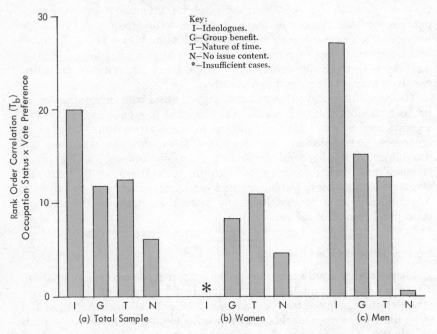

Key:
I—Ideologues.
G—Group benefit.
T—Nature of time.
N—No issue content.
°—Insufficient cases.

(a) Total Sample   *(b) Women*   *(c) Men*

Figure 1 is addressed to such arguments. The graphs indicate the varying degrees of association between objective class position and partisan preference in the 1956 presidential election, as a function of differences in the nature of political belief systems captured by our "levels of

tion between explicit alternatives, which means that conscious belief systems and conscious behavior choices have an important influence—which is *not* to say that these belief systems are not often better understood if one takes account of the sociostructural position of the actor who holds them. It *is* to say that, whether or not they are present is not a matter of indifference for the course of behavior, as we shall see.

conceptualization." If objective locations in the social structure served to produce behavioral consequences regardless of the presence or absence of relevant intervening organizations of conscious beliefs, then we would not expect any particular slope to the progression of bars within each graph. As Figure 1(a) shows for a sample of the adult electorate as a whole, however, the differences in intervening belief organization produce very marked and orderly differences in the degree to which partisanship reflects sociostructural position. Of course, from one point of view, this observation seems only common sense, yet the doctrinaire position that the intervening psychological terms are unimportant or epiphenomenal continues to be argued with more vehemence than empirical evidence.

Since it can be seen that a perfectly functioning opinion-leader model would also produce something approaching a rectangular distribution of bars in Figure 1, the slope depicted in Figure 1(a) can also be taken as a commentary on the practical imperfections with which opinion leader processes operate in this domain. That is, the "ideologues" and "near-ideologues" represented by the first bar of each graph are opinion leaders *par excellence*. While they tend to be disproportionately well educated, they nevertheless include representatives from all broad social *milieux*. Empirically they differ sharply from the less sophisticated in their attention to new political events and in the size of their store of information about past events. They get news firsthand and, presumably, form opinions directly from it. By their own report, they are much more likely than the less sophisticated to attempt to persuade others to their own political opinions in informal communications. Finally, much social data leads us to assume that the bulk of these informal communications is addressed to others within their own social *milieu*. Since social-class questions are important for these opinion leaders and since their own partisan preferences are rather clearly geared to their own class, we would suppose that "opinion leading" should serve to diffuse this connection between status and behavior through less knowledgeable members of their *milieu*, whether or not the more complicated rationales were diffused. In other words, most of what goes on in the heads of the less informed of our respondents would indeed be irrelevant for study if the respondents could at least be counted upon to follow the lead of more informed people of their own *milieu* in their ultimate partisanship. And to the extent that they can be counted on to behave in this way, we should expect Figure 1 to show a rectangular distribution of bars. The departure from such a pattern is very substantial.

Now there is one type of relationship in which there is overwhelming evidence for vigorous opinion-leading where politics is concerned in our society. It is the relationship within the family: The wife is very likely to follow her husband's opinions, however imperfectly she may have absorbed their justifications at a more complex level. We can do a fair job of splitting this relationship into its leader-follower components simply by subdividing our total sample by sex. As Figure 1(b) suggests, our expectation that the presence or absence of intervening belief systems is of reduced importance among sets of people who are predominantly opinion followers is well borne out by the relatively flat and disordered progression of bars among women. Correspondingly, of course, the same slope among men becomes steeper still in Figure 1(c).[26]

The fact that wives tend to double their husbands' votes is, from a broader "system" point of view, a relatively trivial one. If we are willing to consider the family as the basic voting unit, then Figure 1(c) suggests that diffusion of the sociostructurally "proper" behavior without diffusion of understanding of that behavior through simple opinion-leading processes is a very feeble mechanism indeed across the society as a whole, at least where political decisions of this sort are concerned.[27] The organization of partisanship among those who give no evidence of intervening issue content shows no trace whatever of those residual effects that should be left by any systematic opinion-following (and that are visible among comparable women). Thus, while we are in no way questioning the existence of some opinion-leading, it seems doubtful that it represents the dominant, effective phenomenon sometimes supposed, a phenomenon that succeeds in lending shape to mass politics despite the absence of more detailed individual comprehension of the political context.[28]

Much more broadly, we have become convinced that this class of finding—the declining degree of constraint between a term representing social structure and one representing an important political choice as one moves from the more to the less politically sophisticated in the society— is a powerful and general one. It is powerful (for readers not accustomed to the statistics employed) in the simple sense that the variation in constraint as a function of sophistication or involvement is extremely large: There are no other discriminating variables that begin to separate populations so cleanly and sharply as these measures. It is a general finding in at least two senses. First, it replicates itself handsomely across time: In

---

26 The reader is cautioned, in comparing Figures 1(b) and 1(c), that women classed (for example) as "no issue content" are not necessarily the wives of husbands who are also "no issue content." Indeed, the point of the comparison is that wives tend themselves to be qualified at less elevated levels than their husbands but organize their behavior in terms of their husband's "opinion leadership."

27 It should be remembered in assessing Figure 1(c) that the complete absence of this kind of opinion-leading would not produce a graph with a single tall bar at the left and an absence of height for the three other bars. That is, opinion-leading quite aside, we should expect some kind of slope, albeit a steep one, since people represented by the second and (to a fainter degree) the third bars have cruder versions of the intervening images of politics that we are arguing have key behavioral importance. It is only the people represented by the fourth bar who give no evidence of this type of intervening organization at all.

28 The empirical base for this argument becomes even more dramatic than is shown by Figure 1 if we consider all the psychological terms that a class orientation in voting presupposes. That is, Figure 1 treats the relationship between objective status and vote. To the degree that there are ideologues whose class identifications are not what their objective statuses would lead us to expect, they lower the degree of the association. Figure 13–3 of Campbell et al., op. cit., p. 352, which is conceptually parallel to Figure 1 of this paper, shows that ideologues with reported awareness of their social classes have a towering monopoly on the association of *subjective status* and vote partisanship.

every instance within the span of time for which appropriate data are available, the finding is present where class and partisanship are concerned. Secondly, it has some incipient claim to generality where socio-structural terms other than "social class" are concerned: The same sharp finding emerges, for example, when the relationship between religion and partisanship (Protestant *vs.* Catholic) is examined.

And, of course, if class or religious membership is considered to constitute one set of idea-elements and the predispositions that lead to particular partisan preferences and final choice to form another, then the whole phenomenon takes its place as another large class of special cases of the decline of constraints and the narrowing of belief systems to which this paper is devoted.*

X. CONCLUSION

We have long been intrigued, in dealing with attitudinal and behavioral materials drawn from cross-section publics, at the frequency with which the following sequence of events occurs. An hypothesis is formed that seems reasonable to the analyst, having to do with one or another set of systematic differences in perceptions, attitudes, or behavior patterns. The hypothesis is tested on materials from the general population but shows at best some rather uninteresting trace findings. Then the sample is further subdivided by formal education, which isolates among other groups the 10% of the American population with college degrees or the 20% with some college education. It frequently turns out that the hypothesis is then very clearly confirmed for the most educated, with results rapidly shading off to zero within the less educated majority of the population.

We do not claim that such an analytic approach always produces findings of this sort. From time to time, of course, the hypothesis in question can be more broadly rejected for all groups, and, on rare occasions, a relationship turns out to be sharper among the less educated than among the well educated. Nevertheless, there is a strikingly large class of cases in which confirmation occurs only, or most sharply, among the well educated. Usually it is easy to see, after the fact if not before, the degree to which the dynamics of the processes assumed by the hypothesis rest upon the kinds of broad or abstract contextual information about currents of ideas, people, or socity that educated people come to take for granted as initial ingredients of thought but that the most cursory studies will demonstrate are not widely shared. As experiences of this sort accumulate, we

---

* Editor's note: The reader is cautioned that substantial portions of this work have been deleted because of space limitations. The deleted sections are:

VI.   Social Groupings as Central Objects in Belief Systems
VII.   The Stability of Belief Elements over Time
VIII. Issue Publics
IX.   Summary

The deleted sections do not alter the overall conclusions of the chapter but consider other aspects of constraint and its sources. The student is urged to read the total selection.

become increasingly sensitive to these basic problems of information and begin to predict their results in advance.

This awareness means that we come to expect hypotheses about wide-ranging yet highly integrated belief systems and their behavioral consequences to show results among relative elites but to be largely disconfirmed below them. It is our impression, for example, that even some of the more elaborate "ideological" patterns associated with the authoritarian personality syndrome follow this rule. Some recent results that have accumulated in connection with the Protestant-ethic hypothesis of Weber seem to hint at something of the same pattern as well.

In this paper, we have attempted to make some systematic comments on this kind of phenomenon that seem crucial to any understanding of elite and mass belief systems. We have tried to show the character of this "continental shelf" between elites and masses and to locate the sources of differences in their belief systems in some simple characteristics of information and its social transmission.

The broad contours of elite decisions over time can depend in a vital way upon currents in what is loosely called "the history of ideas." These decisions in turn have effects upon the mass of more common citizens. But, of any direct participation in this history of ideas and the behavior it shapes, the mass is remarkably innocent. We do not disclaim the existence of entities that might best be called "folk ideologies," nor do we deny for a moment that strong differentiations in a variety of narrower values may be found within subcultures of less educated people. Yet for the familiar belief systems that, in view of their historical importance, tend most to attract the sophisticated observer, it is likely that an adequate mapping of a society (or, for that matter, the world) would provide a jumbled cluster of pyramids or a mountain range, with sharp delineation and differentiation in beliefs from elite apex to elite apex but with the mass bases of the pyramids overlapping in such profusion that it would be impossible to decide where one pyramid ended and another began.

Norman R. Luttbeg

The Structure of Beliefs among Leaders and the Public*

Concepts such as consensus, social attitudes, political culture, and belief systems appear with increasing frequency in our literature. Since McClosky's seminal piece on party leaders and followers,[1] many have focused on the differences in beliefs between the small group of political activists and the much larger and often apolitical public. This paper focuses on one important hypothesis as to how leaders and the public differ in their beliefs.

Although the leader-follower distinction might at first glance be taken as an indication that society is divided into two groups, a better perspective is of a continuum of differing involvement, knowledge, and concern with political affairs, with leaders and followers representing the poles. With governments that emphasize leadership's responsibility, with the movement toward modernity in developing countries impelled primarily by Western-trained leaders, and for many other reasons, differences among leaders and their publics are important to us.

Philip Converse hypothesizes significant differences between the belief systems of persons of varying degrees of education and political involvement.[2] They differ, he argues, in the degree of constraint between the various elements in their belief systems. While the concept of constraint is operationally simple, derived from the statistical concept of independence, it is conceptually elusive. In his omniscience, the researcher may note that individuals holding one belief also tend to hold certain others; thus, two or more beliefs have constraint between them for an individual if knowing one helps to predict the other. Such a con-

* From *Public Opinion Quarterly*, vol. 32 (Fall 1968), pp. 398–409. Reprinted by permission of the Princeton University Press, copyright owners.

[1] Herbert McClosky, Paul J. Hoffman, and Rosemary O'Hara, "Issue Conflict and Consensus among Party Leaders and Followers," *American Political Science Review*, Vol. 54, 1960, pp. 406–427.

[2] Philip E. Converse, "The Nature of Belief Systems in Mass Publics," in David E. Apter, ed., *Ideology and Discontent*, New York, Free Press, 1964, p. 207.

dition of constraint for an individual can best be noted under conditions of change in his beliefs. If he is forced to change one belief and as a result changes a second, the two beliefs constrain one another. The researcher notes the existence of constraint, but the individual is only occasionally aware of it.[3] The sources of constraint include far more than the normal logical association that one expects of rational behavior. Logically, one might expect a person who believes in the expansion of governmental programs also to favor an increase in taxation. But the very fact that many hold these logically contradictory beliefs, favoring program increases and tax decreases, demonstrates constraint derived from sources other than logic. Of course, the desire for new programs and resistance to taxes may be logical from the point of view of improving one's position relative to others; nevertheless, constraint has many sources. It may be based on two beliefs concerning the same hated or loved object, instrumental to the same desired goal, or learned from the same source. In the average individual's belief system, with its thousands of beliefs, numerous patterns are possible. At one extreme, all beliefs may stand alone with none constraining another. Conversely, the most highly constrained system would be one in which each belief constrains every other. Thus, systems of beliefs vary in structure.

Converse suggests that better educated and more politically involved persons will show greater constraint between the elements of their belief system.[4] Typically, the politically involved will have well-integrated belief systems evidencing substantial constraint, while the belief systems of the less involved will tend to be fragmented, meaning they are characterized by the absence of constraint or any underlying total dimension of attitudes. Thus, it would make some sense to speak of a liberalism-conservatism dimension among leaders in politics but much less sense among the less involved citizens.

Social psychologists frequently make use of the concept of the centrality of beliefs to the individual. This concept focuses upon the intensity with which the individual holds a given belief. Beliefs that are so very close to the central core of the individual that he would, under no circumstances, change them have greater centrality than others, located at the periphery of a belief system, that would occasion only minor dissonance if changed. In this view, the discrepancy between the constraint in leaders' belief systems and in those of the public is most evident among peripheral beliefs.[5]

Converse marshals extensive, convincing evidence in support of his hypothesis. This article presents some additional evidence with which to evaluate its correctness.

MEASURING CONSTRAINT

For a group of individuals, an empirical indication of constraint between two beliefs would be the correlation, or degree of association, be-

---

3 *Ibid.*, pp. 207 and 208.
4 *Ibid.*, p. 213.
5 *Ibid.*, p. 208.

tween them; similarly, the structuring of their belief systems would be indicated by a factor analysis.[6] Thus, if the hypothesis were correct we would expect to find a high intercorrelation among the beliefs of more educated and politically involved persons. Because of this, a limited number of attitude dimensions, such as liberalism-conservatism, internationalism-isolationism, should allow us to describe individual attitude differences among such persons. Since factor anaylsis seeks the minimum number of underlying dimensions necessary to describe individual differences, only a few factors or dimensions should describe leaders' opinions. In contrast, the belief systems of the less involved should show a lesser degree of intercorrelation among beliefs; and a factor analysis of their opinions should lack strong underlying dimensions.

THE STUDY

The data used here came from a study completed in 1959 of two Northwest communities, Eugene and Springfield, Oregon. Two distinct samples of individuals were used in this study. The first, a systematic sampling of both communities and their surrounding suburbs, included a total of 1,226 individuals.[7] This is the "citizen" sample used in the following analysis.

To oversample individuals greatly involved in the communities' politics, the researcher used a reputational technique.[8] The resulting sample, labeled "the leaders," included 117 individuals. Although initially sampled independently, both communities were combined in this analysis in order to achieve a sufficiently large number of cases for a meaningful factor analysis.

One very small part of the interview schedule for both leader and citizen samples included ten questions on issues of concern in the communities for a few years preceding the survey.[9] Approval of each issue

---

[6] *Ibid.*, p. 229.

[7] In Springfield and all the surrounding suburbs, the samples were systematically drawn from a listing of households obtained from local utility companies and the Lane County Planning Commission. A systematic sampling of households was also used in Eugene, where interviewers were told to interview at every kth household on the selected blocks assigned to them. The blocks were chosen to stratify the community roughly on socio-economic bases.

[8] A two-panel reputational technique was used to identify leaders. The method is discussed in Robert E. Agger, Daniel Goldrich, and Bert E. Swanson, *The Rulers and the Ruled*, New York, Wiley, 1964, p. 710. This group of leaders included public officeholders, economic dominants, labor leaders, political party leaders, and candidates for public office. For a detailed analysis of its composition, see Norman R. Luttbeg, "Belief Conflict in the Community: Leader and Follower Differences in Policy Preferences," unpublished Ph.D. dissertation, Michigan State University, Department of Political Science, 1965, Chap. V.

[9] Respondents were asked, "Would you tell us what you feel about the following things or people, whether you strongly approve, approve, are undecided, disapprove, strongly disapprove, or don't care about it?" They were then asked to respond to this list: urban renewal, bringing new industry to the city, annexation to the city of suburban areas, creation of a metropolitan park along the Williamette River, public housing, fluoridation of the community's water supply, spending more money on special education, city-owned parking lots, increasing taxes to provide public kinder-

was measured on a five-point Likert scale varying from strongly approve to strongly disapprove. For the purpose of factor analysis, these alternatives were assumed to constitute an interval scale.[10] Principal-axis factor analysis and Quartermax rotation were used.[11]

THE FINDINGS

The belief systems of the leaders show very little more constraint than do those of the citizens. The five extracted factors for leaders, shown in Table 1, explain some 74 per cent of the variance in their opinions while explaining 65 per cent of the variance in the opinions of the citizens. Converse's hypothesis certainly does not suggest such minor differences.[12]

Focusing on the individual issues and their communalities, it is apparent that 7 of the 10 issues show a higher communality for leaders than for citizens.[13] This would be expected from the hypothesis, but the substantial variations in the differences between leaders' and citizens' communalities merit further consideration. The fact that on 3 out of 10 issues followers have higher communalities than leaders means that the five factors explain more of the variation on these opinions for the citizens than for the leaders. This would suggest that issues vary in the facility with which they are conceptualized. Apparently, on some issues leaders have difficulty in placing their opinions within the total context of their belief systems.

Looking once again at the loading matrix, we find that analysis of the leadership opinions does not permit fullest application of the simple-structure criterion for rotation.[14] If we look at loadings over .300, four issues among the leaders load heavily on more than one factor, while

---

gartens, and increasing local taxes to provide community services. The "don't care" alternative, as well as instances of no answer, were excluded in the calculation of the product-moment correlation.

10 William J. Goode and Paul K. Hatt, *Methods in Social Research*, New York, McGraw-Hill, 1952, pp. 273–275.

11 Therefore, the findings are a unique solution. The Quartermax criterion for rotation was used for no particular reason. Verimax and Equamax solutions were also obtained, but the differences between the various solutions were minor.

12 Converse does not actually attempt a factor analysis of his elite and mass belief systems. He merely presents tables of correlation (Goodman and Kruskal tau-gamma) and notes that the elite matrix is an example of when to use factor analysis (when you have high intercorrelations) and the mass matrix of when not to use factor analysis (when you have low intercorrelations). This would imply that a factor analysis of the mass data would not yield a limited number of factors that would account for a large percentage of the variation (variance) in opinions (Converse, *op. cit.*, p. 230).

13 A communality is the sum of the squares of the loadings on the various factors for a given issue. Moving the decimal point two places to the right, the communality may be viewed as the percentage of variation in opinions on a given issue that is accounted for by the factors. If it is high, this would mean that little other than the five factors is necessary to completely account for variation in opinion on that issue; there is a great deal of constraint.

14 Simple structure is the maximizing of both large and small loading to facilitate interpreting factors.

TABLE 1
Communalities and Factor Loadings for Ten Issues, for Leaders and Citizens

Issue	Communality	Factor				
		1	2	3	4	5
Leaders:						
Attracting industry ..	.908	.030	.085	.037	.095	.943
Annexation	.726	−.087	.296	.701	.374	−.022
Parking lots	.650	.574*	.098	.393	−.200	.341
Special education ...	.726	.230	.771	.215	.017	.181
Fluoridation	.840	.192	.042	.025	.890	.091
Public housing	.700	.819	−.046	.037	.115	−.109
Urban renewal	.668	.640	.272	.239	.353	−.049
Metropolitan park ...	.755	.198	.106	.830	−.118	.041
Public kindergartens	.665	.691	.377	−.179	−.023	.107
Taxes	.832	.147	.889	.119	.050	−.063
Variance explained	74%	20%	17%	15%	11%	11%
Citizens:						
Attracting industry ..	.969	.048	.122	.055	.070	.971
Annexation	.771	.068	.873	.006	−.025	.061
Parking lots	.570	.203	.059	.694	−.164	.133
Special education ...	.591	.750	−.010	.128	−.089	.067
Fluoridation	.420	.592	.095	.018	.231	−.085
Public housing	.679	.057	.033	.792	.200	−.085
Urban renewal	.595	.138	.565	.443	.240	.050
Metropolitan park ...	.868	.203	.109	.089	.895	.077
Public kindergartens	.512	.707	.059	.080	.028	.030
Taxes	.565	.509	.547	.006	.069	.049
Variance explained	65%	18%	14%	13%	10%	10%

* All loadings of .300 or greater have been underlined for emphasis.

only two issues among the citizens do so. In summary, Converse's hypothesis does not hold for these data.

Nevertheless, the relationship may exist within the citizen sample between different levels of political involvement. Certainly, as suggested before, the citizens include both persons who have little or no education or political involvement and those who are well educated and deeply involved in local politics. For purposes of analysis, the citizens were divided into three levels of community political involvement, and each level's attitudes were independently analyzed. This additional analysis does not support the hypothesis that the more politically involved would show a simpler factor structure than the less politically involved. The five factors explain 67 per cent of the variance for the least involved, 65 per cent for the intermediately involved, and 69 per cent for the most involved. Thus, within the citizen sample itself, the degree of constraint within belief systems varies little as one moves to increasingly higher levels of political involvement.

Table 2 shows the communalities of each level on each of the ten issues, and once again, in order to substantiate the hypothesis, we would expect a larger communality with each increase in political involvement.

TABLE 2

Communalities for Ten Issues, by Level of Political Involvement

		Level of Involvement				
Issue	Low		Medium		High	
Attracting industry	.834		.831	<	.905	
Annexation	.524	<	.717		.642	
Parking lots	.842		.518	<	.662	
Special education	.727		.564	<	.708	
Fluoridation	.593		.522	<	.886	
Public housing	.833		.715		.620	
Urban renewal	.603		.587	<	.619	
Metropolitan park	.560	<	.908		.539	
Public kindergartens	.558	<	.640	<	.692	
Taxes	.643		.545	<	.618	

But some support also would be given if this relationship held only for a comparison between two strata of political involvement. Only one issue, public kindergartens, shows the strongest pattern of support, with the communality increasing with each increase in political involvement. For the other issues, even a comparison of each level of political involvement with that of the next lower level of political involvement gives very little support for the hypothesis. Again, there is little evidence to substantiate the hypothesis.

THE MEANING OF THE FACTORS

At least two sets of authors have discovered the usefulness of the concept of ideology in studying their communities.[15] The interpretation of the factors in Table 1 would seem to offer some evidence as to the nature of community ideologies, the assumption being that different ideologies

15 Agger et al., op. cit., and Oliver P. Williams and Charles R. Adrian, Four Cities, Philadelphia, University of Pennsylvania Press, 1963.

would be reflected in different patterns of attitudes on the issues measured. This analysis also allows us to determine whether or not there are significant differences in the content of leaders' and citizens' ideologies. The common elements of the issues heavily loaded on each factor aid in understanding its meaning.

Although the degree of constraint within leaders' and citizens' belief systems is nearly equal, a study of Table 1 shows the structuring of their belief systems to differ greatly. Although interpreting factors involves a great deal of subjectivity, the attempt to do so with these data may help future researchers. The leaders' first factor has heavy loadings from the issues of public parking lots, public housing, urban renewal, and public kindergartens, all issues involving improvements in the communities. This suggests a common liberalism-conservatism dimension, or willingness to undertake local programs, but the surprisingly low loading from the tax question suggests that leaders do not perceive these issues as costly in terms of local taxes. A perceived difference between externally supported and locally supported programs may underlie this dimension.

The special-education and tax issues load heavily on the second factor, as do the public kindergarten and annexation issues to a lesser degree. This dimension might be labeled the school problems dimension. The cost of such programs looms important in this dimension, to judge from the high loadings from the tax question. Annexation may be associated with this dimension because of the perception that annexation may necessitate some reshuffling of school-district boundaries and perhaps entail additional costs in the construction of new schools.

The annexation and metropolitan park issues and, to a lesser degree, the public parking lot issue correlate with the third factor. This suggests a metropolitanism dimension, a willingness to cope with the area's problems. The parking lot issue is associated with the dimension perhaps because it is perceived as an area problem, one affecting both communities. Only the fluoridation issue loads heavily on the fourth factor (although annexation and urban renewal load to a lesser degree), but there are also negative loadings from the public parking lot, metropolitan park, and public kindergarten issues. Although difficult to interpret, the high fluoridation correlation suggests a dimension of willingness to accept or abide by the recommendations of technical experts. The final factor correlates highly only with the attracting of industry issue, and to a lesser degree with parking lots. These correlations, plus the four small negative loadings on annexation, public housing, urban renewal, and the tax-increase issues, suggest the boosterism ideology from the Williams and Adrian study, a desire to make one's community appealing as a location for new industry.

The first factor for the citizen sample shows a sensitivity to the needs of correct child rearing. The heavy loadings from special education, fluoridation, public kindergartens, and a willingness to increase taxes, and a lesser leading on the metropolitan park issue, can be interpreted as possible contributions to the facilities desirable for the proper upbringing of children. The second factor also correlates with the tax issue along with the annexation and urban renewal issues. It is difficult to conceive of the nature of this dimension. Perhaps it reflects a sensitivity to the existing tax burden in the community and the realization of the effects of increasing or decreasing the tax base. Thus, annexation conceivably means that the tax base may be broadened while urban renewal reduces the tax base.

The issues of public parking lots, public housing, and urban renewal have heavy loadings on the third factor. As all these involve improvements in the central part of the cities, apparently this is a core-area improvement dimension. Notably, the loading for the tax issue (.006) indicates that this dimension is independent of considerations of taxes or the level of taxation. This compares with the leaders' first factor.

The fourth factor correlates only with the metropolitan park issue, suggesting a recreation dimension. The large Oregon subculture of sports enthusiasts and persons making use of recreational and camping facilities lends plausibility to this dimension. The fifth factor again has a single loading, and, as with the leaders, it is the attracting of industry issue, suggesting that the public also perceives the booster dimension. Oregon's need to recruit job-providing industry is perceived by both industry and labor. The public apparently shares this concern.

In summary, the dimensions of the belief systems for leaders and citizens are: for leaders, local programs, school taxes, acceptance of technical experts, metropolitanism, and boosterism; and for citizens, child upbringing, tax sensitivity, local programs, boosterism, and recreation. The public's belief structure does not differ generically from that of the leaders. Certainly, the structuring of beliefs by citizens seems more a product of their personal perceptions, compared with the abstractions of leaders, but both evidence a meaningful constraint among beliefs.

CONCLUSION

The data offer very little support for Converse's hypothesis. The leaders and the public differ in the content of their beliefs, but the leaders do not place the ten issues studied on a single unifying dimension. Indeed, their belief systems show a complexity much in contrast to the simplicity suggested by a liberalism-conservatism distinction. The idea of ideologies suggested by Agger, Goldrich, and Swanson and by Williams and Adrian would seem to be necessary to cope with the varieties of leaders' belief systems, rather than the single liberalism-conservatism dimension so frequently used in explaining national opinions. The public also differs from what one would expect if the hypothesis were correct. They show an understandable, if not sophisticated, structuring of their beliefs. Leaders' belief systems differ from those of the public, but not on the variable of constraint.

Then what explains the differences noted between Converse's data and those presented here? Most conspicuously, in Converse's data, the wording of the items presented to the leaders and citizens was not identical: the leaders' items were worded to be more acceptable to the better-educated, while the public received the simply worded items normally given to random samples. Furthermore, the difference between the items in the Survey Research Center's questionnaire used by Converse would tend to support the hypothesis. Although both the leaders' items and those of the public strongly emphasize the generality of the attitude dimension measured, one might argue that the distinct keying concepts in the followers' items cause the public to discount the common threads they perceive.[16] The stimuli encourage independence in responses, which in turn is judged low constraint. For example, one item in the random-sample questionnaire from the Survey Research Center asks about jobs, another about the need for schools, another about Negroes, each of these nouns keying a rather different object for evaluation. Converse himself notes that the general public, in evaluating and giving their responses, will use concepts such as groups to be advantaged and disadvantaged by the proposal.

In contrast, in the present study the samples responded to identical items, which concerned specific rather than general issues. Such specific issues would seem unlikely to affect the responses of individuals with highly constrained and single-dimension belief systems, but an individual using several dimensions to order his beliefs might locate the specific issues on several dimensions and be torn between their favorable and unfavorable aspects. Denied such keying concepts as Negroes and jobs,

---

[16] The items for the elite are:
1. Do you think the federal government ought to sponsor programs such as large public works in order to maintain full employment or do you think that problems of economic readjustment ought to be left more to private industry or state and local government?
2. Do you think the government should provide grants to the states for the construction and operation of public schools or do you think the support of public education should be left entirely to the state and local government?
3. Do you approve the use of federal funds for public housing or do you generally feel that housing can be taken care of better by private effort?
4. Do you think the federal government should establish a fair employment practices commission to prevent discrimination in employment?
5. First, on the foreign economic aid program, would you generally favor expanding the program, reducing it, or maintaining it about the way it is?
6. How about the foreign military aid program? Should this be expanded, reduced, or maintained about as it is?
7. Speaking very generally, do you think that in the years ahead the United States should maintain or reduce its commitments around the world?
     The items for the random sample, "the masses," are:
1. The government in Washington ought to see to it that everyone who wants to work can find a *job*.
2. If cities and towns around the country need help to build more *schools*, the government in Washington ought to give them the money they need.
3. The *government* should leave things like electric power and housing for *private businessmen* to handle.
4. If *Negroes* are not getting fair treatment in jobs and housing, the government should see to it that they do.
5. The United States should give economic help to the *poorer countries* of the world even if those countries can't pay for it.
6. The United States should keep soldiers overseas where they can help countries that are against *Communism*.
7. This country would be better off if we just stayed home and did not concern ourselves with problems in *other parts of the world*.
     Emphasis is added.

the public might be expected to respond entirely randomly. Perhaps the differences in the two sets of questions explain some of the differences noted. Certainly the distinction between the general items and the specific issues should be further explored.

The differences between the Survey Research items and those used in this study suggest an additional analysis. It might be hypothesized that issues become more integrated into belief systems with the passage of time and the intensification of interest. The items used by the Survey Research Center tap enduring controversies, but those used in this study vary in the duration and intensity of their discussion. All the issues used in this study were of considerable concern in at least one of the communities in the period two to three years prior to the study, but there were variations. Thus, the short-term, low-intensity issues in this study may be obscuring the greater degree of constraint among leaders on enduring issues.

Because the two communities are combined in the factor analysis, there is some difficulty in dividing issues into an enduring, high-intensity category and a short-term, low-intensity category. The analysis below focuses only on those issues of enduring and intense interest to both communities. If the issue had been of concern in both communities for more than two years and roused great controversy, it was labeled "enduring." Similarly, short-term and low-intensity issues are labeled "brief."[17] The average communalities for enduring and brief issues, computed for leaders and the public, are as follows:

	Leaders	Public
Enduring	.742	.644
Brief	.727	.713

The higher communalities for leaders than for the public indicate greater constraint in the leaders' belief systems on the enduring issues. This arises from the increase in communalities for the leaders and the decrease for the public between the brief and the enduring issues. It is difficult to explain this decrease for the general public. The modified hypothesis would be strongly supported if the communality of the leaders increased from brief to enduring issues while the public's communality remained constant, but the deviation from this pattern shown above causes some reservations as to its correctness.

If the differences discussed above prove inadequate to explain the differences between the findings of the two studies, another factor may be that Converse's data deal with national issues, whereas the present study deals with local ones. Perhaps the public shows more constraint within local than national belief systems, as a result of the greater simplicity of local issues and the fact that more is known about them and more consideration given to them.

---

17 The issues labeled "enduring" are: annexation, urban renewal, and taxes. The issues labeled "brief" are: special education, public housing, and the metropolitan park issue.

Apparently, belief systems cannot be classified merely as either unidimensional or nonconstrained and fragmented. Rather, it is possible to have multidimensional belief systems as well as unidimensional belief systems, both representing well thought out and constrained belief systems. The application of factor analysis to the interpretation of opinions in belief systems would show the unidimensional belief system as a single factor explaining a rather high percentage of the variance. The multidimensional belief system would be shown by numerous factors explaining a large degree of the variation in opinions. Finally, the fragmented, low-constraint belief system would require a large number of factors to explain only a small amount of the variance in the opinions. These data show that there are nonleadership, noninvolved publics who do have rather well-integrated belief systems, though clearly not unidimensional.

Herbert McClosky, Paul J. Hoffmann, and
Rosemary O'Hara

Issue Conflict and Consensus among Party Leaders and Followers[*]

American political parties are often regarded as "brokerage" organizations, weak in principle, devoid of ideology, and inclined to differ chiefly over unimportant questions. In contrast to the "ideological" parties of Europe—which supposedly appeal to their followers through sharply defined, coherent, and logically related doctrines—the American parties are thought to fit their convictions to the changing demands of the political contest.[1] According to this view, each set of American party leaders is satisfied to play Tweedledee to the other's Tweedledum.

I. PRESSURES TOWARD UNIFORMITY AND CLEAVAGE

Although these "conclusions" are mainly derived from *a priori* analysis or from casual observations of "anecdotal" data (little systematic effort having been made so far to verify or refute them), they are often taken as confirmed—largely, one imagines, because they are compatible with certain conspicuous features of American politics. Among these features is the entrenchment of a two-party system which, by affording both parties a genuine opportunity to win elections, tempts them to appeal to as many diverse elements in the electorate as are needed to put together a

[*] Reprinted from the *American Political Science Review*, vol. 54 (June 1960), pp. 406–27. Copyright 1960, The American Political Science Association.

This article was the first in a series reporting the findings of a national field study of political belief and affiliation among American party leaders and followers. The study was carried out through the Laboratory for Research in Social Relations at the University of Minnesota under grants made to the senior author by the Committee on Political Behavior of the Social Science Research Council, and supplementary grants from the Graduate School Research Fund. The manuscript was prepared at the Survey Research Center, University of California, Berkeley, under a Fellowship in Legal and Political Philosophy awarded to the senior author by the Rockefeller Foundation.

[1] Maurice Duverger, *Political Parties, their Organization and Activity in the Modern State* (New York, 1955), p. 102.

majority.[2] Since both parties want to attract support from the centrist and moderate segments of the electorate, their views on basic issues will, it is thought, tend to converge. Like giant business enterprises competing for the same market, they will be led to offer commodities that are in many respects identical.[3] It is one thing for a small party in a multi-party system to preserve its ideological purity, quite another for a mass party in a two-party system to do so. The one has little hope of becoming a majority, and can most easily survive by remaining identified with the narrow audience from which it draws its chief supporters; the other can succeed only by accommodating the conflicting claims of many diverse groups—only, in short, by blunting ideological distinctions.[4]

Constraints against enlarging intellectual differences also spring from the loosely confederated nature of the American party system, and from each national party's need to adjust its policies to the competing interests of the locality, the state, and the nation.[5] Many party units are more concerned with local than with national elections, and prefer not to be handicapped by clear-cut national programs. Every ambitious politician, moreover, hopes to achieve a *modus vivendi* tailored to the particular and often idiosyncratic complex of forces prevailing in his constituency, an objective rarely compatible with doctrinal purity.[6] Often, too, local politics are largely nonpartisan or are partisan in ways that scarcely affect the great national issues around which ideologies might be expected to form.[7] The development and enforcement of a sharply delineated ideology is also hindered by the absence in either party of a firmly established, authoritative, and continuing organizational center empowered to decide questions of doctrine and discipline.[8] Party affiliation is loosely defined, responsibility is weak or non-existent, and organs for indoctrinating or communicating with party members are at best rudimentary.

Cultural and historical differences may also contribute to the weaker ideological emphasis among American, as compared with European, parties. Many of the great historical cleavages that have divided European nations for centuries—monarchism *vs.* republicanism; clericalism *vs.* anti-

---

[2] The analysis of these and related tendencies associated with the American party system is ably set forth in Pendleton Herring, *The Politics of Democracy* (New York, 1940), p. 102 and *passim*. Also, James M. Burns, *Congress on Trial: The Legislative Process and the Administrative State* (New York, 1949), p. 34.

[3] See especially E. E. Schattschneider, *Party Government* (New York, 1942), p. 92 and *passim;* and V. O. Key, *Politics, Parties, and Pressure Groups*, 4th ed. (New York, 1958), ch. 8; Howard R. Penniman, *Sait's American Parties and Elections*, 5th ed. (New York, 1952), p. 162.

[4] William Goodman, *The Two-Party System in the United States* (New Jersey, 1956), p. 43.

[5] Duverger, *op. cit.*, pp. 187, 418.

[6] Pendleton Herring, *op. cit.*, p. 133.

[7] *American State Legislatures,* ed. Belle Zeller (New York, 1954); but see also Malcolm E. Jewell, "Party Voting in American State Legislatures," *American Political Science Review,* Vol. XLIX (Sept. 1955), pp. 773–91.

[8] Report of the Committee on Political Parties, American Political Science Association, *Toward a More Responsible Two-Party System* (New York, 1950), *passim*.

clericalism; democracy *vs.* autocracy, etc.—have never taken root in this country. Apart from the slavery (and subsequently the race) issue, the United States has not experienced the intense class or caste conflict often found abroad, and contests of the capitalism *vs.* socialism variety have never achieved an important role in American politics. In addition, never having known a titled nobility, we have largely been freed from the conflicts found elsewhere between the classes of inherited and acquired privilege.

Consider, too, the progress made in the United States toward neutralizing the forces which ordinarily lead to sharp social, and hence intellectual and political, differentiation. The class and status structure of American society has attained a rate of mobility equalling or exceeding that of any other long established society. Popular education, and other facilities for the creation of common attitudes, have been developed on a scale unequalled elsewhere. Improvements in transportation and communication, and rapid shifts in population and industry have weakened even sectionalism as a source of political cleavage. Rural–urban differences continue to exist, of course, but they too have been diminishing in force and have become less salient for American politics than the differences prevailing, for example, between a French peasant proprietor and a Parisian *boulevardier.*[9] In short, a great many Americans have been subjected in their public lives to identical stimuli—a condition unlikely to generate strong, competing ideologies.

The research reported here was designed not to refute these observations but to test the accuracy of the claim that they are sufficient to prevent differences in outlook from taking root in the American party system. We believed that the homogenizing tendencies referred to are strongly offset by contrary influences, and that voters are preponderantly led to support the party whose opinions they share. We further thought that the competition for office, though giving rise to similarities between the parties, also impels them to diverge from each other in order to sharpen their respective appeals. For this and other reasons, we expected to find that the leaders of the two parties, instead of ignoring differences alleged to exist within the electorate, would differ on issues more sharply than their followers would. We believed further that even in a brokerage system the parties would serve as independent reference groups, developing norms, values, and self-images to which their supporters could readily respond.[10] Their influence, we felt, would frequently exceed that of ethnic, occupational, residential and other reference groups. In sum, we proceeded on the belief that the parties are not simply spokesmen for other interest groups, but are in their own right agencies for formulating, trans-

---

[9] Data bearing on these generalizations will be presented in companion articles which specifically deal with sectional and rural–urban influences on issue outlook.

[10] *Cf.* James W. Prothro, Ernest Q. Campbell, and Charles M. Grigg, "Two Party Voting in the South: Class vs. Party Identification," *American Political Science Review,* Vol. LII (March 1958), pp. 131–39. Also, Peter H. Odegard and E. Allen Helms, *American Politics: A Study in Political Dynamics* (New York, 1947 ed.), pp. 200–221.

mitting, and anchoring political opinions, that they attract adherents who in general share those opinions, and that through a feedback process of mutual reinforcement between the organization and its typical supporters, the parties develop integrated and stable political tendencies. Other hypotheses will be specified as we present and analyze our findings.

II. PROCEDURES

The questions considered in this paper were part of a large field study made in 1957–1958 on the nature, sources, and correlates of political affiliation, activity, and belief in the American party system (hereafter referred to as the PAB study). Pilot studies on Minnesota samples had led us to suspect that many "settled" notions about party affiliation and belief in America would not stand up under careful empirical scrutiny; further, we felt that little progress would be made in the exploration of this subject until a comprehensive portrait of party membership in America had been drawn. Accordingly, a nationwide study was launched to acquire a detailed description of party leaders and supporters, gathering data on their backgrounds, political experiences, personality characteristics, values, motivations, social and political attitudes, outlooks on key issues, and related matters.

For our samples of party "leaders" we turned to the Democratic and Republican national conventions, largely because they are the leading and most representative of the party organs, their delegates coming from every part of the United States and from every level of party and government activity. Our samples ranged from governors, senators, and national committeemen at the one end to precinct workers and local officials at the other. In the absence of comprehensive information about the characteristics of the party elites in America, no one can say how closely the convention delegates mirror the total party leadership. We felt it fair to assume, nevertheless, that the delegates represented as faithful a cross section of American party leadership as could be had without an extraordinary expenditure of money and labor. Using convention delegates as our universe of leaders also held some obvious advantages for research, since the composition of this universe (by name, address, party, state, sex, place of residence, and party or public office) can usually be ascertained from the convention calls. Of the 6,848 delegates and alternates available to be sampled, 3,193 actually participated; 3,020 (1,788 Democrats and 1,232 Republicans) completed and returned questionnaires that were usable in all respects.[11] The proportion of returns was roughly equivalent for both sets of party leaders.

The rank-and-file sample, which we wanted both for its intrinsic value and for its utility as a control group, was obtained by special arrange-

---

[11] This gratifyingly large number of returns of so lengthy and detailed a questionnaire was attained through a number of follow-up mailings and special letters. These and other procedures designed to check the adequacy of the sample will be fully described in the volume containing the report of the overall study. The difference in the number of returns from the two parties was largely a result of the greater number of Democratic delegates to begin with.

ment with the American Institute of Public Opinion. In January 1958, Gallup interviewers personally distributed our questionnaire to 2,917 adult voters in two successive national cross-section surveys. Some 1,610 questionnaires were filled out and returned, of which 1,484 were completely usable. This sample closely matched the national population on such characteristics as sex, age, region, size of city, and party affiliation, and, though it somewhat oversampled the upper educational levels, we considered it sufficiently large and representative for most of our purposes. Of the 1,484 respondents, 821 were Democratic supporters (629 "pure" Democrats, plus 192 whom we classified as "independent" Democrats) and 623 were Republican supporters (479 "pure" Republicans, plus 144 "independent" Republicans). Forty respondents could not be identified as adherents of either party.

The lengthy questionnaire developed for the study was designed to be self-administered. It contained, in addition to questions on the respondents' personal backgrounds, a number of queries on their political history and experience, their attitudes toward the party system and toward such related matters as party organization, discipline and responsibility, their self-images with regard to social class and liberalism-conservatism, their reference group identifications, and their views on party leadership and ideology. The largest part of the questionnaire consisted of 390 scale items, randomly arranged, which when sorted and scored fell into 47 scales for measuring the personality, attitude, and value characteristics of each of the respondents. We had validated and used all but three of these scales in earlier studies.

The questions most relevant for the present article were those which asked each respondent to express his attitudes toward twenty-four important national issues, and to state whether he believed support for each issue should be "increased," "decreased," or "remain as is." The list of issues and the responses of each sample will be found in Tables H2A through H2E, where for convenience of analysis, the issues have been grouped under five broad headings: Public Ownership, Government Regulation of the Economy, Equalitarianism and Human Welfare, Tax Policy and Foreign Policy.

In tabulating the results, we first scored each individual on each issue and then computed aggregate scores for all the members of a given sample. To begin with, percentages were used to show the proportion who favored increasing, decreasing, or retaining the existing level of support on each issue. But as it was clumsy to handle three figures for each issue, we constructed a single index or "ratio of support" which would simultaneously take account of all three scores. The index was built by assigning a weight of 1.0 to each "increase" response in the sample, of 0 to each "decrease" response, and of .50 to each "remain as is" (or "same") response. Thus the ratio-of-support score shown for any given sample is in effect a mean score with a possible range of 0 to 1.0, in which support for an issue increases as the scores approach 1.0 and decreases as they approach 0. In general, the scores can be taken to approximate the following overall positions: .0 to .25—strongly wish to reduce support; .26 to .45—wish to reduce support; .46 to .55—satisfied with the

TABLE 1

Average Differences in the Ratio-of-Support Scores among Party Leaders
and Followers for Five Categories of Issues

Category of Issues	Democratic Leaders vs. Republican Leaders	Democratic Followers vs. Republican Followers	Democratic Leaders vs. Democratic Followers	Republican Leaders vs. Republican Followers	Democratic Leaders vs. Republican Followers	Republican Leaders vs. Democratic Followers
a. Public ownership of resources	.28	.04	.06	.18	.10	.22
b. Government regulation of the economy	.22	.06	.08	.10	.12	.16
c. Equalitarianism, human welfare ...	.22	.05	.08	.21	.06	.25
d. Tax policy	.20	.06	.06	.20	.04	.26
e. Foreign policy ...	.16	.02	.05	.08	.07	.10
Average differences in ratio scores for all categories	.21	.04	.07	.15	.08	.20

Sample sizes: Democratic leaders, 1,788; Republican leaders, 1,232; Democratic followers, 821; Republican followers, 623.

status quo; .56 to .75—wish to increase support; and .76 to 1.00—strongly wish to increase support. Note that the differences in degree suggested by these categories refer not to the *strength of feeling* exhibited by individuals toward an issue but rather to the *numbers of people* in a sample who hold points of view favoring or opposing that issue.

Because they include the "same" and "no code" as well as "increase" and "decrease" responses, our ratios of support sometimes flatten the differences between groups. Had we employed only the percentage scores for the "increase" or "decrease" responses, the differences between samples would in many instances have seemed larger. Nevertheless, the ratio of support offers so many advantages that we have employed it as our principal measure. For one thing, as the equivalent of a mean score, it takes into account all scores, omitting no respondent from the tabulation. For the same reason it enables us to assess the amount of dispersion or homogeneity exhibited by any sample and makes it easy to calculate significances of difference.[12] Reliance upon a single, uniform statistic

---

[12] The measure of dispersion used for this purpose was the standard deviation, which was computed by using the scores of 0, .50 and 1.00 as intervals in the calculations. To avoid having to calculate separate significances of difference for each of the comparisons we wanted to observe, we simply made the assumption—erring on the side of caution—that the maximum variance of .50 had occurred in each instance. The magnitude of the significance of difference is, in other words, often greater than we have reported. The significance test used in this procedure was the critical ratio. Unless otherwise indicated, all the differences reported are statistically significant at or beyond the .01 level.

also allows us to make ready comparisons not only *between* but *within* samples, and to determine quickly how large the differences actually are. By observing whether a ratio of support is above or below .50 we can see at once whether a particular group predominantly favors or opposes the issue in question, and how strongly it does so. The use of ratio scores also makes it possible to compare issues as well as groups, *e.g.*, to see whether one issue is more preferred than another.

For further information on the meaning of the issue responses, we also compared samples on a number of related scales and items. Tabulating and statistical operations were carried out to control for demographic influences like education, occupation, age, and sectionalism; to ascertain homogeneity of opinion within the several samples; to rank the issues according to the magnitude of the differences between samples; to compare members' positions on issues against official platform statements; and to determine whether leaders and followers are able to name the issues which actually divide the parties. Some of the findings yielded by these operations will be considered here, while others, for reasons of space, will have to be reserved for future publications.

A word of caution before we turn to the findings. The respondents were offered only the twenty-four issues that impressed us in February, 1957, as most significant and enduring. However, they may not all be as salient today as they seemed at that time. Nor, within the limitations of a single questionnaire, could we explore every issue that informed observers might have considered important. Some presumably vital issues such as states rights, political centralization, and expansion of government functions could not be stated explicitly enough within our format to be tested properly. These are issues that are so generalized as to encompass many other specific issues, and so highly charged as to awaken a profusion of symbolic and emotive associations.

The *form* of our issue questions may also be open for criticism, for space limitations prevented our subjects from indicating how strongly they felt and how much they knew about each of the issues. This deficiency, however, may be less important than it appears, since for the groups we most wanted to compare (*e.g.*, Democratic *vs.* Republican leaders), the degree of political knowledge and intensity is likely to be rather similar. The difficulty is greater when comparing leaders with followers, but is somewhat offset by controlling for education and socioeconomic status. Although some subtleties of interpretation are bound to be lost because these variables have been omitted, we are satisfied that our issue questions in their present form furnish a useful measure for assessing *group* (as distinguished from *individual*) opinion.

Finally, one may wonder about the value of opinions stated on a questionnaire compared with the worth of views formally expressed by an organization or implicit in the actions of its leaders. Advantages can be cited on both sides. The beliefs expressed in official party statements or in legislative roll calls, it might be claimed, represent the *operating* beliefs of the organization by virtue of having been tested in the marketplace or in the competition of legislative struggle. Positions taken on issues on which a party stakes its future may be more valid evidence of what the party truly believes than are the opinions expressed by individual members under conditions of maximum safety. On the other hand, the responses to the issue and attitude questions in the PAB study represent the anonymous, private opinions of party leaders and followers, uncomplicated by any need to make political capital, to proselytize, to conciliate critics, or to find grounds for embarrassing the opposition at the next election. Hence they may for some purposes represent the most accurate possible reflection of the "actual" state of party opinion. The controversy over the value of the two approaches is to some extent spurious, however, for they offer different perspectives on the same thing. In addition, considerable correspondence exists between the party positions evident in congressional roll calls and the privately expressed opinions of the party leaders in our study.

III. FINDINGS: COMPARISONS BETWEEN LEADERS

No more conclusive findings emerge from our study of party issues than those growing out of the comparisons between the two sets of party leaders. Despite the brokerage tendency of the American parties, their active members are obviously separated by large and important differences. The differences, moreover, conform with the popular image in which the Democratic party is seen as the more "progressive" or "radical," the Republican as the more "moderate" or "conservative" of the two.[14] In addition, the disagreements are remarkably consistent, a function not of chance but of systematic points of view, whereby the responses to any one of the issues could reasonably have been predicted from knowledge of the responses to the other issues.

Examination of Tables 2A–2E and 3 shows that the leaders differ significantly on 23 of the 24 issues listed and that they are separated on 15 of these issues by .18 or more ratio points—in short, by differences that are in absolute magnitude very large. The two samples are furthest apart in their attitudes toward public ownership and are especially divided on the question of government ownership of natural resources, the Democrats strongly favoring it, the Republicans just as strongly wanting it cut back. The difference of .39 in the ratio scores is the largest for any of the issues tested. In percentages, the differences are 58 per cent (D) vs. 13 per cent (R) in favor of increasing support, and 19 per cent (D) vs. 52 per cent (R) in favor of decreasing support. Both parties prepon-

---

[13] See, for example, the congressional roll-call results reported by Julius Turner, *Party and Constituency: Pressures on Congress*, The Johns Hopkins University Studies in Historical and Political Science Series, Vol. LXIX, No. 1 (1951). The complexities affecting the determination of party votes in Congress are thoroughly explored in David B. Truman, *The Congressional Party: A Case Study* (New York, 1959).

[14] Conservatism is here used not in the classical but in the more popular sense, in which it refers to negative attitudes toward government ownership, intervention, and regulation of the economy; resistance to measures for promoting equalitarianism and social welfare through government action; identification with property, wealth, and business enterprise; etc.

derantly support public control and development of atomic energy, but
the Democrats do so more uniformly.

V. O. Key, among others, has observed that the Republican party is
especially responsive to the "financial and manufacturing community,"[15]
reflecting the view that government should intervene as little as possible
to burden or restrain prevailing business interests. The validity of this
observation is evident throughout all our data, and is most clearly seen
in the responses to the issues listed under Government Regulation of the
Economy, Equalitarianism and Human Welfare, Tax Policy. Democratic
leaders are far more eager than Republican leaders to strengthen en-

TABLE 2A

Comparison of Party Leaders and Followers on "Public Ownership" Issues,
by Percentages and Ratios of Support

	Leaders		Followers	
	Dem.	Repub.	Dem.	Repub.
	N = 1,788	N = 1,232	N = 821	N = 623
Issues		(%s down)		
Public ownership of natural resources				
% favoring: Increase	57.5	12.9	35.3	31.1
Decrease	18.6	51.9	15.0	19.9
Same, n.c.*	23.8	35.2	49.7	49.0
Support ratio	.69	.30	.60	.56
Public control of atomic energy				
% favoring: Increase	73.2	45.0	64.2	59.4
Decrease	7.2	15.3	7.1	10.0
Same, n.c.	19.6	39.7	28.7	30.6
Support ratio	.83	.65	.79	.75
Mean support ratios for the public ownership category	.76	.48	.70	.66

* n.c. = no code.

forcement of anti-monopoly laws and to increase regulation of public
utilities and business. Indeed, the solidarity of Republican opposition to
the regulation of business is rather overwhelming: 84 per cent want to
decrease such regulation and fewer than .01 per cent say they want to
increase it. Although the Democrats, on balance, also feel that government controls on business should not be expanded further, the differences
between the two samples on this issue are nevertheless substantial.

The two sets of leaders are also far apart on the farm issue, the Democrats preferring slightly to increase farm supports, the Republicans wanting strongly to reduce them. The Republican ratio score of .20 on this
issue is among the lowest in the entire set of scores. The magnitude of
these scores somewhat surprised us, for while opposition to agricultural
subsidies is consistent with Republican dislike for state intervention, we
had expected the leaders to conform more closely to the familiar image

[15] Key, op. cit., p. 239.

TABLE 2B
Comparison of Party Leaders and Followers on "Government Regulation of the Economy" Issues, by Percentages and Ratios of Support

Issues	Leaders Dem. N = 1,788	Leaders Repub. N = 1,232	Followers Dem. N = 821	Followers Repub. N = 623
		(%s down)		
Level of farm price supports				
% favoring: Increase	43.4	6.7	39.0	23.0
Decrease	28.1	67.4	27.6	40.3
Same, n.c.	28.5	25.8	33.4	36.7
Support ratio	.58	.20	.56	.41
Government regulation of business				
% favoring: Increase	20.2	0.6	18.6	7.4
Decrease	38.5	84.1	33.4	46.2
Same, n.c.	41.3	15.3	48.0	46.4
Support ratio	.41	.08	.43	.31
Regulation of public utilities				
% favoring: Increase	59.0	17.9	39.3	26.0
Decrease	6.4	17.6	11.1	12.0
Same, n.c.	34.6	64.5	49.6	62.0
Support ratio	.76	.50	.64	.57
Enforcement of anti-monopoly laws				
% favoring: Increase	78.0	44.9	53.2	51.0
Decrease	2.9	0.9	7.9	6.6
Same, n.c.	19.1	46.1	38.9	42.4
Support ratio	.88	.68	.73	.72
Regulation of trade unions				
% favoring: Increase	59.3	86.4	46.6	57.8
Decrease	12.4	4.5	8.9	10.6
Same, n.c.	28.3	9.2	44.5	31.6
Support ratio	.73	.91	.69	.74
Level of tariffs				
% favoring: Increase	13.0	19.2	16.6	15.2
Decrease	43.0	26.3	25.3	21.3
Same, n.c.	43.9	54.5	58.1	63.4
Support ratio	.35	.46	.46	.47
Restrictions on credit				
% favoring: Increase	24.8	20.6	26.1	25.7
Decrease	39.3	20.6	22.2	23.8
Same, n.c.	35.9	58.8	51.8	50.5
Support ratio	.43	.50	.52	.51
Mean support ratios for "government regulation of the economy" category	.59	.48	.58	.53

of the Republican as the more "rural" of the two parties.[16] It appears, however, that the party's connection with business is far more compelling than its association with agriculture. The Republican desire to reduce

[16] The friendlier attitude toward farmers among Democratic leaders than Republican leaders is borne out in the responses to several other questions used in the study. For example, the Republican leaders list farmers as having "too much power" far more frequently than do the Democratic leaders. Equally, the Democrats are significantly more inclined to regard farmers as having "too little power."

government expenditures and to promote independence from "government handouts" prevails on the farm question as it does on other issues, while the Democratic preference for a more regulated economy in which government intervenes to reduce economic risk and to stabilize prosperity is equally evident on the other side. Party attitudes on this issue appear to be determined as much by ideological tendencies as by deliberate calculation of the political advantages to be gained by favoring or opposing subsidies to farmers. Comparison of our findings with Turner's earlier data on farm votes in Congress[17] suggests, in addition, that the sharp party difference on the farm issue is neither a recent development nor a mere product of the personal philosophy of the present Secretary of Agriculture.

Having implied that agricultural policies partly result from principle, we must note that on three other issues in this category (trade unions, credit, and tariffs), principle seems to be overweighed by old-fashioned economic considerations. In spite of their distaste for government interference in economic affairs, the Republicans almost unanimously favor greater regulation of trade unions and they are more strongly disposed than the Democrats toward government intervention to restrict credit and to raise tariffs. Of course, party cleavages over the credit and tariff issues have a long history,[18] which may by now have endowed them with ideological force beyond immediate economic considerations.[19] The preponderant Democratic preference for greater regulation of trade unions is doubtless a response to recent "exposures" of corrupt labor practices, though it may also signify that the party's perspective toward the trade unions is shifting somewhat.

The closer Republican identification with business, free enterprise, and economic conservatism in general, and the friendlier Democratic attitude toward labor and toward government regulation of the economy, are easily observed in the data from other parts of our questionnaire. Republican leaders score very much higher than Democratic leaders on, for example, such scales as economic conservatism, independence of government, and business attitudes. On a question asking respondents to indicate the groups from which they would be most and least likely to take advice, 41 per cent of the Democratic leaders but only 3.8 per cent of the Republican leaders list trade unions as groups from which they would seek advice. Trade unions are scored in the "least likely" category by 25 per cent of the Democrats and 63 per cent of the Republicans. Similarly, more than 94 per cent of the Republican leaders, but 56 per cent of the Democratic leaders, name trade unions as groups that have "too much power." These differences, it should be noted, cannot be ac-

[17] Turner, *op. cit.*, p. 64.

[18] See John B. Johnson, Jr., *The Extent and Consistency of Party Voting in the United States Senate*, Ph.D. thesis, University of Chicago, 1943. By applying the Rice Index-of-Likeness to Senate votes, Johnson finds the tariff to have been the most partisan issue before the Congress in the years 1880–1940.

[19] Corinne Silverman, "The Legislator's View of the Legislative Process," *Public Opinion Quarterly*, Vol. 18 (1954–55), p. 180.

counted for by reference to the greater number of trade union members among the Democratic party leadership, for in the 1956 conventions only 14 per cent of the Democrats belonged to trade unions, and while an even smaller percentage (4 per cent) of the Republicans were trade unionists, this disparity is hardly great enough to explain the large differences in outlook. The key to the explanation has to be sought in the symbolic and reference group identifications of the two parties, and in their underlying values.

Nowhere do we see this more clearly than in the responses to the Equalitarian and Human Welfare issues. The mean difference in the ratio scores for the category as a whole is .22, a very large difference and one that results from differences in the expected direction on all six issues that make up the category. On four of these issues—federal aid to educa-

TABLE 2C

Comparison of Party Leaders and Followers on "Equalitarian and Human Welfare" Issues, by Percentages and Ratios of Support

		Leaders		Followers	
Issues		Dem. N = 1,788	Repub. N = 1,232	Dem. N = 821	Repub. N = 623
				(%s down)	
Federal aid to education					
% favoring:	Increase	66.2	22.3	74.9	64.8
	Decrease	13.4	43.2	5.6	8.3
	Same, n.c.	20.4	34.5	19.5	26.8
Support ratio		.76	.40	.85	.78
Slum clearance and public housing					
% favoring:	Increase	78.4	40.1	79.5	72.5
	Decrease	5.6	21.6	5.8	7.9
	Same, n.c.	16.0	38.3	14.6	19.6
Support ratio		.86	.59	.87	.82
Social security benefits					
% favoring:	Increase	60.0	22.5	69.4	57.0
	Decrease	3.9	13.1	3.0	3.8
	Same, n.c.	36.1	64.4	27.5	39.2
Support ratio		.78	.55	.83	.77
Minimum wages					
% favoring:	Increase	50.0	15.5	59.0	43.5
	Decrease	4.7	12.5	2.9	5.0
	Same, n.c.	45.2	72.0	38.1	51.5
Support ratio		.73	.52	.78	.69
Enforcement of integration					
% favoring:	Increase	43.8	25.5	41.9	40.8
	Decrease	26.6	31.7	27.4	23.6
	Same, n.c.	29.5	42.8	30.7	35.6
Support ratio		.59	.47	.57	.59
Immigration into United States					
% favoring:	Increase	36.1	18.4	10.4	8.0
	Decrease	27.0	29.9	52.0	44.6
	Same, n.c.	36.9	51.7	37.6	47.4
Support ratio		.54	.44	.29	.32
Mean support ratios for "equalitarian and human welfare"					
category		.71	.50	.70	.66

tion, slum clearance and public housing, social security, and minimum wages—the leaders of the two parties are widely separated, the differences in their ratio scores ranging from .36 to .21. The percentages showing the proportions who favor increased support for these issues are even more striking. In every instance the Democratic percentages are considerably higher: 66 *vs.* 22 per cent (education); 78 *vs.* 40 per cent (slum clearance and housing); 60 *vs.* 23 per cent (social security); and 50 *vs.* 16 per cent (minimum wages). The Democratic leaders also are better disposed than the Republican leaders toward immigration: twice as many of them (36 per cent *vs.* 18 per cent) favor a change in policy to permit more immigrants to enter. The overall inclination of both party elites, however, is to accept the present levels of immigration, the Democratic ratio score falling slightly above, and the Republican slightly below, the midpoint.

More surprising are the differences on the segregation issue, for, despite strong southern influence, the Democratic leaders express significantly more support for enforcing integration than the Republicans do. Moreover, the difference between the two parties rises from .12 for the national samples as a whole to a difference of .18 when the southern leaders are excluded. In his study of Congress, Turner found that the Republicans gave more support to Negro rights than the Democrats did.[20] The reversal of this finding in our data does not necessarily mean that a change has occurred since Turner made his study, but only that the votes of the congressional parties do not always reflect the private feelings of the national party leadership. Then, too, southern influence is disproportionately stronger in the Democratic congressional party than in the national Democratic organization as a whole, and disproportionately weaker in the Republican congressional party than in the Republican organization as a whole.

Examination of the actual magnitude of the ratio scores in this category reveals that the Republicans want not so much to abrogate existing social welfare or equalitarian measures as to keep them from being broadened. The Democrats, by comparison, are shown to be the party of social equality and reform, more willing than their opponents to employ legislation for the benefit of the underprivileged. Support for these inferences and for the greater liberalism of the Democrats can be found elsewhere in our data as well. Analysis of the scale results show Republican leaders scoring higher than Democratic leaders on such measures as chauvinism, elitism, conservatism, and right-wing values, and lower on tolerance, procedural rights, and faith in democracy. No differences worth noting, however, were found for ethnocentrism, faith in freedom, or the California F scale. The Democrats had a slightly higher average score on the left-wing scale, but the number of leaders in either party who scored high on this measure was fairly small.

The self-images and reference group identifications of the two parties also should be noted in this connection. For example, many more Demo-

---

[20] Turner, *op. cit.,* p. 54.

cratic than Republican leaders call themselves liberal and state that they would be most likely to take advice from liberal reform organizations, the Farmers' Union, and (as we have seen) from the trade unions; only a small number consider themselves conservative or would seek advice from conservative reform organizations, the National Association of Manufacturers, or the Farm Bureau Federation. The Republicans have in almost all instances the reverse identifications: only a handful regard themselves as liberal or would seek counsel from liberal organizations, while more than 42 per cent call themselves conservative and would look to the NAM or to conservative reform organizations for advice. Almost two-thirds of the Republicans (compared with 29 per cent of the Democrats) regard the Chamber of Commerce as an important source of advice. Businessmen are listed as having "too much power" by 42 per cent of the Democrats but by only 9 per cent of the Republicans. The Democrats are also significantly more inclined than the Republicans to consider Catholics, Jews, and the foreign born as having "too little power." While self-descriptions and reference group identifications often correspond poorly with actual beliefs—among the general population

TABLE 2D

Comparison of Party Leaders and Followers on "Tax Policy" Issues, by Percentages and Ratios of Support

	Leaders		Followers	
	Dem.	Repub.	Dem.	Repub.
	N = 1,788	N = 1,232	N = 821	N = 623
Issues		(%s down)		
Corporate income tax				
% favoring: Increase	32.3	4.0	32.0	23.3
Decrease	23.3	61.5	20.5	25.7
Same, n.c.	44.4	34.5	47.5	51.0
Support ratio	.54	.21	.56	.49
Tax on large incomes				
% favoring: Increase	27.0	5.4	46.6	34.7
Decrease	23.1	56.9	13.8	21.7
Same, n.c.	49.9	37.7	39.6	43.6
Support ratio	.52	.24	.66	.56
Tax on business				
% favoring: Increase	12.6	1.0	24.6	15.9
Decrease	38.3	71.1	24.1	32.6
Same, n.c.	49.1	27.8	51.3	51.5
Support ratio	.37	.15	.50	.42
Tax on middle incomes				
% favoring: Increase	2.7	0.8	4.5	3.0
Decrease	50.2	63.9	49.3	44.3
Same, n.c.	47.1	35.3	46.2	52.6
Support ratio	.26	.18	.28	.29
Tax on small incomes				
% favoring: Increase	1.4	2.9	1.6	2.1
Decrease	79.2	65.0	77.5	69.6
Same, n.c.	19.4	32.1	20.9	28.3
Support ratio	.11	.19	.12	.16
Mean support ratios for "tax policy" category	.36	.19	.42	.38

they scarcely correspond at all, in fact—we are dealing, in the case of the leaders, with a politically informed and highly articulate set of people who have little difficulty connecting the beliefs they hold and the groups that promote or obstruct those beliefs.

Our fourth category, Tax Policy, divides the parties almost as severely as do the other categories. The mean difference for the category as a whole is .20, and it would doubtless have been larger but for the universal unpopularity of proposals to increase taxes on small and middle income groups. Table 2D shows that the differences between the parties on the tax issues follow the patterns previously observed and that tax policy is for the Democrats a device for redistributing income and promoting social equality. Neither party, however, is keen about raising taxes for *any* group: even the Democrats have little enthusiasm for new taxes on upper income groups or on business and corporate enterprises. The Republican leaders are overwhelmingly opposed to increased taxes for *any* group, rich *or* poor. This can be seen in their low ratio scores on the tax issues, which range from only .15 to .24. But while they are far more eager than the Democratic leaders to cut taxes on corporate and private wealth, they are less willing to reduce taxes on the lower income

TABLE 2E

Comparison of Party Leaders and Followers on "Foreign Policy" Issues,
by Percentages and Ratios of Support

	Leaders		Followers	
	Dem.	Repub.	Dem.	Repub.
	N = 1,788	N = 1,232	N = 821	N = 623
Issues		(%s down)		
Reliance on the United Nations				
% favoring: Increase	48.9	24.4	34.7	33.4
Decrease	17.6	34.8	17.3	19.3
Same, n.c.	33.5	40.7	48.0	47.3
Support ratio	.66	.45	.59	.57
American participation in				
military alliances				
% favoring: Increase	41.5	22.7	39.1	32.3
Decrease	17.6	25.7	14.0	15.4
Same, n.c.	40.9	51.6	46.9	52.3
Support ratio	.62	.48	.62	.58
Foreign aid				
% favoring: Increase	17.8	7.6	10.1	10.1
Decrease	51.0	61.7	58.6	57.3
Same, n.c.	31.1	30.7	31.3	32.6
Support ratio	.33	.23	.26	.26
Defense spending*				
% favoring: Increase	20.7	13.6	50.5	45.7
Decrease	34.4	33.6	16.4	15.4
Same, n.c.	44.8	52.8	33.0	38.8
Support ratio	.43	.40	.67	.65
Mean support ratios for "foreign				
policy" category (excl.				
defense spending)	.54	.39	.49	.47

* See footnote 22.

groups. These differences, it should be remarked, are not primarily a function of differences in the income of the two samples. Although there are more people with high incomes among the Republican leaders, the disproportion between the two samples is not nearly great enough to account for the dissimilarities in their tax views.

Of the five categories considered, Foreign Policy shows the smallest average difference, but even on these issues the divergence between Democratic and Republican leader attitudes is significant. Except for defense spending the Democrats turn out to be more internationalist than the Republicans, as evidenced in their greater commitment to the United Nations and to American participation in international military alliances like NATO. Twice as many Democrats as Republicans want the United States to rely more heavily upon such organizations, while many more Republicans want to reduce our international involvements. Both parties are predominantly in favor of cutting back foreign aid—a somewhat surprising finding in light of Democratic public pronouncements on this subject—but more Republicans feel strongly on the subject. Our data thus furnish little support for the claim that the parties hold the same views on foreign policy or that their seeming differences are merely a response to the demands of political competition.[21]

Nevertheless, it would be incorrect to conclude that one party believes in internationalism and the other in isolationism. The differences are far too small to warrant any such inference. Traces of isolationism, to be sure, remain stronger in the Republican party than in the Democratic party—an observation buttressed by the finding that twice as many Republicans as Democrats score high on the isolationism scale. The pattern of Republican responses on both the issue and scale items signifies, however, that the leaders of that party generally accept the degree of "internationalism" now in effect, but shrink from extending it further. Consider too, the similarities in the leaders' scores on defense spending, for despite their greater leaning toward isolationism, the Republicans are no more inclined than the Democrats to leave the country defenseless.[22]

---

[21] Cf. Turner, op. cit., p. 56, in which he found differences on foreign policy difficult to assess in Congress, partly because of its tie with the executive branch; see also, George Belknap and Angus Campbell, "Political Party Identification and Attitudes toward Foreign Policy," Public Opinion Quarterly, Vol. XV (Winter 1951–52), pp. 608–19.

[22] The issue of defense spending has been kept separate from the other foreign policy issues because the magnitude of the scores for some of the leaders and all of the followers were obviously inflated by the launching of Sputnik I in November, 1957. The Sputnik incident occurred between the first and second wave of the leader survey and produced an increase in the number favoring defense spending of 40 per cent for the Democrats and 33 per cent for the Republicans. While this is a fascinating testimonial to the influence sometimes exercised by events on public opinion, its effect in this case was to distort scores in such a way as to make the leader and follower samples non-comparable. With proper caution, however, comparisons can be made between the Democratic and Republican leaders since both samples were affected in roughly the same way by Sputnik. For a similar reason we can also compare the Democratic followers with the Republican followers. Comparisons between leaders and followers on this issue cannot, however, be justified from our data.

In treating issues in the Elmira election study of 1948, Berelson, Lazarsfeld, and McPhee[23] found it helpful to distinguish between "style" and "position" issues. "Style" issues principally yield symbolic, psychological, or subjective gratifications, and have relatively intangible consequences; "position" issues reflect direct, personal and material interests, and have more objective consequences. According to the Elmira report, "position" issues (or what politicians might call "bread and butter" issues) divide voters more sharply than style issues. Most of the issues tested in the present study would have to be classified as "position" issues, but five of them—United Nations, international alliances, foreign aid, immigration, and segregation—could be classified as style issues. Four others—natural resources, atomic energy, education, and slum clearance —contain both symbolic and material elements and can best be described as "mixed."

Although the classification is crude, the findings it yields are generally consistent with the claims of the Elmira study. On the fourteen position issues—taxes, trade unions, tariffs, minimum wages, farm prices, social security, credit restrictions, and the regulation of business, public utilities and monopolies—Democratic and Republican leaders show an average ratio score difference of .21. On the style issues the two parties differ by .13—a significantly smaller difference. Largest of all, however, are the differences for the "mixed" issues, which average more than .30. This result should occasion little surprise, for when ideology and interest are both at work, partisanship is likely to be intensified. Several considerations could account for the superiority of position over style issues as causes of political cleavage: they are "bread and butter" issues, and are thus more often subject to pressure by organized interest groups; they have immediate and tangible consequences, which may lead politicians to pay greater attention to them than they do to issues whose payoff is more uncertain; and, finally, they are not so likely to be part of the common core of values upon which the community structure rests.

Comparison of the magnitude of the differences between groups can be seen in Table 3, where we have ranked the issues, high to low, according to the size of the difference between the groups being compared. By presenting a rank-order of differences for the two leader groups, for the two follower groups, and for the leaders and followers of each party, this table makes it possible to observe not only which issues most and least divide the several party groups, but whether they divide the leaders and followers in the same way.

Notice that the issues commonly thought to be most divisive do not always evoke the greatest cleavage between the parties. Immigration, tariffs, civil rights, monopoly control, and credit regulation fall toward the lower end of the rank order, while farm supports, federal aid to education, slum clearance, social security, minimum wages, public housing, and issues dealing with the regulation and taxation of business fall toward the upper end. Though by no means uniformly, the older, more

---

23 Bernard R. Berelson, Paul F. Lazarsfeld, and William N. McPhee, *Voting* (Chicago, 1954), ch. 9.

TABLE 3. Rank Order of Differences in the Support-Ratio Scores of Party Leaders and Followers*

	Democratic vs. Republican Leaders		Democratic vs. Republican Followers		Democratic Leaders vs. Followers		Republican Leaders vs. Followers	
	Issues	Diff. between Ratio Scores‡	Issues	Diff. between Ratio Scores	Issues	Diff. between Ratio Scores	Issues	Diff. between Ratio Scores
1.	Natural resources	+.39	Farm supports	+.14	Immigration	+.25	Fed. aid to edu.	−.39
2.	Farm supports	+.38	Gov't. reg. of business	+.12	Anti-monopoly	+.15	Taxes—large income	−.32
3.	Fed. aid to edu.	+.37	Taxes—large income	+.10	Taxes—large income	−.15	Taxes—corp.	−.28
4.	Taxes—corp.	+.33	Minimum wages	+.09	Taxes—business	−.13	Taxes—business	−.27
5.	Reg.—business	+.33	Taxes—business	+.09	Reg. pub. util.	+.12	Natural resources	−.23
6.	Taxes—large inc.	+.28	Reg. pub. util.	+.07	Tariffs	−.11	Pub. housing	−.23
7.	Pub. housing	+.27	Taxes—corp.	+.07	Restrict. credit	−.09	Reg. business	−.22
8.	Reg. pub. util.	+.27	Social security	+.07	Natural resources	+.09	Social security	−.22
9.	Social security	+.26	Fed. aid to edu.	+.06	Fed. aid to edu.	−.08	Farm supports	−.22
10.	Taxes—business	+.23	Reg. trade unions	+.05	Foreign aid	+.08	Minimum wages	−.18
11.	Minimum wages	+.22	Natural resources	+.05	Reliance on U.N.	+.07	Reg. trade unions	+.17
12.	Reliance on U.N.	+.21	Public housing	+.05	Minimum wages	−.05	Immigration	−.13
13.	Anti-monopoly	+.20	Taxes—small income	−.04	Social security	−.05	Reliance on U.N.	−.12
14.	Atomic energy control	+.18	American participation, NATO	+.04	Reg. trade unions	+.05	Enforce integration	−.12
15.	Reg. trade unions	−.18	Atomic energy control	+.04	Atomic energy control	+.04	Taxes—middle income	−.11
16.	American participation, NATO	+.13	Immigration	−.03	Farm supports	+.02	Atomic energy control	−.10
17.	Enforce integration	+.12	Defense spending	+.02	Reg. business	−.02	American participation, NATO	−.10
18.	Tariffs	−.11	Taxes—middle income	−.02	Enforce integration	+.01	Reg. public utilities	−.07
19.	Foreign aid	+.10	Reliance on U.N.	+.02	Taxes—middle income	−.01	Anti-monopoly	−.04
20.	Increase immigration	+.10	Tariffs	−.01	Taxes—corporation	−.01	Foreign aid	−.03
21.	Taxes—small income.	−.08	Enforce integration	−.01	Taxes—small income	−.01	Taxes—small income	+.03
22.	Taxes—middle income	+.08	Restriction credit	+.01	American participation, NATO	−.01	Restriction credit	−.01
23.	Restriction credit	−.07	Foreign aid	−.01	Public housing	−.01	Tariffs	−.01
24.	Defense spending	−.03	Anti-monopoly	.00	Defense spending	‡	Defense spending	‡

N's. Democratic leaders: 1,788; Republican leaders: 1,232; Democratic followers: 821; Republican followers: 623.

* The plus sign means that the first group listed in the heading is the more favorable to the issue named in the heading; the minus sign means that the second group is the more favorable.

† Leaders and followers cannot be compared on defense spending, for reasons given in footnote to Table 2E.

‡ Size of difference required for differences to be significant at .01 level: Democratic leaders vs. Republican—.048; Democratic leaders vs. Republican followers—.068; Democratic followers vs. Democratic leaders—.054; Republican leaders vs. Republican followers—.063.

traditional issues appear to have been superseded as sources of controversy by issues that have come into prominence chiefly during the New Deal and Fair Deal.

IV. COMPARISONS BETWEEN FOLLOWERS

So far we have addressed ourselves to the differences between Democratic and Republican *leaders*. In each of the tables presented, however, data are included from which the two sets of party *followers* may also be compared.

The observation most clearly warranted from these data is that the rank-and-file members of the two parties are far less divided than their leaders. Not only do they diverge significantly on fewer issues—seven as compared with 23 for the leader samples—but the magnitudes of the differences in their ratio scores are substantially smaller for every one of the 24 issues. No difference is larger than .14, and on the majority of the issues the disparity is smaller than .05. Insofar as they differ at all, however, the followers tend to divide in a pattern similar to that shown by the leaders, the correlation between their rank orders being .72. All the issues on which the followers significantly disagree are of the "bread and butter" variety, the more symbolic issues being so remotely experienced and so vaguely grasped that rank-and-file voters are often unable to identify them with either party. Policies affecting farm prices, business regulation, taxes, or minimum wages, by contrast, are quickly felt by the groups to whom they are addressed and are therefore more capable of arousing partisan identifications. It should also be noted that while the average differences are small for all five categories, they are smallest of all for foreign policy—the most removed and least well understood group of issues in the entire array.[24]

Democratic and Republican followers were also compared on a number of scales and reference group questions. The results, while generally consistent with the differences between the leaders, show the followers to be far more united than their leaders on these measures as well. Even on business attitudes, independence of government, and economic conservatism, the differences are small and barely significant. No differences were found on such scales as tolerance, faith in democracy, procedural rights, conservatism–liberalism (classical), the California F scale and isolationism. The average Democrat is slightly more willing than the average Republican to label himself a liberal or to seek advice from liberal organizations; the contrary is true when it comes to adopting conservative identifications. Only in the differential trust they express toward business and labor are the two sets of followers widely separated.

---

[24] For comparative data on party affiliation and issue outlooks among rank-and-file voters, see Angus Campbell, Phillip E. Converse, Warren E. Miller, and Donald E. Stokes, *The American Voter* (New York, 1960), especially chs. 8 and 9 dealing with issues and ideology. The test of this important report on the 1956 election study carried out by the Michigan Survey Research Center unfortunately reached us too late to be used to full advantage in the present analysis. The findings of the Michigan and the PAB studies, relative to the role of issues and ideology among the general population, corroborate and supplement each other to a very great degree.

These findings give little support to the claim that the "natural divisions" of the electorate are being smothered by party leaders.[25] Not only do the leaders disagree more sharply than their respective followers, but the level of consensus among the electorate (with or without regard to party) is fairly high. Inspection of the "increase" and "decrease" percentage scores (Table 2A–2E) shows that substantial differences of opinion exist among the electorate on only five of the 24 issues (credit restrictions, farm supports, segregation, and corporate and business taxes). Of course, voters may divide more sharply on issues at election time, since campaigns intensify party feeling and may also intensify opinions on issues. Available data from election studies allow no unequivocal conclusion on this point,[26] but even the party-linked differences found among voters during elections may largely be echoes of the opinions announced by the candidates—transient sentiments developed for the occasion and quickly forgotten.

V. LEADER CONFLICT AND FOLLOWER CONSENSUS: EXPLANATIONS

Considering the nature of the differences between the leader and follower samples, the interesting question is not why the parties fail to represent the "natural division" in the electorate (for that question rests on an unwarranted assumption) but why the party elites disagree at all, and why they divide so much more sharply than their followers.

Despite the great pressures toward uniformity we have noted in American society, many forces also divide the population culturally, economically, and politically. The United States is, after all, a miscellany of ethnic and religious strains set down in a geographically large and diverse country. Many of these groups brought old conflicts and ideologies with them, and some have tried to act out in the new world the hopes and frustrations nurtured in the old. Then, too, despite rapid social mobility, social classes have by no means been eliminated. No special political insight is needed to perceive that the two parties characteristically draw from different strata of the society, the Republicans from the managerial, proprietary, and to some extent professional classes, the Democrats from labor, minorities, low income groups, and a large proportion of the intellectuals.[27] Partly because the leaders of the two parties tend to overrespond to the modal values of the groups with which they are

---

[25] Cf. Stephen K. Bailey, The Condition of Our National Parties (monograph), Fund for the Republic, 1959.

[26] The data reported by the Elmira study of 1948 show the supporters of the two parties to be largely in agreement on issues. See ibid., pp. 186, 190, 194, 211. The findings of the 1956 Michigan Survey suggest strongly that most voters, even at election time, do not know much about issues and are unable to link the parties with particular issues. Campbell and his associates conclude, for example, that "many people fail to appreciate that an issue exists; others are insufficiently involved to pay attention to recognized issues; and still others fail to make connections between issue positions and party policy." The American Voter, op. cit., ch. 8.

[27] For an analysis of the connection between intellectuals and liberal politics, see Seymour M. Lipset, Political Man (New York, 1960), ch. 10; also Paul F. Lazarsfeld and Wagner Thielens, Jr., The Academic Mind (Glencoe, 1958), chs. 1 and 2.

principally identified, they gradually grow further apart on the key questions which separate their respective supporters.[28] The Republican emphasis on business ideology is both a cause and a consequence of its managerial and proprietary support; the greater Democratic emphasis on social justice, and on economic and social leveling, is both the occasion and the product of the support the party enjoys among intellectuals and the lower strata. These interrelationships are strengthened, moreover, by the tendency for a party's dominant supporters to gain a disproportionate number of positions in its leadership ranks.[29]

The differences which typically separate Democratic from Republican leaders seem also to reflect a deep-seated ideological cleavage often found among Western parties. One side of this cleavage is marked by a strong belief in the power of collective action to promote social justice, equality, humanitarianism, and economic planning, while preserving freedom; the other is distinguished by faith in the wisdom of the natural competitive process and in the supreme virtue of individualism, "character," self-reliance, frugality, and independence from government. To this cleavage is added another frequent source of political division, namely, a difference in attitude toward change between "radicals" and "moderates," between those who prefer to move quickly or slowly, to reform or to conserve. These differences in social philosophy and posture do not always coincide with the divisions in the social structure, and their elements do not, in all contexts, combine in the same way. But, however crudely, the American parties do tend to embody these competing points of view and to serve as reference groups for those who hold them.

Party cleavage in America was no doubt intensified by the advent of the New Deal, and by its immense electoral and intellectual success. Not only did it weld into a firm alliance the diverse forces that were to be crucial to all subsequent Democratic majorities, but it also made explicit the doctrines of the "welfare state" with which the party was henceforth to be inseparably identified. Because of the novelty of its program and its apparently radical threat to the familiar patterns of American political and economic life, it probably deepened the fervor of its Republican adversaries and drove into the opposition the staunchest defenders of business ideology. The conflict was further sharpened by the decline of left-wing politics after the war, and by the transfer of loyalties of former and potential radicals to the Democratic party. Once launched, the cleavage has been sustained by the tendency for each party to attract into its active ranks a disproportionate number of voters who recognize and share its point of view.

Why, however, are the leaders so much more sharply divided than their followers? The reasons are not hard to understand and are consistent with several of the hypotheses that underlay the present study.

(1) Consider, to begin with, that the leaders come from the more articulate segments of society and, on the average, are politically more

---

[28] Samuel P. Huntington, "A Revised Theory of American Party Politics," *American Political Science Review,* Vol. XLIV (1950), p. 676.

[29] PAB data supporting this generalization will be presented in a future publication.

aware than their followers and far better informed about issues.[30] For them, political issues and opinions are the everyday currency of party competition, not esoteric matters that surpass understanding. With their greater awareness and responsibility, and their greater need to defend their party's stands, they have more interest in developing a consistent set of attitudes—perhaps even an ideology. The followers of each party, often ignorant of the issues and their consequences, find it difficult to distinguish their beliefs from those of the opposition and have little reason to be concerned with the consistency of their attitudes. Furthermore, the American parties make only a feeble effort to educate the rank-and-file politically, and since no central source exists for the authoritative pronouncement of party policy,[31] the followers often do not know what their leaders believe or on what issues the parties chiefly divide. In short, if we mean by ideology a coherent body of informed social doctrine, it is possessed mainly by the articulate leadership, rarely by the masses.

(2) Differences in the degree of partisan involvement parallel the differences in knowledge and have similar consequences. The leaders, of course, have more party spirit than the followers, and, as the election studies make plain, the stronger the partisanship, the larger the differences on issues. The leaders are more highly motivated not only to belong to a party appropriate to their beliefs, but to accept its doctrines and to learn how it differs from the opposition party. Since politics is more salient for leaders than for followers, they develop a greater stake in the outcome of the political contest and are more eager to discover the intellectual grounds by which they hope to make victory possible. Through a process of circular reinforcement, those for whom politics is most important are likely to become the most zealous participants, succeeding to the posts that deal in the formation of opinion. Ideology serves the instrumental purpose, in addition, of justifying the heavy investment that party leaders make in political activity. While politics offers many rewards, it also makes great demands on the time, money, and energies of its practitioners—sacrifices which they can more easily justify if they believe they are serving worthwhile social goals. The followers, in contrast, are intellectually far less involved, have less personal stake in the outcome of the competition, have little need to be concerned with the "correctness" of their views on public questions, and have even less reason to learn in precisely what ways their opinions differ from their opponents'. Hence, the party elites recruit members from a population stratified in some measure by ideology, while the rank-and-file renews itself by more random recruitment and is thus more likely to mirror the opinions of a cross section of the population.

(3) Part of the explanation for the greater consensus among followers than leaders resides in the nature and size of the two types of groups. Whereas the leader groups are comparatively small and selective, each of the follower groups number in the millions and, by their very size and

---

[30] For the effects of education on issue familiarity, see Campbell, et al., op. cit., ch. 8.

[31] Schattschneider, op. cit.; Toward a More Responsible Two-Party System, op. cit., passim.

unwieldiness, are predisposed to duplicate the characteristics of the population as a whole. Even if the Republicans draw disproportionately from the business-managerial classes and the Democrats from the trade union movement, neither interest group has enough influence to shape distinctively the aggregate opinions of so large a mass of supporters. Size also affects the nature and frequency of interaction within the two types of groups. Because they comprise smaller, more selectively chosen, organized, and articulate elite, the leaders are apt to associate with people of their own political persuasion more frequently and consistently than the followers do. They are not only less cross-pressured than the rank-and-file but they are also subjected to strong party group efforts to induce them to conform. Because their political values are continually renewed through frequent communication with people of like opinions, and because they acquire intense reference group identifications, they develop an extraordinary ability to resist the force of the opposition's arguments. While the followers, too, are thrown together and shielded to some extent, they are likely to mingle more freely with people of hostile political persuasions, to receive fewer partisan communications, and to hold views that are only intermittently and inconsistently reinforced. Since, by comparison with the leaders, they possess little interest in or information about politics, they can more easily embrace "deviant" attitudes without discomfort and without challenge from their associates. Nor are they likely to be strongly rewarded for troubling to have "correct" opinions. The followers, in short, are less often and less effectively indoctrinated than their leaders. The group processes described here would function even more powerfully in small, sectarian, tightly organized parties of the European type, but they are also present in the American party system, where they yield similar though less potent consequences.

(4) Political competition itself operates to divide the leaders more than the followers. If the parties are impelled to present a common face to the electorate, they are also strongly influenced to distinguish themselves from each other.[32] For one thing, they have a more heightened sense of the "national interest" than the followers do, even if they do not all conceive it in the same way. For another, they hope to improve their chances at the polls by offering the electorate a recognizable and attractive commodity. In addition, they seek emotional gratification in the heightened sense of brotherhood brought on by the struggle against an "outgroup" whose claim to office seems always, somehow, to border upon usurpation. As with many ingroup–outgroup distinctions, the participants search for moral grounds to justify their antagonisms toward each other, and ideologies help to furnish such grounds. Among the followers, on the other hand, these needs exist, if at all, in much weaker form.

VI. LEADERS VERSUS FOLLOWERS

In comparing each party elite with its own followers we were mainly interested in seeing how closely each body of supporters shared the point

---

[32] See E. E. Schattschneider, *Party Government, op. cit.,* p. 192.

of view of its leaders, in order to test the hypothesis that party affiliation, even for the rank-and-file, is a function of ideological agreement. In predicting that the parties would tend to attract supporters who share their beliefs, we expected, of course, to find exceptions. We knew that many voters pay little attention to the ideological aspects of politics and that, in Gabriel Almond's phrase, a party's more "esoteric doctrines" are not always known to its followers.[33] Nevertheless we were not prepared for the findings turned up by this phase of the inquiry, for the differences between leaders and followers—among the Republicans at least—are beyond anything we had expected. Indeed, the conclusion is inescapable that the views of the Republican rank-and-file are, on the whole, much closer to those of the Democratic leaders than to those of the Republican leaders. Although conflicts in outlook also exist between Democratic leaders and followers, they are less frequent or severe.

If we turn once again to the table of rank-order differences, we see that the Democratic followers differ significantly from their leaders on twelve of the 23 issues, and that the average difference in the ratio scores of the two samples is .07. Democratic leaders and Republican followers differ significantly on only eleven of the 23 issues, with an average difference between them of only .08. Notice, by contrast, that Republican leaders and followers diverge significantly on 18 of the 23 issues, and show an average difference of .16. To complete the comparison, the Republican leaders and Democratic followers were in disagreement on 19 of the 23 issues, their average difference being .20. As these comparisons make plain, there is substantial consensus on national issues between Democratic leaders and Democratic and Republican followers, while the Republican leaders are separated not only from the Democrats but from their own rank-and-file members as well.

Examination of the Democratic scores shows the leaders to be slightly more "progressive" than their followers on most of the issues on which differences appear. The leaders are, for example, more favorable to public ownership of natural resources, to regulation of monopolies and public utilities, to a reduction of tariffs, and to a liberalized credit policy. They are more internationalist on the foreign aid and United Nations issues and substantially more sympathetic to the maintenance and expansion of immigration. The results showing the relative radicalism of the two samples are not unequivocal, however, for on several issues— federal aid to education, minimum wages, and taxes on business enterprise and large incomes—the followers take the more radical view. Nor are the differences significant on such issues as atomic energy, slum clearance, segregation, farm price supports, government control of business and trade unions, and taxes on middle and small income groups. In general, the followers turn out more radical chiefly on a few of the "bread and butter issues"—a reflection, no doubt, of their lower socioeconomic status. When we control for occupation, the differences between Democratic leaders and followers on these issues largely disappear.

Consideration of the scores of Republican leaders and followers shows

---

[33] Gabriel Almond, *The Appeals of Communism* (Princeton, 1954), pp. 5–6, and ch. 3.

not only that they are widely separated in their outlooks but also that the leaders are uniformly more conservative than their followers. Only on the immigration issue is this trend reversed. The followers hold the more "radical" ideas on the two public ownership issues, on five of the six equalitarian and human welfare issues, on four of the seven regulation-of-the-economy issues, and on four of the five tax policy issues. They are also more willing to place greater reliance upon the U.N. and upon international military alliances. Observe that the largest differences occur on those issues which have most sharply separated New Deal-Fair Deal spokesmen from the hard core of the Republican opposition—federal aid to education, redistribution of wealth through taxes on business, corporations and the wealthy, public ownership of natural resources, public housing, regulation of business, social security, farm price supports, minimum wages, and trade union regulations.

In short, whereas Republican leaders hold to the tenets of business ideology and remain faithful to the spirit and intellectual mood of leaders like Robert A. Taft, the rank-and-file Republican supporters have embraced, along with their Democratic brethren, the regulatory and social reform measures of the Roosevelt and Truman administrations. This inference receives further support from the scores on our Party Ideology scale where, on a variety of attitudes and values which characteristically distinguish the leaders of the two parties, the Republican followers fall closer to the Democratic than to the Republican side of the continuum. Thus, in addition to being the preferred party of the more numerous classes, the Democrats also enjoy the advantages over their opponents of holding views that are more widely shared throughout the country.

Assuming the findings are valid, we were obviously wrong expect that party differentiation among followers would depend heavily upon ideological considerations.[34] Evidently, party attachment is so much a function of other factors (e.g. class and primary group memberships, religious affiliation, place of residence, mass media, etc.) that many voters can maintain their party loyalties comfortably even while holding views that contradict the beliefs of their own leaders.

Still, we are not entitled to conclude that issue outlook has no effect on the party affiliation of ordinary members. It is conceivable, for example, that the Republican party has come to be the minority party partly because the opinions of its spokesmen are uncongenial to a majority of the voters. We have no way of knowing from our data—collected at only a single point in time—how many "normally" Republican voters, if any, have defected to the Democrats or fled into independency because they disapprove of Republican beliefs. At the present stage of the analysis, we have no grounds for going beyond the proposition that political affiliation without conformity on issues is possible on a wide scale. In future analyses we shall attempt to learn more about the nature of the relationship between belief and party affiliation by stratifying voters

---

[34] See the discussion bearing on this conclusion in Campbell et al., op. cit., chs. 8 and 9. Also, Avery Leiserson, *Parties and Politics, An Institutional and Behavioral Approach* (New York, 1958), pp. 162–66.

according to the frequency with which they conform to the beliefs of their party leaders. We hope, in this way, to discover whether those who conform least are also less firm in their party loyalties.

VII. THE HOMOGENEITY OF SUPPORT FOR LEADERS AND FOLLOWERS

So far we have only considered conflict and agreement *between* groups. We should now turn to the question of consensus *within* groups. To what extent is each of our samples united on fundamental issues?

In order to assess homogeneity of opinion within party groups, standard deviation scores were computed on each issue for each of the four samples. The higher the standard deviation, of course, the greater the disagreement. The range of possible sigma scores is from 0 (signifying that every member of the sample has selected the same response) to .500 (signifying that all responses are equally divided between the "increase" and "decrease" alternatives). If we assume that the three alternative responses had been randomly (and therefore equally) selected, the standard deviations for the four samples would fall by chance alone around .410. Scores at or above this level may be taken to denote extreme dispersion among the members of a sample while scores in the neighborhood of .300 or below suggest that unanimity within the sample is fairly high. By these somewhat arbitrary criteria we can observe immediately (Table 4) that consensus within groups is greater on most issues than we would expect by chance alone, but that it is extremely high in only a few instances. Although the Republican leaders appear on the average to be the most united and the Democratic leaders the least united of the four groups, the difference between their homogeneity scores (.340 vs. .310) is too small to be taken as conclusive. The grounds are somewhat better for rejecting the belief that leaders are more homogeneous in their outlooks than their followers, since the hypothesis holds only for one party and not for the other.

While generalizations about the relative unity of the four samples seem risky, we can speak more confidently about the rank order of agreement *within* samples. In Table 4 we have ranked the issues according to the degree of consensus exhibited toward them by the members of each of the four party groups. There we see that the leaders of the Republican party are most united on the issues that stem from its connections with business—government regulation of business, taxes (especially on business), regulation of trade unions, and minimum wages. The Democratic leaders are most united on those issues which bear upon the support the party receives from the lower and middle income groups—taxes on small and middle incomes, anti-monopoly, slum clearance, social security, and minimum wages. The Republican leaders divide most severely on federal aid to education, slum clearance, U.N. support, segregation, and public control of atomic energy and natural resources; the Democratic leaders are most divided on farm prices, segregation, credit restrictions, immigration, and the natural resources issue. Among the followers the patterns of unity and division are very similar, as attested by the high correlation

TABLE 4
Consensus within Party Groups: Rank Order of Homogeneity of Support on Twenty-Four Issues

Average Rank Order°	Issue	Democratic Leaders		Republican Leaders		Democratic Followers		Republican Followers	
		Rank Order	Sigma	Rank Order	Sigma	Rank Order	Sigma	Rank Order	Sigma
1	Tax on small incomes	1	.220	6	.270	1	.224	1	.250
2	Tax on middle incomes	3	.276	4	.248	6	.292	2	.278
3	Social security benefits	5	.282	8	.296	2	.266	3	.286
4	Minimum wages	6	.292	5	.268	4	.276	4	.294
5	Enforcement of anti-monopoly	2	.246	13	.321	8	.324	7	.314
6	Regulation of public utilities	8	.307	10	.300	10	.336	5.5	.310
7	Slum clearance	4	.276	23	.386	3	.274	5.5	.310
8	Regulation of trade unions	12	.356	3	.240	9	.331	15	.345
9	Government regulation of business	17	.376	1	.192	20	.363	8	.315
10	Tax on business	9	.338	2	.236	19	.362	16	.348
11	Level of tariffs	10	.350	16	.344	11	.338	9	.316
12	Public control of atomic energy	7	.302	20	.362	7	.312	13	.340
13	Federal aid to education	13	.360	24	.394	5	.283	11	.322
14	Foreign aid	19	.383	12	.317	12.5	.340	12	.340
15	Tax on large incomes	11	.356	9	.298	17	.358	22	.379
16	American participation in military alliances, NATO	14	.370	18	.351	14	.350	14	.344
17	Immigration into U.S.	21	.399	17	.345	12.5	.340	10	.318
18	Corporate income tax	16	.375	7	.284	21	.371	17	.361
19	Restrictions on credit	22	.400	14	.324	16	.358	18	.362
20	Defense spending ...	15	.371	15	.334	22	.380	21	.366
21	Public ownership of natural resources ..	20	.393	19	.354	15	.352	19	.362
22	Reliance on U.N.	18	.380	22	.384	18	.359	20	.365
23	Level of farm supports	24	.421	11	.306	23	.414	23	.397
24	Enforce integration ..	23	.416	21	.382	24	.418	24	.399

° The range of sigma scores is from .192 to .421, out of a possible range of .000 (most united) to .500 (least united). Hence, the lower the rank order the greater the unity on the issue named.

of .83 between the rank orders of their homogeneity scores. Both Republican and Democratic followers exhibit great cohesion, for example, on taxes on small and middle incomes, social security, slum clearance, and minimum wages. Both divide rather sharply on segregation, farm price support, defense spending, U.N. support, and taxes on large incomes. The two sets of followers, in short, are alike not only in their opinions on issues but in the degree of unanimity they exhibit toward them.

Inspection of the homogeneity data furnishes additional evidence on the between-group comparisons made earlier. Whereas Democratic and Republican followers divide on issues in approximately the same way, the two sets of leaders differ from each other in this respect also (the correlation between their rank orders on homogeneity is only .28). Democratic leaders and followers tend to unite or divide on the same issues for the most part (r equals .77), but Republican leaders and followers are not parallel in this respect either (r equals .30). The pattern of homogeneity and dispersion among Republican followers is, in fact, much closer to that of the Democratic leaders (r equals .75).

In computing scores for homogeneity we were in part concerned to test the belief that political parties develop greatest internal solidarity on those questions which most separate them from their opponents. According to this hypothesis, external controversy has the effect of uniting the members further by confronting them with a common danger. Whether or not this hypothesis would be borne out in a study of small, sectarian parties we cannot say, but it receives no support from the present study of the American mass parties. Comparisons of the rank-order data in Tables 3 and 4 show that there is no consistent connection between interparty conflict and intraparty cohesion. The correlations between the rank orders of difference and the rank orders of homogeneity are in every case insignificant.[35]

SUMMARY AND CONCLUSIONS

The research described in this paper—an outgrowth of a nationwide inquiry into the nature and sources of political affiliation, activity, and belief—was principally designed to test a number of hypotheses about the relation of ideology to party membership. Responses from large samples of Democratic and Republican leaders and followers were compared on twenty-four key issues and on a number of attitude questions and scales. Statistical operations were carried out to assess conflict and consensus among party groups and to estimate the size and significance of differences. From the data yielded by this inquiry, the following inferences seem warranted.

1. Although it has received wide currency, especially among Europeans, the belief that the two American parties are identical in principle and doctrine has little foundation in fact. Examination of the opinions of Democratic and Republican leaders shows them to be distinct communities of co-believers who diverge sharply on many important issues. Their disagreements, furthermore, conform to an image familiar to many observers and are generally consistent with differences turned up by studies of Congressional roll calls. The unpopularity of many of the posi-

---

[35] For an interesting set of comparative data on the relation of internal party cohesion to issue outlook, see Morris Davis and Sidney Verba, "Party Affiliation and International Opinions in Britain and France, 1947–1956," *Public Opinion Quarterly,* Winter 1960–61.

tions held by Republican leaders suggests also that the parties submit to the demands of their constituents less slavishly than is commonly supposed.

2. Republican and Democratic leaders stand furthest apart on the issues that grow out of their group identification and support—out of the managerial, proprietary, and high-status connections of the one, and the labor, minority, low-status, and intellectual connections of the other. The opinions of each party elite are linked less by chance than by membership in a common ideological domain. Democratic leaders typically display the stronger urge to elevate the lowborn, the uneducated, the deprived minorities, and the poor in general; they are also more disposed to employ the nation's collective power to advance humanitarian and social welfare goals (e.g., social security, immigration, racial integration, a higher minimum wage, and public education). They are more critical of wealth and big business and more eager to bring them under regulation. Theirs is the greater faith in the wisdom of using legislation for redistributing the national product and for furnishing social services on a wide scale. Of the two groups of leaders, the Democrats are the more "progressively" oriented toward social reform and experimentation. The Republican leaders, while not uniformly differentiated from their opponents, subscribe in greater measure to the symbols and practices of individualism, *laissez-faire*, and national independence. They prefer to overcome humanity's misfortunes by relying upon personal effort, private incentives, frugality, hard work, responsibility, self-denial (for both men and government), and the strengthening rather than the diminution of the economic and status distinctions that are the "natural" rewards of the differences in human character and fortunes. Were it not for the hackneyed nature of the designation and the danger of forcing traits into a mold they fit only imperfectly, we might be tempted to describe the Republicans as the chief upholders of what Max Weber has called the "Protestant Ethic."[36] Not that the Democrats are insensible to the "virtues" of the Protestant-capitalistic ethos, but they embrace them less firmly or uniformly. The differences between the two elites have probably been intensified by the rise of the New Deal and by the shift of former radicals into the Democratic party following the decline of socialist and other left-wing movements during and after the war.

3. Whereas the leaders of the two parties diverge strongly, their followers differ only moderately in their attitudes toward issues. The hypothesis that party beliefs unite adherents and bring them into the party ranks may hold for the more active members of a mass party but not for its rank-and-file supporters. Republican followers, in fact, disagree far more with their own leaders than with the leaders of the Democratic party. Little support was found for the belief that deep cleavages exist among the electorate but are ignored by the leaders. One might, indeed, more accurately assert the contrary, to wit: that the natural cleavages

---

[36] Max Weber, *Protestant Ethic and the Spirit of Capitalism* (London, 1948), ch. V.

between the leaders are largely ignored by the voters. However, we cannot presently conclude that ideology exerts no influence over the habits of party support, for the followers do differ significantly and in the predicted directions on some issues. Furthermore, we do not know how many followers may previously have been led by doctrinal considerations to shift their party allegiances.

4. Except for their desire to ingratiate themselves with as many voters as possible, the leaders of the two parties have more reason than their followers to hold sharply opposing views on the important political questions of the day. Compared with the great mass of supporters, they are articulate, informed, highly partisan, and involved; they comprise a smaller and more tightly knit group which is closer to the wellsprings of party opinion, more accessible for indoctrination, more easily rewarded or punished for conformity or deviation, and far more affected, politically and psychologically, by engagement in the party struggle for office. If the leaders of the two parties are not always candid about their disagreements, the reason may well be that they sense the great measure of consensus to be found among the electorate.

5. Finding that party leaders hold contrary beliefs does not prove that they *act* upon these beliefs or that the two parties are, in practice, governed by different outlooks. In a subsequent paper we shall consider these questions more directly by comparing platform and other official party pronouncements with the private opinions revealed in this study. Until further inquiries are conducted, however, it seems reasonable to assume that the views held privately by party leaders can never be entirely suppressed but are bound to crop out in hundreds of large and small ways—in campaign speeches, discussions at party meetings, private communications to friends and sympathizers, statements to the press by party officials and candidates, legislative debates, and public discussions on innumerable national, state, and local questions. If, in other words, the opinions of party leaders are as we have described them, there is every chance that they are expressed and acted upon to some extent. Whether this makes our parties "ideological" depends, of course, on how narrow we define that term. Some may prefer to reserve that designation for parties that are more obviously preoccupied with doctrine, more intent upon the achievement of a systematic political program, and more willing to enforce a common set of beliefs upon their members and spokesmen.

6. The parties are internally united on some issues, divided on others. In general, Republican leaders achieve greatest homogeneity on issues that grow out of their party's identification with business, Democratic leaders on issues that reflect their connection with liberal and lower-income groups. We find no support for the hypothesis that the parties achieve greatest internal consensus on the issues which principally divide them from their opponents.

In a sequel to this paper we shall offer data on the demographic correlates of issue support, which show that most of the differences presented here exist independently of factors like education, occupation, age, religion, and sectionalism. Controlling for these influences furnishes much additional information and many new insights but does not upset our present conclusions in any important respect. Thus, the parties must be considered not merely as spokesmen for other interest groups but as reference groups in their own right, helping to formulate, to sustain, and to speak for a recognizable point of view.

Robert W. Jackman

Political Elites, Mass Publics, and Support for Democratic Principles*

Much recent research has concluded that the persistence of responsive and nontyrannical democracies depends upon the maintenance of special political influentials or elites. It is argued that maintaining these groups is essential because they have been socialized, through their participation in the political process, to support democratic principles such as minority rights even when the majority of the polity may not. In fact, many have suggested that this resocialization process is of such magnitude and importance that the end result is a distinctively *political* stratification system, not coterminous with more general patterns of social stratification. Consequently, on phenomena such as support for democratic principles, political elites or influentials demonstrate a level of tolerance *over and above* that which would be expected from a knowledge of their social status alone. This paper questions such broad conclusions about the determinants of political stability primarily by showing that, when compared with members of the mass public in similar social status groups, leaders are not distinctively "tolerant," at least with respect to the principles of minority rights.

THEORETICAL BACKGROUND

Classical democratic theory has long held that effective government requires a citizenry that is involved in and participates in political affairs.

* A slightly modified and abbreviated version reprinted from the *Journal of Politics*, vol. 34, no. 3 (August 1972), 753–73. Copyright 1972.

I should like to thank Charles Cnudde, Douglas Hibbs, Mary Jackman, Donald McCrone, and Brian Silver for their criticisms of and comments on earlier drafts of this paper. The data were kindly made available by the Inter-University Consortium for Political Research through the Data and Program Library Service at the University of Wisconsin. The research was supported in part by the Graduate Research Committee at the University of Wisconsin and by the Political Science Department, Michigan State University.

According to this view, perhaps the basic prerequisite of a stable democracy is general agreement among the electors on both substantive and procedural matters, but with particular emphasis on the latter. The lack of such consensus would mean that there were no constraints on political activity, and hence democratic procedures would break down.[1]

More recently, numerous attempts to revise this view have been made, most notably by the so-called "pluralists." The revisions have been based on two propositions: first, an assumption was made that the United States approximates a democracy sufficiently stable to "test" the model here; and second, recent empirical research (primarily in the United States, but also elsewhere) suggests little consensus on specific democratic procedural norms among the electorate. Where classical theorists would have found these two statements incompatible, the pluralists sought to build a new theory which would help reconcile them. It is useful to outline the steps by which they did so.

While he was not addressing himself specifically to the problem of consensus, Stouffer provided evidence from a national sample suggesting a lack of consensus among the mass public on questions of civil liberties and minority rights.[2] In a similar study of Ann Arbor, Michigan, and Tallahassee, Florida, Prothro and Grigg investigated support for majority rule and minority rights at both abstract and specific levels.[3] Their major conclusion was that a consensus did exist when the questions were phrased abstractly, a consensus that ". . . transcends community, educational, economic, age, sex, party, and other common bases of differences in opinion. . . . When these broad principles are translated into less abstract propositions, however, consensus breaks down completely."[4] They further reported that when they introduced the control variables mentioned above, education appeared to be the most important one, at least with respect to the questions tapping specific applications of the principles. These results are consistent with those of McClosky, who analyzed responses to similar items.[5]

At the same time, some of these authors reported that political elites—that is, those involved actively in political life, whether at the community

---

[1] For examples of the theories involved here, see Ernest S. Griffith, John Plamenatz and J. Roland Pennock, "Cultural Prerequisites to a Successfully Functioning Democracy: A Symposium," *American Political Science Review*, 50 (March 1956), 101–137.

[2] Samuel A. Stouffer, *Communism, Conformity, and Civil Liberties* (New York: Doubleday & Co., 1955), 52.

[3] James W. Prothro and Charles M. Grigg, "Fundamental Principles of Democracy: Bases of Agreement and Disagreement," *Journal of Politics*, 22 (May 1960), 276–294.

[4] *Ibid.*, 286.

[5] Herbert McClosky, "Consensus and Ideology in American Politics," *American Political Science Review*, 58 (June 1964), 361–382. A similar argument is presented by Robert A. Dahl, *Who Governs?* (New Haven, Conn., Yale University Press, 1961), 316–317. Note that in this part of their arguments, McClosky and Dahl are using education primarily to explain variations in tolerance among cross-section samples of the electorate. For a discussion of some British data on the same theme see Ian Budge, *Agreement and the Stability of Democracy* (Chicago: Markham, 1970).

or the national level—appear to be much nearer a consensus over majority rule and minority rights, regardless of whether these questions are asked in specific or abstract terms. Stouffer showed that without exception, each of 14 different types of community leaders were more likely to support the civil liberties of Socialists, atheists, and suspected or self-avowed Communists than was the mass public as a whole.[6] McClosky concluded from his analysis of delegates attending the 1956 Democratic and Republican conventions that "not only do they exhibit stronger support for democratic values than does the electorate, but they are also more consistent in applying the general principle to the specific instance."[7]

An obvious question to ask is: Why this difference? And it is here that the pluralists made their distinctive contribution. First, they compared differences between political elites and the mass public generally in their rates of support for democratic principles within categories of education. The major result was that *within categories of education, elite groups still appeared to be more tolerant than the mass public*. For example, Kornhauser inferred from Stouffer's data that "this difference between leaders and the community at large does not seem to be due simply to education, since 79% of the college educated leaders are among the more tolerant as compared with 66% for the general college educated population."[8] McClosky drew a similar conclusion from his own data: namely, that the political influentials were distinctively more tolerant and supportive of democratic principles. He wrote that "most of the relationships reported in the foregoing have been tested with education, occupation, and sometimes with other demographic variables controlled, but the introduction of these factors does not change the direction of the findings, although it sometimes affects the magnitude of the scores."[9]

In other words, these analysts argued that the usual measures of social stratification by themselves could not explain such elite-mass differentials. Instead, they saw this residual effect as evidence for more directly "political" effects, operating independently of the social stratification system. Increased education would increase tolerance, but only up to a certain point. Beyond that point, the effects of a distinctively political stratification system would operate to produce the observed differences between the elites and the mass public. Key, in particular, spent a good deal of time developing this argument about the separate political stratification system and its special effects, making his case as follows:

---

[6] Stouffer, *Communism*, 57. Similar results are presented by Arnold M. Rose, "Alienation and Participation: A Comparison of Group Leaders and the 'Mass,'" *American Sociological Review*, 27 (December 1962), 834–838.

[7] McClosky, "Consensus," 366.

[8] William Kornhauser, *The Politics of Mass Society* (New York: Free Press, 1959), 67.

[9] McClosky, "Consensus," 373. Similar results are presented for a sample of Berkeley students (1957) by Hanan C. Selvin and Warren O. Hagstrom, "Determinants of Support for Civil Liberties," in *The Berkeley Student Revolt: Facts and Interpretations*, ed. Seymour Martin Lipset and Sheldon S. Wolin (New York: Doubleday & Co., Anchor Books, 1965), 495–518.

. . . the political system is constructed of strata definable in terms of political activity and influence and independent of occupational strata, income levels, and other such readily perceptible indicators beloved of the sociologist and the daily commentator. . . . The . . . political stratum with opinions on many issues and high levels of political activity includes persons at all levels of the occupational hierarchy. Higher occupational strata, to be sure, include larger proportions of persons of above-average political activity and involvement than do the lower occupational strata. *Yet it is the noncongruence of political and occupational strata that is instructive for political analysis.*[10]

Having defined the political stratification system in terms of political activity and as distinct from more general systems of social stratification, the pluralists theorized that political elites would be especially supportive of such rules of the game as the principle of minority rights. As a result, they argued that the observed differences between elite groups and cross-sections of the electorate could be explained by the notion that upward mobility in the political stratification system involves resocialization to the rules of the game,[11] and further that this resocializing would be a result of direct and increased participation in the political process. Kornhauser, for example, concluded that "non-participation results in lack of exposure to information and indoctrination concerning democratic values, and in the lack of habits of discussion, debate, negotiation, and compromise—modes of conduct indispensable to democratic politics."[12] In a similar vein, Key suggested that as people move into leadership ranks ". . . they receive an indoctrination into the mores of the subculture of the political activists," and consequently that "the system can operate as though a fundamental consensus prevailed for the reason that a governing elite happens to be imbued with particular habits and values of action."[13] Dahl argued that the maintenance of democratic consensus is a dynamic, ongoing process of interaction among the various political strata. To be sure, those with more formal education show more support for the rules of the game, but the greater support from political elites is generated and maintained by their socialization into politics as well. "Because they are more involved in, concerned with, and articulate about politics, they invest more time and effort in elaborating a consistent ideology. Because they participate more extensively in politics, they more frequently express and defend their views, encounter criticism, and face the charge of inconsistency. They know more about politics, read more, experience more, see more."[14] The dynamics of this political resocialization process experienced by elites were also stressed by McClosky, who

[10] V. O. Key, Jr., *Public Opinion and American Democracy* (New York: Alfred A. Knopf, 1961), 197–199. Italics added.

[11] An alternative hypothesis to the resocialization effects model might have been formulated in terms of selective recruitment. Cf. Kenneth Prewitt, "Political Socialization and Leadership Selection," *The Annals*, 361 (September 1965), 96–111.

[12] Kornhauser, *Mass Society*, 73.

[13] Key, *Public Opinion*, 52.

[14] Dahl, *Who Governs?*, 320.

suggested that the difference in levels of adherence to democratic principles between the "political stratum" and others could be explained by the notion that the former ". . . are unavoidably exposed to the liberal democratic values which form the main current of our political heritage. The net effect of these influences is to heighten their sensitivity to political ideas and to unite them more firmly behind the values of the American tradition."[15]

On the basis of such conclusions, the pluralists derived the new position that political stability depends on the continued effectiveness of this resocialization process, without which the political elite and its distinctive values cannot be perpetuated.[16] Key, for example, argued that "if a political order is to be democratic, political activists must be sprinkled in some such manner through all levels of the economic-occupational hierarchy."[17] In his final chapter he elaborated on this point in this way:

> By various analyses, none founded on completely satisfactory data, we have shown that in the United States the political activists—if we define the term broadly—are scattered through the socio-economic hierarchy. The upper income and occupational groups, to be sure, contribute disproportionately; nevertheless, individuals of high political participation are sprinkled throughout the lesser occupational strata. Contrast the circumstances when the highly active political stratum coincides with the high socio-economic stratum. Conceivably the winning of consent and the creation of a sense of political participation and of sharing in public affairs may be far simpler when political activists of some degree are spread through all social strata. The alternative circumstance may induce an insensitivity to mass opinion, a special reliance on mass communications, and a sharpened sense of cleavage and separatism within the political order.[18]

On the same grounds, Dahl suggested that political elites ". . . might properly be called [the] democratic 'legitimists',"[19] while Milbrath wrote that "it is vital that the recruits [to this stratum] be socialized to elite norms and customs, especially basic democratic principles and the rules of the political game."[20]

The purpose of the following analysis is to suggest that such conclusions are suspect because there is no evidence of a special resocialization effect unique to a political elite. Instead, the democratic attitudes of the so-called political stratum do not seem to be distinguishable from those of the wider social elite from which they are drawn. We shall also

[15] McClosky, "Consensus," 375.

[16] I am hardly the first to note the subtle change in emphasis from democracy to stability. For an excellent discussion on this point, see Jack L. Walker, "A Critique of the Elitist Theory of Democracy," *American Political Science Review*, 60 (June 1966), 285–295.

[17] Key, *Public Opinion*, 199.

[18] *Ibid.*, 541.

[19] Dahl, *Who Governs?*, 320.

[20] Lester W. Milbrath, *Political Participation* (Chicago: Rand McNally, 1965), 150.

note that some problems arise with taking many of these measures of support for democratic principles at face value, especially among less-educated groups.

DATA AND ANALYSIS

The analysis is based on Stouffer's surveys from the summer of 1954, during which he interviewed both a national sample of community leaders and a national sample of the population. The latter sample was done by both the American Institute of Public Opinion (AIPO) and the National Opinion Research Center (NORC) with identical results. This paper relies on the NORC data. Like all cross-sectional data, these are time-bound, but 1954 is appropriate for two reasons: most of the pluralists' hypotheses are based on data collected in the 1950s, and given that these data were collected in the immediate "post McCarthy era," we might perhaps expect items designed to tap adherence to democratic norms to be of particular salience in this period.

A possible objection to the Stouffer data is that the sample of community leaders includes individuals like newspaper editors, who do not occupy exclusively "political" roles—that is, it includes those who are not holders of elective office. Their inclusion does not affect the analysis, however, for even if we adhere to this narrow definition of political roles, we may note that with respect to the dependent variable, the scores of the politicians (for example, mayors and the chairmen of the county committees of both major parties) are close to the mean tolerance score of all community leaders. The highest scoring groups are newspaper editors and presidents of bar associations and library boards, and the lowest are the presidents of women's clubs, the American Legion, and the Daughters of the American Revolution.[21] Moreover, it is important to remember that most of the theories we have reviewed were based on the Stouffer data. Of the four major writers discussed above, only McClosky drew his conclusions from another data set.[22] Consequently, we feel that we are not misrepresenting their definitions of political elites—definitions expressed in terms of levels of political activity.

Finally, there is no reason to expect that a multivariate analysis of McClosky's elite sample of delegates to the two 1956 national party conventions would yield different results. Data reported in several studies would lead us to believe that the majority of convention delegates have usually not previously attended a convention, and that of the minority who have, only a few have attended more than one other.[23] On the other

[21] For full details on this subject, see Stouffer, *Communism*, 26–57.

[22] See Kornhauser, *Mass Society*, 67; Key, *Public Opinion*, 52; and Dahl, *Who Governs?*, 312, for the references to Stouffer. McClosky's data are as yet unavailable for further analysis.

[23] For discussion of the activity of convention delegates in 1952 and 1956, see Paul T. David, Ralph M. Goldman, and Richard C. Bain, *The Politics of National Party Conventions* (Washington, D.C.: Brookings Institution, 1960), 349–351. For more recent data, see John W. Soule and James W. Clarke, "Amateurs and Professionals: A Study of Delegates to the 1968 Democratic National Convention," *American Political Science Review*, 64 (September 1970), 893.

hand, these same studies indicate that convention delegates have typically been involved in politics at a local level for long and sustained periods of time, so that the elites interviewed by Stouffer and McClosky have experienced the same kinds of involvement in politics and are therefore comparable for our purposes. This is not to say that all possible political elites are covered in this analysis or in the studies reviewed. Indeed, the attitudes of higher-level elites such as congressmen may be different. But the Stouffer data allow for a fair test of the elite resocialization hypothesis, because that hypothesis was initially generated from the same (or comparable) data.

The dependent variable is based on the 15 items used by Stouffer in his "willingness to tolerate non-conformists" scale (see the Appendix), which measures specific support for civil liberties and the principles of minority rights, two of the more delicate elements of the democratic creed.[24] The index used in the present study was created by expressing the number of tolerant responses as a percentage of all tolerant or intolerant responses. Out of a possible maximum of 100, the mean tolerance score on this index for the mass sample is 56.8, while for the elite it is 74.8.

Of the three basic independent variables chosen, education is the most important theoretically, and many analysts have argued that this variable is one of the major determinants of such phenomena as tolerance. As Figure 1 shows, the mass and elite samples do differ considerably in their distributions on this variable. The other variables were included because their distributions are different in the two samples. This difference in itself would not matter were it not for the fact that Stouffer reported that they are all related to the dependent variable. Consequently, these variables are used not so much for their intrinsic theoretical interest, but rather so that we can "standardize" the two samples with respect to these characteristics before we compare them on other dimensions. Accordingly, region is included (South vs. other) because southern respondents are slightly less tolerant than others, and also because the proportion of southerners in the mass sample is greater than it is in the elite sample, which inflates the difference in tolerance scores between the two, thus reducing their comparability. For similar reasons, sex is also included as an explanatory variable: 53 percent of the mass sample are women, whereas women constitute only 23 percent of the elite sample. Because the elite sample is drawn from cities only, while the mass sample includes respondents from rural areas, an urban/rural variable is added to the model for the latter sample only.[25]

The model proposed specifies that the tolerance score for a given individual is the algebraic sum of four components for the elite sample and five for the mass sample. In the elite sample, the four components are as

---

[24] For a discussion of the scale, its component items, and comparisons with other related scales, see John P. Robinson, Jerrold G. Rusk, and Kendra B. Head, *Measures of Political Attitudes* (Ann Arbor, Mich.: Survey Research Center, 1968), 161–186.

[25] The regional, sex, and urban-rural differences are all reported by Stouffer, *Communism*, 130, 155. Note that none of these differences is large, although they are all persistent.

FIGURE 1

Distribution of Education in Each of the Two Samples

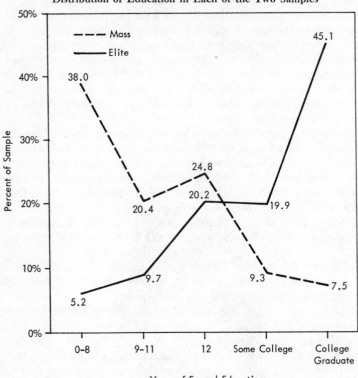

Years of Formal Education

follows: one common to all individuals; one common to all members of a given educational category; one common to all members of a given region; and a final component taking the sex of the respondent into account. For the mass sample, the five components include (in addition to the four just listed) a component taking the population-size of the area of residence into account. Both models are expressed as dummy-variable, multiple-regression equations.[26]

Before considering the differences between the elite and mass samples, their tolerance scores differed by 18 percent (the means were 75 and 57 percent respectively). After introducing the controls in Figure 2 which make the samples more comparable (that is, controls for region, sex, and—for the mass sample only—city size), we see that there is no substantial difference between the tolerance scores of the two samples *within educational categories*. In fact, the direction of the differences that do exist is not even consistent. Moreover, the differences are so small that

---

[26] For full details on the specification of these models, see the original version of this article (*Journal of Politics,* 34 [August 1972]) at pp. 762–764. The regression coefficients of these equations are:

it would be difficult to attach any meaning to them other than the possibility of measurement error. Clearly, there is little evidence here for the possible existence of special attitudes belonging to a distinctive political stratum because we have no residual category that requires labeling. As a result, theories that attempt to account for the differential rates of support for minority rights among elites and the mass public by invoking the notion that elites undergo some unique resocialization process are basically superfluous.

An important lesson to learn from this part of the analysis is that before we compare two samples, one of which is drawn from a population subset of the other, we must consider the effects of the characteristics that differentiate the two samples, and which affect the phenomenon we are trying to explain. In this case, those characteristics are sex, region of residence, and the population-size of the area of residence. If we fail to take into account these aspects of the samples that reduce their comparability, we are in effect systematically inflating differential scores on the dependent variable under consideration. For this research problem, the failure of previous studies to utilize a multivariate design was bound to leave some of the difference in levels of tolerance between the two samples unexplained. It also raised the temptation to give a label to that residual difference (that is, the resocialization or leadership effect).

	Mass	Elite
a	86.78	85.06
b_4	−7.58	−7.59
b_3	−15.61	−11.24
b_2	−20.41	−15.39
b_1	−28.09	−22.28
c	−10.54	−7.74
d	−5.16	−7.82
e_1	−8.30	−−−
e_2	−8.66	−−−
e_3	−6.20	−−−
R	.4403	.3685
R^2	.1939	.1358
N	2,450	1,500

° Both models are statistically significant by the F-test beyond the .001 level.

The zero-order relationships between support for minority rights and each of the independent variables for each sample are as follows:

	Mass	Elite
Education	.356	.305
Sex	.086	.154
Region	.251	.156
City-size	.211	−−

The seven coefficients in this table are actually the multiple correlation coefficients (R) obtained from seven separate regression equations, a procedure made necessary by the use of dummy variables.

FIGURE 2

Mean Tolerance Scores within Educational Categories for the Mass
and Elite Samples with Region, Sex, and
(for the Mass Sample Only) City Size Controlled[*]

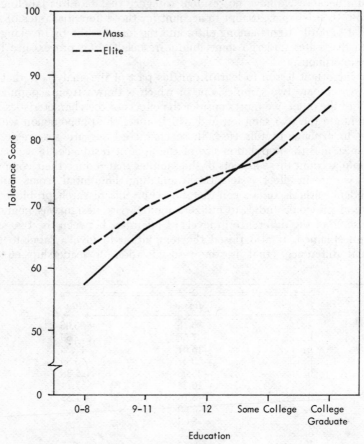

[*] Note that the lines joining the points in this figure are offered for heuristic purposes only.

However, a pronounced, monotonic difference in tolerance scores between educational categories exists, ranging from approximately 59 in
the lowest category to 87 for college graduates.

DISCUSSION

These results are largely consistent with those reported by Alford and
Scoble for their Wisconsin data.[27] They argued that education is more

27 Robert R. Alford and Harry M. Scoble, "Community Leadership, Social Status,
and Political Behavior," *American Sociological Review,* 33 (April 1968), 259–271.

important than leadership with regard to the quality or direction of political beliefs. The major difference in the present analysis is that the question has been phrased in a different way. They examined the *relative* importance of leadership and education on tolerance, but this formulation does not take into account the fact that these two explanatory variables are intercorrelated (see Figure 1), which makes it difficult to separate out their "independent" effects on the dependent variable, either conceptually or statistically.[28] We know that people generally receive their formal education *before* they become leaders. By implication, then, leadership is not one of the determinants of support for democratic principles to the extent that within educational categories, leaders are not distinctively tolerant. Consequently, education is the important variable, while the variable leadership can be omitted from the theory.

But this formulation raises further questions, of which the most theoretically important are: (a) Why does this relationship between education and tolerance exist? and (b) What conceptual meaning do we attach to the variable "years of formal education"? Alford and Scoble answer the second question by saying that education is a good indicator of social status—clearly, it *is* one such indicator, and has been used as such in the main part of this paper. But looking at it in another way helps us to deal with the first question in more detail. Many analysts have argued that education is an important variable to the extent that it measures an individual's capacity to think abstractly and to conceptualize problems. According to this view, those with some college education have been trained to think about the world in a way that those with only an elementary-school education cannot.[29] The greater one's education, the more one has a relatively well-organized belief system, an integrated world view.[30]

This line of thinking leads us to entertain the notion that perhaps the better-educated in these samples are responding more to the *content* or *substance* of the items designed to tap support for minority rights, while the less-educated are responding more to the *form* of the question. That is to say, the responses of the better-educated and those of the less-educated may represent different *kinds* of underlying cognitive processes. The authors of *The American Voter* argued that this is what was happening on their authoritarianism items, which led them to believe that they were really obtaining reasonably valid measures of authoritarianism

---

[28] In fact, their formulation leaves them open to the charge of the "partialling fallacy" as it is discussed by Robert A. Gordon, "Issues in Multiple Regression," *American Journal of Sociology,* 73 (March 1968), 592–616. Also note the problems associated with the statistical estimation of the "relative importance" of any two variables for a third variable (apart from the question of multicollinearity). Glen G. Cain and Harold W. Watts, "Problems in Making Policy Inferences from the Coleman Report," *American Sociological Review,* 35 (April 1970), 228–241.

[29] Stouffer, *Communism,* 89–108; and Gabriel A. Almond and Sidney Verba, *The Civic Culture* (Boston: Little, Brown & Co., 1965), 299–306, 315–324.

[30] Philip E. Converse, "The Nature of Belief Systems in Mass Publics," in *Ideology and Discontent,* ed. David Apter (New York: Free Press, 1964).

among the better-educated only, since this was the group responding to the substance of the items.[31]

If we are confronted with these problems when we try to measure concepts such as authoritarianism, it is a reasonable inference that the index being used in this study may suffer the same limitations, because authoritarianism and tolerance of minority rights are closely related concepts. That is, we may have a special kind of systematic measurement error, where education is related positively to the ability to respond substantively to questions, while this second variable (the measurement error) intervenes in the following sequence: education ———> ability to answer question ———> tolerance.[32] Moreover, we might expect this kind of effect whenever we attempt to measure basic beliefs about the society or the "system," feelings that normally require a relatively highly constrained belief system to be meaningful at all.[33]

It is also worth noting that the literature we are discussing largely assumes a close relationship between attitudes and behavior because elite tolerance is held to imply a behavioral commitment. Otherwise the grounds for depending on elites for the preservation of democratic forms and values would be shaky indeed. Now if we view attitudes generally as indicating a predisposition to action, then of course this relationship follows by definition. Indeed, this conception of a one-to-one relationship is often reasonable, although there may be some theoretical settings in which we might want to question it. However, when dealing with *measured* attitudes, we are almost forced to conclude that this relationship may be far from perfect.

---

[31] Angus Campbell, Philip E. Converse, Warren E. Miller, and Donald E. Stokes, *The American Voter* (New York: John Wiley & Sons, 1960), 512–515. This problem is related to the question of acquiescence "response-set" bias discussed by McClosky, "Consensus," 379–380. His answer is that those who acquiesce have distinctive "personality and cognitive" traits, and thus that the effect of the response set may not be entirely artificial. However, we should note that the measures of the personality and cognitive traits mentioned by McClosky are themselves subject to the same acquiescence response-set bias. As a result, much of the covariance between these traits and acquiescence may be a result of correlated error. Other problems associated with controlling for acquiescence are discussed by Franz Samuelson and Jacques F. Yates, "Acquiescence and the F Scale: Old Assumptions and New Data," *Psychological Bulletin*, 68 (August 1967), 91–103.

[32] Discussions of random measurement error raise the issue of the reliability of the instrument (in this case, the measure of tolerance), but in raising the question of non-random or systematic measurement error, I am arguing that we may be confronted with the much more fundamental and critical issue of the *validity* of the instrument. Consequently, instead of reflecting a *true* effect, the *observed* effect of education on an invalid measure of tolerance may simply reflect the effect of education on ability to respond substantively to questions. The results of a recent analysis of the relation between education, response-set, and anti-Semitism are consistent with this argument: see Mary R. Jackman, "Education and Prejudice or Education and Response-Set?" *American Sociological Review*, 38 (June 1973). On the distinction between reliability and validity, see George W. Bohrnstedt, "Reliability and Validity Assessment in Attitude Measurement," in *Attitude Measurement*, ed. Gene F. Summers (Chicago: Rand McNally, 1970), 80–99.

[33] Converse, "Belief Systems," 255–256.

In this context one final possibility should be discussed: namely, that these data may overestimate the tolerance (in a behavioral sense) of the better-educated, including the leaders. Converse has reported a general tendency for people to respond to survey items as though they were intelligence tests,[34] the responses to which of course may be either correct or incorrect. Consequently, we might expect the better-educated, who are much more aware of the appropriate or "correct" norms, to appear particularly tolerant on minority-rights items.[35] In other words, their responses may reflect socially-approved responses rather than a behavioral commitment. While the literature on the relationship between attitudes and behavior is slim, a recent study in the area of racial discrimination provides some support for the notion that we may be overestimating the potential tolerance of the better-educated.[36]

In short, this discussion should heighten our sensitivity to the possibility that the relationship between education and support for minority rights may not be altogether meaningful.[37] If so, the analysis reported earlier in this paper may only show that the better-educated appear more tolerant simply because they know how best to answer the questions. In this context, the leaders look best simply because they are the best educated.

CONCLUSION

In review, this analysis leads us to conclude that little evidence favors the special political socialization hypothesis suggested by many theorists to account for the apparent differential rates of support of minority rights between political elites and the mass public. Those elites do not seem to be characterized by a distinctive, uniquely political set of values with respect to these norms. As a result, we are led to question hypotheses about democratic stability that place emphasis on a special political stratification system. In fact, this study should act as a caution against the notion that patterns of socialization to specialized political roles will always be distinguishable from patterns of socialization to more general social roles.

---

[34] Philip E. Converse, "Attitudes and Non-Attitudes: Continuation of a Dialogue," in *The Quantitative Analysis of Social Problems*, ed. Edward R. Tufte (Reading, Mass.: Addison-Wesley, 1970), 177.

[35] We should note in this context that some analysts have argued that conventional measures of authoritarianism and tolerance lack the capacity to distinguish variation among the better-educated or those who fill decision-making positions. See John P. Robinson and Phillip R. Shaver, *Measures of Social Psychological Attitudes* (Ann Arbor, Mich.: Survey Research Center, 1969), 213.

[36] Lawrence S. Linn, "Verbal Attitudes and Overt Behavior: A Study of Racial Discrimination," *Social Forces*, 43 (July 1965), 353–364. For a general review of the attitude-behavior literature, see Icek Ajzen, Russel K. Darroch, Martin Fishbein, and John A. Hornik, "Looking Backward Revisited: A Reply to Deutscher," *American Sociologist*, 5 (August 1970), 267–273.

[37] Similar considerations may also apply to the much-cited "working-class authoritarianism" hypothesis. See Seymour Martin Lipset, *Political Man* (London: Heinemann, 1960), 97–130.

Along with this basic result, and in view of the results of other research, it appears that major problems are associated with assuming that we have in fact measured support for a basic and central democratic principle. Moreover, the theories under consideration require that such support imply some behavioral commitment, a conclusion that may not be met with the current data. As a result, it may be difficult with those data to accept the proposition that continued political stability depends upon elite or any other norms.

Leaving to one side the considerations of the last paragraph, one might still object that, in spite of the basic result of this analysis, the leaders remain collectively more tolerant than the electorate at large on the simple univariate distributions, and that it is this fact that has important political consequences. In a sense, this kind of proposition is not unreasonable, but it is not as interesting theoretically because it ignores the *dynamics* of the processes involved. Central to the theories of democratic stability discussed in this paper is the notion of a special elite socialization pattern into politics and the related concept of a distinctive political stratification system. We have suggested that there is little evidence for the existence of any such distinctive process or system. Consequently, the determinants of political stability and democratic stability must be sought elsewhere.

APPENDIX: ITEMS USED IN THE WILLINGNESS TO TOLERATE NON-CONFORMISTS SCALE

The 15 items below are designed to tap the degree of willingness to tolerate non-conformists of the following types: self-proclaimed Communists, atheists, Socialists, and Communist "suspects" (recall that the data were collected in 1954).

Now, I should like to ask you some questions about a man who admits he is a Communist.

1. Suppose this admitted Communist wants to make a speech in your community. Should he be allowed to speak, or not?*
2. Suppose he wrote a book which is in your public library. Somebody in your community suggests the book should be removed from the library. Would you favor removing it, or not?†
3. Suppose this admitted Communist is a radio singer. Should he be fired, or not?†
4. Now suppose the radio program he is on advertises a brand of soap. Somebody in your community suggests you stop buying that soap. Would you stop, or not?†
5. Should an admitted Communist be put in jail, or not?†

There are always some people whose ideas are considered bad or dangerous by other people. For instance, somebody who is against all churches and religion.

6. If such a person wanted to make such a speech in your city (town,

community) against churches and religion, should he be allowed to speak, or not?*

7. If some people in your community suggested that a book he wrote against churches and religion should be taken out of your public library, would you favor removing this book, or not?†

Or consider a person who favored government ownership of all the railroads and all big industries.

8. If this person wanted to make a speech in your community favoring government ownership of all the railroads and big industries, should he be allowed to speak, or not?*

9. If some people in your community suggested that a book he wrote favoring government ownership should be taken out of your public library, would you favor removing the book, or not?†

Now I would like you to think of another person. A man whose loyalty has been questioned before a Congressional committee, but who swears under oath he has never been a Communist.

10. Suppose he is teaching in a college or university. Should he be fired, or not?†
11. Should he be allowed to make a speech in your community, or not?*
12. Suppose this man is a high-school teacher. Should he be fired, or not?†
13. Suppose he has been working in a defense plant. Should he be fired, or not?†
14. Suppose he is a clerk in a store. Should he be fired, or not?†
15. Suppose he wrote a book which is in your public library. Somebody in your community suggests the book should be removed from the library. Would you favor removing it, or not?†

---

* A *positive* response to this item (i.e., agreement with the question) indicates the tolerant answer.

† A *negative* response to this item (i.e., disagreement with the question) indicates the tolerant answer.

Section VI
The Role-Playing Model

In their early study of the legislatures of California, New Jersey, Ohio, and Tennessee, the authors of *The Legislative System* dealt extensively with legislators' perceptions of how a legislator should deal with others involved in the making of public policy. Only one of the roles they conceptualized interests us here—that concerning how the legislator felt he should represent his constituency. Many legislators thought of themselves as "trustees" of the people, elected to follow what they think to be right and just rather than merely voicing their constituents' opinion in the legislature. Only an average of 28 percent of representatives in legislatures studied thus far conceive of themselves as "delegates" enacting constituency's wishes at all times even in those instances in which the representative personally opposes the act.[1] The role-playing model, which is dependent on the delegates' motivation to seek out his constituency's opinions and to vote them, seems challenged by the minority sentiment among legislators to do so.

Perhaps even more challenging is the prevalence of the sentiment among legislators noted by Kenneth Prewitt in the section on the competitive parties model. In the first legislative study of roles discussed above, 38 percent failed to mention interactions with their constituents when describing the job of the legislator, suggesting the little attention they devote to this task.[2] The "volunteerism" noted by Prewitt would make the representative less concerned with being a delegate.

A study of the 1967 Iowa legislature provides us with evidence on the importance of the different representational role orientations of legislators as well as their accuracy in correctly perceiving public opinion.

---

[1] Robert S. Erikson and Norman R. Luttbeg, *American Public Opinion; Its Orgins, Content, and Impact* (New York: Wiley, 1973), p. 262.

[2] Kenneth Prewitt and Heinz Eulau, "Political Matrix and Political Representation: Prolegomenon to a New Departure from an Old Problem," *American Political Science Review*, vol. 63 (June 1969), p. 427.

Ronald Hedlund and H. Paul Friesema in the first selection report variations in the accuracy of legislator's estimates of the success of four referenda in their districts, but role orientations show little effect. Trustees correctly predict that outcome in the district slightly better than delegates (80 percent versus 62 percent). A study of the first Florida presidential primary further supports their conclusions. Voters were invited to express their opinions on three issues—banning school bussing solely for purposes of integration, allowing prayer in the classroom, and support for providing equal education for all. These were quite salient issues to the public at the time, often forcing the candidates to take positions. Representatives erred on average only 7 percent in guessing the support their constituencies would give to bussing and only 12 percent and 13 percent, respectively, on the other two. This accuracy confirms Hedlund and Friesema's speculation that more salient and local issues would get more accurately assessed. With many cues representatives better know their constituents. Again on the average, trustees show the greater accuracy in gauging their constituencies' opinions.

The fact that a representative may know his constituency's opinions need not mean that he acts consistently with them. In their second selection Friesema and Hedlund assess whether delegates act more consistently with constituency opinions. While the issues may not be the most salient issues in public opinion, delegates prove no more responsible to their constituency.

Warren Miller and Donald Stokes offer the most exhaustive assessment of the ties between the representative's perceptions of his constituency's opinion, actual constituency opinions, the representative's personal opinions, and most importantly his votes. While the representatives accurately perceive and vote their constituents' attitudes on civil rights, the other two areas show substantial error in perceiving constituency opinion and much less success in accurately representing the opinions of their constituencies. The only area of representational success then comes by way of the representative voting his perceptions of constituency opinion. We do not know, of course, whether he does so for fear of losing his seat in the next election or whether despite his safety from such threats he feels he should represent his constituents.

The representative in a democracy is subject to a din of opinions each claiming to represent a concerned minority if not a majority of the public. He receives letters, petitions, telephone calls, visits to his offices, opinions from audiences where he speaks, opinions from pressure groups, and probably even opinions from his children. Which give the real public sentiment and which are self-serving narrow opinions? We know little about the process by which the representative goes about getting an accurate assessment of public opinion; but the existing studies have consistently found intense opinions predominate in the many channels for communicating to one's representative.

Looking for the source of Goldwater's election strategy in 1964 which clearly ran in the face of the evidence available in opinion polls, Philip Converse, Aage Clausen, and Warren Miller found sharp differences in the opinions of those who troubled themselves to write and those who did not.[3] Goldwater may well have taken cues received from conservative idealogues as accurate of "real" public opinion not realizing that idealogues are more apt to communicate by way of available channels of communication. A later study by Sidney Verba and Richard Brody confirms the bias in various expressions of public opinion.[4] Respondents in this study gave both their attitudes toward the war in Vietnam and their extent of activity in communicating with their leaders. While 18 percent of the public could be labeled "hawks" by the nature of their responses, 26 percent of those who had tried to change the opinions of others, 30 percent of those had written a letter, and one of the eight persons who admitted to participating in a demonstration (13 percent) were hawks. Six of the eight demonstrators held "dove" preferences compared with 12 percent of the public. Thus the representative who heeded letter opinions would think the public was decidedly more hawkish than was actually the case, and the representative taking the demonstrations as indications of public opinion would also be erring, but in the opposite direction.

Not unexpectedly, politicians are increasingly turning to polls to find the prevalence on nonintense opinions. In the period between 1954 and 1970, the use of polls by members of the House of Representatives increased from 11 percent to 74 percent.[5] Clearly, representatives are placing more confidence in such assessments, but they need to be cautious of the "nonopinion" noted by Converse. Even the task of learning public opinion is full of pitfalls.

---

[3] Philip E. Converse, Aage Clausen, and Warren E. Miller, "Electoral Myth and Reality: The 1964 Election," *American Political Science Review*, vol. 59 (June 1965), p. 334.

[4] Sidney Verba and Richard Brody, "Participation, Policy Preferences, and the War in Vietnam," *Public Opinion Quarterly*, vol. 34 (Fall 1970), p. 330.

[5] Erikson and Luttbeg, *American Public Opinion*, p. 268.

Ronald D. Hedlund and H. Paul Friesema

Representatives' Perceptions of Constituency Opinion*

Contemporary research capabilities have opened the prospect for rigorous systematic analysis of the basic and staple political question concerning political representatives and those they are supposed to represent. Some of the most impressive political science research of the recent decade has been devoted to delineating this relationship.[1] In this area of contemporary scholarship, as in few others, there are clear ties between contemporary research and earlier political science scholarship —ties particularly apparent in connection with Edmund Burke's ideas about the roles and responsibilities of political representatives.

This contemporary scholarship is so well-known that an extensive review seems superfluous, yet the research leaves open some important questions, and in some ways it even deepens the mystery about representative institutions because it tends to raise new questions.

Many studies have examined alternate or overlapping connections between representatives and constituents. Such ties have come to be called *linkages*. Norman R. Luttbeg has said, "A linkage between the

* Reprinted from the *Journal of Politics*, vol. 34, no. 3 (August 1972), pp. 730–52. Copyright, 1972.

The authors would like to acknowledge the assistance of the University of Iowa Computer Center and Laboratory for Political Research. Support has also come directly and indirectly from the University of Iowa Graduate School, University of Wisconsin-Milwaukee College of Letters and Science and Graduate School, the National Science Foundation, and the Social Science Research Council. We would particularly like to acknowledge the coding and technical assistance of Kathy Nelson, Ted Hebert, and Reinhold Knopfelmacher. Also Larry Margolis of the Citizens Conference on State Legislatures made available studies of public opinion in Iowa on these four issues.

[1] Some of the most important contemporary efforts include John C. Wahlke et al., *The Legislative System* (New York: John Wiley & Sons, 1962); Raymond Bauer, Ithiel Pool and Lewis A. Dexter, *American Business and Public Policy* (New York: Atherton Press, 1963); Warren E. Miller and Donald E. Stokes, Constituency Influence in Congress," *American Political Science Review*, 57 (March 1963), 45–56.

public and its leaders is the mechanism that allows public leaders to act in accordance with the wants, needs, and demands of their public."[2] He classifies studies by the possible alternate ways in which political leaders, and particularly political representatives, may be linked and restrained by their constituents and by institutions presumed to be mediators between political leaders and followers.[3] The primary models he identifies are: the *rational-activist*, in which constituents are issue- and policy-conscious and exercise control over their representatives' behavior through the electoral process; the *competitive-political-parties*, in which the parties serve to organize and focus public opinion and to compel legislators to act in response to the electoral market place; the *pressure-group*, in which real or potential groups organize interests of the public and through their real or potential participation insure responsiveness of political authorities; the *belief-sharing* or *consensus*, in which the people who achieve representative positions come to be responsive to their constituents' views and values by acting out their own views and values, which they share with those whom they represent; and the *role-playing*, in which an internalized value, or set of values, causes a representative to seek out and follow constituent opinion even without the prospect of constituent sanctions being imposed.

All of these models may help to explain why political representatives vote and act as they do. They may be useful in the understanding how legislators *translate* demands which are placed upon them and may also explain how they combine these translated demands with their personal goals into some kinds of legislative outputs. The models may identify important correlates of legislative behavior. But democratic theory raises a more fundamental set of empirical questions about representative institutions. How closely do constituent attitudes and opinions and representative behavior match? How adequately do the linkages work in insuring responsive legislative behavior? These are the basic representational questions for democratic theory.

It seems very likely that the necessary preconditions for Luttbeg's first four models—the rational-activist, competitive-party, pressure-group, and belief-sharing—are not adequately met if concern is focused upon the more fundamental requirement of democratic theory: the insuring of close relationships between constituent attitudes and opinions and representative behavior. For example: 1) the rational-activist model seems insufficient because, among other things, voters are not aware of policy issues and do not reward and punish on the basis of rational evaluation of legislative performance; 2) the parties seem to be insufficient linkages because, among other things, they are frequently not competitive within legislative districts, they imperfectly aggregate interests, and they do not present clear-cut policy alternatives; 3) the interest groups seem insuffi-

---

[2] "Political Linkage in a Large Society," in Norman R. Luttbeg, ed., *Public Opinion and Public Policy: Models of Political Linkages* (Homewood, Ill.: Dorsey, 1968), 2. The concept of "linkage" was developed by V. O. Key, Jr., *Public Opinion and American Democracy* (New York: Alfred A. Knopf, 1964).

[3] Luttbeg, "Political Linkage," 1–9.

cient linkages because, among other things, many people are unorganized on many issues, leaders and activists only imperfectly represent the views of even their own memberships; 4) belief-sharing seems unlikely because leaders, including, undoubtedly, legislators, hold substantially different views on issues than do followers.[4] Luttbeg's fifth model, role-playing, needs explication before it can be regarded as an adequate mechanism for insuring a fairly high degree of representative responsiveness to constituency opinion.

CONSTITUENT-REPRESENTATIVE RELATIONSHIP

The basic empirical question about the viability of representative democratic theory starts with constituent opinions and attitudes and concerns the relationship between such opinions and attitudes and the legislative behavior of representatives. The processing of constituent opinions and attitudes through various complementary or alternative mediating linkages is, of course, critical. The pattern can be illustrated in a very simple diagram:

FIGURE 1

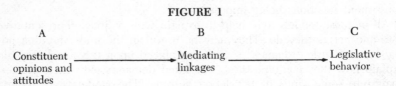

A	B	C
Constituent opinions and attitudes	Mediating linkages	Legislative behavior

If representative democracy is to be viable, it seems clear that there must somehow be a fairly strong relationship between A and C. But most of the recent evidence and analysis focuses primarily on relationships between B and C, paying little attention to relationships between A and B, or, indeed, to the broader question of relationships between A and C.

That the focus of much of this research is limited is quite understandable. Predicting or explaining legislative behavior (particularly roll-call behavior) is an important research endeavor, even though it is only a part of the empirical issue of representative democracy. The tools of the behavioral revolution are particularly useful in predicting legislative output from institutional variables. But the new standard research techniques, particularly the sample survey, are not as easily applied to gathering data about relations between constituency opinions and attitudes and legislative behavior. As V. O. Key, Jr., has written, "Sampling the opinions of a congressional district—so strange are the properties of survey methods—amounts to almost as great a task as sampling the people of the nation. Hence, given the data now available, any treatment of how any representative links opinion in his constituency to the governing process must be less than exact."[5] The problems of gathering sufficient informa-

---

[4] See evidence cited in Luttbeg, *Public Opinion.*
[5] *Ibid.*, 483.

tion in enough separate constituencies so as to have an adequate sample of constituencies seemed (and still seems) Herculean. Of course, efforts have been made to compare roll-call behavior with constituency *characteristics*. But constituency characteristics (*e.g.,* percent non-white, degree of urbanization, and so on) cannot easily be treated as surrogate indicators of constituency attitudes and opinions—or even needs.

A few systematic efforts undertake to treat this representational question. Wilder W. Crane, Jr., provides an important example when he examines the question, "Do Representatives Represent?" by comparing legislative roll-call votes with subsequent referendum results upon the same issue.[6] His use of referendum results within a constituency as a measure of constituency opinion on that issue seems reasonable. A daylight-savings time bill was voted by the Wisconsin Legislature and shortly thereafter by a statewide popular referendum. Approximately 85 percent of the legislators voted as their constituencies did. Most explained or justified their vote in terms of following constituency opinion. Many legislators who voted differently from their district explained the discrepancy by saying that they misjudged constituency opinion. Crane did not attempt to examine what let to correct or incorrect assessments of constituency opinion.

Warren E. Miller and Donald E. Stokes's article, "Constituency Influence in Congress," developed a model of the relationship between constituency attitudes and representative roll-call behavior and tested the model with data from the Survey Research Center's study of representation.[7] This study included interviews with United States congress-

FIGURE 2

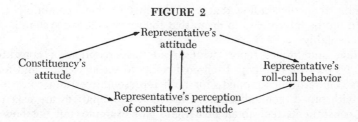

men and a national sample survey which produced discrete data for over 100 congressional districts. Figure 2 represents the connections they postulated between a constituency's attitude and the representative's roll-call behavior. This impressive study indicated that in three distinct issue areas—civil rights, social welfare, and foreign affairs—a high relationship existed between the representatives' roll-call behavior on specific issues and both their own generalized attitude toward the issue areas and their perceptions of constituency attitudes. Moreover, when the two independent variables (representatives' own attitudes and representatives' perceptions of constituency attitudes) were taken together, they predicted

[6] *Journal of Politics,* 22 (May 1960), 295–299.

[7] "Constituency Influence," 46.

roll-call voting quite successfully. The multiple correlation is 0.7 for social welfare, 0.6 for foreign involvement, and 0.9 for civil rights.[8] However, the relationship between representatives' estimates of constituency opinion and the constituencies' actual opinion, as measured in the sample survey, was much lower. On civil rights, the correlation was .63, but on foreign affairs it was .19 and on social welfare .17. So it appears that representatives' perception of constituency influence was very critical in explaining their roll-call behavior, but at the same time in two of the three issue areas the representatives were quite inaccurate in assessing constituency opinion. Miller and Stokes conclude, "Therefore, although the conditions of constituency influence are not equally satisfied, they are met well enough to give the local constituency a measure of control over the actions of the Representative."[9]

Their conclusion seems overstated. Representative democracy requires at least a fairly high level of accurate information about constituency attitudes and opinions. Without that, legislative institutions may provide the stamp of legitimacy and perform other functions, but they do not provide a decision-making system that reflects the views and values of the citizenry, no matter how the issue is judged. While there is no absolute standard against which to test findings about the accuracy of representatives' perceptions (what one would accept as good enough), Miller and Stokes's reported findings seem so low that it is *not* a matter of some people seeing a glass of water half-full while others see it half-empty. If it is a requisite for a responsive representative system that (1) representatives' roll-call behavior is influenced by their perceptions of public opinion, and (2) representatives' perceptions of public opinion are tolerably accurate, then the finding that *only* the first of these conditions is met should not be interpreted to mean that the representative system is working acceptably.

Miller and Stokes report widespread misperception of constituency attitudes on issues ranging from civil rights to social welfare and foreign affairs. The attitudes tapped (for both representatives and constituents) deal with broad, generalized issue areas. Representatives are asked how their constituents feel about civil rights, for example, but not how they feel about specific legislative issues the representatives must act upon (open housing, public accommodation, voting rights, and the like). This

---

[8] There are obvious interaction effects between these two variables. But Cnudde and McCrone, in a re-analysis of the intercorrelation on the civil rights dimension have tested the causal links and indicated that the perception of constituency opinion influences representatives' own attitudes rather than the reverse. "These analyses indicate that constituencies do not influence civil rights roll calls in the House of Representatives by selecting Congressmen whose attitudes mirror their own. Instead, Congressmen vote their constituencies' attitudes (*as they perceive them*) with a mind to the next election. Constituency influence is not provided by candidate recruitment but by the elite cognitions." (Italics added.) Charles F. Cnudde and Donald J. McCrone, "The Linkage Between Constituency Attitudes and Congressional Voting Behavior: A Causal Model," *American Political Science Review*, 60 (March 1966), 66–72.

[9] "Constituency Influence," 56.

procedure may seem perfectly reasonable, given the voting population's lack of precise cognitive information about current legislation. But, in terms of assessing the responsiveness of the representatives to constituency opinion, the assumptions inherent in this procedure are hazardous. The major assumption, of course, is that the representative is able to take his perceptions of how his constituency feels about a broad issue area (civil rights, social welfare, foreign affairs) and translate these into an equally valid assessment of how his constituency feels (or would feel, if it were aware of this issue) about some specific legislative proposal. While it may be reasonable to presume that representatives themselves derive their attitudes toward specific legislative proposals from broad evaluative dimensions, this presumption is less reasonable for the general public. The lack of consistency among the public between general abstract principles of democracy and specific action, as reported by Prothro and Grigg is well-known.[10] It seems quite reasonable to say that when one wants to know what a constituency feels about open-housing legislation and whether a representative can accurately assess constituency opinions on that specific issue, evidence about the generalized attitude and perception of that attitude toward "civil rights" is somewhat removed. Perhaps what one must do is find out specifically about opinions on open housing, a task which obviously raises a different set of measuring problems.

The data, if not the interpretations, in the Miller-Stokes article raise profoundly disturbing questions about the ability of representative institutions in a democracy to perform their most manifest function. They should provide a decision-making structure that reflects and responds to public opinion. The Miller-Stokes article, as well as the Cnudde and McCrone reanalysis of the civil rights issue, indicates the critical importance of representatives' perceptions of constituent opinion. But these works provide little to explain the variation, from issue to issue and from representative to representative, in the capacity to understand constituent opinion. Do representatives who adopt varying representational roles differ in perceiving and responding to constituent opinion?[11] Does the perceptual accuracy of representatives increase or decrease if they are geared in to one or another linkage mechanism? These would seem to be critical questions in the effort to examine and reflect upon the prospects for representative democracy.

THE RESEARCH SETTING

Events in the 1967 Iowa General Assembly, and subsequently in the whole state, provided an economically feasible opportunity to explore

---

[10] James W. Prothro and Charles M. Grigg, "Fundamental Principles of Democracy: Bases of Agreement and Disagreement," *Journal of Politics*, 22 (May 1960), 276–294. See also Robert Axelrod, "The Structure of Public Opinion on Policy Issues," *Public Opinion Quarterly*, 31 (Spring 1967), 51–60.

[11] For a discussion of the various representational roles, see Wahlke, *Legislative System*, 267–286.

many dimensions of the relations between legislators and constituents. Members of the 1967 legislature were interviewed in a major legislative research project.[12] The legislative agenda for that session included voting for the second passage of a series of constitutional amendments, which, if approved, would be submitted to statewide referenda.

In the course of the interview, legislators were asked to predict their own district results and the state referendum results on each constitutional amendment. The four amendments which passed the legislature and were subsequently approved in popular referenda, dealt with home rule for municipalities, reapportionment, annual sessions of the legislature, and item veto for the governor. The interviews also sought information about the roles adopted by the representatives, their ties to linkage institutions, personal attributes, and other variables.

If we make the reasonable stipulation that the referenda results will be the measure of constituent opinion, constituent opinion on a district-by-district basis not only becomes economically available, but this constituent opinion deals with the specific issue of legislative action. Thus, we need not infer constituent opinion on specific legislative issues from statements made regarding their underlying attitudes. The four issues were salient to the legislators at the time of the interview because they were required to act on the issues then, even though the statewide referenda would not take place for over a year.[13]

While the issues were salient to the legislators, who had to act on them, it might be questioned whether they were of significant interest to the general public so that a legitimate test of the relationships could be made. For example, one might argue that these issues were *not* so noticeable to the public that representatives could legitimately be expected to know their constituents' opinions; or if they did not know their constituents' preferences, that anything could be said about the validity of representative institutions. This argument is rejected on two grounds. First, substantial anecdotal evidence indicates that home rule, reapportionment, and annual sessions, at least, had been important issues. They had been considered by several prior sessions of the Iowa General Assembly, the legislature having, in fact, discussed and voted on all four amendments in 1965. The ensuing public debate and media coverage of these issues served to awaken public interest on the topics before the legislature began voting in 1967. Further, Iowans had observed intense public discussion, legislative debate, and lobbying effort over the issue of reapportionment since at least 1963. The well-respected Iowa Poll noted in 1965 that reapportionment ranked third behind school aid and taxes in a statewide survey of important issues facing that session of the

---

[12] The principal investigators in the Iowa Legislative Research Project are Samuel C. Patterson, G. Robert Boynton, and Ronald D. Hedlund. A series of articles has appeared.

[13] Legislative estimates were gathered in the late spring of 1967. The referenda were held in November, 1968. No abnormal intervening events were apparent between the legislative action and the referenda. Public opinion polls taken between the legislative interviews and the referenda indicate little net change in opinion on a *statewide level* during the interim.

General Assembly.[14] As early as 1961 the Iowa Poll indicated that annual sessions were popular among a cross-section of the public with 58 percent favoring such a policy, 26 percent opposed, and 16 percent having no opinion.[15] If one considers an absence of an opinion on an issue as a rough indicator of low issue salience, then the proportion of no opinions on that issue should measure its level of public interest. Results from the 1968 pre-election Iowa Poll indicate that about four out of five respondents had an opinion on item veto, home rule, and annual sessions. On reapportionment the comparable rate was two out of three.[16] Finally, if one considers voter participation on these amendments in the 1968 election, one finds that over 60 percent of those voting for president also voted on each constitutional issue. This rate is comparable to or exceeds that observed for previous constitutional amendments.[17] For these reasons public interest on these issues seems to have been at least as high as that observed for all but the most emotional issues in this period.

The argument that these four issues are not sufficiently salient is also rejected because it begs the question. Notions of representation and democracy do not hold that a representative is to be responsive to his constituency on *only* the emotional issues. If this were the case, then representation at the state level might be operative only on daylight-savings time, legalized bingo, and colored oleomargarine. We argue that the level of public interest on home rule, reapportionment, annual sessions, and item veto is probably more typical of that found on the entire range of legislative issues. Thus a representative's perception of constituent opinion on these amendments is probably more typical of his daily functioning on the vast majority of legislative decisions. These constitutional issues are precisely the type of issues which are most appropriate for examining the relationships between constituents and representatives.

THE PREDICTION OF CONSTITUENT RESPONSE

All four constitutional amendments were passed in the referenda. Home rule and reapportionment were passed with substantial margins, but annual sessions and the item veto were closer contests. More than a majority of legislative districts favored each amendment.

Before the referenda were held, legislators were asked to predict whether the majority vote in their district would support or oppose each amendment. Iowa legislators were not uniformly accurate in their prediction of district outcome on the four constitutional amendments. There

---

[14] "Iowans Put School Aid First, Poll Shows," *Des Moines Sunday Register*, Jan. 31, 1965.

[15] "Poll Finds 51% of Iowans for Reapportionment," *Des Moines Sunday Register*, Feb. 12, 1961.

[16] "Iowans Favor State Constitutional Changes," *Des Moines Sunday Register*, Sept. 8, 1968.

[17] George B. Mather, *Effects of the Use of Voting Machines on Total Votes Cast: Iowa—1920–1960* (Iowa City: Institute of Public Affairs, University of Iowa, 1964), 41.

was substantial variance from amendment to amendment. More than 90 percent of the estimates of constituent reaction to home rule were accurate, while less than 60 percent of the estimates concerning annual sessions were.[18] Home rule and reapportionment were, by general consensus of observers and participants, highly charged political issues which attracted wide-scale public attention and much partisan and interest-group activity. Controversy over annual sessions of the legislature and the item veto was more muted, since these were perceived as more technical and procedural. The legislators were substantially better predictors of constituency response on the two more politically-charged issues of home rule (91.5 percent accurate) and reapportionment (81.7 percent) than they were on annual sessions (58.9 percent) and item veto (64.3 percent).

Only one-third of the legislators accurately predicted constituent response to all four issues; another third predicted constituent response on three of the four issues. Four legislators out of 181 failed to predict correctly any of the referenda results in their own district. The accuracy of the predictions in the two chambers of the Iowa Legislature did not differ significantly. The senators, who represent larger districts, were slightly better predictors than were the members of the lower house, who represent smaller population districts.

ROLE ORIENTATIONS AS POTENTIAL LINKAGES

Legislative role orientations vis-à-vis constituents have been identified by Wahlke, et al., in *The Legislative System*. The three roles are well-known: *delegate*, where legislators perceive their voting behavior to be bound by constituency opinion; *trustee*, where legislators, when a conflict appears, are bound finally to conscience and their own legislative expertise rather than to constituency opinion; and *politico*, where these clear-cut options are defined by the legislators as essentially situational— that is, upon some issues they follow constituency opinion, but not on others.[19] These role types are identified and defined in terms of legislators' self-perceptions, without any indication of how they are implemented. But as Luttbeg observes, "although these different roles relate to the competitiveness of their districts, no inquiry is made about whether the delegates—those who believe they should follow instructions from their constituency—succeed in reflecting their constituencies' opinions

---

[18] In measuring the ability to predict accurately constituent opinion (the dependent variable), more than one indicator, employing the same information, was used. The simplest and most useful measure was the legislator's estimate of majority voter response to each amendment. But as a summary measure of the ability to predict across all four issues, the proportion of correct predictions of each legislator was also tried. Since there were relatively few non-responses to any of the four questions and since most of those were of an "I don't know" nature, it does not seem inappropriate to use the number of correct predictions as another measure of accuracy of predicting constituent opinion.

[19] Wahlke et al., *Legislative System*, 267–280. These are, of course, variations and specifications of the concepts of Edmund Burke.

better than other legislators. This of course would be expected if the role-playing model were an effective linkage."[20]

When Iowa legislators were classified by their legislative role orientation elicited during their interviews, the delegates, presumably putting greater stress on constituency opinion, were *least* able to predict constituency opinion (Table 1).[21] If three or four correct predictions (out

TABLE 1

Number of Correct District Predictions by Representational Role
(percent by columns)

| Number of Correct Predictions | Representational Role | | | Total |
	Trustee	Politico	Delegate	
None	1.1	—	6.8	2.2
One	4.4	9.7	13.6	7.7
Two	16.3	26.8	29.6	22.7
Three	38.0	31.7	27.3	33.7
Four	40.2	31.7	22.7	33.7
Total %	100.0	99.9	100.0	100.0
N	92	41	44	177
$X^2 = 10.32$	$df = 8$	$P > .05$		

of four) are defined as reasonably accurate, 78.2 percent of the trustees, 63.4 percent of the politicos, and an even 50 percent of the delegates were reasonably accurate in predicting their districts' responses to these four constitutional issues. In other words, half of those legislators who indicated that their voting behavior should be determined by what their constituents wanted did not accurately know what their constituents wanted on more than two of the four issues. This pattern, of delegates being least accurate in their assessment of constituency opinion, was consistent across all four constitutional issues.

On other questions, which also assess the different perceptions of legislators toward their constituents, the same type of pattern appears. The legislators were asked what they thought they should do if there were a conflict between their district and their own consciences. Some 71.3 percent who opted for following their own consciences were reasonably accurate in judging their constituents' desires (three out of four instances) while only 57.1 percent of the legislators opting to follow their districts' opinion were that accurate. The legislator-respondents were also asked how important they thought it was for a legislator to know the will of the people of his district. Here again, legislators indicating it was very

---

[20] *Public Opinion*, 391.

[21] In deriving this indication of legislator role perceptions, representatives were asked to indicate which of three verbal descriptions of representational behavior came the closest to describing how a legislator should act when making important decisions. The verbal descriptions were synopses of those given in Wahlke, *Legislative System*, 267–280.

important to know the will of the district were less accurate in actually knowing that will than were legislators who placed less stress on it.

It seems patent that legislators adopting the delegate role are not thereby particularly aware of actual constituency opinion. While role orientations may, or may not, affect how legislators vote on roll calls, the Iowa evidence is that delegates were *less* sensitive to constituency opinion than legislators adopting other role orientations. If the delegate-role linkage is to provide a reasonable mechanism for translating constituent opinions and attitudes into legislative action, we would presuppose that legislators adopting this orientation would know their constituents' preferences. But our evidence indicates that the role linkage provides no reasonably adequate mechanism for insuring that constituent opinions and attitudes will be translated into legislative action, even by the minority of legislators who consciously try to reflect constituent views.

OTHER POTENTIAL LINKAGES

Political parties are important reference points for legislators, especially in explaining their roll-call behavior. It was possible that party identification might help to account for the variation in the ability to assess constituent opinion accurately. Democrats were better in their estimates than Republicans. Strong party identifiers were also somewhat better predictors than weak party identifiers, a finding which may mean that the legislators more involved with political parties were thereby slightly more attuned to grass-roots opinion. But the differences were small, and the relationship between the legislators' responses to questions about whether they considered themselves strong or weak Democrats (or Republicans) and the political parties as linkages between legislators and constituents seems obscure. Those legislators who acknowledged working closely with interest groups did not differ significantly in their ability to predict constituency opinion from legislators who indicated that they kept their distance from, or ignored, interest groups. So degrees of legislative involvement with these two institutionalized linkages between constituents and legislators do not explain much of the difference between accurate and inaccurate assessments of constituent opinion.

The extent to which the voting public exacts an electoral toll for misperceiving its preferences toward political issues was also examined. Even if the electorate is not issue conscious, perhaps through other means it comes to reward more sensitive representatives while punishing less sensitive ones. Charles Merriam listed a high degree of sensitivity to opinion as one of the "aptitudes" of the successful political leader.[22] Table 2 presents a comparison of the number of correct predictions leg-

---

22 Charles E. Merriam, *Political Power: Its Composition and Incidence* (New York: McGraw-Hill Book Co., 1934), 40. This clearly does not require that a legislator or other successful political leader *follow* his correct assessment of public opinion. Indeed, Carl Friedrich's "law of anticipated reactions" might correctly include calculations that a legislator could vote against constituency wishes but escape any electoral accountability for his actions.

TABLE 2

Number of Correct District Predictions by 1968
Election Outcome
(percent by columns)

Number of Correct Predictions	Election Outcome			Total
	Re-Elected	Defeated	Other	
None	0.0	13.6	1.3	2.2
One	8.9	9.1	6.3	7.7
Two	24.1	27.3	20.3	22.7
Three	39.2	18.2	31.6	33.7
Four	27.8	31.8	40.5	33.7
Total % ..	100.0	100.0	100.0	100.0
N	79	22	79	180

$X^2 = 24.85$ $df = 8$ $p < .01$

islators made and the electoral outcome in the following (1968) election. Legislators who were re-elected seem to be somewhat better in predicting their districts' responses to the constitutional amendments than were legislators who suffered defeat. But, anomalously, legislators who did not run for another term, because of voluntary retirement, primary defeat, or other reasons, were slightly better estimators than legislators who were reelected.[23]

The only reasonable—if tentative—conclusion that can be drawn from this examination of legislators' ties to political parties and interest groups and their political success or skill as measured by subsequent election returns is that these things do not explain much about variation in the ability of legislators to understand correctly their constituents' opinions and attitudes. The linkage models, as classified by Luttbeg, do not insure that political representatives will accurately take account of constituent opinion.

But if the ties to linkage institutions do not differentiate between legislators who are sensitive to constituent opinion and those who are not, what might explain the variation which occurs?[24]

---

[23] It is possible, of course, that the reason the defeated legislators were slightly poorer estimators might be that they represented marginal districts. Hence their poor estimates and electoral defeat could both stem from the same thing: opinion in their district was rather evenly divided. Indeed, that or something else may even "explain" the relative inability of delegates to reflect constituency opinion. But regardless of such explanation the role model does not provide a basis for adequate responsiveness of legislative institutions to public opinion.

[24] One answer to this question might well be that the legislator's own opinion on these issues influences his perceptions of constituent opinion. We do not have any data on the legislator's own opinion, except, of course, for his roll call. But his roll-call vote may or may not reflect his own opinion. It is not reasonable to treat a legislator's vote on a bill as an indication of his own opinion when so many legislators adopt delegate and politico roles. This seems true, even though we treat constituent votes as indicators of their opinions. The relations between the roll-call vote and the constituency vote will be analyzed in a future paper.

ALTERNATE EXPLANATIONS: MULTIVARIATE ANALYSIS

If the bivariate analysis of the linkages between political representatives and constituents not only does not turn up much to explain legislators' predictions (with some of the relations taking an unexpected direction), perhaps a more exploratory procedure could turn up relationships upon which other linkages could be defined. In the entire survey from which these data are drawn, some 95 separate variables conceivably could be related to the predictive ability of the Iowa legislators. When this array was tested through bivariate analysis, a total of 20 significant relationships was found between the proportion of correct district predictions and possible explanatory variables. (See Table 3.) Eighteen of these variables were identified through Pearson's product-moment correlation coefficient and two through the chi-square test of statistical significance.[25] While some of these have already been discussed, others

TABLE 3
Independent Variables Significantly Related with Proportion of Correct Predictions

Variable Name	Correlation Coefficients	
	Simple	Partial
1. Strength of political party identification	−.157	.003
2. Importance of knowing district's will	−.196	−.185
3. Influence by farm bureau	−.212	−.031
4. Influence by insurance companies	−.170	−.013
5. Size of place of residence	−.317	−.020
6. Number of Democratic legislators elected from district since 1960	−.201	.020
7. Legislator's vote on item veto	.213	.138
8. Population of district, 1966 estimate	.368	−.081
9. Population change in district, 1950–60	.435	.145
10. Percent urban population in district, 1960 ...	.452	−.059
11. Percent black population in district, 1960 ...	.336	.106
12. Percent district population over 65, 1960 ...	−.414	.073
13. Percent district population with high school diploma, 1960	.324	.016
14. Percent district population employed in manufacturing, 1960	.372	−.155
15. Percent district population employed in white collar occupations, 1960	.406	−.078
16. Percent district households with income under $5,000, 1960	−.519	−.280
17. Percent district houholds with income exceeding $10,000, 1960	.434	.049
18. Percent district area in farm land	−.211	−.082
19. Election outcome, 1968	$X^2 = 24.85$	df = 8
20. Should represent/district or conscience	$X^2 = 13.64$	df = 4

° This partial correlation coefficient computed with the other variables held constant.

[25] With an N = 175, the probability of a product moment correlation r = .148 is less than .05. All coefficients equal to or greater than .15 are included in Table 3 on subsequent multivariate analysis.

seem unrelated to any of the linkage models. Some of the variables discarded as statistically unrelated to predictive ability were: the legislator's educational level; faith in people; political ideology (as measured on two conservatism scales); support and commitment to the legislature; political socialization; political ambitions; and level of organizational activities.

As a first step in the search for one or more alternate linkage models, the significant bivariate relationships were submitted to multivariate analysis. One goal was to identify possible spurious relationships through partialling techniques. A product of this operation would be a reduction in the number of variables needed to account for variation in legislators' predictive ability, and thus a more parsimonious explanatory model.

Table 3 lists the correlations between the independent variables and the legislators' proportion of correct predictions. The multiple R for the 18 independent variables is .6187, indicating that by using all the variables it is possible to explain 38.3 percent of the total variance in the dependent variable. However, the highly interrelated nature of all district demographic variables—numbers 8 to 18—raises questions of multicollinearity.[26] Consequently the most representative district demographic variable—households with income under $5,000—was selected to indicate the relationship of these eleven variables to the representatives' predictive ability in the multivariate analysis with the other seven independent variables. In this subsequent multivariate analysis a large number of spurious relationships apparent in the resulting small partial correlation coefficients indicates that the number of independent variables can be drastically reduced without much effect upon the ability to explain variance. Such a small loss indicates that many of the original list of statistically significant variables are not, of themselves, very important in explaining legislators' ability to predict their districts' opinion on the four constitutional issues.

If the model is reduced to two explanatory variables—district households with income under $5,000, and legislators' feeling about the importance of knowing the district's will—the multiple R is .5441 and the explained variation is 29.6 percent. So in reducing the independent variables to two, the percentage of explained variance has gone from 38.3 percent to 29.6 percent. Finally, if only the variable about district households with income below $5,000 is used, with an r of −.519, the explained variance of 26.9 percent, a loss from the original model of 11.4 percent.

In the two-variable model, the more sensitive variable of the two (the households with income under $5,000) indicates that the larger the percentage of poor households in the district, the less accurate are the legislators' assessments of constituent opinion. Perhaps poor constituents are less visible to legislators, even in districts in which they are concentrated. The second important variable, the legislators' assertion about the im-

---

26 See Dennis J. Palumbo, *Statistics In Political and Behavioral Science* (New York: Appleton-Century-Crofts, 1969), 215, and H. M. Blalock, "Correlated Independent Variables: The Problem of Multicollinearity," *Social Forces*, 42 (December 1963), 233–237.

portance of knowing the will of the district, with its perplexing negative relationship to accuracy of knowing constituency opinion, is harder to explain. But it is important to note that even when controlling for the effects of other variables, legislators expressing more of a delegate orientation seem less able to assess constituent opinion accurately than other legislators—the reverse of what would be expected.

The importance of the multivariate analysis lies as much in those variables excluded as in those which remain. Such political variables as party identification, legislators' roll-call voting, influence by private interest groups, and personal characteristics of the legislators drop out. The characteristics of the constituent district seem more critical.

Because variables related to the nature of the district accounted for more than 25 percent of the total variance, we felt that the search for alternate explanation of the linkage variability might well concentrate on some new measure of the commonalities in social characteristics as between representatives and constituents—perhaps conceived as the social distance between legislators and their constituents. In an effort to assess, tentatively, the reasonableness of this alternative, the relationship between the representatives' predictive ability and one indicator of social distance which could be reconstructed from the survey data was examined. The analysis proved inconclusive. The educational difference—defined as the number of years of formal schooling separating a representative and the median for his district—had an insignificant relationship with the representatives' ability to predict. Legislators whose educational level was lower than or equal to that of their constituents were slightly better predictors than were legislators with a higher educational level than their constituents. If better measures of social distance and representative-constituent commonality were available, a more adequate test of this alternative linkage would be possible.

While it is clear from the accumulated literature on recruitment that political representatives *as a whole* tend to be of substantially higher SES than those they putatively serve, it is far less clear what difference this makes in their representational behavior, or what are the consequences of variance in the social distance from legislators to constituents.

CONCLUSIONS

If the data in this survey are sufficient to sustain the analysis and if the perceptual skills of the Iowa legislators are similar to the skills of other political representatives, then there seems to be need for some fundamental rethinking about representative democracy. If we are truly interested in democracy, perhaps other mechanisms for insuring popular control and participation in our political system are necessary.

For instance, the great debate since Burke's time about the role of the political representative vis-à-vis his constituency seems to be largely unreal, or at least not grounded within the empirical possibilities of contemporary American legislative experience. If legislators who perceive their role to be delegates cannot assess the wishes of their constituents with any more accuracy than did the Iowa legislative delegates, then there is little possibility that delegate legislators can mirror their constituents' wishes when acting upon the myriad issues with which modern American legislators must cope. Moreover, legislators who look upon themselves as trustees feel that they need not, even if they could, be responsive to constituent opinion. Thus the hope and assumption of representative democratic theory that legislative institutions provide an adequate means to insure legislative responsiveness to public opinion—the minimal condition for representative democracy—does not appear to be met.[27]

It is comforting, perhaps, to know that legislators seem to be more reasonably accurate in assessing constituency opinion on major issues than on less major ones, as the Miller-Stokes data on United States congressmen and the Iowa legislative analysis both suggest. But political representatives deal with so many issues which intervene in the lives of the people that their relative inability to perceive constituent opinion on issues like these reported here would seem to be a most serious limitation.

Furthermore, neither increasing nor decreasing legislators' ties to political parties or interest groups, two presumably important linkages, would seem to offer an adequate prospect for making legislators more sensitive to their constituents—that is, without fundamentally changing the linkage institutions themselves. Nor does the election machinery seem to be an effective vehicle for insuring legislative accountability. So what are the alternatives if one wants a responsive democracy? Perhaps one can try to redefine constituency so that it is no longer a small territorial subunit of a larger jurisdiction. Perhaps representatives could reasonably take into account statewide or nationwide public opinion (or party identifiers' opinion).[28] This is a prospect which seems worth pursuing, for, among other things, technological innovations and present-day research capabilities could conceivably give legislators reasonably accurate information on public opinion for many issues. Or perhaps the evolution of a type of political decision-making more similar to the plebiscite, or the institution of a more formal instructed delegate system of representation, or even the further political decentralization of political authority, as the New Left would have it, might increase the democratic input into American political systems. Of course, any of these might not. By now, political scientists ought to have substantially better ways to evaluate the consequences of basic structural changes than were available when American representative institutions were created. Some of the major settled questions about American political practices may have to be reopened. The option may be to confirm and perpetuate an essentially elitist decision-making system which takes account of public opinion only in a substantially distorted manner.

---

[27] On the elitist premise of the trustee position, see Kenneth Prewitt, "Political Ambitions, Volunteerism, and Electoral Accountability," *American Political Science Review*, 64 (March 1970), 16.

[28] The Iowa legislators also predicted the statewide referenda responses to the four constitutional issues. While the data analysis is incomplete, they were not notably better predictors of the statewide results than they were of their legislative district results.

All of these speculations are too grand for the data analysis. Perhaps the issues and the analysis in Iowa were wrongly conceived, or possibly the referenda results are inadequate measures of constituent opinion. Perhaps the fact that, after all, a majority of legislators were accurate on each issue means that the interpretations in this paper are overly pessimistic. And it may be that political representatives in other legislative settings have different and more accurate linkages with their constituents. We can fervently hope that this is the case even as we doubt it.

H. Paul Friesema and Ronald D. Hedlund

The Reality of Representational Roles

The value of role theory for the analysis of American legislative behavior has been forcefully argued, and debated, since the publication of the four state comparative legislative study, *The Legislative System*.[1] Of all the possible legislative roles and role orientations, one has come under the closest scrutiny—the role orientation of legislators vis-à-vis their electoral constituency. This is probably because the usual formulation of alternate role orientations toward electoral constituents (delegate, politico, trustee) is derived from Edmund Burke, and directly related to one of the persistent normative questions about representative democracy—whom should the legislator represent, his constituents (delegate) or his own conscience (trustee). While the intermediate category, "politico," is constructed from indeterminate legislative responses and is ambiguous, the terms "delegate" and "trustee" are traditional intellectual constructions which, happily, have appeared to correspond, or be relevant, to contemporary actors' definitions of their own roles. So it has seemed.

In the preceding article, we presented an analysis of some legislators' perceptions of their constituencies' opinions.[2] In that analysis we demonstrated that the putative delegates in the Iowa legislature, perceiving themselves bound by constituency desires, were not very accurate in their perceptions of constituency opinion. We suggested that "the great debate since Burke's time about the role of the political representative vis-à-vis his constituency seems to be largely unreal, or at least not grounded within the empirical possibilities of contemporary American legislative experience."[3] Nonetheless, a legislator's role orientation toward his electoral constituency could still be very significant in affecting his own activities and particularly his voting behavior. But the evi-

---

[1] John C. Wahlke, et al., *The Legislative System* (New York: John Wiley and Sons, 1962).

[2] Ronald D. Hedlund and H. Paul Friesema, "Representatives' Perceptions of Constituency Opinion," *Journal of Politics*, 34 (1972), pp. 730–752.

[3] *Ibid.*, p. 750.

dence is quite limited. As Malcolm E. Jewell has written in his assessment of legislative role research:

> This research has explored a number of variables that may help to explain the role concepts of various types of legislators, but it has added little to our knowledge about the effects of roles on behavior of legislators. . . . Role analysis may be useful for conceptual clarification, but legislative scholars need tools of analysis that will also contribute to explanation and prediction of legislative behavior. They may agree that logically there must be a link between role concepts and behavior of legislators. But they want to know how that link can be measured empirically, how strong it is, and whether knowledge concerning the linkage can add significantly to what we already know about the causes of legislative behavior.[4]

Because we have the roll call votes of the Iowa legislators for each of the constitutional issues, as well as their representational role orientations, and their constituents' opinion (as reflected in the referenda), we are able to explore the relationships between role orientations and legislative behavior. Table 1 presents a comparison of the legislators' roll call

TABLE 1

Consistency between Legislator's Voting and District Voting

Type of Relationship	Issues				
	Home Rule	Item Veto	Annual Sessions	Reappor- tionment	Total
Consistent	89	63	59	74	71
Inconsistent	11	37	41	26	29
Total % ...	100	100	100	100	100
N	179	176	176	174	705

° A "consistent" relationship is one where the legislator's vote (yea or nay) is the same as the district vote (yes or no). An inconsistent relationship is one where the legislator's vote is the opposite of the district vote.

votes for each of the constitutional amendments with the subsequent referenda votes in the legislators' districts. A significant majority of consistent votes between legislators and their constituents is observed on each issue. Over 70 percent of all votes are consistent. Table 2 compares legislators' roll call votes on the constitutional amendments with the legislators' *estimates* of how their constituents would vote on the referenda. In this instance even higher agreement is seen between legislators' roll call votes and what *they think* their constituents will do (from 71 percent of consistent votes, with regard to actual referenda results to 82 percent for *anticipated* referenda results). Therefore, it seems reasonable to conclude that legislators' perceptions of constituency opinion have an important effect upon their own roll call behavior.

[4] Malcolm E. Jewell, "Attitudinal Determinants of Legislative Behavior: The Utility of Role Analysis," in Kornberg and Musolf (eds.), *Legislatures in Developmental Perspective* (Durham: Duke University Press, 1970), pp. 460–461.

TABLE 2

Consistency between Legislator's Voting and Legislator's Prediction
of District Voting

Type of Relationship	Issues				
	Home Rule	Item Veto	Annual Sessions	Reapportionment	Total
Consistent	97	79	80	73	82
Inconsistent	3	21	20	27	18
Total % ...	100	100	100	100	100
N	179	168	167	172	686

When the legislative respondents are divided into their representational role orientations (Table 3), the delegates, supposedly bound by constituency opinion, in fact, have roll call records which are far more inconsistent with their districts than do the trustees or politicos, who, logically, should feel less commitment to their electoral constituency. This disconcerting outcome could result because, as previously discussed, the delegates were significantly less accurate than other legislators in assessing constituency opinion. But, Table 4 adds further difficulty. The delegates, who verbally express a commitment to voting their districts' wishes, are less likely to vote the way they believe their constituents will vote than are the trustees who express a legitimacy and willingness to vote on the basis of criteria other than their constituents' wishes. If this pattern is not a fluke of some kind, it raises very serious questions about the continued value of some very important scholarly pursuits of recent years. If the identified delegates are less aware than other legislators about their constituents' opinions, through naïveté or whatever, and also are less likely than other legislators to vote as they perceive their constituents would want, thus apparently acting against their expressed

TABLE 3

Consistency between Legislator's Voting and District Voting,
by Representational Roles

Type of Relationship	Home Rule			Item Veto			Annual Sessions			Reapportionment			Total		
	T*	P*	D*	T*	P*	D*	T*	P*	D*	T*	P*	D*	T*	P*	D*
Consistent ...	92	90	80	67	69	53	69	55	43	75	74	68	76	72	61
Inconsistent ..	8	10	20	33	31	47	31	45	57	25	26	32	24	28	39
Total % ..	100	100	100	100	100	100	100	100	100	100	100	100	100	100	100
N	91	40	44	90	39	43	90	38	44	88	38	44	359	155	175

* Role orientations:
   T—trustee.
   D—delegate.
   P—politico.

TABLE 4

Consistency between Legislator's Voting and Legislator's Prediction of District Voting, by Representational Roles

Type of Relationship	Issues														
	Home Rule			Item Veto			Annual Sessions			Reappor- tionment			Total		
	T°	P°	D°	T°	P°	D°	T°	P°	D°	T°	P°	D°	T°	P°	D°
Consistent ...	98	95	98	86	74	70	84	71	84	74	76	65	85	79	79
Incon- sistent ..	2	5	2	14	26	30	16	29	16	26	24	35	15	21	21
Total % ..	100	100	100	100	100	100	100	100	100	100	100	100	100	100	100
N	91	40	44	86	35	43	86	34	43	88	37	43	351	146	173

° Role orientations:
  T—trustee.
  D—delegate.
  P—politico.

values, future use of at least the trustee-politico-delegate pattern variable in legislative research would seem rather pointless. Of course, replicating these findings and explaining them are important future tasks.

DISCUSSION AND CONCLUSION

It is possible, of course, that the interviewing or coding procedure for this study was inadequate, so that the explanation for the unexpected inverse relationship between a legislator being categorized as a delegate and voting what he thought were his constituents' views is simple research error. But this project followed accepted procedures and used the standard coding conventions of much past legislative role research. The legislative respondents were asked to indicate which of three verbal descriptions of representational behavior came the closest to describing how a legislator should act when making important decisions. The verbal descriptions were synopses of those given in Wahlke, *The Legislative System*.[5] Those responses were the basis for the assignment of legislative role orientations. (When other independent measures of role were used, e.g., a series of forced response questions, a similar pattern of results was obtained.) A more likely explanation of these unexpected findings may be that the respondents, or at least many of them, were simply providing verbal responses to questions which were of little consequence or meaning to them. If so, one would want to know if this was a peculiar response pattern for legislators (or politicians, perhaps) or whether it might even be very specifically related to the categorization of legislative role orientation toward constituents. One can think of plausible reasons why legislators might be especially likely to give what they perceived to be the politically proper answer, whatever the depth of their commitment to the behavior which flowed logically from the asserted value. The ability

---

[5] Wahlke, et al., pp. 267–280.

to give such answers, or make such statements, might even be a cultivated characteristic of some legislators. It is also possible that the anomaly is a product of an attempt by scholars to impose too rigid a categorization upon people whose views are more obtuse than the Burke construction can capture. Unlike most role research, the trustee-politico-delegate categorization does not flow solely from grouping the respondents' expressed views, and then appropriately labeling the category (in the manner of naming some factor loading). The role categories (delegate and trustee) are products of a classic intellectual tradition concerning representative democracy, which may or may not be of any immediate saliency to contemporary legislators.

The answers to such questions are basic to any consideration of the future utility of legislative role research. It is clear to us that this first effort to link legislative role orientations with legislative roll call behavior has produced results which throw into serious doubt the continued value of an important research effort of legislative scholars. For if ostensible legislative delegates do not know the will of their districts, and do not even vote according to their perceptions about their constituents' views as much as other legislators, this role category is virtually useless in accounting for legislative behavior. Further, the utility of representational role as an explanatory variable for legislative behavior or as a linkage mechanism between representative and constituent is probably nonexistent.

Warren E. Miller and Donald E. Stokes

Constituency Influence in Congress*

Substantial constituency influence over the lower house of Congress is commonly thought to be both a normative principle and a factual truth of American government. From their draft constitution we may assume the Founding Fathers expected it, and many political scientists feel, regretfully, that the Framers' wish has come all too true.[1] Nevertheless, much of the evidence of constituency control rests on inference. The fact that our House of Representatives, especially by comparison with the House of Commons, has irregular party voting does not of itself indicate that Congressmen deviate from party in response to local pressure. And even more, the fact that many Congressmen *feel* pressure from home does not of itself establish that the local constituency is performing any of the acts that a reasonable definition of control would imply.

I. CONSTITUENCY CONTROL IN THE NORMATIVE THEORY OF REPRESENTATION

Control by the local constituency is at one pole of *both* the great normative controversies about representation that have arisen in modern times. It is generally recognized that constituency control is opposite to the conception of representation associated with Edmund Burke. Burke wanted the representative to serve the constituency's *interest* but not its *will*, and the extent to which the representative should be compelled by

* Reprinted from the *American Political Science Review,* vol. 67 (March 1963), pp. 45–56. Copyright 1963, The American Political Science Association.

The research reported here was made possible through grants of the Rockefeller Foundation and the Social Science Research Council, whose support is gratefully acknowledged. The authors are indebted also to Ralph Bisco and Gudmund R. Iversen for invaluable assistance.

[1] To be sure, the work of the Federal Convention has been supplemented in two critical respects. The first of these is the practice, virtually universal since the mid-19th Century, of choosing Representatives from single-member districts of limited geographic area. The second is the practice, which has also become virtually universal in our own century, of selecting party nominees for the House by direct primary election.

electoral sanctions to follow the "mandate" of his constituents has been at the heart of the ensuing controversy as it has continued for a century and a half.[2]

Constituency control also is opposite to the conception of government by responsible national parties. This is widely seen, yet the point is rarely connected with normative discussions of representation. Indeed, it is remarkable how little attention has been given to the model of representation implicit in the doctrine of a "responsible two-party system." When the subject of representation is broached among political scientists the classical argument between Burke and his opponents is likely to come at once to mind. So great is Burke's influence that the antithesis he proposed still provides the categories of thought used in contemporary treatments of representation despite the fact that many students of politics today would advocate a relationship between representative and constituency that fits *neither* position of the mandate-independence controversy.

The conception of representation implicit in the doctrine of responsible parties shares the idea of popular control with the instructed-delegate model. Both are versions of popular sovereignty. But "the people" of the responsible two-party system are conceived in terms of a national rather than a local constituency. Candidates for legislative office appeal to the electorate in terms of a *national* party program and leadership, to which, if elected, they will be committed. Expressions of policy preference by the local district are reduced to endorsements of one or another of these programs, and the local district retains only the arithmetical significance that whichever party can rally to its program the greater number of supporters in the district will control its legislative seat.

No one tradition of representation has entirely dominated American practice. Elements of the Burkean, instructed-delegate, and responsible-party models can all be found in our political life. Yet if the American system has elements of all three, a good deal depends on how they are combined. Especially critical is the question whether different models of representation apply to different public issues. Is the saliency of legislative action to the public so different in quality and degree on different issues that the legislator is subject to very different constraints from his constituency? Does the legislator have a single generalized mode of response to his constituency that is rooted in a normative belief about the representative's role or does the same legislator respond to his constituency differently on different issues? More evidence is needed on matters so fundamental to our system.

---

[2] In the language of Eulau, Wahlke et al., we speak here of the "style," not the "focus," of representation. See their "The Role of the Representative: Some Empirical Observations on the Theory of Edmund Burke," *American Political Science Review*, Vol. LIII (September 1959), pp. 742–756. An excellent review of the mandate–independence controversy is given by Hanna Fenichel Pitkin, "The Theory of Representation" (unpublished doctoral dissertation, University of California, Berkeley, 1961). For other contemporary discussions of representation, see Alfred de Grazia, *Public and Republic* (New York, 1951), and John A. Fairlie, "The Nature of Political Representation," *American Political Science Review*, Vol. XXXIV (April–June 1940), pp. 236–48, 456–66.

II. AN EMPIRICAL STUDY OF REPRESENTATION

To extend what we know of representation in the American Congress the Survey Research Center of The University of Michigan interviewed the incumbent Congressman, his non-incumbent opponent (if any), and a sample of constituents in each of 116 congressional districts, which were themselves a probability sample of all districts.[3] These interviews,

---

[3] The sampling aspects of this research were complicated by the fact that the study of representation was a rider midway on a four-year panel study of the electorate whose primary sampling units were not congressional districts (although there is no technical reason why they could not have been if the needs of the representation analysis had been foreseen when the design of the sample was fixed two years before). As a result, the districts in our sample had unequal probabilities of selection and unequal weights in the analysis, making the sample somewhat less efficient than an equal-probability sample of equivalent size.

It will be apparent in the discussion that follows that we have estimated characteristics of whole constituencies from our samples of constituents living in particular districts. In view of the fact that a sample of less than two thousand constituents has been divided among 116 districts, the reader may wonder about the reliability of these estimates. After considerable investigation we have concluded that their sampling error is not so severe a problem for the analysis as we had thought it would be. Several comments may indicate why it is not.

To begin with, the weighting of our sample of districts has increased the reliability of the constituency estimates. The correct theoretical weight to be assigned each district in the analysis is the inverse of the probability of the district's selection, and it can be shown that this weight is approximately proportional to the number of interviews taken in the district. The result of this is that the greatest weight is assigned the districts with the largest number of interviews and, hence, the most reliable constituency estimates. Indeed, these weights increase by half again the (weighted) mean number of interviews taken per district. To put the matter another way: the introduction of differential weights trades some of our sample of congressional districts for more reliable constituency estimates.

How much of a problem the unreliability of these estimates is depends very much on the analytic uses to which the estimates are put. If our goal were case analyses of particular districts, the constituency samples would have to be much larger. Indeed, for most case analyses we would want several hundred interviews per district (at a cost, over 116 districts, of several small nuclear reactors). However, most of the findings reported here are based not on single districts but on many or all of the districts in our sample. For analyses of this sort the number of interviews per district can be much smaller.

Our investigation of the effect of the sampling variance of the constituency estimates is quite reassuring. When statistics computed from our constituency samples are compared with corresponding parameter values for the constituencies, the agreement of the two sets of figures is quite close. For example, when the proportions voting Democratic in the 116 constituencies in 1958, as computed from our sample data, are compared with the actual proportions voting Democratic, as recorded in official election statistics, a product moment correlation of 0.93 is obtained, and this figure is the more impressive since this test throws away non-voters, almost one-half of our total sample. We interpret the Pearsonian correlation as an appropriate measure of agreement in this case, since the associated regression equations are almost exactly the identity function. The alternative intraclass correlation coefficient has almost as high a value.

Although we believe that this analysis provides a textbook illustration of how misleading intuitive ideas (including our own) about the effects of sampling error can be, these figures ought not to be too beguiling. It is clear that how close such a correlation is to 1.0 for any given variable will depend on the ratio of the between-district variance to the total variance. When this ratio is as high as it is for Republican

conducted immediately after the congressional election of 1958, explored a wide range of attitudes and perceptions held by the individuals who play the reciprocal roles of the representative relation in national government. The distinguishing feature of this research is, of course, that it sought direct information from both constituent and legislator (actual and aspiring). To this fund of comparative interview data has been added information about the roll call votes of our sample of Congressmen and the political and social characteristics of the districts they represent.

Many students of politics, with excellent reason, have been sensitive to possible ties between representative and constituent that have little to do with issues of public policy. For example, ethnic identifications may cement a legislator in the affections of his district, whatever (within limits) his stands on issues. And many Congressmen keep their tenure of office secure by skillful provision of district benefits ranging from free literature to major federal projects. In the full study of which this analysis is part we have explored several bases of constituency support that have little to do with policy issues. Nevertheless, the question how the representative should make up his mind on legislative issues is what the classical arguments over representation are all about, and we have given a central place to a comparison of the policy preferences of constituents and Representatives and to a causal analysis of the relation between the two.

In view of the electorate's scanty information about government it was not at all clear in advance that such a comparison could be made. Some of the more buoyant advocates of popular sovereignty have regarded the citizen as a kind of kibitzer who looks over the shoulder of his representative at the legislative game. Kibitzer and player may disagree as to which card should be played, but they were at least thought to share a common understanding of what the alternatives are.

No one familiar with the findings of research on mass electorates could accept this view of the citizen. Far from looking over the shoulder of their Congressmen at the legislative game, most Americans are almost totally uninformed about legislative issues in Washington. At best the average citizen may be said to have some general ideas about how the country should be run, which he is able to use in responding to particular questions about what the government ought to do. For example, survey studies have shown that most people have a general (though differing) conception of how far government should go to achieve social and economic welfare objectives and that these convictions fix their response to various particular questions about actions government might take.[4]

What makes it possible to compare the policy preferences of constituents and Representatives despite the public's low awareness of leg-

---

and Democratic voting, the effect of the unreliability of our constituency estimates is fairly trivial. Although the content of the study is quite different, this sampling problem has much in common with the problem of attenuation of correlation as it has been treated in psychological testing. See, for example, J. P. Guilford, *Fundamental Statistics in Psychology and Education* (New York, 1956), pp. 475–78.

[4] See Angus Campbell, Phillip E. Converse, Warren E. Miller, and Donald E. Stokes, *The American Voter* (New York, 1960), pp. 194–209.

islative affairs is the fact that Congressmen themselves respond to many issues in terms of fairly broad evaluative dimensions. Undoubtedly policy alternatives are judged in the executive agencies and the specialized committees of the Congress by criteria that are relatively complex and specific to the policies at issue. But a good deal of evidence goes to show that when proposals come before the House as a whole they are judged on the basis of more general evaluative dimensions.[5] For example, most Congressmen, too, seem to have a general conception of how far government should go in the area of domestic social and economic welfare, and these general positions apparently orient their roll call votes on a number of particular social welfare issues.

It follows that such a broad evaluative dimension can be used to compare the policy preferences of constituents and Representatives despite the low state of the public's information about politics. In this study three such dimensions have been drawn from our voter interviews and from congressional interviews and roll call records. As suggested above, one of these has to do with approval of government action in the social welfare field, the primary domestic issue of the New Deal–Fair Deal (and New Frontier) eras. A second dimension has to do with support for American involvement in foreign affairs, a latter-day version of the isolationist–internationalist continuum. A third dimension has to do with approval of federal action to protect the civil rights of Negroes.[6]

Because our research focused on these three dimensions, our analysis of constituency influence is limited to these areas of policy. No point has been more energetically or usefully made by those who have sought to clarify the concepts of power and influence than the necessity of specifying the acts *with respect to which* one actor has power or influence or control over another.[7] Therefore, the scope or range of influence for our

---

[5] This conclusion, fully supported by our own work for later Congresses, is one of the main findings to be drawn from the work of Duncan MacRae on roll call voting in the House of Representatives. See his *Dimensions of Congressional Voting: A Statistical Study of the House of Representatives in the Eighty-First Congress* (Berkeley and Los Angeles: University of California Press, 1958). For additional evidence of the existence of scale dimensions in legislative behavior, see N. L. Gage and Ben Shimberg, "Measuring Senatorial Progressivism," *Journal of Abnormal and Social Psychology,* Vol. XLIV (January 1949), pp. 112–17; George M. Belknap, "A Study of Senatorial Voting by Scale Analysis" (unpublished doctoral dissertation, University of Chicago, 1951), and "A Method for Analyzing Legislative Behavior," *Midwest Journal of Political Science,* Vol. II (1958), pp. 377–402; two other articles by Mac-Rae, "The Role of the State Legislator in Massachusetts," *American Sociological Review,* Vol. XIX (April 1954), pp. 185–94, and "Roll Call Votes and Leadership," *Public Opinion Quarterly,* Vol. XX (1956), pp. 543–58; Charles D. Farris, "A Method of Determining Ideological Groups in Congress," *Journal of Politics,* Vol. XX (1958), pp. 308–38; and Leroy N. Rieselbach, "Quantitative Techniques for Studying Voting Behavior in the U.N. General Assembly," *International Organization,* Vol. XIV (1960), pp. 291–306.

[6] The content of the three issue domains may be suggested by some of the roll call and interview items used. In the area of social welfare these included the issues of public housing, public power, aid to education, and government's role in maintaining full employment. In the area of foreign involvement the items included the issues of foreign economic aid, military aid, sending troops abroad, and aid to neutrals. In the area of civil rights the items included the issues of school desegregation, fair employment, and the protection of Negro voting rights.

analysis is the collection of legislative issues falling within our three policy domains. We are not able to say how much control the local constituency may or may not have over *all* actions of its Representative, and there may well be pork-barrel issues or other matters of peculiar relevance to the district on which the relation of Congressman to constituency is quite distinctive. However, few observers of contemporary politics would regard the issues of government provision of social and economic welfare, of American involvement in world affairs, and of federal action in behalf of the Negro as constituting a trivial range of action. Indeed, these domains together include most of the great issues that have come before Congress in recent years.

In each policy domain we have used the procedures of cumulative scaling, as developed by Louis Guttman and others, to order our samples of Congressmen, of opposing candidates, and of voters. In each domain Congressmen were ranked once according to their roll call votes in the House and again according to the attitudes they revealed in our confidential interviews. These two orderings are by no means identical, nor are the discrepancies due simply to uncertainties of measurement.[8] Opposing candidates also were ranked in each policy domain according to the attitudes they revealed in our interviews. The nationwide sample of constituents was ordered in each domain, and by averaging the attitude scores of all constituents living in the same districts, whole constituencies were ranked on each dimension so that the views of Congressmen could be compared with those of their constituencies.[9] Finally, by considering

---

[7] Because this point has been so widely discussed it has inevitably attracted a variety of terms. Dahl denotes the acts of *a* whose performance *A* is able to influence as the *scope* of *A's* power. See Robert A. Dahl, "The Concept of Power," *Behavioral Science*, Vol. II (July 1957), pp. 201–15. This usage is similar to that of Harold D. Lasswell and Abraham Kaplan, *Power and Society* (New Haven: Yale University Press, 1950), pp. 71–73. Dorwin Cartwright, however, denotes the behavioral or psychological changes in *P* which *O* is able to induce as the *range* of *O's* power: "A Field Theoretical Conception of Power," *Studies in Social Power* (Ann Arbor: Research Center for Group Dynamics, Institute for Social Research, The University of Michigan, 1959), pp. 183–220.

[8] That the Representative's roll call votes can diverge from his true opinion is borne out by a number of findings of the study (some of which are reported here) as to the conditions under which agreement between the Congressman's roll call position and his private attitude will be high or low. However, a direct confirmation that these two sets of measurements are not simply getting at the same thing is given by differences in attitude–roll call agreement according to the Congressman's sense of how well his roll call votes have expressed his real views. In the domain of foreign involvement, for example, the correlation of our attitudinal and roll call measurements was .75 among Representatives who said that their roll call votes had expressed their real views fairly well. But this correlation was only .04 among those who said that their roll call votes had expressed their views poorly. In the other policy domains, too, attitude–roll call agreement is higher among Congressmen who are well satisfied with their roll call votes than it is among Congressmen who are not.

[9] During the analysis we have formed constituency scores out of the scores of constituents living in the same district by several devices other than calculating average constituent scores. In particular, in view of the ordinal character of our scales we have frequently used the *median* constituent score as a central value for the constituency as a whole. However, the ordering of constituencies differs very little according to which of several reasonable alternatives for obtaining constituency scores is chosen. As a result, we have preferred mean scores for the greater number of ranks they give.

only the constituents in each district who share some characteristic (voting for the incumbent, say) we were able to order these fractions of districts so that the opinions of Congressmen could be compared with those, for example, of the dominant electoral elements of their districts.

In each policy domain, crossing the rankings of Congressmen and their constituencies gives an empirical measure of the extent of policy agreement between legislator and district.[10] In the period of our research this procedure reveals very different degrees of policy congruence across the three issue domains. On questions of social and economic welfare

---

[10] The meaning of this procedure can be suggested by two percentage tables standing for hypothetical extreme cases, the first that of full agreement, the second that of no agreement whatever. For convenience, these illustrative tables categorize both Congressmen and their districts in terms of only degrees of favor and assume for both a nearly uniform distribution across the three categories. The terms "pro," "neutral," and "con" indicate a relative rather than an absolute opinion. In Case I, full agreement, all districts relatively favorable to social welfare action have Congressmen who are so too, etc.; whereas in Case II, or that of no agreement, the ordering of constituencies is independent in a statistical sense of the ranking of Congressmen: knowing the policy orientation of a district gives no clue at all to the orientation of its Congressman. Of course, it is possible for the orders of legislators and districts to be *inversely* related, and this possibility is of some importance, as indicated below, when the policy position of non-incumbent candidates as well as incumbents is taken into account. To summarize the degree of congruence between legislators and voters, a measure of correlation is introduced. Although we have used a variety of measures of association in our analysis, the values reported in this article all refer to product moment correlation coefficients. For our hypothetical Case I a measure of correlation would have the value 1.0; for Case II, the value 0.0. When it is applied to actual data this convenient indicator is likely to have a value somewhere in between. The question is where.

Case I: Full Policy Agreement
Constituencies:

Congressmen:	Pro	Neutral	Con	
Pro	33	0	0	33
Neutral	0	34	0	34
Con	0	0	33	33
	33	34	33	100%

Correlation = 1.0

Case II: No Policy Agreement
Constituencies:

Congressmen:	Pro	Neutral	Con	
Pro	11	11	11	33
Neutral	11	12	11	34
Con	11	11	11	33
	33	34	33	100%

Correlation = 0.0

there is considerable agreement between Representative and district, expressed by a correlation of approximately 0.3. This coefficient is, of course, very much less than the limiting value of 1.0, indicating that a number of Congressmen are, relatively speaking, more or less "liberal" than their districts. However, on the question of foreign involvement there is no discernible agreement between legislator and district whatever. Indeed, as if to emphasize the point, the coefficient expressing this relation is slightly negative (-0.09), although not significantly so in a statistical sense. It is in the domain of civil rights that the rankings of Congressmen and constituencies most nearly agree. When we took our measurements in the late 1950s the correlation of congressional roll call behavior with constituency opinion on questions affecting the Negro was nearly 0.6.

The description of policy agreement that these three simple correlations give can be a starting-point for a wide range of analyses. For example, the significance of party competition in the district for policy representation can be explored by comparing the agreement between district and Congressman with the agreement between the district and the Congressman's non-incumbent opponent. Alternatively, the significance of choosing Representatives from single-member districts by popular majority can be explored by comparing the agreement between the Congressman and his own supporters with the agreement between the Congressman and the supporters of his opponent. Taking *both* party competition and majority rule into account magnifies rather spectacularly some of the coefficients reported here. This is most true in the domain of social welfare, where attitudes both of candidates and of voters are most polarized along party lines. Whereas the correlation between the constituency majority and congressional roll call votes is nearly $+0.4$ on social welfare policy, the correlation of the district majority with the non-incumbent candidate is -0.4. This difference, amounting to almost 0.8, between these two coefficients is an indicator of what the dominant electoral element of the constituency gets on the average by choosing the Congressman it has and excluding his opponent from office.[11]

These three coefficients are also the starting-point for a causal analysis of the relation of constituency to representative, the main problem of this paper. At least on social welfare and Negro rights a measurable degree of congruence is found between district and legislator. Is this agreement due to constituency influence in Congress, or is it to be attributed to other causes? If this question is to have a satisfactory answer the conditions that are necessary and sufficient to assure constituency control must be stated and compared with the available empirical evidence.

---

[11] A word of caution is in order, lest we compare things that are not strictly comparable. For obvious reasons, most non-incumbent candidates have no roll call record, and we have had to measure their policy agreement with the district entirely in terms of the attitudes they have revealed in interviews. However, the difference of coefficients given here is almost as great when the policy agreement between the incumbent Congressman and his district is also measured in terms of the attitudes conveyed in confidential interviews.

III. THE CONDITIONS OF CONSTITUENCY INFLUENCE

Broadly speaking, the constituency can control the policy actions of the Representative in two alternative ways. The first of these is for the district to choose a Representative who so shares its views that in following his own convictions he does his constituents' will. In this case district opinion and the Congressman's actions are connected through the Representative's own policy attitudes. The second means of constituency control is for the Congressman to follow his (at least tolerably accurate) perceptions of district attitude in order to win re-election. In this case constituency opinion and the Congressman's actions are connected through his perception of what the district wants.[12]

These two paths of constituency control are presented schematically in Figure 1. As the figure suggests, each path has two steps, one con-

FIGURE 1

Connections between a Constituency's Attitude and
Its Representative's Role Call Behavior

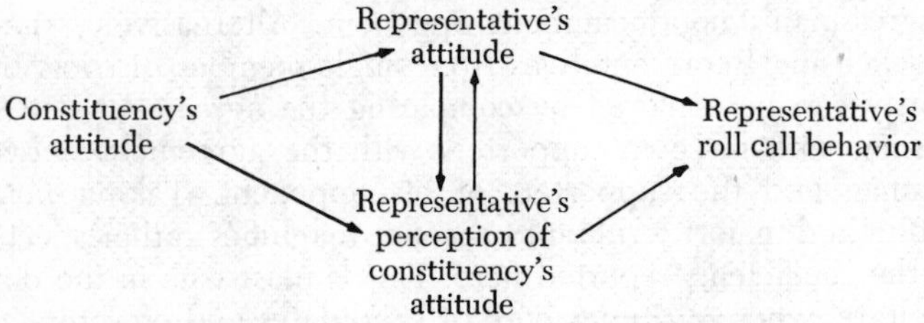

necting the constituency's attitude with an "intervening" attitude or perception, the other connecting this attitude or perception with the Representative's roll call behavior. Out of respect for the processes by which the human actor achieves cognitive congruence we have also drawn arrows between the two intervening factors, since the Congressman probably tends to see his district as having the same opinion as his own and also tends, over time, to bring his own opinion into line with the district's. The inclusion of these arrows calls attention to two other possible influence paths, each consisting of *three* steps, although these additional paths will turn out to be of relatively slight importance empirically.

Neither of the main influence paths of Figure 1 will connect the final roll call vote to the constituency's views if either of its steps is blocked. From this, two necessary conditions of constituency influence can be

---

[12] A third type of connection, excluded here, might obtain between district and Congressman if the Representative accedes to what he thinks the district wants because he believes that to be what a representative *ought* to do, whether or not it is necessary for re-election. We leave this type of connection out of our account here because we conceive an influence relation as one in which control is not voluntarily accepted or rejected by someone subject to it. Of course, this possible connection between district and Representative is not any the less interesting because it falls outside our definition of influence or control, and we have given a good deal of attention to it in the broader study of which this analysis is part.

stated: *first*, the Representative's votes in the House must agree substantially with his own policy views or his perceptions of the district's views, and not be determined entirely by other influences to which the Congressman is exposed; and, *second*, the attitudes or perceptions governing the Representative's acts must correspond, at least imperfectly, to the district's actual opinions. It would be difficult to describe the relation of constituency to Representative as one of control unless these conditions are met.[13]

Yet these two requirements are not sufficient to assure control. A *third* condition must also be satisfied: the constituency must in some measure take the policy views of candidates into account in choosing a Representative. If it does not, agreement between district and Congressman may arise for reasons that cannot rationally be brought within the idea of control. For example, such agreement may simply reflect the fact that a Representative drawn from a given area is likely, by pure statistical probability, to share its dominant values, without his acceptance or rejection of these ever having been a matter of consequence to his electors.

IV. EVIDENCE OF CONTROL: CONGRESSIONAL ATTITUDES AND PERCEPTIONS

How well are these conditions met in the relation of American Congressmen to their constituents? There is little question that the first is substantially satisfied; the evidence of our research indicates that members of the House do in fact vote both their own policy views and their perceptions of their constituents' views, at least on issues of social welfare, foreign involvement, and civil rights. If these two intervening factors are used to predict roll call votes, the prediction is quite successful. Their multiple correlation with roll call position is 0.7 for social welfare, 0.6 for foreign involvement, and 0.9 for civil rights; the last figure is especially persuasive. What is more, both the Congressman's own convictions and his perceptions of district opinion make a distinct contribution to his roll call behavior. In each of the three domains the prediction of roll call votes is surer if it is made from both factors rather than from either alone.

Lest the strong influence that the Congressman's views and his perception of district views have on roll call behavior appear somehow foreordained—and, consequently, this finding seem a trivial one—it is worth taking a sidewise glance at the potency of possible other forces on the Representative's vote. In the area of foreign policy, for example, a number of Congressmen are disposed to follow the administration's advice, whatever they or their districts think. For those who are, the multiple

---

[13] It scarcely needs to be said that demonstrating *some* constituency influence would not imply that the Representative's behavior is *wholly* determined by constituency pressures. The legislator acts in a complex institutional setting in which he is subject to a wide variety of influences. The constituency can exercise a genuine measure of control without driving all other influences from the Representative's life space.

correlation of roll call behavior with the Representative's own foreign policy views and his perception of district views is a mere 0.2. Other findings could be cited to support the point that the influence of the Congressman's own preferences and those he attributes to the district is extremely variable. Yet in the House as a whole over the three policy domains the influence of these forces is quite strong.

The connections of congressional attitudes and perceptions with actual constituency opinion are weaker. If policy agreement between district and Representative is moderate and variable across explained much more in terms of the second condition of constituency control than the first. The Representative's attitudes and perceptions most nearly match true opinion in his district on the issues of Negro rights. Reflecting the charged and polarized nature of this area, the correlation of actual district opinion with perceived opinion is greater than 0.6, and the correlation of district attitude with the Representative's own attitude is nearly 0.4, as shown by Table 1. But the comparable correlations for

TABLE 1

Correlations of Constituency Attitudes

| | Correlation of Constituency Attitude with | |
Policy Domain	Representative's Perception of Constituency Attitude	Representative's Own Attitude
Social welfare	.17	.21
Foreign involvement	.19	.06
Civil rights	.63	.39

foreign involvement are much smaller—indeed almost negligible. And the coefficients for social welfare are also smaller, although a detailed presentation of findings in this area would show that the Representative's perceptions and attitudes are more strongly associated with the attitude of his electoral *majority* than they are with the attitudes of the constituency as a whole.

Knowing this much about the various paths that may lead, directly or indirectly, from constituency attitude to roll call vote, we can assess their relative importance. Since the alternative influence chains have links of unequal strength, the full chains will not in general be equally strong, and these differences are of great importance in the relation of Representative to constituency. For the domain of civil rights Figure 2 assembles all the intercorrelations of the variables of our system. As the figure shows, the root correlation of constituency attitude with roll call behavior in this domain is 0.57. How much of this policy congruence can be accounted for by the influence path involving the Representative's attitude? And how much by the path involving his perception of con-

FIGURE 2

Intercorrelations of Variables Pertaining to Civil Rights

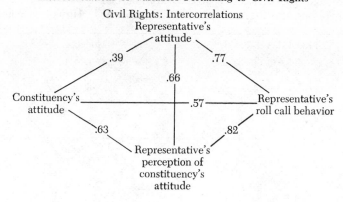

Civil Rights: Intercorrelations

stituency opinion? When the intercorrelations of the system are inter-preted in the light of what we assume its causal structure to be, it is influence passing through the Congressman's perception of the district's views that is found to be preeminently important.[14] Under the least

---

[14] We have done this by a variance-component technique simliar to several others proposed for dealing with problems of this type. See especially Herbert A. Simon, "Spurious Correlation: A Causal Interpretation," *Journal of the American Statistical Association*, Vol. 49 (1954), pp. 467–79; Hubert M. Blalock, Jr., "The Relative Importance of Variables," *American Sociological Review*, Vol. 26 (1961), pp. 866–74; and the almost forgotten work of Sewall Wright, "Correlation and Causation," *Journal of Agricultural Research*, Vol. 20 (1920), pp. 557–85. Under this technique a "path coefficient" (to use Wright's terminology, although not his theory) is assigned to each of the causal arrows by solving a set of equations involving the correlations of the variables of the model. The weight assigned to a full path is then the product of its several path coefficients, and this product may be interpreted as the proportion of the variance of the dependent variable (roll call behavior, here) that is explained by a given path.

A special problem arises because influence may flow in either direction between the Congressman's attitude and his perception of district attitude (as noted above, the Representative may tend both to perceive his constituency's view selectively, as consistent with his own, and to change his own view to be consistent with the per-ceived constituency view). Hence, we have not a single causal model but a whole family of models, varying according to the relative importance of influence from at-titude to perception and from perception to attitude. Our solution to this problem has been to calculate influence coefficients for the two extreme models in order to see how much our results could vary according to which model is chosen from our family of models. Since the systems of equations in this analysis are linear it can be shown that the coefficients we seek have their maximum and minimum values under one or the other of the limiting models. Therefore, computing any given coefficient for each of these limiting cases defines an interval in which the true value of the coefficient must lie. In fact these intervals turn out to be fairly small; our findings as to the relative importance of alternative influence paths would change little according to which model is selected.

The two limiting models with their associated systems of equations and the for-mulas for computing the relative importance of the three possible influence paths under each model are given below.

favorable assumption as to its importance, this path is found to account for more than twice as much of the variance of roll call behavior as the paths involving the Representative's own attitude.[15] However, when this

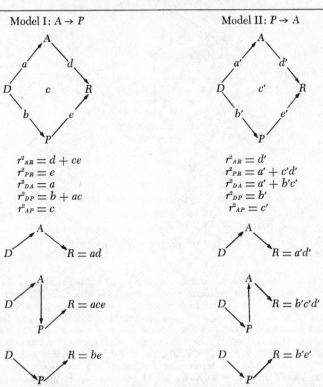

Model I: $A \rightarrow P$ ⁣ ⁣ ⁣ ⁣ ⁣ ⁣ ⁣ ⁣ ⁣ Model II: $P \rightarrow A$

$r^2_{AR} = d + ce$ $r^2_{AR} = d'$
$r^2_{PR} = e$ $r^2_{PR} = a' + c'd'$
$r^2_{DA} = a$ $r^2_{DA} = a' + b'c'$
$r^2_{DP} = b + ac$ $r^2_{DP} = b'$
$r^2_{AP} = c$ $r^2_{AP} = c'$

$R = ad$ $R = a'd'$

$R = ace$ $R = b'c'd'$

$R = be$ $R = b'e'$

[15] By "least favorable" we mean the assumption that influence goes only from the Congressman's attitude to his perception of district attitude (Model I) and not the other way round. Under this assumption, the proportions of the variance of roll call behavior accounted for by the three alternative paths, expressed as proportions of the part of the variance of roll call votes that is explained by district attitude, are these:

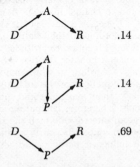

.14

.14

.69

Inverting the assumed direction of influence between the Congressman's own attitude and district attitude (Model II) eliminates altogether the effect that the Representative's attitude can have had on his votes, independently of his perception of district attitude.

same procedure is applied to our social welfare data, the results suggest that the direct connection of constituency and roll call through the Congressman's own attitude is the most important of the alternative paths.[16] The reversal of the relative importance of the two paths as we move from civil rights to social welfare is one of the most striking findings of this analysis.

V. EVIDENCE OF CONTROL: ELECTORAL BEHAVIOR

Of the three conditions of constituency influence, the requirement that the electorate take account of the policy positions of the candidates is the hardest to match with empirical evidence. Indeed, given the limited information the average voter carries to the polls, the public might be thought incompetent to perform any task of appraisal. Of constituents living in congressional districts where there was a contest between a Republican and a Democrat in 1958, less than one in five said they had read or heard something about both candidates, and well over half conceded they had read or heard nothing about either. And these proportions are not much better when they are based only on the part of the sample, not much more than half, that reported voting for Congress in 1958. The extent of awareness of the candidates among voters is indicated in Table 2. As the table shows, even of the portion of the public that was sufficiently interested to vote, almost half had read or heard nothing about either candidate.

Just how low a hurdle our respondents had to clear in saying thay had read or heard something about a candidate is indicated by detailed qualitative analysis of the information constituents *were* able to associate with congressional candidates. Except in rare cases, what the voters

TABLE 2
Awareness of Congressional Candidates
among Voters, 1958

		Read or Heard Something about Incumbent*		
		Yes	No	
Read or Heard Something about Non-Incumbent	Yes	24	5	29
	No	25	46	71
		49	51	100%

* In order to include all districts where the House seat was contested in 1958 this table retains ten constituencies in which the incumbent Congressman did not seek re-election. Candidates of the retiring incumbent's party in these districts are treated here as if they were incumbents. Were these figures to be calculated only for constituencies in which an incumbent sought re-election, no entry in this four-fold table would differ from that given by more than two percent.

---

[16] Under both Models I and II the proportion of the variance of roll call voting explained by the influence path involving the Representative's own attitude is twice as great as the proportion explained by influence passing through his perception of district attitude.

"knew" was confined to diffuse evaluative judgments about the candidate: "he's a good man," "he understands the problems," and so forth. Of detailed information about policy stands not more than a chemical trace was found. Among the comments about the candidates given in response to an extended series of free-answer questions, less than two percent had to do with stands in our three policy domains; indeed, only about three comments in every hundred had to do with legislative issues of *any* description.[17]

This evidence that the behavior of the electorate is largely unaffected by knowledge of the policy positions of the candidates is complemented by evidence about the forces that *do* shape the voters' choices among congressional candidates. The primary basis of voting in American congressional elections is identification with party. In 1958 only one vote in twenty was cast by persons without any sort of party loyalty. And among those who did have a party identification, only one in ten voted against their party. As a result, something like 84 percent of the vote that year was cast by party identifiers voting their usual party line. What is more, traditional party voting is seldom connected with current legislative issues. As the party loyalists in a nationwide sample of voters told us what they liked and disliked about the parties in 1958, only a small fraction of the comments (about 15 percent) dealt with current issues of public policy.[18]

Yet the idea of reward or punishment at the polls for legislative stands is familiar to members of Congress, who feel that they and their records are quite visible to their constituents. Of our sample of Congressmen who were opposed for re-election in 1958, more than four-fifths said the outcome in their districts had been strongly influenced by the electorate's response to their records and personal standing. Indeed, this belief is clear enough to present a notable contradiction: Congressmen feel that their individual legislative actions may have considerable impact on the electorate, yet some simple facts about the Representative's salience to his constituents imply that this could hardly be true.

In some measure this contradiction is to be explained by the tendency of Congressmen to overestimate their visibility to the local public, a tendency that reflects the difficulties of the Representative in forming a correct judgment of constituent opinion. The communication most Congressmen have with their districts inevitably puts them in touch with organized groups and with individuals who are relatively well informed about politics. The Representative knows his constituents mostly from dealing with people who *do* write letters, who *will* attend meetings, who

---

[17] What is more, the electorate's awareness of Congress as a whole appears quite limited. A majority of the public was unable to say in 1958 which of the two parties had controlled the Congress during the preceding two years. Some people were confused by the coexistence of a Republican President and a Democratic Congress. But for most people this was simply an elementary fact about congressional affairs to which they were not privy.

[18] For a more extended analysis of forces on the congressional vote, see Donald E. Stokes and Warren E. Miller, "Party Government and the Saliency of Congress," *Public Opinion Quarterly*, Vol. 26 (Winter 1962), pp. 531–46.

have an interest in his legislative stands. As a result, his sample of contacts with a constituency of several hundred thousand people is heavily biased: even the contacts he apparently makes at random are likely to be with people who grossly overrepresent the degree of political information and interest in the constituency as a whole.

But the contradiction is also to be explained by several aspects of the Representative's electoral situation that are of great importance to the question of constituency influence. The first of these is implicit in what has already been said. Because of the pervasive effects of party loyalties, no candidate for Congress starts from scratch in putting together an electoral majority. The Congressman is a dealer in increments and margins. He starts with a stratum of hardened party voters, and if the stratum is broad enough he can have a measurable influence on his chance of survival simply by attracting a small additional element of the electorate —or by not losing a larger one. Therefore, his record may have a very real bearing on his electoral success or failure without most of his constituents ever knowing what that record is.

Second, the relation of Congressman to voter is not a simple bilateral one but is complicated by the presence of all manner of intermediaries: the local party, economic interests, the news media, racial and nationality organizations, and so forth. Such is the lore of American politics, as it is known to any political scientist. Very often the Representative reaches the mass public through these mediating agencies, and the information about himself and his record may be considerably transformed as it diffuses out to the electorate in two or more stages. As a result, the public— or parts of it—may get simple positive or negative cues about the Congressman which were provoked by his legislative actions but which no longer have a recognizable issue content.

Third, for most Congressmen most of the time the electorate's sanctions are potential rather than actual. Particularly the Representative from a safe district may feel his proper legislative strategy is to avoid giving opponents in his own party or outside of it material they can use against him. As the Congressman pursues this strategy he may write a legislative record that never becomes very well known to his constituents; if it doesn't win votes, neither will it lose any. This is clearly the situation of most southern Congressmen in dealing with the issue of Negro rights. By voting correctly on this issue they are unlikely to increase their visibility to constituents. Nevertheless, the fact of constituency influence, backed by potential sanctions at the polls, is real enough.

That these potential sanctions are all too real is best illustrated in the election of 1958 by the reprisal against Representative Brooks Hays in Arkansas' Fifth District.[19] Although the perception of Congressman Hays as too moderate on civil rights resulted more from his service as intermediary between the White House and Governor Faubus in the Little Rock school crisis than from his record in the House, the victory of Dale

---

[19] For an account of this episode see Corinne Silverman, "The Little Rock Story," Inter-University Case Program series, reprinted in Edwin A. Bock and Alan K. Campbell, eds., *Case Studies in American Government* (Englewood Cliffs, 1962), pp. 1–46.

Alford as a write-in candidate was a striking reminder of what can happen to a Congressman who gives his foes a powerful issue to use against him. The extraordinary involvement of the public in this race can be seen by comparing how well the candidates were known in this constituency with the awareness of the candidates shown by Table 2 above for the country as a whole. As Table 3 indicates, not a single voter in our sample of Arkansas' Fifth District was unaware of either candidate.[20] What is

TABLE 3
Awareness of Congressional Candidates among
Voters in Arkansas Fifth District, 1958

		Read or Heard Something about Hays		
		Yes	No	
Read or Heard Something about Alford	Yes	100	0	100
	No	0	0	0
		100	0	100%

more, these interviews show that Hays was regarded both by his supporters and his opponents as more moderate than Alford on civil rights and that this perception brought his defeat. In some measure, what happened in Little Rock in 1958 can happen anywhere, and our Congressmen ought not to be entirely disbelieved in what they say about their impact at the polls. Indeed, they may be under genuine pressure from the voters even while they are the forgotten men of national elections.[21]

V. CONCLUSION

Therefore, although the conditions of constituency influence are not equally satisfied, they are met well enough to give the local constituency a measure of control over the actions of its Representatives. Best satisfied is the requirement about motivational influences on the Congressman:

---

[20] The sample of this constituency was limited to twenty-three persons of whom thirteen voted. However, despite the small number of cases the probability that the difference in awareness between this constituency and the country generally as the result only of sampling variations is much less than one in a thousand.

[21] In view of the potential nature of the constituency's sanctions, it is relevant to characterize its influence over the Representative in terms of several distinctions drawn by recent theorists of power, especially the difference between actual and potential power, between influence and coercive power, and between influence and purposive control. Observing these distinctions, we might say that the constituency's influence is *actual* and not merely *potential* since it is the sanction behavior rather than the conforming behavior that is infrequent (Dahl). That is, the Congressman is influenced by his calculus of potential sanctions, following the "rule of anticipated reactions" (Friedrich), however oblivious of his behavior the constituency ordinarily may be. We might also say that the constituency has *power* since its influence depends partly on sanctions (Lasswell and Kaplan), although it rarely exercises *control* since its influence is rarely conscious or intended (Cartwright). In the discussion above we have of course used the terms "influence" and "control" interchangeably.

our evidence shows that the Representative's role call behavior is strongly influenced by his own policy preferences and by his perception of preferences held by the constituency. However, the conditions of influence that presuppose effective communication between Congressman and district are much less well met. The Representative has very imperfect information about the issue preferences of his constituency, and the constituency's awareness of the policy stands of the Representative ordinarily is slight.

The findings of this analysis heavily underscore the fact that no single tradition of representation fully accords with the realities of American legislative politics. The American system *is* a mixture, to which the Burkean, instructed-delegate, and responsible-party models can all be said to have contributed elements. Moreover, variations in the representative relation are most likely to occur as we move from one policy domain to another. No single, generalized configuration of attitudes and perceptions links Representative with constituency but rather several distinct patterns, and which of them is invoked depends very much on the issue involved.

The issue domain in which the relation of Congressman to constituency most nearly conforms to the instructed-delegate model is that of civil rights. This conclusion is supported by the importance of the influence-path passing through the Representative's perception of district opinion, although even in this domain the sense in which the constituency may be said to take the position of the candidate into account in reaching its electoral judgment should be carefully qualified.

The representative relation conforms most closely to the responsible-party model in the domain of social welfare. In this issue area, the arena of partisan conflict for a generation, the party symbol helps both constituency and Representative in the difficult process of communication between them. On the one hand, because Republican and Democratic voters tend to differ in what they would have government do, the Representative has some guide to district opinion simply by looking at the partisan division of the vote. On the other hand, because the two parties tend to recruit candidates who differ on the social welfare role of government, the constituency can infer the candidates' position with more than random accuracy from their party affiliation, even though what the constituency has learned directly about these stands is almost nothing. How faithful the representation of social welfare views is to the responsible-party model should not be exaggerated. Even in this policy domain, American practice departs widely from an ideal conception of party government.[22] But in this domain, more than any other, political conflict has become a conflict of national parties in which constituency and Representative are known to each other primarily by their party association.

It would be too pat to say that the domain of foreign involvement conforms to the third model of representation, the conception promoted by Edmund Burke. Clearly it does in the sense that the Congressman looks

---

[22] The factors in American electoral behavior that encourage such a departure are discussed in Stokes and Miller, *loc. cit.*

elsewhere than to his district in making up his mind on foreign issues. However, the reliance he puts on the President and the Administration suggests that the calculation of where the public interest lies is often passed to the Executive on matters of foreign policy. Ironically, legislative initiative in foreign affairs has fallen victim to the very difficulties of gathering and appraising information that led Burke to argue that Parliament rather than the public ought to hold the power of decision. The background information and predictive skills that Burke thought the people lacked are held primarily by the modern Executive. As a result, the present role of the legislature in foreign affairs bears some resemblance to the role that Burke had in mind for the elitist, highly restricted *electorate* of his own day.

Section VII
Failures in the Process: Alienation, Electoral Turnover, and Civil Strife?

The final two selections deal with the impact of the failure of political leaders to give their constituents representation. Not knowing which model of political linkage serves to achieve political linkage and not knowing whether different models work in different policy areas or at different levels of government, any assessment of the quality of political linkage must be most superficial or crude. Norman Luttbeg and Richard Griffin focus on whether linkage failure (operationalized here as a large difference between representatives' policy preferences and those of their constituents) causes a loss of public support for the political system. They do indeed find support decreases with the loss of representation, but the relationship is quite weak. The finding in their study of public school systems that the loss of public support is manifested more in voluntary activities than in support for elected officials and that the public seems most attentive to the nonelected leader, the principal, may hold only for educational politics. But it suggests that we need to be alert to implications of the loss of public support other than thinking unresponsive elected officials will be the only victims of the failure in political linkage.

Arthur Miller, Thad Brown, and Alden Raine note a sharp change in the cynicism Americans express in such questions as, "Would you say the government is pretty much run by a few big interests looking out for themselves or that it is run for the benefit of all the people?" In 1958 only 17 percent thought it benefited big interests, but by 1972 more than 50 percent agreed.[1] Miller assesses whether this dissatisfaction or cynicism is more common among those favoring a solution to social problems which have been rejected by government. Cynicism, he finds is related to differences between what one wants government to do and what government is actually doing. Notably, neither party is seen as the solu-

---

[1] Arthur H. Miller, Thad A. Brown, and Alden S. Raine, "Social Conflict and Political Estrangement, 1958–1972," a paper presented at the Midwest Political Science Association meeting, Chicago, 1973.

tion to this personal failure to get what you want, which of course implies the failure of the political parties model for these people. With dissatisfaction rising both among those who favor less government involvement and among those favoring more government involvement than is presently the case, Miller sees a threat to the system.

Norman R. Luttbeg and Richard W. Griffin

Public Reactions to Misrepresentation: The Case of Educational Politics

This analysis focuses on the systemic consequences of misrepresentation by elected public officials. While representation of a constituency is but one of many standards that can be applied in evaluating the performance of an elected official, democratic theorists, the public, and representatives themselves agree that it is a crucial standard if the governmental system is to be a democracy.[1] Technical considerations, long term planning, efficiency, and sensitivity to human values such as avoiding the persecution of minorities, of course, hopefully can also be accommodated by the representative in making his decisions, but his very name, "representative," suggests the primacy of the criterion of whether

---

[1] Henry B. Mayo, *An Introduction to Democratic Theory* (New York: Oxford University Press, 1960), chapter 4 gives what we take to be the expectations of representation from the elected official. Similarly, numerous studies of representatives find them giving at least lip-service to the importance of their being representative, as Miller and Stokes find 85% of Congressmen interviewed in 1958 felt their personal record and standing in Congress was quite or very important to their re-election. Warren E. Miller and Donald E. Stokes, "Party Government and the Saliency of Congress," *Public Opinion Quarterly*, 26 (Winter, 1962), p. 542. Also see John W. Kingdon, *Candidates for Office: Beliefs and Strategies* (New York: Random House, 1966), p. 24. The analysis of legislator's representative roles, however, shows less concensus as Prewitt and Eulau report 38% of the legislators in one study failed to think of their representational duties when asked about the job of the legislator. Kenneth Prewitt and Heinz Eulau, "Political Matrix and Political Representation: Prolegomenon to a New Departure from an Old Problem," *American Political Science Review*, 63 (June, 1969), p. 427. This would suggest that the concern with representing the public is less than consuming to the legislator. Also one public sample finds 69% agree with the need for the representative to voice his constituency's opinions, but 46% agree to the statement "An elected legislator (Congressman) should decide what he thinks is best, and always vote accordingly, even if it is not what his district wants." Carl D. McMurray and Malcolm B. Parsons, "Public Attitudes Toward the Representational Roles of Legislators and Judges," *Midwest Journal of Political Science*, 9 (May, 1965), p. 170.

439

he is responsive to his constituency or not. Lacking such representation, the system not only encourages the charge that it is undemocratic but potentially even risks the loss of public support. Our hypothesis, however, is that in reality the low salience of politics for the average man means that the lack of representation in no way affects the level of public support for the political system.

More specifically, our study attempts to compare across many systems the level of representation enjoyed by publics and the support they give to the system. As such, our work accepts Pitkin's conclusion that representation must be evaluated by assessing the representation given by a legislature for its citizens rather than the representation given by a representative to a constituent.[2] And we judge a legislature to be more representative of its citizens if the opinions of the representatives on a broad spectrum of relevant issues closely parallel those of the citizens on the same issues. It is quite possible for representatives to act consistently with public opinion by voting their perception of those opinions while personally disagreeing.[3] We lack data on this aspect of representation, but studies of this less direct process of representation suggest its severe limitation because representatives act mainly on their personal opinions, have difficulty in getting unbiased opinions from their constituents, and seem less than totally concerned with this aspect in their duties.[4]

THE EDUCATIONAL SYSTEM

Our data comes from a study of Florida educators' and public opinions on issues relevant to the governance of public high schools. Issues such as bussing to achieve integration, open classroom discussion of controversial subjects, and the question of students' role in choosing subjects, retaining teachers, and deciding what is passing work among the many issues affecting public schools all suggest the importance of politics in the schools and difficulty of reaching decisions in such controversy. The dynamics of representation and public support are assessable within school systems as they are within municipal, county, state, and national governments. We have little information as yet that would permit us to assess the differences in the public's roles at different levels of government, but if consistency in opinions is taken as an indicator of the public's ability to play an active role in monitoring its representatives, public education would seem to be the arena of greatest public competence.[5] Furthermore, the scale investment of public money in public education, the nearly universal pattern of separating public education from other

2 Hanna Fenichel Pitkin, *The Concept of Representation* (Berkeley: University of California Press, 1967), p. 221.

3 Luttbeg suggests this in his "Role Playing Model." Norman R. Luttbeg (ed.) *Public Opinion and Public Policy* (Homewood, Illinois: Dorsey, 1968), p. 8.

4 For a summary of the empirical research on this subject, see Robert S. Erikson and Norman R. Luttbeg, *American Public Opinion: Its Origins, Content, and Impact* (New York: Wiley, 1973), chapter 8.

5 Norman R. Luttbeg, "The Structure of Beliefs Among Leaders and the Public," *Public Opinion Quarterly*, 32 (Fall, 1968), p. 403.

local governmental decisions, and the overwhelming preference for elected rather than appointed school officials all suggest that representation is seen as crucial in school governance.[6]

Two recent studies have laid the groundwork for empirically evaluating the process of representation in a democracy. One studies city councilmen in San Francisco Bay area municipalities and the other a national sample of school boards.[7] Neither study has an independent measure of public opinion, which could be used as a standard to judge the representativeness of councilmen's or board member's opinions, but instead both focus on the representative's professed sensitivity to his constituency, his representative style. Both studies also lack an independent assessment of levels of public support for the political system relying instead again on the councilmen's or school board members' judgment of the level of public support they enjoy from their constituency. Boards and councils that see themselves as responding to groups feel they lack public support; but in the school board study, those boards that cite individuals rather than specific groups as the most useful source of information on public attitudes also perceive broad public support for their efforts.[8] Our public attitude information permits us to measure representation rather than professed representational style, and our independent measures of public support for the system free us from troublesome speculation about whether the representative's perception of his responsiveness is distinct from his judgment of public support for his efforts and whether either representative style or perceived support accurately parallel reality in his district or city.

METHODS

Questionnaires and Interviews. The great diversity of Florida from the metropolitan Dade city-county in the far south to the sparsely populated, rural, and heavily black Gadsden county in the northern panhandle offers a great variety of types of school districts within which we can assess the importance of representation. To assure a representative sample, we assigned interviews to each county based on its proportion of the total state population. But in the interest of expense we pooled the interviews of the less populated counties entitled to fewer than thirty interviews, assigning a minimum of twenty to each of sixteen smaller counties representing eight homogeneous strata on the basis of the size of their largest town, their location in the state, and their proportion of non-white residents. Area random sampling was used within counties to further define the household in which the interview was to be completed by our

[6] U.S. Bureau of the Census, *Census of Governments, 1967*, Vol. 6, No. 1: *Popularly Elected Officials of State and Local Governments* (Washington D.C., 1968), p. 3.

[7] Prewitt and Eulau; and M. Kent Jennings and Harmon Zeigler, "Response Styles and Politics: The Case of School Boards," *Midwest Journal of Political Science*, 15 (May, 1971), pp. 290–321.

[8] Prewitt and Eulau, p. 440; and Jennings and Zeigler, p. 303.

professional interviewers. In this study the public interviews of each of the twenty-seven counties in which we completed interviews stand as a sample of its public.

From the pool of all public schools offering courses to ninth through twelfth graders in the twenty-seven counties, we sampled 275 schools. Principals in each school were mailed a questionnaire identical to the public questionnaire except for a few deletions and some additional personal information relevant only to principals. Finally, all school board members and superintendents throughout the state were mailed a questionnaire, but only those within the twenty-seven county frame are used in this study.[9]

Data for empirical analysis concerning these counties may be classified into two general categories: (1) the attitudes of important educational decision-makers and their constituents; and (2) indicators of the degree of public support for those decision-makers evident in votes, turnouts, and other available public aggregate data. The questionnaire designed for use with all samples asks for the respondent's evaluation of current educational policies and the quality of education in the county and state, his conception of the legitimate substantive content of education, and his position as to the proper locus of decision-making within the school system. Identical data were gathered from the educator samples.

Educational Leadership. We chose to identify educational leaders on the basis of their holding official elective or appointive decision-making positions within each educational system. This positional identification method is a common technique in political science and is in no way a solution to the difficulty of identifying those with actual influence.[10] As a result the reader should be alert to the possibility that the "true" influentials in county educational decision-making may differ dramatically from those holding the formal positions. Many of the theoretical models by which democracy is said to function, however, assign important roles to those holding formal decision-making positions and many of the pro-

---

[9] In short, the public sample is a close approximation of an area random sample. Although we aimed at getting 1,000 interview opportunities, largely because of the datedness of the 1960 Census of Housing in a state that has grown by nearly 35% in ten years, only 856 respondents were approached with 703 or 82% completing the interview. The sample of school principals is an even looser approximation of an area random sample but includes no systematic basis. One hundred fifty-five or 56% of the principals returned their questionnaires, but all 27 superintendents did. Sixty-six of the 136 school board members (49%) in these 27 counties returned completed questionnaires. Interviews with the public were completed by professional interviewers trained by the Survey Data Center of Florida State University.

[10] The identification of community leaders has been a perplexing and highly disputed methological issue for students of community politics for a number of years. Traditionally, the conflict has fundamentally revolved around assumptive and ideological variations of researchers representing different disciplines in social science. Examining a three variable model of discipline, methodology, and empirical findings, John Walton, for example, has discovered the operation of a "developmental sequence" in which the discipline of the researcher tends to affect his choice of the methodological technique employed in any particular study and this, in turn, determines the characteristics of the leadership structure identified by that study. John Walton, "Discipline, Method and Community Power: A Note on the Sociology of Knowledge," *American Sociological Review*, Vol. 31 (October, 1966), pp. 684–689.

posed models by which "influentials" control public decision-making have the formal decision-makers serving as pawns directly implementing the decisions of the informal elites. Thus knowing the relative impact of formal decision-makers and the public on public educational policy does not allow us to make generalizations about the "true" leaders who might not hold public office.

In selecting the leadership sample we sought to identify holders of authoritative roles in the educational system. Byron G. Massialas has proposed that

> . . . since the decisions of the school board are authoritative and legitimate, they are political decisions and they affect the organization, administration, and functioning of the schools.[11]

Those holding school board positions were thus given a central role in our analysis.

Another office of formal authority within each school system is that of the "chief school officer," or as it is referred to in Florida, the County Superintendent. Because the County Superintendent performs the role of "shifting and blending the pressures among the board of education members, among central staff assistants among line personnel," he is involved in the educational policy process and, thus, occupies a pertinent position within the "influence system" of the "local school District."[12] Therefore, the Superintendents of Public Instruction in each county included in the sample were identified as fulfilling authoritative activities in the county educational system and were, like the school board, requested to complete the attitude survey.

Finally, school principals completed our sample of educational decision-makers. Principals function as authoritative sources through the performance of routine, day-to-day administrative and classroom activities. It is here that policy decisions are eventually implemented, and as Agger, *et al.*, have pointed out, policy effectuation assumes a final, key stage in the decision-making process.[13] As effectuators of educational policies and because of their great visibility to the public, principals have thus been included in the list of decision-makers in order to examine more comprehensively the relationship between educator attitudes and public support for educations.

Opinions and Representational Quality. Out of more than one hundred measured items in the questionnaire we shall attend here to ten opinions that are embroiled in the controversy over public schools, including: (1) desire to ban a course from the schools; (2) approval of open classroom discussion of the shortcomings of democracy; (3) approval of open discussion of differences among candidates for public offices; (4) belief that

---

11 Massialas, p. 14.

12 Luvern L. Cunningham, "Community Power: Implications for Education," in Robert S. Cahill and Stephen P. Hencley (eds.), *The Politics of Education in the Local Community* (Danville, Illinois: The Interstate Printers and Publishers, Inc., 1964), pp. 47–48.

13 Robert E. Agger, et al., *The Rulers and the Ruled: Political Power and Impotence in American Communities* (New York: John Wiley and Sons, Inc., 1964), pp. 40–51.

an adequate rather than equal education is sufficient; (5) belief that minorities will do as well as others given equal opportunities and education; (6) approval of allowing teachers to join unions; (7) support for investing in making schools better to assure poor children an education equal to others; (8) belief that students are justified in being angry at our country's failures; (9) support for bussing to achieve school integration; and (10) support for schools without grades but with children grouped on different subjects by competence. With the exception of the item on banning subjects from the classroom, all items are 5-point Likert scales with an "undecided" midpoint. The banning question is a dichotomy between willingness and unwillingness to have any course banned.

The measurement of representative quality was straight-forward with the mean on each opinion computed for each of the 27 districts for both the public and the three educator samples.[14] The size of the gap between each of the three educator samples and their constituency for each district on each issue became our gauge of representative quality. Only the *magnitude* of the leader-public difference, not the direction of the difference, was assessed.

Public Support for Education.   We chose thirteen indicators of public support for education. They include: (1) superintendent victors' margin of electoral victory; (2) school board victors' margin of victory; (3) superintendent incumbents' margin of victory; (4) school board incumbents' margin of victory; (5) the percentage of times in which superintendent incumbents were re-elected; (6) the percentage of school board incumbents' re-elected; (7) voter turnout in superintendent elections; (8) voter turnout in school board elections; (9) the percentage of school bond elections successful; (10) the amount of present operating property tax millage; (11) Parent Teacher Association participation rate; (12) public school/private school attendance ratio; and (13) the percentage of successful millage increase elections.[15] These variables measure a broad range of public support and are sensitive to the various ways in which a citizen may express his evaluation of leadership.

While public support is often seen as vital to a democratic system, previous research offers no guidance as to which of the multitude of assessments of public support merit closest attention.[16] In an exploratory

---

[14] We are assuming therefore that the Likert Scales are interval level data. See: William J. Goode and Paul K. Hatt, *Methods in Social Research* (New York: McGraw-Hill Book Co., 1952), pp. 273–275; and Helen Peak, "Problems of Objective Observation," in Leon Festinger and Daniel Katz (eds.), *Research Methods in the Behavioral Sciences* (New York: Holt, Rinehart and Winston, 1966), p. 253.

[15] These data were collected from the Elections Division of the Florida Secretary of State. Data concerning the elected offices of superintendent and school board members cover the nine year period of 1960–1968, while those involving school board elections are from 1945 to 1968.

[16] Marian D. Irish and James W. Protho, *The Politics of American Democracy* (Englewood Cliffs, New Jersey: Prentice-Hall, Inc., 1968), pp. 9–11. For excellent discussions of support as an input into the political system, see Gabriel A. Almond, "An Approach to the Analysis of Political Systems," *World Politics*, Vol. 9 (April, 1957), pp. 383–400; and William A. Gamson, *Power and Discontent* (Homewood, Illinois: The Dorsey Press, 1968), p. 41.

study such as this, one might decide that the inclusion of all measures would assure the greatest and most valid insight into relationships; but with 13 support variables and 10 attitude gaps for each of three educators in 27 districts, we would have an awkward 390 possible relationships. We choose therefore to reduce the number of support variables by factor analyzing them.[17] In the analysis of the relationship between public support and representation, factor scores on each of the four support dimensions were used rather than the initial raw data on all thirteen items.[18]

The first two factors in Table 1, "Superintendent Electoral Support" and "School Board Electoral Support," are indicators of the level of public support for both groups of elected educational officials during the nine-year period.[19] The dimensions are not strictly parallel, however, as the "voter turnout in school board elections" variable is a component of the "Participation—Willingness to Spend" factor. "Participation—Willingness to Spend" involves both the degree of public participation and the public's disposition toward funding for the educational system.[20] Evidently, the extent of public turnout for superintendent elections rather than the division of that vote among candidates reflects public support. Finally, the percentage of millage elections which are successful fails to cluster with any other variables. It then becomes our fourth dimension of public support, "Millage Support."

THE FINDINGS

Table 2 presents the Pearsonian correlations between representativeness and public support on the four dimensions, for all those correlations exceeding ±.30. This is an arbitrarily chosen value, which if exceeded, means 10 percent of the variance in support is attributable to misrepresentation. Lesser relationships seem to us to be theoretically meaningless.

---

[17] Factor Analysis identifies underlying variables. It is, more precisely, a method which permits the researcher to "discern the regularity and order in phenomena" by illuminating the patterns in those phenomena as they co-occur in space or in time" and by plotting "distinct patterns" among independent "co-occuring phenomena." See R. J. Rummel, "Understanding Factor Analysis," *Journal of Conflict Resolution*, Vol. 11 (December, 1967), p. 445.

[18] The four factors explained a total of 64% of the variance on the twelve items or 23, 17, 15, and 9% respectively. Varimax rotation on the Biomedical X72 Factor analysis program was used in this analysis.

[19] The reader should be aware that not all Superintendents of Public Instruction in Florida are currently elected. Fortunately for us, however, the appointed Superintendent is a relatively new trend. Of the 27 counties, 17 held elections through 1968, 4 more through 1964, and 4 more through 1960. We were thus unable to determine the extent of "Superintendent Electoral Support" for only 2 counties.

[20] This dimension is closely associated with the "Demography" dimension ($r = +.82$), to be discussed in the next section. This association explains the positive factor loading for "Private school public school attendance ratio" on "Participation-Willingness to Spend," as low demographic counties in Florida are characterized by an absence of private schools. See, Florida State Department of Education, *Florida Educational Directory* (Tallahassee, Florida: Florida State Department of Education, October, 1969), pp. 207–237.

TABLE 1
The Dimensions of Public Support

Dimension	Factor Loading	Component Variables
Superintendent-electoral support	+.62	Superintendent victor's margin of victory
	+.91	Superintendent incumbent's margin of victory
	+.88	Percentage of superintendent incumbents victorious
	+.59	Voter turnout in superintendent elections
School board-electoral support	−.79	School board victor's margin of victory
	−.95	School board incumbent's margin of victory
	−.78	Percentage of school board incumbents victorious
Participation-willingness to spend	+.81	Private school/public school attendance ratio
	+.75	Parent Teacher Association participation
	+.46	Voter turnout in school board elections
	+.48	Amount of present operating millage
	+.65	Percentage of school bond elections successful
Millage support	−.67	Percentage of millage elections successful

While all but one of the presented correlations support the hypothesis that public support will be lost with misrepresentation, 10 of the 26 significant relationships involve the non-elected principals on a dimension of public support not related to voting for or against office holders. Only the Participation and Willingness to Spend dimension seems to be consistently associated with dissatisfaction with the misrepresentation of educators. This dimension involves PTA participation, voting turnout, and successful bond elections, all conceivable forms of public expression of dissatisfaction—but all also characteristically middle-class activities, as we will discuss later.

Although restricting our consideration to relationships of relatively large magnitude yields the surprising result of the principal's apparently great influence on one non-electoral form of public support, the consistency of the relationships as shown in Table 3 much more strongly supports the importance of representations to public support. Only 29 of the total of 120 relationships show popular support increasing with misrepresentation. The Table consistently shows that the smaller the principal-constituency gap . . . the greater the popular support (except on the Superintendent Electoral Support dimension, where principals' misrepresentation helps a superintendent's election chance perhaps by way of the "support me to control them" appeal). The school boards and superintendents each contribute 11 of the exceptional cases, while the principals

TABLE 2
The Relationship between Misrepresentation and Public Educational Support

Educator Sample and Issue	Dimensions of Public Support			
	School Board Electoral Support°	Superintendent Electoral Support	Participation and Spending Support	Millage Support°
School board				
Ban courses§				
Shortcomings of democracy				
Differences in candidates			−35(02)	
Adequate education ..			−43(−22)	
Minorities do as well .			−39(−24)	−42(−25)
Teachers unions			−61(−26)	
Equal education				
Anger at failures			−48(00)	
Bussing			−60(−10)	−38(−47)
Ungraded classes	−49†(−32)‡			
Principal				
Ban courses			−54(13)	
Shortcomings of democracy			−70(−14)	
Differences in candidates			−67(−09)	
Adequate education ..			−66(−16)	
Minorities do as well .			−74(−37)	
Teachers unions			−71(−44)	
Equal education			−71(−15)	
Anger at failures			−73(−36)	
Bussing			−72(−22)	
Ungraded classes			−72(−49)	
Superintendent				
Ban courses		45(40)		
Shortcomings of democracy		−56(−53)		
Differences in candidates	−33(−24)			
Adequate education ..			−33(−40)	
Minorities do as well .				
Teachers unions		−37(−15)		
Equal education		−34(−17)		
Anger at failures				
Bussing				
Ungraded classes		−35(−26)		

( ) Partials controlling demography.
° The signs of the factors have been reversed to correspond with meaning.
† Cell entries are product moment correlations between the difference in opinion noted between the public mean and that for the educator and the public support for the educational system.
‡ Correlations in parentheses are partials controlling for "demography."
§ The wording of the items is:
Are there any subjects which should not be taught in our schools?
Open discussion of any shortcomings of democracy in the U.S.
Open discussion of differences among candidates for public office.
If schools in poorer areas do an adequate job, we should not be greatly concerned that schools in wealthy areas are better equipped and get better teachers.
Given opportunities and education, such minorities will do just as well as other Americans.
Teachers in your community should be allowed to join unions if they want to.
More money should be spent on better buildings and teachers and on special catch up classes to be sure that poor children get a good schooling as others.
Although our country may have given students much which they should be thankful for, they are right in being angered by its failures.
Bussing students from one school to another as a solution to integration in our schools.
Grouping children in large classes with many teachers which are then divided into discussion groups thus allowing children to advance as fast as they can, doing away with the 1st grade, 2nd grade, etc.

TABLE 3
Signs of the Relationships between Educator Misrepresentation and Public Educational Support

Opinion Question	Support Dimension Educator Sample											
	Superintendent Electoral Support			School Board Electoral Support			Participation and Willing to Spend Support			Millage Support		
	Bd.	Prin.	Sup.	Bd.	Prin.	Sup.	Bd.	Prin.	Sup.	Bd.	Prin.	Sup.
Ban courses	+*	+										
Shortcomings of democracy		+							+	+		
Differences in candidates												+
Adequate education	+	+		+			+			+		
Minorities do as well	+	+	+	+		+						
Teachers unions	+	+		+		+			+			
Equal education		+		+								
Anger at failures		+				+			+			
Bussing												
Ungraded classes			+			+			+			
Totals	4	7	2	4	0	4	1	0	4	2	0	1
Totals by support dimensions		13			8			5			3	

Total by educators ..... School board 11   Principal 7   Superintendent 11

* Only positive relationships are shown. All others are negative, supporting the hypothesis that support declines with misrepresentation.

contribute 7, all coming on the Superintendent Electoral Support dimension. Also, from the perspective of which issues show a consistent pattern of loss of public support with misrepresentation, clearly bussing and open classroom discussion of candidates for public office draw greatest public attention. Less controversial internal school affairs, such as teachers unions, using adequacy rather than equality as a standard, and optimism that minorities will do as well show little consistency, suggesting that the public is not watching.

Because of the broad literature suggesting that both differences in political style and levels of public investment in policies are directly related to the wealth and social make-up of an area, we considered the importance of a multitude of district characteristics that might alternatively explain our findings.[21] In particular we included measures of income, education, and occupation of the population of each district, along with urbanness, percentage born in Florida, and percentage registered

---

[21] Ira Sharkansky and Richard L. Hofferbert, "Dimensions of State Policy," in Jacob and Vines (eds.) *Politics in the American States: A Comparative Analysis*, 2nd ed. (Boston: Little Brown, 1971), p. 315.

to vote. Again because of the number of such variables we turned to factor analysis to attempt to develop a summary measure of middleclassness or wealth. All variables loaded heavily on a single factor, which we labeled "demography." The loadings of each variable on this factor are shown in Table 4. In Florida middle class districts tend not only to be wealthier, better educated, and urban, but also are the largely white districts settled by large numbers of people from outside the state. Regionally, such districts predominate in the southern and central parts of the state. As with the public support dimensions, factor scores were assigned, and these scores proved related to the support dimensions.

TABLE 4
The Demography Dimension

Dimension	Factor Loading	Component Variables
Demography	+.74	Per capita income
	+.92	Median family income
	+.84	Percentage of white collar employees
	+.94	Median years of education
	−.87	Percentage of population born in Florida
	−.58	Percentage of population registered to vote
	+.84	Percentage of urban population

Middle class districts give more support to the school system in all areas, but especially in participation in school affairs and giving greater financial support to education. The correlations between "demography" and "support" are: .18 for Superintendent Electoral Support; .32 for School Board; .82 for Participation; and .22 for Millage. As Table 5 indicates, demography also correlates highly with the level of misrepresentation in the district. With only four exceptions, middle class districts enjoy substantially better representation, especially from their principals. Misrepresentation on bussing, adequacy as a standard of education, and banning some courses proves to be most highly correlated with differences in demography.

These results suggest an alternative conclusion. Even the limited pattern of relationships between public support for the political system and the quality of representation may be spurious by way of middle class districts both granting more support and enjoying better representation. If this were the case, controlling for the demography of the district would reveal little correlation between public support and representation. As we see in Table 2, this control sharply reduces the magnitude of the relationships previously noted. While twelve relationships previously showed misrepresentation to explain at least 25 percent of the variance in public support, only two remain in this range once the effects of Demography are removed.

TABLE 5

Relationships between Misrepresentation of the Three Samples
of Educators and the Demographic Character of a School District

Opinion Question	Representational Quality		
	School Board	Principal	Superintendent
Ban courses	−21°	−54	−29
Shortcomings of democracy	−06	−61	28
Differences in candidates	−33	−43	−07
Adequate education	−46	−56	−30
Minorities do as well	−37	−56	−07
Teachers unions	−51	−61	30
Equal education	−01	−49	−01
Anger at failures	−53	−66	−07
Bussing	−56	−65	−21
Ungraded classes	16	−63	08

° Cell entries are product moment correlations between differences in public and educator opinion and the "demography" of the districts.

The overall pattern of relationships in Table 3 also attenuates with Demography controlled, as 39 of the 120 relationships now run counter to the hypothesized relationship between representation and public support. Except on the Millage Support dimension the school principal continues to show the fewest inconsistencies. Discussion of differences among candidates in the classroom and bussing to achieve integration remain the most salient items, with only two instances in which public support does not decrease as a result of misrepresentation by educators.

CONCLUSIONS

While the overall pattern of relationships shows public support to decline with greater misrepresentation, the strength of the pattern is limited, typically explaining no more than 10 percent of the variance in public support. As Table 3 indicates, the strongest and most consistent are found with non-elected principals in the non-election aspect of public support, Participation and Willingness to Spend.

While public education consumes a major proportion of our tax dollar and has traditionally been decentralized to allow it to be closer to its local public in the interest of making it representative of local opinions, it has increasingly come under attack. Gittell and Hollander, for example, conclude,

. . . public education . . . has over the years become perhaps the most nonpublic of governmental services. Public school systems have removed decision-making from the agents closest to the school child—the teachers and parents . . . the concept of public accountability has been abandoned. The school professionals have convinced the various public interests that only they are qualified to make policy . . . The insulation of public education is two-fold: bureaucratic centralization (or more accurately over-centralization) which is a product of size, reinforced by an ideological rationale of professionalism, which is a product of the vested interests of the educationalists.[22]

The data of this study certainly confirms the above argument. According to Table 6, while less than a majority of the public sample felt the performances of its local teachers and schools were at least "good," more than 80 percent of the educational leadership groups typically rated their performances as "good" or "very good." Yet, nearly every member of the

TABLE 6
Percentage of Each Sample Evaluating
Performance of Local Teachers and
Schools as Good or Very Good°

Group	Local Teachers	Local Schools
Public	49	49
Superintendents	81	81
School boards	81	78
Principals	90	89

° The wording of the question was:
Are your local teachers (local schools) doing a:
1) Poor job   3) Good job   5) Don't know.
2) Fair   4) Very good job

public (93 per cent) stated that he would probably deal directly with school officials either personally, as a member of a group of citizens, or through friends or connections who knew the officials if he felt local schools were run poorly. And 94 per cent of the public would not resort to organizing a protest demonstration, going to court, or threatening school officials with the ballot box to correct the situation. It appears, then, that the public has indeed bought the story of the school professional that "only they are qualified to make policy," since alternative political controls such as voting and court action are seen as inappropriate ways to shape educational policy.

More importantly, when asked a series of questions concerning the proper locus of educational decision-making, the public minimized its own policy-making impact to the advantage of the professionals. As Table 7 illustrates, only on the issue of the need for new school buildings, which certainly taps the Willingness to Spend dimension, was the public willing to give itself any meaningful degree of responsibility, and even here less than a majority would demand their say.

[22] Marilyn Gittell and T. Edward Hollander, *Six Urban School Districts: A Comparative Study of Institutional Response* (New York: Frederick A. Praegger, Publishers, 1968), pp. 196–197.

TABLE 7

Percentages of Each Sample Feeling the Community
Should Make Educational Decisions°

Group	What Is Taught	Who Is Retained	What Is Passing Work	When New School Buildings Are Needed
		Decisions on:		
Public	25	11	1	45
Superintendents	34	2	0	14
School boards	22	1	1	12
Principals	36	0	1	18

° The wording of the questions was:
1) Who should have the most say as to what is taught?
2) Who should make decisions as to which teachers will be retained?
3) Who should make decisions as to what is passing work for a student?
4) Who should make decisions as to whether new school buildings are needed?
The respondents were given the following choices on each of these four questions:
1) Mostly the teachers   3) Mostly the school board
2) Mostly the principals and administrators   4) Mostly the community
Thus, 100% minus the percentage shown in the table indicates the percentage of the
sample feeling a particular decisional area should be left to educational professionals.

The generalizability of these data to other areas of public decision-making may be limited because of the educational professionalism causing this misrepresentation. But our analysis reveals that the public's support for decision-makers is hardly responsive to misrepresentation—except perhaps on two issues of a highly controversial nature: bussing to achieve racial balance and discussing candidate qualifications (partisanship) in the classroom. Their responsiveness to the non-elected principals perhaps suggests the futility of thinking about who should be elected apart from whom the public monitors. Under its new constitution, Florida now permits appointive superintendents and local option elections dealing with this change typically center on this issue of professionalism versus public accountability. Perhaps the best elected educators would be the principals who together would appoint a central administrator with no school board involved. Such a system would put accountability where the public seems capable of using it.

Finally, we should note that the salient dimension of public support tends to be Participation and Willingness to Spend; and not the electoral dimensions. Apart from a few local referenda on bond indebtedness, annexation, and flouridation and the occasional use of state referenda, most public elections focus upon the choice of who will hold public office. The above data, however, suggest the lack of utility of such opportunities for public expression. If further research confirms the limited nature of the public reaction to misrepresentation noted above, perhaps local, state, and national referenda would be most conductive to the public's fulfilling its obligation to monitor its representatives.

Arthur H. Miller

Public Policy and Political Cynicism: 1964–1970*

RECENT TRENDS OF POLITICAL ALIENATION

A democratic political system cannot survive for long without the support of a majority of its citizens. When such support wanes, underlying discontent is the necessary result, and the potential for revolutionary alteration of the political and social system is enhanced.[1] That previous change in the United States has been absorbed with minimal damage gives credit to the flexibility of the system. It has, in fact, been argued that a minority of politically apathetic individuals (who are presumably satisfied with the status quo) adds to that flexibility.[2] However, when dissatisfaction with the existing situation leads to pervasive distrust of government, this flexibility is greatly curtailed,[3] thereby increasing the potential for radical change.

A situation of widespread, basic discontent and political alienation is the existing condition in the United States today. Support for this contention can readily be found in the daily reports of the mass media, in an examination of recent political events—witness the substantial support for George Wallace in both the 1968 election and the 1972 primaries—

* This paper is a revision of a longer paper, "Political Issues and Trust in Government: 1964–1970," *American Political Science Review*, forthcoming.

Thanks are extended to Warren E. Miller for his sponsorship and valuable advice, and to C. Richard Hofstetter, John Kessel, John Stucker and Herbert Weisberg for comments on an earlier draft, as well as to Thad Brown and Alden Raine of the Institute for Social Research and Gary Gartin of The Ohio State University for their assistance in the data analysis.

[1] William A. Gamson, *Power and Discontent* (Homewood, Illinois: Dorsey Press, 1968), Chapter 9.

[2] Bernard R. Berelson, et al., *Voting* (Chicago: University of Chicago Press, 1954), Chapter 14.

[3] Gamson, *Power and Discontent*, pp. 42–48.

and in the 1972 political campaign rhetoric. But, more convincingly, it is also found in national survey data.

Survey questions dealing with political efficacy and political trust, two dimensions of alienation, provide evidence substantiating this contention.[4] Converse has recently reported a steady decline in political efficacy, the feeling that an individual can have an impact upon the political process, between 1960 and 1968, despite large overall increases in education.[5] In 1960, for example, nearly 42 per cent of the population disagreed with the following statement: "Sometimes politics and government seem so complicated that a person like me can't really understand what's going on." In 1968, the comparable figure was 30 per cent and in 1970, it was only 26 per cent.

A similar and equally dramatic change was found in five survey questions designed to measure political trust.[6] The percentage distribution of responses to these items is presented in Table 1. These data reveal a strong trend of increasing political cynicism for the general population between 1964 and 1970. The change in the responses to all but one of the items is somewhat more than 20 percentage points in the direction of increased distrust of the government. Even with all five items, the average increase in cynical responses was slightly over 17 percentage points. The magnitude of this change can be better appreciated in light of the finding that responses to the same five items showed an average change of only two percentage points in a cynical direction during the previous six-year period from 1958 to 1964. That some segment of American society believes that officials violate legal procedures in dealing with the public or in arriving at policy decisions is not surprising. What is startling, and somewhat alarming, is the rapid degree of change in this basic attitude over a period of only six years.

The Study of Political Cynicism

Political trust has been defined as a basic evaluative orientation toward the government.[7] It is a general attitude toward the government and, more specifically for this study, the government in Washington.[8]

[4] For a discussion of the dimensions of political alienation, see Ada W. Finifter, "Dimensions of Political Alienation," American Political Science Review, XLIV, 2 (June 1970), 389–410.

[5] Philip E. Converse, "Change in the American Electorate," in Angus Campbell and Philip E. Converse, eds., The Human Meaning of Social Change (New York: Russell Sage Foundation, 1972).

[6] John Robinson, et al., Measures of Political Attitudes (Ann Arbor, Michigan: Institute for Social Research, 1968), pp. 626–647.

[7] Donald E. Stokes, "Popular Evaluations of Government: An Empirical Assessment" in Harlan Cleveland and Harold D. Lasswell, eds., Ethics and Bigness: Scientific, Academic, Religious, Political and Military (New York: Harper & Brothers, 1962), p. 64.

[8] See Joel D. Aberbach, "Alienation and Political Behavior," American Political Science Review, 63 (1969), 36–99 for a discussion of the importance of a specific referent when measuring political alienation. See also Kenneth Keniston, The Uncommitted: Alienated Youth in American Society (New York: Harcourt, Brace & World, 1965), pp. 453–455.

TABLE 1

Responses to Cynicism Items, 1964–1970

How much of the time do you think you can *trust* the government in Washington to do what is right—*just about always, most of the time,* or *only some of the time?*

	1964	1966	1968	1970
Always	14.0%	17.0%	7.5%	6.4%
Most of the time	62.0	48.0	53.4	47.1
Only some of the time°	22.0	31.0	37.0	44.2
Don't know	2.0	4.0†	2.1	2.3
Total	100.0%	100.0%	100.0%	100.0%
(N)‡	(4658)	(1291)	(1557)	(1514)

Would you say the government is pretty much run by *a few big interests* looking out for themselves or that it is run for the *benefit of all* the people?

	1964	1966	1968	1970
For benefit of all	64.0%	53.0%	51.8%	40.6%
Few big interests°	29.0	34.0	39.2	49.6
Other; depends; both checked	4.0	6.0	4.6	5.0
Don't know	3.0	7.0	4.3	4.8
Total	100.0%	100.0%	100.0%	100.0%

Do you think that people in the government waste *a lot* of the money we pay in taxes, waste *some* of it or *don't waste very much of it?*§

	1964	1966	1968	1970
Not much	6.5%	–	4.2%	3.7%
Some	44.5	–	33.1	26.1
A lot°	46.3	–	57.4	68.7
Don't know; not ascertained	2.7	–	5.3	1.5
Total	100.0%	–	100.0%	100.0%

Do you feel that almost all of the people running the government are smart people who usually *know what they are doing,* or do you think that quite a few of them *don't seem to know what they are doing?*§

	1964	1966	1968	1970
Know what they're doing	68.2%	–	56.2%	51.2%
Don't know what they're doing°	27.4	–	36.1	44.1
Other; depends	1.9	–	1.8	2.3
Don't know; not ascertained	2.5	–	5.9	2.4
Total	100.0%	–	100.0%	100.0%

Do you think that *quite a few* of the people running the government are a little crooked, *not very many* are, or do you think *hardly any* of them are crooked at all?§

	1964	1966	1968	1970
Hardly any	18.2%	–	18.4%	15.9%
Not many	48.4	–	49.3	48.8
Quite a lot°	28.0	–	24.8	31.0
Don't know; not ascertained	5.4	–	7.5	4.3
Total	100.0%	–	100.0%	100.0%

° Indicates response interpreted as "cynical."
† Includes 1% coded "It depends."
‡ The sample size for each of the years applies to all five items. The 1964 N is weighted.
§ These items were not included in the 1966 election study interview schedule.

Hypothetically, the dimension of trust runs from a great deal of positive affect, that is, high trust in the government, to a substantial degree of negative affect, that is, distrust or high political cynicism. Cynicism thus refers to degree of negative affect toward the government and is a statement of the belief that the government is not functioning and producing outputs in accord with individual expectations.

As noted, cynicism and efficacy have been viewed as components of the more general concept of political alienation.[9] Empirical studies utilizing these concepts are increasing in number. Generally, they tend to emphasize either background and personality characteristics or, to a lesser extent, reactions to political decisions as the main explanations of political trust and cynicism.[10] The focus of this paper is on the impact that reactions to political issues and public policy have on the formation of political cynicism.

The Data

The data used in this report are based on The University of Michigan Survey Research Center election studies (now conducted by the Center for Political Studies) of a national cross section of eligible voters for the years 1964, 1966, 1968, and 1970.[11] Each of these surveys included a

---

[9] Cynicism and efficacy correspond very closely to Seeman's conceptualizations of normlessness and powerlessness and have been treated as theoretically separate components of political alienation by a number of analysts. Melvin Seeman in "On the Meaning of Alienation," *American Sociological Review*, 24, 6 (December 1959), 783–791 defines normlessness as ". . . a high expectancy that socially unapproved behaviors are required to achieve given goals." Gabriel A. Almond and Sidney Verba, *The Civic Culture* (Boston: Little, Brown & Co., 1965) have emphasized the difference between these two concepts by drawing the distinction between "input affect," that is, political efficacy, and "output affect," or political cynicism (discussed in terms of trust). Gamson, in *Power and Discontent*, p. 42, has likewise stressed their conceptual differences. He notes that the efficacy dimension of political alienation refers to "people's perception of their ability to influence." There currently exists an extensive body of literature dealing with the conceptual problem of studying political trust, political efficacy and, more generally, political alienation. See, in particular, Aberbach, "Alienation and Political Behavior," and Finifter, "Dimensions of Political Alienation."

[10] The empirical literature investigating trust is characteristically lacking in two respects: longitudinal considerations are rarely entertained, and little use is made of political issues as explanatory variables. Furthermore, an overwhelming majority of those few studies dealing with any form of relationship between issues and cynicism were either based upon restricted populations, such as college students or particular cities, or done under special conditions, such as at times of riots. Some studies that have dealt with issues but used limited samples are: William A. Gamson, "The Flouridation Dialogue: Is It an Ideological Conflict?," *Public Opinion Quarterly*, 25, 2 (Winter 1961), 526–537; Edgar Litt, "Political Cynicism and Political Futility," *Journal of Politics*, 25, 2 (May 1963), 312–323; Joel D. Aberbach and Jack L. Walker, "Political Trust and Racial Ideology," *The American Political Science Review*, 64, 4 (December 1970), 1199–1219.

[11] The sample of respondents for each study is representative of a cross section of eligible voters living in private dwelling units within the continental United States. In 1970 the sample also included 18 to 20 year olds although they were not at the time eligible to vote. In the analyses making comparisons across the four different studies, only eligible voters were used. However, the 18 to 20 year olds were included

battery of questions dealing with public policy on race relations, foreign affairs, and a variety of domestic problems. These issues provide a wealth of data on which to test the hypothesized relationships between public policy and cynicism.[12]

Throughout this paper percentage difference indices will be used in the presentation of data. A percentage difference index (PDI) value indicates the preponderance of one type of response over another at a given time point for a single variable. For example, a trust in government PDI based on the first item of Table 1 may be computed by subtracting the per cent of "most cynical" responses ("only some of the time") from the per cent of "least cynical" responses ("always"). Resulting negative index values indicate a preponderance of "most cynical" responses over "least cynical" responses, while positive index values indicate the reverse. The possible range of PDI values is from +100 to −100. In the specific example for Table 1, the magnitude of the negative value indicates the *degree* of political cynicism; conversely, positive values indicate trust. If all respondents said they could trust the government "only some of the time," the resulting PDI value would be −100, whereas a +100 would result if all respondents said they can "just about always" trust the government to do what is right. The actual values that would result for the item from Table 1 are:

	1694	1966	1968	1970
PDI	−8.0	−14.0	−29.5	−37.8

These PDI values very clearly and parsimoniously display the trend toward increased cynicism previously discussed with respect to Table 1.

POLICY POSITION AS AN EXPLANATION OF CYNICISM

The first hypothesis which may be entertained as a possible explanation of political cynicism is that individuals are cynical because they prefer an unpopular policy alternative on some political issue or issues. Key has described the distribution of public attitudes on political issues in terms of two general models of consensus and conflict.[13] According to Key, the development of public opinion is from conflict to consensus, with consensus resulting either out of compromise and the movement of

---

in any analysis which dealt with the 1970 data alone. The data were made available by the Inter-university Consortium for Political Research. Neither the Center for Political Studies nor the Consortium bear any responsibility for the analyses or interpretations presented here.

[12] Factor analysis (with about 20 items for each study) indicated that for each of the four election studies under consideration, the five trust items formed a single dimension. They were measured by means of a Guttman scale ranging from least cynical (score of zero) to most cynical (score of five). Whenever performing statistical analysis requiring fairly substantial numbers of respondents in each category from which to make reliable inferences, the six categories of the cynicism scale were collapsed into three by combining $0 + 1$, $2 + 3$, and $4 + 5$.

[13] V. O. Key, Jr., *Public Opinion and American Democracy* (New York: Alfred A. Knopf, 1965) Chapters 2 and 3.

individuals to a middle position on the issue or coalescense in favor of one policy alternative. Presumably, the majority opinion would be enacted into policy and, according to the hypothesized relationship, the dissenting minority would fall into the most cynical category because their alternative was not adopted.

Racial Issues

Public policy dealing with racial integration provides a prime subject area for analysis here because the government's policy position, and even more so it's rhetoric, can be equated with active enforcement of integration since passage of the 1964 Civil Rights Act. Hypothetically, therefore, individuals in agreement with an integration position should be least cynical while those opposed should be most cynical, leading one to expect a correlation between cynicism and issue position. The correlation (gamma) between political cynicism and racial issues dealing with the role of the government in racial integration, as well as the style and progress of the Civil Rights Movement, are displayed in the final column of Table 2.

TABLE 2
Cynicism Percentage Difference Indices and Racial Issues for 1964 and 1970

Do you think the government in Washington should see to it that White and Negro children are allowed to go to the same schools or should the government stay out of this area as it is not its business?*

	Same Schools	Other; Depends	Stay Out	Gamma
1964 PDI †	57.9	29.3	25.7	.32
1970 PDI	−0.6	−1.0	−15.6	.07
Change	(58.5)	(30.3)	(41.3)	

Do you think the civil rights leaders are trying to push too fast, are going too slowly, or are they moving about the right speed?*

	Too Fast	About Right	Too Slowly	Gamma
1964 PDI	36.1	57.9	48.7	−.22
1970 PDI	−10.8	13.3	−27.3	−.08
Change	(46.9)	(44.6)	(76.0)	

* Full wording of the question can be found in the 1964 or 1970 SRC-CPS election study questionnaires.
† Negative values of the cynicism PDI indicate degree of cynicism; positive values indicate degree of trust.

The difference in the pattern of correlations for 1964 and 1970 is strikingly obvious. The 1964 correlations are moderate in size and fit the prediction of the hypothesis. For the 1970 data, however, the relationships are very weak.

What are we, therefore, to conclude from the 1970 racial integration items? Had the Civil Rights Movement become so integral a part of the

American consciousness that a depoliticization of the issue had occurred through the simple acceptance of integration as a way of life? And, more significantly, were even the dissenters no longer cynical? Most likely not, since such an interpretation would completely negate what is readily apparent from even a cursory examination of the racial situation in America today. On the contrary, a much different phenomena appears to have occurred, altering the basic form of the relationships between political cynicism and racial issues.

The percentage difference indices (PDI) presented in Table 2 more completely describe the relationships between racial issues and cynicism and clearly display the changes which have occurred in this relationship between 1964 and 1970. In 1964, those opposed to government intervention in race relations were considerably more cynical than those favoring such intervention. For example, in 1964, the 38 per cent of the population believing that integration of schools was not the federal government's business had a PDI value of 25.7; for the 41 per cent in favor of government intervention, it was 57.9; and for the seven per cent favoring a compromise position, 29.3. In 1970, the most cynical group of respondents were still those who opposed government integration of schools, but the difference between these individuals and those favoring intervention had narrowed appreciably. Indeed, the difference in degree of cynicism between those favoring a compromise position and those favoring government intervention had disappeared.

The change in the attitude of trust indicated in Table 2 suggests that the increase in cynicism from 1964 to 1970 for supporters of government intervention in school integration was considerably greater than that for opponents of intervention. Also, cynicism seems to have increased at a slower rate among that subset of the population favoring a compromise position ("other; depends" category).

Turning to the questions dealing with the style and progress of the Civil Rights Movement, a similar pattern of change can be noted. In 1964, those who thought the Movement had been going "too slowly" and those who thought it was going at "about the right speed" were considerably less cynical than the 63 per cent believing that civil rights leaders were pushing "too fast." By 1970, a curvilinear pattern had developed with those finding the progress of the Movement too slow being much more cynical than people who thought it had been going too fast; those who felt that the Movement was going at about the right speed were still the least cynical. By far the largest increase in cynicism (indicated in Table 2 by a "change" value of 76.0) occurred among respondents impatient with the progress being made by the Civil Rights Movement.

In summary, it can be said that consensus has not occurred on racial issues. In 1970, despite a gradual shift in a pro-integrationist direction,[14] attitudes on school integration were still distributed in a bimodal fashion, particularly for whites. There had not been a coalescing of support for

---

[14] Angus Campbell, *White Attitudes toward Black People* (Ann Arbor, Michigan: Institute for Social Research, 1971).

enacted policy, as has so often been the case with controversial programs such as, for example, the sweeping social welfare programs of the New Deal era. Nor has the discontent among the dissenters subsided. On the contrary, political cynicism has consistently been most prevalent among those favoring segregation and believing that the federal government should not play a role in the integration of schools and public accommodations. However, the surprising phenomena disclosed by the data analysis, and in need of explanation, is that individuals in favor of forced integration have also become discontented and apparently at a faster rate.

A clue to a partial explanation of the increase in discontent and cynicism among blacks and white integrationists is suggested by the pattern of change presented in Figure 1.[15]

FIGURE 1

Index of Trust in Government by Race, 1964–1970

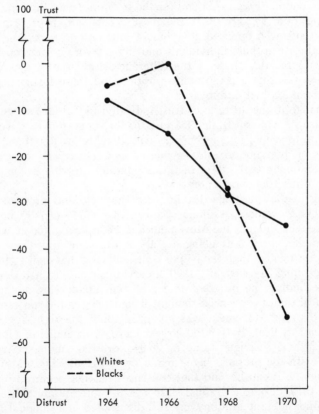

---

[15] The item asking "How often can you trust the government in Washington to do what is right?" was selected for this portion of the analysis because it was one of the two items asked in all four years. It is also very much an "average" item for the set and has the most face validity as a measure of political trust.

Blacks demonstrated more trust in the government than whites prior to 1968, with a sharp divergence and reversal occurring between the races after 1968. During the two-year period from 1964–1966, while blacks were registering more faith in the government, whites exhibited a rapid decline in trust. Since 1966, however, political cynicism has apparently been increasing among blacks and whites, although the rate of change for whites has been at a somewhat slower pace.

Trust in the government may have increased among blacks between 1964 and 1966 out of a reaction to the Civil Rights Bill of 1964; the decrease for whites may also be similarly explained. The Bill may have increased the hope among blacks and white integrationists that a real change in racial integration, along with a reduction in discrimination, would be forthcoming. At the same time, the security of white segregationists might have been threatened by the fear that their social and economic positions would be challenged by blacks with the support of the government. Or, they may have been resentful at the thought that "the government is helping the blacks, why doesn't it help me?" Such reactions would partially explain the change in cynicism between 1964 and 1966 while setting the stage for the changes which ensued after 1966.

It is suggested that actual modification of the racial situation and the conditions of racial discrimination have not paralleled the rising expectations of the black community or those sympathetic to their plight, nor have they at the same time been as drastic as feared by white segregationists. Trust in the government may have thus declined sharply among blacks after 1966 because of frustration arising out of the unfulfilled expectation of more active government involvement in the area of integration.[16] Coincidentally, the Civil Rights Movement was making blacks, as a whole, increasingly more aware of the real constraints and discrimination existent in the system, thereby increasing their discontent and reaffirming for them even more staunchly the notion that only a change in the system would improve the "black condition."[17] On the other hand, those opposed to integration were also dissatisfied with

---

[16] This explanation is lent additional support by the degree of change in political trust found for blacks who felt the Civil Rights Movement was going too slowly. In 1964, 27 per cent of the blacks fell into this category; six years later, the figure was 39 per cent. The growing impatience on the part of the blacks appears to be reflected in their increased cynicism, as indicated by the respective cynicism index values of 57.8 and −45.2. The magnitude of attitude change suggested by the difference between these two values is extraordinary, particularly for such a basic and presumably stable attitude as political trust. The aggregate increase in distrust of the government was substantially less for the 63 per cent of black respondents who felt that civil rights was moving at about the right speed. In 1964, the cynicism index value for these blacks was 53.6—not very different from impatient blacks—but by 1970 the blacks who were satisfied with the speed of the Movement (now down to 54 per cent) were very much less cynical (−19.6) as a group than blacks who thought progress was too slow.

[17] Patricia Gurin, et al., "Internal-External Control in the Motivational Dynamics of Negro Youth," *Journal of Social Issues*, 25, 3 (1969) investigates whether an individual places the blame for social or economic failure among blacks on the individual or the system.

governmental performance in this area, presumably in part because between 1968 and 1970 the Nixon administration did not attempt to, nor could it, completely reverse the process of integration.

The Vietnam Issue

While significant differences in the degree of cynicism have been found to exist among people favoring alternative policy positions on racial issues, these issues do not completely explain all the increase or the variation in cynicism occurring since 1964. The Vietnam war, an issue with steadily increasing political potency since the early 1960s, appears also to be related to the attitude of trust in government. Table 3 presents the distribution of support for Vietnam policy alternatives from 1964 to 1970. A percentage difference index for the Vietnam issue, computed by

TABLE 3
Support for Vietnam Policy, 1964–1970

Which of the Following Do You Think We Should Do Now in Vietnam?	1964	1966	1968	1970
Pull out of Vietnam entirely	8.3%	9.1%	19.8%	32.3%
Keep out soldiers in Vietnam but try to end the fighting	25.0	35.6	36.0	32.0
Take a stronger stand even if it means invading North Vietnam ...	31.6	35.9	33.5	24.2
Other; depends	0.1	2.2	3.3	5.1
Don't know; not ascertained	35.0	17.2	7.4	6.4
Total	100.0%	100.0%	100.0%	100.0%
(N)	(4658)*	(1291)	(1557)	(1514)
Percentage Difference Index†	23.3	26.8	13.7	−8.1

* Weighted N.
† Negative values indicate more support for withdrawal; positive values indicate greater support for escalation.

subtracting the per cent of respondents favoring withdrawal from the per cent favoring escalation whereby a negative value indicates greater support for withdrawal, is also presented.

The Vietnam index in Table 3 summarizes the trend in attitude among the general population on this issue. This trend toward support for withdrawal certainly comes as no surprise as it has previously been documented by various polling agencies and publicized extensively in the mass media. However, the source of increased support for withdrawal requires more careful attention. From 1964 to 1970, the percentage of individuals favoring withdrawal from Vietnam increased by 24 per cent while the percentage preferring escalation remained relatively stable, except for an approximate 9 per cent decline from 1968 to 1970. This suggests that most of the increased preference for withdrawal from Vietnam may have come less from converting "hawks" to "doves" than either from attitude changes among those preferring a compromise position or from the uninformed public taking a dovish position as the Vietnam issue became more salient.[18]

A model that relates policy dissent with discontent would predict that dissenting doves are more cynical than hawks. Such a relationship would help explain the increase in cynicism occurring between 1964 and 1970, the same period during which the ranks of the doves increased. The trust in government (from Figure 1) and Vietnam percentage difference indices were plotted with respect to each other for whites and blacks and are presented in Figure 2.

Figure 2 reveals a very similar pattern of change in support for withdrawal from Vietnam and trust in government, especially for blacks who have been consistently more dovish than whites. The slight increase in support for escalation for both groups in 1966 probably reflects a leadership effort that rallied early support for Johnson's policy before attitudes on Vietnam became more informed. This would seem to be particularly true for blacks as about 29 per cent of them did not have an opinion on Vietnam in 1966, compared to 16 per cent of the whites. After 1966, however, the black community quickly moved in the direction of support for withdrawal, with only about 9 per cent of the total black population in favor of escalation and 50 per cent supporting withdrawal.

The whites, on the other hand, have been more reticent in their support for withdrawal. Furthermore, a closer look at the Vietnam and trust curves for whites reveals certain discrepancies at odds with the original hypothesis. Not only are the Vietnam and trust curves less parallel for whites than for blacks, but there is also a definite divergence of the two curves for whites in 1966. While support for escalation was increasing relative to support for withdrawal among white respondents, trust was declining. Inspection of the relationships between Vietnam policy preference and political cynicism for 1964 and 1970 provides a partial explanation for these discrepancies. Table 4 presents the percentage responses and cynicism index for the Vietnam question for whites only for these years.

The most immediate observation made from Table 4 is that the original prediction that the most cynical would be those favoring withdrawal

---

[18] Two pieces of information lend credence to this interpretation. First, the very substantial decrease in the per cent of respondents saying "don't know" corresponds more closely to the percentage increases in the middle and withdrawal categories than it does to the percentage fluctuation found in the escalation category. Secondly, as Morris Rosenberg, *et al.*, point out in *Vietnam and the Silent Majority: The Dove's Guide* (New York: Harper & Row, Publishers, 1970), p. 55, it is the "hawks" who have been the more informed on the Vietnam issue; hence, their attitudes on Vietnam would be more crystalized and less susceptible to change. What these data suggest, therefore, is that while there has been a trend toward support of withdrawal from Vietnam, there has not been a concurrent reduction in the polarization of attitudes on Vietnam policy. Continued conflict over Vietnam policy is understandable, given the continued dissent among opinion leadership—identified by Richard A. Brody and Sidney A. Verba in "Hawk and Dove: The Search for an Explanation of Vietnam Policy Preferences," scheduled for publication in *Acta Politica* in 1972, as among the most important independent variables in explaining opinions on Vietnam—as well as changes in official policy, a factor which tends to reduce the impact "current policy" would have on a converging policy preference.

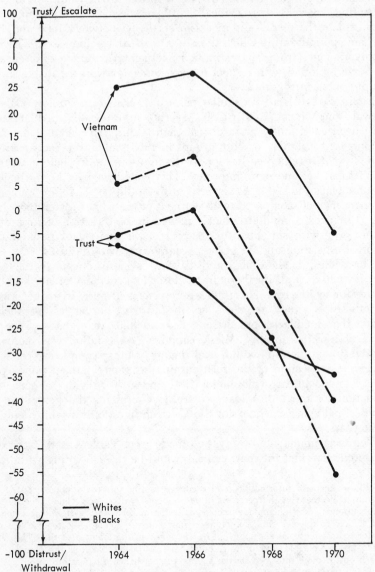

FIGURE 2

Indices of Trust in Government and Support for Withdrawal
from Vietnam, 1964–1970

was partly false. In 1964, respondents favoring escalation were less trusting of the government (cynicism index value of 27.5) than those preferring withdrawal (37.1); in 1970, the reverse was true (−7.2 and −12.6,
respectively). The most striking difference found in Table 4 is not, however, between those supporting withdrawal and those preferring escalation, but rather between the latter two groups and those wanting to keep

TABLE 4

Current Vietnam Policy Preference in Relation to
Trust in Government for Whites, 1964 and 1970

Trust in Government	Vietnam Policy Preference: 1964		
	Withdraw	Maintain	Escalate
High	58.3%	74.6%	53.8%
Medium	20.4	14.9	19.9
Low	21.3	10.5	26.3
Total	100.0%	100.0%	100.0%
(N)	(108)	(315)	(433)
Percentage Difference Index°	37.1	64.1	27.5
	Vietnam Policy Preference: 1970		
High	29.5%	46.8%	32.5%
Medium	28.4	28.4	27.8
Low	42.1	24.8	39.7
Total	100.0%	100.0%	100.0%
(N)	(437)	(455)	(363)
Percentage Difference Index°	−12.6	22.0	−7.2

° Negative values of the cynicism percentage difference index indicates degree of political cynicism; conversely, positive values indicate trust.

the soldiers in Vietnam while trying to end the fighting. Respondents choosing this category were definitely less cynical than either the hawks or the doves, both in 1964 and in 1970. Hence, a curvilinear rather than a linear relationship is found between Vietnam policy preference and political trust, thereby increasing the complexity of the interpretation.

As Rosenberg and others[19] have demonstrated, individuals preferring escalation have often been dissatisfied with Vietnam policy even while a stronger stand was being taken because in their opinion the escalation was not sufficient. Increased dissatisfaction with the intensity of the escalation may explain the increase in cynicism among hawks in 1966 and thus the divergence noted in Figure 2. Cynicism among doves can similarly be explained on the basis of dissent in 1964 and on the basis of growing impatience in 1970.

"CYNICS OF THE LEFT" AND "CYNICS OF THE RIGHT"

The preceding analysis clearly demonstrates that no monolithic description of cynicism arises out of policy preferences for the issues investigated. Rather, what evolves is that those who preferred a middle-of-the-road or compromise policy were the least cynical, and that the most cynical formed two ideologically distinct types that may be labeled "cynics of the left" and "cynics of the right." Operationally, cynics of the left and cynics of the right can be defined as those both most cynical and preferring opposing policy alternatives on five contemporary issues: ur-

---

[19] Rosenberg, et al., *Vietnam and the Silent Majority;* as well as Philip E. Converse, et al., "Continuity and Change in American Politics," *American Political Science Review*, 63 (December 1969), 1083–1105.

ban unrest, Vietnam, campus demonstrations, protecting the rights of individuals accused of crime, and government aid to minorities. Such an operational definition provides fairly pure types of cynics, with 11 per cent of the population ($N = 176$) classified as "most" cynical on the left and 19 per cent ($N = 290$) on the right.

Cynics of the left may be described as predisposed to social and political change. Witness their support of policy alternatives indicating that solutions to contemporary social problems lie in the alteration of the existing system: the prevention of riots in cities by solving the problems of unemployment and poverty, government aid to improve the social and economic conditions of minority groups, a pro-integrationist stand on civil rights, and protection of the rights of the accused. This predisposition is supported by their apparent belief that constraints in the system, rather than individual shortcomings, are to blame for the failure of people, particularly minority groups, to "get ahead" in society. This system-blame attitude is evident in their strong preference for government action to improve the social and economic conditions of minority groups as well as that of all those who suffer from poverty and unemployment. As is further suggested by their responses to the student unrest issue, they appear to be somewhat favorably inclined toward the use of collective action for obtaining that change; hence, they are sympathetic with demonstrating students.

Cynics of the right, may, on the other hand, be described as more predisposed toward social control[20] than social change. That is, they are bent upon maintaining the system as it exists and are supportive of authorities and policies which act to control those who may be potentially disruptive of the orderly functioning of the system. They were inclined toward segregation policies and policies tending to disregard the rights of the accused in an attempt to prevent crime, and were strongly in favor of complete military victory in Vietnam. The Protestant Ethic seems engrained in cynics of the right as evidenced by their greater stress on the individual rather than the system for one's failure to attain social status; they were firmly against government assistance aimed at improving the social and economic position of minority groups. Their corresponding support for using police force against demonstrators suggests that since they apparently believed that unsuccessful attempts at social advancement were individual shortcomings, such disruptive actions were attempts by a few to gain special privileges for themselves.

The two types of cynics were as different demographically as they were in terms of policy preferences. One-third of the cynics of the left were under 30 whereas only 12 per cent of the most cynical on the right were young. Blacks comprised 38 per cent of the former group; 99.7 per cent of the latter were white. While cynics of the left tended to identify more with the Democratic (71 per cent) than the Republican party (12 per cent), those on the right were more evenly split: 48 per cent were Democrats and 35 per cent were Republicans. The cynics of the right had

---

[20] For a definition of social control, see Gamson, *Power and Discontent*, pp. 11–19.

higher incomes, with only 21 per cent making less than $4,000 a year; 38 per cent of those on the left were below that figure. However, those on the left were much better educated: 28 per cent had some college training or held a college degree, as compared with only 18 per cent among those of the right. Again, with blacks removed, the percentage of those of the left who had had some college rose to 38 per cent.

In retrospect, the explanation for the curvilinearity in the relationship between policy preference and trust may arise out of increased political awareness and the type of issues prevalent today rather than the distribution of preferences. These issues are very close to the individual's immediate experience and seem to affect the very basic values and fears that form the foundation of everyday existence for the average citizen. Attitudes on these issues would, therefore, tend to be well crystallized and more firmly held than on issues more remote from an individual's daily existence. It is thus understandable that respondents with the most completely formed attitudes—presumably those favoring the extreme alternatives[21]—should be the most cynical. It is they who would be most dissatisfied were their well-formulated policy expectations not only left untended but also threatened by enactment of opposing policies. By 1970 Americans had, to a considerable degree, withdrawn some of their trust from the government because they had become widely divided on a variety of issues, for in the normal attempt to satisfy the greatest numbers, the government had generally followed a more or less centrist policy which in reality appears to have displeased a substantial proportion of the population.

Issue position was, therefore, found to be related, in a complex manner, to political cynicism. There is, however, nothing intrinsic in support for a particular policy alternative, or even a pattern of policy preferences, which provides a theoretical interpretation for such a finding. It was hypothesized that dissenters, that is, those favoring the policy alternative endorsed by a minority of individuals, would be the most dissatisfied and thereby the most cynical. This hypothesis proved to be totally inadequate in predicting or explaining either the widespread distrust of government in 1970 or the increase in distrust occurring between 1964 and 1970. Alternatively, it may be hypothesized that cynicism is related to political expectations and policy dissatisfaction.

POLICY DISSATISFACTION

Gamson contends that distrust of the government arises out of "the nature of the decisions made and the satisfaction or dissatisfaction with them . . ."[22] particularly when dissatisfaction is generalized across a number of decisions which result in undesirable outcomes. This contention leads to several testable hypotheses. The first states that discontent may be related to dissatisfaction with the perceived policies of the party in

---

[21] Angus Campbell, et al., *The American Voter* (New York: John Wiley & Sons, Inc., 1960), p. 178.

[22] Gamson, *Power and Discontent*, p. 178.

power on issues that are relevant to the values of a substantial segment of the population. Secondly, if discontent has been evident over an extended period of time, as it has in America, it may also be somewhat related to the policies of the opposition party. This should be especially true if that party was just recently voted out of office. Finally, given the first two hypotheses, it may be that political cynicism is related to *dissatisfaction with both parties*. That is, an individual may be dissatisfied with the policies of both parties and thus be alienated because neither party offers him an acceptable policy alternative.

To test these hypotheses with the 1970 issue questions (see Appendix), policy dissatisfaction was operationalized in terms of the distance between the individual's own policy preference and the policy alternative that he identified with a particular party. Underlying this is the assumption that if an individual completely agrees with the policy alternative of a particular party as he perceives it (that is, when a respondent places both himself and the party at the same point on an issue scale), he is more satisfied with the party's policies than he would be if he identified the party with a policy some distance from his own position on the issue.

An indicator of policy dissatisfaction on an issue can be computed as the absolute difference between the respondent's issue scale value and the scale value associated with the position where the respondent has placed the party. This distance measure, as used here, would have a range of scores from zero, minimum policy dissatisfaction, to four, maximum policy dissatisfaction. An average measure of policy dissatisfaction, as indicated by a mean distance score for the eight issues, was used in the analysis because it captures the effects of dissatisfaction that may be cumulative across the several issues.

The data which directly test all three hypotheses simultaneously are presented in Table 5 which displays a 25-celled cross-classification of the total cross-section sample determined by distance from both the Republican and Democratic parties' perceived policies. The cell entries are average cynicism scores which can range from zero, or least cynical, to five, for most cynical. The percentage of the total population falling into the particular cell is indicated in parentheses and these percentages total to the corner.

If cynicism is related to dissatisfaction with the perceived policies of the party in power (Republicans in 1970), the average cynicism scores should increase as distance from the Republican party increases, that is, going down the columns of the table. If cynicism is related to dissatisfaction with the Democratic party policies, the cell entries will increase going across the rows. Finally, the average cynicism values along the diagonal from the 0,0 cell toward the 4,4 cell will increase if discontent is related to dissatisfaction with the policies of both parties.

It is apparent from even a cursory glance at the mean cynicism scores going down the columns that a substantial increase in cynicism accompanies increased dissatisfaction with Republican party policies on the issues. Are we to conclude from this that discontent in America would be reduced by replacing the Republican administration and Republican

TABLE 5

Mean Cynicism by Distance from Both Parties

Distance from Republican Party	Distance from Democratic Party					Total
	0	1	2	3	4	
0	1.69° (5.9%)	1.60 (4.1)	2.50 (1.7)	1.50 (0.6)	2.10 (0.7)	13.0%
1	1.84 (6.1)	2.19 (18.3)	2.56 (8.4)	2.33 (3.0)	2.85 (0.9)	36.7
2	2.19 (4.6)	2.71 (9.8)	2.67 (11.4)	3.00 (3.1)	3.24 (1.2)	30.1
3	2.79 (2.4)	3.25 (4.2)	2.88 (3.5)	3.46 (2.5)	3.50 (0.6)	13.2
4	3.46 (2.0)	3.10 (2.1)	4.40 (1.1)	4.37 (0.9)	4.69 (1.0)	7.1
Total	21.0%	38.5	26.1	10.1	4.4	(100.0%) $N = 1401$

Eta = .32

° Cell entries are mean cynicism values. The cynicism scale ranged from 0 = least to 5 = most cynical.

policy alternatives with the Democratic alternative? Not necessarily. The column marginal percentages for Table 5 clearly demonstrate that in 1970 a substantial proportion of the population was also dissatisfied with the policy alternatives they perceived the Democratic party as pursuing to solve the problems reflected by contemporary issues. Nearly 60 per cent of the population fell into the two "least dissatisfied" categories (0 and 1) of Table 5, compared to 50 per cent who were equally satisfied with Republican policies. Thus, while there was somewhat less dissatisfaction, in general, with Democratic policies, a sizable fraction of the population will still somewhat in disagreement with perceived Democratic policy alternatives. This is indeed a surprising finding, given that Democrats generally outnumber Republicans nearly two-to-one. Furthermore, that cynicism was related to dissatisfaction with Democratic policies can be readily ascertained from the increase in the means going across the rows of Table 5.

The results of Table 5 also clearly demonstrate the degree to which distrust of the government increases as dissatisfaction with the policies of both parties increases. Those individuals who were completely satisfied with the perceived policies of the Democratic and Republican parties (cell 0,0) were the most trusting of the government (mean cynicism of 1.69), whereas those who were most dissatisfied with both parties (cell 4,4) were dramatically more cynical (mean of 4.69). These data thus provide strong evidence in support of the contention that those who feel that neither party offers viable solutions to contemporary social problems are among the most cynical, distrustful and alienated citizens in the United States today.

Policy Dissatisfaction and Cynicism: An Explanation

How is the relationship between policy dissatisfaction with both parties and political cynicism to be explained? And how does this finding correspond to the increase in cynicism between 1964 and 1970? A possible explanation, inspired by the concepts of party identification and relative deprivation, is that Democrats would tend to be dissatisfied with Republican policies, and thereby more distrusting of the government, because they do not believe that Republican policies benefit them. This party-based interpretation would, however, lead to the prediction of no correlation between cynicism and Democratic policies, a prediction not supported by the data. Another interpretation which would seem theoretically reasonable, but similarly unsupported by these data, is that a negligible relationship between cynicism and dissatisfaction with Republican policy would be found for Democrats because their expectations during a Republican administration would be low and policy dissatisfaction would thus not lead to increased cynicism. Perhaps the reason these explanations do not fit the data is that contemporary social issues are not closely related to party identification, and what appears confusing when approached from a party focus becomes more meaningful from another vantage point.

An investigation of policy dissatisfaction for cynics of the left and cynics of the right produces a partial reduction in the confusion and a clearer explanation. It appears that the Democratic cynics of the left $(N = 122)$ were dissatisfied with the Democratic and Republican parties because, to a certain extent, they perceived both of them as being too far to the right: 38 per cent placed the Democratic party further to the right than their own policy preference and nearly 96 per cent saw the Republican party as more conservative on the issues than they were themselves. Their average distance from the Democratic party was 1.4, from the Republican party, 3.2, thus illustrating a greater degree of discontent with Republican than Democratic policies. The Democratic cynics of the right $(N = 138)$, however, were equally as dissatisfied with both the Republican and Democratic policies: 74 per cent perceived both parties as further left than their own policy preference. On the average, the Democratic cynics of the right placed the Democratic party 1.9 units away from their own policy position, while their mean distance from the Republican party was 2.4.

Republican cynics of the left, were also equally dissatisfied with both parties. Their average distance from the Democratic party was 1.8, compared to 1.6 from the Republican party. The Republican cynics of the left perceived Republican party policies as somewhat more conservative than their own preferences but very centrist; on the average, 61 per cent placed the party at point 4 on the issues. Surprisingly, they perceived Democratic policies as somewhat more to the right than Republican policies. Unfortunately, there were only 25 respondents so classified, thus making inferences about Republican cynics of the left rather tenuous. In contrast, Republican cynics of the right $(N = 102)$ were more dissatisfied with Democratic party policies (average distance of 2.7) which they perceived as being further left than Republican policies. Nevertheless, 57 per cent placed the Republican party further to the left (average distance of 1.8) than their own policy preference, implying a distrust for the government because of too liberal administration policies.

In short, both Democratic and Republican cynics of the right perceived partisan solutions to contemporary social problems as too liberal. It is important to add that individuals preferring centrist policy alternatives, regardless of whether "centrist" is defined as points 3 to 5 or only 4 on the scale, were proportionately more likely to perceive both the parties in the center; hence they were less dissatisfied and correspondingly less alienated. Besides demonstrating which Democratic and Republican subgroups were dissatisfied more with one party than the other, or with both equally, these data support a reformulated explanation of how policy dissatisfaction corresponds to the recent increase in political distrust.

When approached from the left-right cynicism perspective, the data strongly imply that the increased distrust of government in 1970 was the result of a combination of unfulfilled expectations on the part of some, and for others, the perception that their situation, which was already one of deprivation and discrimination, had actually worsened relative to others. For example, in 1968 Richard Nixon promised to end the war, but respondents in that year's study who perceived him as tending toward a policy of complete military victory outnumbered, by 2 to 1, those who saw him as favoring withdrawal. By 1970, U.S. involvement in Vietnam had not ended, and Vietnamization—a centrist approach to the war—had been declared the official policy of the Republican administration. Furthermore, a larger proportion (34 per cent) of the cynics of the right, who on the whole were very hawkish, perceived Nixon as favoring withdrawal in 1970 than did in 1968 (23 per cent). In contrast, the most dovish of the doves, the blacks, perceived Nixon, despite his promises to end the war, as more in favor of a complete military victory in 1970 (52 per cent) than they did in 1968 (42 per cent). Thus, the expectations of both hawks and doves, regardless of their party identification, had not been met, resulting in a decline in confidence for both groups.

The failure of the Republican administration to meet the expectations of the Democratic cynics of the right may have led them to the view that the Republicans are just as bad as the Democrats. Such an interpretation would coincide well with the close correspondence between dissatisfaction with Democratic policy and dissatisfaction with Republican policy that was found earlier for Democratic cynics of the right. It would also explain why Republican cynics of the right were dissatisfied with Republican policies. However, their party identification, which was somewhat stronger than that of the Democratic cynics of the right, would be expected to keep them from perceiving Republican and Democratic policies as identical; exactly what the analysis demonstrates.

Similarly, the combined effects of party identification, unmet expectations, and the belief that social and economic conditions had deteriorated under the Republican administration can also explain increased cynicism among those on the left. Further, the relationship found between distrust of the government and dissatisfaction with the policies of both parties suggests that discontent in 1970 was related to an earlier dissatisfaction with the policies of the previous (Democratic) administration.

In summary, it has been demonstrated that support of the federal government decreased substantially between 1964 and 1970. Data presented suggested that this increased distrust of the government was partially related to changing attitudes on the issues of racial integration and U.S. involvement in the Vietnam war. A curvilinear relationship was found to exist between policy preference on these issues and political cynicism, with those favoring centrist policies being less cynical than those preferring non-centrist opposing policy alternatives. This complex relationship between cynicism and policy preference was later explained by dissatisfaction with the policies of both political parties.

The dissatisfied non-centrists formed two highly polarized and very different types of cynics, cynics of the left and cynics of the right. It was established that cynics of the left preferred policies bringing social change, while those on the right favored social control policies. The data suggested that increased cynicism could be explained for cynics of the left in terms of frustrations arising out of unmet political expectations for social change, an impatient desire for the alteration of existing policies in order to solve social problems more rapidly, and the belief that the policies of the Republican administration, elected in 1968, had brought a deterioration in the social and economic position of certain groups in society. Increased cynicism on the right has similarly been explained in terms of unmet expectations but for greater social control (a hoped-for Vietnam victory, a slowing of racial integration, a more forceful stand on law and order), and fear arising out of what were perceived as the "too liberal" policies of both parties which threatened to negate their values, as well as undermine their social and economic position.

Finally, the data analysis suggests that the individual evaluates the policies of the parties with respect to his own preference, and if he is dissatisfied with those policies it is more likely that he will feel alienated from the political system. There is, however, nothing inherent in his own policy preference that would result in his being less trusting of the government. If an individual takes a centrist position on an issue and perceives the policies of the parties to be in disagreement with his desires and expectations, he is as likely to be distrusting of the government as the individual who prefers a more extreme policy position. Since public opinion on the issues is polarized and because the parties are perceived by a sizable proportion of the population to offer centrist policy alternatives as solutions to contemporary problems,[23] it follows that those who prefer non-centrist policies are more dissatisfied and thereby the most alienated.

---

[23] The proportion of the total population perceiving the Democratic party as taking a centrist position (#'s 3–5) on the eight issues ranged from 51.9 to 66.5 per cent. In comparison, 60.7 to 68.9 per cent placed the Republican party in positions #3–5 on the eight issues.

CONCLUSION

This study demonstrates that the widespread discontent prevalent in the United States today arises, in part, out of dissatisfaction with the policy alternatives that have been offered as solutions to contemporary problems. The findings strongly suggest that policy alternatives more acceptable to the total population will be exceedingly difficult to discover in the future because of the existing degree of issue polarization. This polarization implies that, on the one hand, there is growing discontent among some individuals because of an unfulfilled desire for social change, while on the other hand, there is an even larger group of alienated individuals who are fearful of change. Those desirous of change, and particularly blacks—since the contemporary problems so directly affect their lives—are those most in need of the use of political influence to obtain that change; however, they perceive the legitimate means of attaining such influence as ineffective. This suggests, for blacks at least, that other means, whether peaceful or violent, legal or illegal, will have to be found to bring about the desired modifications. A move on the part of the administration to make its policies more responsive to the needs of blacks and other minority groups would undoubtedly reduce cynicism among those on the left, but as the data suggest, this would at the same time increase the size of the cynical group on the right and probably intensify its distrust. The current political dilemma arises out of such issue polarization and also out of the difficulties implicit in maintaining government responsiveness and providing for orderly change without the occurrence of intense political conflict under such conditions. Discontent can be functional for a political system if it acts as a catalyst for orderly change, but when the normal channels are perceived as ineffective, the probability that the conflict may burst forth in the form of extra-legal behavior increases.

One goal of the U.S. political system is to contain protest and rage within the electoral process, and parties generally provide a vehicle for such protest. However, investigation of the data has demonstrated that people lack confidence in the ability of the existing parties to bring about responsive government. The fact that a great deal of dissatisfaction with the policies of both parties exists implies that conditions are highly conducive to party realignment and reformation or a third party movement. What appears necessary to reestablish confidence in the parties is a wave of populism and party reforms which will allow those who normally lack access to legitimate power but want change to bring about desired modifications. Whether the current reforms of the primary system and the Democratic party will have a substantial impact on confidence in parties remains to be seen. The results of the study suggest that 1972 may prove to be a critical period of change in the attitude of political trust. There are some indications that the distrust of the government might increase beyond the 1970 level. However, in a system as stable as that in the United States, it is difficult to conceive of the trend in trust continuing to decline at the same rate that it has from 1964 to 1970. A slowing in the rate of decline could certainly be expected to accompany a settlement of the Vietnam conflict, improvement in the economic condition of the country, the easing of racial tensions, and a reduction in turmoil in schools and on university campuses.

What happens if the policies of the administration elected in 1972 bring no reduction in dissatisfaction? Likewise, what happens if present policy is maintained in the future? The trends in the data suggest that trust of the government would continue to decline, increasing the difficulty for leaders to make binding political decisions, as well as raising the probability of the occurrence of radical political change. This would again seem to be particularly true for blacks, for whom the very means of legitimate political control and change are now on trial. Further increases in alienation would presumably bring into question the very philosophy and goals of the political system, as well as the viability of the political community itself, and a "desire for political separation may develop."[24]

The importance of political trust is often couched in terms of a discussion of social control or the necessity for influence. It is argued that without a sufficient degree of political trust, political leaders cannot freely make decisions and commit resources to attain collective goals. Likewise, as cynicism increases, the desire for change increases; if confronted with an immobile leadership, this can lead to need for radical change. Both of these concerns have important implications for the political system and merit attention. However, such analysis almost strikes of an insensitivity to the questions about the quality of life which must have led to such discontent in the first place. The use of political trust as a simple barometer of satisfaction with the political system is too often ignored or buried beneath a series of esoteric arguments and theoretical concerns. The disenchantment and dissatisfaction of individuals who feel politically inefficacious and cynical about the government is real and it arises out of a reaction to real conditions of life. The use of political cynicism as an indicator of the quality of American life is, in and of itself, an important justification for its continued study. Hopefully, continued study will bring a better understanding of those conditions which lead to political cynicism and the basic information from which solutions to the problems may be found.

The distribution of policy preferences on contemporary issues, and the curvilinear relationship between preferences and discontent implies that these solutions will be difficult to come by. It is, however, important that these problems be solved and this importance is underscored by the consensus among experts that the three major types of contemporary civil violence—urban riots, campus disturbances and crime—all flow from the wellsprings of unsolved social problems. Solutions to these problems necessitate change, but if alterations of the current social system are to be forthcoming, the resistance and fear which often deter change must be dealt with. The findings of this study suggest that a reduction of alienation among those favoring change can be brought about

---

[24] Gamson, *Power and Discontent*, p. 52.

by creative and constructive action in domestic areas that will benefit the majority of people and diminish feelings of frustration and relative deprivation. But once again, the caveat must be added that these policies need to be designed to solve existing social problems without further alienating a substantial proportion of the population. The vast opinion leadership potential of the president would have to be fully exploited if this were to be realized under the current situation of opinion polarization. A president initially viewed as a moderate or centrist ought to have a much better chance of mobilizing broad support for reform policies under these circumstances than a president who is viewed as a non-centrist. However, the leadership role cannot rest with the president alone; the decrease of discontent among those preferring social control policies would require that constructive programs of social change be administered by leaders not only sensitive to the fears evoked by change, but are also capable of dealing with the resulting resistance to such programs. These programs would require educating the public so that they will better understand the need for social change and the benefits which would evolve from such change. Whether the necessary modifications of the social and political system, and the style of leadership necessary to bring about these changes with minimal conflict will be forthcoming is, again, yet to be realized. The results of this study however, clearly imply that current discontent in America will not be reduced with a continuation of centrist policies, or centrist politics, especially if such politics include numerous promises which give rise to expectations that are never fulfilled.

APPENDIX ISSUE QUESTIONS FOR 1970

Urban Unrest

And now I would like to talk to you about some problems which are important in America today.

1.* There is much discussion about the best way to deal with the problem of urban unrest and rioting. Some say it is more important to use all available force to maintain law and order—no matter what results. Others say it is more important to correct the problems of poverty and unemployment that give rise to the disturbances. And, of course, other people have opinions in between. Suppose the people

Solve Problems of Poverty and Unemployment						Use All Available Force
1	2	3	4	5	6	7

a. Where would you place yourself on this scale? _____
b. Where would you place the Democratic party? _____
c. Where would you place the Republican party? _____
d. (Where would you place) Richard Nixon? _____
e. (Where would you place) Edmund Muskie? _____
f. (Where would you place) George Wallace? _____

who stress doing more about the problems of poverty and unemployment are at one end of this scale—at point number 1. And suppose the people who stress the use of force are at the other end—at point number 7.

Vietnam

2.* There is much talk about "hawks" and "doves" in connection with Vietnam, and considerable disagreement as to what action the United States should take in Vietnam. Some people think we should do everything necessary to win a complete military victory, no matter what results. Some people think we should withdraw completely from Vietnam right now, no matter what results. And, of course, other people have opinions somewhere between these two extreme positions. Suppose the people who support an immediate withdrawal are at one end of this scale at point number 1. And suppose the people who support a complete military victory are at the other end of the scale at point number 7.

Campus Demonstrations

3. Some people are pretty upset about rioting and disturbances on college campuses and in high schools. Some feel sympathetic with the students and faculty who take part in these disturbances. Others think the schools should use police and the national guard to prevent or stop disturbances. And others fall somewhere between these extremes.

Government Aid to Minority Groups

4. Some people feel that the government in Washington should make every possible effort to improve the social and economic position of Negroes and other minority groups. Others feel that the government should not make any special effort to help minority peoples but they should be expected to help themselves.

Inflation

5. There is a great deal of talk these days about rising prices and the cost of living in general. Some feel that the problem of inflation is temporary and that no government action is necessary. Others say the government must do everything possible to combat the problem of inflation immediately or it will get worse.

---

* Only these two items were used in the 1968 election study.

Protecting Rights of Accused

6. Some people are primarily concerned with doing everything possible to protest the legal rights of those accused of committing crimes. Others feel that it is more important to stop criminal activity even at the risk of reducing the rights of the accused.

Ecological Pollution

7. There are many sources of air and water pollution; one of them is private industry. Some say the government should force private industry to stop its polluting. Others believe industries should be left alone to handle these matters in their own way. Given these two approaches. . . .

Government Health Insurance

8. There is much concern about the rapid rise in medical and hospital costs. Some feel there should be a government health insurance plan which would cover all medical and hospital expenses. Others feel that medical expenses should be paid by individuals and through private insurance like Blue Cross.